WHY YOU NEED THIS UPDATE

Converging Media's Third Edition 2013–2014 update covers modern-day global, political, economic, and cultural issues while increasing its focus on media literacy.

- Guide to how the content in *Converging Media* relates to each of the twelve core values and competencies of the **Accrediting Council on Education in Journalism and Mass Communications (ACEJMC)**. Visit us online at www.oup.com/us/pavlik for more information on how we provide this content.

- Six new current and compelling chapter-opening vignettes provide students with chapter previews and learning objectives:
  - *The Huffington Post*'s Pulitzer Prize win (pp. 266–268)
  - Digital piracy including the controversy with SOPA and PIPA (pp. 400–402)
  - eBook pricing (pp. 71–72)
  - China's internet censorship (pp. 199–200)
  - Impact of Super PACs on elections (p. 463)
  - Critics' reactions to personalized online news sites, such as Paper.li (p. 3)

- Up-to-date discussions of topics in the mass media:
  - The Facebook IPO (p. 254)
  - The role of the media in the 2012 election process and results (pp. 474–484)

2013-2014
Update

THIRD EDITION

CONVERGING MEDIA

A NEW INTRODUCTION TO MASS COMMUNICATION

John V. Pavlik
Rutgers University

Shawn McIntosh
Columbia University

New York   Oxford
OXFORD UNIVERSITY PRESS

Oxford University Press is a department of the University of Oxford. It furthers the University's
objective of excellence in research, scholarship, and education by publishing worldwide.

Oxford New York
Auckland Cape Town Dar es Salaam Hong Kong Karachi
Kuala Lumpur Madrid Melbourne Mexico City Nairobi
New Delhi Shanghai Taipei Toronto

With offices in
Argentina Austria Brazil Chile Czech Republic France Greece
Guatemala Hungary Italy Japan Poland Portugal Singapore
South Korea Switzerland Thailand Turkey Ukraine Vietnam

For titles covered by Section 112 of the US Higher Education Opportunity
Act, please visit www.oup.com/us/he for the latest information about
pricing and alternative formats.

Published in the United States of America by
Oxford University Press
198 Madison Avenue, New York, NY 10016

Library of Congress Cataloging-in-Publication Data

Pavlik, John V. (John Vernon)
  Converging media : a new introduction to mass communication / John V. Pavlik, Rutgers University, Shawn
McIntosh, Columbia University.—Third edition. 2013-2014 update.
    pages cm
  Includes bibliographical references and index.
  ISBN 978-0-19-996846-6 (main text : alk. paper)—ISBN (invalid) 978-0-19-985992-4 (instructor's manual :
alk. paper)—ISBN (invalid) 978-0-19-985991-7 (instructor's resource CD)—ISBN (invalid) 978-0-19-985990-0
(companion website) 1. Mass media. 2. Digital media. 3. Internet. I. McIntosh, Shawn. II. Title. III. Title: New
introduction to mass communication.
  P90.P3553 2013
  302.23--dc23
                                    2012043555

Printing number: 9 8 7 6 5 4 3 2 1

Printed in the United States of America
on acid-free paper.

To my wife, Jackie, and my daughters, Tristan and Orianna   —J.V.P.

To my parents, Dennis and Kathie   —S.M.

BRIEF CONTENTS

CONTENTS

MEDIA LITERACY IN THE DIGITAL AGE 34

PRINT MEDIA: BOOKS, NEWSPAPERS, AND MAGAZINES 70

FEATURES

FEATURES

7 NETWORKS AND DIGITAL DISTRIBUTION   198

8 SOCIAL MEDIA AND WEB 2.0 **236**

PART 4   MEDIA PERSPECTIVES

9   JOURNALISM: FROM INFORMATION TO PARTICIPATION **266**

10 ENTERTAINMENT **300**

11 ADVERTISING AND PUBLIC RELATIONS: THE POWER OF PERSUASION 336

PART 5 MEDIA AND SOCIETY

MEDIA ETHICS **374**

COMMUNICATION LAW AND REGULATION
IN THE DIGITAL AGE **400**

14 MEDIA THEORY AND RESEARCH: FROM WRITING TO TEXT MESSAGING **432**

15 MASS COMMUNICATION AND POLITICS IN THE DIGITAL AGE 462

FEATURES

Egypt's former president Hosni Mubarak witnessed first-hand the power of media convergence in the spring of 2011. Thousands of students and other citizens mobilized via social media such as Twitter, Facebook, and YouTube and mobile communication against his long-standing regime, ousting the dictator after weeks of well-organized protest.

What the world has come to know as the Arab Spring demonstrates not only the influence of media convergence but also the increasingly global nature of media in the digital age. As citizen protests surged, words, pictures, and video traveled almost unobstructed from Cairo's Tahrir Square and elsewhere throughout North Africa and the Middle East to the rest of world. Professional journalists reported the story via traditional and new media, providing context to complement the real-time data streaming via citizens' cell phones and social media.

Meanwhile, the continuing transformation of media into digital form has continued unabated. Digital distribution is now the dominant format for music, television, and radio, whether terrestrial, satellite, or Internet-delivered. Thanks to tablet devices such as the iPad, the Kindle, and the Nook, the rise of the ebook has seen a dramatic surge in the popularity of digital book distribution. Newspapers and magazines, which have experienced significant declines in print circulation, are nonetheless seeing growth in tablet, smartphone, and online distribution. Digital motion picture distribution is also becoming mainstream, especially as 3D movies grow in popularity and movie distributors such as Netflix move into the online arena to complement their DVD business model.

To best understand how convergence affects our lives on many levels, we need to understand traditional mass media forms and industries, which still largely determine what content we get. Research shows that we spend more time watching television, about thirty hours a week, than with any other medium. In fact, by the time most of us turn seventy-five, we will have spent fourteen years of our lives watching television. In contrast, we spend an average of about eighteen hours a week online. This translates into about nine years of our lives online by age seventy-five. If we add in the myriad other screens we spend time with today, including movies, computers, tablets, PDAs, or smartphones, the numbers grow even greater. Today's digital natives spend far more time staring at screens in one form or another than older generations, and as we utilize even more media in digital form, this trend is sure to continue.

Rarely have there been such differences in media usage between the digital natives and those who grew up in a pre-Internet era of mass communication. One group may enjoy reading a printed newspaper over breakfast; the other may get their news on a tablet—if they get any news at all. One group may have impressive collections of CDs and DVDs; the other group may have their music and movie collections in the digital, online "cloud" and accessible from any location or on their portable devices. The younger group may worry how increased product placement may affect the type of shows that are produced; the older group may wonder what product placement is and why it matters. One group may believe that it is nobody's business what their relationship status is; the other group may publicly post that and much more personal information on social-networking sites.

Interestingly, this media divide is often represented in the college classroom, where college students are the digital natives and their professors are from an older mass media tradition. Yet the two parties converge, just like the media discussed in this book, to form a greater understanding of where media has been, where it is today, and where it is going.

One way to look at the state of mass communication today is that convergence is bringing us the kinds of tools that audiences have long wanted with their media—the ability to have greater control over what they watch, read, or listen to; and the ability to share their stories and their lives with others. And, as some embattled Egyptian revolutionaries might tell us, convergence brings us the ability to connect with others and change the world when needed.

▲▼ *Converging Media*, Third Edition: An Updated Introduction to Mass Communication

Change is a constant in the mass communication industry and in recent years this transformation has rocketed forward with surprising speed. Students are changing. The field is changing. The world is changing. Yet these changes go largely unnoticed in most textbooks. An introductory textbook should provide a foundation of knowledge for students learning a new field. But when the foundation sits on a bed of shifting sand, the introduction needs to be revised continually.

Converging Media: A New Introduction to Mass Communication embraces the metamorphosis of today's mass communication system and examines the changes even as it prepares students for what comes tomorrow. This book represents the beginning of a third wave in mass communication textbooks, building on the earlier waves of case studies and critical-cultural approaches. This new approach demands a more balanced and nuanced understanding of the role that technology and digital media have played in our mass communication environment.

The third edition of *Converging Media* follows the class-tested formula of the previous edition by offering:

- **A Fresh Perspective.** Through the lens of convergence, our book shows how different aspects of media are parts of a whole and how they influence each other. Digital media are not relegated to special features or an isolated chapter; they are integrated throughout every chapter. This better reflects the world as students live in it and prepares them to understand the changes that are taking place. This organization invites students and professors to engage in timely discussions of media within a larger framework of understanding traditional mass communication topics.

- **Comprehensive Coverage of Traditional Media.** In order to understand the present, we have to study the past. We cover the development and historical influences of print and electronic media, and the issues these media face today. The communication professions of journalism, advertising, and public relations are viewed from historical, societal, and career perspectives, giving students insights into how they interact and influence each other. Basic information on computers and networks also gives students a clear understanding of the media they use every day.

- **Unique Coverage of Social Media.** As the first introductory mass communication textbook to devote a chapter to this emerging area, we place social media within a larger media and sociocultural context while explaining basic principles of social networks and why they are important for a basic understanding of today's mass communication. Popular social media tools used widely by people today are given a historical context and thematically connected to older online communication tools. Social media are such an integral part of the media mix for so many people that they must be covered in an introductory course, not introduced in an upper-division media and technology course.

- **Cutting-edge Examples.** We have chosen examples that are diverse, interesting, and up to date. We have written *Converging Media* with students always in mind—understanding the changing world they live in today. Taken from popular media that are familiar and relevant to undergraduates, the examples illustrate how the landscape of media has evolved—and is still evolving.

- **Cultural Context.** Mass communication, media technologies, and convergence take place firmly within a sociocultural milieu that simultaneously affects and is affected by these forces. Understanding this cultural context is vital for a complete grasp of convergence and today's media environment. The authors emphasize the cultural influences and implications of media technologies while explaining how they work and how they were developed.

- **Emphasis on Ethics.** The book now has a new chapter devoted entirely to ethics (Chapter 12) and continues to thread ethics-related discussions throughout other chapters, as appropriate. Students should learn that ethical considerations are tightly linked to a full understanding of mass communication and media. Ethics can also help guide us in the complex and often confusing world of converging media, giving a basis for sound and humane decisions on media use and production and new technologies, and the way they affect people.

- **Integration of International Perspectives.** In a global media environment, it is hard to package all things international in a stand-alone chapter. As with ethics, global issues affect domestic media and vice versa, and this text highlights international perspectives in feature boxes and in the text itself. Through comparisons and contrasts, students obtain an appreciation for different media systems throughout the world and how they work.

◤▼ Features for Students

We have kept features limited and focused on a few key areas that will help bring out interesting and relevant aspects of the content discussed in the book.

- **Convergence Culture** boxes showcase how media impact our social, political, and popular culture in sometimes dramatic ways.
- **Convergence Context** boxes explore hard-to-understand concepts in fresh and engaging ways, making them easier to grasp and more relevant to students' lives.
- **International Perspectives** boxes take a global perspective on chapter topics, showcasing how media and technology use and media industries are similar to or different from the U.S. context and why that is so.

- **Timelines** provide a history, or even pre-history, of different media, such as newspapers, television, or social networking site launches, giving the context for their development.
- **Media Pioneers** boxes offer personal mini-biographies of visionaries and leaders in the world of media both historically and in the contemporary scene.
- **Ethics in Media** boxes, appearing in select chapters, discuss timely issues related to ethical practices and issues in mass media.
- **Media Quizzes** provide a lighthearted yet pedagogically sound way to measure students' knowledge of traditional and digital media and to give them a new awareness of their media usage.
- **Discussion Questions and Further Reading** assignments round out each chapter.

▲▼ Changes from the Second Edition

This third edition has undergone several major changes to keep pace with the rapidly evolving world of media.

- **New Chapters and Revised Organization.** We have divided the previous chapter on media literacy and ethics into two stand-alone chapters to expand the discussion of each of these critical topics. Media literacy comes first as Chapter 2, while ethics opens Part 5 of the book on media and society, as Chapter 12. Among the updates to the ethics chapter is a close examination of the *News of the World* hacking case in London, England, which dominated much of the media world's attention in mid-2011 and led to the downfall of that 167-year-old newspaper.
- **New Digital Media Coverage.** Chapters 3, 4, and 5 have undergone major updating, as the digital revolution has swept through those industries. In Chapter 3, *tablet technologies* in the form of the iPad, Kindle, and the like have made the *ereader* and *ebooks* viable and increasingly popular among both consumers and media entrepreneurs. In Chapters 4 and 5, the music, radio, motion picture, and television/video industries have undergone sweeping changes in recent months and years.
- **New Social Media Revolution.** Part 3 reflects the changing media environment, especially advances in the realm of social media and Web 2.0 and digital distribution. *Social networks* have taken center stage in much of the media world and this edition of the book incorporates this development. A new feature box, **Media Pioneers**, offers students a helpful glimpse via personal mini-biographies into the lives and contributions of the innovators and leaders who have shaped and continue to shape the world of media.
- **Reflections on News, Entertainment, and the Impact of Media on Society.** We have made extensive updates to Parts 4 and 5. Chapter 9 contains new material on *citizen journalism,* as well as the integration of social media in online news outlets like the *Huffington Post,* which won a Pulitzer in 2012. Chapter 10 features new material about *video and video games,* as well as developments in *reality television* and other parts of television and the movie business. In addition to featuring a new chapter on *media ethics,* Part 5 has been substantially updated throughout all of its chapters. Chapter 13 has considerable updates on developments in *communication law and regulation,* as important FCC policies and Supreme Court rulings have been incorporated. The recent debates over measures to fight Internet piracy (SOPA and PIPA) also appear. Insights garnered from recent media investigations have been synthesized and added to Chapter 14 on media theory

and research. Finally, we have added fresh perspectives on the evolving influence of mass communication, including social media, on politics in the digital age.

How the Book Is Organized

Converging Media has the comprehensive mission of explaining not only the world of digital media and social media but also the basics of communication theory, ethics, and traditional mass-communication forms, while also assisting in the development of media literacy skills. It does this using a class-tested, multipart structure.

Part 1: The Changing Media Landscape

Chapter 1 not only explains the multifaceted nature of convergence (and disputes over its definition) but looks at *theories of communication* in general to see how the nature of mass communication is changing. **Chapter 2** discusses *media literacy,* which helps meet students' need for solid critical-thinking skills in the twenty-first century's complex and fast-changing digital media environment. Providing an early foundation in media literacy is a good way to insure students will bring a critical perspective to the remainder of the book.

Part 2: Mass Communication Formats

Chapter 3 begins the exploration of traditional media with a discussion of the print industry and the digital dynamics to which it is now subject. **Chapter 4** explores sound—namely, the recording industry and radio. The recording industry has of course been at the forefront of changes that digital media have brought to their industry through music file sharing, and radio is increasingly facing questions about its role as people come to expect music on demand and there are more options for bands to promote their music, such as in video games and on television shows. **Chapter 5** looks at visual media—photography, movies, and television—and how each of these developed and influenced the ways that we see media. Photography is often ignored in books such as this but is an important aspect of the development of our media usage. Technological advances in photography not only led directly to motion pictures, but contributed to the increased importance we place on visual media today.

Part 3: How Digital Media Are Changing Our World

The part of the book containing **Chapters 6, 7**, and **8** is unique to this course. We explain how *storage capacity, user interface,* and *interactivity* play fundamental roles in the development of media, especially digital media, the subject of **Chapter 6**. **Chapter 7** explores the nature of telecommunication networks and how digital distribution and government policies have influenced the development and use of the Internet and other broadband delivery media in different countries. **Chapter 8** addresses *social media* and *Web 2.0* and basic concepts around social networks. Even if specific companies that are popular today fail, the principles discussed in this chapter will apply to whatever new social media take their places.

▲▼ Part 4: Media Perspectives

Chapters 9, 10, and **11** examine the history of the communication professions, and the changes now taking place. Journalism, the subject of **Chapter 9**, is probably the field most threatened by the digital democratization of news reporting. Yet it is also an exciting field to enter precisely because of the nature of social media and journalism's important role for democracy and people who want more democratic forms of government. *Entertainment* is the subject of **Chapter 10**, and it is hard to ignore as a powerful force when considering the role it plays in terms of culture and economics. Intertwined with and supporting both journalism and entertainment are *advertising* and *public relations,* the subjects of **Chapter 11**. These two areas are also facing drastic changes in some of their basic professional assumptions, in part because the public can now talk back to media producers and companies and because advertisers face more fragmented audiences with greater media choices than in the past.

▲▼ Part 5: Media and Society

The purpose of Part 5 is to show connections between media and society. **Chapter 12** examines media ethics, providing an in-depth discussion of the ethical issues each profession faces. We explore the unique dilemmas raised by digital technologies, including the threats to privacy and the digital divide. **Chapter 13** explores *legal and regulatory aspects of media*, especially as related to the First Amendment. For students interested in gaining a deeper understanding of media or who are considering a career in academia, **Chapter 14** provides a good introduction to some of the media theories and introduces the communication professional to different types of research and the strengths and weaknesses of each. **Chapter 15** makes a thorough examination of *politics and communication,* an area that, in introductory books, is often confined to examining U.S. election coverage. We introduce the notions of the *public sphere* and *public opinion* and look at the media's role in democratic and nondemocratic countries throughout the world.

▲▼ Supplements

Adopters of the third edition of *Converging Media* will be pleased to know that Oxford University Press offers a comprehensive support package for both students and instructors, for all kinds of introductory mass-communication courses.

▼ FOR STUDENTS

- The **Companion Website** at **www.oup.com/us/pavlik** offers a wealth of study and review resources including activities, flashcards for key terms in the book, interactive self-tests, objectives, summaries, and web links to a variety of media-related websites.

▼ FOR INSTRUCTORS

- **Instructor's Manual and Test Bank**, by Tamara Henry of the University of Maryland, College Park, provides teaching tips, exercises, and test questions that will prove useful to both new and veteran instructors. The Instructor's Manual includes chapter objectives, detailed chapter/lecture outlines, discussion topics, and suggested activities for each chapter. The comprehensive Test Bank offers numerous exam questions for each chapter in multiple-choice, true/false, and essay formats.

- **Instructor's Resource CD with Computerized Test Bank**, available to adopters, includes the full Instructor's Manual and Test Bank, as well as computerized testing software and new PowerPoint-based lecture presentations by Michael Evans of Indiana University.
- **Instructor's Companion Website** at **www.oup.com/us/pavlik** is a password-protected site that features the Instructor's Manual, PowerPoint-based lecture slides, and links to supporting materials.
- **Course cartridges** for a variety of e-learning environments allow instructors to create their own course websites with the interactive material from the instructor and student companion websites. Contact your Oxford University Press representative for access or for more information about these supplements or customized options.

Acknowledgments

Creating a book such as this is very much a collaborative effort, and the authors have benefited greatly from the advice and wisdom not only of the reviewers, listed below, but of those who adopted the first and second editions of the book. These early adopters, in all senses of the word, sometimes had to work hard to persuade colleagues and departments that *Converging Media* was the text to use to introduce students to mass communication. We can only hope that the argument is easier to make with the third edition as we witness a growing number of books about media convergence in the market.

We would also like to thank the adopters who wrote to us over the years asking when a revised edition would be published, and who offered encouraging words about the usefulness of the book when there were still plenty of professors who were not convinced that a new approach to teaching mass communication was needed, or who thought that only minor tweaks to curricula would do the trick.

John truly appreciates the love and support of his family, especially his wife, Jackie, and daughters, Orianna and Tristan. Shawn is similarly grateful for the love and support of his wife, Naren, and son, Altan, who was good at reminding him that there is always time for tickling and "wrestle-fighting."

We want to especially thank the editors at Oxford University Press with whom we worked: Mark T. Haynes and Peter Labella, our editors; Thom Holmes, development manager; Danielle Christenson, development editor; Caitlin Kaufman, assistant editor; Kate McClaskey, editorial assistant; and Erin Brown, marketing manager. They immediately understood and shared our vision of what this textbook should and could be to introductory mass-communication courses. Their insights, advice, and willingness to accept sometimes drastic changes to the organization and structure of the text helped this book surpass our expectations. We are also grateful for the fine job of the production group: our managing editor, Lisa Grzan; project manager, Kate Scully; art directors, Paula Schlosser and Betty Lew; and designer, Binbin Li. Copyeditor Deanna Hegle also helped clarify and simplify and made great improvements throughout the book.

And last but certainly not least, we wish to thank the following reviewers for the detailed and insightful feedback on various chapters of this book:

Lonny J Avi Brooks, *Cal State East Bay*
Ovril Patricia Cambridge, *Ohio University*
Skye Dent, *Fayetteville State University*
Marie Dick, *St. Cloud State University*
Paul Glover, *Henderson State University*
Chandler Harriss, *Alfred University*
Myleea D. Hill, *Arkansas State University*
Hans Ibold, *Indiana University*
Daekyung Kim, *Idaho State University*
Viktoria Kreher, *Southern Illinois University Carbondale*
Carole McNall, *St. Bonaventure University*
Robert M. Ogles, *Purdue University*
Ted Satterfield, *Northwestern Oklahoma State University*
Lauren Reichart Smith, *Auburn University*
Elyse Warford, *Georgia State University*
Scott Winter, *University of Nebraska–Lincoln*

SECOND EDITION REVIEWERS
Charles Apple, *University of Michigan–Flint*
Charlyne Berens, *University of Nebraska–Lincoln*
William R. Bettler, *Hanover College*
Joseph S. Clark, *Florida State University*
David Cundy, *Iona College*
James Ettema, *Northwestern University*
Michael Robert Evans, *Indiana University*
Thom Gencarelli, *Manhattan College*
Roger George, *Bellevue College*
Donald G. Godfrey, *Arizona State University*
David Gore, *Eastern Michigan University*
Margot Hardenbergh, *Fordham University*
Chandler Harriss, *Alfred University*
Karima A. Haynes, *Bowie State University*
Jeffrey B. Hedrick, *Jacksonville State University*
Tamara Henry, *American University*
Patricia Holmes, *University of Louisiana–Lafayette*
Seok Kang, *University of Texas–San Antonio*
Greg Lisby, *Georgia State University*
John Madormo, *North Central College*
Charles Marsh, *University of Kansas*
Stephen J. McNeill, *Kennesaw State University*
Olivia Miller, *University of Memphis*
James E. Mueller, *University of North Texas*
Robert M. Ogles, *Purdue University*
Selene Phillips, *University of Louisville*
Marshel D. Rossow, *Minnesota State University–Mankato*
Ted Satterfield, *Northwestern Oklahoma State University*
Randall K. Scott, *University of Montevallo*
Brad Schultz, *University of Mississippi*
Arthur L. Terry, *Bethel University*
Mina Tsay, *University of Kentucky*

About the Authors

John V. Pavlik is professor and chair of the Department of Journalism and Media Studies at the School of Communication and Information, Rutgers, the State University of New Jersey. He is also director of the Journalism Research Institute at Rutgers and faculty associate at the Columbia Institute for Tele-Information. Having published widely on the impact of new technology on journalism, media, and society, Pavlik has also authored more than a dozen computer software packages for education in journalism and mass communication. He is co-developer of the situated documentary, a new type of digital storytelling using mobile augmented reality. He is a former senior fellow at the San Diego Supercomputer Center and was the inaugural Fulbright Distinguished Chair in Media Studies in 2008 at the Academy of Fine Arts, Vienna, Austria. He received his PhD and MA in mass communication from the University of Minnesota and is a 1978 graduate of the School of Journalism and Mass Communication at the University of Wisconsin at Madison.

Shawn McIntosh is a lecturer in strategic communication at Columbia University's School of Continuing Education, where he teaches graduate courses in critical thinking, ethics, and digital media. He was an adjunct faculty member at Iona College, where he taught online journalism, website publishing, feature writing, and information visualization; he has taught a course on media ethics at Rutgers University. McIntosh was an editor and freelance writer for ten years for various newspapers and magazines in the UK, United States, and Japan. He was also co-site manager and senior producer at Fathom, an online educational website consortium of leading academic institutions, museums, and research organizations in the United States and England. His research interests include social media; media, power, and democracy; and citizen journalism. He received a BS in microbiology from the University of Idaho and an MS in journalism from the Graduate School of Journalism at Columbia University.

THE **NEXT STEP** IN THE EVOLUTION OF THE
INTRODUCTORY MASS COMMUNICATION TEXTBOOK

C H A P T E R S

"FIRST WAVE" | INDUSTRY	"SECOND WAVE" | CULTURE	"THIRD WAVE" | CONVERGENCE
Focus on **industry** analysis and on careers in mass communication; formats covered separately in different chapters; discussions of the Internet and new media are treated historically, not as central forces in communication.	Focus on **culture**—media formats still divided into different chapters, but now most chapters include a cultural component. Sequence is variable; history and intro merge; discussion of Internet moves up but still treated as separate media.	Focus on **convergence**—the *industrial, cultural,* and *technological* synthesis of media in the digital age; similar formats discussed in the same chapter, giving rise to new chapters on implications of digital media; ethics and literacy now have their own separate chapters to underscore their importance; cultural contexts and global perspectives integrated throughout. (Pavlik/McIntosh)

FIRST WAVE	SECOND WAVE	THIRD WAVE	Notes
Introduction	Introduction & History	Mass Communication and its Digital Transformation	
Industry History	The Internet & New Media	Media Literacy in the Digital Age	*Now up front in its own chapter, due to importance in today's media*
Newspapers	Newspapers & Journalism	Print Media: Books, Newspapers, and Magazines	
Magazines	Magazines & Specialization	Audio Media: Music Recordings, Radio	*The same formats are discussed—but they are now grouped together to enable a more in-depth discussion of the impact of digital media convergence*
Books	Books & the Power of Print	Visual Media: Movies and Television	
Radio	Radio & Popular Broadcasting	Information Overload, Usability, and Interactive Media	
Sound Recording	Sound Recording & Music	Networks and Digital Distribution	
Motion Picture	Movies & the Impact of Images	Social Media & Web 2.0	*Unique Chapters*
Broadcast Television	Television & Visual Culture	Journalism: From Information to Participation	
Cable, Satellite, Wireless	Cable & the Wireless World		
The Internet and the World Wide Web			
News Reporting	Journalism and Ethics	Entertainment	
Public Relations	Public Relations	Advertising and Public Relations: The Power of Persuasion	*Unique*
Advertising	Advertising	Media Ethics	
Global Media	Global Media & Economics		*Global perspectives are integrated into **Converging Media** chapters via "International Perspectives" sections, rather than a standalone chapter on Global or International Media*
Ethics	Media Effects & Research	Communication Law and Regulation in the Digital Age	*Theory & research discussed together*
Cultural Effects of Media		Media Theory and Research: From Writing to Text Messaging	
	Legal Controls and Freedom of Speech	Mass Communication and Politics in the Digital Age	*Unique*

*Cultural issues are now integrated throughout textbooks that focus on culture; this integration continues with **Converging Media***

1

MASS COMMUNICATION AND ITS DIGITAL TRANSFORMATION

LEARNING OBJECTIVES

By the end of this chapter
you should be able to:

- Define convergence.

- Discuss the main types
  of convergence and
  their implications for
  communication.

- Explain the eight major
  changes taking place
  in communication
  today because of
  convergence. Define mass
  communication.

- Describe the basic theories
  of mass communication.

- Identify the basic
  components and functions
  of the mass-communication
  process.

One concern critics have long had about the Internet and digital media is our ability to create "The Daily Me," a highly personalized online newspaper that contains only information that the user is interested in. The concern with The Daily Me is that we may self-select such a unique range of interests that it leaves us unable to discuss in a meaningful way with others matters of broader public importance.

Some sites have taken the notion of The Daily Me one step further, making it easy for users to create personalized, automatically updated online newspapers based on Twitter or Facebook feeds. Sites like Paper.li, TweetedTimes, and PostPost all work basically the same way. They let users select certain types of content based on keywords or hashtags and create their own news feeds, or allow them to choose material that comes to their personalized site that matches their search criteria. What's more, users can then send their social media "newspaper" to their social network, letting their friends get the same summary.

There is nothing exactly new about aggregating and distributing news content—print magazines like *Time* were created on the same principles. But what has changed is that now anyone can do much the same thing with social media. Some see this as a good thing, letting us efficiently cut through the clutter of information to see meaningful aggregations of content. Others see it as an echo-chamber of trivial information.

"At its best, the Internet can educate more people faster than any media tool we've ever had," wrote journalist Thomas Friedman. "At its worst, it can make people dumber faster than any media tool we've ever had."[1]

The media of mass communication have long played a fundamental role in people's lives. The media inform, persuade, entertain, and even sell. Media can provide companionship. They can shape perception. They are fundamental to an informed and educated public.

We will examine the nature of mass communication and how it is changing in the so-called digital age, the age of computerization of the media in a world connected by electronic networks. Far more than just a technological change, this change is cultural, social, and economic. Journalists, public relations professionals, advertising practitioners, and content creators, as well as media consumers, are facing a new world of media symbols, processes, and effects.

Few communications technologies better encapsulate the fundamental aspects of convergence than two seemingly very different devices, the telephone and the television. We will first look briefly at the history and evolution of the telephone as a communications device, as it touches on almost every important issue that we are dealing with today in terms of the Internet and digital media. Furthermore, the phone continues to be at the heart of some of the most innovative changes taking place in how we communicate with each other and how we interact with the world and with media. At the end of the chapter we will take a brief look at the television and how it continues to be at the forefront of convergence and how it is changing our relationship with the media.

▲▼ Telephony: Case Study in Convergence

Although we may take the mobility of the cell phone for granted, this mobility has important repercussions for a wide range of activities. First, we are no longer tied to a specific place when making or answering a phone call. The question "Are you at home now?" when calling someone on a landline does not make sense—of course the person is home, otherwise they would not be able to answer the phone.

By being able to communicate anywhere and any time, you are able to coordinate with others in a much more fluid and spontaneous fashion than in the past. Prior to widespread use of cell phones, if you had a sudden change of plans (or change of heart) regarding a planned meeting with someone, you had very limited ways to let them know you would not show up. Coordinating meeting times and places among several people in a group took much more planning and did not allow for last-minute changes. Also consider how much more we talk on the phone when we carry it with us as opposed to those days when you had to travel to the location of the phone (e.g., at home, at a phone booth) to use it. This makes us more likely to

The Nature of "Intermass" Communication

Even before the Internet era, scholars were asking how mass media and interpersonal communication affected each other.[2] Where is the dividing line between interpersonal and mass communication in your media world?

1. Do you have a Facebook, LinkedIn, or other social-networking site page?
2. When did you create the page? Why?
3. How often do you update or add content to the page, and what prompts you to do so?
4. How would you feel if your professor or a potential employer visited your page?
5. Have you ever created a blog? What was it about?
6. Have you ever created a website? How many page views did it receive at its peak?
7. Have you ever responded to spam (unsolicited email advertising messages)?
8. Are you typically on the Internet when you watch TV, or do you use the Internet to find information on your favorite shows?
9. Do you typically text message or chat online with friends watching the same program?
10. Have you ever uploaded music or other content to file-sharing sites?

If you're like most college students, you will have done many if not most of these activities. This shows that the line between interpersonal and mass communication for you is a blurry one indeed. If you have created a page on a social-networking site, created a blog or website, or uploaded music to a file-sharing site, then you were essentially participating in mass communication, even if the reasons for doing any of these were profoundly personal or you only intended to share your site with friends.

call someone and share information on the spot than if we had to wait to get home to make a phone call. However, it also can mean that we are less likely to interact with those around us as we talk to distant others.

Our familiarity with the phone belies its revolutionary character from a communications perspective. Before the phone, people could not talk directly to others whom they could not physically see. If there was an emergency, the only way to inform the proper authorities was to physically go to where they were and let them know. The phone played a major role in changing our patterns of communication with each other and thereby changing social relations. But it was the telegraph, not the telephone, that first revolutionized our speed of communication.

The telegraph was the first means of electronic communication, using a series of dots and dashes on a keypad to spell out words. These signals were transmitted over telegraph wires connecting one location to another. Telegraph operators were specially trained to code and decode messages and the result was a thriving new industry that grew during the mid- to late nineteenth century. This innovative form of instantaneous communication led to entirely new kinds of business enterprises; personal messaging services and "newswire" services such as Reuters and Associated Press are examples.

Telephones adopted the principles discovered with telegraphy but allowed voice to be transmitted. Although Alexander Graham Bell is the inventor of record for the telephone in 1876, others were also working on how to transmit voice electronically through wires, and there is some evidence that Bell's invention may have borrowed liberally from existing patents by inventors trying to build similar devices. Still, after years of lawsuits, it was Bell who won out. This parallels the many suits and countersuits seen today as companies claim patent infringement on Internet or software inventions and technologies.

Regardless of who can claim credit for inventing the telephone, it was easier for the general public to use than the telegraph. Even so, it was not immediately thought of as an interpersonal communication device, largely because it was expensive and difficult to connect every single household to the telephone network. This parallels the "last mile" issue we see today regarding broadband, or high-speed, Internet connections coming directly into homes and touches on the importance of networks in our communication environment. It also highlights how new communications technologies often do not have "obvious" contemporary uses that seem apparent only much later. How they may be used or adopted is very much an open question that relies not only on the technology itself but on a range of economic, social, and cultural issues at the time.

As the telephone network spread, telephone lines started to clutter the landscape.

Despite the dramatic changes to communications the phone would bring, it was initially either ignored or thought of as simply a novelty when it was unveiled by Bell in 1876. Once some technological improvements were made, however, making it easier to hear and increasing the number of voices that could be carried on a single wire, the telephone became more widely accepted. The ring of the telephone was a death knell for most telegraph companies, just as later media technologies rendered earlier technologies from which they were built obsolete, changing entire industries.

Initially, especially in Europe, the telephone acted as a kind of early radio. Wealthy patrons paid a fee to listen to music performances that were sent along the wires, and some public venues would pipe in sermons or performances for their patrons.[3] For several years in Budapest, Hungary, Telefon Hírmondó delivered news over the telephone, with subscribers dialing in at certain times to listen to someone reading the news of the day. A similar service was also tried in 1911 in Newark, New Jersey, but only lasted for a few months before closing.

Delivering news over telephone wires therefore is not something new with the Internet, and it also shows how long before video recorders or TiVo were used that people recognized a desire for information and entertainment "on demand" by the public. What was still missing at that time was an economic model that could support a business like telephone newspapers. This issue is commonly dealt with today by media companies that need to see a return on investments before they are willing to experiment with new ways of doing business.

The decision whether to make the telephone a government-run agency or a private enterprise was an important crossroad, and the choices made in Europe (government) differed from those made in the United States (private enterprise). These choices had profound repercussions even into the twenty-first century that have influenced the development and perceptions of the control and use of the

Internet. This shows how new technologies often inherit and carry with them the baggage of historical decisions made much earlier.

In the United States, leaving the early development of telephone systems up to private enterprise resulted in many incompatibilities between competing systems. Local telephone companies sold their own telephones and these were often incompatible with other telephone systems. This might have prevented a person from calling somebody who used a competing phone provider. The issue of compatibility between systems is still seen today in the form of competing computer operating systems, gaming systems, Internet browsers, and other electronic devices including ebooks and tablet computers.

During the formative years of the telephone industry, the U.S. government sought to eliminate such incompatibilities in the phone network by granting one company, AT&T, a monopoly on the telephone system. This too had important repercussions for later developments in telecommunications. Just as the monopoly telegraph company Western Union had done in the late 1800s when it became apparent the telephone was a threat to its business, AT&T in the 1960s and 1970s tried to hamper the development of a new kind of network that would potentially hurt its business. The network that was needed for development of the Internet was not compatible with the system that AT&T used. Even though AT&T realized the new network was more efficient, the telephone company feared losing dominance and initially refused to adopt it.

Issues of government regulation and private enterprise, monopoly powers, and business interests at the expense of the public interest are still very much with us today. How much we pay for services, what companies charge and how they set up payment plans, and a variety of other business decisions are influenced by the laws and regulations that have been created, sometimes as a result of industry lobbying efforts.

Just as payment amounts and methods may influence how we use the telephone, social and cultural factors play an equally important role in determining whether a technology is adopted. With almost any new technology, people do not know how to act or interact with it. There is a story that in the early days of the telephone a farmer came to town to place an order for supplies. The store clerk told him to place his order directly with the company over the phone, so the farmer dutifully wrote out his order, rolled it up carefully, and then jammed the rolled note into one of the holes of the phone handset and waited.

If this seems too silly to be true, consider your own reactions when you are given a friend's phone to use or have to use a remote control that you are not familiar with. The variety of functions seen in phones today stretches the very definition of "phone" compared to even twenty years ago. For young people today, it would seem odd to have a phone that does not take pictures or contain an address book or video games. This can be seen in some of the complaints about the Apple iPhone, which cannot show video.

In short, the phone is continuing to evolve as a multifunctional communications device that connects us to the world of information through the World Wide Web as well as to our friends. It provides an almost seamless interface between interpersonal and mass communication, as we access the Web from it to read reviews on a restaurant we pass by, and as we snap a photo while in the restaurant and upload it to the Web or even post our review on the spot, after which it can be seen potentially by millions of people.

All these aspects of the development and use of the phone, ranging from the technical, legal, and regulatory to the economic, social, and cultural, touch on the

Today's cell phones typically have a variety of functions that have nothing to do with traditional functions of the phone.

notion of media convergence. But as we will see, "convergence" is a debated concept and has multiple layers of meaning. We will start to unpack these layers and will define it to show how it encompasses some of the most dramatic transformations taking place in communications today.

◣◥ Three Types of Convergence

Convergence is known broadly as the coming together of computing, telecommunications, and media in a digital environment. It is important to study and understand convergence because what would seem like technology or media issues have had profound influences on our economic, social, and cultural lives.

There is some disagreement among scholars over a single definition of convergence, an indication of the far-reaching consequences of the changes taking place in mass communication today. Indeed, these changes speak to the fact that there are many forces changing in ways that we do not yet have adequate descriptions for, nor do we fully understand yet how these changes will affect us. For now, the term "convergence" seems to come closest to encompassing many of these forces. Some argue that convergence has already happened, and in many respects you could say that is true. But we believe that convergence is an ongoing phenomenon that continues to shape the world of traditional media.

We can look at three main categories of convergence as ways to frame our understanding of the changes taking place today in the media industries: technological convergence, economic convergence, and cultural convergence. As you will see, these three categories actually overlap in many respects.

▼ TECHNOLOGICAL CONVERGENCE

Perhaps the most easily visible aspect of convergence is the rise of digital media and online communication networks. Technological convergence refers to specific types of media, such as print, audio, and video, all converging into a digital media form. Such types of convergence are becoming increasingly apparent in news organizations, for example, where today's journalists often need to be able to tell stories in text, audio, video, and even interactive media.

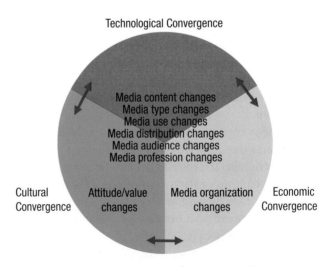

FIGURE 1-1 Three types of convergence and their influence on media.

Digital media often change the very nature of their traditional counterparts and affect how we use and perceive them. For example, although you can look at reading a book on Kindle as simply "print online," the fact is that a Kindle book alters the reading experience. One obvious way is that because of its storage capacity you can easily carry many books in one device, allowing you to move back and forth between books or to cross-reference passages quickly. Furthermore, you are able to change the text size to make reading more comfortable for you, look up words with a built-in dictionary, annotate and index sections, and even purchase new books on the spot through a wireless Internet connection. The notion of page numbers also becomes meaningless on a Kindle—much to the chagrin of students who realize they need to cite quotations taken from a book.

If most of these activities, such as looking up a word you don't know in a dictionary, seem like things that exist already with printed books, that is because they do. The difference is that you can do these activities within a single device rather than carrying a separate dictionary with you, or permanently marking in a book. Activities that used to be separate or cumbersome are now easier and folded into the media experience. It is not simply a matter of convenience—these changes fundamentally alter how we interact with our media. We may be far more likely to look up a word in Kindle than if we had to walk to the shelf to get the dictionary, for example. The music, television, and film industries, which we will look at in later chapters, provide other examples of how our media use changes thanks in part to changes in technology.

This form of convergence is very relevant today for communications professionals, but it is not the only way to think of convergence. The changes that come from new technologies also affect business models and established industries, which often see the upstarts as threats to their dominance. Sometimes, these upstarts become larger and more powerful than established companies; Google is a case in point. Because of the importance of networks in today's world, it is often advantageous for a company to control not only media content but the means of distributing that content through the networks, which is part of what economic convergence is about.

Ebooks like the Kindle have functions that help make for a unique reading experience.

▼ ECONOMIC CONVERGENCE

Economic convergence refers to the merging of Internet or telecommunications companies with traditional media companies, such as Comcast with NBC Universal. Traditional media companies have grown fewer and much larger in the past fifty years through mergers and acquisitions, a process we define as **consolidation**, not convergence. However, there is an element of economic convergence involved in many such consolidations when formerly independent and dissimilar media enterprises find themselves in the position of furthering the success of one another because they fall under the same corporate umbrella. Entertainment companies may own news stations; large corporations traditionally outside of the media business, such as GE, may purchase media companies like NBC. This can result in conflicts of interest when corporate parents don't want some aspects of their businesses covered in the news or when a news outlet gives prominent coverage to a movie coming out that is from the studio also owned by the corporate parent. The latter occurred in 2000, when *Time* magazine made a cover story out of Stanley Kubrick's last movie, *Eyes Wide Shut,* starring Tom Cruise and Nicole Kidman, which also got prominent play on other Time Warner media news outlets such as CNN's *Larry King Live.* The movie was from Warner Brothers studios.

consolidation

The process of large companies merging with each other or absorbing other companies, forming even bigger companies.

User-Generated Content: Creativity or Piracy?

With the ease of copying and altering digital content, almost anyone can take media content and make it into something different. Two or three popular songs from different artists can be combined and made into a new song; an artist's paintings can be manipulated digitally and mixed with one's own work.

Is this kind of content creation original art or is it copyright infringement, since it relies on preexisting art owned by someone else? What are the ethical and legal obligations of the creator who uses others' works?

Some make arguments that almost any creative work has been influenced by previous works encountered by the artist and that digital content simply makes it easier to make "mash-ups" of content. They argue that notions of copyright—essentially a government-granted monopoly to the content creator (or owner of the copyright, as is often the case with recording labels where the artists don't own the copyright)—is anachronistic in the digital age and increasingly stifles creativity through steep licensing or copyright fees. Copyright reduces the amount of creative material in the public domain, thus reducing the pool of works freely available.

However, copyright is still a cornerstone of media industries and a fundamental way in which media companies generate revenues. It is hard for most media industries, especially in entertainment, to envision a world with no copyright that would still allow them to create the kind of content they do.

Creative Commons has made a range of "copyleft" contracts for content creators that help ensure creative works remain in the public domain. Under the various contracts, content creators allow their content to be used by anyone for free, but they may make certain stipulations, such as that they must be credited or that the content can only be used if it isn't sold. One common stipulation within the community, however, is that people using the content must allow it to remain free for public use.

WEB LINK
Creative Commons
www.creativecommons.org

Economic convergence also has important repercussions for the nature of the media, telecommunications, and computing industries. A telecommunications company that also owns a media company can bolster the user experience for its own content at the expense of content from other companies by doing something as simple as speeding up transmission of its content and slowing that of other content. It could also control the type of content its customers see by blocking material from certain websites.

The Internet is not causing this type of behavior, as there are many historical examples of media owners censoring content that they did not like or blocking access by the public. But what makes this issue bigger and more prominent is the combination of consolidated media giants and ever bigger audiences. In other words, despite the explosion of channels and media content, our choices may not always be as broad as we may think. Consider the increasingly frequent temporary blackouts of channels as cable companies and media conglomerates fight over television licensing fees and let their agreements lapse. For example, over 3 million households on the East Coast missed the first two games of the 2010 World Series as Cablevision and Fox Networks fought over the terms of a new licensing agreement and Fox channels were suspended for Cablevision subscribers.

It is difficult to tell who won that battle in the court of public opinion, despite the fact that interactive media and the Internet have given the audience louder and more powerful voices than ever before. A kind of cultural shift is taking place, still in fits and starts, in which the relationship between the audience or public and media producers is changing.

▼ CULTURAL CONVERGENCE

Culture refers to the values, beliefs, and practices shared by a group of people. Culture may refer to a population at large, such as American culture, or to subgroups within a larger group, such as the traditions and practices shared by a specific professional group.

From this definition, one aspect of cultural convergence comes from the process of globalization of media content. Cultural convergence occurs, for example, when an HBO series like *Sex and the City* becomes wildly popular among female office workers in Thailand, or when a Mexican telenovela, or soap opera, finds avid mass audiences in Russia. The popularity of such shows across a variety of cultures demonstrates that there is some aspect to them that foreign audiences identify with or aspire to and indicates that there may be more in common between a young professional woman in Bangkok and one in New York City than would first appear.

But we can also look at cultural convergence from the perspective of how we consume, create, and distribute media content. The shift from a largely passive and silent audience that consumes media produced by large-scale media companies to an audience with nearly equal ability to produce and distribute its own content is one of the major themes of this book and a crucial aspect of cultural convergence.

A central premise of this kind of convergence is that although there will continue to be mass communication, in the sense that media companies and others will continue to produce messages for large audiences, audiences will more frequently receive personalized messages tailored to the needs of individuals. Furthermore, what was traditionally considered interpersonal communication, such as email, can be distributed through online networks in the same way that mass communication can, making the dividing line between interpersonal and mass communication increasingly hard to distinguish. The ability to better target audiences with personalized advertising and messages raises important issues of privacy, consumer rights, and media business economic models. Whether audiences will become more active in media production than in the past remains open to debate, although there are many examples throughout the book that substantiate this trend.

Digital technology has allowed more people to create professional-quality videos and other media content.

◢◤ Implications of Convergence

Whether society ultimately will be better served by an Internet-connected world is impossible to say. However, there is no doubt digital media are changing and will continue to change the relationship between mass-communication industries and the public. Media organizations face many challenges, but so do media consumers as the nature of our media environment changes. Some general trends can be discerned that will provide a better perspective on how our digital-media use is changing our media world and, by extension, our social and cultural worlds.

It is clear that the changes brought about by convergence have dramatic implications. Within the larger framework of the three types of convergence we see, these implications fall into eight areas of change:

1. Media organization changes
2. Media type changes
3. Media content changes
4. Media use changes
5. Media distribution changes
6. Media audience changes
7. Media profession changes
8. Attitude and value changes

These eight areas of change are recurrent themes throughout this book.

▼ MEDIA ORGANIZATION CHANGES

In the preconverged world, centralized media organizations created and published or broadcast content on predetermined schedules. A newspaper was printed and distributed daily or weekly; a television show appeared at a certain time on a certain day. "Centralized" media organizations are ones where content production and distribution, as well as marketing and other functions, are controlled by a central unit or individual. The economics of the media system throughout most of the twentieth century heavily favored a mass production model leveraging centralized control to produce efficiencies. The costs of content creation, production, marketing, and distribution were simply too great except for large companies.

Internet-based media can be less centralized, partly because many of the costs of the predigital era have been greatly reduced. Of course movies, television shows, and many other types of mass-produced media still rely on the old production and distribution models, but now there are new avenues for marketing and distribution over the Internet that make it easier for smaller media companies and even individuals to mass distribute their media products.

Most media companies throughout the world try to make a profit, with the exception of public service media. Many media companies are among the most profitable private enterprises in the world, with average profit margins often in excess of 20 percent a year—double the average for other industries. Advertising is one of the main means by which media companies earn revenues, but with the growing popularity of the Web, advertisers are spending less in traditional media than they used to. Furthermore, they are not making up the difference with online advertising. This has put a lot of pressure on many media companies, especially print media, which has seen the largest drop in advertising, and has led to layoffs, reduced printing and pages of newspapers and magazines, closings, and buyouts of struggling companies.

Concentration of media ownership, or consolidation, has been a growing trend even before digital media. Convergence is in some ways fuelling media consolidation by leading traditional media giants such as Time Warner to join with a former online colossus such as America Online, giving rise in 2001 to the short-lived AOL Time

Warner. In 2010, AOL, long jettisoned from Time Warner, bought one of the most popular blogs on the Web, *The Huffington Post,* showing once again how the differences between traditional technology companies and media companies are blurring.

The trend is clear; analog and digital media are rapidly being consolidated into the hands of a few very large, very powerful, and very rich owners, an economic structure referred to as an **oligopoly**. These media enterprises today are increasingly likely to be part of large, global media organizations publicly owned and accountable to shareholders whose main interest is the financial bottom line. When traditional telecommunications companies, like Comcast, join with large media companies, like NBC Universal, it gives the companies a great deal of centralized control over what access and content is available to media consumers, which is problematic.

Related to how media organizations are changing, the types of media or ways in which we get our media content are also changing. Although it may seem irrelevant for most of us whether we watch a television program on a TV or on a mobile device, it actually has far-reaching consequences for media organizations, advertising, and audiences.

oligopoly

An economic structure in which a few very large, very powerful, and very rich owners control an industry or collection of related industries.

▼ MEDIA TYPE CHANGES

Just what constitutes a television or radio receiver, or TV or radio programming, is in a state of flux. Once it was simple. Radio programming was what a listener heard on a radio. Today, however, there are radio stations that transmit their programming via the Internet or by satellite and listeners tune in via their computers. Moreover, these radio station websites can include images, graphics, text, and video, and listeners can choose what they want to hear or see when they want. The audience can sometimes even choose how they want to get content, such as watching a video, listening to the podcast, or reading the story. A growing number of print and radio reporters have been trained in digital video shooting and editing and can now be "VJs," or video journalists, webcasting their stories visually as well as through audio.

Defining media types reaches beyond whether we choose to watch a video or read the transcript. Entire media empires have been built on owning certain types of media, and complex laws and regulations have been created by the government to regulate different media industries and media ownership. For example, in the United States, print media enjoys more free speech protections than electronic broadcast media, which is more tightly regulated, and cable providers are treated differently than broadcast networks in terms of laws and regulations. This raises the question regarding how text on the Internet should be treated—does it have the same First Amendment protections as its print counterpart since it is simply words? Or should it be treated as electronic media since it is delivered electronically? And now as more people watch TV on their computers, what responsibility does the Internet provider play in all of this, since it is simply the channel and is not creating the content itself? Many of these questions have yet to be settled.

▼ MEDIA CONTENT CHANGES

Stories told in a digital, online medium can make connections with other types of content much more easily than in any other medium. This is done primarily through the use of **hyperlinks**, or clickable pointers to other online content. For example, online interactive advertisements permit visitors to click on the ads and go to the sponsor's website, or to play a game or take a survey. Or, in entertainment

hyperlink

Clickable pointer to other online content.

programming, hyperlinked content allows a viewer to explore a story in a nonlinear narrative, where the outcome of a story may be determined by the links the user chooses to click.

Moreover, on-demand content has become increasingly popular. In the traditional media world, news, entertainment, and marketing information was broadcast or published on a schedule solely determined by the publisher or broadcaster. Children growing up in an on-demand media world of YouTube, podcasting, and digital video recorders (DVRs) may not readily understand why the same rules don't always apply while listening to the radio or a traditional television channel that has not yet adopted on-demand features.

Digitization is transforming both how and when media organizations distribute their content. They no longer distribute content solely through traditional channels but instead deliver it via the Internet, satellite, and a host of other digital technologies. They are increasingly making that content available twenty-four hours a day, with news organizations updating the news almost continuously, and to a worldwide audience.

The production cycle and process is similarly being transformed by digital technology, as Figure 1-4 on page 28 shows. In fact, the transformation may be even deeper in terms of media-content production. Whether in Hollywood motion pictures, television shows or news, books, magazines, newspapers, or online, the process of producing media content is rapidly becoming almost entirely digital. Movies are shot using digital cameras and edited on computers. Reporters working for television, radio, newspapers, or any other news operation capture their raw material with digital devices as well, editing their stories digitally. Even book authors typically write on a computer, with words increasingly remaining digital throughout the entire production process, being read on e-readers.

Our understanding of most types of media content as static or unchangeable, such as a book, is being challenged by digital media. This can be seen especially in a

digitization

The process in which media is made into computer-readable form.

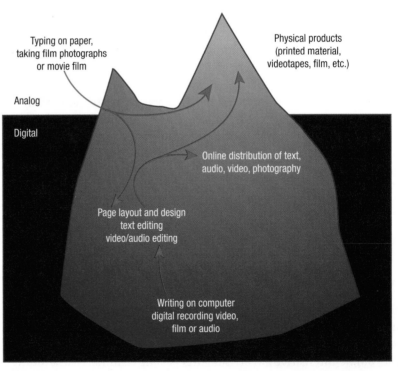

FIGURE 1-2 "Media Iceberg"

wiki. This is a type of website that can be edited by anyone, and the growing popularity of wikis, thanks in part to the success and attention of Wikipedia, shows that there was a pent-up demand among Web users for such a function. Now, that most staid form of print media, the authoritative encyclopedia article, begins to blur the line between news and encyclopedia as breaking news developments are added to Wikipedia articles.

wiki

A type of website that can be edited by anyone.

Of course content was never actually unchangeable; it just seemed that way. A book could be reprinted as a new edition, yet for most readers the changes made between editions were practically speaking impossible to discern. A book can now be seen as a much more fluid and changeable document online, with discussion forums on book material incorporated into the contents, ongoing discussions between the author and readers on a website, and interactions between readers.

Similarly, the idea of mash-ups of existing media has become common, thanks to digital editing tools for music and video. Any popular item produced from mass media (e.g., advertisements, movie trailers) has the potential of being transformed very quickly into a number of user-generated parodies or send-ups, most done simply for the fun of creating something rather than for commercial gain. Online discussions and mash-ups both share an important change taking place in digital media in that they show audience participation and are two of the ways in which people are changing their media use habits.

▼ MEDIA USE CHANGES

The pervasiveness of the media system means that wherever one goes there will likely be unprecedented access to mass communication. With today's global satellite communications, it is not possible to truly "escape" anywhere on the planet. In May 1996, climber and guide Rob Hall was trapped high on Mt. Everest for more than a day after a sudden storm hit. Unable to descend, unable to be rescued, and knowing he would die there, he was able to talk to his pregnant wife in New Zealand by satellite phone.[4]

A 24/7 media environment had begun to emerge even before the arrival of the Internet, and now it is fully here. This media environment has had several implications for how we use and what we expect from media, as well as for media industries. Media companies have to find content to fill the time, and thus we are seeing more "encore" performances of hit shows or movies on channels like TNT, showing the same movie two or three times in a row and on multiple nights. This is as much a nod to filling programming time as it is to understanding that viewers want more flexibility in their viewing schedules.

Portable media devices and flat-screen technologies mean that we can take our media with us and access it in places where we previously did not encounter media. Video displays in elevators or at checkout registers are two examples of how advertisers are using technology to reach captive audiences. Playing video games or watching videos on smart phones adds to the pervasiveness of media content in our lives.

Pervasive mass communication means better access to entertainment, information, and news—in theory. It can also mean that media organizations can turn us into super-consumers of media of questionable social or civic value. One can question the value of being able to watch a lowbrow reality show on your mobile phone while riding the bus, or of tuning others out with your iPod.

All of the activities mentioned here make a large assumption—that individuals either have ready access to computers, a broadband Internet (wired or Wi-Fi) connection, and the knowledge and skills to know how to use them. It is a world that

Mapping Sex Offenders

In April 2011 a female Hollywood executive sued online dating site Match.com after she was sexually assaulted by a man she met on the site. Her suit claimed that if the company had performed a background check on their members they would have discovered that the man, Alan Wurtzel, was a convicted sex offender for prior assaults on women he had met through the Internet.

Match.com responded the following week by promising to run sex offender background checks on all current and new members, even as the company expressed doubts about the reliability of the sex offender database.

The role of surveillance in our society becomes especially important when the public has easy access to data that used to be stored only in institutions. It strikes close to home when users can type in an address or zip code and see on a map where registered sex offenders live and work. Such sites include not only the addresses of the offenders but their pictures and information such as offense, year released from prison, and personal attributes like height, weight, and identifying marks. Users can sign up to receive email alerts when a sex offender registers or changes address in their neighborhood.

WEB LINK
Family Watchdog
www.familywatchdog.us

WEB LINK
Vision 20/20
www.thevision2020.com

Such sites have been lauded by parents' groups and child-safety organizations, yet they also raise some thorny ethical questions regarding rights of privacy and the potential for vigilante justice. One such case occurred in Evansville, Indiana, in early 2008 when would-be vigilantes tried to burn down the house of a registered sex offender—except they set fire to the wrong house.

Cases like this one reveal the power of personalized and localized information in surveillance when combined with easy access, but they also demonstrate the dangers of wrongly accusing people of crimes they did not commit.

many in advanced, industrialized countries may take for granted, but it is still far from a universal condition, even within developed countries.

Better Internet access has not come evenly to all, nor allowed everyone to benefit equally from that access. People in lower socioeconomic groups in industrialized countries have lagged in almost every category of Internet access. The high cost of telecommunication services, including broadband Internet, keeps many from being able to develop the skills and knowledge that can help them fully participate in society.

The United States has been slipping in high-speed Internet penetration and affordability for the services that are available and for Internet speed for users. The United States ranked twenty-fifth in 2010 in terms of Internet speed, trailing Romania, and Americans' average Internet speed was more than ten times slower than first-ranked South Korea.[5]

▼ MEDIA DISTRIBUTION CHANGES

Content is much more fluid, dynamic, and rapidly transmitted throughout the globe in an online environment. However, this is not without its dangers, as events in distant places can have far-reaching repercussions to others because of the reach of global media and instantaneous communications. False rumors about companies or company leaders, such as the email in late 2008 that falsely claimed that Steve Jobs had had a heart attack and that sent Apple's shares down for much of the trading day, demonstrate the power and danger of rapid global communication.

The Internet enables audiences around the world to participate in a global dialog about the world's events and issues and can bring individuals into direct contact with each other though they are separated by thousands of miles and political and cultural boundaries. It is not clear what the net effect of this sea change in communication will be, but it is clear the foundation is being laid for a more connected and engaged global public. However, this does not mean that increased connectivity and engagement among people will naturally lead to rational discussions or debates. It is likely the opposite will occur as people from different cultures discover that what they take as cultural "common sense" may be considered heresy by someone else. Consider the amount of vitriol seen in many discussion groups even among people who are from the same culture but who have differing opinions.

Audiences are increasingly active in their communication with each other and with the creators of mass-communication content. This gives them much greater control over what media they consume and shifts some of the power away from media organizations. Through **viral marketing**, or the online equivalent of word-of-mouth advertising, a popular website, product, or piece of content can potentially reach millions of online users in a very short time, all without corporate promotion or advertising dollars. The success of **peer-to-peer** (or P2P) file-sharing programs shows how an Internet audience shifts the balance of power away from media organizations, even though those organizations created and provided that content in the first place.

Digital media make it easier than ever for the public to create and distribute media content, whether it is **user-generated content** (UGC) such as an original drawing done using illustration software, an animation or video, or a song sampled and mixed from current hits by famous recording artists. Writing and music have led the way in media consumers creating content—especially music, where remixes of previously recorded (and copyrighted) material are common. This is not to say that the average person now has the same ability to produce and create a hit song as a major recording label, as an individual does not have the marketing and promotion capabilities that a recording label has at its disposal, but the basic capability of producing and distributing at least exists. Nevertheless, media companies have tried unsuccessfully to control the channels of media distribution like they used to, as the Internet has threatened their business models. It has also led to important changes in how audiences view and use content, and changed the relationship between media companies and their audiences.

▼ MEDIA AUDIENCE CHANGES

Traditionally, mass communication is largely one-way, from the source of a message to the receiver, or audience. The audience is relatively large, heterogeneous, and anonymous. Audience members have relatively few means by which to communicate either with each other on a mass scale or with the creators and publishers. Audiences in the age of convergence can now communicate via email, online forums, and other interactive media more easily and quickly with each other and

viral marketing

Spreading news and information about media content through word of mouth, usually via online discussion groups, chats, and emails, without utilizing traditional advertising and marketing methods.

peer-to-peer [P2P]

A computer communications model in which all users have equal abilities to store, send, and accept communications from other users.

user-generated content [UGC]

Content created by the general public for distribution by digital media.

with those who create and publish mass-communication content. In addition, they can create the content themselves and reach far larger audiences for much lower costs than they could have with traditional media. They are generally not anonymous, as they can be tracked through user names or IP addresses.

Audiences aren't willing to wait for the evening news or the next day's paper for developments in a breaking story. Audiences can get their information and entertainment from literally thousands of sources around the world. Audiences aren't content to sit back and listen in silence to what the media report; they actively seek the most recent information through blogs, instant messaging, and other informal communication channels. There have been cases of employees finding news of their company's planned layoffs through websites hours before the company officially announced the layoffs.

Digital media do not cause people to become active media producers, or "**produsers**," as they are sometimes called in an attempt to capture how we use (not just consume) and produce media content now. However, they do give people ready tools to produce media if they wish and to do so far more cheaply and easily than analog media. Active audiences have two important implications for media companies: they compete for limited time among the potential audience, and they can become more critical media consumers of the mass communication they do receive, which is relevant in media literacy, the topic that will be covered in the next chapter.

As produsers, audiences also learn to become more critical media consumers and to raise questions on the quality of news, information, and entertainment they get. The channels available through interactive media let the public speak directly to traditional media producers in a public way, thereby giving a sense of shared experience, even perhaps community, as people see that others may feel as they do that an advertisement was offensive or that a news story was inaccurate.

Active audiences are more likely to organize and work together on common problems, especially if they have developed trusted relationships through interacting with each other, than if they perceive themselves as isolated individuals or anonymous faces in a crowd who have no choices in determining what media they get.

These changes are not without some dangers, however. Actively choosing the media you want to see, hear, or read can narrow the scope of news items or entertainment that you may encounter by accident that unintentionally inform or entertain. Former MIT Media Lab director, the late Michael Dertouzos, called the specialization of news to one's specific interests "The Daily Me." This phenomenon could fragment audiences into small groups of like-minded individuals who do not interact with other groups and choose to receive only the news and information that reinforce their beliefs and values. Media fragmentation has already been a trend in analog media, and digital media can easily accelerate that trend. However, personalization and localization of news does have benefits in potentially getting the public to become more engaged in news and in helping people become better informed about current events.

▼ MEDIA PROFESSION CHANGES

With all the changes brought to mass communication because of convergence, it is obvious that the way communications professionals do their jobs is also changing. Just as print, video, and audio become absorbed as types of digital media, so the divisions will disappear between print and electronic journalists and between

produsers

The notion that audiences cannot simply be considered consumers anymore but also often take an active role in producing content or information.

advertising and public relations professionals. Newsrooms increasingly expect reporters to know how to use video and audio to tell stories as well as to write effectively. Advertising and public relations professionals will have to learn how to best attract the attention of a public that encounters ever more media and in which the public is more active than in the past.

But in order to take advantage of digital media, new skills will have to be learned and it will be more important than ever that the fundamental principles and ethics of each profession are not abandoned in the march toward the digital environment. This is no easy order given the pressure by corporate parents to blur the lines between news and entertainment, or news and promotion.

Giving the audience a chance to talk back and interact with journalists, as well as provide news coverage themselves in the form of **citizen journalism**, is another important development in journalism today. A mistake in a story can be publicly countered or corrected in the discussion section of the story and, if shown to be correct, can then be incorporated in a revised version. Citizens can provide news content or report on stories of relevance to their locales that big news operations may not deem newsworthy.

citizen journalism

Audience-generated feedback and news coverage.

▼ ATTITUDE AND VALUE CHANGES

Changes in audience interactions have had repercussions on what the public expects from its companies in general and media companies in particular. Members of the public are coming to expect a certain amount of transparency in their communications with each other and with leading organizations, including media organizations. There have been a growing number of cases in which organizations have been caught deceiving the public and have suffered damage to their reputations. One such example was Edelman, a global PR firm that financed the "Wal-Marting Across America" blog in 2006. The blog was ostensibly done by a couple traveling around the country in an RV, who liked to stay at Wal-Mart parking lots because of the free services offered for RVs. Of course, the couple had nothing but good things to say about Wal-Mart and its employees. When the truth was revealed that the couple was actually being paid by Edelman, whose client was Wal-Mart, debates raged on how ethical it was to have such a blog and not state who was funding it.

Because most people on the Web do not physically make contact with each other and know one another only through their online interactions and communication, establishing a sense of trust has become crucial. There are a growing number of reputation systems on the Web that attempt to help Web users do this, ranging from rankings such as on Amazon or eBay to the "karma points" on Slashdot, a popular technology news and discussion website.

This idea of managing one's reputation online, and how that may affect the offline world (imagine the consequences of getting bad reviews on eBay if you are trying to make a living selling items on the site), becomes important not only for companies but for individuals as well. Companies can fall prey to disinformation campaigns, and monitoring blogs and online discussions of a company become important.

At the heart of reputation and transparency is the idea of building relationships based on trust and respect. Media companies that do not realize this will suffer in the digital media world in the long run. For many, it means a shift in corporate policies or philosophies and a loss of the control they have enjoyed through much of the mass-communications era. There is a conventional wisdom among some executives that employees are more willing to spend company time doing personal things, like

Television dating shows have become very popular in China, offering viewers a titillating mix of sharp tongues, attractive young women, discussions about sex, and rampant materialism. In the most popular show, *If You Are the One,* produced by Jiangsu TV, a female contestant won notoriety when she was asked by a bachelor if she would like to ride on his bicycle with him. She said she would "rather cry in the back of a BMW" than be smiling on the back of a bicycle.

Another female contestant told the panel that if anyone other than her boyfriend wanted to hold her hand it would cost them $30,000.[6] These kinds of comments—combined with on-screen and off-screen scandals—have drawn the ire of China's television censors, who claim shows like these are corrupting China's youth with vulgarity and crass materialistic values. As a result, some shows were canceled, and those that stayed on the air toned down the more flamboyant aspects of the programs.

The popular dating shows form part of China's burgeoning commercial television industry. China's state-run television allowed commercial stations to start in the 1990s, but now may have created a dragon they cannot fully control.

Despite their periodic efforts to set strict guidelines to discourage materialism among Chinese youth, the effectiveness of their efforts is questionable. In April 2012, Chinese media reported that several people were arrested for being involved in a scheme in which a 17-year-old teenager donated a kidney because he wanted to buy an iPad and iPhone.[7]

shopping online, than they were in the past. But on the other hand companies are also expecting employees to stay longer at work and must realize that the blurring of company time and private time is a large-scale trend.

The convergence of digital media has led to confusion over our traditional notions of privacy, both for individuals and for companies. Although there have been a number of clear violations of privacy laws, even by traditional standards, there is also a lot of confusion over what is acceptable or even legal and what is not.

For example, a person writing a blog may consider it a private journal, or something intended for only a select audience of friends, and thus feel like her privacy was invaded and get angry when a potential employer mentions inappropriate postings during a job interview. Similarly, information that always has been public, such as property deeds or arrests by the police, but that has generally been cumbersome to retrieve, can now be easy to find online.

One component of privacy is the ability to be left alone, and this has become increasingly difficult in an age of pervasive media. Maintaining a sense of privacy can be difficult when we are getting barraged with updates from friends through social media or receiving text messages.

Wireless communication between devices, without the need for specific human direction—such as swiping a debit card at a supermarket checkout—makes it easy to paint a picture of a person simply through her electronic transactions over a short period of time. The ability to track consumers with such accuracy, especially on the Web, means that we can get more relevant or personal media content, but it also means we have provided a great deal about our personal habits and interests, not all of which we may wish to share with companies or advertisers who use that information for **behavioral targeting** in their advertising campaigns.

Mass-communication organizations can keep detailed and updated records on their audiences by tracking their paths within their websites through intelligent software agents and programs known as **cookies**.

Cookies allow a website to recognize when a previous user returns and to offer personalized content. Cookies provide invaluable information for media organizations to better understand an audience's media behaviors, preferences, and habits. Advertisers on websites also add cookies to your computer so they can track your browsing behavior as well. Surveillance is an increasingly powerful tool that is necessary to optimize content and to give advertisers a high return on their investment, even as it raises serious concerns about our eroding privacy.

So far we have discussed how convergence has been changing the media industries and their business models, the issues communications professionals have faced that are brought by new technologies, the nature of the relationship between media producers and audiences, and legal matters that have yet to be addressed. You have gotten a glimpse of the powerful transformations taking place today in mass communications and the media and will see even more examples in greater detail in subsequent chapters.

But before we can move forward we have to take a step back and look at what mass communication itself is and even how media scholars theorize how communication works. We will then be able to use these foundations to better understand the changes taking place today.

behavioral targeting

The use by advertisers of consumer buying patterns and preferences in advertising campaigns.

cookies

Information that a website puts on a user's local hard drive so that it can recognize when that computer accesses the website again. Cookies are what allow for conveniences like password recognition and personalization.

interpersonal communication

Communication between two or more individuals, usually in a small group, although it can involve communication between a live speaker and an audience.

mass communication

Communication to a large group or groups of people that remains largely unknown to the sender of the message.

Interpersonal communication takes place between two or more people, is interactive, and can happen face-to-face or through a medium.

◤◢ Mass Communication in the Digital Age

The traditional mass-communication model differs from other forms of communication, such as **interpersonal communication**, which is communication between two or more persons. Interpersonal communication often interacts with and intersects **mass communication**.

▼ INTERPERSONAL COMMUNICATION

Interpersonal communication is usually interactive, or flowing at least two ways, is generally one-to-one, and tends not to be anonymous. Think of chatting with a friend or talking with a small group of friends. Responses are generally immediate and the speaker or speakers will often adjust their messages based on the responses they receive.

These same principles apply to live public speaking, even though this is a one-to-many model and opportunities for audience feedback will be more limited than in a casual small-group setting. The speaker and audience can communicate through a variety of nonverbal cues, such as facial expressions, physical contact, or body language. If speakers see looks of boredom or audience members yawning, they can react to that feedback and try to make their presentations more interesting.

Interpersonal communication can also take place through a **medium**, or communication channel, such as talking on the telephone, instant messaging, or writing back and forth in a chat room. Note how the mediation limits some aspects of interpersonal communication compared to face-to-face interactions. There are no visual cues either on the telephone or online (unless using a webcam), and meanings can be misconstrued by text messages. The online medium also blurs the line between interpersonal and mass communication, as a chat room can have hundreds or thousands of participants.

medium
_____

A communication channel, such as talking on the telephone, instant messaging, or writing back and forth in a chat room.

▼ MASS COMMUNICATION

Media of mass communication refer to any technologically based means of communicating between large numbers of people distributed widely over space or time.

Since Johannes Gutenberg invented the Western world's first mechanical printing press in Germany in 1455, the media of mass communication have been characterized by a single, overarching model. This model has had the following four main characteristics:

1. Communication flow is largely one-way, from sender or source to receiver or audience.

2. Communication is from one or a few to many (i.e., one or a few sources generate and distribute content to large, heterogeneous audiences).

3. Communication is anonymous (sources generally do not know their audiences and audiences do not know the sources, except at a general level).

4. Audiences are largely seen as passive recipients of the messages distributed by the media, with little opportunity for feedback and practically no opportunity for immediate feedback or interaction with each other.

In other words, media companies create content they believe the audience will want and distribute that content to an audience that has very few ways to provide immediate feedback. This model has characterized all media of mass communication, whether books, magazines, newspapers, broadcast television or radio, cable or satellite TV, recorded music, or motion pictures. Digital media, however, are radically changing that model, as we will see throughout this book.

In the traditional mass-communication model, content creators play a fundamental role in society by representing and defining reality (as done by journalists or other communication professionals), or by authoring fictional narratives to explain, interpret, or entertain (as done by artists, authors, and film auteurs). Authors and artists create stories about issues and events, they write books and articles, they create music or motion pictures, and then they publish, broadcast, or present those stories at set dates or times and in set locations.

Some mass-communications models, such as live television or radio, are **synchronous media**. Synchronous media require the audience to be assembled simultaneously with the broadcast, transmission, or event. Others are asynchronous. **Asynchronous media**, such as newspapers or magazines, do not require the audience to assemble at any given time. Audio and video recording devices let people **time shift** and record a live concert or performance so it can be watched anytime, thereby turning synchronous media into asynchronous media.

▼ MASS COMMUNICATION AND CONVERGENCE

Digital media and online networks have blurred the line between interpersonal and mass communication. The media companies built on mass-communication models, despite facing many challenges in the digital era, are not disappearing anytime soon, and neither will certain fundamental aspects of mass communication.

What is changing, however, is the interplay between mediated interpersonal communication and mass communication: interpersonal communication is capable of adopting some characteristics of mass communication, and mass communication is trying to adopt certain characteristics of interpersonal in an attempt to remain relevant to audiences. Let's consider some examples.

Email is considered a form of mediated interpersonal communication, yet as anyone who has had their inbox clogged with forwarded jokes from Aunt Gertrude can attest, it can also be broadcast to many recipients, following the one-to-many model typical of mass communication.

Weblogs, or **blogs**, often feel interpersonal in tone and scope, yet some blogs have become very influential among the public or among decision makers, with readership greater than many well-established mainstream publications. Blogs may allow immediate feedback or discussion from readers, who often must be registered in order to write feedback and are therefore not anonymous—thereby weakening two of the linchpins in the definition of mass communication. Yet it is hard to claim that the most popular blogs are not a type of mass communication because of the numbers of audience members reading them and the lack of interaction between the blog author and a respondent.

Twitter also follows a blended mass communication and mediated interpersonal communication model, as people broadcast their tweets to thousands or even millions of followers, yet the followers can re-tweet and interact with each other and their followers.

Similarly, the fragmented nature of audiences on the Web makes defining a "mass" extremely difficult. Some websites have small but dedicated followings, while others have millions of visitors a month, reaching far more people than your typical local newspaper. Yet the local newspaper would be traditionally defined as a type of mass communication, whereas a YouTube video such as "Charlie bit my finger—again!," with over 296 million views almost three years after being posted and over two thousand various remixes and spoofs, would generally not be.

It is important to remember that much of the interaction and conversation that takes place between members of the public online does so because of the

synchronous media

Media that take place in real time, such as live television or radio, that require the audience to be present during the broadcast or performance.

asynchronous media

Media that do not require the audience to assemble at a given time. Examples of asynchronous media are printed materials and recorded audio or video.

time shift

Recording an audio or video event for viewing later rather than when the event was originally broadcast. Setting a VCR to record a favorite program while one is out is an example of time shifting.

blog

Short for "weblog," a type of website in which a person posts regular journal or diary entries with the posts arranged chronologically.

information and entertainment generated from mass communication. Although there are a handful of "Charlie Bit My Finger" fan clubs on Facebook (including a Mexican one), a TV series such as *Star Trek,* which ran for only three seasons in the late 1960s, continues to have a thriving fan subculture that creates—and consumes—content about the series and the actors in it, not to mention the various movies and television-series spin-offs from the original *Star Trek.* The daily mix of news, information, and entertainment that we consume through mass-communication channels gives us the fodder from which to create remixes, to blog, to interact with each other—and to talk back to the media producers who are giving us the content.

◥◣ Functions of Mass Communication

Defining mass communication was once a relatively straightforward matter. The media were relatively stable and well known. The functions of mass communication in society were also relatively well understood and thoroughly researched. Studies by Harold D. Lasswell, Charles Wright, and others suggest that these functions have tended to fall largely into four broad categories.[8] These functions can be a useful lens through which to understand how the various forms of mass communication work.

▼ SURVEILLANCE

surveillance

Primarily the journalism function of mass communication, which provides information about the processes, issues, events, and other developments in society.

Surveillance refers primarily to journalism, which provides information about the processes, issues, events, and other developments in society. This can include news on the latest military developments, weather alerts, and political scandals. Surveillance can also include aspects of advertising and public relations, as well as educational aspects of communication.

One weakness in the surveillance function is that too much news about disasters, murders, or other unusual events can skew the audience's perception of what is normal in society. Another weakness is that too much information can make the audience apathetic. Consider how media coverage of a scandal regarding a sports figure such as Yankees baseball player Alex Rodriguez can take on a life of its own and seem to continue forever, until we are truly sick of seeing any more stories about A-Rod.

The example may seem trivial in the case of celebrity scandals, but it takes on greater importance when one considers coverage of wars or disasters, especially in developing countries.

Journalists covering conflicts overseas represent one important aspect of the surveillance function of mass communication.

▼ CORRELATION

correlation

The ways in which media interpret events and issues and ascribe meanings that help individuals understand their roles within the larger society and culture.

Correlation refers to the ways in which media interpret events and issues and ascribe meanings that help individuals understand their roles within the larger society and culture. Journalism, advertising, and public relations all shape public opinion through comments, criticism, or even targeted marketing campaigns. Individuals may learn what others think about an issue through polls or surveys and thus get a sense of where their views fit within mainstream opinions. Some people may even subtly shift their views or beliefs to better correlate with a social group they aspire to. By correlating one's views with other groups or perceived notions of general public opinion, the media can help maintain social stability, although this function can be taken too far and the media can thwart social change or block a full range of views from being disseminated to a mass audience.

Interpretation can also tend to favor established business or elite interests over disadvantaged or minority groups, lending a sense of credibility and authority to certain views that may not be fair to all members of society.

▼ CULTURAL TRANSMISSION

Cultural transmission refers to the transference of the dominant culture, as well as its subcultures, from one generation to the next or to immigrants. This function includes socialization, which the media perform in helping persons learn society's rules or how to fit into society. This function is especially important for children but also is performed for adults who may have recently immigrated to a new country with a different culture.

The other side of the coin regarding the cultural-transmission function is a criticism that it creates a homogenized culture that promotes mindless consumerism as a means to achieve happiness, rather than imparting more humanistic, and ultimately more rewarding, values to people.

▼ ENTERTAINMENT

The entertainment function is performed in part by all three of these activities (surveillance, correlation, and cultural transmission) but also involves the generation of content designed specifically and exclusively to entertain. Although some say that this function helps raise artistic

Wartime propaganda posters provide windows into how public opinion can be shaped.

Commercials can be highly influential in shaping public tastes and fashions.

Entertainment is one of the most important functions of mass communication partly because of the cultural meanings it often transmits.

cultural transmission

The transference of the dominant culture, as well as its subcultures, from one generation to the next or to immigrants, which helps people learn how to fit into society.

and cultural taste among the general populace, critics argue that mass media encourage lowbrow entertainment at the expense of fine art, encourage escapism, and do not help raise the cultural level of society. It is also important to note that entertainment is often imbued with powerful cultural values and symbols that can easily be taken for granted but that play a role in transmitting specific sets of values.

Entertainment can also perpetuate certain stereotypes about various groups, wittingly or unwittingly. These can be especially hard to notice as they are often part and parcel of a story line or characters and can often seem "natural" in terms of the show.

◣◥ Theories of Communication

Underlying the functions of mass communication is a rich history of thinkers who have tried to understand how communication itself works and what exactly "communication" is. They have proposed a variety of theories on communication in their attempts to explain it. One of the earliest communication theorists was the philosopher Aristotle, who in 300 BCE called the study of communication "rhetoric" and spoke of three elements within the process: the speaker, subject, and person addressed. His basic ideas laid an enduring foundation for communication research, even today.

The need to better understand communication from a theoretical perspective arose with the importance that mass communication began to have in people's lives, especially as electronic communication such as radio and television became so dominant.

▼ TRANSMISSION MODELS

In 1949, scientists Claude E. Shannon and Warren Weaver formulated an influential model of communication.[9] It is known as a transmission model of communication and is closely related to communication theorist Harold Lasswell's famous question about media effects, which he posed in 1948. Lasswell asked, "Who says what in which channel to whom with what effect?" This model has allowed for many general applications in mass communication.

The Shannon and Weaver mathematical theory of communication, as they described it, is based on a linear system of electronic communication. The original formulation of the model included five main elements:

- Information source
- Transmitter
- Channel
- Receiver
- Destination

In this model, an information source formulates a message. A transmitter encodes the message into signals. The signals are delivered via a channel. A receiver decodes the signals, "reconstructing" the original message, which reaches its destination. The communication flow in this model is decidedly one-directional, from the sender to the receiver. The system has a limited capacity to provide feedback from the receiver to the information source: to acknowledge receipt of the

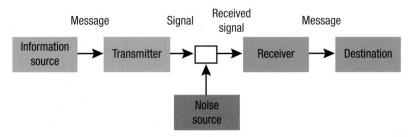

FIGURE 1-3 Shannon and Weaver. Mathematical Theory from *The Mathematical Theory of Mass Communication*. C. Shannon and W. Weaver. Copyright 1949, 1998 by Board of Trustees of the University of Illinois Press. Used with permission of the University of Illinois Press.

message, to indicate whether the message has been understood, and to communicate the receiver's reaction. The communication process can be adversely affected by noise, or interference, from the environment, possibly by way of competing, or distracting, messages, or even electrical interference. The original Shannon and Weaver mathematical theory of communication, or model, is depicted in the diagram in Figure 1-3.

The model clearly explains how a telephone works. The information source speaks (encoding a message), the phone (transmitter) transforms the sound waves into electrical impulses (the signal), which are sent over the channel (the tiny box in the center), and those electrical impulses are turned back into sound waves by the phone (receiver) at the other end of the line, where they are heard and (one hopes) understood (decoded) by another person (destination). "Noise" is any interference anywhere along the way.

The Shannon and Weaver model is especially technological in its orientation and therefore limited in its utility for understanding traditional mass communication because it does not fully reflect the role of humans in the process—specifically, how meaning is created. Moreover, the advent of digital, networked communication media is greatly expanding the interactive nature of communication, making the limited feedback capacity of the model more problematic even by its own standards.

Adapting the Shannon and Weaver model and integrating concepts from Aristotle, pioneering communication scholar Wilbur Schramm in 1954 developed a **simplified communications model** in the book *The Process and Effects of Mass Communication.*[10]

In the Schramm model, communication requires three main elements:

1. a source, who encodes

2. a message, or signal, which is transmitted (via the media or directly via interpersonal communication) to

3. a destination, where the receiver decodes it.

Significantly, Schramm envisioned the importance of understanding as part of human communication. Schramm realized that another important aspect of the traditional communication model needed correcting. In human communication, mediated or not, communication is not a one-way process. Schramm wrote, "In fact, it is misleading to think of the communication process as starting somewhere and ending somewhere. It is really endless. We are little switchboard centers handling and rerouting the great endless current of information." As a result, Schramm and Charles Osgood developed a circular model of communication. The

simplified communications model

Developed by Wilbur Schramm in 1954 and based on the mathematical theory of communication. It includes a source, who encodes a message, or signal, which is transmitted (via the media or directly via interpersonal communication) to a destination, where the receiver decodes it.

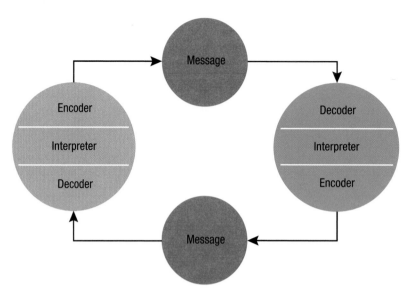

FIGURE 1-4 Schramm-Osgood Model. From *The Process and Effects of Mass Communication.* Wilbur Lang Schramm, ed. Copyright 1954 by Board of Trustees of the University of Illinois Press. Used with permission.

participants exchange roles of source/encoder and receiver/decoder. This model is depicted in Figure 1-4.

However, even this model, based on certain concepts derived from the transmission model, has its limitations for some scholars. A transmission model-based theory of communication that conceives of people as switchboards of information processing simply does not adequately explain how an advertisement may tug at our heart strings and evoke deep-ranging yet differing emotions in people, or how people may see the same message very differently. For that we have to look at other theoretical traditions.

▼ CRITICAL THEORY AND CULTURAL STUDIES

A typical critique of transmission models of communication (made by others outside the critical-theory tradition as well as within) is that it treats communication as some kind of separate, independent phenomenon outside of the people who are engaging in communication. Its technological orientation may explain an electronic signal well, but it falls far short when trying to explain the deeper meaning behind someone reading a morning paper. To define humans as a type of "switchboard center" when it comes to communication, as Schramm does, is to leave us unable to explain how media economics may influence what paper we are able to read or if we even have an Internet connection—nor does it help us to better understand the role that power, identity, and a host of other factors can play in how we make and share meaning through communication.

Critical theory is a theoretical approach broadly influenced from Marxist notions of the role of ideology, exploitation, capitalism, and the economy in understanding and eventually transforming society. There are many branches of critical theory, not all of which focus on media and mass communication, and they often disagree with each other on certain fundamental points. We will explore **cultural studies**, which tends to focus more on mass communication than some of the other types of critical theory.

critical theory

A theoretical approach broadly influenced from Marxist notions of the role of ideology, exploitation, capitalism, and the economy in understanding and eventually transforming society.

cultural studies

A framework in studying theories of culture and communication that shuns the positivist scientific approach used by scholars in the empirical school and that tries to examine the symbolic environment created by mass media.

To understand a cultural-studies approach to the subject of communication, it is important to first see its intellectual heritage through the lens of critical theory and to know how it differs from "traditional," or positivist, social science. Critical theorists criticize positivist researchers for inappropriately applying physical science research methods to human behavior. They do not agree that by using various statistical techniques, and with enough research, various "natural laws" of society and behavior can be determined.

Critical theorists not only say that the process of scientific creation of "fact" is a social and variable process like any other (consider how Pluto has gone from being considered a planet to now being asteroid 134340), but they refute that natural laws can be discovered that can explain human behavior. They see the drive to better predict and control society as one more form of oppression. In short, critical theorists would say positivists ask uninspiring questions and get uninteresting—if not misleading—answers that largely describe the societal and cultural status quo as unproblematic.

Cultural-studies researchers join critical theorists in rejecting the positivist scientific approach. They try to examine the symbolic environment created by mass media and to study the role that the mass media play in culture and society by utilizing a host of disciplines ranging from anthropology and sociology to political science and literary theory. For cultural-studies researchers, a television commercial can be a rich source of cultural codes and representations that tell us in subtle and not-so-subtle ways how we should be acting and thinking as members of society.

Communications scholar **James Carey** was a leading cultural-studies theorist and developed what he calls a ritual view of communication. He claims that "communication is a symbolic process whereby reality is produced, maintained, repaired, and transformed."[11] From this view, the act of reading a newspaper has less to do with receiving information than with participating in a shared cultural experience that portrays and confirms the world in a certain way. By reading the paper, we are actually participating in a ritual that produces and reproduces certain sociocultural norms that are played out through our actions and interactions with others.[12] The same dynamic can be said to take place with online media, such as posting photos on MySpace or IMing a friend—you are not simply transmitting information but are sharing ways of doing things and ways of thinking that actually create the society we live in through our repeated actions.

James Carey was one of the most influential media and communications scholars of the twentieth century.

James Carey

Communications scholar and historian who has shaped a cultural-studies approach to communication theory.

Television: The Future of Convergence

We started this chapter by looking at the telephone, an example of a communication technology in which you may not have considered the role that convergence has played. We will end by looking briefly at television and how convergence has shaped television today and how it will affect the future of television.

We will discuss the invention and development of television in Chapter 5 and focus here on the role convergence has played for this quintessential mass communication technology. Television's dominance as a mass media in the latter half of the twentieth century continuing through to today means it has been much discussed, debated, and studied. Television has been blamed for everything from a decline in reading by young people to a rise in violence in society. Few mass communications technologies better show the influence on our culture and society, even if one disagrees with the degree of effects television may have. Nevertheless, the fact that many people believe television has detrimental (or beneficial) effects has influenced everything from government regulation to the kinds of commercials and programming we see. The popularity of television also means it can be highly influential in terms of teaching people culture and social norms—or at least idealized norms.

Television viewing habits changed with the advent of the remote control, meaning viewers did not have to get up to change the channel. Thus, channel-surfing was born, making it easy for people to later name and understand the process of Web surfing that we do on the Internet.

Changes in viewing habits through the use of digital video recorders (DVRs) has led to concern by advertisers that viewers will skip commercials. The use of **product placement** has grown in response to the fears that viewers fast-forward through commercials when watching programming that was recorded on DVRs. Product placement shows a convergence of programming with advertising content in which advertising is essentially mixed with normal programming and that is often not recognized as an advertisement by the viewer.

Television has been able to adapt to new methods of distributing content over the years. Over-the-air broadcast towers used to be the primary way that people received their television signals, even though today cable and satellite systems are dominant. However, cable television systems were first created in 1948 so viewers in areas where over-the-air signals could not easily reach could get television programming, long before most households had cable systems.

The first transatlantic satellite signal was sent in 1962, when television as a mass medium was still not even fifteen years old.[13] Entertainment, especially movies and sports programming, played a role in encouraging the growth of cable and satellite-cable partnerships in the 1970s.

In 1978, Ted Turner launched WTBS Atlanta as a national **superstation**. A superstation is a local TV station that reaches a national audience by beaming its programming nationwide via satellite to local cable systems, which then transmit the program to local subscribers. In 1980, Turner employed the same technological combination to launch the first twenty-four-hour TV news network, the Cable News Network (CNN).

Today, many countries use similar systems for their own national broadcasting. In a country like Indonesia, which has hundreds of islands, a cable system is simply not practical between islands. Using satellite to beam programming to local cable operators, who connect viewers in their areas with cable, has proven to be an economical solution.

Television is a major communications industry in its own right, but when it began as a mass medium from the late 1940s its rapid rise in popularity was seen as a threat by the film industry, which promised to blacklist actors if they performed on television shows. It took several years for the film industry to realize that television could replace the second- and third-run movie theaters as a source of additional revenues for older films. The specter that the movie industry feared of mass audiences staying home and watching television instead of going to movie theaters never materialized; people still went to movies in droves.

Today the tug-of-war between the movie industry and television for attracting audiences continues, even as some film companies own television channels through the process of consolidation. The latest battles have been taking place in the area of 3-D, which used to be seen solely in movie theaters. Not only has 3-D

product placement

A form of advertising in which brand name goods or services are placed prominently within programming content that is otherwise devoid of advertising, demonstrating the convergence of programming with advertising content.

superstation

A local TV station that reaches a national audience by beaming its programming nationwide via satellite to local cable systems.

viewing technology for movies gotten better, but television screens have rapidly caught up and now 3-D television is also on the market.

Perhaps one of the biggest areas of convergence that we are seeing is the melding of the television and the personal computer. Television is becoming more interactive, encouraging viewers to do things like vote for their favorite *American Idol* contestants (though still not through the television—they use their mobile phones for that). At the same time, a growing number of people are watching television programming on their PCs. In the future, it may not matter much whether we think of the television as merged with the PC or the PC as merged with the television; we will simply have a high-definition screen that we can interact with, accessing the Web or chat or our email even as we watch our favorite programs.

This book takes the premise that mass communication as we have known it is fundamentally changing, perhaps to the point where it no longer is a relevant or even accurate descriptive term for our communication and media landscape. That day, however, is still not here. Convergence is, broadly speaking, the process with which we are seeing these changes taking place on technological, economic, and sociocultural levels. Many of the ramifications of the changes taking place today through convergence will likely not be realized or fully known for years to come, while others seem to have immediate and dramatic effects.

What we have today is a fascinating and confusing mixture of mass-communication industries and business models combining with various emerging digital technologies and communications practices that simultaneously threaten and hold great promise for traditional media companies and the communications professions. Issues of consumer privacy, of copyright, of affordable access to the Internet, and other legal, regulatory, and ethical issues have still to be worked out.

Moreover, the leaders of the industries in the media business have a unique opportunity to transform their media enterprises into institutions that better serve society. Rather than follow the familiar path of the commercially dominated media industry, journalists and other communication professionals can take this opportunity to reinvent media enterprise and help lead troubled industries into a renaissance. But in order to do that it takes money, and media companies for the most part have still not figured out new business models that work with digital media, at least none that would still leave them with the same kind of control they have enjoyed over selling and distributing media content. To date, few media organizations seem willing to relinquish that control.

The public, or audience, may finally have some say in the matter in the new digital media environment. Through communication tools that give the public unprecedented power to share information with each other and to "talk back" to those in power, people are able to connect and organize on any number of issues that are important to them, affecting policy changes through online and offline means. We have already seen the power that online organizing has had for various politicians in terms of getting donations and getting young people more engaged in political campaigns. Will the Internet and other digital media flourish and lead to a rich blend of eclectic voices, or will the emerging global media system be a homogenous blend of commercial banality where news and entertainment are little more than commodities that sit with equally insipid user-generated content? It is still an open question, but dealing with issues like these responsibly is the moral mandate of mass communication in the digital age. This book hopes to give you the tools to do so.

DISCUSSION QUESTIONS

1. Keep a media diary for a day of the media you consume (and create). Include what sources you get your news from, what types of online communication you use with friends and family, and how often you are on the phone. What did you learn from the diary?

2. Discuss any media content you have created and what happened if you put it online. It could be a video clip, a music mash-up, blog, etc.

3. What effect do you think the United States' lag in broadband access and Internet speed will have on the country? Why? What could business, government, and citizens do to improve the ranking of the United States?

4. Discuss the three main types of convergence and which one you think may be the most important or relevant for mass communications.

5. Discuss ways in which audiences can engage with each other and with media organizations. Do you think this has made audiences more active? Why or why not?

6. What are some ethical implications of the changes in privacy that have occurred because of social media like Facebook?

7. In which direction do you think digital media are more likely to go—toward a more open, diversified, and democratic medium or toward a more corporate, commercialized, and centrally controlled medium? Why?

8. List some changes you have seen in the past few years on the Internet in terms of your own use of digital media, and explain why you think these changes came about and whether you feel they are for better or for worse.

FURTHER READING

Convergence Culture: Where Old and New Media Collide. Henry Jenkins (2008) NYU Press.

The Coming Convergence: Surprising Ways Diverse Technologies Interact to Shape Our World and Change the Future. Stanley Schmidt (2008) Prometheus Books.

Understanding Media Convergence: The State of the Field. August Grant, Jeffrey Wilkinson (eds.) (2008) Oxford University Press.

Media Organizations and Convergence: Case Studies of Media Convergence Pioneers (Lea's Communication Series). Gracie Lawson-Borders (2005) Lawrence Erlbaum Associates.

The History of the Telephone. Herbert Casson (2006) Cosimo Classics.

America Calling: A Social History of the Telephone to 1940. Claude Fischer (1994) University of California Press.

The History of Wireless: How Creative Minds Produced Technology for the Masses. Ira Brodsky (2008) Telescope Books.

Speaking into the Air: A History of the Idea of Communication. John Durham Peters (1999) University of Chicago Press.

Understanding Media Theory. Kevin Williams (2003) Oxford University Press.

Understanding Media Cultures: Social Theory and Mass Communication, 2nd ed. Nick Stevenson (2002) Sage Publications.

Theories of Communication: A Short Introduction. Armand Mattelart, Michele Mattelart (1998) Sage Publications.

Communication Theories: Origins, Methods, and Uses in the Mass Media, 5th ed. Werner J. Severin, James W. Tankard Jr. (2001) Addison Wesley Longman.

Being Digital. Nicholas Negroponte (1995) Alfred A. Knopf.

What Will Be: How the New World of Information Will Change Our Lives. Michael Dertouzos (1997) HarperEdge.

2

MEDIA LITERACY IN THE DIGITAL AGE

LEARNING OBJECTIVES

By the end of this chapter
you should be able to:

- Define media literacy.

- Use basic skills to improve
  critical-thinking ability
  when consuming mass-
  communication content.

- Explain three elements of
  media literacy: historical
  development of media,
  media grammar, and
  commercial forces that
  shape media content.

- Describe what makes
  digital media ubiquitous
  and different from other
  types of media.

- Examine how traditional
  types of media content are
  changing, and will likely
  change further, in a world
  of digital media.

- Understand business
  models currently being
  tried with online media.

C hannel One News is seen daily by 6 million children in nearly eight thousand middle schools and high schools throughout the United States. The fast-paced 12-minute news programs have won various journalism awards and helped launch careers for people like CNN's Anderson Cooper, among others. In exchange for agreeing to run the program on at least 90 percent of school days, schools receive free televisions, satellite dishes, and video equipment. Students get to watch professionally produced news segments about events throughout the world with news from content partners including NBC and CBS.

Proponents of Channel One News tout how it helps inform students about world events and spurs classroom discussions on important news and issues of the day. Students can engage with Channel One News through several online websites, including *You Tell It* and *Your Turn*, where students are encouraged to post video news themselves or comment on news. Learning about media through producing media is a crucial component of media literacy education, placing this aspect of Channel One News firmly within the context of media literacy programs throughout the United States.

Channel One News also has its critics. The Media Education Foundation created a documentary titled "Captive Audience" that critiques growing commercialism in schools. Some studies have shown that students better remember the commercials from Channel One News than the news content. Other researchers and teachers criticize the programming content itself, saying that for every award-winning news segment that Channel One News produced there is much more lighter fare, or "fluff," that often has promotional purposes or product tie-ins disguised as news.

Critics worry that Channel One News is simply one more channel that advertisers are using to reach what has formerly been a largely advertising-free zone: our public schools. Between vending machine deals, advertising in textbooks, and examples like Channel One News, many educators are concerned that our school children are learning more about how to be good consumers than good citizens.

We live in a media society. Mass media surround and influence our world in a variety of ways. They entertain us, they inform us, and they sell us everything from household products to political candidates. Although we often tend to study media and mass communications as something separate from our culture, society, and lives, the fact is media are just as real as the "real world."

With the pervasiveness of media in modern life, it is more important than ever to understand how media messages may influence us. We must look critically at all media we receive and understand something about how media organizations work as businesses, how they fit into other aspects of society, and how they influence culture and can manipulate public opinion.

This chapter explains some basic principles behind media literacy while teaching you to critically analyze the media messages you encounter. We take an especially close look at digital media throughout the chapter, as digital media underscores many media-literacy issues that we encounter in all types of media.

◢▽ Education and Media

In school we learn to read, write, and do arithmetic. We learn about history, other cultures, literature, science, and politics. We learn athletic skills and teamwork; we can even learn art, mechanics, computer programming, and how to cook.

But we also learn much from our daily and extensive interactions with media content—some may argue we even learn more of practical value from media than from the typical school day spent in classes. If we think back to the four functions of mass communication mentioned in the previous chapter—surveillance, correlation, cultural transmission, and entertainment—the common component that runs through all of these functions is that they essentially educate and inform us.

This raises the question that if media are so pervasive in our lives, why aren't we studying them in the same way that we study geography or biology? Why can we take a class in high school on how to dismantle a car engine, but we do not have a class that teaches us how to deconstruct our modern systems of media and mass communications?

The question highlights two interesting issues. First, it shows that "education," like media, is not something that we can easily set aside as a thing separate from our lives. We are learning all the time, even when not in a formal academic setting such as a classroom or doing homework.

How Media Literate Are You?

Because of widespread media exposure, most young people have a relatively high level of media literacy in some areas. Although you may have seen every movie your favorite actor has been in and can swap MP3 music files with friends over the Internet, it doesn't necessarily mean you have an adequate level of media literacy in today's world.

Get a general idea of how media literate you are by taking the following quiz. Be sure to try this quiz again at the end of the semester and see if your media literacy has improved.

1. Can you name the number one song in the pop chart right now by title and artist?
2. Name other hit songs the group or artist may have had.
3. Name the recording company this artist or group is signed to and who owns the label, if the recording company is a subsidiary of a larger recording label.
4. (T/F) The World Wide Web and the Internet are the same thing.
5. Name at least three movies made from Stephen King's books.
6. Describe the last time you saw product placement in a movie or television show.
7. (T/F) It is legal for employers to read employees' emails sent from work computers.
8. (T/F) Web-analytics software can determine what type of computer you have and what Web browser.
9. (T/F) The United States leads the world in broadband penetration and Internet affordability.
10. (T/F) Apple can enter your iPhone remotely and "kill" any application you have installed on it without your knowledge.

Second, if we are learning all the time through our interactions with each other and with media content, then how can we ensure that what we are learning is accurate and useful if we do not have the skills to consider where that learning is coming from and how it may be affecting our thought processes?

Educators have recognized a growing need to teach **media-literacy** skills to school-age children, starting as young as kindergarten or elementary school and continuing to high school graduation. Some countries, such as Canada and Australia, have taken the lead in media-literacy education, while the United States generally lags behind in teaching media literacy. However, it is changing, and a growing number of states, such as New Jersey, have implemented statewide media-literacy guidelines for K–12 schools.

media literacy

The process of interacting with media content and critically analyzing it by considering its particular presentation, its underlying political or social messages, and ownership and regulation issues that may affect what is presented and in what form.

▲▼ What Is Media Literacy?

Being able to read a book, understanding how to navigate a website or send an email attachment, and realizing a scary part of a movie is coming up when the background music changes are all types of media literacy. Some fall under what we would consider the traditional meaning of the term "literacy," and others can be classified as visual literacy or computer literacy. Media literacy encompasses all these skills and much more.

THE FILTER BUBBLE

ETHICS IN MEDIA

We have talked about The Daily Me as something that an Internet user may create, a personalized online "newspaper" that brings pre-selected news topics, but what happens when The Daily Me is created for us automatically, based solely on our online behavior and topics of discussion in social media?

In his 2010 book *The Filter Bubble: What the Internet Is Hiding From You*, Eli Pariser discusses the implications of activities such as Google's customized search results for users, a program begun in 2009. Rather than giving a user general search results, Google provides the results, based on the data they have collected about you, that they think you are most likely to click on.

This practice raises ethical concerns because, rather than creating a personalized page on your own, you are receiving filtered results without even knowing it, which potentially hampers your ability to find the information you actually want. You can test this for yourself: Do a Google search for some term when you are signed into Google, and then sign out, clear your cache, enter the same term into Google without signing in (Google would see your computer as a "general user"), and compare the differences in the search results.

Google is not the only company trying to create a more personalized Web for users. Notice how when you look at products on retail sites, you then see ads for similar products when you return to a page like My Yahoo!. Or notice how you see ads that may be related to topics you discussed in Web-based email accounts. Computers are scouring the emails and search terms, finding what the algorithms think are relevant matches, and then sending those to you on subsequent pages.

The idea behind this is to deliver personalized ads and content that makes the user experience better on the Web. However, the practice also raises serious concerns about privacy, about how sites could use the information they collect about your online behavior, and about how they could combine the data to create a more complete profile of you than you could ever imagine.

Media literacy in the digital world raises a whole range of new issues and scenarios to consider.

Media literacy can be defined as the process of critically analyzing media content by considering its particular presentation, its underlying political or social messages, and ownership and regulation issues that may affect what stories are presented and in what form. While this discussion focuses on media consumption, understanding media from a critical standpoint also enables those who create their own media content to do so with a more informed frame of mind.

Media consumers should always question what they see, hear, or otherwise experience when receiving or interacting with mediated communication. Is a news story biased? How might the story be slanted through word choices or the people interviewed in ways that do not accurately reflect the situation? Why is it even news? Does a popular television show or video game encourage gender or racial stereotypes? What is an advertiser really trying to sell and to whom? Does the

Learning media-literacy skills has become even more important for students today.

placement of articles and photos in a newspaper fairly represent the relative importance of those items as news? These are just a sample of the kinds of questions critical media consumers should ask.

Developing media literacy is an ongoing process, not a goal. There is no qualification test in media literacy to differentiate the media literate from the media illiterate. You will never receive a certificate in "media literacy." If you do, you should apply your newfound critical-thinking skills and ask whether it is worth the paper it is printed on.

Even though you cannot ever attain "perfect media literacy," it is possible to always improve your level of media literacy and thus be a wiser media user. The importance of media in contemporary society makes it imperative that audience members exercise critical thinking in their consumption of media content so they can better control their actions and not be controlled by media messages. Learning new skills in creating media, such as taking courses on graphic design or video production, can further help your media literacy.

Media-literacy scholar W. James Potter talks about building "knowledge structures" to improve one's level of media literacy.[1] A knowledge structure is simply a way to visualize building one's level of knowledge on a given topic or topics. For example, if you have a basic understanding of the history of the World Wide Web and someone tells you they had created their first website in the 1980s, you can be confident that they are incorrect because the Web did not exist until 1991.

It might seem like an impossible task to be truly media literate in today's complex media environment. However, three basic categories represent the foundation for critical media consumption. These are

1. Historical development of media

2. Media grammar

3. Commercial forces on media content

From these foundations, it is possible for us to better navigate the complex interplay of traditional media and digital media that we encounter today. We will look at each of these in a general context first and then focus on how they apply to some of the unique differences that digital media brings.

◢◣ Historical Development of Media

It is important to understand that there is nothing "natural" about how we use media today and how our current media system operates or has evolved. We tend to think of the evolution of media technologies as going from a more primitive state to our current, more advanced state—which of course we see as the best—until a new development comes along.

However, this is a mistaken way to think of media and mass communication. Of course there are improvements in media technologies and changes in media-usage habits that can do things like provide easier and cheaper access to more people, or that provide information or entertainment in new ways, but it should not be thought of as some kind of inevitable evolution.

When looking at the historical development of media and media technologies there are many times when something we take for granted today could have developed very differently. It will become obvious even with the brief examples below that there were many other possible outcomes to the development of media besides what we currently take for granted. This knowledge can be especially liberating, as it can help us think more deeply about what is right and wrong about today's media systems and make us aware of forces that could change things for better or worse in the future.

▼ REGULATORY FACTORS

Regulations and laws created by politicians or government agencies such as the Federal Communications Commission (FCC) can have profound effects on what type of media are available and what type of content we see. Regulations can directly affect the level of competition in an industry by making it difficult or impossible for potential competitors to enter a market.

An example of regulatory control over media is the restrictions on monopoly ownership of a newspaper, television station, and radio station in a single market. Although these restrictions have gradually been easing, it still generally is not allowed for a single owner to have all three within a specific locale. This regulation was created to ensure that the public could get a diversity of voices through the media.

net neutrality

A principle that states that broadband networks should be free of restrictions on content, platforms, or equipment and that certain types of content, platforms, or equipment should not get preferential treatment on the network.

The debates around **net neutrality**, which will be discussed in more detail later in the book, are another example of the powerful role that regulations play. Telecommunications companies want to start charging content providers for certain types of content being sent over their networks or charging more for heavy users of bandwidth.

Critics argue that this will lead to telecommunications firms favoring media content that comes from a parent media company, for example, and slowing down content that comes from competing media companies. Despite denials by telecommunications firms that this would happen, there have already been examples of firms favoring some content over others in the past few years. Consider how different your Web browsing experience may be if your Internet Service Provider (ISP) allows music videos from Universal Music Group artists to reach you easily while slowing down how fast you can download music from Warner, or charges you more to be able to download Warner's content at the same rate as Universal's.

Calls for new regulations or deregulation must be watched closely, as such calls are often prompted by industry lobbyists who want to give their clients a business advantage at the expense of competitors—and often the general public. The issues are often complex and couched in bureaucratic or scientific language, but the effects can be far-reaching.

One example is the case of low-power FM (LPFM), which allows for communities or groups to create nonprofit, hyperlocal FM stations. Despite the potential for such stations to create a range of voices in the media and to offer more choices to the public for radio listening, LPFM advocates faced a long struggle against the broadcast industry—including National Public Radio—which saw a threat to its interests if LPFM was allowed. Regulations or lobbying efforts are not always responsible for hampering new technologies, of course. Sometimes the reasons are more engrained in society or culture.

▼ SOCIOCULTURAL FACTORS

Sometimes perfectly good or sensible technologies do not get adopted simply because people do not seem to be ready for them or because using them breaks certain sociocultural practices or norms. Consider the development of video conferences in business settings. Video conferences over broadband Internet offer much in terms of cost and time savings for businesses yet still have not replaced business trips. Despite making it possible to see and hear the people at the other end, a video conference cannot replace the kind of interaction we expect in face-to-face interpersonal communication.

Similarly, sociocultural norms may change over time to accommodate new media technologies and new media uses. Consider the example of the telephone in the previous chapter and how it went from initially being considered a novelty, in Victorian times, to what it is today. Even now we struggle with establishing social norms of polite behavior with mobile phones when talking in public places. Think of our reactions when we hear someone in a restaurant, bus, train, or other public space speaking loudly on the phone. We generally don't show the same annoyance when two people are talking with each other equally loudly, but we do not like it when we hear only one side of the conversation.

Social norms regarding activities like texting or talking on cell phones change over time.

There are often unintended consequences of new media and examples of how the media are used that were likely not imagined by their creators. The inventors of video on mobile phones no doubt did not think that it would lead to "happy slapping," or groups of youth in England and elsewhere videotaping and posting with their phones their friends attacking total strangers just for the fun of it.

In short, it is important to remember not only that technology may affect sociocultural practices and norms but that those norms may have an effect on how that technology is used and perceived, which in turn could have an effect on things like new laws being made to regulate the new behaviors.

▼ TECHNOLOGICAL FACTORS

We often want the latest and the best technology, and some people make sure they have the latest, lightest, or fastest high-tech gizmo to show off. Even though we may think we have the best technology, the history of media and technology is littered with the ghosts of better technologies that were never successful.

The classic example of this was the battle in the 1970s between two competing video formats, Betamax, by Sony, and VHS, by JVC. Betamax tapes were smaller and had better picture quality than VHS yet ultimately failed in the marketplace as VHS became the standard, primarily because VHS had a better distribution and marketing network and thus reached a wider audience first. Once people owned a VHS video player, they were unlikely to also purchase a Betamax player and replace their videotapes.

Within the past several years a similar struggle took place between competing high-definition (HD) DVD formats, Toshiba's HD-DVD and Sony's Blu-ray. Initially, HD-DVD was more widely adopted and seen as the better technology, but within four years of being released Blu-ray discs outsold HD-DVD and eventually became the accepted standard.

Another example is the competition between Apple computers and PCs. Although Apple computers were in many ways superior to PCs in terms of usability and capability, they only captured a small part of the market share. Similarly, Microsoft crowded out Netscape in a few short years during the 1990s with its Internet Explorer web browser that came bundled with the Windows operating system. Internet Explorer was not a vastly superior browser to Netscape Navigator, yet within six years Internet Explorer captured over 90 percent of the web browser market, essentially pushing Navigator out of the market. In early 2008 AOL, which at that time owned Netscape Navigator, announced they would no longer offer any support for the browser and recommended users to switch to a different browser such as Firefox.

How did Microsoft do it? Although marketing played a role, by and large it was simply a combination of inertia and lack of computer literacy on the part of most computer users. Nothing prevented people from downloading the Netscape Navigator browser (after connecting to the Internet through the already-loaded Internet Explorer), but many people learning to use computers in the mid-1990s simply thought that using Internet Explorer was the only way to see the Web or didn't want to bother trying a new web browser once they became familiar with Internet Explorer.

Why doesn't the best technology always win? Why can't consumers recognize the better product and simply buy or use that one? It can be especially difficult with new media technologies that do not have a track record or long history of use. Most people do not want to spend a lot of time learning how to use new devices, or changing their media consumption, and will stay with what is familiar. Companies that come to market with new technologies that threaten old ones always have to deal to some extent with complacency from the general public. They also have to deal with large-scale economic and business factors ranging from distribution to changes in media formats (such as a new DVD) that could have repercussions far beyond a particular new technology.

Text Messaging and the Thumb Tribe

Text messaging is a prime example of how regulatory, sociocultural, technological, and economic factors all come together to affect whether something gets adopted and how it is used.

In many parts of the world, text messaging has become a predominant way to use a cell phone, and there have been instances of large crowds mobilizing for protests in a very short time through text messages. This happened in Manila in 2001 when Filipinos wanted to oust President Joseph Estrada, who was accused of corruption. Texting also played an important role in the protests and revolutions in the Arab world in early 2011, along with social media sites.

Text messaging is also popular in Japan, where crowded public spaces make speaking on the phone especially bothersome to others and do not allow a private conversation to take place. Young Japanese have become so proficient at texting that they have been dubbed "the thumb tribe" by some social commentators.

Yet text messaging was much slower to catch on in the United States than in other countries, though it is now widespread. Why the difference?

The cell phone network in the United States, partly for technological reasons and partly for regulatory reasons, makes phone calls relatively cheap compared to some other countries. The cost of making a phone call, compared to the cost of a text message, is not an issue for most Americans.

Americans generally have more private space than some other countries, as well, making it easier to talk on the phone without worrying about sharing private information with strangers.

Finally, until phones with keyboards came out, texting was cumbersome on most cell phones compared to simply calling, so until the technology caught up, Americans tended to disfavor texting.

Of course, with the rise in popularity of texting comes a range of unintended problems and issues. One such is issue is texting while driving, which greatly increases the risks of accidents. In other countries such as Japan, public transportation is used much more than in the United States, so these kinds of issues did not surface to the same extent as they have in the United States.

Sexting, or sending pornographic pictures or comments, has also become an issue. Recently, some states have been planning to enact laws that keep minors who send pornographic pictures of other minors from getting a record as a sex offender or being charged with trafficking in child pornography, which they are currently subject to.

▼ ECONOMIC FACTORS

Economic factors very closely affect how we use media and even what type of media we get. Many towns throughout the United States now only have one newspaper where there used to be two or more competing dailies. Economic pressures forced the others to close or to merge with the remaining paper. The high cost of publishing a newspaper or starting a television station prevented most people from even considering starting such ventures.

Economics can be at the heart of industry lobbying efforts to change regulations so they are more favorable to the industry. It can be an important factor, through licensing or marketing deals, in making an inferior technology more popular than a better one, such as the case with Apple. Unlike Windows and PC makers, Apple did not license its operating system to other companies to make Apple or Mac clones, thus limiting the availability of Macs while keeping the cost relatively high in comparison to PCs. Cheaper costs of PCs and number of software programs that were written for PCs helped push the PC to the huge majority it has today.

Economic factors also play a key role in the types of programming we see today and the types of information we receive. It is relatively cheap to produce reality shows, which may account in part for their proliferation in recent years. It is also cheaper to produce news on light, entertainment-oriented topics rather than conduct in-depth investigative pieces on complex social issues, and entertainment news tends to attract larger audiences. Economics is also driving media consolidation, which further affects the types of content available when media owners or corporations make programming decisions based on their own business interests rather than the public interest.

Media Grammar

Being a critical consumer of media messages begins with understanding the grammar of the media—the underlying rules by which a medium presents itself and is used and understood by the audience. Each medium of mass communication presents its messages uniquely. With mediums that we are familiar with through widespread use or exposure, we often do not think about the role media grammar plays in what we see, how we see it, and what our perceptions are. In many ways, it becomes "background," but it nevertheless can have profound implications for our understanding of media content. We become more aware of media grammar when we encounter a new media type that we do not know the "rules" for yet.

We perhaps become even more aware of media grammar when we create media content, as each particular media grammar gives us the building blocks from which to make larger works, just as grammar helps us build sentences when we write. Once we learn certain grammatical rules, we can create an amazing variety of new sentences applying those rules. The same applies for understanding media grammar.

Here we will look briefly at the main forms of media and explore some basics about each particular form of media grammar and what it means for our perceptions and expectations of that medium.

▼ PRINT MEDIA

Print media, partly due to their long history compared to other types of mass communication, have developed a very sophisticated media grammar. Everything from the physical dimensions of a book to whether it contains pictures or not, the size and style of the typeface, whether it is hardcover or paperback, and the artwork on the book jacket conveys important messages to the potential book buyer beyond the actual content. Within a book itself, there are several aspects of media grammar that have evolved over the years. Spacing between words to aid reading comprehension is an early example, as are page numbering, tables of contents, indexes, and chapter headings. We take many of these conventions for granted, but most took years before they were widely adopted and became standard in books.

Newspapers have their own types of media grammar that have also evolved over time and that continue to change. An obvious example is the amount of color photos and graphics used in newspapers today compared to forty years ago. Since space is limited in a newspaper, more graphics means less room for text. Many media critics and journalists have complained that this "packaging" of news into relatively short, easy-to-read units accompanied by splashy pictures or graphics does readers a disservice by not providing them with the depth of information they need in today's world. Proponents of the trend say that newspapers must compete with television and other visual media for audience attention and so must present news in a way that suits people's busy lifestyles.

Most newspapers are organized into sections such as sports, business, and local news. These not only act to help organize information so readers can quickly find stories that interest them, but they create subconscious parameters for readers on what types of stories to expect in those sections. The sections also help define where certain advertisers prefer to appear in the paper. The editorial pages and op-ed pages are where newspaper readers expect to hear opinions on events, either from the newspaper staff or publisher (editorials) or from guest columnists.

In terms of size, newspapers conform largely to the rules of either tabloid (typically more sensational in tone) or broadsheet (more serious). They use headlines to capture attention and "teasers" on the front page or front-section pages to entice readers to see articles inside the paper. They use a variety of graphic techniques to attract and guide the reader's eye. More important stories usually appear "above the fold," or on the upper half of the broadsheet paper, so when it is stacked in a newsstand those stories and graphics are what people first see.

Newspapers typically present hard news using an inverted pyramid organization (most important items first) in the body of the text report, although this structure is slowly starting to change to resemble that of a feature story. Sources, or people interviewed, are quoted to establish the credibility of what is being reported, enliven the report, and show that it's not just the reporter offering his or her views. Photos and illustrations are accompanied by a brief tagline that explains what the artwork is about. Features, such as human-interest stories or profiles, are written in a different style, sometimes starting with a vignette that helps humanize the story and hook the reader.

Magazines similarly use sophisticated graphic and design techniques, even more so than newspapers, and feature more long-form writing, often with just one or two articles per page and multipage articles. Advertising in magazines often takes up a full page, and in some magazines it is hard to immediately tell if something is an ad or graphics at the beginning of a feature. In some ways magazines combine elements of books and newspapers in their media grammar. Because of their length, they usually have a table of contents (many also have an advertiser index), which helps readers find specific articles quickly. Like newspapers, they are often divided into subject-related sections within their topic areas, which usually contain short, newsy items.

We can often tell what kind of newspaper a foreign paper is, even without knowing the language, simply from the look of the publication.

With hundreds of years to develop the grammar for print media, it is perhaps surprising to see how quickly we have adapted to the rise of electronic media, especially audio and, later, video.

▼ RADIO AND RECORDED MUSIC

Radio and recorded music similarly have their own grammar, one based only on sound. Radio uses a combination of audio techniques to achieve different ends. Among these techniques are volume changes, multiple audio tracks, **actualities** (i.e., edited audio clips from people interviewed), sound effects, and **voice-overs**, all of which can be used to convey information, capture attention, evoke a mood or scene, or achieve some other purpose.

Recorded music typically conforms to particular stylistic conventions, especially with regard to length (less than five minutes a song) and music format. Popular music genres, such as hip-hop, rock, country, or swing, have certain rhythms, lyrical styles, and sounds that make them clearly distinguishable. This underlying media grammar of specific categories or genres makes it easier to market and promote artists. Radio stations brand themselves by the genres of music they generally play, making it easier for audiences to pick stations that play music they like.

However, putting music into genres like this has its drawbacks. Someone with a sound or style that does not easily fit into well-established genres may therefore find it harder to get listened to, as radio stations are hesitant to play something that does not fit nicely into their established formats. An artist may also find it harder to get a recording contract in the first place, as a recording label will not want to sign someone it believes will have difficulty getting promoted on the radio.

Even a format as apparently chaotic as talk radio has a well-defined media grammar. Despite the interactive nature of call-ins from the audience—talk radio is one of the few traditional mass-communication formats to include such a high degree of interactivity between media producers and the audience—the callers are obviously in a subordinate position in terms of how long they are allowed to speak, what they may say, and the fact that they can be disconnected at any time by the host or producers.

Although radio developed years before television became a mass medium, and some of the earliest television shows were taken directly from popular radio programs, media producers and audiences had already developed a fairly sophisticated visual grammar thanks in large part to the popularity of movies.

▼ FILM AND TELEVISION

Although film and television have much shorter histories as media than print, they have already developed a sophisticated media grammar that is based on editing, camera angles, lighting, movement, and sound.

For example, in the early history of film, most movies were only a few minutes long and either simply recorded daily activities or were essentially filmed short stage plays. Although the short length of movies was more a function of the limited technology at the time, audiences soon tired of the novelty of watching silent filmed plays and wanted something more interesting.

Filmmakers started producing more sophisticated storylines for their short films and introduced a technique that was unique to film at the time—crosscut

actualities

Edited audio clips from people interviewed.

voice-over

An unseen announcer or narrator talking while other activity takes place, either on radio or during a television scene.

scenes. By crosscutting different scenes to simulate simultaneous events happening in two different locations (think of the classic scenes of a train heading down the tracks and a woman tied to the tracks by the villain), filmmakers were able to tell much more complex and dramatic stories. Further, increasing the speed between crosscut scenes helped increase dramatic tension in the audience.

Today's filmmakers have many more such tools at their disposal and are able to give audiences a lot of information, all with visual or audio techniques. Think of the combination of low music and strong shadows in many horror movies, or how we understand an on-screen dream sequence or flashback, or how we differentiate "good" from "bad" characters even before they have spoken or revealed their characters through the narrative plot.

The media grammar of television fiction uses many of the same techniques seen in movies, although of course television production budgets are much smaller than movie budgets. Consider the media grammar of your average sitcom—it is usually shot on a set, with perhaps less than half a dozen "locations" generally used, and the actors come and go as if on a stage. The camera is usually stationary, although multiple camera angles are used, and punch lines are reinforced by a **laugh track**, which in some sitcoms can almost be timed with clockwork precision (even if the line isn't particularly funny).

laugh track

A device used in television sitcoms that generates prerecorded laughter, timed to coincide with punch lines of jokes.

Other types of television shows have their own types of media grammar, such as game shows, soap operas, talk shows, and news. Although we tend to think of the news as objective—or at least the media grammar used in news shows tries to encourage that kind of thinking by the audience—it is important to understand how camera angles, lighting, distance from the subject and interviewer, sound, and intercut scenes all affect our perceptions of the news.

The "objective point of view" used in television news-reporting interviews treats the viewer as an observer. Typically, the camera is kept still, with shots over the shoulder of the journalist interviewing a subject. Prior to the interview, the subject is instructed by the journalist to never look directly into the camera. Rather, only the news anchor or field reporter in his or her stand-up, often used as a means to summarize or conclude the report, is allowed to look directly into the camera and thereby establish eye contact with the audience. This grammar establishes the authoritativeness and objectivity of the journalist and helps the viewer recognize the difference between the subject and the reporter.

It has been interesting to see how television news, especially, has borrowed some elements of media grammar from the online world—which originally had borrowed heavily from television when graphical user interfaces such as windows and digital video started appearing online. Multiple windows on the television screen

Fake news shows use the conventions of journalism and the media grammar of news shows to make ironic or humorous points.

showing different kinds of information, scrolling news across the bottom of the screen giving updates, and icons such as blinking cursors are just some examples of how television news is borrowing from the interactive online world and thus adding new types of media grammar.

▲▼ Commercial Forces on Media Content

Even in open and democratic societies with a free press, economic factors and corporate decisions often influence what is and is not covered in the news and what kind of entertainment is created and shown to the general public. Rarely do average media consumers think of how commercial forces are shaping the content they see every day, but these forces affect everything from what types of shows are produced to whether a news report critical of an important advertiser is downplayed or even pulled by a media corporation.

These activities happen at the local, national, and international levels. At the local level, reducing the number of reporters at a news organization to help save money can result in a noticeable drop in local coverage, such as coverage of area schools. The newspaper company may save money, but the public is poorer for the lessened coverage of local issues. A company that advertises heavily in a local newspaper may gain undue influence in the decision by the paper whether to publish articles critical of it by threatening to withdraw its advertising. A publisher with business interests in other industries, such as local tourism, may influence the types of coverage in the newspaper it owns in order to further these other business interests.

But this kind of manipulation of media content is not confined to small-town media outlets. In 1998, Chris Patten, former British governor of Hong Kong, had his book contract cancelled by HarperCollins, which is a subsidiary of Rupert Murdoch's News Corporation. Patten's book, *East and West,* was reportedly going to be highly critical of China's policies, and Murdoch at the time was trying to get China to accept Murdoch's Star TV satellite and cable programs. Similarly, a few years prior to that he removed the BBC from Star TV when Chinese leaders expressed displeasure at the BBC's reports on the killings in Tiananmen Square in June 1989.

These incidents are not meant to show that Rupert Murdoch and News Corporation are particularly greedy or selfish; similar stories of corporate decisions influencing what we see or do not see can be told about all of the major media corporations and will be covered in more detail throughout the book, especially in the chapter on media ethics.

Media scholar Robert McChesney has written several books that show how corporate media have adversely affected the quality of communications content we receive and how media companies have lobbied the government to further their own corporate interests at the expense of the public interest. He claims that today's corporate media giants actually harm our democracy and political processes in a number of ways, ranging from poor news coverage that largely does not challenge the status quo (especially when it comes to media companies' own business interests), to banal entertainment that dulls our senses, to incessant advertising that implies that we can find happiness through consumerism. McChesney's organization, Free Press, is dedicated to trying to reform media in the United States in order to create a better democracy.

▼ PROFIT AND NONPROFIT MEDIA

As McChesney points out, basic to all mass media is the underlying commercial nature of mass communication. As such, there are two main systems for funding media. One system relies on the commercial marketplace, where print and electronic media are run to make money, just like any other business. The other system is not for profit and can rely on a combination of public funding, or support from government or other public institutions, corporate gifts and sponsorships, and audience contributions. This system is used primarily for electronic media. For example, in Britain the public pays a tax on its television or radio receivers, which then is used to fund media programming on the BBC channels.

In the for-profit model, ownership plays a key role in determining the nature of the media enterprise. For-profit media companies are either publicly held companies or privately owned operations. For publicly held media companies, shares are bought and sold on the stock market, just like any other company. The people who run these companies are responsible to their shareholders, who, by and large, expect their investments to return a profit.

In recent history, media businesses have been among the most profitable of any industry, with profit margins typically around 20 percent on an annual basis. Sometimes, profit pressures lead media companies, especially publicly traded companies, to focus on the short term—cutting costs, laying off staff, or making decisions that can increase near-term profits but that negatively influence the quality of a product, such as news coverage. The result can be an immediate increase in profitability, but that profitability is not sustainable.

On the other hand, making money can also be an incentive for media companies to produce a better-quality product. The Disney Company, for example, is among the most profitable of major publicly owned media companies in the United States, and it is recognized for its quality entertainment products, including award-winning motion pictures, recorded music, and television (it owns the ABC television network and ESPN, the most profitable channel on television).

The influence of this commercial foundation is especially evident in entertainment media, such as in much television programming and many motion pictures. Most of the television schedule is organized with commercial breaks on the hour and throughout each program so advertisers can insert their commercial messages. Broadcast television, although thought of as "free" television, is still essentially paid for by the consumer as companies have to recoup their expenses for advertising and marketing. Commercials are the most obvious result of for-profit media, but advertisers can also influence the content of shows and motion pictures directly.

▼ COMMERCIAL FORCES IN PUBLIC SERVICE MEDIA

Although the U.S. media system includes public service broadcasting, even that is increasingly influenced or shaped by commercial forces. In the United States, a portion of the funding for public service broadcasting comes from corporate sponsors, and those sponsors tend to be most interested in programming that is consistent with the image they want to cultivate among public broadcasting's generally upscale audiences. In 2009, the Public Broadcasting Service (PBS), which produces and distributes public television and public radio through National Public Radio (NPR), received 16 percent of its funding from businesses—nearly the same amount as the 15 percent it receives from the appropriation from the Corporation for Public Broadcasting, its parent organization. The largest portion, 28 percent, came from member donations. Large, philanthropic foundations provided 8 percent, the same as state colleges and universities. Federal sources of funding make up 18 percent of PBS's total funding.[2]

PBS has faced especially tough competition from some of the specialized cable channels, which produce targeted or niche educational programming on sciences, nature, or history much like that shown by PBS. PBS also has to face political critics who want to cut its government funding. In 2010 and 2011, some lawmakers threatened to cut federal funding for public broadcasting in order to try to reduce the deficit. PBS and NPR must occasionally respond to conservative lawmakers who claim the networks have a liberal bias and say that the public should not have to pay for that kind of programming.

▼ PRODUCT PLACEMENT AND CORPORATE SPONSORSHIP

product placement

The practice of advertisers paying for actual products to be used and shown prominently in television shows and movies.

Influencing the content of shows and motion pictures can happen in at least two ways. First is **product placement**, where advertisers pay to have their product displayed in a movie or show with the brand name highly visible to the audience. A character driving a name-brand car or drinking from a popular brand of soda is an example of product placement. Second, advertisers or marketers sometimes work directly with media organizations to sponsor specific programs on television or special sections in newspapers. A brand of beer or soft drink sponsoring a concert tour that is televised on MTV is an example of this, as is Ford sponsoring a commercial-free hour of a popular TV show such as *24*.

Even entire channels of content are based on corporate sponsorship. An example is the Hallmark Channel. Launched in August 2001 by Hallmark Cards and Crown Media Holdings, the Hallmark Channel features dozens of series and specials, movies, and miniseries, ranging from *The Martha Stewart Show* to reruns of *The Golden Girls*. The Hallmark Channel is widely distributed through 1,700 cable systems and direct-to-home satellite services, across the United States, and worldwide to one hundred international markets, where it is seen by more than 85 million subscribers globally.[3] It's worth noting that simply because a program or channel is advertiser sponsored, it isn't necessarily flawed. In fact, advertising sponsorship has produced some of the best programming on television, including the Hallmark Channel, which features a library of 4,500 hours of programming that has won nearly two hundred Emmy Awards.

▼ CONCENTRATION OF MEDIA OWNERSHIP

Regardless of ownership, there are incentives for media companies to seek economies of scale. Strictly speaking, "economy of scale" refers to the decrease in unit manufacturing cost that results from mass production. In the context of media, it means essentially that media enterprises can reduce costs and increase profit by getting larger and reaching a larger market with their content. Of course, just getting bigger doesn't necessarily translate into greater economies of scale, but it is the basic reason behind a fundamental trend in media over the past half century. Successful media enterprises have acquired, either through purchase or merger, other media enterprises and have thereby become larger in size and scope. Newspaper companies have bought other newspaper companies; radio-station groups have bought other radio-station groups. Cross-media enterprises have acquired other media enterprises, sometimes extending internationally as well. The result is a media system that is increasingly large, multifaceted, and international in ownership. These companies compete with other large media enterprises and across international borders.

Some critics have argued that despite the possible economies of scale, there is a significant downside to media conglomerates or media monopolies (i.e., when in a community there is just one media organization serving the public). Greater concentration of ownership, or fewer owners owning more media, results in less diversity of media voices, and the public is thus poorly served. Minority voices and non-mainstream views are silenced.

One of the most vocal critics of concentrated media ownership is Ben H. Bagdikian. In his book *New Media Monopoly*, Bagdikian presents evidence that during the 1990s a small number of the country's largest corporations purchased more public communications power than ever before. In 1983, the biggest media merger in history was a $340 million deal involving the Gannett Company, a newspaper chain, which bought Combined Communications Corporation, whose assets included billboards, newspapers, and broadcast stations. In 1996, Disney's acquisition of Capital Cities/ABC was a $19 billion deal—fifty-six times larger. In 2001, AOL's acquisition of Time Warner dwarfed even this deal at $160 billion, or nearly ten times the price of the 1996 Disney deal.

These companies, Bagdikian contends, have built a communications cartel within the United States. A cartel is a group of independent businesses that collaborate to regulate production, pricing, and marketing of goods by the members of the group. In this case, the group is controlling not just industrial products such as gasoline, refrigerators, or clothing. At stake are the symbols—the words and images—that define and shape the culture and political agenda of the country.

"Aided by the digital revolution and the acquisition of subsidiaries that operate at every step in the mass communications process, from the creation of content to its delivery into the home, the communications cartel has exercised stunning influence over national legislation and government agencies, an influence whose scope and power would have been considered scandalous or illegal twenty years ago," writes Bagdikian.

Bagdikian further notes that 99 percent of the daily newspapers in the United States are the only daily in their cities. All but a few of the nation's cable systems are monopolies in their cities. Most of the country's commercial radio stations are part of national ownership groups, and just a half-dozen formats (e.g., all news, rock, hip hop, adult contemporary, oldies, easy listening) dominate programming in every city. The major commercial television networks and their local affiliates carry programs of essentially the same type all across the country. By looking at media from this perspective, it seems that perhaps there is not as much diversity in media channels as would first appear.

This system is called a **media oligopoly**. A media oligopoly refers to a marketplace in which media ownership and diversity is severely limited and the actions of any single media group substantially affect its competitors, including determining the content and price of media products for both consumers and advertisers.

Dominating the media worldwide are eight diversified global media giants. These corporations are international conglomerates, many of which are either themselves part of a larger company comprising nonmedia business interests or contain in their financial portfolio significant nonmedia commercial properties

media oligopoly

A marketplace in which media ownership and diversity are severely limited and the actions of any single media group substantially affect its competitors, including determining the content and price of media products for both consumers and advertisers.

and investments. They include a wide range of media or channels of distribution. Of special note is that three of the eight started as technology companies and that Google didn't even exist until late 1998.

Much of what we see, hear, or read in traditional media, or interact with on the Web, comes from one of these eight companies. Of course, these are not the only media companies in the world, as there is what McChesney calls a "second tier" of about fifty large media companies operating at the national or international level, each doing more than $1 billion of business a year. Any of these second-tier companies, in and of themselves, can be considered a huge media power with an array of business interests, but their revenues pale in comparison to the big eight.

The trend of media concentration continues, even among the top eight (in 1999 there were nine, and that doesn't include the addition of Yahoo!, Apple, and Google since 1999). In 2007 and starting again in late 2008, Microsoft approached Yahoo! with the idea of a friendly takeover. The merger of Yahoo! and Microsoft would make a software and Web-content powerhouse to rival the juggernaut that is Google, but it would further concentrate the channels by which the public receives news, entertainment, and information. Although that deal appears dead, it is likely to arise again either with these two companies or with a similarly large media company. The image in the gatefold insert at the back of this book shows the evolution of the concentration of media ownership over approximately twenty-five years.

The concentration of media ownership and consolidation of media companies into ever larger companies is not simply about learning "the inside scoop" on who owns what. As Bagdikian, McChesney, and other scholars have pointed out, it has serious repercussions for our politics, society, and culture because of the power that media have in our lives. This is becoming even more important as social media sites such as Facebook become ever more popular sources of information and content.

◢▼ Historical Development of Digital Media

Digital media are not simply an improvement on or enhancement of other forms of media, in the same way that radio could be thought of as "wireless telegraphy," or broadcast television could be thought of as "radio with moving images," for example.

For many people it will not matter that a song was created, produced, and even distributed digitally. But digitization of media alters and threatens existing media business models, creates new opportunities for media-content creators, and causes shifts in how media consumers access, use, and interact with media.

Digital media are those that have been created in or transformed into machine language, or computer-readable form. Computers can only understand "on" or "off" states, or the presence or absence of information, represented by either a 1 or 0, called a "bit." Each bit of information (the term "bit" is a shortening of "**b**inary dig**it**") in a computer is stored in what is called "binary code." Eight bits make a byte (pronounced BITE).

A series of bits, a byte, or a series of bytes can represent any information. Each letter of the alphabet is one byte, so capital A is represented in computer-readable code as "01000001," for example. Every digital word, image, song, or movie is represented by nothing but a string of 0's and 1's, or electronic on–off states. A computer makes no distinction between a digital video clip and a digital text document, except for the differing amount of memory each takes up in the computer. The process in which media is made into computer-readable form is called **digitization**.

The term **analog media** derives from the world of audio recording, in which the modulation of the sound carrier wave is analogous to the fluctuations of the sound itself. Because of the on–off nature of digitization, it can never exactly capture a sound in the way analog media can; the best it can do is sample the original data and get as close to the original as possible.

Analog media work differently than digital media. Consider, for example, how Thomas Edison's original phonograph worked. Created in 1877, Edison's phonograph was an analog-media device that required the user to speak into a sound horn while rotating an attached tin cylinder. A needle, attached to a diaphragm that vibrated in corresponding fashion to the sounds of the speaker's voice, "recorded" or scratched onto the tin cylinder a pattern analogous to the sounds emitted by the speaker. Playing back the sound required the needle to move over the groove etched during the recording. The needle would vibrate as it moved over the groove, which caused the diaphragm to vibrate and emit via the sound horn a replica of the original voice. Modern phonographs use essentially the same principles, although helped greatly by improvements in materials, design, and the use of electronic rather than mechanical amplifiers.

 ## Discussing Digital Media: Networks Are Key

It became obvious to early computer pioneers that having a network that connects computers or media devices to each other so they can communicate would be essential. We will look at the development of the Internet and other communication networks in Chapter 7, so will provide only some basics here.

There are many kinds of networks, but we will concentrate primarily on the Internet and the World Wide Web here. All data that pass through the various networks—telephone, cable, or satellite—are at one or more stages digital, but we will use the term "digital media" to refer to networked, or online, digital media.

The broader topic of online communications, of which the Internet is a vital part, must be clarified. Although many may consider the term "online" synonymous with the Internet, "online" is in fact a term with a larger meaning. "Online" refers to the interconnected, networked media that permit the direct, electronic exchange of information, data, and other communications. Everything from local area networks (LANs) to wide area networks (WANs), such as the Internet, is part of the online world. In other words, the Internet and the World Wide Web are part of the online communications world; they are not the entire online world. However, the Internet and the Web are among the most important parts of the online world for mass communication because they are where much media content resides and where most of the public gets its digital content.

Out of all modern media, the Internet/World Wide Web reached 50 percent of U.S. households faster than any other media technology. It is important to note here, however, that the Internet is more complex in its requirements for adoption than other media. One can't simply go out and "buy an Internet" as one could with a radio or TV. Instead, one must first have a computer and a means of connecting it to the Internet, plus a higher level of technical media literacy to use the computer than is required for a television or VCR, so direct comparisons with older media

digitization

The process in which media is made into computer-readable form.

analog media

Term originally used in audio recording for media analogous to the sound being re-created. It now refers to all nondigitized media, such as print media, audio and video recordings, photography, and film.

TABLE 2-1

Number of Years to Reach a 50 Percent
Penetration of U.S. Households

Technology/Medium	Years
Newspapers	100+
Telephone	70
Phonograph	55
Cable Television	39
Personal Computer	19
Color Television	15
Radio	9
Broadband Internet[4]	9
Internet/World Wide Web	7
Tablet Devices (e.g., iPad)[5]	7

Adapted from John Carey ("The First 100 Feet for Households: Consumer
Adoption Patterns," paper presented to "The First 100 Feet: Options for
Internet and Broadband Access" conference by the Freedom Forum in
Arlington, VA [October 29–30, 1996]. Retrieved June 20, 2002, from http://
www.ksg.harvard.edu/iip/doeconf/carey.html); Electronic Industry Association;
U.S. Dept. of Commerce

types can be problematic. Nevertheless, even with these technological hurdles,
Table 2-1 shows the relatively rapid adoption rate of the Internet.

The World of Digital Media

Digital media did not simply spring from the ether, untouched by the existing
media environment. Rather, the development of digital media has been influenced
by traditional media businesses and the types of media content available, just as it
has influenced that content.

Discussing online mass communication means talking about all of mass communication. Today, countless offline mass-communication products, whether print
or electronic, also exist in some form online, or the physical product can be bought
online. It is unusual today if a newspaper, magazine, recording artist, television
network or station, or even individual movie does not have its own website, Facebook page, or Twitter handle.

Even companies not traditionally involved with mass communication have
found that maintaining their own websites is an excellent way to communicate directly to a large audience. For many young people, especially, who are comfortable
online, if an organization does not have a website or social media presence, then for
all intents and purposes it does not exist.

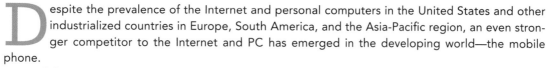

Mobile Telephony in the Developing World

INTERNATIONAL PERSPECTIVES

Despite the prevalence of the Internet and personal computers in the United States and other industrialized countries in Europe, South America, and the Asia-Pacific region, an even stronger competitor to the Internet and PC has emerged in the developing world—the mobile phone.

Mobile telephony holds several advantages over the Internet in many developing countries. First, the telecommunications infrastructure in these countries is often in poor condition, making land-line phone calls expensive and sporadic at best for those who have phones.

Without adequate phone lines, let alone consistent electric power, it is nearly impossible to depend on a PC or have regular Internet service, even a dial-up service. Needless to say, many of these countries do not have cable television industry wires, relying instead on satellite transmission of cable content, when allowed by the governments. (In countries like Malaysia, owning a satellite dish is a crime.)

Mobile telephones provide an easy and relatively cheap way for people to communicate with each other, and text messaging allows further mass coordination so that the phone becomes part of a larger, ad hoc mass-communication system.

There are even cases of mobile telephones helping foster a sense of community among phone users. In Nigeria, for example, women generally run the various market stalls throughout urban areas. By using mobile phones, they were able to easily coordinate prices with each other in different parts of the city. What's more, they recognized that they shared common interests and had common grievances, joining together to try to alleviate some of the problems they faced as sellers in markets.

The following discussion describes the current state of digital media as well as emerging trends among the major forms of mass communication. In subsequent chapters the history and development of these forms will be explored to show how they have influenced digital media today.

▼ DIGITAL PRINT

The printed word was the forerunner, just as it was in the traditional media world, to mass communication online. Limited computing power and slow Internet connection speeds have favored, for much of the history of the Internet, the use of text over audio or video. Although this has changed with the rise of broadband services in recent years, allowing audio and video to play more prominent roles on the Internet, text will always continue to be important for Web users.

Digital Books

Digital books offer a variety of advantages over printed books, including permitting the reader to not only read the text but to make electronic annotations and bookmarks, access the content of the book via an interactive table of contents, and search the entire text by keyword. Digital books and their sale online also point to a fundamental issue in the future of how mass-communication industries will derive much if not most of their revenue: from online transactions, or what is called ecommerce.

In the late 1990s, major publishers prepared for a surge in consumer demand for electronic books, and many experimented with the online sale and distribution of digital books. However, after the economic slowdown in 2000 that hit technology and Internet companies particularly hard, and a subsequent slowdown in sales of digital books, publishers started to adopt a slower, more cautious approach.

The launch in 2007 of Amazon's Kindle ebook reader, which stores up to two hundred titles, was heralded as the latest technology breakthrough that may finally be the tipping point toward digital books. Major publishers such as Random House, Simon & Schuster, and HarperCollins have embraced ebook readers like Kindle, the Sony Reader, and Barnes & Noble's Nook, making many more titles available for downloading. The growing popularity of tablet computers like the iPad have also increased the market for ebooks.

Free sample chapters and other marketing techniques will also likely help aid the growth of digital books, as will improvements in technology such as screen clarity. The growth in digital books, though only making up 9% of total book sales, has been remarkable in recent years. In 2008, ebook sales totaled $61.3 million. In 2009 they more than doubled to $169.5 million, and from January to August 2010 alone ebook sales had already surpassed 2009's sales at $263 million, a 193% increase from the same period the year before.[6]

Digital Newspapers and Magazines

One notable difference between online and offline newspapers is that the online "newspaper" sites are in direct competition with the leading national "broadcast" and "cable" television news sites. In fact, with growing calls for converged newsrooms and wider broadband access among the general public, newspaper websites increasingly contain audio, multimedia features, and video clips.

Online newspaper sites also face direct competition on a number of other fronts in the online arena, such as blogs, growing numbers of **citizen journalism** websites, news aggregators like Yahoo! News or Google News that combine news stories from a number of sources, and social media sites.

Advertising, especially classified ads, is another big area in which newspaper companies are threatened by the Internet. Classified ads make up a large portion of advertising revenues for most newspapers, but online classified-ads aggregators can allow people to search far more ads than are usually covered in a newspaper's circulation area. Similarly, users can visit an online auction site like eBay and reach a nationwide group of potential sellers or buyers, communicating with them directly.

There are very few online magazines that were created to be solely online: Slate.com and Salon.com are two of the most prominent ones. However, a growing number of print-based magazines have ceased publishing and moved to online-only versions in response to rising production costs and slowing readership growth.

There are several likely reasons online magazines have fared poorly in the digital world. One of the main reasons is technological: computer screens, especially mobile devices with small screens, still cannot match the clarity of the printed page, although this is starting to change with better and larger screens such as in tablet computers.

Changing behavior among members of the public in how they consume media is another factor weighing against long-form, text-based narratives like those found in the *New Yorker* or the *Atlantic Monthly*. With greater competition for their attention during the day, people seem less willing to spend the time necessary to read long articles. In an online environment, readers are also more likely to click on hyperlinks to get more information rather than wait for the author to fully explain

citizen journalism

Journalism done by amateurs or volunteers, either with citizen journalism websites, blogs, or as part of a mainstream news organization's website.

a point. Likewise, an article may be a starting point for a much more robust discussion among Web users in the form of online discussion groups, further detracting from the controlled narrative of a single author.

However, there could be an important niche for magazines to provide a measure of distance and perspective on issues and to thereby be a voice of authority in their specialized area. If a magazine is perceived as having suitable authority and is respected highly enough by its readers, it seems the public is willing to pay for an online subscription. Consumer Reports Online is one of the few success stories in the online-magazine world, when it comes to subscriptions, with over six hundred thousand subscribers who can access archived articles and reviews on various products.

▼ DIGITAL AUDIO

The MP3 file format represents an interesting example of how the new networked digital marketplace could work. It's indicative of how the recording industry will likely sell much of its music in the future, as the recording industry has been at the forefront of dealing with issues of piracy and other threats to traditional media business models. There are few case studies that better highlight the changes digital media are bringing to traditional mass-communication companies.

The MP3 file format is used to compress near-CD-quality audio, which then lets the files, which generally range between 2 and 4 MB in size, be distributed easily over the Internet. There is nothing inherently illegal in the MP3 file format itself; it is simply the technology used to compress audio files.

The problems with the recording industry arise because consumers can copy, download, and distribute music largely for free through file-sharing services. The recording industry has long held that it is acceptable for an individual who purchases a CD to make a copy for personal use, and it is of course not uncommon for friends to exchange copies of music among themselves.

File sharing of online music takes these exchanges to completely new levels, however. At any given time during the day, it is not unusual for millions of users to be on a file-sharing service, exchanging hundreds of millions of files. These are not simply audio, of course, and can include video, text, and images as well, but it would be safe to say most of the files being shared are music files.

Peer-to-peer file-sharing systems have been at the core of this phenomenon and have faced the brunt of the recording industry's wrath, though the industry has not been afraid to periodically threaten and even sue its own customers or push institutions like universities to take action in trying to stem the tide of file sharing. The issues surrounding peer-to-peer networking and the public sharing of music online are discussed in more detail in later chapters.

For now, suffice it to say that the major labels and everyone else in the recording industry value chain are enormously threatened by this development. They lose significant control, and, they say, their profits and investments are being reduced through the piracy of their intellectual property. It was not until 2001 that the major record labels finally began getting into the online music business themselves, even as they maintained their lawsuits against file-sharing services.

Finding new songs and artists you like may become more difficult than ever in the digital age as production and distribution costs decrease, allowing more people to create their own professional-sounding (although not necessarily good) recordings and distribute them digitally. One emerging solution is the use of intelligent agent-based collaborative filtering, a sort of music club for the digital age. Amazon.com and other ecommerce organizations already are making use of collaborative filtering to alert their customers to new books and music that they would likely find appealing, based on previous purchases and the purchasing patterns of people with similar buying tastes.

Radio has traditionally been the main avenue by which songs and artists are promoted. Yet in the digital world, the concept of radio is starting to change as consumers become used to being able to listen to music on demand through **podcasts** or downloaded music. In that way, online "radio" is technically audio programming, not true over-the-air broadcasting, and in some ways will seem much closer to the current state of on-demand online music downloads, even though the term "radio" may stay with us.

Web radio would seem to offer the best of both worlds—a radio format that provides access to any number of songs whenever a user wants to listen to them—yet a ruling in 2002 by the U.S. Copyright Office declared that webcasters must pay royalties for songs based on the number of their listeners. The ruling forced many webcasters from the Internet, as they could not afford to pay the backdated royalty payments from 1998.

Online radio stations must abide by the **Digital Millennium Copyright Act**, however, which prohibits the advance posting of playlists, which would permit users to plan when to copy songs. Even before the 2002 rulings on royalty payments for webcasts, some online radio stations paid royalties to one of the two music licensers in the United States, the American Society of Composers, Authors and Publishers (ASCAP), or Broadcast Music Inc. (BMI).

Live transmissions of sports events have emerged as an important part of online radio. In the case of Major League Baseball, Internet users must pay a fee to listen to live audio webcasts of professional baseball games.

Satellite radio, though not technically online, is also competing with traditional radio programming. Largely free of advertising and based on a subscription model, satellite radio offers many specific programs of sports, entertainment, talk radio, and music.

▼ DIGITAL VISUAL MEDIA

The Internet has proven a valuable means of distribution for movies, especially independent and short films, which have traditionally found distribution to be the most vexing bottleneck in becoming successful. Because independent and short films vary widely in quality and style and are produced outside the mainstream of Hollywood, few theaters, or theater chains, have been interested in showing them. The low cost of online distribution and the potential to build audiences over time and space has let a growing number of websites provide an extensive selection of independent and short films online.

Digital video has also been a godsend for low-budget directors, who can shoot professional-quality footage at a fraction of what it would cost for actual rolls of film. Editing and other postproduction work can also be done on computers or dedicated editing workstations.

There is a growing variety of sources of video content online, ranging from the popular YouTube to many video-sharing sites cloning the YouTube model. Most television stations and all major networks maintain websites with some of their television coverage online for viewing, and sites like Hulu have entire episodes from a number of networks as well as clips of shows.

As more people get broadband access, it is clear that video content will be shared in the same way music has been shared, and the film and video industries

podcast

A program that is usually audio or video that lets users easily subscribe, much like subscribing to a blog.

Digital Millennium Copyright Act

A copyright law in the United States that makes it a criminal act to circumvent or alter digital rights management technologies that protect copyrighted works.

have tried to learn the hard lessons from the recording industry in dealing with the potential threat to their business models.

Television stations seem to be taking a more conciliatory approach toward video-sharing sites than the recording industry did with music, though not after some initially negative reactions and demands to remove content. Realizing that YouTube was actually serving a useful function in promoting a network's shows, more networks began allowing clips from shows to be uploaded. In 2008, CBS agreed to have entire shows available on YouTube, no doubt hoping that the YouTube traffic would generate interest among the public to watch the shows on television as well.

◭▽ Digital Media Grammar

We may be thoroughly familiar with and comfortable using the Internet and online media, but there are still many people throughout the world who have limited or no contact with the online world. In addition, online media are still new enough that the grammar is still developing. The Web of 2002 bears little resemblance to the Web today and will look even more different in ten years.

Imagine a media world in which we have to teach someone how to turn pages in a book, or where people try to use a remote control on a magazine or are afraid to change the channel lest they break the television, or where they see a different kind of image on their TV compared to their neighbors because they have a different model. That is roughly the state of online media in the early twenty-first century, and it is unlikely to change anytime in the near future.

However, some media-grammar elements are starting to form. **Hypertext**, for example, is generally either underlined or otherwise set apart typographically or graphically from nonlinked text. More and more web designers are following an unwritten rule to have a website logo in the upper-left corner of the screen linked to return to the website's home page. Icons are increasingly used to create a visual, interactive "language" that transverses websites in order to allow computer users to quickly learn new types of programs or to utilize interactivity on a website, such as an **RSS feed** or letting someone "**digg**" a story. Other examples include more or less standardized icons for functions such as printing, opening a document, sending a file, emailing a document, and manipulating images (such as zooming in or out), where applicable.

Mass communication in an online digital environment increasingly exploits a full range of storytelling and communication tools, including text, audio, video, graphics, and animation. This broadened set of tools enables communication professionals to tell each story in a manner uniquely suited to that story. Because of the lack of experience of new online-media users and the ever-changing state of technological improvements, it still can be a challenge to guide users to access that information.

There are four main concepts that underlie the digital media world—multimedia, interactivity, automation, and ethereality. Some of these are not unique to digital media, as there are examples in the analog media world as well, but digitization makes them easier than ever before. Each plays an important role in giving digital media the power that they have.

hypertext

Text online that is linked to another web page, website, or different part of the same web page by HTML coding.

RSS feed

Short for really simple syndication, it lets users easily subscribe to feeds from a blog or website.

"digg"

A popular website in which users submit material (called "digging") to be voted on by other users, with the most popular material appearing on the home page.

▼ MULTIMEDIA

When all information consists of bits, it becomes easy to juxtapose various media types that could not coexist in the analog media world. There will never be an option to watch a video clip in a print newspaper or listen to the interview of the

Ebook readers allow for multimedia in books as well as greater levels of interactivity than traditional print media.

story; the nature of print as a medium and physical laws of nature simply will not allow it. The best that can be done is to read and perhaps look at a photograph or use other media such as a radio or television to supplement the reading. Likewise, it is impossible to retrieve the written lyrics of a song directly from the radio.

The idea of **multimedia**, or combining various media types into one package, is not new. Putting photographs with text is a type of multimedia, but a better example is the combination of moving pictures and sound, as in film and video. In the digital world, however, there are more opportunities for multimedia. Video can sit side by side with a text transcript, and audio can play while the media consumer reads the lyrics of a song or reads information about the artist or even watches a concert by the artist.

▼ INTERACTIVITY

Interactivity is a crucial aspect of digital media but is, ironically, extremely hard to define to everyone's satisfaction. There is no doubt that the term is misunderstood, misused, and abused. According to WhatIs? online encyclopedia, it is defined this way:

> In computers, interactivity is the dialog that occurs between a human being (or possibly another live creature) and a computer program. . . . In addition to hypertext, the Web (and many non-Web applications in any computer system) offers other possibilities for interactivity. Any kind of user input, including typing commands or clicking the mouse, is a form of input. Displayed images and text, printouts, motion video sequences, and sounds are output forms of interactivity.[7]

Media and Internet scholar Sheizaf Rafaeli states that interactivity is "the condition of communication in which simultaneous and continuous exchanges occur."[8] In other words, interaction involves two or more parties to a communication engaging in an ongoing give-and-take of messages.

For our purposes, we will define interactivity as having the following elements:

1. A dialog that occurs between a human and a computer program (this includes emails, online chats, and discussion groups, as at either end of the communication flow it is a human interacting with a computer program—the Internet is simply the channel).

2. The dialog affects the nature or type of feedback or content that is received, changing as the dialog continues.

3. The audience has some measure of control over what media content it sees and in what order (getting personalized or localized information, magnifying an image, clicking on a hyperlink, etc.).

These three components of interactivity include almost all of the activities that we typically engage in with digital media and make interaction with digital media fundamentally different than that with traditional media. Turning the pages of a magazine may be considered "interactive" by some, but the reader is unable to engage in dialog with the article, cannot change the size of text or personalize the information in the article, and the article itself will remain unchanged no matter what the reader writes in the margins.

multimedia

A combination of different types of media in one package; thus, film or video with sound is a type of multimedia because it combines visual and audio elements. Web pages that combine text, video, animation, audio, or graphics are another type of multimedia.

interactivity

Although an exact definition is still being debated, for digital-media purposes interactivity can be defined as having three main elements: (1) a dialog that occurs between a human and a computer program, (2) a dialog that occurs simultaneously or nearly so, and (3) the audience has some measure of control over what media content it sees and in what order.

▼ AUTOMATION

Computers can be programmed to automate many complex and time-consuming tasks, which are made easier since all data exists in essentially the same format. Search engines and other elements that make computers and the Web relatively easy to use are all possible through automation. Automation enables computers to draw 3-D objects, it makes computer games engaging, and it is changing the way journalists and other media professionals do their work. But automation also makes it much easier for companies to find and track individuals and makes media use no longer anonymous.

Automation plays a crucial role in the ability of online media to be **personalized** and **localized** or to provide user-specific or geographic-specific information. Users can specify what kinds of news or information they want to receive based on any number of factors, such as geography, interests, or specific topics. With automation, computer programs can even select media content that is more likely to be of interest to a specific user simply based on tracking of websites or type of content the user has visited.

personalization

The ability of media-content producers to provide content that is of interest to a specific user based either on criteria the user has selected, such as a zip code, or on automated tracking of their Web-viewing habits.

localization

The ability of media-content producers to provide content based on a user's locale, either done automatically based on an ISP or after the user has provided information such as a city name or zip code.

▼ ETHEREALITY

We've already said how digital media is made up of representations of 1's and 0's. In some ways digital information is better without a physical presence, as often the need to put it in some sort of physical form makes it lose its natural digital characteristics.

The "immaterial" quality of digital information has far-reaching consequences for distribution of content, media companies, the law, and society. Digital libraries will not need time limits for books that are checked out, as online visitors simply download a perfect copy to their own computer. In fact, the concept of "checking out" a book becomes meaningless. The concept of watching a show broadcast at 8 p.m. on a certain night of the week is similarly meaningless. The shows are available, all the time, and can be accessed and watched on demand. Endless copies of media content can be made and easily distributed, as file-sharing services have shown.

With all of digital media's capabilities, it is easy to forget that digital information has no real form.

◣◤ Commercial Forces on Digital Media Content

Traditionally, media enterprises, like other industrial-age businesses, required heavy capital investment. Capital was required to build the transmission towers for television and radio stations. It was required to buy printing presses and to build cable systems. Not only was the infrastructure expensive, but it created enormous barriers to entry for prospective competition.

In the digital age, these rules are changing. Some of the most significant barriers to entry are shrinking. Capital costs are reduced, as almost anyone who is online can create a website and potentially compete with established media companies. It is part of why relative newcomers such as Google, Yahoo!, and Craigslist have been so successful. Moreover, few media enterprises have found a formula for making profits in the online world, as most people seem unwilling to pay for content and traditional advertising has not been very effective.

Most large online media outlets have the backing of traditional media companies, such as MSNBC.com, a joint venture between NBC and Microsoft, or CNBC.com. With advertising and other revenues generated from the parent companies, these online endeavors can afford to take losses for a while as online revenue models are tried and tested. Many smaller, independent, dot-com media companies were not so fortunate, especially after the economy and stock market spiralled downward from spring 2000. Some severely scaled back their business plans, and others, such as award-winning crime-news website APBnews.com, went out of business.

Although the Web today is largely commercial, the roots of computing and the Internet were based on nonmarket principles. The earliest computing and Internet pioneers instead shared an ethos of collaboration and sharing information, and this tradition lives on in the form of the open-source movement, also called the free-software movement.

▼ THE OPEN-SOURCE MOVEMENT

One of the biggest challenges to the usual business models has come from the open-source movement. The open-source, or free-software, movement began with creating software and programs that were freely available for anyone to use. Further, the source code, or code that created the programs, was purposely left accessible so others could tinker with it and improve the program, sharing it with yet more people to do the same. This was the spirit of community and sharing on nonmarket principles that embodied the early development of computers and the Internet.

Today, the public benefits from a range of high-quality open-source software, most available for free or at a fraction of the cost of similar software. The operating system Linux is one example, as is OpenOffice, the software suite that includes word processing, spreadsheet, database, presentation, and drawing software. With capabilities that rival if not surpass what Microsoft Office offers, it has the added advantage of being free to download and without the requirement for subsequent purchases of updates or new releases, as they are free as well. The open-source web browser Firefox has slowly taken away from the market share of Microsoft's Internet Explorer browser, and for every commercial software product or service you are able to find several open-source projects.

The notions of the open-source movement have moved to content production as well, with Wikipedia being a prime example of how many volunteers can come together on their own and create something far grander than any individual or smaller group could create, all for no monetary compensation. The logic seems to defy explanation in an economic system that has been based on producing commodities (including media) that are bought and sold, yet it has become a powerful competitive force for mainstream computer makers and for media companies.

For example, some countries have adopted OpenOffice as the standard office-suite software for all government agencies, which can easily lead large-scale organizations such as educational institutions to also adopt OpenOffice in order to have compatible file types when communicating with the government agencies that oversee them. This of course is a threat to Microsoft's business model of selling its proprietary software Microsoft Office and then charging customers for periodic updates. In order to counter OpenOffice, Microsoft has provided computers (loaded with Microsoft Office, of course) free to libraries in some developing countries. The hope is that once people become familiar with a certain type of software, they will be reluctant to switch. Microsoft, with its billions of dollars in revenues,

Open-source software such as Linux gives users for free the same capabilities as proprietary software and has seen more widespread adoption by institutions and even governments.

Wikipedia in Our Cites: The Trouble with Collaborative Knowledge

Wikipedia has become an amazing cultural phenomenon and source for knowledge in a very short time, surpassing traditional encyclopedias in both scope of topics covered and speed with which information is updated. Furthermore, one study showed that Wikipedia was comparable to the venerable Encyclopaedia Britannica in terms of accuracy.[9]

In March 2012 the 244-year-old *Encyclopaedia Britannica* announced that it would no longer print its encyclopedias anymore after its 2010 edition. The decision reflected the dramatic changes in how people search for information today, a change that Wikipedia also illustrates.

Wikipedia is a type of **wiki**, or website in which pages can be created and edited by anyone. The scope and depth of knowledge demonstrated by individuals making small contributions to Wikipedia has astounded even skeptics of the idea of just how much the general public actually knows.

With so much information in one place, and accuracy that is purported to match established and well-respected encyclopedias, the question often arises from dismayed college students why they are not allowed to cite Wikipedia in their papers. The best way to use Wikipedia when doing research is as a first stop to get an overview of a subject and to quickly find relevant links to sources that you can trust. Then go to those sources to find more in-depth information and verify the facts presented.

In Wikipedia, although the overall information of any specific article may be accurate, there could be inaccuracies, either by mistake or put there deliberately by mischievous contributors, that have gone unnoticed. Without knowing where a specific piece of information came from, it is impossible to verify its accuracy.

However, the Wikipedia community does have a robust system in place to catch errors, both through human editors and through automatic means. People caught vandalizing entries have their IP addresses blocked and then cannot edit Wikipedia. Sources must be properly cited or are flagged for citations if they are not, and Wikipedia's policy is to only include information that has already been published elsewhere.

Wikipedia is part of the not-for-profit Wikimedia Foundation. It has been trying to solicit small donations from readers in increasingly strident ad campaigns, including large banner ads across the top of article pages that showcase contributors or the founder, Jimmy Wales.

WEB LINK
Wikipedia
www.en.wikipedia.org

can take a small loss initially in giving away computers with the goal of attracting long-term customers.

For media companies such as Encyclopaedia Britannica or Microsoft's now-defunct Encarta, an open-source encyclopedia free for anyone to use was a direct threat to their subscription business model. Of course, the open-source challenger would have to be as accurate and have the same high quality as the products that a person would normally pay for. This has not been an issue by and large with Wikipedia, where the self-correcting mechanisms of many volunteers working together have helped make it a dynamic and relevant source of information.

▼ REVENUE MODELS FOR DIGITAL MEDIA

One of the most significant challenges all commercial online media properties face is building a revenue stream to not only cover costs but to return a profit. There are several ways online media companies can generate revenues—at least in theory.

wiki

A type of website that can be edited by anyone.

These include traditional methods such as advertising, subscriptions, and syndication, as well as methods that are either unique or feasible in an online environment, such as ecommerce or joint offline and online activities. However, none so far have proven to be inherently better than other methods, and companies are still experimenting with ways to earn profits. It is likely that more advanced technology will open the door to creative revenue-generating models that are unavailable today.

For the time being, the revenue streams that appear most viable for content sites involve a combination of advertising, subscription, ecommerce, and leveraging content or data in partnerships online and offline.

Advertising

Traditional banner advertising has proved disappointing in generating revenues for all but the largest sites that attract millions of visitors. Media companies both offline and online charge advertisers for the cost per thousand (**CPM**) of audience members. This means a magazine with a circulation of one hundred thousand can receive more for carrying ads than a magazine with a circulation of ten thousand.

Banner ads still exist but have largely been superseded by other types of ads. A **banner ad** is one that sits at the top or along the side of a web page. They have had a history of very low **click-through rates (CTR)**, or the rate at which people click on the ad.

In the online media environment, technology allows website owners to not only see exactly how many people have visited a given page on the site, but to track whether people clicked on the advertisement on that page or not. When advertisers are able to see how low the click-through rates are, they question the effectiveness of the ads in attracting customers.

Online companies have tried a number of things to improve click-through rates on ads and thereby increase revenues. Larger ads, animated ads, and pop-up and pop-under ads have all been tried. Some show slightly higher click-through rates than static banner ads, but they also run the risk of annoying Web users who do not want to have to click "close" on a number of ads just to get to the content they initially wanted.

Search engine advertising has become the most important form of advertising on the Web, and the most successful. Based on the fact that people increasingly go to search engines such as Google as the first place to start looking for content, the placement on a search-results page can be the difference between success and failure for a company. **Search engine marketing (SEM)** involves paying a search engine to have a listing in a specific part of a search-results page, while **search engine optimization (SEO)** uses careful keyword choices, site design, and linking strategies to get a site listed higher in a search engine's ranking.

Subscriptions

The most successful revenue-producing media sites have been those that have carved out an important content niche, produced original, quality content, and designed an effective, efficient online presence—and charged a subscription for their site. The two best examples are The Wall Street Journal Interactive and Consumer Reports Online. Consumer Reports Online provides all the content from its well-known magazine, plus additional customizable information and reports on product testing and ratings. With a fee of less than fifty dollars a year, Consumer Reports Online has captured over six hundred thousand paid subscribers. This is only a fraction of its 3 million paid subscribers to the printed magazine,

CPM

Cost per thousand. The standard unit for measuring advertising rates for publications, based on circulation.

banner ad

An advertisement across the top or along the side of a website, and the original form of advertising on the Web.

click-through rate [CTR]

Rate at which people click on the ad.

search engine marketing [SEM]

Paying a search engine such as Google to have a listing appear prominently when searched.

search engine optimization [SEO]

A strategy that utilizes website design, careful choice of keywords, links, and other techniques to show prominently in online searches.

The rise in popularity of tablet computers has given publishers new opportunities for online versions of their publications.

but it is nevertheless a significant number and revenue stream (nearly $30 million a year).

Most other sites that have tried subscription models, however, have not been as successful. Even the esteemed *New York Times* failed in its experiment with a partial subscription model, its Times Select product, in which op-ed columnists could not be accessed unless a subscription fee was paid. This essentially quarantined some of the most popular content of its online newspaper, and after two years the *Times* announced it was abandoning Times Select. In early 2010 the *Times* announced it was moving to a **freemium** model. Non-subscribers could read up to twenty articles per month for free from the site and after that would have to subscribe, while subscribers would have unlimited access to all the content all the time. Partial subscription models like these are being tried by a number of online media companies as they look for what types of content the public is willing to pay for in a medium that started out with, and still has, most of its information available for free.

Ecommerce

Ecommerce refers to the electronic commercial environment that emerged in the 1990s, primarily on the Internet. Ecommerce presents an interesting opportunity in the long run for media businesses operating in the digital age. The online arena is an environment in which consumers can not only get information about products on demand, but, conversely, media and other organizations can collect vast amounts of data on the behavior of their online visitors. This data can be extremely valuable to advertisers that want to reach specific audiences.

Further, through **behavioral targeting**, users can receive ads based on their online profiles, their past browsing behavior, and even through what friends in

freemium

A subscription type in which subscribers can receive some content for free but if they want to take advantage of all the site has to offer they must pay a monthly subscription.

behavioral targeting

A technique used to increase the effectiveness of their campaigns by using information collected on an individual's web-browsing behavior to select which advertisements to display to that individual.

their social network have browsed, bought, or recommended. Proponents of behavioral targeting say that it gives users more relevant ads, while critics say that it invades users' privacy, especially when their browsing or buying behavior is being shared among their social network without their knowledge.

Related to behavioral targeting but on a simpler level, a variety of media and nonmedia products can be packaged with media content and promoted. For example, a book review may have a link to Amazon or some other bookseller, making it easy to purchase the book, or have titles within the genre in an ad alongside the book review. It would seem to be a convenient way for a reader who likes the review to buy the book, and it is. However, if the website is an "affiliate member" of Amazon, a common program in which a member receives a commission on each book sold if consumers come to Amazon through a link on the member's site, then the website's or reviewer's journalistic objectivity could be called into question. It is in their best financial interest to get people to buy that book, making it appear less likely that a reviewer would give a negative review. This kind of behavior, for which several large media organizations have been called to task in the past several years, further erodes public trust in content produced by media companies.

Related to making ecommerce successful is that media companies must show a willingness to surrender some of the control they have had over packaging media content. Allowing customers to buy individual songs rather than an entire CD is one simple example of something recording labels showed remarkable resistance to until the past several years. Allowing a good deal more "try before you buy" free trial samples, such as Kindle's free book chapters, is another business practice that will have to be encouraged for online customers.

WEB LINK
Last Page of the Internet
www.1112.net/lastpage.html

LOOKING BACK AND MOVING FORWARD

Media literacy is not a goal to reach but an ongoing process in which one can always improve in order to become a better mass media consumer and user. Media literacy involves critically thinking about the media. By developing a better understanding in three key areas—the historical development of media types, media grammar, and how commercial forces shape media content—we can be aware of when mass media are trying to manipulate us and can act accordingly.

It is perhaps hardest for us to recognize how commercial forces shape the type of content we see, largely because we see the end product and not the processes that have taken place behind the scenes to make that media product. But it is arguably the most important aspect of media literacy and of being a critical media user to consider how commercial forces may not always have the best interests of the public at heart, even when media companies claim they are serving the public or simply giving the people what they want.

Broadband digital media present both an opportunity and a threat for those in the media and communication industries. On the one hand, long-standing corporations, institutions, and entire industries are being turned upside down by the digital revolution. Businesses built on analog technologies of production and distribution are trying to figure out how to adapt in the digital age. New efficiencies of creating and delivering content in a digital, networked environment are emerging throughout the world. Long-held, highly profitable business models based on the analog world are less viable in a digital marketplace.

Nevertheless, the new digital world means new business opportunities. It means opening new markets that formerly were restricted by political, economic, and geographic boundaries. It means new storytelling formats that bring true interactivity to television and radio. It means creating immersive audio and video on demand for consumers who want their media, in all its forms, customized not only according to their preferences but to their current geographic location and many other factors.

The changes that we are witnessing with convergence, especially the rise of user-generated content and collaborative media, are perhaps the most direct challenge to some of the traditional media companies who have enjoyed largely unquestioned dominance of the public's attention throughout most of the twentieth century. The way the public is creating media, often on nonmarket principles and simply for the joy of sharing and interacting with others, belies the notion that the public is as happy with its mainstream media content as media conglomerates would have us believe.

As some open-source advocates are discovering, profits do not necessarily have to come from the sale of packaged media products such as books. Seth Godin, a noted author on Internet advertising and marketing, makes his books freely available for download on the Internet. This would appear to be the fast track to the poorhouse, but Godin's success stems from the fact that his strategy helps get his books in the hands of many influential people, including business leaders and conference organizers, who then invite him (and pay him) to speak at events and conferences.

The conflict between open-source philosophies in the realm of cultural production and proprietary business models based on traditional, industrial-era models of media production is one of the main ideological struggles taking place today regarding the Internet. At stake are notions of intellectual property protection, the availability of cultural material in the public domain, and the future of the audience as either passive media consumers with limited choices or active produsers in a vibrant, interactive community.

Companies' efforts to keep the public satiated with a never-ending stream of media content (that it continues to pay for), and to maintain the largely one-way flow of content from media producer to audience, will continue and even intensify. Scholars such as McChesney are skeptical that the Internet will live up to its promise as a transformational communication technology that can improve democracy and better engage citizens. Whether it does or not will largely depend on how media literate the public becomes and how well we can develop our moral reasoning and ethical thinking to make sure that we do indeed create the kind of society we want to live in, not just have to live in.

DISCUSSION QUESTIONS

1. Go to the library and look at a newspaper from forty years ago (likely only available on microfilm now) and compare the front page with the same paper for the year you were born and that of today. What differences do you notice? What is your first impression of each one? Which one provides more information?

2. If online news websites merged into combined newspaper/radio/television news stations or channels, which group do you think would be better prepared to learn new skills—print journalists learning broadcast skills or broadcast journalists learning print skills? Why do you think so?

3. What do you think the popularity of "reality TV" says about U.S. society and media literacy? Is it a change for the better or for the worse?

4. Would you be willing to pay a mandatory annual television licensing fee if television networks and cable companies promised to show fewer commercials? If so, how much would you be willing to pay? What advantages or disadvantages could there be to a stronger public-supported media presence in the United States?

5. Imagine a media system that is entirely publicly funded and that does not allow commercials of any kind. What problems may arise with a publicly-funded media system and how do you think programming may be different?

6. What open-source software do you use? Where did you first hear about it? Why did you decide to try it? Why do you still use it?

7. Which revenue models have the most potential to be successful for digital media? Why?

8. Describe your vision of how the media world will be for most people five years from now. Discuss how and where people would access news, entertainment, and other media content, and examine what media companies may be important.

FURTHER READING

Media Literacy, 5th ed. W. James Potter (2010) Sage Publications.

Approaches to Media Literacy: A Handbook, 2nd ed. Art Silverblatt, Jane Ferry, and Barbara Finan (2009) M.E. Sharpe.

Digital and Media Literacy: Connecting Culture and Classroom. Renee Hobbs (2011) Corwin Press.

The New Media Monopoly. Ben H. Bagdikian (2004) Beacon Press.

The Political Economy of Media: Enduring Issues, Emerging Dilemmas. Robert W. McChesney (2008) Monthly Review Press.

Rich Media, Poor Democracy: Communication Politics in Dubious Times. Robert McChesney (1999) The New Press.

The Problem of the Media: U.S. Communication Politics in the Twenty-First Century. Robert McChesney (2004) Monthly Review Press.

Jamming the Media: A Citizen's Guide to Reclaiming the Tools of Communication. Gareth Branwyn (1997) Chronicle Books.

Citizen Muckraking: How to Investigate and Right Wrongs in Your Community. The Center for Public Integrity (2000) Common Courage Media.

The Conquest of Cool: Business Culture, Counterculture, and the Rise of Hip Consumerism. Thomas Frank (1997) The University of Chicago Press.

Convergence Culture: Where Old and New Media Collide. Henry Jenkins (2008) NYU Press.

New Media Old Media: A History and Theory Reader. Wendy Hui Kyong Chun and Thomas Keenan (2007) Taylor & Francis.

Wikinomics: How Mass Collaboration Changes Everything. Don Tapscott and Anthony Williams (2008) Portfolio Hardcover.

The Wealth of Networks: How Social Production Transforms Markets and Freedom. Yochai Benkler (2007) Yale University Press.

Bodies in Code: Interfaces with Digital Media. Mark Hansen (2007) Routledge.

Infotopia: How Many Minds Produce Knowledge. Cass Sunstein (2007) Oxford University Press.

Of course the answers to some of the questions will depend on when students take the quiz, but as far as the timeless answers go, here they are:

4. False.

5. *The Green Mile, The Shining, It, Salem's Lot, Hearts in Atlantis, Cujo, Carrie,* just to name some.

7. True.

8. True.

9. False.

10. True.

3

PRINT MEDIA: BOOKS, NEWSPAPERS, AND MAGAZINES

LEARNING OBJECTIVES

By the end of this chapter you should be able to:

- Describe the functions of print media in general, and distinguish between books, magazines, and newspapers.

- Trace the historical development of print media.

- Think critically about current business issues affecting the industries for each print medium.

- Outline the financial model for each print medium, including sales, circulation, readership, and distribution.

- Identify forces—including political, cultural, economic, technological—likely to affect the future of the print media.

The announcement by the Justice Department in April 2012 had several of the biggest book publishers shaking in their boots—and others shaking their heads.

The antitrust suit filed by the government accused Apple and five major publishers of colluding to secretly set prices of ebooks from 2010 so that no publisher could undercut Apple. When Amazon's Kindle was practically the sole ebook reader, ebooks typically cost $9.99. However, consumers noticed that ebook prices jumped to $14.99 after Apple's iPad came out, which could also act as an ebook reader.

After the suit was filed, three of the publishers—HarperCollins, Hachette, and Simon & Schuster—settled with the government, while Penguin and Macmillan, along with Apple, vowed to fight the suit. The chief executive of Macmillan said the company had done nothing wrong and had colluded with no one.

Amazon controls about 60 percent of the ebook market.[1] An already tense relationship with publishers soured further when Amazon announced that they would enter the publishing business, which would put them in direct competition with book publishers rather than just acting as a retailer of publishers' ebooks. In order to break Amazon's near-monopoly on ebooks through its Kindle reader, the government's suit claims, the publishers decided to secretly work with Apple to promote non-Kindle ebooks.

Ironically, the antitrust suit actually puts Amazon in an even stronger position than before, with one industry analyst saying that a perceived monopoly has now been replaced with a real monopoly. With its commanding position in the field of ebooks, Amazon can afford to take losses on ebook sales as it attracts more Kindle buyers, thus locking in the market, critics charge.

In the short term, consumers will see a drop in prices in ebooks, which will no doubt make them happy. The lawsuit claims that consumers lost $100 million over the past two years because of the price-fixing scheme.[2]

Supporters of the book-publishing industry, including many bookstore owners, are not so sure the shift in power is good in the long run, as without competition there is little incentive for a company like Amazon to continue to innovate or keep prices as low as they are.

At the heart of the matter here is a classic confrontation between industries built around the traditional business models—in this case, book publishing—and a bold new competitor that says it wants to encourage reading while being willing to adjust to new distribution methods and new pricing models.

Shelves full of books, racks brimming with magazines, and newsstands overflowing with newspapers are familiar. Yet print media are undergoing momentous changes as they transform from analog to digital. This chapter examines the history, business models, and current challenges of print media.

Print media represent the beginning of mass communication. Their origins lie in the "typographical era" of the Middle Ages. Mass forms of mechanical printing and typography played a role in sweeping social change in Europe, including mass literacy and the Renaissance. Print media challenged society's ability to adapt to technological change, just as modern society is struggling to adapt to digital media.

Some scholars, such as noted communication scholar **Marshall McLuhan**, even claim that reading printed words has changed the way we think. Reading, as opposed to viewing or listening, lets us ponder what the author is saying. We can go back and reread and think about passages of text, and develop arguments over time in response to points that are made, in ways that we simply cannot do when watching or listening to someone speak. The format of the printed word, some scholars claim, helps us develop solid critical-thinking skills and encourages us to refine arguments using logic. It is interesting to consider how electronic media and the Internet could be affecting our thinking just as much. What McLuhan wrote about electronic media in 1962 in *The Gutenberg Galaxy* could equally be applied to the effect of digital media: "We are today as far into the electric age as the Elizabethans had advanced into the typographical and mechanical age. And we are experiencing the same confusions and indecisions which they had felt when living simultaneously in two contrasted forms of society and experience."

Marshall McLuhan

A communication scholar who wrote *Understanding Media* and *The Gutenberg Galaxy,* among other books. He is perhaps most famous for creating the "global village" metaphor regarding electronic media and his often-misunderstood phrase "the medium is the message."

Print Media

1. What was the last book you read for pleasure? What made you decide to read it?
2. Where did you buy your latest book that was not a textbook?
3. What is the oldest book you own?
4. Did you read a print newspaper today? If not, when was the last time you read a print newspaper?
5. Compare the print version of your local newspaper with its online version. Are there stories found in one format but not the other?
6. Did you read any news today from a website? If so, describe at least one story.
7. Do you subscribe to any magazines? Which ones?
8. If you subscribe to a magazine, describe how you typically read it. For example, do you read some sections first and jump around, or cover-to-cover? Do you read it over a month, or soon after getting it?
9. What do these reading patterns say about your relationship with the magazine?
10. What makes you decide to print out an article you read online rather than read it on the screen?

Functions of Print Media

From a child's first beginner book throughout adult life, print media, in the form of books, newspapers, and magazines, serve many social functions. Among the most important are the transmission of culture from generation to generation, the diffusion of ideas and knowledge, and entertainment. These ideas overlap, but are important for explaining social meaning.

▼ TRANSMISSION OF CULTURE

From childhood on, people learn the language, values, and traditions of a culture from all types of media. Although not the sole means of transmitting culture, books, newspapers, and magazines teach what is considered right or wrong in a society, what is socially acceptable and what is unacceptable. Immigrants often learn about the rules and norms of a society from reading. In learning how to read, children absorb the basic principles and practices of a culture. On a grander scale, consider the lasting impact of ancient religious texts such as the Bible, Koran, or Torah in imparting cultural mores and values.

▼ DIFFUSION OF IDEAS AND KNOWLEDGE

Culture is especially transmitted through education. Books lay the foundation for formal education and are central to many people's lifelong formal and informal education. Textbooks and other works of nonfiction impart everything from scientific knowledge to psychological self-help. Books teach not only how to do things, but explain what is known about the arts, literature, history, contemporary society, and social and natural sciences.

Newspapers and magazines keep us informed of the latest events and interpret those events in order to help us make sense of the world. We read about new discoveries, fashions, trends, and other parts of the world through newspapers and magazines. Special-interest magazines give us knowledge of specific fields or hobbies and help us connect with others who share our interests.

▼ ENTERTAINMENT

Sometimes we intend to learn something specific, but reading is often done purely for the joy it provides. Reading can offer escape or diversion, and readers travel to exotic places or faraway planets, or experience fantastic creatures and memorable characters, all through the printed page. For many people there is often a sense of disappointment when they see a movie version of a favorite novel, as the characters do not seem to be how they pictured them in their mind.

Comic books and picture books provide children some of their first experiences in reading, and the stories are meant to be entertaining in order to engage young readers and encourage them to read. Short stories or nonfiction writing in magazines and books can both inform and entertain us.

Just because something is read primarily for entertainment does not mean that it cannot also impart knowledge to the reader. We can gain access to what the ancients thought through their books, often making connections across centuries as we find commonalities in the human condition. Great literature can elevate our senses and make us feel new emotions as characters come to life. Readers who may not otherwise know or care how our legal system works, or what it is like to be in military intelligence, nevertheless can learn a lot when they read legal thrillers such as *The Firm* by John Grisham or military action stories such as *The Hunt for Red October* by Tom Clancy.

However, there have been some studies in recent years that show a marked drop in reading among the American public, with fewer than half of American adults saying they read literature. The steepest decline in reading literature is among young people, although reading has declined across all age groups.[3]

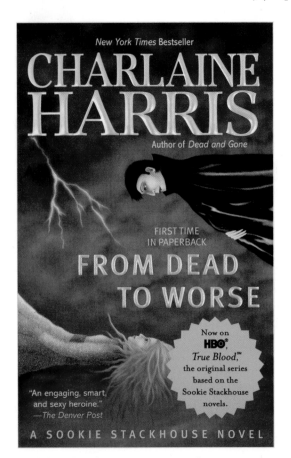

Books have long been a main source of entertainment for the reading public.

◣ Distinctive Functions of Books

Books have played an important role throughout history. Even before there were books in the form that we know them today, compiling a large volume of knowledge and putting it in one document (scroll or book) was seen as a vital, even sacred endeavor for imparting human knowledge and values. Consider religious books and the role they have played in shaping our beliefs and world views of what is right and wrong, and the wars that have been fought over conflicting belief systems. Some books are still considered sacred today, as can be seen by protests and killings in Afghanistan after members of a Florida church burned copies of the Koran, the Muslim holy book, in March 2011.

The social and cultural significance of books can also be seen in numerous book burnings throughout history, right up to modern times. Some groups have burnt library books they deem to have a corrupting influence on children, including books widely considered literature classics. Other books have been banned by governments for sexual content or political messages that criticize the government. Although banning books was more common in the early to mid-twentieth century, we still see it in recent times with Lebanon's ban of the controversial 2003 novel *The Da Vinci Code,* for example.

Even textbooks, which are primarily supposed to impart knowledge, can also transfer values, as much by what they omit as by what they contain. Consider the debates in the United States about whether to include both evolution and creationism in high school science textbooks. Or notice the criticisms from China and Korea when Japanese history textbooks either ignore or euphemize Japan's military atrocities during World War II. Even books written for entertainment can cause controversy because of cultural values they supposedly do or do not impart. Some have criticized the Harry Potter children's book series, written by J. K. Rowling, for not featuring stronger female characters in central roles, and others have said the books promote witchcraft.

These examples show the important cultural place books hold in our society as authoritative and relevant, even in today's world of electronic media and the Internet. Newspapers and magazines do not have the same sense of established knowledge or compiled wisdom that books provide, nor do they allow for complex or long stories to unfold. The growing popularity of e-readers attests to the role that books still play in our lives, no matter the format in which we choose to read them.

History of Books to Today

Since the Sumerians of 3500 BCE pressed marks into wet clay tablets to create what some scholars consider the first form of books, authors have been writing long-form text narratives to record and convey their ideas. Many innovations came from developing packages more portable than clay tablets. By 2500 BCE writers in western Asia were using animal skins to publish books in scroll form. The ancient Egyptians wrote the *Book of the Dead* in 1800 BCE on papyrus. Between the first century BCE and the sixth century CE the **codex**, or manuscript made of bound individual pages, began replacing the scroll-form book and established the modern book form. Book publishing continued to evolve through new inventions: block printing in China by 600 CE; movable copper-alloy type in Korea in 1234; and the Western world's first mechanical printing press in Germany in 1455.

codex

A manuscript book of individually bound pages.

▼ MONASTIC SCRIBES

Until the invention of printing, books had to be laboriously copied by hand. In the Middle Ages, this work was done by specially trained monks called scribes, who worked in monastic writing rooms called *scriptoria*. Scribes copied religious and classical works, and work in a scriptorium was considered an important task dedicated to promoting the ideas of the Christian Church. Many of the books published in the Middle Ages were written in beautiful calligraphy and are richly illustrated.

Early books were published in scroll format, and then codexes. Until paper arrived from China via the Middle East in the later Middle Ages, European scribes

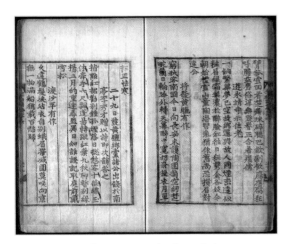

Korean copper-alloy type was the first printing to use metal plates, hundreds of years before Gutenberg's European press.

Johannes Gutenberg

German printer credited with creating the first mechanical printing press in Europe in 1455.

Gutenberg Bible

One of a handful of surviving Bibles printed by Johannes Gutenberg; considered the first mechanically printed works in Europe.

wrote on parchment or vellum, made from specially treated hides of goats, sheep, or calves. Copying and illustrating books by hand was extremely time-consuming and creating parchment was expensive, so books were generally not widespread before the end of the Middle Ages.

▼ JOHANNES GUTENBERG

As the Christian Church grew in Europe, the need for religious texts grew as well. It was out of this need that **Johannes Gutenberg** found his inspiration for the invention of printing with lead, using movable type, in 1455 CE. Gutenberg's invention pressed oil-based ink onto paper using a converted wine press.

Johannes Gutenberg (1400–c.1468) was born to an upper-class merchant family in Mainz, Germany. Gutenberg met the silversmith Waldvogel in Avignon in 1444, who taught the craft of "artificial writing," as early printmaking was called. In 1450, Gutenberg formed a partnership with the wealthy Mainz burgher Johann Fust in order to complete his own printing invention and to print the famous Gutenberg "forty-two-line Bible." The publication of the **Gutenberg Bible** in 1455 is considered the beginning of mechanical printing.[4]

Even with the new printing technology available, the handmade tradition continued. Books were still bound by hand, and illustrators embellished printed pages with drawings and artistic flourishes to match expectations of handwritten manuscripts. By combining a printing press with existing book binding technology, it was possible to begin the mass production of books at a fraction of the time and cost it took to produce an equal number of hand-copied books. The printing press spread rapidly, and was initially met with enthusiasm by the church and the cultural centers of Europe.

The Gutenberg Bible, like most books of the period, had lavish hand-colored illustrations alongside the printed text.

▼ BEGINNINGS OF MASS COMMUNICATION AND MASS LITERACY

The printing press had an important role in the growth of Renaissance culture. Scientific discoveries and religious beliefs spread—some of which challenged the authority of the Catholic Church. Many books copied by scribes, especially scientific works, were printed in Latin, which effectively reduced readership to elites who were educated in the classics. Printers rapidly discovered that books and other material such as broadsheets printed in the local common languages (the vernacular) had an eager audience, and more common people learned to read. Books had left the quiet monastic scriptoria and entered the bustling commercial world of printmakers and the average person.

Despite this increase in books and printed materials from the Renaissance onward, literacy was not universal. Most Europeans and Americans remained illiterate until the nineteenth century. In the American colonial era, education was available largely to the wealthy who could afford to hire and house private tutors for their children. Increased public education in the early 1800s helped reduce illiteracy among the general population, and textbooks played a crucial role in the public education system.

One of the first textbooks published in America was the *New England Primer,* published initially in about 1690 by Benjamin Harris. The textbook introduced children to the English alphabet, the rudiments of reading, and basic Christian religious values. Noah Webster, known today for his *Webster's Dictionary,* wrote his 1783 textbook, *A Grammatical Institute of the English Language,* as a reaction to the textbooks imported from England that were commonly used and that taught English cultural values. Known popularly as the "Blue Back Speller," Webster's textbook provided tutorials on language, religion, morals, and domestic economy. McGuffey Readers, first published in 1836, became standard reading books for schoolchildren throughout the nineteenth century.

Textbooks of the 1800s reflected the social mores of contemporary society, just as modern textbooks reflect today's mores. Issues like slavery or racism were not challenged in textbooks in the nineteenth century. Today we see debates about textbook content as it relates to teaching evolution, or certain historical topics such as the Civil War. In order to appeal to the widest cross-section of society, textbooks generally avoid controversial subjects and embrace perspectives and bodies of knowledge in which there is general agreement among members of the dominant group.

Noah Webster is most famous for his dictionary, but he also published a grammatical textbook widely used throughout much of the nineteenth century.

▼ CHEAPER AND SMALLER BOOKS

Successful publishing has always been driven by wider distribution and lower costs. The printing press and digital books—and all the trends in between—appeared as a result of these forces. One way to make money publishing is to publish a book that many people want to buy and read, which usually means publishing books that entertain people (wider distribution). Another way is to make the book affordable for many people to buy (lower prices). The dime novel and, later, mass-market paperbacks satisfied both these criteria.

Dime Novels

The **dime novel** was the first paperback book form and, as its name suggests, sold for ten cents. This made it accessible even to the poor. Introduced in 1860 by Irwin P. Beadle & Company, the dime novel initially featured stories of Indians

dime novel

The first paperback book form, which cost ten cents. This made it accessible even to the poor.

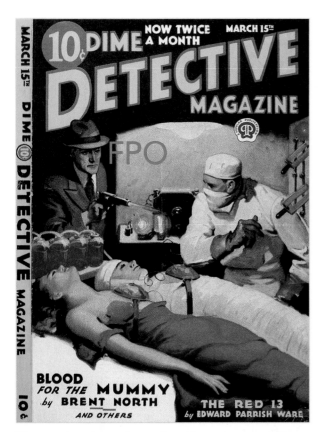

Dime novels and magazines such as this one were much like paperback novels in that they made stories more accessible to the public.

The Internet Archive's Bookmobile is an example of how print-on-demand can bring a huge variety of books to communities that do not have easy access to them.

and pioneer tales that were often nationalistic in tone. Ann S. Stephens wrote the first dime novel, *Malaeska: The Indian Wife of the White Hunter.* Within a year of publication, *Malaeska* sold more than three hundred thousand copies. By the 1870s, dime novels included melodramatic fiction, adventures, detective stories, romances, and rags-to-riches tales.

Mass-Market Paperbacks

Mass-market paperbacks were introduced in the United States in 1939 by Robert de Graff's company Pocket Books. Pocket Books, with its familiar kangaroo mascot Gertrude, published a line of plastic-laminated books priced at twenty-five cents each that were small enough to be carried in a back pocket. The paperback revolution came from offering books to the public in places like drugstores and supermarkets, an alternative mass-distribution network to established bookstores.

The post–World War II baby boomers who became the students of the 1950s and '60s were dubbed "the paperback generation." They were raised on Dr. Benjamin Spock's best-selling paperback, *Dr. Spock's Baby and Child Care,* and influenced by paperback books such as J. D. Salinger's *Catcher in the Rye* and Kurt Vonnegut's *Slaughterhouse Five.*

Print-on-Demand

One interesting development in printing that began in the late 1990s is **print-on-demand (POD)**. High-quality color laser printing and binding machines can print a single book in a few minutes at a fraction of the cost it would take for a traditional print run. These tiny print runs can make books available cheaply that otherwise would be out of print or hard to obtain.

POD enables writers to publish using low-cost printers and sell their paperback books online or even in some bookstores. The combination of low-cost, digital, and online technologies has released a flood of POD authors publishing their own books in recent years. In 2009, over 764,000 books were self-published, according to bibliographic information company Bowker, three times the number of titles published by traditional publishing houses for that year. A growing number of POD publishers, such as Xlibris, Virtual Bookworm, and Lulu Publishing, let authors publish their books for as little as four hundred dollars.

In 2002, the Internet Archive formed, a group dedicated to digitizing and archiving all kinds of media. In its first year, it started a publicity venture called the Internet Bookmobile, consisting of a Ford minivan with a computer and POD printer in the back. It toured U.S. cities, giving people access to more than twenty thousand public domain books in its digital archive, all available in a matter of minutes for a fraction of the cost of similar books sold in bookstores. The Internet Archive hoped it might prove to be a cost-effective option for libraries as compared to the cost of pursuing late books and reshelving them.

◢◤ Current Book Industry Issues

Publishing is a global industry. In 2009, the book-publishing industry's annual U.S. sales were $40.32 billion, a 1 percent increase from 2008.[5] Although it is an enormous global market, there has been tremendous consolidation of ownership in the book publishing industry worldwide, which has significant repercussions for the diversity of book titles and perspectives that are published.

There are at least three significant trends affecting the business of book publishing. First, mergers and consolidation in the industry enable publishers to reduce operating costs, including the costs associated with warehousing, marketing, and sales, and thus increase profit margins. Size also gives the publishers more leverage in negotiating terms with the dominant retail giants Barnes & Noble and Amazon.com. Such negotiations include obtaining good display locations in bookstores and on the Web.

Second, the book publishing industry is intertwined with the global media and the entertainment industry. All of the biggest publishers derive an increasing part of their profits from selling technology products and services, such as electronic databases or educational testing, rather than only selling printed books. Likewise, some books are published and subsequently adapted or licensed for film or TV, from Mary Wollstonecraft Shelley's *Frankenstein* (published in 1818 and made into movies many times) to Steven Gould's debut novel *Jumper,* published in 1992 and made into a movie starring Hayden Christensen in 2008.

Third, book sales and distribution are being transformed by the emergence of online booksellers, electronic books, and on-demand printing. Online booksellers such as Amazon.com, bn.com, and others are capturing an increasing portion of total book sales. Moreover, these and other online booksellers are distributing electronic books. As electronic books and online book sales grow, the future of traditional brick-and-mortar bookstores is uncertain. Megabookstores like Borders and warehouse shopping outlets selling discounted books were thought to have the needed economies of scale to compete with online enterprises. However, Borders, the second biggest bookstore chain in the U.S., announced in February 2011 that it would be closing over 200 of its stores nationwide and filed for bankruptcy protection, and in July 2011 announced it would close all its stores. Independent bookstores are also suffering, even large ones like Portland-based Powell's, which has laid off workers and undergone other changes to cope with changes in consumer book buying.

Thomson Reuters was considered the world's largest publisher after Thomson acquired news giant Reuters and sold its textbook division in 2007, but has moved to third place behind Pearson. This is a clear example of the way mergers and digital media are affecting the publishing industry, as Thomson Reuters earns the majority of its revenue from information collected in electronic databases, not printed books or journals.

Only eleven of the top fifty book publishers worldwide have their parent company headquartered in the United States, although there are several with joint Canadian/U.S. ownership or European/U.S. ownership.[6] Publishers whose names you may recognize, such as Random House and Penguin, are owned by overseas companies (Bertelsmann, based in Germany, and Pearson, based in England, respectively). McGraw-Hill Education is the top-ranked U.S. company, ranking eighth in the world in 2009, followed by Scholastic in twelfth place. The smallest American publisher on the list, Marvel Entertainment, ranked thirty-eighth and generates revenues from books, comics, and licensing deals.

In countries with literacy rates that approach 100 percent, it is hard for people to understand the devastating effect that illiteracy can have on a country's development. Without even basic literacy skills, large swaths of the population remain trapped in cycles of poverty, unable to participate in larger public discussions that take place in the pages of newspapers or magazines, or to better their lives through reading books and educating themselves. Furthermore, the public becomes easy to manipulate by cynical leaders who use easy-to-understand catchphrases or slogans to garner support from the uneducated masses.

UNESCO estimates that there are 774 million adults worldwide who lack basic literacy skills, and 64 percent of them are women. In 2000, UNESCO launched the Education for All 2015 project, with 164 governments making a pledge at a conference in Senegal to vastly expand educational opportunities for people worldwide.

WEB LINK
One Laptop Per Child
http://laptop.org/en/

Through an annual commissioned Global Monitoring Report, UNESCO has been able to track the progress of various efforts toward providing education to children, youth, and adults. There have been tremendous strides in many countries, creating mandatory child-education laws and abolishing tuition for elementary schools, thereby removing one of the major barriers that kept many children from attending schools.

One part of this effort is getting affordable computers into the hands of school children. One Laptop Per Child (OLPC) encourages people to donate rugged, specially made cheap computers to children in the developing world to help with education, literacy, and simple computer skills.

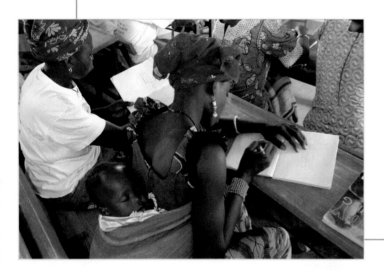

However, there is still a long way to go in many countries. A lack of schools, teachers, and supplies remains a top concern, and efforts to educate adults have generally lagged behind the education of children. It is important for adults to recognize the value of literacy so they can encourage learning among their children as well.

Out of 177 countries, 17 have adult literacy rates below 50 percent. These range from Pakistan, at 49.9 percent, to last-place Burkina Faso, at 23.6 percent. Fourteen of the 17 countries are in Africa, with Nepal and Bhutan completing the list.

◤▽ Sales and Readership of Books

For more than twenty years, the patterns of book sales have been unsteady. The industry has grown slightly overall, but total revenue varied up and down a few percent every year, and different categories sold well or poorly.

Categories are the most important concept in book sales. Each has different markets and different strategies for reaching their audiences. As Figures 3-1 and 3-2 show, only looking at sales or the number of units sold can give a misleading picture of the industry. Net dollar sales would suggest that the professional category is on par with the adult trade category, but when looking at units sold it is

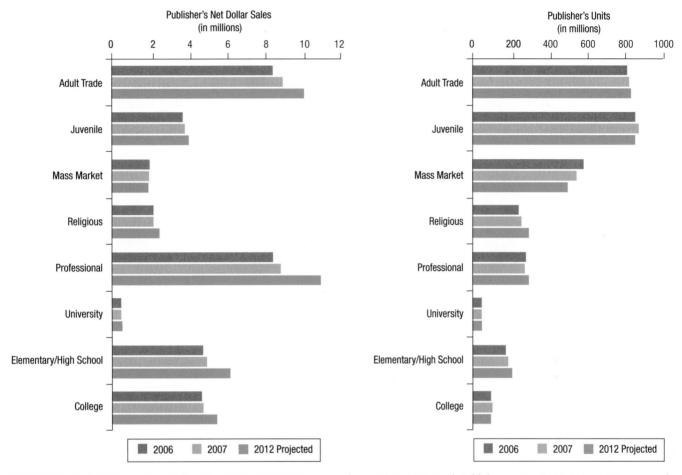

FIGURE 3-1 Book Publishers' Net Dollar Sales: 2006, 2007, 2012 projected. *Book Trends*, 2008.

FIGURE 3-2 Book Publisher's Units: 2006, 2007, 2012 projected. *Book Trends*, 2008.

clear that far fewer professional books are sold than adult trade books. Professional books are much more expensive than most adult trade books, meaning fewer books can be sold to equal the same dollar amount of much cheaper books.

Within traditional publishing, trade books, or books intended for general readership, produce the greatest revenues and are second only to juvenile books in terms of units sold. Paperbacks used to dominate the trade book industry, but in recent years hardcover books have made a comeback. There has been a seesawing in yearly sales between hardcover and paperback books, and rapid rises in ebook sales.

Outlook for Books

The recession hurt the book industry just as it did other industries, and the changes brought by digital media have affected few industries as greatly as book publishing. One area that has shown remarkable growth in the past few years has been ebooks, even though their total sales in 2010 still made up only a little over 8 percent of total book sales, according to the Association of American Publishers (AAP). Even so, there was dramatic growth in sales compared to 2009 for AAP members (which includes many, but not all, U.S. book publishers), from $166.9 million to $441.3 million in 2010. This growth in ebook sales is even more remarkable when considering that ebooks only accounted for just over 1 percent of total book sales in 2008.

Different categories increase or decrease slightly year on year. In 2010, most book categories saw small decreases in sales over 2009, especially hardcover and paperback trade titles and mass market paperbacks. University press paperbacks and professional titles saw slight increases in 2010 over 2009.

Another area of growth for book publishing has been in audio books, both digitally downloaded audio books and physical audio books. Downloaded audio books increased 38.8 percent in 2010 to $81.9 million, while sales of physical audio books fell 6.3 percent to $137.3 million, still greater than downloaded audio book sales.[7]

Even with the increase in ebook sales, publishers are still trying to find ways to get more revenue more quickly. What price consumers are willing to pay for ebooks is still an open question, with different publishers trying different pricing structures such as offering older titles at deeply discounted prices, around $2.99, and newer titles around $12.99 or more. In March 2011, HarperCollins Publishing angered many librarians when it announced a change in their ebook purchasing policy for libraries. Previously, libraries could purchase an ebook and, like a printed book, make it available for patrons forever. However, HarperCollins' new policy says that ebook purchases by libraries can only be used for 26 checkouts of the book before it has to be purchased again.

◢◣ Distinctive Functions of Newspapers

Newspapers, as most everyone knows, consist largely of words, photos, and graphics printed on lightweight, inexpensive paper stock. They are very portable and inexpensive. They are typically printed either daily or weekly. Although they are called "news" papers, most newspapers consist primarily of advertising. The typical daily newspaper in the United States, for example, is roughly 60 percent advertising and about 40 percent editorial content. Similarly, about 65 percent of the cost of producing a newspaper goes into printing and distribution, and only about 35 percent goes into the actual creation of the "news" (reporters' salaries, etc.).

The most important function newspapers serve in modern society is **surveillance**, or informing the public of important events taking place. However, they also play a role in the **correlation** and **entertainment** functions. Typically, the front page of a newspaper is all "news," with section front pages similarly constructed, and most news placed "above the fold," or on the top half of the page, on other pages.

Newspapers have tended to serve communities defined by geographic, political, cultural, or economic borders. Correspondingly, newspapers are generally organized into sections often defined by geography, including local, national, and international news; and topic, including business, culture, health, science, sports, and technology.

▼ LOCAL NEWSPAPERS

The vast majority of newspapers in the United States serve local geographic communities (usually city based, but with "zoned" editions for the suburbs). Local newspapers tend to cover the local communities they serve, monitoring the activities of local government, law enforcement, business, religion, education, the arts, and other area institutions. They also carry some regional, national, and international news, although most of this tends to come from other, better equipped news-gathering organizations, including the news services like the Associated Press and Reuters. Local papers also tend to serve as the legal record of public communications in their communities, running obituaries and various legal announcements.

surveillance

Primarily the journalism function of mass communication, which provides information about the processes, issues, events, and other developments in society.

correlation

The ways in which media interprets events and issues and ascribes meanings that help individuals understand their roles within the larger society and culture.

entertainment

A function of mass communication that is performed in part by all three of the other four main functions (surveillance, correlation, cultural transmission) but also involves the generation of content designed exclusively to entertain.

They are also an important part of the local community's economic infrastructure, carrying extensive advertising for local products, services, and businesses with local interests and markets.

▼ NATIONAL NEWSPAPERS

A few newspapers have emerged as truly national newspapers, with readership throughout the country. These include the *New York Times, USA Today,* and the *Wall Street Journal.* Each of these papers offers its own distinctive brand of news. The *New York Times,* known as the "paper of record" in the United States, as well as the "Old Gray Lady," offers especially strong coverage of international events and issues. The *Wall Street Journal,* bought by Rupert Murdoch's News Corp. in 2007, is the nation's leading newspaper covering business and finance. Many in the world of business or finance consider the *Journal* a must-read for their work.

Japan's *Yomiuri Shimbun* is the largest circulation newspaper in the world.

USA Today offers a strong mix of general-interest news packaged in well-designed, colorful, easy-to-read sections. Launched in 1982, *USA Today* was the brainchild of newspaper mogul Al Neuharth. The paper took ten years to become profitable, but in the meantime transformed the look and feel of most newspapers in the United States and many around the world. Prior to *USA Today's* launch, many twentieth-century newspapers were dull in appearance and filled with long columns of text. *USA Today* introduced colorful graphics and an overall design that was inspired by television and easy to read.

Most significantly, *USA Today* was printed on a new economic model. Using the then-new satellite communication technology, the paper's content was sent electronically to printing and distribution centers throughout the country. This model was cheaper than traditional printing and distribution methods, and allowed a daily paper to distribute nationwide. Today, the *New York Times* and *Wall Street Journal* use similar methods to distribute their papers nationwide.

Despite the relatively large circulation of the *Wall Street Journal* and *USA Today* (2.1 million and 1.8 million, respectively, in early 2012) compared to most U.S.

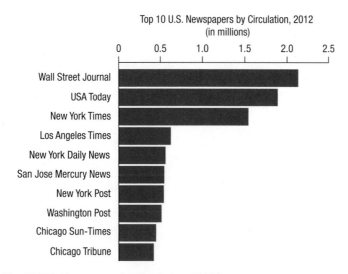

FIGURE 3-3 Top 10 U.S. Newspapers by Circulation, 2012.[8]

newspapers, they are dwarfed by the circulation numbers of the world's largest dailies in Japan, the *Yomiuri Shimbun* (over 10 million), the *Asahi Shimbun* (over 8 million), and the *Nikkei Keizai Shimbun* (over 3 million), the latter of which is similar in coverage to the *Wall Street Journal*. About 75 percent of the top 100 best-selling papers are in Asia, with the largest English-language newspaper the *Times of India* (7.3 million). In the United Kingdom, the three top dailies are all sensationalist tabloids, *The Sun* (3.1 million), *The Daily Mail* (2.1 million), and the *Daily Mirror* (1.8 million).

▲▼ History of Newspapers to Today

The precursors to newspapers were news pamphlets or brochures, printed in Germany in the 1400s. From the early 1600s newspapers or news sheets were printed in Germany, Holland, and England. Printers often faced government censors and even imprisonment, so few publications were printed on regular schedules. The first English-language newspaper published in what is today the United States was *Publick Occurrences, Both Foreign and Domestick*. It was only published once: on September 25, 1690, in Boston. After that beginning, more newspapers caught on. The American colonial press took two forms: commercial papers and political papers.

Publick Occurrences, although only published once, is considered the first newspaper in colonial America.

▼ THE COMMERCIAL PRESS AND PARTISAN PRESS

The commercial papers, with names such as the *Boston Daily Advertiser* and the *Daily Mercantile Advertiser*, were published by merchants. They printed reports on the arrivals and departures of ships, contents of their cargo, weather, and other information useful to commercial enterprises.

After independence and prior to the 1830s, most United States newspapers were affiliated with a political party or platform. Political papers were sponsored by political parties, with names like the *Federal Republican* and *Daily Gazette*, and the articles were often written by political figures, usually anonymously. The partisan press, as it was called, did not subscribe to the modern notions of good journalism, free of bias and impartial in its coverage of daily events. The newspapers of the late eighteenth and early nineteenth centuries were decidedly opinionated and took a position not only on their editorial pages but throughout the entire papers.

TIMELINE

History (and Pre-History) of Newspapers

200 BCE	*Tipao* gazettes distributed among Chinese officials.
59 BCE	Julius Caesar orders publication of first daily news sheet, *Acta Diurna* (*Daily Events*)—Rome.
748 CE	First printed newspaper—Beijing, China.
1502	*Zeitung* ("newspaper") published in Germany.
1513	Earliest known English-language news sheet and first illustration in a news sheet—*Trewe Encountre*.

1609 First regularly published newspaper in Europe (Germany)—*Avisa Relation oder Zeitung*.

1620 First English-language newspaper—*The new tydings out of Italie*, published in Amsterdam.

1621 First English-language newspaper printed in England—*Corante, or, Newes from Italy, Germany, Hungarie, Spaine and France.*

1638 First printing press arrives in what later became the United States—Cambridge, Massachusetts.

1665 First issue of the *Oxford Gazette* published at Oxford, England, offering first use of double columns in a news publication. Considered the first true newspaper.

1666 The *Oxford Gazette* becomes the *London Gazette* and is published continuously for more than 300 years.

1690 First newspaper published in what is now the United States, in Boston—*Publick Occurrences, Both Foreign and Domestick*.

1702 First daily newspaper—the *Daily Courant*, published in London.

1704 North America's first regular newspaper—the *Boston News-Letter.*

1721 First independent newspaper in North America, the *New England Courant*, published by James Franklin, Benjamin Franklin's brother.

1764 The *Hartford Courant* established, the oldest continuously published newspaper in the United States.

1784 First daily newspaper in the United States—the *Pennsylvania Packet.*

1800 First iron hand press—Stanhope, England.

1830s First steam-powered rotary press makes mass distribution possible; prints on both sides of paper, 4,000 sheets per hour. Prior hand presses printed just 200 sheets per hour.

1880s–1900s "Yellow journalism" is coined as competition between Pulitzer's and Hearst's New York papers leads to flashy and often inaccurate stories to gain readership; the precursor to today's tabloid journalism.

1932–1944 Despite most newspaper editorials being against President Franklin Roosevelt and his New Deal policies, he wins election a record four times, using the power of radio to talk to Americans directly through his "fireside chats."

1971 Newspapers switch from hot metal letterpress to offset printing.

1977 *Toronto Globe and Mail* offers public access to newspaper text database.

1982 *USA Today* founded; typeset in regional plants by satellite commands.

1995 *Metro*, distributed free to subway commuters in Stockholm, Sweden, launches what becomes a worldwide newspaper chain that focuses on younger, urban readers.

2005 The *New York Times* acquires About.com, a leading online site of consumer information, for $410 million.

2008 The New York Times Company, Tribune Company, Gannett, and Hearst Corporation announce creation of quadrantONE, an online sales organization for national advertisers.

2011 U.S. newspapers gain $1 in digital advertising revenue for each $7 they lose in print revenue.

2012 The Pew Research Center's Project for Excellence in Journalism reports there are about 1,350 U.S. English-language daily newspapers, down from roughly 1,400 in 2007.

WEB LINK
Media History Project
www.mediahistory.umn.edu/

▼ COLONIAL READERSHIP AND FINANCES

Both commercial and political papers were sold by subscription at a cost of eight to ten dollars per year, or about six cents an issue. Since the average worker made just eighty-five cents a day, the subscription price of most newspapers put them out of reach of the masses. Readership was also limited in at least two ways. First, readership was largely limited to those who supported or agreed with the political position of the paper. Second, readership was largely limited to society's elite, well-educated, land-owning, and economically advantaged groups. By 1750 most colonists who could read had access to a newspaper, although literacy was generally limited to the elite.

▼ THE GOLDEN AGE OF NEWSPAPERS

Beginning in the 1830s technological developments transformed newspapers. A "golden age" for newspapers in America emerged. This golden age lasted until about 1930 when radio began to dominate.

The *New York Sun* was the first of the penny papers.

Freesheets: Riding the Rails of Newspapers' Future?

It looked like a crazy idea, even back in 1995. At a time when newspapers were already struggling with rising costs and budget crises, and just starting to understand the threat that the World Wide Web would have on their readership, Pelle Tornberg launched a free daily newspaper in Stockholm targeted to subway commuters.

The paper, called the *Metro,* was created to be read in fifteen minutes. Tabloid sized and colorful, with short articles covering a variety of topics, *Metro* aimed squarely at an elusive yet lucrative readership for advertisers—young, affluent, and urban. This was also precisely the demographic that had largely stopped reading newspapers.

Now there are 210 free newspapers in 50 countries, with a total worldwide circulation of 40 million. The *Metro* chain of freesheets has expanded throughout Europe, Latin America, and Asia and into New York, Boston, and Philadelphia in the United States. They now are in 100 cities in 20 countries and publish in 18 languages.[9]

Free newspapers remain the fastest-growing segment of newspapers worldwide, although growth has slowed in some key markets. The *New York Metro* and its competitor, *amNewYork,* have been struggling to gain the kind of popularity of the freesheets in Europe. Even in Europe, however, freesheets have had to close down in some cities.

Freesheets have shown themselves to be sustainable and popular, with the worldwide *Metro* chain claiming to be the largest newspaper in the world. With the rise of tablet computers, however, it is still unclear if freesheet readers will transfer to paid-circulation newspapers and whether reading freesheets will instill a lifetime habit of reading newspapers, online or offline.

Prior to the 1830s, printing presses were powered by hand (and briefly by horses), and could print from two hundred to six hundred one-sided sheets per hour. This severely limited the circulation of the papers of the day. But in the 1830s steam-powered printing presses were developed. These could print up to four thousand sheets per hour printed on both sides. This made mass-scale printing possible.

Seizing the opportunity, publisher **Benjamin Day** launched the *New York Sun,* on September 3, 1833. This daily newspaper sold for only one cent, carried by newsboys in the streets instead of traditional subscriptions. This **penny press** truly offered news for the masses, with sensationalized stories written to appeal to the lowest common denominator. It was massively successful, reaching a circulation of eight thousand almost immediately, and thirty thousand within three years, astounding contemporary publishers.

In many ways, the penny press's effect was analogous to the social shift from Gutenberg's printing press some four centuries earlier. News was no longer for the political or commercial elite; it was for everyone.

Benjamin Day

Publisher of the *New York Sun,* he ushered in the era of the penny press when, on September 3, 1833, he began offering his paper on the streets for a penny.

penny press

Newspapers that sold for a penny, making them accessible to everyone. They differed from older newspaper forms in that they tried to attract as large an audience as possible and were supported by advertising rather than subscriptions.

The penny press changed the business of news by employing reporters to seek out stories, not just publish items that came into the office. The penny press also brought a new marketing function to newspapers. The price for a newspaper did not cover printing and distribution costs, but because the penny press brought large audiences, businesses seeking to sell their products to mass markets saw potential in advertising. The penny press began advertising medicines, entertainment, and jobs, as well as items the commercial and partisan press frowned upon, such as ads for theaters, lotteries, or abortionists. Advertising emerged as the primary revenue source in the modern newspaper business model. Today, about 70 percent of newspaper revenue typically comes from advertising.

Newspapers multiplied rapidly in the Golden Age, feeding the appetite for news in large eastern cities such as New York, Boston, and Philadelphia. Between 1870 and 1900, the U.S. population doubled, the urban population tripled, and the number of daily newspapers quadrupled. The 1880 U.S. Census counted 11,314 newspapers (by 2006 there were 2,344). Metropolitan newspapers sprouted throughout the nation, led by press innovators whose names still resonate, such as James Gordon Bennett, Horace Greeley, Joseph Pulitzer, William Randolph Hearst, and E. W. Scripps.

▲▼ Current Newspaper Industry Issues

After World War II, U.S. society shifted from the urban population that supported the penny press to a suburban society. A population spending much of its time commuting by automobile came to rely more on radio, TV, and eventually the Internet as its primary source of news. It became very easy for tired suburban commuters to watch television for both news and entertainment in the evenings. This especially drove afternoon-published papers into decline.

At one time, cities usually had two or more competing daily newspapers, but now many cities have only one newspaper or a morning and evening paper. The **Newspaper Preservation Act of 1970** was intended to preserve a diversity of editorial opinion in communities where only two competing, or independently owned, daily newspapers exist. The two papers are ostensibly competitors but can sometimes be owned by the same company or work under a **joint operating arrangement**, or JOA, provided for by the Act. A JOA is a legal agreement that permits newspapers in the same market to merge their business operations yet maintain separate editorial operations. Today, ten cities in the United States are served by two or more major daily newspapers operating under a JOA, with eleven cities served by different newspapers under common ownership. Critics argue, however, that JOAs essentially allow virtual monopoly control of a market.

Modern newspapers are still changing significantly, including marked changes in their news and advertising content. Even leading newspapers are more likely to pander to popular taste to maintain circulation numbers. Departing from the editorial tradition (established after the penny press days) of selecting newsworthy topics regardless of general appeal, many newspapers are deferring to marketing polls and focus groups when setting standards for content, tone, and layout. Brightly colored photos and graphics like those pioneered in *USA Today* can, when they are done properly, actually help readers understand the news more easily. However, when done poorly, they can trivialize the news and even be confusing or misleading.

Newspapers have been experimenting with the electronic delivery of news to news consumers since the late 1970s, when newspapers like the *Globe and Mail*

Newspaper Preservation Act

Created in 1970, it is intended to preserve a diversity of editorial opinion in communities where only two competing, or independently owned, daily newspapers exist.

joint operating arrangements [JOAs]

Legal agreements that permit newspapers in the same market or city to merge their business operations for reasons of economics yet maintain independent editorial operations.

(Toronto) allowed public access to their news databases. Most of these early efforts were not very successful, however, in the days before widely available personal computers or Internet access. Reading text on computer screens was also very tiring.

As the Internet has grown as a medium of public communication, most daily newspapers have launched online news operations. They have increasingly used this new medium as a vehicle for serving an audience no longer limited to or defined by geographical, political, or even cultural or linguistic boundaries. Still, most newspapers have seen the Internet as a bigger threat to their business model than a boon in terms of gaining paid subscribers or advertisers. As a sign of trends to come, two major newspapers, the *Christian Science Monitor* and the *Seattle Post-Intelligencer,* announced in late 2008 and early 2009 that they would no longer publish papers and would exist only online. Other newspapers will likely follow suit, either scaling back their print publishing operations or closing them down altogether. Most proposals to make printed newspapers more valuable to their audiences—and more viable businesses—involve some combination of an expanded online presence for the newspaper and greater interactivity with the audience, including user-generated content, that begins to blur the line between the traditional conceptions of professional journalist and audience.

▼ NEWSPAPER CHAINS

The other approach to a viable business model has been through the newspaper chain. Traditionally in the United States, newspapers were owned by families, individuals, or political parties. These owners generally lived in the communities their newspapers served. In the twentieth century, both in the United States and around the world, ownership was increasingly concentrated. In other words, most newspapers today are part of newspaper groups or chains, whether privately held or publicly traded companies.

The newspaper business has traditionally been highly profitable, with profit margins often in the range of 20 percent of gross revenues in the 1990s. This made the newspaper industry among the most profitable in any sector of the economy, earning double the average profit margin of other industry sectors. Newspapers became a desirable target for investors. Furthermore, there are certain economies of scale that newspapers can enjoy through chain ownership. Large newspaper chains have successfully bought up smaller independent local or regional newspapers and newspaper groups, which faced declining audiences and advertising revenue, as well as rising costs for newsprint and other necessary resources. Even so, today the profit margin for newspapers is only 5 percent.

Benefits of Chains

One of the benefits for smaller, struggling newspapers is gaining access to the resources of the entire chain. This can be especially important in communities where a single advertiser or industry controls an especially large share of the advertising revenues. A single advertiser can threaten the commercial viability of the local newspaper by reducing or removing advertising. Subject to this influence, the newspaper can find itself in the compromising position of not reporting as rigorously on an advertiser as may be warranted.

Chains also offer newspapers the advantage of shared resources for news gathering, especially when covering regional, national, or international stories—much as newspapers have benefited from the shared news-gathering resources made

FIGURE 3-4 Major Newspaper Chains in the U.S.

THE MCCLATCHY COMPANY

The McClatchy Company became the third-largest newspaper publisher in the United States after its purchase of Knight Ridder in 2006 and after selling its largest newspaper property, the *Minneapolis Star Tribune.* It owns thirty newspapers in twenty-nine markets and has focused on owning newspapers in fast-growing markets. Its purchase of Knight Ridder also gave the company some nondaily newspapers and added ten foreign news bureaus as well as expanding the Washington, D.C., news bureau.

Newspapers include: *Anchorage Daily News, Sacramento Bee, Fresno Bee, Modesto Bee, Miami Herald, El Nuevo Herald, Idaho Statesman* (Boise, ID), *Wichita Eagle, Kansas City Star, News & Observer* (Raleigh, NC)

Website: **www.mcclatchy.com**

TRIBUNE COMPANY

Tribune Company is the second-largest newspaper publisher in the United States, though it has been struggling with a large debt load after going private in 2007. A merger with the Times Mirror newspaper group in 2000 added the *Los Angeles Times,* the *Baltimore Sun,* New York–based *Newsday,* and several other Times Mirror newspapers. The company also owns twenty-three television stations, a radio station, and the Chicago Cubs baseball team.

Newspapers include: *Chicago Tribune, Baltimore Sun, Los Angeles Times, Newsday, Orlando Sentinel, Newport News* (VA)

Website: **www.tribune.com**

E. W. SCRIPPS

The E. W. Scripps Company is a publicly traded company under family control. Family trusts own 60 percent of the company and control 90 percent of the votes. The Cincinnati, Ohio–based chain owns seventeen newspapers in fifteen markets, as well as the Scripps Howard News Service and Scripps Media Center in Washington, D.C. Its television group has six ABC-affiliated stations and three NBC-affiliated stations.

Newspapers include: *Rocky Mountain News* (Denver), *Commercial Appeal* (Memphis), *News Sentinel* (Knoxville, TN)

Website: **www.scripps.com**

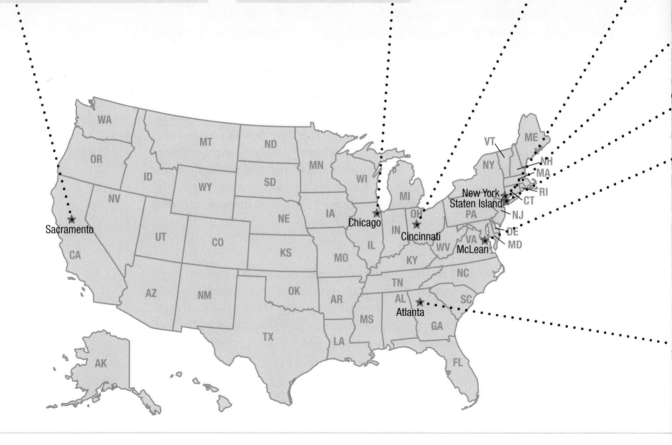

THE NEW YORK TIMES COMPANY

The New York Times Company also is publicly traded, but it is controlled by the Sulzberger family. It owns twenty daily newspapers, including the *New York Times,* the *Boston Globe,* half of the *International Herald Tribune,* and eighteen other regional daily newspapers through two regional media groups, as well as eight network-affiliated television stations, two New York radio stations, and more than forty websites, including About.com.

Newspapers include: *New York Times, Boston Globe*

Website: **www.nytco.com**

ADVANCE PUBLICATIONS

Advance Publications Inc. is a private, family-controlled company, led by chairman and CEO Samuel I. "Si" Newhouse Jr. Advance owns newspapers in twenty-two cities, Conde Nast Publications, Parade Publications, the Golf Digest companies, and has interests in cable television and the Internet.

Newspapers include: *Newark Star-Ledger, Times* (Trenton), *Birmingham News, Huntsville Times, New Orleans Times-Picayune, Plain Dealer* (Cleveland), *Oregonian* (Portland)

Website: **www.advance.net**

THE HEARST CORPORATION

The Hearst Corporation's diverse media properties include television, radio, cable network programming, online services, and twelve daily newspapers, eighteen weeklies, and sixteen consumer magazines.

Newspapers include: *Houston Chronicle, Seattle Post-Intelligencer, Seattle Times*

Website: **www.hearst.com**

GANNETT

Gannett, a publicly controlled chain, publishes ninety-five daily newspapers, including *USA Today,* in forty-one states and the United Kingdom, and owns more than three hundred nondaily newspapers and shoppers. It also owns several magazines and twenty-two television stations nationwide.

Newspapers include: *Greenwich Time* (CT), *Florida Today* (Melbourne), *Honolulu Advertiser, Indianapolis Star, Des Moines Register, Courier-Journal* (Louisville, KY), *Detroit Free Press, Clarion-Ledger* (Jackson, MS), *Reno Gazette-Journal, Home News Tribune* (East Brunswick, NJ), *Statesman Journal* (Salem, OR), *Argus Leader* (Sioux Falls, SD), *Tennessean* (Nashville, TN), *Burlington Free Press* (VT)

Website: **www.gannett.com**

COX ENTERPRISES ATLANTA

Cox Enterprises is a global media giant whose interests include fifteen daily newspapers and almost a dozen nondailies through ownership of newspaper groups in Austin, Texas; North Carolina; and Ohio. Cox's flagship newspaper is the *Atlanta Journal-Constitution.*

Newspapers include: *Atlanta Journal-Constitution, Palm Beach Daily News, Palm Beach Post, Daily Sentinel* (Grand Junction, CO)

Website: **www.coxenterprises.com**

possible through the Associated Press news service. As the JOAs demonstrate, also combining business operations can help newspapers save money as they reduce operating costs, as the chain has greater bargaining power when buying equipment and supplies because of economies of scale.

Problems with Chains

Chains, especially those that are publicly owned and traded on the stock market, can pressure local newspapers within the chain to bring in higher profits. One common strategy is to cut editorial costs by eliminating reporters and filling the news hole with wire service copy or material from the chain's other papers, to produce a less expensive newspaper of the same size.

For the communities they serve, chain-owned newspapers weaken the connection between the local media and the local communities. As local reporting gets squeezed out by cheaper wire service or chain-produced content, communities are being forced to look elsewhere for local news and information. This sets up a spiral of decline—as readership drops, so does advertising, which makes the newspaper less profitable, forcing it to cut more costs either through fewer pages or staff, which makes it seem even less relevant to readers.

▼ LEADING NEWSPAPER CHAINS

In the late 2000s, mergers and sales between chains changed the business landscape. In 2006, The McClatchy Company, the eighth-largest chain in the United States, paid $4.5 billion to buy Knight Ridder, the second-largest newspaper chain, which was well-known in the industry for its innovative expertise with new technologies.

Knight Ridder was itself a merger of two family-run companies that had both gone public in 1969. It published thirty-one daily papers in twenty-eight markets, including many respected papers such as the *Miami Herald,* the *Philadelphia Inquirer,* and the *San Jose Mercury News.* Shareholders were pressuring the company to cut costs and raise profits, and some press critics charged that the papers had been sacrificing quality.

Antitrust laws required the new merged firm to sell off papers where it now dominated the entire local market. Some papers sold to other media chains, while others, like the *Philadelphia Inquirer,* sold to private investor groups from the local area. The big difference between private ownership of newspapers in the past and the private equity groups buying newspapers today is that the investors were doing so largely because of the potential they saw for profits, despite the current problems in the industry, not because they wanted to return a paper to its roots as an important local voice for news. Today, seven of the top twenty-five newspapers are owned by hedge funds, which live or die by the returns they give their investors.

In 2007, the news world was shaken when the Bancroft family, owners of Dow Jones and the *Wall Street Journal,* agreed to sell the paper to Rupert Murdoch's News Corporation (News Corp.). Many journalists feared that Murdoch would meddle with the content, as he has done with other papers he has bought, and quit in protest. Murdoch promised he would not, and to date he has kept his promise and allowed the venerable *Wall Street Journal* to maintain its standards of high journalistic quality. In July 2011, Les Hinton, CEO of Dow Jones and who oversaw the *Wall Street Journal,* resigned to take responsibility for his role in the phone hacking scandal that closed down Britain's *News of the World.*

▼ DECLINING NUMBER OF DAILY NEWSPAPERS

Since 1940, the total number of daily newspapers has dropped more than 21 percent, with 1,422 daily papers in the United States in 2007. Most of the decline has been in evening papers, which decreased 51 percent since 1940. In 2000, for the first time the number of morning dailies exceeded the number of evening papers, and it has remained that way since then. Since 1940, the number of morning papers has increased over 100 percent, doubling since 1980 to 867 morning daily papers, with 565 afternoon daily papers in 2007. The number of Sunday papers increased 65 percent since 1940, reaching a high of 917 papers in 2005, but falling to 907 by 2007.[10]

 ## Sales and Readership of Newspapers

The cost of the printing press, the newsprint paper, the ink, the press operators (or "pressmen," as they are known in their union), the delivery trucks and drivers, and the maintenance of subscriber databases, as well as various other non-news-related production and distribution costs, make up roughly two-thirds of the overall cost of publishing a newspaper. It is ironic that most of the cost of a newspaper goes to functions other than producing news—which represents an interesting opportunity for newspapers in the digital age.

However, newspapers are having trouble adjusting to changes in the digital era. Newspaper readership, circulation, and advertising have continued to decline even before digital media, along with the number of daily newspapers. The declines in circulation have made newspapers less appealing to advertisers, who have gone online to sell ads—although not necessarily to the online sites of the newspapers.

▼ CIRCULATION AND READERSHIP

Newspaper **readership** refers to the number or percentage of people who read a newspaper, which is larger than the **circulation** number (number of copies sold or distributed) because some copies are read by more than one person. This is called "pass-along readership." Because the U.S. population is growing, the actual number of persons reading newspapers does not show a large decline. However, the percentage of the U.S. population that reads a daily paper has been declining, and the amount of time people spend reading newspapers has been slipping as well. Readership among the young is lower than for people between thirty-five and sixty-five and has been showing sharp declines in recent years, though some statistics by the newspaper industry have shown that the young are reading news online in higher numbers than they were. Of course, many of these online sources are published by daily-newspaper parent organizations.

readership

The number or percentage of people who read a newspaper, which may be larger than the actual number of copies sold because a single copy may be read by more than one person.

circulation

The number of copies of a newspaper that are sold or distributed.

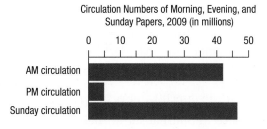

FIGURE 3-5 Circulation Numbers of Morning, Evening and Sunday Papers, 2009.

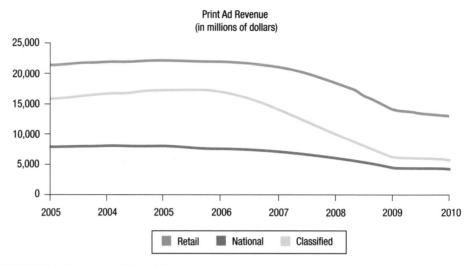

Print Ad Revenue
(in millions of dollars)

| Retail | National | Classified |

FIGURE 3-6 Newspaper Print Ad Revenue Declines. *Newspaper Association of America.*

▼ ADVERTISING

Close to two-thirds of the revenue generated by newspapers in the United States comes from advertising, with the rest from subscriptions. In other countries such as Japan, subscription prices are higher and the revenue split is closer to 50-50. Since 2006, advertising revenues for newspapers have fallen 48 percent, although the decline was a modest 6.3 percent in 2010 compared to 2009's 26 percent decline, according to the Pew Research Center's Project for Excellence in Journalism *State of the News Media 2011* report. Online ad revenues had grown quickly before 2008, although they still fell far short of making up for the lost print-based ad revenues, and also declined slightly between 2008 and 2010.

As Figure 3-6 shows, advertising in all three main categories for newspapers—retail, national, and classifieds—were down sharply since 2003. Classified ads, down 67 percent since 2005, have traditionally made up a large portion of newspaper advertising revenues, but sites like Craigslist or eBay and services like Groupon have siphoned away many classifieds advertisers. Job recruitment is one category of classifieds that has fallen the greatest, according to the Newspaper Association of America. Newspapers received revenues from recruitment classifieds of $8.7 billion in 2000, but only $760 million in 2010.

There is a general sense among newspaper publishers that although online advertising could continue to grow, it likely will not be enough to support the publications in the same way that print advertising did, and thus publishers are still exploring revenue options through advertising and other means.

◆▼ Outlook for Newspapers

"The rumors of my death have been greatly exaggerated," once quipped American novelist, humorist, and former journalist Mark Twain, after reading his own obituary in a local newspaper. This may have been true for Twain, but can the same be said for newspapers?

Six major trends became apparent to the authors of the Pew Research Center's Project for Excellence in Journalism in their *State of the News Media 2011* study. One trend is that more newspaper executives are coming from outside the newspaper industry, with little appreciation or understanding of the unique aspects of the newspaper industry. Another trend is slow progress for online subscription models. There has been a growing willingness for readers to pay for online subscriptions, but these are often bundled with other incentives such as receiving a Sunday paper. Local news is becoming increasingly important, but at the same time as newspapers have cut back on staff it makes it harder to provide adequate local coverage. Various experiments have been tried using citizen-journalists for hyperlocal news, which will be examined in Chapter 9. Understanding audiences better and how to measure them will also be a key issue for newspapers, especially in the online world where clicks or page views are becoming less relevant because of social media. Similarly, another trend is that newspaper companies will have to consider alternative revenue streams that are likely smaller but more numerous than the traditional advertising and subscription-based models they have used. As Figure 3-6 shows, ad revenues have declined sharply with newspapers in general. The last trend is the role that the government bailout of the U.S. auto industry had for advertising, as auto companies dramatically increased advertising across all media channels. Political advertising also greatly helped all media, not just newspapers, as the Supreme Court relaxed restrictions on certain types of political advertising.

In our media-saturated world with 24/7 news cycles and constant news updates, newspapers will have to adjust their content to better fit audiences' information needs. Newspapers may have to change to be more interpretative, or to analyze news events, or to include full, interactive multimedia to a greater extent than they do now. However, this could bring them into direct competition with news magazines, both print and online. As we will see in the next section, magazines are facing their own demons as audiences read less and seem to prefer shorter articles when they do read.

▲▼ Distinctive Functions of Magazines

There are three factors that most clearly distinguish magazines and newspapers. First, magazines tend to feature more long-form writing, whether in the form of news and analysis, or of features and human-interest articles. Magazines gained popularity in the 1800s with serial novels—stories released one chapter at a time through many issues—or excellent short stories. The great English writer Charles Dickens, author of *A Tale of Two Cities, A Christmas Carol,* and *Oliver Twist,* had many of his classics first published as serials, typically one chapter at a time. American writer and sometime-journalist Edgar Allan Poe, whose dark tales are still popular today, also had most of his stories first published in magazines. His *Murders in the Rue Morgue,* said to be the first modern detective story, was published in the April 1841 issue of George Rex Graham's *Lady's and Gentleman's Magazine,* whose circulation jumped from five thousand to twenty-five thousand the year Poe started writing for it. Many contemporary writers also use magazines, both in print and online, to introduce their books, either by featuring chapters and other excerpts for new readers or by creating books out of a series of magazine articles they have written. Samuel Huntington's influential book *The Clash of Civilizations* began as a 1993 magazine article.

Second, magazines are published at regular intervals but tend to be published less frequently than newspapers, most typically on a monthly basis, although weeklies and quarterlies are also common. This contributed to the writing style of magazines, typically less time sensitive, often more analytical or interpretative, creative, or fictional.

Finally, magazines often have been published on higher-quality paper stock than newspapers and are often designed to be kept considerably longer than dailies. Magazines have tended to be printed on paper that is eight and a half by eleven inches. However, certain clever magazine publishers have sometimes reduced the size of their magazines—known as the "trim size"—by a quarter inch or half inch in order to save money on printing costs, yet maintained the same cost to advertisers and subscribers. On the other hand, some magazines, such as *Rolling Stone* and *ESPN Magazine,* print on larger stock, which helps make them stand out on crowded shelves.

In their definitive book *The Magazine Publishing Industry,* Charles P. Daly, Patrick Henry, and Ellen Ryder outline several additional qualities of magazines, most importantly that magazines have a defined audience. Although this is true today in a general sense, it has not always been true. General-interest magazines of the mid-twentieth century such as *Look* and *Life* are two notable exceptions. There is also no reason why a magazine could not exist without a defined audience, except that it may be problematic for attracting advertisers.

Magazines serve several important functions in society, especially surveillance, correlation, entertainment, and marketing of goods and services. Surveillance is the most basic function magazines perform. However, unlike most newspapers, magazines tend to specialize by subject matter rather than geographic area (travel or regional-interest magazines are notable exceptions). They cover relatively narrow topics, such as science, health, or sports. Some concentrate on extremely specialized topics, such as doll collecting, harness racing, or scuba diving.

Many magazines have national, regional, or even international readership and distribution. A few major news magazines, such as *The Economist* and *Time,* can provide information in greater detail than newspapers because they tend to feature longer stories. Since magazines are typically printed on higher-quality paper, they can provide exceptionally effective photography and illustration, making them well suited to covering fashion, nature, entertainment, and science.

Many magazines are either exclusively or largely designed to provide entertainment and are mostly read as a leisure activity. Magazines such as *People* or *Entertainment Weekly,* with their coverage of celebrities and Hollywood, are illustrative of magazines that emphasize the entertainment function.

Almost all magazines serve a vital marketing function for a broad cross-section of goods and services. It often happens that readers spend more time looking at ads than reading editorial content as they browse a magazine. This is especially true of fashion magazines, such as *Vogue, Glamour,* or *GQ,* which often feature not just the latest news on designer clothes but the hottest advertising.

In the latter nineteenth century, national magazines helped the growing United States establish a common sense of identity and culture.

◤ History of Magazines to Today

In some ways, the early histories of magazines and newspapers are interwoven, with technological, business (i.e., advertising), and journalistic/entertainment functions overlapping between the two. It was not until 1731 that the first English-language periodical used the word "magazine" in its title: *The Gentleman's Magazine,* published in London. Benjamin Franklin published *Poor Richard's Almanack* in 1732, a predecessor of the modern-day magazine. The first magazine published in North America was the *American Magazine, or A Monthly View of the Political State of the British Colonies,* published in 1741 in Philadelphia. The first newsweekly magazine was *Niles' Weekly Register,* first published in 1811.

In the nineteenth century, magazines helped a young United States define itself, as they reached a nationwide audience. Newspapers were primarily metropolitan or local in scope.

Also important in this period were Frank Leslie and Miriam Florence Folline Leslie. Frank founded a variety of periodicals, including one of the first influential newsweeklies, *Frank Leslie's Illustrated Newspaper,* launched in 1855. In 1871 Leslie hired Miriam as editor of *Frank Leslie's Lady's Journal;* the two married in 1874. Frank's business went bankrupt in 1877, but after he died in 1880, Miriam took it over and skillfully restored the enterprise to financial health. She became one of the wealthiest and most powerful women in journalism and bequeathed some $2 million to the cause of women's suffrage.

Important magazine developments in the late 1800s and early 1900s include the 1888 debut of *National Geographic,* founded by the National Geographic Society. *National Geographic* introduced color plates in 1906. Time Inc., founded by Henry Luce, bought humor and general interest *Life* magazine in 1936 and made it into a weekly news magazine with a large format and excellent photography. Some of our most iconic images of the mid-twentieth century come from photos in *Life.* After several years of declining circulation, it ceased publication as a weekly magazine in 1972. It had different iterations in subsequent years; a themed news magazine, a monthly news magazine, a Sunday newspaper supplement, and finally as a website from 2009 with many of its famous images.

◤▼ Current Magazine Industry Issues

In the 1940s and 1950s, the public appetite for general-interest magazines and afternoon newspapers declined dramatically, and advertising dollars fled from these media to television. Television quickly drew national advertisers seeking large audience reach. As a result, general-interest magazines such as *Life* and *Look* saw their business base dissolve.

Magazine publishers had to adapt in order to survive. Overall, they stopped publishing general-interest magazines in favor of specialized magazines on almost every conceivable topic, with highly targeted audiences. Advertising returned to the appealing target marketing possible in specialized publications. Targeted advertising has continued in the online arena. There are nearly eighteen thousand specialized magazines available in print and online.

One entrepreneur who decided to do something to serve the media needs of African Americans in the mid-1900s was John H. Johnson. His hometown high school in Arkansas City, Arkansas, was "whites only," so Johnson's family moved to Chicago, where he got his formal high school education. His mother funded his business by pawning her household furniture and giving her son five hundred dollars to start *Ebony* magazine in 1945. *Ebony* has become one of the leading magazines targeting the interests of African Americans, with a circulation of more than 1.5 million. Johnson became one of the leading cross-media owners in the United States, with a book publishing company, a nationally syndicated television program, and two radio stations.[11] Johnson was the first African American to appear on

John H. Johnson, founder of *Ebony* magazine, started his media empire by borrowing $500 from his mother.

the Forbes 400 Rich List, and when he died in 2005 he was estimated to have a fortune of $500 million.

Specialization in the magazine industry divides into several major topic areas. In fact, Bacon's annual directory of magazines lists 225 "market classifications." Ten of the most important, at least in terms of circulation, are news, fashion, women (with at least three major subgroups: middle-aged and older women, women under thirty-five, and teenage girls), families (especially aimed at parents of children under age twelve), sports (with some general interest, but many specialized by type of sport), ethnic, medical/health, political, farm (*Farm Journal* alone has a circulation of 815,000), and lifestyles (many by type of home, region, or cooking).

◣◥ Sales and Readership of Magazines

Contemporary magazines, like all media, are increasingly subject to ownership consolidation and media concentration. In contrast to the newspaper industry, the magazine industry did not suffer the same steep drops in circulation and advertising during the recession, although they did suffer and the recession did claim some notable victims, such as *U.S. News & World Report,* which stopped publishing in 2010 and went entirely online except for its college and hospital ranking issues. *Newsweek* also underwent dramatic changes between 2007 and 2010 as its revenues declined by 38 percent, it suffered large drops in circulation and subscribers, and it cut staff and changed its format. None of these were successful, and finally The Washington Post Company sold *Newsweek* to Tina Brown's The Daily Beast.

Circulation and advertising revenue were both down slightly in 2010 for the industry. The total number of ad pages sold were down only 0.1 percent in 2010, while in 2009 they were down 25.9 percent. Newsstand sales, which industry experts believe is a more accurate way to determine the health of the magazine industry, continued to decline even as subscriptions remained steady.

Despite a generally flat outlook until at least 2012, every year hundreds of new magazine titles are published. Most do not survive more than two years. Even well-established or big-name titles go out of business each year or move to online-only editions, as Hearst Publications did in 2008 with *CosmoGirl.* In general, the teen-girl magazine market has seen a narrowing of titles in the past few years, reflecting the changes in reading habits of the target audience from print to online. In August 2008 *Playgirl* announced it was going online only.

The leading circulation magazines reflect the general trends in magazine publishing. The top magazines target specific audiences. They cover specialized subjects in depth, and with quality. However, not even these titles are immune to changes in readership or to the unwillingness to purchase or subscribe to print magazines. Those with the largest circulation appeal to large and growing audience segments such as aging baby boomers, who are more likely to read a print magazine than younger people.

Table 3-1 compares the top ten paid-circulation magazines in the United States in 1972 and 2010. Both *AARP The Magazine* and *AARP Bulletin* are publications of the American Association of Retired Persons (AARP). *AAA Tourbooks* is a publication of the Automobile Association of America, while *Costco Connection* is published by mega-chain store Costco. One notable shift in the top ten

TABLE 3-1

Top Ten Paid-Circulation Magazines in the U.S. in 1972 and 2010

	1972		2010	
	TITLE	**CIRCULATION**	**TITLE**	**CIRCULATION**
1	Reader's Digest	17,828,000	AARP The Magazine	23,748,475
2	TV Guide	16,411,000	AARP Bulletin	23,574,132
3	Woman's Day	8,192,000	AAA Tourbooks	13,069,703
4	Better Homes and Gardens	7,996,000	Costco Connections	8,364,738
5	Family Circle	7,890,000	Better Homes and Gardens	7,677,497
6	McCall's	7,517,000	Reader's Digest	5,533,037
7	National Geographic	7,260,000	Game Informer	5,073,003
8	Ladies' Home Journal	7,014,000	National Geographic	4,493,024
9	Playboy	6,401,000	Good Housekeeping	4,418,398
10	Good Housekeeping	5,801,000	Woman's Day	3,895,814

circulation magazines is that in 1972 most of the magazines were either women's or general interest magazines that people specifically subscribed to. In 2010, the top four magazines not only have circulations far greater than the remaining ones, but are sent to members of the organizations that publish them so in that respect people are joining an organization that includes a magazine along with other benefits.

◢◤ Outlook for Magazines

Magazines face several pressures but continue to maintain some important advantages over newspapers in terms of staying relevant as print-based products.

Working against magazines are the online reading trends toward relatively short pieces as opposed to long, in-depth features. Directly transferring print content to their online counterparts may not be as successful as creating new, shorter content better geared to the online environment. There are exceptions to this, most notably online-only magazines such as *Slate,* but these are not the rule.

As readers expect to be able to interact with authors and with each other through discussion forums, blogs, and chat rooms, the long-form, authoritative or idiosyncratic authorial and noninteractive voice of many magazine features may seem antiquated or limiting. Readers may feel that they are being forced to listen to a long lecture rather than take part in a conversation.

Will Printing on Dead Trees Ever Die?

It is easy to think in the digital age that printed materials will soon be seen only behind glass cases or in musty libraries. However, there is strong evidence that this will not happen. The "paperless office" was widely touted as offices became computerized and connected by networks, yet paper use increased dramatically thanks in part to the availability of photocopiers and cheap printers.

Printed materials also maintain several advantages over their electronic brethren, the main ones being portability, disposability, and durability. Although electronic readers match the portability of books and actually exceed books in terms of the amount of material they can hold, printed matter still holds the advantage in the other two areas. Forget your newspaper at a coffee shop and you shrug it off; leave your laptop or Kindle there and it can ruin your week. Similarly, printed materials never need recharging and hold up much better to being dropped than most electronic devices. But this too may change as electronic readers become more rugged or disposable.

The relative importance of printed materials may change, however, with printed newspapers, especially, becoming less common than they were in the past, but it is unlikely that they will completely disappear anytime in the near future.

Before you lament the decline of print too loudly, however, remember how environmentally unfriendly the publishing industry is. Paper is of course made from trees, and it is estimated that one tree can make 2,700 thirty-five-page newspapers. Today, printers use more recycled paper and tree pulp for paper, but pulp mills are some of the worst polluters among modern industries. Combine the papermaking process with the many harmful chemicals used in inks, and the environmental damage caused by fleets of delivery trucks, and it adds up to a large environmental footprint, although some publishers have been trying to reduce the amount of pollution printing creates.

WEB LINK
Salon
www.salon.com

Publishing is a resource-intensive enterprise, requiring not only pulp and paper mills but printing plants, inks and dyes, and a large distribution network.

On the economic side, with full-color pages and generally high-quality, glossy paper, magazines are both expensive to produce and environmentally unfriendly, even when using recycled paper and vegetable inks.

However, the pages of magazines may also be their saving grace, as they remain more visually enticing and more readable than any mobile electronic screen can yet be, despite great gains in visual clarity with tablet computers. It may only be a few years before this is not the case, but for now high-quality print still beats out what a similarly sized screen can show. Advertisements can be works of graphic art in and of themselves, and the portability and relatively low cost of magazines make them almost as disposable as newspapers so consumers do not feel like they are making a major investment when buying one at a newsstand.

The generally interpretative nature of many magazines may also help them survive, as they may provide a perspective on issues of the day that could be hard to foster in an online environment. Though the same content could be found online in the magazine's website, of course, strong forces may support the desire for a portable, nonelectronic magazine that interprets rather than just reports the news of the day.

Some magazines can also serve an important social function that is likely to keep people subscribing for a long time. Although reading a newspaper may not indicate one's social aspirations or intelligence (especially in one-newspaper towns), publicly reading the *New Yorker* or the *Atlantic Monthly* imparts a very different impression of the reader than *Popular Hot Rodding* or *Guns & Ammo*. In fact, magazines considered prestigious (either because of their content or their excellent graphics) can often be used as subtle social markers by being displayed on the coffee table in the home or office (even if the magazine is never actually read).

Over the long term, however, it is likely that print magazines will lose their relative importance as a form of delivering content as more and more readers make the online environment their primary source for information and entertainment. Better screens on tablet computers may give magazines a new lease on life and help them migrate more to the digital space. The type of magazine content we see today may not change much, but the way in which we see it will, though this change will likely be slower than that occurring with newspapers.

In a world of eye-catching multimedia, flashy graphics, and media saturation, it would seem that gray, boring, and quiet print media will take a backseat. Indeed, some studies have shown a worrisome decline in reading among adults and especially young people. If print has improved our ability to think logically and rationally, as some scholars believe, that raises questions about how today's digital media may be affecting our thinking, adversely or otherwise.

However, even with so many other media options, reading remains an important component of our media consumption—some may say it even could become more important, especially if media literacy and critical-thinking skills decline.

From an economic perspective, media industries that have relied on printing on paper are facing grave challenges. This is not because what is written has become irrelevant, but because the packaging that the content comes in is changing. Just as scrolls gave way eventually to books, and in the change the form of writing also changed, printed books are beginning to give way to online formats such as tablet computers and mobile phones, and the changes in appearance and content could be equally revolutionary.

Similarly, newspapers and magazines are facing drastic changes brought on by digital media. There is nothing sacred or magical about the form of the modern newspaper (although for people who grew up reading newspapers it may seem so), and if newspapers are to survive, they very well may need to move from paper to digital-only formats—which we are already starting to see with some major newspapers. This change is not simply one of form: it will alter the nature of the newspaper and likely even the nature of news itself and will allow print to sit alongside audio, video, and multimedia. Whether this reduces the importance of the written word, or how it alters it in our minds, remains to be seen.

Print published on paper will never disappear entirely, of course, just as sailboats did not disappear with the rise of steamships and horseback riding did not disappear with the invention of railroads and cars. But the changes that will inevitably occur will alter our society and culture, and the records that will be kept—most likely in written form—will give historians of the future a rearview mirror that will tell far more about us than we realize today.

DISCUSSION QUESTIONS

1. Do you think that, with the Internet and digital media, we are in the midst of a media revolution as far-reaching as that brought on by the printing press? Why or why not? What are some societal and technological similarities or differences between now and the mid-1400s that will support your argument?

2. If you were to travel into the future to a postapocalyptic world to build a new civilization, what three books might you bring and why?

3. If you had to make a choice today for the rest of your life to receive your textual news and knowledge about the world only from printed materials or only from online sources, which would you choose? What are your reasons?

4. How did the development of the penny press change the nature of mediated communication in the nineteenth century?

5. Why have magazines seemed to adjust better than newspapers to societal and technological changes brought on primarily since World War II? Create a brief outline of a business plan that a twenty-first-century newspaper could follow in order to survive, including its target audience and type of content.

6. What forces led to the specialization of magazines in the years following World War II? What factors will shape the future of magazines in the twenty-first century?

7. Magazines survived by moving from general-interest to niche markets, a trend followed by cable television today. Given that fact, what would a good marketing strategy for magazines be?

8. Local advertisers can exert undue control over small, independently owned papers by threatening to reduce or stop advertising. What factors could hurt public-service journalism in an age of media concentration by companies whose primary business interests are not journalism?

FURTHER READING

A History of Reading. Alberto Manguel (1997) Penguin.

An Introduction to Book History. David Finkelstein and Alastair McCreely (2005) Routledge.

The Smithsonian Book of Books. Michael Olmert (1992) Smithsonian Press.

The Evolution of the Book. Frederick G. Kilgour (1998) Oxford University Press.

Preserving the Press: How Daily Newspapers Mobilized to Keep Their Readers. Leo Bogart (1991) Columbia University Press.

-30-: The Collapse of the Great American Newspaper. Charles M. Madigan (ed.) (2007) Ivan R. Dee.

The Vanishing Newspaper: Saving Journalism in the Information Age. Philip Meyer (2004) University of Missouri Press.

The Death and Life of American Journalism: The Media Revolution That Will Begin the World Again. Robert McChesney and John Nichols (2010) Nation Books.

The Magazine from Cover to Cover. Sammye Johnson and Patricia Prijatel (2006) Oxford University Press.

Magazines: A Complete Guide to the Industry. David Sumner and Sherril Rhoades (2006) Peter Lang.

Pulp Culture: The Art of Fiction Magazines. Frank Robinson and Lawrence Davidson (2007) Collectors Press.

4

AUDIO MEDIA: MUSIC RECORDINGS, RADIO

LEARNING OBJECTIVES

By the end of this chapter
you should be able to:

- Define the nature and
  functions of the recording
  arts (i.e., music).

- Discuss the history of the
  recording arts.

- Describe how the recording
  industry works.

- Identify the changes
  digitization, the Internet,
  and file-sharing services
  have brought to the
  recording-industry business
  model.

- Understand the basic
  functions served by radio.

- Discuss the history of radio.

- Describe how the radio
  industry works.

The woman waiting for the bus, fiddling quietly with her iPod to get the song she wants to listen to, may seem quiet and removed from the world around her, but in fact she is at the center of a transformation taking place today in the music industry.

Whether she downloaded the songs for free from a file-sharing service or paid for them a la carte from iTunes, her actions challenge the major record labels to come up with new ways of marketing and distributing their product.

The newfound freedom among music lovers to discover new music or artists that may only be heard on college radio stations or in a rare indie music shop seems like a boon to the recording industry. Sites like Pandora, which through their Music Genome Project lets users create their own music "stations" and recommends artists similar to the style of music a user is listening to, make finding new musical genres and artists even easier. Yet it is exactly this kind of freedom that the industry fears.

The recording industry has been built on a model of mass-producing albums by a select number of artists and using its marketing might to convince consumers to buy the product. This still works to some extent, but it is not nearly as powerful as it was before digital media and the Internet. Furthermore, the record labels have been unable to stop the flood of free versions of songs found on file-sharing services, giving little incentive to many consumers to buy physical CDs.

Independent artists would seem to be the main beneficiaries of this new system, but in taking advantage of a more level playing field to distribute music, they have created a din that is nearly impossible to break through. Ironically, this makes marketing and promotion even more important in order to get noticed by the public. Furthermore, their songs are just as likely to be shared for free as those from an international pop star, which means it may be just as difficult as it has been for artists to make a living from their music.

The recording industry has been at the vanguard of where established media business models and digital media clash, and the recording industry has not been shy about voicing its concerns or protecting its interests. It has been watched closely by other media industries, who have so far been able to avoid many of its mistakes. From enabling through inaction the rampant use of file-sharing services to suing its customers for copyright infringement, the recording industry has made its share of poor decisions and suffered in the spotlight of public opinion.

Radio is the most familiar and far-reaching medium of mass communication in the world. Just about everyone listens to radio. Unlike computers, radio doesn't require any particular technical skill from the listener—and doesn't even need an electrical connection, with hand-cranked or battery-powered radios. Unlike print media, radio doesn't even require literacy; all you have to do is listen.

One principle in particular has guided the development of radio and other wireless communication media in the twentieth century: that the airwaves belong to the public, that they are a public good, and that those who use them have a responsibility to serve in the public interest. This concept, in tandem with the notion that the airwaves are a limited resource, laid the foundation for the regulation of radio and other electronic wireless media. Important changes to this principle are happening in the twenty-first century, however, as digitization transforms the potential use of the broadcasting spectrum and commercial interests increasingly dominate the character of radio and other wireless communications.

◢◤ The Recording Industry

The recording industry has shown the best and the worst of what mass communication and entertainment can offer. On the one hand, the public has been exposed to a much greater variety of music than before. We are all familiar with stories of recording artists from humble origins being discovered and becoming wildly successful entertainers. On the other hand, careers and lives have been ruined because of the excesses that come with fame that the recording industry is partly responsible for encouraging. Despite the variety of music we have available to us, the industry itself has made it especially hard for artists who do not fit established genres or styles of music to get contracts and be heard by a mass audience.

The recorded-music industry has similarities to other large media entertainment companies. It is an industry controlled mostly by a few very large firms (which are often subsidiaries of even larger media corporations), and it has been primarily promoted through radio, television, and movies. Today, video games, television commercials, and mobile phone ringtones are increasingly popular venues to promote music. Because of this strong mass-market emphasis, recording labels do not have any benefit in promoting music that will not have large numbers of sales. This leads to a certain homogenization of music styles that are often formulaic and sound much the same. This situation is beginning to change with the emergence of online music distribution, in which fans can find music styles and artists that would not be available in the traditional marketing and distribution structure because they would not make enough money for the labels.

Distinctive Functions of the Recorded-Music Industry

Recorded music serves a variety of functions, primarily **entertainment** and **cultural transmission**. The principal service to the audience is to provide musical entertainment. From children to senior citizens, just about everyone in contemporary society finds at least some recorded music to their liking. Although largely a commercial enterprise driven by a profit motive, the recording industry has helped produce art, as well. Whether recordings of jazz, opera, or even hip-hop,

entertainment

Providing or being provided with amusement or enjoyment.

cultural transmission

The process of passing on culturally relevant knowledge, skills, attitudes, and values from person to person or group to group.

phonograph

First patented by Thomas Edison in 1877 as a "talking machine," it used a tinfoil cylinder to record voices from telephone conversations. Successive technological improvements in electronics and the type of material the sounds were recorded on made sound quality better.

graphophone

An improvement on Thomas Edison's phonograph in recording audio, it used beeswax to record sound rather than tinfoil. Developed by Alexander Graham Bell and inventor Charles Tainter.

gramophone

Developed by inventor Emile Berliner, it used a flat disc to record sound rather than the cylinder that was used up to that time.

It was a technological challenge to record sound on devices that would be easy for the public to use.

many recorded musical performances and studio productions have achieved a cultural impact or enduring quality that critics have praised or acknowledged.

Music can also be a powerful force in transmitting culture, especially in terms of new fashion styles that cross ethnic or socioeconomic boundaries, and can introduce listeners to new words and phrases that, along with fashion, help people define their identities as belonging to certain groups. Further, song lyrics can be powerful influencers of people's emotions, subtly instructing us how to think about romantic love or relationships. Lyrics can also be lightning rods of culture, especially when some groups find some songs offensive either because of the language used or what they promote, such as treating women as sex objects. The public discussions that arise from these complaints can help shape our cultural norms as to what is acceptable and not acceptable.

Another type of cultural transmission that recorded music provides is how it can educate. Children, especially, listen to recorded music, sometimes the same songs over and over, learning vocabulary, musical rhythms, and the pleasure of dancing.

◤◥ History of Recorded Music

The recorded-music industry, or the recording arts, is the first medium of mass communication not based on print. Having begun to develop as a mass medium in the 1870s, the recording arts predate even the development of cinema, which did not develop as a mass medium until the turn of the century. Radio, which was invented in the 1890s, did not develop as a mass medium until the 1920s.

Audio recording began when Thomas Edison patented his first "talking machine" in 1877, the **phonograph**, using a tinfoil cylinder as a way to record telephone messages. Edison held a monopoly in the recording industry for nine years until telephone pioneer Alexander Graham Bell and inventor Charles Tainter developed an improved audio-recording device called the **graphophone** that used beeswax rather than tinfoil cylinders. Based on their invention, the American Graphophone Company was launched in 1887.

The Columbia Phonograph Company soon entered the scene, launching its own technology to sell recordings on wax cylinders that could be played on coin-operated machines. The Victor Talking Machine Company was also launched, employing technology developed by inventor Emile Berliner called the **gramophone**, which used a flat disc to record sound rather than a cylinder, as proposed by Edison.

Certain technological hurdles hampered the development of audio recording. In order to record sound, it first has to be accurately captured. A microphone gathers sound energy and converts it to electrical energy with similar wave characteristics.

History has obscured the exact origins of the microphone. Some suggest that D. E. Hughes of England invented it in 1878, although some evidence indicates that Scottish inventor Alexander Graham Bell may have been the one. Bell had been interested in the education of the deaf, which led him to invent in 1876 his "electrical speech machine," now known as a telephone.

There were very few dramatic changes in recording-arts technology over the first one hundred years of its existence. Even the creation of vinyl long-play (LP) albums at 33⅓ rpm, or revolutions per minute, in the mid 1950s, which allowed playing times of forty to forty-five minutes rather than the two-and-a-half minutes of the shellac 78 rpm albums, were simply improvements in existing production processes and sound quality rather than radical new technologies.

The dog Nipper "listening to his master's voice" is a widely recognized symbol of what started as the Victor Talking Machine Company.

Electromagnetic tapes such as eight-track tapes, and later cassettes, created in 1965, actually provided poorer sound quality than LPs, but consumers were willing to trade audio quality for portability.

Compact discs, developed in 1980, were the first conveyor of digitally recorded songs and the first real technological breakthrough in the recording arts since Edison's time. Digital technology not only can improve the sound quality of older recordings by removing unwanted noise such as pops and hisses, but it has also allowed for easy creation of "duets" by live and dead singers, such as the song "Unforgettable" by Nat King Cole and his daughter Natalie.

◣◥ The Recorded-Music Industry Today

By 1909 a handful of companies controlled the recording-arts industry. Recording-arts scholar Geoffrey P. Hull notes that although the companies went through major changes, a three-way corporate oligarchy dominated the music industry until the 1950s, when a variety of industry-wide changes set in. The growth of rock and roll music introduced much greater competition into the recording industry, with the emergence of various new recording labels such as Detroit's Motown, although it was relatively short-lived diversity.

Through extensive merger and acquisition activity, the 1990s saw the reemergence of tight oligarchy control in the recording arts. The Internet and online music distribution has triggered a titanic struggle to redefine this structure, however. Today, the recording-arts industry is perhaps best thought of as the world of musical recording and distribution for profit. The industry is dominated globally by four companies, the **major labels**. They are Sony Music Entertainment, EMI, Warner Music Group, and Universal Music Group. Similar to other media companies, the record labels have been consolidating. In 1998 there were six major labels, and in 2004 there were five, which included Bertelsmann Music Group (BMG). In 2008, BMG was absorbed into Sony Music, leaving the four remaining major labels.

Each of the big-four recording-industry giants is either a subsidiary of a larger media empire or has other media and entertainment interests that stretch beyond music. Combined, these companies control much of the recording and entertainment industries. Universal Music Group alone controls 25 percent of the worldwide market for recorded music.

major labels

The four biggest recording-arts companies that control much of the music industry partly through their powerful distribution channels and ability to market music to mass audiences. They are Universal Music Group, Sony Music, EMI, and the Warner Music Group.

Alexander Graham Bell is credited with inventing the telephone, although historians disagree on how much his invention relied on several other inventors' patents.

TABLE 4-1
The Major Record Labels and Their Main Subsidiary Labels

MAJOR LABELS	Universal Music Group	Sony Music	EMI	Warner Music Group
Subsidiary labels (and select artists)	Interscope Geffen A&M (Beck, Black-Eyed Peas, Lady Gaga, Marilyn Manson, New Kids on the Block, Weezer) The Island Def Jam Music Group (Rihanna, The Killers, Kanye West) Universal Motown Republic Group (Amy Winehouse, Lil Wayne, 3 Doors Down, Nelly) Universal Music Group Nashville (Shania Twain, Trisha Yearwood, Ryan Adams, Willie Nelson) Decca Label Group (Andrea Bocelli, Boyz II Men) The Verve Music Group (Billie Holiday, Ella Fitzgerald, John Coltrane) Universal Records South (Allison Moorer, Dean Miller, Bering Strait) Universal Music Latino (Juanes, Café Tacuba, Luis Fonsi) A&M/Octone (Flyleaf, Hollywood Undead, Dropping Daylight)	Arista/J Records (Alicia Keys, Boxie, Santana) Arista Nashville (Brooks and Dunn, Brad Paisley, Alan Jackson) RCA Records (Kelly Clarkson, Foo Fighters, Kings of Leon) RCA Records Nashville (Martina McBride, Jake Owen, Chris Young) BNA Records Label (Kenny Chesney, Pat Green, Craig Morgan) Burgundy Records (America, Chaka Khan, Julio Iglesias) Columbia (AC/DC, Adele, Bruce Springsteen, System of a Down) Columbia Nashville (Keith Anderson, Montgomery Gentry, Gretchen Wilson) Epic (Brandy, Ben Folds Five, Michael Jackson) Zomba-Jive Label Group (Britney Spears, Chris Brown, Justin Timberlake) Legacy Recordings (Johnny Cash, The Clash, Miles Davis) Sony BMG Latin (Alicasto, Calle 13, Marc Anthony) Masterworks (Leo Bernstein, Yo-Yo Ma, Beverly Sills)	Owns Capitol Music Group, Virgin Music Group, and Blue Note Music Group, among others (Barenaked Ladies, Beastie Boys, Bebe, Trouĺble Andrew, The Decemberists, Coldplay, Elvis Costello, Amy Grant, Norah Jones, REM, Bob Seger, Snoop Dogg, Spice Girls, Trace Adkins)	Atlantic Records Group (Kid Rock, Matchbox Twenty, Staind) Rhino Entertainment (Aretha Franklin, Chicago, Black Sabbath) Rykodisc (Frank Zappa, Joe Jackson, Freezepop) Warner Bros. Records (Red Hot Chili Peppers, Linkin Park, Seal)

TABLE 4-1

The Major Record Labels and Their Main Subsidiary Labels

MAJOR LABELS	Universal Music Group	Sony Music	EMI	Warner Music Group
Subsidiary labels (and select artists) (cont'd)		Provident Label Group (Annie Moses Band, Jars of Clay, Pillar) Verity (gospel) Windham Hill (New Age)		
Other interests or parent companies	Parent company is Vivendi, involved in publishing, TV and film production, and video games	Parent company is Sony		Parent company is Time Warner, involved in publishing, TV and film production

Independent labels—ranging from small local companies producing and distributing music from even a single artist or two to large labels such as Disney—produce the majority of music titles, estimated at about 66 percent by SoundScan and the Recording Industry Association of America (RIAA), yet have only about 20 percent of the sales.

Similar to book publishing, the vast majority of recorded-music releases sell less than 5,000 copies per year, with only a handful of recordings, numbering in the hundreds, selling more than 250,000 a year. Yet these few account for over half the total sales volume, and most are released by the major labels.

How do the major labels manage to produce so many of the big hits? There are at least two answers, and no one knows for sure which is correct. One answer is that they produce the best music from the best artists, market it the best, and reap the rewards. Although there is no doubt at least some truth to this, answer number two also rings at least partly true. The major labels so dominate the entire production and distribution process that even if they produce collectively only marginal-quality recorded music, they will also dominate music sales because of their ability to market what they do produce.

Regardless of which reason you believe, one thing that everybody has agreed on is the steep decline in recorded music sales since 2001, which recording industry executives call the beginning of the "digital piracy era." In 2010, global music sales were $15.9 billion, down 8.4 percent from 2009 when they were $17.4 billion, according to the International Federation of the Phonographic Industry (IFPI), a London-based organization that represents the interests of the recording industry worldwide. The RIAA and IFPI claim that file-sharing services that encourage illegal downloads are to blame for the decline in sales, though other industry observers say the picture is more complex than that.

First, about two-thirds of music sales globally in 2010 were still CDs, making up $10.4 billion out of the total $15.9 billion in sales. CD sales declined 14.2 percent, or $1.8 billion, between 2009 and 2010. However, digital sales increased 5.3 percent, for a total of $4.6 billion in 2010, according to IFPI. Digital sales

independent labels

Any small record-production and distribution companies that are not part of the four major-label companies. They include companies producing only one or two albums a year, as well as larger independents such as Disney. The independent labels produce 66 percent of the albums each year but only 20 percent of the sales.

worldwide were a third of the total music sales, but in the United States digital accounted for 49 percent of music sales in 2010, up from 43 percent in 2009.

Although the rise in digital music sales is encouraging for the music industry, the declines in CD sales year after year are still bigger than what digital revenues can make up for. Moreover, the music industry is getting caught in a downward distribution cycle with major retail chains like Best Buy and Wal-Mart, where 65 percent of all CD sales occur. As CD sales drop, retailers devote less floor display space to CDs, making it even harder for the record labels to distribute all the new CDs they produce. However, even this picture is muddied by the fact that some bands have had exclusive distribution deals with major chains like Wal-Mart. For example, in 2008 AC/DC's *Black Ice* was sold through an exclusive distribution deal with Wal-Mart and was the fifth highest-selling album of the year.

Independent releases have risen dramatically, especially with the rise of the Internet and digital distribution, but sales continue to be small compared to most major-label releases. Some websites have dedicated themselves to promoting and selling independent artists, although their marketing might pales in comparison to the resources of the major labels. Marketing is not the only reason that independent labels are at a disadvantage compared to the major labels. Despite changes in the industry, the basic business model remains largely the same.

▲▼ Recording-Industry Business Model

Throughout much of the twentieth century, the basic business model in the recorded-music industry could be divided into three main parts: creation, promotion, and distribution. Even in the digital world these main parts have not changed, though components of the parts have of course changed with digital technology and the Internet.

▼ CREATION

The major record labels sign artists and financially back those artists in the creation and recording of the music. Because of their financial investment in the process, the recording labels have historically received the majority of the financial rewards, with most artists receiving royalty payments of approximately 10 percent of gross, or overall, sales for their endeavors. Since recording labels obviously want to sign artists whose music will sell well, they can be seen as a gatekeeper or filter of talent, although not necessarily a perfect one, much like book publishers can be filters of writing talent.

Being signed to a major label may seem like a struggling band has finally "made it," but remember that most music sells fewer than 5,000 copies annually, with only a handful selling more than 250,000 copies. When seen this way, 10 percent of sales, or about $2 per album sold, actually does not seem like much income for a band. For every Adele selling millions of copies of an album, each year there are thousands of signed artists who release albums under major or indie labels who only sell a few thousand albums and who never get heard on the radio.

▼ PROMOTION

Promoting artists and their music is crucial to an album's success. There are several venues for promoting music to fans and the public. Artists perform in concerts, for which additional royalties are received, but radio is a primary promotional vehicle for music. Radio is where the major labels have huge advantages over the indie labels in getting their artists airtime. In the past two decades, music videos have also become an important promotional vehicle, and the use of music from new bands on TV shows, video games, and ringtones in recent years has become an important way to help bands reach wider audiences.

The record labels traditionally provide the radio stations and television programmers with free copies of the recorded music and music videos in exchange for playing them on their stations and channels. Sometimes certain unscrupulous programmers or disc jockeys in major markets have demanded illegal cash, gifts, or other payments under the table—known as **payola**—from the labels in exchange for promoting a song by playing it more frequently than other songs. The labels have sometimes paid this fee because of the importance of radio, especially certain major stations, as a promotional vehicle. Payola was very big in the 1950s, until the FTC ruled it was unfairly stifling competition. Payola favors the major labels over small labels, because small labels lack the financial resources to make these payments. Moreover, payola reduces the potential for diversity on the air.

Perhaps the most famous case of radio payola involved rock-radio DJ Alan Freed. Freed is credited with naming the emerging rhythm and blues–type music "rock and roll" while working for WJW-AM in Cleveland in the early 1950s. His career in radio was ruined in 1964 when he was convicted in New York on commercial bribery charges for accepting payoffs, or payola, to play certain records. After a series of radio jobs in various cities and a worsening drinking problem, Freed died in Palm Springs, California, in 1965. In 1986, Freed was inducted into the Rock and Roll Hall of Fame.[1] Today, payola, or what is now called "pay for play" (and some suspect still done extensively), is punishable with a fine or even imprisonment and is enforced by the FCC. Record labels have devised ways to get around a clear "pay for play" format by doing things like having artists visit radio stations for interviews in exchange for promoting their music, special events in certain markets, and other types of promotions such as concert ticket giveaways or backstage passes in which the labels and radio stations work together.

payola

Cash or gifts given to radio disc jockeys by record labels in exchange for greater airplay given to the label's artists or most recent songs. The practice is now illegal after several scandals involving payola in the 1950s.

DJ Alan Freed, who was at the heart of the payola scandals between the record labels and radio stations.

▼ DISTRIBUTION

Although recorded music has appeared in different ways over the years—first as tin or beeswax cylinders, then on grooved plastic as albums, then on magnetic tape as eight-tracks and audio cassettes, then in optical form on compact discs—the method of distribution has essentially remained unchanged. The record labels make copies of the music from a master copy and send the albums, tapes, or CDs to local retail outlets that sell them to consumers. Online stores, such as Amazon, act much like their real-world counterparts, except consumers receive the CDs at their homes and Amazon does not have to be concerned about display space in stores.

Because online stores such as Amazon do not have to worry about display space, they are able to carry a larger number of CDs than retail stores, which lets them carry CDs that are far less popular. This is an example of what is called the **long tail**, where businesses are able to succeed by selling a greater variety of items but selling fewer of each item.

long tail

The notion that selling a few of many types of items can be as profitable or even more profitable than selling many copies of a few items. The concept works especially well for online sellers such as Amazon or Netflix.

Another aspect of digital media and the Internet has been changing distribution much more radically. Consumers do not even have to buy a physical product and are able to download songs either through a subscription service or a la carte. Not only can songs be copied and distributed easily by the general public, but flawless copies can be created with no loss in sound quality. This is having profound effects on the very business models the recording industry uses in distributing music, which will be examined below.

▼ PRICING STRUCTURE

A major source of debate in the industry is the pricing structure for recorded music. Price, of course, is a major determining factor in both sales and profitability for the label and royalties for the artist, as well as income for all others in the distribution chain. In the 1970s, when vinyl LPs were the standard means of distributing recorded music, list prices (what the consumer paid) were about $6 (about $26 in 2010 dollars). In the 1980s, the compact disc was introduced as the new means of distributing music, and CDs as a percentage of album sales gradually increased from just 22 percent in 1988 to 91 percent in 2001. List prices for CDs were about $19 in the early 1980s (about $39 in 2010 dollars), with wholesale prices about $12.

Over time, with increases in production volume, the cost of producing CDs has fallen, and as a result, wholesale prices have fallen to about $10, with list prices at about $15 or often less when promotional discounts are used. Inside the labels, manufacturing costs are today about $1 per CD, with artist and producer royalties about $2 per album (roughly 10–20 percent of the list price) and distributor charges about $1.50. Marketing costs (roughly 50¢) tend to be quite low, because most of the promotion is provided free by radio stations and music television. Thus, a label typically has a gross profit of $5 per CD sold. This is a simplified model, but it illustrates the immense profitability in the recorded-music industry.

▲▼ Outlook for the Recording Industry

The recording industry got some good news in 2011 when Nielsen SoundScan and Billboard announced that music sales had increased 3.5 percent in the first half of 2011, the first sales increase since 2004.[2] Whether the increase is sustainable or will continue is still hard to say, but it does point to the role that digital media has played in both the music industry's decline and, potentially, in its regrowth. On one hand, there are new revenue streams that simply did not exist in the predigital era, such as ring tone sales, and new ways to sell music to consumers, including online subscription services. On the other hand, illegal downloading of songs for free continues, which the music industry has blamed on the continued decline in sales the past several years.

▼ DIGITAL RIGHTS MANAGEMENT AND
ILLEGAL FILE SHARING

Critics of the music industry and major record labels say they only have themselves to blame as they scramble to stop the general decline in music sales. Rather than embracing the potential of digital technologies and the Internet for generating new kinds of revenue streams early on, they fought it in a number of ways that proved later to be valuable lessons for television networks and movie studios.

Security of copyrighted material remains a prime concern to the record labels, and many of their past initiatives in **digital rights management** (DRM) have been heavy-handed and raised the ire of customers, such as limiting the number of digital copies a customer can make of purchased music. Most DRM efforts for physical media like CDs have also proved short-lived, as hacks have quickly emerged to break the security codes. By 2009, none of the major record labels used DRM on their music CDs, saying the costs associated with DRM did not justify the results.

DRM is far more common with online music, although not all online sellers use DRM. For downloaded music, DRM restricts either the types of devices that can play the downloaded song, the length of time the song can be played, or limits access to the song in some other way, such as requiring an ongoing subscription, like with Kazaa. Generally, the music services that do offer DRM versions of songs online offer them at lower price points than non-DRM songs, which do not have the same restrictions regarding copying files between devices or having different formats.

digital rights management [DRM]

Various technologies or security codes used to protect copyrighted works from being illegally copied.

Since 2001, the recording industry has sued various file-sharing services and Internet Service Providers (ISPs), successfully shutting down and eventually bankrupting music file-sharing pioneer Napster. The RIAA even sued several thousand individuals who were sharing files, creating a huge amount of bad publicity for the record industry. At the end of 2008 it announced it would stop suing individual file sharers and would instead put pressure on the ISPs to cut off those people from the Internet.

Electronic Frontier Foundation

The EFF is a non-profit organization that focuses on issues of privacy and developments in communications technologies.

Many ISPs have blocked access to file-sharing services because of both threatened lawsuits and the heavy load that such sharing can place on networks, thus slowing the networks down even for users not sharing files. Universities, with their fast Internet connections and large groups of music-loving young people, have been prime targets of the RIAA, which has pushed for special ethics education for incoming students to discourage music-file sharing and to remind them that sharing copyrighted works is illegal.

The recording industry has also been more aggressive in pursuing file-sharing services themselves. In late 2010 popular file-sharing service Limewire, with 50 million users monthly, was ordered shut down by a federal judge, the result of a four-year-old court case by the RIAA. After the shutdown, Bearshare, another file-sharing service, saw a sharp rise in users. This shows how difficult it is for the recording industry to stop file sharing, because as soon as one service is closed other services get used more or new services spring up.

Lobbying efforts by the recording industry have resulted in some politicians proposing legislation that would further strengthen the legal positions of the recording industry, with suggestions such as requirements for electronic-equipment manufacturers to install digital security devices in their products. Manufacturers are resisting such directives, and groups like the Electronic Frontier Foundation and others also fight these efforts from a citizen or consumer rights perspective.

▼ NEW BUSINESS MODELS EMERGING

Despite the continued popularity of illegal file sharing, the increase in music sales in the first half of 2011 may help reinforce the point that the music industry's critics have long made about the music industry not doing enough to develop new

freemium

Subscriptions in which subscribers can receive some content for free but if they want to take advantage of all the site has to offer they must pay a monthly subscription.

amplitude modulation

How the audio signal is encoded on the carrier frequency

frequency modulation

Refers to the modulation of the length of the wave

Global Positioning System

A system of satellites that provide location information anywhere in the world

broadcast

The original usage was agricultural, referring to casting seeds widely in a field rather than depositing them one at a time. The notion was transferred to the fledgling electronic medium of radio and later television.

ways to sell music that match consumers' interests and ways of using media. There are two main business models that seem to be emerging today: downloads and subscription services.

Downloading music, as the discussion on illegal file sharing shows, is hardly new. It was not until 2003 with Apple's iTunes, however, that the music industry finally seemed to be able to get consumers to pay for downloading music. Many in the recording industry, including artists themselves, worried that a la carte song downloads would mean the death of the album. However, this has not been the case, as in 2010 sales of digital albums outpaced single-song downloads, accounting for 17.5 percent of total album sales in the UK and 26.5 percent in the United States, according to IFPI's Digital Media Report 2011. Various artists entice consumers to download an entire album by including additional content like behind-the-scenes footage, exclusive interviews, and games. Downloading ring tones has also been a new source of revenue. Although small compared to song and album downloads, it demonstrates how songs may be popular in a variety of formats, including formats that normally would never have been considered as mass media.

Subscription services have shown remarkable growth in recent years and offer great potential for a variety of new types of revenue streams. Many subscriptions operate on a **freemium** model, in which subscribers can receive some content for free, but if they want to take advantage of all the site has to offer they must pay a monthly subscription. There are a number of models being experimented with in the freemium model, such as advertising-supported content for the free service but no ads for the premium service. Other ways to differentiate the free and paid tiers include allowing access to special content for paying subscribers or providing songs that subscribers can download to other devices.

In North America, Slacker Radio and Pandora are two of the biggest music subscription services, and both have seen huge growth in recent years. Pandora has more than 75 million registered users, up from 25 million in 2008, and claims 500,000 paying subscribers. Sweden-based Spotify, launched in 2008 and the second most popular digital music service in Europe after iTunes, was available in the United States in July 2011, adding to a growing field of competitors in the music subscription space. As the names and functions of these services suggest, the line between "Internet radio" and an "online music subscription service" is very blurry, making it hard to define exactly where radio ends and downloading songs begins.

From an industry perspective, the recording industry is looking at forming partnerships with ISPs, some of which choose to offer their own branded music subscription services to ISP customers. They are also looking to increase partnerships with mobile operators, which will let consumers more easily get songs and music content from their mobile devices.

In short, the music industry finds itself caught between old models of doing business and new ways for customers to get what they want that do not always look like the ways the industry has traditionally used. Although its problem is not unique, the music industry has been at the forefront of this revolution and made numerous strategic mistakes that have hurt the industry's public image, as well as revenue opportunities. Other media industries, especially the film and television industries, have been watching and learning from the recording industry's mistakes, and we will look at what they are doing in the next chapter.

Giving consumers more choice in how they get their music has been a difficult adjustment for the major record labels.

The Alphabet Soup of Spectrum Allocation

Since the electromagnetic spectrum used for wireless communications is a limited resource, the FCC allocates various portions of it to different uses so these applications do not interfere with each other. Electromagnetic waves are divided into cycles per second, or hertz. If a radio station is at 99.5 on the radio tuner, this means its transmitter is oscillating at 99,500,000 cycles per second, or 99.5 megahertz (MHz).

"AM" stands for amplitude modulation and refers to how the audio signal is encoded on the carrier frequency. AM radio broadcasts between 535 kilohertz (kHz) and 1,700 kHz (1.7 MHz), and was the only radio signal to reach the public for a number of years.

"FM" stands for frequency modulation; this refers to the modulation of the length of the wave. FM radio broadcasts in the 88–108 megahertz (MHz) portion of the radio spectrum. This band is used exclusively for FM radio.

Other portions of the wireless bandwidth spectrum are used for other applications, such as Global Positioning System (GPS), a system of satellites that provide location information anywhere in the world, between 1,227 and 1,575 MHz. Citizens band, or CB, radio (26.96 to 27.41 MHz) enjoyed short-lived popularity among the public in the 1970s and is still commonly used by long-haul truckers today. It was also the spectrum used by Sputnik, the first satellite ever launched into space.

WEB LINK
How Stuff Works
electronics.howstuffworks.com/radio3.htm

WEB LINK
U.S. Frequency Allocation Chart
www.ntia.doc.gov/osmhome/allochrt.html

What Is Broadcasting?

The term **broadcast** was used much earlier than the development of radio or television broadcasting as we know them today, as far back as 1883. The term "broadcasting" was borrowed from agriculture, where it referred to a form of planting seeds by casting them widely in a field rather than depositing them one at a time.

In its early days, wireless communications, which was initially only radio, provided point-to-point communication where telegraph lines were impractical or unreliable. The main purpose early wireless inventors saw was ship-to-ship communications or ship-to-shore communications, which would allow ships to communicate emergencies quickly to others. Subsequently, radio technology was developed to permit the broadcasting of messages through wireless means to multiple locations to distribute information widely. The subsequent development of television broadcasting dozens of years later offered the opportunity to transmit moving pictures as well as audio via wireless technology.

Whether it is radio or television, however, broadcasting works essentially the same way. A transmitter sends messages over a part of the electromagnetic spectrum to a receiver, or antenna, which translates the message to a device such as a radio or television. The electromagnetic waves, whether they are audio or images, are then decoded by the receiving device so they can be heard or seen.

Early radios were often built to fit in with other living room furniture.

◣◤ Radio

Radio is the most widely available medium of mass communication around the world. It is also the most heavily used medium in the United States, where people listen to radio on average over 2.5 hours per day, although there are sometimes great disparities in reported radio listening depending on how the research is done. For example, when filling out a diary of radio usage compared to observational studies, people tend to greatly underreport their radio listening. This is likely because radio is often playing "in the background" while they do other things, even while they consume other media such as reading a book or going online, and they tend not to think about it.

At least 99 percent of all U.S. households have at least one radio receiver and there are similar levels of penetration in most industrialized countries. Even developing nations have a relatively high radio penetration. Radio is less expensive to produce, transmit, and receive than television; radio receivers are highly portable—even wearable—and radio doesn't require literacy to understand. There are basically three types of radio broadcasting, AM, FM, and satellite radio. However, satellite radio, like so-called Internet radio, is an entirely different method of delivering audio programming and is not the same form of broadcasting as traditional AM and FM, even though some in the industry call it "radio." Its method of delivery makes it more akin to audio programming like that in an airplane than true broadcasting, although both are "broadcast" in the sense that they reach mass audiences.

◣◤ Distinctive Functions of Radio

Around the world, radio is a medium of entertainment as well as of news and information, or surveillance, and marketing. Even in remote rural areas, radio is used to disseminate important news and information, as it can distribute instructions for farming and agriculture easily, cheaply, and rapidly. Radio is also used as an emergency broadcast medium in all parts of the world, for such events as severe storms, natural disasters, or military conflict, largely because of its portability and flexible power source. Radio is especially well suited for emergencies, when electrical power may be lost, since radio receivers can easily operate for long periods on battery power alone.

In industrialized societies, radio offers a diverse array of functions, perhaps more diverse than any other of the traditional analog media. Talk radio provides information, debate, and even limited audience interactivity with listeners calling in. News programming offers breaking news reports as well as traffic and weather reports, school closings, and more. The mainstay of commercial radio has been the broadcasting of recorded music for entertainment. This latter function also serves artists and the recording industry, who want their music promoted.

◣◤ History of Radio

Radio is a medium with a remarkable history. Technically, economically, and programmatically, radio has evolved considerably since its early development, and it continues to evolve as we enter the digital age. The following discussion reviews the development of radio, from its early days in the late nineteenth century to the early twenty-first century.

▼ WIRELESS TELEGRAPHY

Many inventors and scientists around the world were experimenting with radio technology at almost the same time. In 1884, German **Heinrich Hertz** began experimenting with electromagnetic waves, and in 1885 he demonstrated the existence of radio waves. His discovery was based on earlier theoretical notions proposed by Carl Friedrich Gauss and James Clerk Maxwell. Hertz's work set the stage for the development of modern wireless communications, both fixed and mobile, a portion of which Americans have come to know as radio. In much of the rest of the English-speaking world, radio has been known as "the wireless." The measurement unit of electromagnetic frequencies was named for Hertz.

Another scientist experimenting with radio technology was African American **Granville T. Woods**, who in 1887 invented what is known as "railway telegraphy." His invention allowed messages to be sent between moving trains, and between moving trains and a railroad station, reducing the frequency of railway collisions and informing engineers of obstructions ahead on tracks.[3]

At the twilight of the nineteenth century, in 1899, Italian **Guglielmo Marconi** invented radio telegraphy, what he called "the wireless." Marconi's invention made possible real-time transmission of audio, although in the form of dots and dashes of Morse code, over distance without a wired connection; it was what might be called the first real radio transmission.

Guglielmo Marconi invented radio telegraphy, or the wireless telegraph, in 1899.

As is typical for notable inventions, there is some debate regarding whether Marconi can be credited as the inventor of radio. Marconi was not the only inventor at the time working on wireless communications technology. Called by some the *real* inventor of radio, Kentucky farmer Nathan B. Stubblefield created and demonstrated in 1892 a wireless communications device that could even transmit voice and music over a short distance, about five hundred feet. Stubblefield was a mysterious figure who made his invention available to the Wireless Telephone Company, which proved to be a fraud, and Stubblefield never patented his device. He ultimately failed to reap the commercial rewards of his invention and in 1928 died of starvation, alone and penniless on the dirt floor of a shack.[4]

▼ EXPLORING RADIO'S EARLY POTENTIAL

In the United States, the Department of Agriculture saw radio's potential and in 1900 financed Canadian Reginald A. Fessenden's early research for gathering reports and then for distributing them over a broad area. Fessenden in 1901 obtained a U.S. patent for his new radio transmitter engineered to use a high-speed electrical alternator to produce "continuous waves." His design is the basis for today's AM radio. The USDA started using radio broadcasting to transmit weather reports in 1912, although its initial transmissions were in telegraphic code, not in human voice.

▼ VOICE TRANSMISSION

In 1906, Swedish-born inventor Ernst Alexanderson was among the first to build a working high-frequency, continuous-wave machine capable of transmitting a radio broadcast of the human voice and other sounds. His invention permitted the station to transmit a radio broadcast featuring a human voice and a violin solo.

Heinrich Hertz

Demonstrated the existence of radio waves in 1885, which set the stage for the development of modern wireless communications. The measurement unit of electromagnetic frequencies was named for Hertz.

Granville T. Woods

Inventor of railway telegraphy in 1887, a type of wireless communication that allowed moving trains to communicate with each other and with stations, greatly reducing the number of railway collisions.

Guglielmo Marconi

Italian inventor and creator of radio telegraphy, or wireless transmission, in 1899.

Milestones in Early Radio Technology Development

1839 Carl Friedrich Gauss proposes the Earth's atmosphere contains a conducting layer.

1864 James Clerk Maxwell predicts the existence of electromagnetic or radio waves that use the conducting layer in Earth's atmosphere (i.e., that electric waves can travel through the air).

1885 Heinrich Rudolf Hertz demonstrates the existence of radio waves, based on Maxwell's prediction.

1887 Granville T. Woods invents railway telegraphy, which allows messages to be sent between moving trains.

1892 Nathan B. Stubblefield creates and demonstrates a wireless communications device that can transmit voice and music.

1893 Nicola Tesla demonstrates a wireless communications device.

1899 Marchese Guglielmo Marconi invents radio telegraphy, which he calls "the wireless."

1901 Reginald A. Fessenden obtains a U.S. patent for his new radio transmitter engineered to use a high-speed electrical alternator to produce "continuous waves." It will be the basis for amplitude modulation, or AM (medium-wave), radio.

1906 Ernst Alexanderson builds a working high-frequency, continuous-wave machine capable of transmitting a radio broadcast of the human voice and other sounds.

1907 Lee de Forest develops a reliable transmission technology for radio broadcasting of human voice, for both point-to-point communication and broadcasts of entertainment and news.

Lee de Forest, one of the three "fathers" of radio.

Although much of the early work on radio was done by Italian Marconi and Canadian Fessenden, a U.S. pioneer in radio was **Lee de Forest**, who developed a unique transmission technology for radio broadcasting of human voice. His arc transmitter for voice transmissions proved reliable for both point-to-point communication and broadcasting, and by 1907 de Forest's company supplied the U.S. Navy's Great White Fleet with arc radiotelephones for its pioneering around-the-world voyage. This helped establish de Forest as the "father" of radio, although in reality, radio had at least three "fathers."

▼ RADIO BEFORE, DURING, AND AFTER WWI

Despite evident practical uses for radio, radio technology still needed to improve before it could become a mass medium. With considerable financial support from and direction by the U.S. military, research on the vacuum tube helped produce a reliable radio transmitter and receiver by about 1915. Using the perfected vacuum-tube radio transmitter, de Forest's Highbridge Station 2XG introduced nightly broadcasts, which offered listeners a so-called wireless newspaper for amateur radio operators.

All this activity ended with the entrance of the United States into World War I in April 1917. At this point, all radio stations were either taken over by the U.S. government or shut down completely. For the duration of the war it was illegal for private citizens to own or operate a radio transmitter or receiver without special permission. The military continued to conduct research on radio technology, and with the end of the war in late 1918 radio restrictions were lifted.

Commercial broadcasting in the United States began in 1920, as well as the first election-night coverage. Regular commercial radio broadcasts began when AM station KDKA of Pittsburgh, Pennsylvania, reported results of the Harding–Cox presidential election.

▼ WIDESPREAD PUBLIC ADOPTION OF RADIO

In the early 1920s in the United States there were roughly 6,000 licenses for amateur radio stations and 4,600 commercial stations, or stations run for profit. Up to this point, general public interest in radio had been slow to develop. There were amateur enthusiasts, who could be likened to the computer geeks in the early days of personal computers and the Internet, but to most members of the public, radio was a bit of a novelty whose application to their lives was limited.

However, a sporting event on July 2, 1921, would help establish radio as a major medium of mass communication. People across the country were keenly interested in the heavyweight boxing title fight between champion Jack Dempsey and challenger Georges Carpentier.[5] Radio networks did not yet exist, however, so only one station, a temporary long-wave station, WJY, broadcast the bout live, with technical help from the Radio Corporation of America (RCA). RCA, of course, had a financial incentive to see the success of the event. As a manufacturer of radio receivers, it wanted to see a radio set (or two) in every American household.

Organizers of the broadcast telegraphed a transcript of the commentary to pioneering station KDKA in Pittsburgh, which then broadcast the fight to its listeners on a slightly delayed basis. Because most people did not have their own radio receivers at this time, most listeners were in halls where local organizers, including volunteer amateur radio operators, set up receivers and charged admission to offset costs. Because of the sensational nature of the event, much subsequent media commentary was given to the technical breakthrough and promise of the new medium of radio, helping propel radio as a medium of mass communication.

A broadcasting boom began after the Dempsey–Carpentier fight, with hundreds of radio stations springing up across the country, similar to how web servers became widespread in the mid-to-late 1990s. Radio receivers were selling as fast as RCA and others could manufacture them. American Telephone and Telegraph Company (AT&T) drafted a plan to create a national radio network. AT&T began implementing the programming for its national network in 1922 with flagship station WEAF in New York City and quickly set the standard for the entire industry.

Lee de Forest

Considered the "father" of radio broadcasting technology because of his invention that permitted reliable voice transmissions for both point-to-point communication and broadcasting.

▼ FM RADIO, EDWIN HOWARD ARMSTRONG, AND DAVID SARNOFF

Edwin Howard Armstrong

Inventor of FM radio transmission; Columbia University engineering professor.

David Sarnoff

Head of RCA. He helped push the development of television as a mass medium yet blocked the development of FM radio for years because its adoption would hurt AM listenership and reduce demand for AM radio receivers, which RCA produced and sold.

In 1934, an important breakthrough in radio transmission technology occurred when Columbia University engineering professor **Edwin Howard Armstrong** (1890–1954) invented FM (frequency modulation) radio, and later stereo FM radio, with his colleague, John Bose.

Armstrong completed his first field test on June 9, 1934, sending an organ recital, via both AM and FM, from an RCA tower on top of the Empire State Building to the home of a trusted old friend on Long Island. The FM organ came through loud and clear. The AM version had much more static.

Armstrong and **David Sarnoff**, head of RCA, had started out as friends, both seeing the great potential of radio broadcasting. But RCA had made much of its fortune from the mass sales of AM radio sets, called "radio music boxes." FM radio threatened to destroy the RCA empire.

Once Sarnoff realized the magnitude of the invention, he blocked Armstrong by ordering RCA engineers to ask for more tests, lobbying federal regulators to deny Armstrong a license to test his invention, and even trying to obtain Armstrong's patent. Armstrong responded as best he could, filing suit against RCA and many other radio companies who were infringing on the Armstrong FM radio patent.

Tragically, Armstrong never reaped the commercial rewards of his invention and ultimately committed suicide virtually penniless in 1954 over his long-running legal battles with Sarnoff and other companies, as well as the end of his marriage. Ironically, his many lawsuits were settled shortly after his death, leaving a fortune to his widow and the Armstrong Foundation.

The story of Armstrong's invention and Sarnoff's machinations to protect the RCA business model mirrors some of the developments that have taken place with the Internet, in which sometimes legal wrangling or threatened business interests have prevented the better technologies from winning out.

For most of the first half of the twentieth century, AM radio listenership far exceeded FM listenership. But in the late 1970s this turned around, and today FM listenership is far greater than AM listenership, just as the number of FM stations exceeds AM stations. The ascendancy of FM radio in the 1970s was due to a number of factors, among them the inclusion of an FM dial in most automobile radio receivers, changes in programming, and regulatory changes, combined with the fact that FM has less static.

Edwin Howard Armstrong, inventor of FM radio, spent much of the latter part of his life battling companies that tried to squash FM radio because it threatened their business models that were based on AM radio.

▼ CREATING A VIABLE BUSINESS MODEL FOR RADIO

Just as with the Internet, the question of how to make a viable business out of radio broadcasting would prove a complex and controversial subject. Many stations in the United States experimented with commercial sponsorship, but through the mid-1920s there were many outspoken critics of advertising on the public airwaves. The May 1924 issue of *Radio Broadcast* magazine sponsored a five-hundred-dollar contest for the best essay on "Who is to Pay for Broadcasting—and How?" The fact that the magazine ran this contest suggested it wasn't convinced on-air advertising was a viable solution.

However, a confluence of commercial interests, government decisions (sometimes influenced by commercial interests), and lack of coordination among advocates of publicly supported broadcasting made privately owned stations with on-air advertising the standard radio-broadcasting business model that continues to this day. As a result, the engine that drives profits is audience size, especially among key demographic groups that are attractive to the advertisers who provide sponsorship.

▼ THE RISE OF RADIO NETWORKS

During the 1920s the first commercial broadcasting networks were formed, initially as radio networks—affiliated radio stations in multiple cities all broadcasting a common core set of programming—and later as national television networks. Prior to the passage of the **Radio Act of 1927** and the creation of the **Federal Radio Commission (FRC)**, the predecessor to the **Federal Communications Commission (FCC)**, broadcasting was lively but haphazard and not well organized. There were numerous stations competing with each other on the same or nearby frequencies, which often caused reception interference. There were also few regulations regarding the power of transmitters, so powerful transmitters could drown out with a stronger signal the lower-powered, local transmitters. The FRC revoked thousands of radio broadcast licenses and instituted a system that favored fewer, high-power stations over smaller but more numerous local low-power stations. This policy benefited large commercial broadcasting companies over educational, religious, and small, private broadcasters.

The National Broadcasting Network, or NBC, was the first network to form, having been created in 1926 when RCA, under the leadership of Sarnoff, purchased New York station WEAF (now WNBC) from AT&T for $1 million. That same year, NBC bought WJZ (licensed to Newark, New Jersey, but transmitting in New York) from Westinghouse and thus created the first network.

CBS was the second network to be formed, first as the United Independent Broadcasters in 1927 and then, after going on the air with a partner, the Columbia Phonograph and Records Company, becoming the Columbia Broadcasting System. In 1928, cigar maker Sam Paley bought CBS for $400,000 and installed his son, William, as its head, moving the network's headquarters from Philadelphia to New York. Under William's longtime leadership, and later under that of his corporate heir Frank Stanton, CBS held to the number-one position among the networks and described itself as the Tiffany Network—although others sometimes called it Black Rock, in partial reference to the black marble façade of its midtown Manhattan headquarters.

By 1935, fifty-eight of sixty-two stations nationwide were part of either the NBC or the CBS network. It was not until the 1940s that a third competing commercial network emerged, in television: ABC.

▼ CONSOLIDATION IN RADIO STATION OWNERSHIP

Throughout most of the twentieth century, ownership of radio in the United States was relatively diverse. This was partly a result of federal laws that prohibited any one person or organization from owning more than twenty FM stations and twenty AM stations nationwide.

Regulatory changes in 1992 and the passage of the Telecommunications Act of 1996 resulted in new FCC radio-ownership rules. These new rules put no limit on the number of radio stations that can be owned or controlled by a single entity

Radio Act of 1927

An act of Congress that created the Federal Radio Commission and that was intended to help establish some sort of regulation and order over the chaos of the largely unregulated airwaves. It helped establish the principle that the airwaves were a limited public good and that companies using those airwaves had a duty to act responsibly toward the public in terms of the type of material they broadcast.

Federal Radio Commission [FRC]

Formed by the Radio Act of 1927, the commission was the precursor to the FCC and created a policy that favored fewer high-power radio broadcasting stations rather than more numerous low-power stations.

Federal Communications Commission [FCC]

The principal communications regulatory body at the federal level in the United States, established in 1934.

nationwide, although it is still required that the owner be a U.S. citizen. Since the passage of the act, more than 4,400 radio stations have changed ownership, and the radio industry has become more of an oligopoly, in which fewer companies own a greater number of radio stations.

Regulatory changes altered the FCC's "duopoly rules" on local station ownership. Duopoly rules refer to a prohibition on any one person or group owning, operating, or controlling more than two AM stations and two FM stations in the largest markets. The rules had also restricted the combined audience share of the co-owned stations to 25 percent, with smaller markets having even more restrictive limits. The act ended these duopoly restrictions and the FCC now permits a single entity to own substantially more in the same service market than it could in the past.

This shift in regulatory policy led to a trend in the 1990s and early twenty-first century toward increasing consolidation of radio ownership. For most of the first fifty years of radio broadcasting, radio was a small business, with owners longtime residents of the towns in which the stations operated, even if they were affiliates of a national network. Although many stations in smaller towns are still locally owned and operated, most radio stations in big cities have become corporate enterprises.

Increasingly, with the end of the duopoly rules, some groups now control eight or more stations in a single market, and most of the big, highly profitable stations are owned by the most powerful media groups. Those who support the

TABLE 4-2

Top Radio Groups in the United States by Number of Stations Owned, 2010

OWNER	# OF STATIONS	TOTAL RADIO AUDIENCE (MILLIONS)
Clear Channel	844	167
Cumulus Broadcasting	303	9.14
CBS Radio	130	96.5
Entercom	112	24.6
Salem Communications Corp.	91	6.37
Saga Communications	88	3.51
Cox Enterprises	84	23.1
Univision Communications	74	22.7
Regent Communications.	69	2.94
Radio One	52	16.1

Source: PEW Research Center's Project for Excellence in Journalism, March 2010. http://stateofthemedia.org/media-ownership/audio/?srt=2&so=-1&compare=. Retrieved April 13, 2012.

changes in station ownership say consolidation is a good thing for many reasons, including increased efficiency; more economical, centralized production; larger budgets that permit greater programming experimentation and development; and more effective management. Critics argue that group ownership typically means less sensitivity to local concerns because owners are often remotely located.

There has been an interesting trend in the past few years toward radio groups deconsolidating and selling some of their vast holdings; Clear Channel is the most obvious case, as it sold almost half of its 1,200 radio stations and all of its 51 television stations since 2007, partly because of its announcement to become a privately held company and partly because of FCC regulations. Even with these sales, Clear Channel is still by far the largest of the radio groups, with its number of stations and number of markets more than the next three radio groups combined. Cumulus Broadcasting, the fourth-largest radio group in 2009 by revenues, also went private in 2008.

Table 4-2 provides a breakdown of the top radio groups in the United States by number of stations owned. Although the move away from consolidation may seem like a good thing for the radio industry, the shift from publicly traded companies to privately held firms may also mean that the new owners make decisions based purely on the bottom line rather than considering the role that radio stations play for the public.

◣◥ The Radio Industry Today

The U.S. radio industry revenues had been declining every year since 2006, but in 2010 rose 5.4 percent to $14.1 billion, according to BIA/Kelsey, a group that tracks and advises the radio industry. This was in part due to a rise in digital revenues, something industry experts believe will continue to grow in the years to come.

There are approximately 10,000 commercial radio stations and 2,500 noncommercial stations in the United States. Noncommercial stations include NPR-affiliated stations, college radio stations, and community and religious stations.

All stations in the United States are assigned call letters, which designate the station and its geographic location east and west of the Mississippi River. For stations east of the Mississippi, W is the first call letter, and for stations west of it K is the call letter, although there are some exceptions that used call letters before the boundaries were determined, such as KDKA in Pittsburgh. Under an international agreement issued at the London International Radiotelegraphic Conference in 1912, different countries were awarded different letters. The United States received "KDA" to "KZZ."

▼ RADIO STATION PROGRAMMING

Perhaps the most fundamental development in commercial radio in the twentieth century was its eventual specialization. Radio grew in its early years to become a dominant medium of mass communication. Large audiences assembled to listen to individual programs during much of the first half of the twentieth century. But with the rise of television as a medium of mass communication in the years following World War II, radio fell from a position of media dominance and, like magazines, adapted to the new media landscape by specializing.

The caller with the hilarious question or perfect rant to your favorite drive-time radio show that sparks call-in responses for the next hour may not be a fellow listener at all but a paid voice actor. And he may not even be calling live; his script may have been prerecorded and is being used to sound like he called in live so the DJs can launch into their own funny asides about the situation raised by the "caller."

Premiere On Call, a new service launched by Clear Channel Communications subsidiary Premiere Networks, seeks and auditions voice talent to read scripts or do on-air calls for radio stations. Actors who are hired ($40 an hour) must sign confidentiality agreements and not divulge that they are paid or who they are working for. Instead, they are to act like ordinary citizens calling in even though they have set scripts to read.

When the story broke in February 2011 by *Tablet*, a Jewish lifestyle magazine, it created a minor ethics controversy in radio.[6] Questions arose regarding whether Rush Limbaugh and Sean Hannity, who work for Clear Channel, had ever used Premiere On Call. Limbaugh vehemently denied ever using the service, stating that all his callers are real listeners, and saying he thought it unlikely that the service was used at all for any of the popular news talk formats. It was more likely, he said, that the service was used by the types of morning or afternoon drive-time shows that focus on comedy and entertainment.

Premiere Networks refused to admit that their service was unethical, saying that they simply provided a service for commercial radio stations and how the stations chose to use the content they received was up to them.

What Premiere Networks—and the stations that used their content—ignored was the erosion of trust among the listening public that such practices created. If a service like Premiere On Call demands secrecy from its voice actors, and radio stations do not inform the public about such arrangements, then how are we to know if a caller is an actual listener or not or simply a paid actor reading from a script just to spark some heated discussions among actual listeners?

What responsibilities do radio stations or their owners have to inform the public regarding whether callers are real or not, or when a DJ is actually based locally or is remote, another common practice among the large radio station groups?

daypart

A segment of time used by radio and television program planners to decide who the primary audience is during that time of day or night.

This specialization takes a number of forms, including program formats, time of day for certain formats, and especially audience demographics. In radio, a day is broken up into different time segments called "dayparts." The 6 a.m. to 10 a.m. **daypart**, for example, is a time when most people listen to the radio as they get ready for work or school or are commuting. Therefore, the programming emphasizes frequent news, traffic, and weather reports as well as some of the more outspoken talk radio shows such as *Imus in the Morning*.

Radio stations are organized according to the type of programming they air. There are dozens of radio-programming formats.[7] Formats vary widely in terms of the audience they draw. Contemporary hit radio, for example, draws a much different audience than the country format, which is by far the most popular radio format in the United States. Over 1,900 stations are devoted to country music, as Table 4-3 shows.

In order to reduce operating costs, more and more stations are relying on computerized automated systems that use remote DJs and set music programming. Although the DJs' chatter may sound like they are in the local studio at the time

NPR and PRI: America's Public Radio Networks

National Public Radio (NPR) is a not-for-profit membership organization with 490 member public radio stations nationwide and a weekly audience of 17 million.[8] It produces and distributes news, cultural, and informational programs for public radio in the United States, linking the nation's noncommercial radio stations into a national network.

Public Radio International (PRI) produces and distributes additional public radio programming, such as *Marketplace* and Garrison Keillor's *A Prairie Home Companion,* to nearly 600 affiliate stations in the United States, Puerto Rico, and Guam, as well as international programs including the BBC World Service.[9]

NPR debuted on April 19, 1971, with live coverage of the Senate Vietnam hearings, and a month later broadcast *All Things Considered,* establishing NPR as an important provider of news and information programming. Today, NPR broadcasts each week one hundred hours of original programming.

Public radio distinguishes itself from commercial radio in a number of ways, including more extensive, impartial, and original audio news, especially long-form audio reporting, as heard on *Morning Edition* and *All Things Considered.* NPR also offers extensive music programming in classical and folk music, jazz, and opera, featuring a variety of live transmissions of the performing arts from theaters and concert halls. Evening programs include ones that introduce listeners to classical music as well as international musicians and unique musical formats beyond the standard genres.

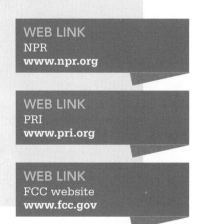

WEB LINK
NPR
www.npr.org

WEB LINK
PRI
www.pri.org

WEB LINK
FCC website
www.fcc.gov

TABLE 4-3
Most Popular Radio Programming Genres

FORMAT	# OF STATIONS (UNITED STATES)
Country	1,991
News/Talk/Information	1,453
Spanish	810
Sports	673
Classic Hits	653
Oldies	623
Adult Contemporary	618
Contemporary (CHR Top 40)	542
Classic Rock	474
Hot Adult Contemporary	426

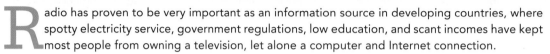
Radio has proven to be very important as an information source in developing countries, where spotty electricity service, government regulations, low education, and scant incomes have kept most people from owning a television, let alone a computer and Internet connection.

Radios, however, are nearly ubiquitous thanks in part to their portability, low cost, and ability to run on batteries, solar power, or by hand cranks.

Maasai women listening to the Prime radio provided by Lifeline Energy (www.lifelineenergy.org)

A survey conducted overseas in 2009 by the International Center for Media Studies found that people in the developing world tended to trust radio more than any other source of information. Muslim respondents even said they trusted radio more than their religious leaders and that they were five times more likely to trust radio to tell them "how to live life" than other forms of media.

The implications of these findings are important for NGOs (non-governmental organizations) and others working in the developing world, as they highlight how important it is for those from developed nations to not take for granted certain cultural assumptions about media and how they are used. For example, an award-winning print-advertising campaign about disease prevention in the United States or Europe may not be understood or even seen by wide swaths of the population in a developing country, whereas a radio ad could reach many more people and have a greater effect as a trusted source of information.

and choosing songs as they go along, in fact it is likely that they may never have actually visited the city they are ostensibly broadcasting from, with a playlist that has been generated by computer program.

This can cause problems during times of emergency, such as what happened in 2002 when a train carrying ammonia derailed in Minot, North Dakota. With no staff actually at the six Clear Channel radio stations (out of nine stations in the city), and emergency services in disarray and power out in many places, the stations continued with their regular programming rather than broadcasting evacuation or safety information to desperate residents.

▲▼ Outlook for the Radio Industry

Radio industry experts remain cautiously optimistic about the radio industry and predict slight growth in the future, thanks in part to an expected large increase in digital revenues, which will remain a fraction of overall revenues.

Terrestrial radio stations will continue to exist, despite the rise of popularity of music subscription services and downloadable music, and will continue to play an important role in promoting music. Although sales of stations to the top radio station groups has been relatively steady in recent years, thanks in part to the poor economy, further consolidation will likely continue among the groups. Radio groups are also acquiring music subscription services, such as Clear Channel's acquisition of Thumbplay in March 2011. Thumbplay was not even a year old when it was acquired.

Sites like Slacker, Pandora, and Spotify, among others, often promote themselves as personal radio stations. Along with their ability to let users create and save their own playlists, these sites often use radio terminology in promoting their services, such as "My Stations" or "Channels" for saved libraries of songs. Their on-demand nature actually makes them more like personalized audio programming than what has traditionally been considered radio, but it highlights the blurring online of music subscription services, downloadable audio, and traditional radio.

Radio plays an integral role in promoting music and making some recording artists top stars.

Podcasting and satellite radio are also affecting our perceptions of traditional radio. Most radio stations have websites where they promote their shows and provide extra content to listeners as podcasts, or let users listen live to shows. Satellite radio has been hyped as the future of radio by its proponents and dismissed as an unsustainable business model that will eventually disappear by its skeptics.

▼ PODCASTING

Podcasts began to rise in popularity from 2004, and they differ from other media formats such as downloads or streaming media. Although podcasts are downloaded in one respect, the technology that interfaces with the user's computer is different than a direct download of a file. One difference between podcasts and direct downloads is that podcasts often have an episodic nature to them, or belong to a series of related content such as a news program or investigative report. They are also easy to get and download, acting much as RSS feeds do with blogs, in sending subscribers new content automatically.

Podcasts provide radio stations with greater flexibility in delivering content to listeners. No longer does a listener have to be listening at the time of a certain report, nor do they have to get online and visit the website to download an audio file. Now they can simply subscribe to receive podcasts and are able to listen at their convenience on their computer or mobile device. Podcasts have proved popular not only for talk-based radio, such as NPR features, but also for sports and music. In an interesting twist that harkens back to the earliest days of radio, when it was primarily used to provide weather and farm news, several companies have been created in recent years that specialize in podcasting farm news, giving farmers information on weather, commodity prices, and other news of interest to them.

The ease and low cost of creating podcasts could provide new ways for local radio news to once again be heard by people in communities where the terrestrial radio stations are all owned by distant, large radio conglomerates.

▼ SATELLITE RADIO

More akin to audio programming than to traditional broadcast radio, satellite radio uses digital radio signals broadcast from a satellite, beaming the same programming across a much wider swath of territory than what terrestrial broadcast stations can do. With up to fifty channels of CD-quality music in a variety of formats and a variety of third-party news, sports, and talk radio programs (most of them commercial free because it is a subscription-based service), satellite radio has won a loyal following of over 18 million listeners in the United States. Because it is subscription based, like cable television, it does not have the same restrictions regarding content that terrestrial broadcasters face.

Sirius Satellite Radio, which started out as CD Radio in the early 1990s, launched its satellites for its radio service in 2000 and began broadcasting in 2002. XM Satellite Radio launched soon after, and the two companies competed vigorously in offering exclusive access to various sports channels, hosted music channels, and noted talk radio hosts.

In 2004, shock jock Howard Stern signed an exclusive five-year, $500 million contract with Sirius, to begin in 2006. The signing was widely debated by media watchers, some saying it signaled a sea change in the importance of satellite radio in comparison to terrestrial radio and others saying it was reminiscent of the wasteful spending seen during the dot-com boom of the late 1990s and that Stern would essentially disappear from the public's eye (or ear) because he would not be reaching nearly the same number of people on satellite radio.

In mid-2008 Sirius completed its acquisition of former competitor XM Satellite Radio and became Sirius XM Radio. The company almost filed for bankruptcy in early 2009 as large debts came due, but was rescued at the last minute by Liberty Media, owner of DirecTV, who acquired 40 percent of Sirius XM Radio. Sirius XM Radio continues to innovate and provide better receivers and new technologies for subscribers, including mobile phone apps so people can listen on their mobile devices.

Radio shock jock Howard Stern's move to satellite radio was hailed by some and criticized by others.

LOOKING BACK AND MOVING FORWARD

It is still unclear whether Sirius XM Radio will survive, and, if it does not, whether another satellite radio service will take its place and try to pick up where it left off. However, even if the future is not in the heavens, it will be grounded in certain behaviors and consumer desires that have become readily apparent across all media but especially regarding music.

First, although the way radio is transmitted and the devices the public uses to listen to it will change, radio itself—or, more accurately, the transmission of audio content to a mass audience—will remain an important form of mass communication. A primary reason for this is that radio, almost alone among mass media, allows people to easily engage in other activities while listening. No matter how advanced or portable media technology becomes, there is no way that we can watch TV or read a book or newspaper while driving safely, as we can do when listening to audio content.

However, as with other digital media, the shift to an on-demand media environment will become more important. This is one shift that satellite radio has signaled already, along with the various music subscription services or personal radio stations. A service like Pandora, Slacker, or Spotify may well be where the future of radio lies: a highly personalized system that not only responds to your musical tastes but uses special algorithms and collaborative filtering to suggest new artists who play similar styles of music. These kinds of changes may so drastically alter how radio stations think of their programming that the term "radio" may technically become obsolete or come to mean something very different.

Of course, tied closely to the future of radio is the recording industry, which has relied largely on radio as a promotional vehicle for new music. Until the advent of digital media, the recording industry had little incentive to change its business model or ways of creating, promoting, and distributing music. Although advances in technology helped both the sound quality and portability of recorded music, little changed regarding basic business policies.

This radically changed with the MP3 format, which made music files small enough to easily be sent via the Internet and stored on computers. The recording industry has become a poster child for other entertainment companies worried about a similar fate for their products, as file-sharing services make illegally copying and sharing of copyrighted material easy.

There are two main camps, or schools of thought, regarding the state of the music industry today. One camp claims that the music industry has only itself to blame in not realizing earlier that digital media would alter established business models and that it would need to adapt rather than try to bully consumers and the government with lawsuits and legislation benefiting the industry at the expense of the public. They point to growing sales of digital downloads of a la carte songs, music subscription services, and ringtone sales as areas in which record labels can find new revenue streams.

Spotify has become a huge success in the United States and in Europe.

However, these new revenue streams are still far from making up for the decline in music sales seen over recent years, which the recording industry blames on illegal file sharing of music. The interest in music remains as strong as ever, but music sales have declined. Supporters of the recording industry say that illegal file sharing hurts not only corporations but more importantly the artists who rely on royalties to survive and that file sharing is theft, pure and simple.

These two schools of thought are not confined only to the world of recording artists; there are echoes of this found especially in other entertainment, such as television and film.

1. The public appetite for recorded music is great, but especially so among teenagers. Why do you think music is generally more important for teenagers than for people in their forties, for example?

2. In what ways have MTV and the music video influenced the recording-arts industry and popular music?

3. What suggestions would you make to a record-label executive regarding creating a successful business model in the digital age?

4. If you were an emerging artist starting to build a following of fans online, would you offer your songs for free download on your website? Why or why not? If not, what would you charge for your songs?

5. Which do you think was more important in the development of radio: the shift in its early days to favor large-scale, powerful commercial stations over small, independent stations or the shift from terrestrial radio stations to online personal radio stations?

6. Listen to your favorite radio station with a critical ear and list the techniques it uses to give a certain character to the music format and the station itself. Listen for things like use of sound effects, how promos are done, and tone of the DJs. Now find a station of similar genre elsewhere in the country (via the Internet), listen to it, and find similarities and differences.

7. Look at your music library and count how many songs you have that you have downloaded for free. Now put a value on each song of ninety-nine cents and calculate how much you would have spent if you'd purchased the songs legally.

8. Look at your music library and determine how many downloaded songs from new artists persuaded you to purchase that artist's CD or to buy digital downloads of their songs or their album.

All You Need to Know About the Music Business, 6th ed. Donald Passman (2008) Hal Leonard Corp.

The Business of Music, 10th ed. William Krasilovsky, Sidney Shemel, John Gross, Jonathan Feinstein (2007) Billboard Books.

The Future of Music: Manifesto for the Digital Music Revolution. David Kusek (2008) Berklee Press.

Appetite for Self-Destruction: The Spectacular Crash of the Record Industry in the Digital Age. Steve Knopper (2009) Free Press.

The Listener's Voice: Early Radio and the American Public. Elena Razlogova (2011) University of Pennsylvania Press.

Empire of the Air: The Men Who Made Radio. Tom Lewis (1993) Harper Perennial Library.

Hello, Everybody! The Dawn of American Radio. Anthony Rudel (2008) Houghton Mifflin Harcourt.

Sound Business: Newspapers, Radio, and the Politics of New Media. Michael Stamm (2011) University of Pennsylvania Press.

Censorship: The Threat to Silence Talk Radio. Brian Jennings and Sean Hannity (2009) Threshold Editions.

Something in the Air: Radio, Rock, and the Revolution That Shaped a Generation. Marc Fisher (2007) Random House.

Right of the Dial: The Rise of Clear Channel and the Fall of Commercial Radio. Alex Foege (2009) Faber and Faber.

MEDIA QUIZ ANSWERS

4. False.

5. Mississippi River.

6. Country music.

7. Because it was originally called wireless telegraphy.

8. True.

VISUAL MEDIA:
MOVIES AND TELEVISION

LEARNING OBJECTIVES

By the end of this chapter you should be able to:

- Explain the role photography has played in our visual culture and its continued importance within mass communication.

- Understand the impact technological changes have had on the film and television industries and their content.

- Recognize the ways business models and structures have influenced the film industry.

- Understand the development of television from its origins to digital TV.

- Explain the differences between terrestrial, cable, and satellite broadcasting and what they mean for viewers.

- Understand the implications of the convergence of telecommunications and content companies.

Aptly named Yap.TV delivers on its promise, letting television viewers easily tune into a universe of social media chat and talk about shows in real-time with private circles of friends. The iPhone or iPad app shows the viewer a real-time Twitter feed and has polls to participate in for those who want to see what the public (or the Tweeting public, at least) is saying.

Yap.TV and similar apps demonstrate yet again how convergence is taking place. Growing numbers of people typically multitask when interacting with media content, and texting friends or tweeting while watching a network television show like *American Idol* is simply one example of that. It may not be too many years from now when a show that does not have some sort of interactivity built into the program will be seen as a throwback to a different age in television, when "interactivity" meant yelling at the television set.

However, just as we are growing accustomed to being able to interact with each other as we watch television, advertisers are also learning to watch us. Our viewing behavior is recorded by cable and satellite companies that we belong to, and some companies have used that data in combination with other demographic data or information gleaned from our daily transactions to create viewer profiles that are then matched with specific advertisements.

In the future, this may mean that although you and a friend may be watching the same program and texting with each other about it, you each may receive different advertisements depending on what advertising profile you match.

If this feels very Big Brother, *1984* to you, you are not alone. But, television advertisers are simply trying to do what Internet advertisers have been doing for some time now in their ability to track specific behavior and provide highly targeted ads based on that behavior.

Photographs and film have played a fundamental role in framing our world through journalism, entertainment, and art and giving us a sense of the importance of the visual in our lives. Even as digitization dramatically alters aspects of visual media, in other ways these media continue to shape our perceptions of what we create in a digital environment. Photojournalists, cinematographers, and videographers have used the frame of the photographic lens to place a defining structure on the linear narrative of visual storytelling.

The visual media grammar that filmmakers have created in the past hundred years of filmmaking provides the foundation for digital videographers as they explore the limits of the new medium with more portable equipment and more sophisticated editing tools.

The Internet and online consumption of video, film, and television are only starting to have serious ramifications on our understanding of the role of television in the future, but the changes are happening rapidly. Already for many people the Internet is a more important medium than television, which is still the dominant medium for the majority of people.

Although technological advances in visual media have been linked to entertainment genres and media content, in this chapter we will focus primarily on the role that technology has played with photographic, film, and television industries and business models and touch only briefly on the impact that it has had on content. We will look more carefully at the role content has played in these and other mediums in Chapter 10, when we discuss entertainment.

◢◤ Photography

Still images, or photographs, have long been important to mass communications. Still images have performed—and continue to perform—two main functions, that of **surveillance** and **cultural transmission**. Photos and other images can provide verification of factual claims. While words might provide the narrative, photos confirm the truth of what those words say, whether it is a plane crash, an alleged extramarital affair, or a mass grave in a war-torn part of the world. Although photos can of course be doctored digitally, they are still one of the surest ways to verify facts. Photographs transmit culture by what they show, how they show it, and what emotions can be stirred from them. A photograph can tell a story or convey information quickly. Photos can engage, entertain, or elicit emotion in a way that words alone might not. At a glance, a reader can scan the photos

surveillance

The inherent nature of photography for verifying factual claims through visual evidence.

cultural transmission

The way in which photographs convey beliefs, values, and practices by what they show, how they show it, and the emotions that are stirred in the process.

or images in a newspaper or magazine. Seeing photos of people suffering in a remote part of the world can stir feelings that mere verbal descriptions might never produce.

▼ HISTORY OF PHOTOGRAPHY

The principles involved in creating photographs had been known and used for hundreds of years before photography was invented, so in one respect it was perhaps surprising that photography had not been developed earlier. The earliest recorded use of a **camera obscura**, a dark box or room with a small hole in it that allowed an inverted image of an outside scene to be shown on the opposite inner wall, is in the writings of Leonardo da Vinci. He explained how a camera obscura can be an aid to drawing scenery, as one simply moves a sheet of paper around until the scene comes into sharp focus and then traces the scene.

The other important element is understanding how light can affect certain chemicals, which was also known for hundreds of years before the first photograph was developed. Although some scientists could produce photographs by using various light-sensitive chemicals, they had no way to make the images permanent. In June 1827, Joseph Niépce created a picture using an asphalt-like material that hardened after being exposed to light. However, the picture was very unclear and required an exposure time of eight hours.[1]

Photography can often capture powerful emotion moments in ways few other media can.

camera obscura

A dark box or room with a small hole in it that allows an inverted image of an outside scene to be shown on the opposite inner wall.

WEB LINK
Mathew Brady's Portraits
ww.npg.si.edu/exh/brady/index2.htm

In 1829 Niépce agreed to go into partnership with fellow Frenchman **Louis Daguerre**. Although Niépce died in 1833, Daguerre continued to experiment and in January 1839 unveiled the **daguerreotype**, a method of creating a positive image on a metal plate. He had reduced the exposure time from eight hours to thirty minutes or so.[2] Exposure time and image quality, along with the ability to take color photographs, were the fundamental drivers of advances in photography over the next 150 years. As cameras became more portable and easier to use, they became accessible to the general public.

In the early days of photography, when specialized knowledge was still needed to take photographs, **Mathew B. Brady** was highly acclaimed for his Civil War photos and portraits of famous people. It is through Brady's work that many of the day's greatest and most popular figures are best known to us today. Brady did not always subscribe to the standards of impartial photojournalism expected of photojournalists today. Historians have criticized Brady for sometimes "arranging" his subjects, including battlefield corpses, for dramatic photocomposition purposes.

Such a practice is considered unethical in modern journalism. Nevertheless, the photography of Brady and others during the Civil War, the first war to have been documented by photography, played an important role in helping the public—which saw the war through the window of the press—understand the conflict.

▼ SEEING BEYOND THE HUMAN EYE

Early applications of photography were not limited to journalism, of course. One of the most notable was Eadweard Muybridge's use of photography for scientific documentation. Muybridge took a famous photo series through which he was able

The Civil War was the first war to be documented by photography, with many enduring photographs taken by Alexander Gardner.

Development of Photography

1839 Louis Daguerre and Joseph Niépce develop the daguerreotype, a method of printing photographs.

1850s "Pictorial" newspapers begin widely publishing photographs and other illustrations of news events and subjects.

1860s Mathew Brady uses photographs to document the Civil War, helping bring more visual news coverage of war to the public.

1878 Eadweard Muybridge's innovative use of serial photographs sees what the human eye cannot: the rapid movement of a running horse.

1884 George Eastman, founder of the Eastman Kodak Company, invents roll film, which makes it more practical for newspapers to publish timely news photos and makes photography something that can be done by the general public.

1912 The modern process of color film is developed after decades of trying to make color photography without success. The process would be perfected in the 1930s and remain in use until today for roll film.

1948 The first instant camera, the Polaroid Model 95, starts a boom in sales of instant cameras by Polaroid.

1981 Sony releases the Sony Mavica, the first electronic still camera for commercial use that stores images on a minidisc rather than film. Although not a true digital camera, it heralds the rise of digital cameras.

1991 Kodak, after developing variations of digital camera systems throughout the mid-1980s, releases the first professional digital camera system.

1994 The Apple QuickTake 100 camera is the first consumer-level digital camera that allows connection with a home computer system via a serial cable. Kodak, Casio, and Sony release similar cameras in subsequent years.

1999 The peak of sales of roll film. After 1999, sales of roll film drop an estimated 25–30 percent per year as more consumers buy digital cameras. Many retail stores will then shut down their film-development services and instead offer self-printing kiosks that allow customers to download their photos and choose which to print out on the spot.

Louis Daguerre.

Horse running.

Early-model Kodak camera using roll film.

to document, for the first time, how a horse runs. Such applications of photography are of great importance in mass communications, especially where they can help us see things that human eyes, unassisted, would be unable to see. This is an opportunity taken to new heights in the digital age. Today, not only photographs of the microscopic can captivate us but images of the heavens as well. Some scientific images have even been considered visual art.

Photography remains an especially important component of modern magazines, even reaching high art in some cases, and has had powerful effects on what we perceive as ideals of beauty or fashion (which few of us can ever reach). The power of the image can persuade just as effectively as it can educate.

Recent years have seen the growth of imagery and video from satellites. Remote-sensing satellite imagery has since the end of the cold war grown dramatically to become an almost daily part of media content.[3] On the Web, through

THE PHOTOJOURNALIST'S DILEMMA: SUDAN, STARVATION, AND SUICIDE

ETHICS IN MEDIA

On March 23, 1993, the *New York Times* ran a photo taken by South African photojournalist Kevin Carter that seemed to epitomize the human suffering and anguish in Africa.

A small, starving Sudanese girl tried to crawl to a feeding station in a remote area while a vulture stood nearby, waiting for her to die. Carter said he waited for about twenty minutes, positioning himself for the best shot and careful not to disturb the bird, hoping it would spread its wings. When it did

not, he snapped some pictures, chased the bird away, and watched as the little girl resumed her struggle. A friend and colleague of Carter's said that afterward Carter was depressed and kept saying he wanted to hug his own young daughter. The photo touched many who saw it, and hundreds of people asked the *Times* if the girl had survived, but there was no way the *Times* could find out the girl's fate.

On April 12, 1994, Carter learned that he won the Pulitzer Prize for photography, even as some colleagues and media outlets strongly criticized him. The *St. Petersburg* (Florida) *Times* said, "The man adjusting his lens to take just the right frame of her suffering might just as well be a predator, another vulture on the scene."

Carter was painfully aware of the photojournalist's dilemma but said, in describing photographing a gunfight, that one simply had to think visually first and think about the other issues later. American photojournalist James Nachtwey, who often worked with Carter and his photojournalist friends, says, "Every photographer who has been involved in these stories has been affected. You become changed forever. Nobody does this kind of work to make themselves feel good. It is very hard to continue."

This was apparently the case for Carter, who committed suicide by carbon monoxide poisoning in his truck on July 27, 1994, near a park where he used to play as a child. He was 33.[4]

What responsibility, if any, does a photojournalist have to help the subjects he or she photographs? What implications could there be if photojournalists regularly helped people during conflicts or in times of tragedy?

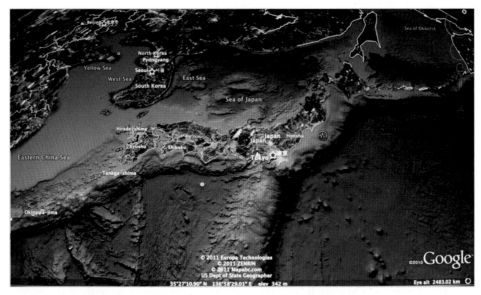

Satellite imagery like Google Earth's has helped the public see the world in new ways but sometimes raises privacy concerns.

applications like Google Earth, members of the public can see satellite images of their homes and even in many cases street-level photographs.

Just as early photography raised new ethical issues for photojournalism regarding capturing actual scenes and creating more visually compelling scenes, digital photography combined with social media like MySpace or Facebook have created new ethical debates among the general public around privacy issues. It is a testament to the continued power of the visual image that these debates arise when there are new ways to see things or when more people have access to photographs.

▼ PHOTOGRAPHIC INDUSTRY TODAY

Despite the continued importance of photographs in today's highly visual media world, the photographic industry as such does not play the same role in mass communications as the movie industry or television industry, so we will keep our discussion on it brief. The photographic industry has been altered just as much as print, radio, movies, or television, however.

Consider the effect that digital cameras have had on professional photographers, the photographic film industry, and consumers. In only ten years after the peak of photographic film sales in 1999, Kodak, one of the largest and most well-known film companies, announced it would stop making its Kodachrome color film by the end of the year. Despite seeing the shift to digital cameras and attempting to position itself to take advantage of that shift through selling digital cameras and photo printers, Kodak has continued to lose money.

Fujifilm, headquartered in Tokyo, is the world's largest photographic and imaging company. It too has seen declines in its photographic film business, but Fujifilm integrated digital imaging technology into its business model more effectively than Kodak and today has a range of popular digital cameras as well as inkjet and laser photo paper. Fujifilm is also a main supplier of movie film.

Today, professional photographers have more powerful cameras than ever before, and digital cameras give professional and amateur photographers more functions to be able to take professional-quality pictures without needing to make manual adjustments to the camera.

▲▼ Movies

Even before the invention of daguerreotype photography, inventors had tried to re-create the perception of motion through a variety of devices that were as awkwardly named as they were difficult to use. Most were never more than novelties. If still images proved important to mass media of the mid-nineteenth century, then the development of motion pictures at the end of the nineteenth century dramatically transformed the nature of mass communications and entertainment in the twentieth century. The introduction of motion pictures meant that for the first time activity could be recorded. More importantly for the movie industry, the technology could re-create reality and *create* visual "realities" that never could exist in the real world.

▼ THE FUNCTIONS OF THE MOVIE INDUSTRY

The primary function of motion pictures is to entertain, with many millions of movie watchers enjoying the sweeping epics, slapstick comedies, romance, and action and adventure they see in feature-length films. However, as with much entertainment, the function of cultural transmission also is important.

Many fans and critics alike consider the cinema to be more than simple entertainment and appraise its value and function as a serious visual art form comparable to painting, sculpture, or architecture, with a history of important social influence. As such, motion pictures hold a special place among other forms of mass communications, with perhaps the exception of literary books and some recorded music. Nevertheless, it would be an oversimplification to imply that movies are primarily a medium of high art. Most commercially produced motion pictures in the United States are made to make money, and it is the exception that rises to serious art form.

▲▼ History of the Movie Industry

In 1891, **Thomas Alva Edison** created his Kinetoscope, a "peep-show" precursor to the motion picture viewer. Edison's failure to patent this technology allowed two Frenchmen, Louis and Auguste Lumière, to manufacture a more portable camera, film processing unit, and projector, which they patented in 1895. Their invention was suitcase sized and enabled the Lumières through a single device to shoot footage in the morning, process it in the afternoon, and project it for an audience in the evening. It soon became the rage all over France. They called their invention the Cinématographe, and it was clearly based on Thomas Edison's peep-show machine. The critical difference between Edison's Kinetoscope and the Lumières' Cinématographe was the Cinématographe's ability to display motion pictures to many people at the same time.[5]

On December 28, 1895, the Lumières debuted their process to a paying audience at the Grand Café in Paris, showing a series of ten fifteen- to sixty-second glimpses of real scenes recorded outdoors.

Perhaps this is the first form of the documentary. Louis Lumière did not envision the Cinématographe as a medium for news or entertainment; he typically documented some aspect of ordinary, daily life, almost like an anthropologist with a camera. Louis Lumière's first film was the arrival of the express train at La Ciotat, France—a visual experience so jarring for some in the audience that they leapt out of their chairs as the train approached. His other films included a man hammering a wall, people enjoying a picnic along a river, and parents feeding their child.

Spike Lee, whose films often tackle controversial and sensitive subjects related to race, discrimination, and society.

Thomas Alva Edison

Inventor whose inventions include the electric light, the phonograph, and the Kinetoscope. Edison's lab in Menlo Park, New Jersey, had over sixty scientists and produced as many as four hundred patent applications a year.

The Lumière brothers failed to recognize the value of their invention. Their approach to filmmaking attempted to reproduce reality rather than tell a story, and Louis Lumière felt that the novelty of watching moving images on a screen that could just as easily be seen by walking outside would eventually wear off. This mind-set was distinctly different from that of other film pioneers such as Thomas Edison and Georges Méliès, who saw that film could change reality as well as reproduce it.

The Lumière brothers, who generally made short films showing daily life.

▼ SILENT ERA: NEW MEDIUM, NEW TECHNOLOGIES, NEW STORYTELLING

Early cinema history began with silent films, as the ability to add sound to film was still not technologically feasible at the time. Silent films had an advantage in that they could more easily cross language barriers than their "talkie" descendants because the few words that the silent movies did include, usually presented as placards on the screen to read, could easily be translated into the local language and inserted in place of the originals.

The storytelling aspects of the earliest films were quite limited and short in duration (a few minutes in length). Nevertheless, Cinématographes were soon in the hands of filmmakers around the world, and the motion picture age began. It did not take long for early moviemakers to experiment with new ways of visual storytelling, many of which are still used today and taken for granted in movies.[6]

Georges Méliès and D. W. Griffith

One filmmaker who pioneered the use of film as a medium of the imagination was the Frenchman **Georges Méliès** (1861–1938). In contrast to the Lumière brothers, who saw the cinema as a device for recording reality, Méliès used the medium almost as a vehicle for magic, to conjure and create illusions. Méliès was the first to use film to create special effects, such as to make objects suddenly appear or disappear or to transform them into other objects. Among his most memorable examples was the celluloid transformation of a carriage into a hearse. Méliès pioneered a variety of innovative special effects, including the first double exposure (*La Caverne maudite,* 1898), the first split-screen shot (*Un Homme de tête,* 1898), and the first dissolve (*Cendrillon,* 1899).

Georges Méliès

An early French filmmaker who pioneered the use of special effects in film in order to show imaginative stories.

Méliès notwithstanding, many silent films were little more than novelties. But by the 1910s, the medium began to evolve as an important storytelling vehicle. One of the most important silent films of this era was D. W. Griffith's 1915 American classic, *Birth of a Nation. Birth of a Nation* was the first major full-length film and introduced many innovative cinematic techniques. Griffith used crosscutting (parallel editing) and other techniques to portray battle scenes highly effectively. He often depicted the action in one set of shots moving from right to left, while another set of shots showed action moving from left to right. Griffith's classic, however, does contain overt racism; it is a screen adaptation of the racist novel *The Clansman,* a book glorifying the Ku Klux Klan (KKK).

F. W. Murnau and Sergei Eisenstein

Innovation in filming, lighting, editing, and storytelling techniques continued throughout the silent era. In 1922, two silent-film classics were released. German director F. W. Murnau created *Nosferatu,* an unforgettable adaptation of the Dracula tale penned by Bram Stoker. Through *Nosferatu,* Murnau helped to develop the language of film. Also in 1922, American Robert Flaherty directed *Nanook of*

The Odessa Steps sequence in the film *Battleship Potemkin* is still considered a masterpiece of editing.

the North, the first great documentary film, which depicted the life of an Eskimo whaler. It is a film still often shown in college anthropology courses. Flaherty lived among the Eskimos for six months filming his classic, subsequently editing the film upon his return to New York.

Russian filmmaker Sergei Eisenstein pioneered the use of fast cuts between scenes in film, similar to the type of editing we commonly see in music videos. Prior to Eisenstein, most filmmakers kept the camera stationary and had scenes take place within the confines of the picture frame.

In 1925 he released *Battleship Potemkin,* a silent film that depicts the 1905 revolt in Odessa by Russian sailors on the battleship *Potemkin* and their subsequent defeat by czarist troops. The movie is particularly known for an editing sequence referred to as "the Odessa Steps." In this sequence, shots of townspeople trapped by czarist troops are intercut with shots of the troops firing upon the crowd, creating a very emotionally charged scene that has been imitated as a kind of tribute in several films, including the 1987 Brian De Palma film *The Untouchables.*

▼ SOUND AND COLOR COME TO MOVIES

Although movie technology was a revolutionary step in capturing daily activity and in creating imagined realities, it still didn't fully re-create what people saw and heard because there was no sound or color. Making films more accurately reflect what we see and hear needed advances in technology and is a process that continues today.

By the turn of the century, several alternative methods for producing color motion pictures had been developed, but each was complex and cumbersome, such as hand tinting or hand coloring scenes. In about 1920 a system was developed that used a beam splitter with a prism to divide light entering the lens, capturing the different color on alternating frames. Using this technology produced the first successful feature-length color films in the 1920s.

Technicolor Motion Picture Corporation was founded in 1922 and became the standard for color motion pictures for the next three decades. Among the earliest

Selected Milestones in Early Motion Pictures

1898   Georges Méliès, director. First double exposure (*La Caverne maudite*), an advance in special effects

1915   D. W. Griffith, director. *Birth of a Nation*, the first major full-length film

1919   Oscar Micheaux, director. *Birth of Race*, African American response to the racial stereotypes portrayed in *Birth of a Nation*.

1922   Robert Flaherty, director. *Nanook of the North*, the first great documentary

1925   Sergei Eisenstein, director. *Battleship Potemkin*, a silent film particularly known for its editing sequence "the Odessa Steps"

1925   Technicolor Corp.; Douglas Fairbanks, actor. *The Black Pirate*, among the first successful color major motion pictures

1927   Al Jolson, actor. *The Jazz Singer*, the first commercially successful motion picture with sound

1928   Walt Disney, animator, voice, director. Disney's first animated hit, *Steamboat Willie*, introduced Mickey Mouse

1932   Walt Disney, director. *Flowers and Trees*, the first color cartoon

1934   MGM, motion picture company; Maureen O'Sullivan, actress. *Tarzan and His Mate* reveals a scantily clad "Jane" and a prolonged underwater nude scene, contributing to a public backlash and the strict enforcement of the Hays morals code in movie content

---

Technicolor films were *The Black Pirate* with Douglas Fairbanks in 1925 and *Gone with the Wind* and *The Wizard of Oz*, both released in 1939. It was not until the 1950s that the motion picture cameras capable of capturing color without prisms, beam splitters, or alternating frames were developed and thus color films became more common.

Figuring out how to add sound to movies turned out to be much easier. Even in the earliest days of movies, "silent" movies were not actually silent. Live pianists, actors speaking out parts, and even whole orchestras were used during shows to add sound. Actors in the films sometimes accompanied shows as well, talking about their roles and answering audience questions before or after the showing of the film. The first sound film short was shown before a paying audience in Berlin in 1896.

In 1927, Al Jolson starred in *The Jazz Singer*, the first commercially successful motion picture with sound. This popular "talkie" was not a sound movie by contemporary standards. Rather, like other early talkies, *The Jazz Singer* contained little dialog. It had subtitles and recorded music played back. This technology was soon replaced by the superior sound-on-film systems (i.e., an optical soundtrack).

WEB LINK
Al Jolson website
www.jolson.org/

Al Jolson in a scene from *The Jazz Singer*, the first "talkie" that was a commercial hit.

The first motion picture to synchronize sound was produced in 1925, but this film was not as much a commercial endeavor as a technical experimentation.

By 1929 it had become more practical to record and play back sound synchronously with the recorded image. Very few silent films were made after this time, the most notable exceptions being those by Charlie Chaplin in the 1930s. His character "The Tramp," whom he had invented in the 1910s and 1920s, was still popular among the viewing public.

But the silent era had come to an end, which brought with it many changes to the movie industry. Some silent-era stars could not adjust to sound, either because of heavy foreign accents or unappealing voices. Screenwriting and filming techniques changed dramatically as well, as stories were written increasingly for the spoken word rather than visual effect. Slapstick comedy was out and witty one-liners and joke telling were in. Because of cumbersome microphones, cameras also became more stationary and experimentation with moving cameras, innovative editing, and interesting camera angles became less common. Although there were winners and losers with the development of sound in motion pictures, the industry itself was unfazed by the changes in technology. In the words of Al Jolson, "You ain't heard nothin' yet."

▼ THE BIRTH OF HOLLYWOOD

The United States motion picture industry began on the eastern seaboard, especially New York, but soon moved to Los Angeles, where the powerful movie moguls of the early 1900s created Hollywood. The main reason the industry started in New York was because at the time it was the center of entertainment in the United States, with its Broadway and vaudeville theaters. Thomas Edison's laboratories were also located nearby in New Jersey.

There were many reasons for the move to Hollywood, not the least of which was better weather. Actors, producers, and directors found their way to the growing movie-making center, creating a split between the theater (and later television) in New York and film in Hollywood that largely continues to this day. Most television shows are now filmed in Hollywood studios as well, even the comedies and police dramas ostensibly set in New York, with only exterior or location scenes shot in New York.

The warm, dry weather in Hollywood allowed filmmakers to produce films year-round to feed the hungry distribution chains a nonstop flow. Success bred more success, and today the U.S. movie industry is securely based in Hollywood, although there are a number of regional centers for movie production across North America, including Toronto and Vancouver, Canada.

Since its birth, the industry has grown to a multibillion-dollar giant that, with a distinctly American influence, not only provides global entertainment but also shapes global culture, commerce, and imagination. The development of the Hollywood movie industry very much reflects the social, business, and political climate of the times and continues to be heavily influenced by technological changes that bring about different business models. One example of how intertwined commerce and pop culture are in the movie industry can be found in the development of the Hollywood studio star system and its dismantling.

Hollywood Star System

Today we often feel that the term "movie star" is synonymous with a glamorous lifestyle and even with Hollywood itself. But for the first several years of movies, actors' and actresses' names did not even appear in the movie credits. However, it

3-D Movies: What Will Be the Impact?

Movie studios have been promoting 3-D movies as The Next Big Thing, but this time several noted directors are also cheerleaders, including Steven Spielberg, Peter Jackson, and James Cameron, all of whom have released 3-D movies. Some proponents even claim that 3-D will revolutionize cinema in the same way that sound revolutionized the early film era.

By 2013, 3-D movies had even moved from the realm of hype to mainstream. Many mainstream movies are now released both in conventional format and in 3-D, and are available for viewing at 3-D cinemas across the U.S. In 2012, blockbuster 3-D movies such as Dr. Seuss's *The Lorax* or *Journey 2: The Mysterious Island* offered high quality immersive viewing experiences. These 3-D movies were both commercial successes at the box office, with *The Lorax*, for instance, bringing in more than $39 million in box office receipts in its first weekend of release, on a ticket price of $11.50 for an adult and $8.50 for a child.

3-D movies are also available for a vast array of titles on Blu-Ray DVDs for home viewing. For instance, in 2012, some of the 3-D Blu-Ray titles include

The Adventures of Tintin, Hugo, Immortals, The Three Musketeers, Puss in Boots, Scorpions, and *A Very Harold & Kumar 3-D Christmas.*

In either case, 3-D movies still require viewers to wear special glasses. However, the quality of the viewing experience has improved dramatically in recent years. Viewers are less uncomfortable wearing the glasses during the movies to access the immersive 3-D experience. As a result, the popularity of 3-D movies has risen to such heights that script writers are now adapting their scripts to consciously incorporate 3-D effects. "You build sequences differently when you know things have to pop out and jump at you," says Kieran Mulroney, one of the script writers for Warner Bros.' Sherlock Holmes sequel, as reported in the *Los Angeles Times.*[7]

The next generation of 3-D movies will likely be even more popular, as it is expected that viewers will no longer be required to wear special glasses to see the 3-D effects. Like previous technological changes, the spread of 3-D will probably change the moviegoing experience in ways not yet foreseen.

was not long before audiences showed an interest in learning not only the names but also the personalities and histories of the people they were watching on-screen. Fan magazines helped stoke interest in stars. Shrewd studio heads created and cultivated personas for their popular stars, even giving them false histories in order to better market them. Although not as blatant as in early years, the embellishment of stars' backgrounds for marketing purposes continues today.

In the early 1930s a new era began in American film and lasted until 1949. This was the era of the Hollywood studio star system. Paramount Pictures (1912), Columbia Pictures (1920), Metro-Goldwyn-Mayer (1924), Warner Brothers (1923), and 20th Century Fox (1935) all held long-term contracts on star directors and

Films made by production companies outside the main Hollywood studios.

actors and built their success on those stars. Many are still familiar today, more than a half century after the era ended.

During this era, stars were unable to seek their own contracts for individual films, but they could be loaned from one studio to another, often in exchange for other stars. Stars were also expected to be highly productive, often starring in five or six films a year. Warner Brothers' Humphrey Bogart starred in forty films between 1934 and 1943, and perhaps his most famous, *Casablanca,* was just one of four films he made in 1943.

Many of the films of this era, including *Casablanca,* were not made as great works of cinematic art. Rather, they were made as popular entertainment to make profits for the studios. These films made a great deal of money for the studios, which also typically owned large theater chains where the films were shown. People often went to see these films for the stars they had come to know and for the characters they often represented. Gary Cooper, star of *Mr. Deeds Goes to Town* (1936) and *Meet John Doe* (1941), was known as a tall, clumsy, and humble man who may have been naive but was also a man of integrity. He was the quintessential American, the strong, silent type. Jimmy Stewart was in many ways the same kind of character, immortalized in Frank Capra's *It's a Wonderful Life* (1945), now a holiday classic on American television.

The studios also imported much of their talent from abroad, including not only the star of *Gone with the Wind,* Vivien Leigh, from the UK, but also the great English director, Alfred Hitchcock. Hitchcock became Hollywood's master of the thriller genre but began his career in the UK in 1919 working on silent films at Paramount's Famous Players-Lasky studio in London.

The studio star system came to an end in the late 1940s, when several forces converged. First, in 1948 the U.S. Supreme Court forced the studios to divest themselves from their theater empires because of monopolistic practices brought to light in *United States v. Paramount Pictures.* This drastically cut into the power of the studios to control the means of production and distribution of motion pictures in America.

It meant that **independent films**, or films produced outside the major studios, could be shown in large numbers of theaters, thereby giving independent films financial viability. However, studios still found a way to give themselves an advantage by having theaters agree to book a studio's films in blocks, making it cheaper for a theater to show several popular films from a studio rather than take a chance on showing a single independent film that might not be as popular.

Second, the rise of television as a medium of popular entertainment drew audiences away from theaters, especially theaters that ran second- or third-run films. Although in the earliest days of television studio heads threatened to blacklist any actor who moved to television, this ban was soon lifted and stars such as Bob Hope and Lucille Ball helped give the new medium early star power. Similarly, actors who first made their names in television series, such as Clint Eastwood, became successful film stars. Today, we often see television as a proving ground for actors, many of whom have made the move from popular shows such as *SNL* or situation comedies to movies.

Citizen Kane has been hailed as one of the greatest films of all time.

Partly because of these changes, it was no longer as profitable for studios to keep actors under long-term contracts. The high labor costs associated with studios also gave them incentive to rent themselves out to smaller, independent producers who worked with large studios on a per-project basis and allowed studios to still use their extensive distribution networks to earn income.

◤◢ Movie Industry Today

Today's motion picture industry contrasts significantly from the one using the star system more than half a century ago, when the movie companies were vertically integrated entertainment companies that owned not only the means of production but also the distribution system, i.e., the movie theaters. The Supreme Court's antitrust decision of 1948 forced the studios to sell their theaters, and today much more power rests in the hands of the artists making the films, especially directors and high-paid actors and actresses, than in the past.

That is not to say that the major studios have lost all their power. They have found ways to adapt to changing conditions and still maintain an inordinate amount of power when it comes to deciding which movies to make and promote. With the high costs of making a movie, including several million dollars spent in marketing, and the specialized knowledge required for the high production standards that U.S. moviegoers expect, it still requires large organizations like the movie studios to bring everything together.

Like other media industries, the major studios are parts of much larger media conglomerates, as Table 5-1 shows. The major studios make movies under a variety of subsidiary production companies, some of which when taken on their own can still be considered quite large film companies. Although movie studios do not have the same kind of vertical integration and control they once enjoyed, they are able to utilize their sister companies within their media family. For example, it is not unusual to see a Paramount picture appearing in the news on CBS (both are owned by Viacom),

TABLE 5-1

Major Film Studios, Ownership, Subsidiary Studios

FILM STUDIO	SUBSIDIARY STUDIOS	PARENT COMPANY
Warner Bros. Pictures	New Line Cinema, HBO Films, Castle Rock Entertainment, Turner Entertainment, Warner Bros. Animation	Time Warner
Paramount Pictures	Nickelodeon Movies, MTV Films	Viacom
Columbia Pictures	Sony Pictures Animation	Sony
20th Century Fox	20th Century Fox Animation, Fox Faith	News Corporation
Universal Studios	Universal Animation Studios	General Electric, Vivendi SA
Walt Disney Pictures/ Touchstone Pictures	Disneynature, Disney Animation Studios, Pixar Animation Studios	Walt Disney

or a Pixar picture such as *Cars 2* on an ABC news show (both are owned by Disney), or a 20th Century Fox picture appearing on Fox News (both are owned by News Corp.).

The average cost of making a motion picture is over $70 million, although movies often top $100 million, especially when there are special effects or big Hollywood stars involved, and that does not include marketing costs, which can add another $30 to $50 million to the total costs. Production costs for movies are the largest single expense category, usually equal to about 25 percent of the total budget, and are used for a variety of purposes including the construction of sets, filming on location, printing copies of the completed movie for distribution, and the salaries of all crew members. Almost all workers involved in a film, from actors to screenwriters to cinematographers to carpenters, belong to unions, which have standard salary rates and rules that must be followed.

A movie can be developed in several different ways, though most often a filmmaker approaches a movie studio with a script or story pitch for a movie he or she wants the studio to bankroll. The script may be an original story, but it also often comes from a novel or real-life story adapted by a screenwriter.

A studio will often demand changes, sometimes major changes, to the script before agreeing to bankroll and distribute a movie. This often leads to creative differences that can kill projects before they start or force filmmakers to seek support from other major or independent studios. Actor and director Stanley Tucci rejected studio support for his critically acclaimed 1996 independent film *Big Night* because studio executives insisted that he add mob characters to the movie about two Italian American brothers who owned a restaurant. The movie *Rain Man* (1988), starring Tom Cruise and Dustin Hoffman, was almost never made because studio executives demanded that there be some sort of action-packed car and motorcycle chase involving Hoffman's autistic character.

Once a project finally has been approved and the actors' contracts and schedules agreed upon, shooting can begin. This can take several weeks or even several months, depending on schedules and other issues that may arise. After shooting is done, the filmmaker is still looking at several more months of postproduction work and editing the hours and hours of footage into a typical movie length. This too can often lead to serious creative differences, as studio executives may demand a more upbeat or otherwise different ending based on early audience feedback, which often means deleting some scenes or even in some cases reshooting scenes or shooting entirely new scenes. The Ridley Scott classic *Blade Runner* (1982) is perhaps one of the most famous cases in which the director's ending did not meet with the studio's approval after early audience testing and had to be redone to be more upbeat. Of course, several versions of the movie were later released, including a "director's cut" that more closely adhered to Scott's vision of the movie. Postproduction is also the phase during which musical scores are added and dubbing and voice-overs put in.

▲▼ Marketing and Distribution for Movies

Marketing and distribution are quite expensive and are often the keys to a movie's success. A well-attended movie that debuts in one thousand theaters nationwide simply will not earn as much at the box office as a movie that fills half the seats but that is distributed to over three thousand theaters. This is where the power of the major studios still comes into play, as they can more easily get a movie distributed widely than an independent film company.

The main channel for marketing movies is advertising on television. Most movies are heavily advertised during the two weeks before release, because it is nearly impossible for a movie to become popular after it has poor attendance when it is released. A lot of research, effort, and expense go into creating movie trailers and packaging movies so they reach the right target audience and look as appealing as possible. Although movie studios also advertise in other outlets, such as newspapers, radio, and billboards, almost 60 percent of spending on marketing is on network and cable television advertising. There have been cases for some movies, such as *Paranormal Activity,* where the Web and word-of-mouth marketing have played important roles in marketing the movie, but for the most part the Web is still a small part in the overall mix of marketing movies.

Movies have a regular pattern of exhibition "windows," or places where they are shown, that help increase revenues. When studios were at their strongest, they could control theatrical releases to what were deemed "first-run" theaters; then, after the movies lost their appeal at those, they were placed in second-run theaters. Movie studios determined which theaters were first-run and which were second-run and had agreements with theater owners that ensured theaters would have exclusive showing privileges within a certain geographic area for a certain amount of time. However, studios also often forced theaters to buy package deals of movies that included a few hits but also many lower-quality films that would not be as popular. This is one of the practices that became forbidden in the 1948 *Paramount* antitrust case.

The movie industry boycotted television when it first arrived, refusing to provide movies that could be shown on television and even blacklisting actors who acted on television. Studios felt that television would draw audiences away from theaters and thus ruin the movie industry. This resistance to technological change has become a common pattern among entrenched media-entertainment industries.

However, it was not long before the movie industry realized that television could be used to give new life to movies that had run through their life cycle in theatrical release, and they started selling their previously released movies to the television networks. What's more, they could license showings of their older movies, many of which had not been seen in theaters for years. A similar pattern of resistance, and then belated acceptance, by the studios occurred as they saw more revenue opportunities with VCRs and cable television. Until recent years, studios had been hampering development of digitally delivered video-on-demand or movies-on-demand for fear of piracy like that seen with music.

The usual exhibition windows for movies start with domestic theatrical release then proceed to international release, video, on-demand, pay cable channels (HBO, Showtime, etc.), network or cable TV, and then syndicated TV. Each of these windows has a specified time for its showing, and windows generally do not overlap. However, in recent years different exhibition windows have been used, such as releasing likely blockbuster movies simultaneously in the United States and select countries worldwide. Depending on the success of a movie, it may get released to video earlier than usual in order to take advantage of residual popularity of the theatrical release, or if the movie is deemed not worthy of theatrical release, it gets the "straight to video" label and heads directly to video stores. As video-on-demand becomes more widespread, it will likely become the first window after theatrical release even though today it often appears simultaneously with the video release.[8]

▲▼ Movie Industry Business Model

In basic terms, the movie industry business model seems simple: get as many people as possible to pay to watch a movie. This quickly gets more complicated when considering the ways that people can watch movies today other than in movie theaters, and how important a movie's box office popularity is to attracting viewers in later exhibition windows. Adding to the complexity, there are other means by which studios can generate revenue for a movie, including licensing deals and product placement and promotional tie-ins.

Most movies end up losing money, partly because they are so expensive to make and market. However, movies also have a chance to make great profits, and Hollywood is rife with tales of movies such as the independent film *Napoleon Dynamite* (2004) that cost $400,000 to make and that grossed $46 million worldwide. The high costs and high risk in making a movie leads to a mindset among Hollywood studios that seeks safety in the form of blockbusters, thus the usual spate of sequels of popular movies and the generally formulaic stories and characters in most Hollywood movies.

Audiences have been steadily declining at the U.S. box office over the past several years even as U.S. box office revenues have continued to rise, thanks mostly to increasing ticket prices of about 5 percent a year. This has been helped by 3-D movies, which can charge about three dollars more than non-3-D movies. In 2010 gross U.S. box office revenues were $6.44 billion, up 4.5 percent from 2009, even though audiences declined by over 5 percent from the year before.[9]

U.S. box office revenues are not nearly as important from a financial standpoint as they used to be, as today international box office sales are often greater than U.S. sales. DVD rentals and sales are usually the biggest money generator for movies, long since surpassing box office revenues. However, sales have dropped in recent years as consumers seem to prefer renting movies over buying them, and are increasingly getting them through video-on-demand (VOD) services such as Netflix or through their cable operators.

Licensing deals can also generate revenue for movies. For popular movies, such as the *Toy Story* series, the studio can license the rights to make toys, blankets, pajamas, and other goods based on the characters in the movies, for which the studio gets royalties based on sales. For the manufacturer, they have a chance to generate greater sales of their items because of the association with a popular movie. This relationship works best, of course, when a movie turns out to be a blockbuster or is based on popular characters. Some licensing deals have turned out poorly when a movie does not do well at the box office, leading some companies in recent years to be more cautious about the deals they enter with movie studios.

Promotional tie-ins, such as with fast food chains, can help generate some revenue even as they help generate interest in the movie. **Product placement**, or using or showing real-life products in a movie in exchange for payment from the product maker, can also create some revenue for a movie, although the overall amount is small compared to the money received from box office sales or video rentals.

product placement

A form of advertising in which brand name goods or services are placed prominently within movie content that is otherwise devoid of advertising, demonstrating the convergence of programming with advertising content.

▲▼ Outlook for the Movie Industry

Digitization has had profound effects on the movie industry, some of which are already being seen both in the industry itself and in theaters. Amazing special effects can be created, using digital technology, that far surpass previous special-effects efforts. As computer power increases, computer artists and program- mers continue to improve their skills to render surfaces like snow and fur more realistically. Computer-created charac- ters have become increasingly lifelike, although studies have shown that audiences begin to feel repulsed when animated characters become too similar to humans.[10]

Digital distribution of films also promises cost sav- ings for movie studios. It costs up to two thousand dollars to produce, duplicate, and ship one forty-pound celluloid film print to a movie theater, and most studios ship prints to three thousand theaters nationwide if they hope the movie can be a blockbuster. That means $6 million just in distribution costs for a major film.[11] A digital film, on the other hand, would simply be sent over satellite or through broadband to a movie theater, thereby avoiding all the costs associated with shipping a bulky physical product. In addition, endless perfect copies could be made, just as

Digital technology has allowed filmmakers to combine live actors with computer-generated animation to produce interesting new effects.

with other digital media, eliminating the need to receive even more prints when film breaks or loses its quality after repeated showings. Some industry experts estimate it could save movie studios $600-$800 million per year.

The movie industry has been relatively slow to wholly embrace digital technol- ogy on the distribution end, however, for a number of reasons. One reason is the high cost of outfitting theaters with digital projector systems, computer servers, and satellite dishes or high-speed wiring. Theater owners argue that since it is the movie studios that will get the greatest savings through digital distribution, they should pay at least part of the cost of upgrading theaters to digital systems. In 2008, five of the major studios struck a deal with three of the main movie-theater chains to convert thousands of theaters to digital projection systems. Financing was secured for the project in 2010 to convert 14,000 theaters to digital.

Another reason the movie industry has been slow in moving to digital technol- ogy, despite potential cost savings, is its concern over piracy and subsequent loss of revenues. The studios have watched the music industry's battles with file-swapping services such as Napster and realize that they are prime targets for similar practices because of the popularity of movies and growing numbers of people with broad- band connections.

Assuming that the movie industry does eventually adopt digital technology at all levels of production, it is likely that the moviegoer will see great changes not only in digital effects, such as improved picture quality (including 3-D) and better sound, but in the availability of types of movies as well. Independent movies may more likely be shown in major theaters, as the theaters or studios will not be bank- ing on the same large audiences to break even since production and distribution costs will be lower. Some theaters could even promote local or regional digital film festivals, giving audiences exposure to films they would normally never be able to see, let alone see in a mainstream movie theater.

◣◥ Television

Television (from the Latin terms for "distance" and "viewing") is a much-loved and much-hated medium. Unlike many other media of mass communications, televi- sion draws as many critics as fans. Despite the rise of the Internet and other new media, people still spend more time watching television than they spend with any other medium. According to the Kaiser Family Foundation, children between eight and eighteen spend more time (6.5 hours a day on average) in front of some kind of screen—TV, computer, cell phone—than with any other activity except sleeping. The average viewer today who lives to be seventy-five will have spent eleven years watching television.

Many think television watching is largely a waste of time and worry what too much time in front of one screen or another will do for social skills and physical fitness. They see television as offering little of redeeming social value and as largely mindless entertainment. Others point to the many hours of educational television, news, and cultural programming as examples of quality content worth watching. Moreover, television is a big business.

Terrestrial, or over-the-air broadcast, TV has traditionally been the most common way people received television programming. But today the most common way to get TV is via cable, with two-thirds of homes receiving their TV this way. Many homes get satellite-delivered TV, which is actually digital but, until 2009, when all U.S. television went digital, was transferred back to analog format via a set-top converter box. Moreover, most households watch DVDs, videocassettes, or video-on-demand (VOD) via their televisions. Consumer recording devices for television were an important development for a number of reasons. One is that they allowed the audience to **time shift**, or watch a program anytime after it was originally broadcast and when it suited them, rather than be held hostage by a broadcaster's scheduling.

Time shifting was an important step in moving the balance of power toward the audience in choosing media content—a trend that will continue as TV has switched to a digital format. Digital media in fact will complicate the very definition of television, much as the definition of radio has blurred, as televisions take on more interactive programming and converge with the PC.

▼ FUNCTIONS OF TELEVISION

Television serves the entertainment, surveillance, correlation, and cultural transmission functions, mostly because of its widespread use and the range of content that is on television. More U.S. households have television sets than telephones—98 percent have at least one TV—and it is the most influential medium of mass communications.

More Americans say they get their news from television than from any other source, making the surveillance function for TV preeminent. More Americans get their entertainment from television than from any other mass medium as well. Entertainment programming plays an important role in cultural transmission and in influencing new trends and social norms.

Since the advent of television as a medium of mass communication, only one development has caused TV viewership to drop—the Internet. But despite this, TV is still number one in most population groups' media use. The trend does seem to be changing to some extent, however. In 2009 a nationwide survey by the Kaiser Family Foundation found that young people are increasingly spending time watching television content that is not live programming. This includes watching DVDs or VOD and also watching television programming on computers or mobile devices.

Television became a mass medium much faster than film, music, and radio. As it became more widespread, television displaced radio—which had displaced national magazines—as the medium providing a common set of experiences. Although this effect may be reduced with more channels and growing audience fragmentation,

time shift

The recording of an audio or video event for listening or viewing later, rather than at the time of the original broadcast. Setting a VCR to record a favorite program while one is out is an example of time shifting.

there is no doubt that television continues to have a profound effect on people's attitudes about a variety of social and cultural issues.

◣◥ History of Television

Unknowingly laying the basis for the development of television, a British telegrapher, Louis May, discovered in 1873 what some consider to be the basics of photoconductivity, a critical foundation for the electronic transmission of visual and audio information. He discovered that, when exposed to light, selenium bars conduct electricity and that the level of conduction varies in relationship to the amount of light hitting the bars. In 1881, British inventor Shelford Bidwell transmitted silhouettes using both selenium and a scanning system and called his device the "scanning phototelegraph." These technologies contributed to the development of modern television by outlining an electrical method for scanning objects.

Most TV sets and computer displays traditionally used a **cathode-ray tube (CRT)** for displaying video images. The cathode-ray tube is not a modern invention. The CRT was conceived in 1859 by Julius Plücker, a German mathematician and physicist, and the first functional CRT was built in 1878 by William Crookes, a British chemist. In 1897, German physicist Karl Braun improved the cathode-ray tube, demonstrating how cathode rays could be controlled by a magnetic field.

▼ SEEING THE LIGHT: THE FIRST TELEVISION SYSTEMS

In 1884 German inventor Paul Nipkow developed a concept for mechanical television that used a rotating disk. In 1923, Scottish inventor **John Logie Baird** invented Baird Television, the first mechanically scanned television device to earn any money from sending pictures through the air. Baird's thirty-line TV is considered by some to be the first high-definition TV because it contained many more lines of resolution than other early TV systems and thereby displayed finer visual detail.

In 1923, Russian immigrant **Vladimir Zworykin** invented a more advanced cathode-ray tube he called the "iconoscope" (meaning "a viewer of icons"), which still serves as the basis of many modern television display tubes. The iconoscope was an electronic camera pickup tube and represented perhaps the first important tangible device that would eventually lead to what is now called television. In 1929, Zworykin also invented the first totally electric camera tube.

In 1927, Philo T. Farnsworth transmitted the image of a dollar sign across his San Francisco apartment using the scanning-beam and synchronization-pulse technologies he invented. This was the first electronic wireless transmission of an image, the first step in the development of electronic television. His first "broadcast" transmitted images from a Jack Dempsey/Gene Tunney fight and scenes of Mary Pickford combing her hair (from *Taming of the Shrew*). Farnsworth and Zworykin became entangled in bitter legal battles over television patents, each claiming to have been the first to develop electronic television.

▼ MODERN TELEVISION TAKES SHAPE

If television was going to become a popular mass medium for broadcasting images, then much better image resolution was needed than what the earliest attempts had produced. With a CRT screen, the greater the number of scanned lines, the clearer

cathode-ray tube [CRT]

A device, still used in most television screens and computer monitors, in which electrons are transmitted to a screen for viewing.

John Logie Baird

Scottish inventor who created the first mechanically scanned television device, in 1923. His thirty-line TV had better resolution than the first attempts at electronic televisions.

Vladimir Zworykin

Inventor of an improved cathode-ray tube he called the "iconoscope" that is the basis for the CRTs still used today in television sets and many computer monitors. He is considered one of the fathers of electronic television.

Philo T. Farnsworth transmitted the first wireless electronic image, the first step toward electronic television.

David Sarnoff unveiled television to the public at the 1939 World's Fair in Queens, New York.

the picture is. In 1939, a 441-line TV technology was demonstrated by David Sarnoff at the New York World's Fair.

The 1939 demonstration brought national and international attention to the new medium of television. That same year, TV broadcasting began in the United States when the National Broadcasting Company (NBC) started regularly scheduled broadcasts to only four hundred sets in the New York area. The development of television was interrupted by the start of World War II in late 1939.

The government lifted its wartime ban on the construction of new TV stations and TV sets in October 1945. There were just seven thousand receiving sets in the United States at the beginning of 1946 and only nine stations on the air. By 1949, there were ninety-eight stations in fifty-eight market areas. In 1950, there were 3.88 million households with television, or 9 percent of the total 43 million U.S. households.

There were initially four commercial television networks: NBC, CBS, ABC, and DuMont, although DuMont failed in 1955. By the end of 1955, the number of TV households had grown to 30.7 million, or 64.5 percent of U.S. households, and U.S. advertisers spent more than $300 million on TV time. By 1960, only about fifteen years after wartime bans on television were lifted, 45.7 million U.S. households (87.1 percent) had at least one television set.

Color television broadcasting debuted in 1951 in the United States with a live CBS telecast from Grand Central Station in New York. Unfortunately, only twenty-five receivers could accommodate the mechanical color technology, while viewers of the 12 million existing black-and-white sets saw a blank screen. In 1953, color broadcasting had its official start in the United States, when the FCC approved a modified version of an RCA system that was compatible with existing screens. The development of color television was only one step in the never-ending process to give viewers sharper and better pictures. Another step was to create new types of displays.

◤▼ Digital Television: Preparing the Way for Convergence

Although electronic television has always utilized a video display terminal, it has evolved in terms of picture and sound quality. In the 1950s, the video display was relatively small, black and white, and with monophonic, low-fidelity sound (i.e., no directionality and not high quality). In the 1960s and 1970s, color television and stereophonic sound were developed, greatly increasing the realism of the viewing experience. All the while, the level of resolution of the display was relatively unchanged.

In 1981, NHK (Japan Broadcasting Corporation) engineers demonstrated analog **high definition television (HDTV)**, calling it Hi-Vision. HDTV was a significant advance because it presented a much higher resolution image, sharper color, a wider aspect ratio, and superior audio. NHK had begun its research on HDTV in 1973, long before the digital revolution was on the global radar screen.

In 1990, General Instrument Corporation proposed an all-digital television system, something initially deemed technically impossible, especially for over-the-air broadcasting. But this proved not to be the case. **Digital television (DTV)** became the accepted global standard for next-generation TV. It is important to note that DTV and HDTV are not the same thing. HDTV as invented by the Japanese was analog in format. DTV was invented in the United States as a response to the

high definition television (HDTV)

Modern television technology that produces a much higher resolution image, sharper color, a wider aspect ratio, and superior audio to traditional television. The term was first used by the Japanese organization NHK to describe a system they called Hi-Vision.

digital television (DTV)

An all-digital television system in which all information, broadcast by cable or through the air, is in digital or computer-readable form.

Japanese invention of HDTV. HDTV can be digital, and digital TV can be HDTV, but the two were not always synonymous.

Since June 2009, all television broadcast signals in the United States were switched to digital. Digital TV enables the convergence of computing, television, and telecommunications and brings the possibility of interactivity. This means that with DTV new storytelling techniques are possible, as well as the ability to link to **multicast** (also known as multiplex), which means simultaneously transmitting multiple channels of compressed content, or in some cases the same content but at different times. DTV brings possible functions to the television set that have been used in recent years on computers and the Web, taking yet another step toward converging the TV and PC.

multicast

The simultaneous transmission of multiple channels of compressed content, or in some cases the same content but at different times.

▼ THE RISE OF FLAT-PANEL DISPLAYS

Two main types of flat-panel displays for televisions have gradually overtaken the CRT television: liquid crystal displays (LCDs) and plasma displays. Besides the obvious space-saving features, flat-panel displays have better picture and color clarity as well as more efficient energy use.

We see LCD screens in digital alarm clocks, laptops, and tablet computers. They use much less power than the traditional CRT display, and of course there could be no such thing as a laptop computer without some sort of portable, thin screen. At the end of 2007, LCD televisions outsold CRT sets worldwide for the first time, and in 2008 they became the majority of sets sold, at just over 50 percent, and their sales continue to grow. It is quite likely that your children will be reading about the CRT display in the same way you read about the black-and-white television: as a part of television history.

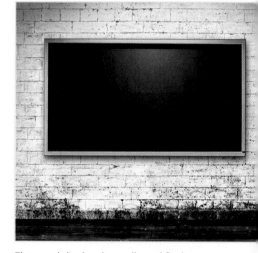

The technology behind LCDs goes back to the latter nineteenth century and was developed by various engineers throughout the first half of the twentieth century. But it was not until 1972 that the first liquid crystal display was created. Even so, because of technological limitations, it was widely believed until the last several years that LCD screens could only be smaller than forty inches. That has since been proven wrong, and television manufacturers have started ramping up production of large-screen LCD television sets.

Flat-panel displays have allowed for larger, yet less obtrusive, television sets in homes.

Plasma displays, created around the same time as the early LCD screens, seemed to have a number of advantages over LCDs in terms of picture quality, viewing angle, and size of screen. With LCDs able to nearly match the size of plasma displays, however, and with LCD costs generally lower, plasma screens have become less popular for large-screen, HDTV viewing than they once were.

Regardless of the type of screen that becomes most popular, the fact is that large-screen, flat-panel, high-definition displays have changed the television-viewing experience, bringing nearly theater-quality sound and picture clarity to living rooms, and even 3-D viewing.

Television Distribution

The quality of the image on a TV screen matters little if there is no way to distribute content to a large audience—thus the importance of television networks in the earliest days of television. These networks came directly from the existing national radio networks. There are three primary means of distributing television programming. These are broadcasting, cable, and direct-to-home satellite. The Internet has rapidly become an important medium for television distribution as well, as more people watch clips of shows or entire programs online. The numbers on online television viewers have risen fast, and perhaps in a short time the Internet will prove to be the most popular way to watch television programming.

▼ BROADCAST TV

Broadcasting (terrestrial wireless) is the traditional means of over-the-air distribution of television programming. This is the way the network-owned and affiliated stations and most other local stations broadcast their programming. ABC, CBS, and NBC were all originally radio networks, while Fox, launched in 1986, became the fourth national network and is owned by News Corp. Although in the early 1970s terrestrial TV dominated the viewing landscape, today that is far from the case. Today, just 15 percent of U.S. households receive terrestrial TV signals on their primary TV set. The broadcasting networks dominated television programming and viewing until the 1980s, when cable and satellite TV and other programming alternatives made program and audience fragmentation inevitable.

Today, most households' primary TV sets are connected to cable or satellite. That's not to say viewers don't see the programming carried on broadcast stations, since those stations are also carried on cable TV and many on satellite TV. In fact, the three traditional commercial networks still have a cumulative weekly audience reach of more than 70 percent.[12]

▼ CABLE TV

Many think cable TV was invented in the 1980s, when in fact the first cable television systems were created in the United States much earlier. The first systems, called **Community Antenna Television**, or **CATV**, were built noncommercially in Mahoney City, Pennsylvania, and Astoria, Oregon, in 1948. The main function of these early CATV systems was to bring TV signals into communities where over-the-air reception was nonexistent or poor due to hilly terrain or distance.

Although the first cable systems were built in the late 1940s, the cable system nationwide didn't begin expanding rapidly until the 1970s, when the number of local cable systems grew from about two thousand in 1970 to more than four thousand in 1980.

Coaxial cable, which is an insulated and layered conducting wire typically about a half-inch thick, is the material traditionally used for delivering cable television to the home. The first use of coaxial cable was for undersea telephone transmission. Most early cable TV systems were based on coaxial cable, but today they increasingly consist of optical fiber. **Optical fiber** is a much faster, higher-capacity, transparent filament, usually made of glass or plastic, using light to carry media content or information (including audio and video) rather than the electrical impulses used in coaxial cable.

Cable television underwent some dramatic changes in the 1980s. The government began deregulating the cable industry, permitting cable companies to buy cable television systems nationwide. Early cable giant Tele-Communications, Inc. (TCI), now a subsidiary of AT&T Broadband, was among the most aggressive in taking advantage of this deregulation, spending $3 billion for 150 cable companies across the United States. By the end of the decade, 50 percent of U.S. households

community antenna television (CATV)

Also known as cable television, it was developed in 1948 so communities in hilly or remote terrain could still access television broadcasts.

coaxial cable

An insulated and conducting wire that is typically used for most cable television connections.

optical fiber

A transparent filament, usually made of glass or plastic, that uses light to carry information. This makes transmission of information much faster and with much greater capacity than twisted-pair copper wires or coaxial cable.

were wired for cable TV, setting the stage for the decline of network television and over-the-air broadcasting, as well as spurring audience fragmentation.

▼ SATELLITE TV

Direct-broadcast-satellite (DBS) emerged in the United States in the 1990s as a serious competitor to traditional terrestrial broadcast and cable television. Although DBS was already a viable commercial television alternative in Europe, efforts made for more than a decade to launch a viable national DBS commercial TV service in the United States failed until the 1994 launch of DirecTV. Prior to that year, most of the direct-to-home satellite systems required expensive, large three-meter dishes.

DirecTV and other 1990s DBS entrants introduced inexpensive, compact eighteen-inch dishes that could be installed without professional help and an annual subscription price that rivals cable alternatives. With its 19 million subscribers, DirecTV ranks second only to cable MSO Comcast in terms of subscribers, while rival Dish Network, with 14 million subscribers, ranks third.

In a country like Indonesia, where many islands make it difficult to lay cable for TV, satellite TV plays a major role.

◣◥ Television Industry Today

Ownership of television stations has continued to consolidate since the passage of the 1996 Telecommunications Act, which relaxed ownership limits. Among the newly expanded limits is the 35 percent rule, which permits groups to own stations that nationwide reach up to 35 percent of television households and to own two stations in major markets.

Despite the fact that there are more than ten thousand local cable systems, consolidation in the cable industry has resulted in a relatively small number of companies—roughly six hundred multiple system operators (MSOs)—controlling cable television for more than 90 percent of Americans who subscribe to cable TV. As Table 5-2 shows, the top ten MSOs have nearly three-quarters of all cable TV subscribers, with Comcast by far the largest, almost double its nearest rival, Time Warner.

Since 2008 most cable operators have lost subscribers as consumers "cut the cord" from cable and choose either satellite, fiber-optic through telcos like Verizon or AT&T, or simply watch terrestrial television or television online. Comcast lost nearly 2 million subscribers between 2008 and 2010, and second-place Time Warner lost almost five hundred thousand during the same period. The decline has been especially notable in urban areas, where the telcos have started offering fiber-optic services in competition with the cable companies.

▼ CABLE SYSTEM STRUCTURE

The typical cable system features what is called a tree-and-branch architecture. A head-end, or main office, is the center, with fiber or coaxial cable trunk lines, feeder lines, and drops to end users.

TABLE 5-2

Top Ten Cable TV MSOs in the United States, 2010

CABLE MSO	# OF SUBSCRIBERS
Comcast Corporation	22,802,000
Time Warner Cable	12,422,000
Cox Communications	4,916,000
Charter Communications	4,520,000
Verizon Communications, Inc.	3,472,000
Cablevision Systems Corp.	3,314,000
AT&T Inc.	2,987,000
Bright House Networks	2,177,000
Suddenlink Communications	1,216,000
Mediacom Communications Corp.	1,193,000

Source: National Cable and Telecommunications Association (Dec. 2010)

Most cable systems have been undergoing a significant transformation since the 1990s from analog to digital technology, with upgrades costing most MSOs, or what are normally called cable companies, millions or billions of dollars to not only improve and expand channel capacity but to add interactive features, such as two-way capacity (for program ordering, for example), and cable modems and set-top box converters for high-speed Internet services. In 2011, 84 percent of American households subscribed to pay-TV services at an average basic subscription cost of $86.[13]

▼ SATELLITE VS. CABLE

DBS offers more than three hundred digital programming channels, compared to nearly two hundred for cable. DBS subscriptions are usually cheaper than cable subscriptions, even for basic cable, but there are usually installation costs involved with the satellite dishes and equipment needed to view satellite.

The greatest problem DBS systems have faced is their inability to carry a full array of local programming. Local programming is important for delivering local news, weather, and other programming. Although the DBS systems have great channel capacity, they cannot carry every local station. Instead, they carry local channels in the largest markets and require subscribers to pay a fee to watch the local broadcasting channels available in their region. If DBS viewers opt not to pay the fee and still want local programming, they must maintain a basic cable service or another antenna to get local channels.

Cable companies have been strongly criticized over the years for their increasing monthly subscription costs and their track records of poor customer service. In most areas there is still only a single cable provider, although this is starting to change in some urban or heavily populated areas. The extra choice, combined with increased TV viewing on the Internet, has helped people decide to stop their subscriptions to cable. Cable companies have begun introducing a greater range of services, such as VOD, DVRs, and video gaming in order to compete with both satellite and the Internet.

◣◤ Television Industry Business Model

There is no single television business model, but multiple models depending on how the television signal is delivered. Traditionally, the terrestrial broadcasting networks relied primarily on selling advertising, which was shown during programs. One-minute or thirty-second advertisements would be shown periodically during programs, taking up between sixteen and twenty-two minutes of an hour-long program.

Advertising revenues not only generated profits for the networks, but they essentially subsidized the development of new shows. They also created a culture among networks that was very similar to that in Hollywood—a risk-averse mindset that sought hit television shows in order to attract the largest number of viewers, which would then let the networks charge more for commercials during those time slots. This mindset is what television's critics tend to complain about most, because it lead to networks taking very few risks on new types of programming content and lent itself to a copycat culture, where a hit show would soon be emulated the next season by the other networks, with slight variations in the formula.

The importance of tracking audiences led to the Nielsen ratings, a way to measure how many people in various markets were watching a particular show. Nielsen ratings became the yardstick by which shows were judged successful, and small drops in viewership could have profound consequences for shows, such as moving them to different days or time slots or canceling them completely.

▼ CABLE AND SATELLITE SERVICES AND PROGRAMMING: OVERCOMING AUDIENCE FRAGMENTATION

With cable television, audiences became enormously fragmented, making the Nielsen ratings an inaccurate yardstick by which to determine audience reach and share. Even cable shows that are considered hits usually have audiences smaller than a low-rated network television show. Luckily for cable, they do not rely entirely on advertising to earn revenues.

Cable services are typically offered in tiers, much like satellite services: varying program packages at varying rates. The main types of cable services, or tiers, are basic service, premiere channel service, and per-program service, which can either be pay-per-view or VOD. Basic service is the minimum level of cable service. As required by the FCC, basic service must include all local over-the-air television broadcast signals and all public, educational, or government access channels mandated by the cable system's franchise agreement. Basic cable channels air commercials even as they charge a monthly subscription fee, which lets them get two streams of revenue. However, because of the smaller audiences, advertising rates are much lower than for network television.

Subscribers to premium cable channels do not have commercials and can subscribe to bundles of premiere channels like HBO and Cinemax or Showtime, as well as specialized channels and foreign-language channels. Depending on the packages being offered and the cable provider, monthly fees for premium content can be anywhere from $4.99 a month to $16.99 a month. Pay-per-view services include being able to watch certain programs such as fights or sporting events, usually for around $50, while VOD has become increasingly popular for television viewers and costs anywhere from $2.99 to $16.99 to buy and download a movie. Some services offer free content on-demand along with paid programming.

VOD services will continue to grow, especially as television networks, cable operators, and satellite operators compete with online television services and services like Netflix, which let users view movies and some television series episodes on their computers or television.

▲▼ Outlook for the Television Industry

The long-awaited shift of all television signals in the United States to digital finally occurred in June 2009, but not without some problems. It turned out that there were not enough digital converter devices to be distributed to all households that still had analog television sets and no connection with cable. It also turned out that many consumers, despite a massive advertising campaign to inform the public, still did not realize that they would need converters to continue watching television.

The switch to an entirely digital signal has several important implications. First, it frees up some areas of bandwidth that were used by analog signals. Second, it creates opportunities for broadcasters and cable operators to offer new products, including video-on-demand and other interactive services that have been dramatically changing the television-viewing experience. Third, it reiterates that "digital" is not something standing separate from traditional signal types but encompasses, as well as changes, those types because everything will be or already is digital.

Although cable and satellite operators have had to adjust to changes brought by digitization, network television has arguably been affected the greatest. Not only have they seen advertising revenues decline as audiences are pulled away to other viewing options, but they have faced challenges from programming as cable channels offer edgier or more innovative shows.

Networks are experimenting with online viewing, such as with Hulu.com, founded in 2007. Co-owned by NBC Universal, News Corp., and Providence Equity Partners, Hulu was able to easily add a lot of content from subsidiary companies Fox, NBC, Sony Pictures Television, Warner Brothers Television, and others. Furthermore, they have made a notable effort to have high-quality streaming video online, which is quite different than the varying and generally poorer-quality videos found on YouTube.

Supported by an advertising model, it is yet one more example of how media companies are realizing that the old models of business simply will not work and that if they do not do something online, other upstart companies simply will.

WEB LINK
Hulu
www.hulu.com

A Brief History of Interactive TV

Almost as soon as the TV became a mass medium, people were looking for ways to improve interactivity with the television set. The technology itself does not allow for true interactivity between viewers and media producers. Nevertheless, there have been some notable attempts at interactive TV (ITV), and earlier than you may assume.

The first regularly scheduled television show that encouraged interactivity was called *Winky Dink and You* and was produced for CBS in 1953.[14] It was interactive by inviting children to help the animated character Winky Dink escape from situations (such as being chased by wild animals) by drawing things (like a bridge over a yawning chasm) on a piece of wax paper placed on the screen. The show was short-lived, partly because children frequently failed to put the wax paper up before drawing the bridges, rope, ladder, or whatever else Winky Dink needed, and drew directly on the screen.

Warner Amex's QUBE experiment, the first two-way cable TV system, launched in 1978 in Columbus, Ohio. The interactive video system permitted viewers in their homes to participate in public opinion polls by punching buttons on a device. Warner concluded the experiment in 1984 after winning the local cable franchise and deeming it no longer necessary to continue an expensive showcase experiment to demonstrate their superiority over competing cable companies.

A trial of ITV in the early 1990s by Time Warner in Orlando, Florida, called the Full Service Network, collapsed under its own weight because of high costs and the creation of the World Wide Web, which had interactivity built into it.

After initial enthusiasm for ITV and glowing promises of how it would transform the audience experience, the cable and ITV industries have toned down their rhetoric markedly in recent years, though talk of the promise of ITV is once again on the rise.

WEB LINK
Winky Dink and You Kit
www.tvparty.com/requested2.html

WEB LINK
The Wall Street Journal Interactive
www.wsj.com

WEB LINK
Consumer Reports Online
www.consumerreports.org/

LOOKING BACK AND MOVING FORWARD

The mergers and consolidation in the cable industry in recent years were made possible by deregulation and the passage of the Telecommunications Act of 1996, which among other things expanded competitive alternatives in the communications industries. Cable TV is now permitted to offer telephone and Internet services, which are being introduced via a number of cable modem services, such as Time Warner's

Road Runner and Comcast. These and other companies offer consumers bundled packages of telephone, cable television, and Internet service. Verizon, traditionally a telecommunications company, has begun offering its direct-to-home fiber-optic lines, called FiOS, in a greater number of regions in the United States. This has proved popular among consumers and has contributed in part to the decline in cable subscribers in the past few years.

Many interesting questions arise in the convergence of cable TV and telephony. If consumers use a cable provider for their telephone service, which rules and regulations apply to them—cable TV regulations or laws created to regulate telephone companies? Why should an email sent by dial-up modem over telephone wires be treated differently from a legal perspective than an email sent by cable modem? Cable and DBS, both of which compete in the digital video and Internet services domains, are regulated to a less stringent standard than broadcasters. Since the computer industry does not operate a system of video delivery, it is not regulated at all with regard to these issues, although it is certainly an increasingly important player in the digital video marketplace.

Consumer issues also arise when primarily media-content companies, such as Time Warner, merge with technology or Internet companies, such as AOL. After the merger, business pundits predicted a media environment in which AOL's subscribers would have ready access to the myriad of media content from Time Warner, both through AOL's dial-up service and through Time Warner's broadband Road Runner service. Others worried that this type of convergence would favor one provider's content over another's. Because of the difficulties faced by AOL Time Warner, the company split its AOL unit off as a stand-alone company again, but these issues have arisen in the form of the debates about Net neutrality, covered in a later chapter.

DISCUSSION QUESTIONS

1. With the existence of film and television, do you think still photography is as relevant as it used to be? Why or why not?

2. The ability of the earliest filmmakers to tell stories was hampered by technological limitations that kept film reels short, so only a few minutes of filmed footage could be shown at a time. In what ways could current technological limitations hamper our ability to tell stories through the Internet?

3. Recent movies seem to consistently break box office records. Why do you think this is so?

4. Could a group of young digital filmmakers revolutionize the industry and dominate movie production and distribution like the Hollywood movie moguls did in the earliest days of Hollywood? Why or why not?

5. Discuss new ways movie theaters might be able to use their large screens and space to show digital film not only from big-name moviemakers but from local artists as well. What effects might this have for the local movie theater and for its role in the community?

6. Keep a diary for a week of the television shows you watch, how long you watch them, and how (TV, computer, video-on-demand, etc.). What patterns do you see and what implications do they have, if any, for your media consumption?

7. Research one of the top ten cable MSOs (or top twenty-five) and find out what people are saying about it in online discussions such as forums and blogs. Compare your findings with classmates.

American Photography: A Century of Images. Vicki Goldberg, Robert Silberman (1999) Chronicle Books.

Film Art: An Introduction, 8th ed. David Bordwell, Kristin Thompson (2008) McGraw-Hill Higher Education.

Hollywood! A Celebration. David Thomson (2001) DK Publishing.

The Film Snob's Dictionary: An Essential Lexicon of Filmological Knowledge. David Kamp, Lawrence Levi (2006) Broadway.

Film: A Critical Introduction, 2nd ed. Maria Pramaggiore, Tom Wallis (2007) Allyn & Bacon.

The Film Encyclopedia: The Complete Guide to Film and the Film Industry, 6th ed. Ephraim Katz (2008) Collins.

The Business of Television. Howard Blumenthal, Oliver Goodenough (2006) Billboard Books.

The Columbia History of American Television. Gary Edgerton (2009) Columbia University Press.

Career Opportunities in the Film Industry. Fred Yager, Jan Yager (2009) Checkmark Books.

1. True.

2. Make photography accessible to the general public.

3. No.

4. Because they took film of people doing everyday activities and they felt the novelty of watching such things on screen would soon wear off.

5. *The Untouchables,* among others.

6. Because they generally do not get large audiences and are not profitable.

7. 11 years.

8. Cable.

9. False.

10. June 2009.

6

INFORMATION OVERLOAD, USABILITY, AND INTERACTIVE MEDIA

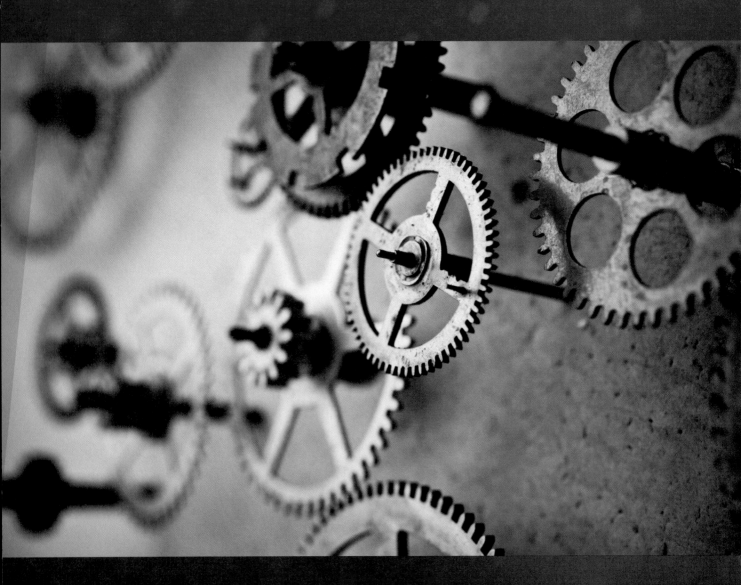

LEARNING OBJECTIVES

By the end of this chapter you should be able to:

- List the five fundamental principles that make something a storage technology and how they relate to mass-communication issues.

- Compare and contrast various historical and current storage technologies in terms of how well they meet the five fundamental principles.

- Describe the consequences of storage technologies for mass communication and society.

- Describe why user interface is important to mass communication.

- Explain how emerging trends will affect user interface and the way we use media.

- Define the elements of interactivity.

- Describe the importance of interactivity in terms of modern media.

Imagine a world without paper. No books, magazines, or newspapers as we know them. There are still libraries to store knowledge, of course, but they are likely vastly bigger to store the material in whatever form is most common—probably something similarly portable to paper but perhaps harder to use, perhaps more fragile, or more expensive to make.

Now imagine a world much like ours today except with no digital media. Instead, our computers and other technologies are all mechanical and steam-powered, much like what is seen in the sci-fi subgenre known as steampunk. No sleek iPods that slip unobtrusively into a pocket, no slim laptops that fit easily in a bag, and no hand-held camera phones that send information wirelessly to others.

Consider a world in which you look at a TV-like screen but with no buttons or switches of any kind—no way to understand how to turn it on, how to change channels, or perhaps even understand what it does, exactly.

These three examples show how important the type of storage technology and the interface we get accustomed to using are to our media environment, and to our lives in general. They affect how we access and think about information, how we use media devices, and even how we communicate with each other and socialize.

A common thread with the examples is the idea of interactivity—the notion of how we engage with the media and the devices we use. This, too, greatly affects our position in relation to media: interactive media can change us from passive media consumers to potentially active users—and creators—of media content.

T his chapter focuses on three major aspects of digital media that make them different than traditional media: storage technology, user interface, and interactivity. Understanding these three characteristics will help you develop a more thorough understanding of digital media and today's world of mass communication in general.

The term "**storage technology**" simply refers to any type of device or medium in which information can be kept for later retrieval. An ideal storage technology will be strong in five components common to all storage technologies: longevity, capacity, portability, accessibility, and reproducibility.

However, throughout history various technologies have been strong in some aspects but not others, and attempts to find a perfect balance continue today. In addition, digital technology and the importance of information in the modern age bring their own unique issues to storing and retrieving content in a mass-communication context.

Even if media content is stored, there still remains the important question of how to easily access the information we want when we want it. Related to this is the problem of the relative newness of digital media and our lack of understanding of how to use it in even basic ways sometimes. This is why user interface is so important in today's media. Poor user-interface design can keep people away from websites or content and can affect how subsequent technologies are developed. Similarly, good interface design can enhance the user experience and open up new realms of information and entertainment.

Interactivity is a key aspect differentiating today's digital media from traditional media. The power that interactivity has to engage and involve users changes our relationship with media and raises new ethical issues, which will be explored in this chapter.

◣◥ Characteristics of Storage, Representation, and Retrieval

How information is stored is critical to communication, whether analog or digital. Since only a portion of media content is distributed live, or without storage, an overwhelming amount of the media content we read, see, or hear has first been stored for subsequent editing, distribution, and access. Whether through letters on a page, a magnetic tracing on a computer disk, or etchings on an optical drive, information must be represented in a fashion that allows for people to access it. The following discussion identifies the five concepts of longevity, capacity, portability, accessibility, and reproducibility that help to define the nature and quality of stored information.

MEDIA QUIZ

Searching for Knowledge

1. (T/F) Kilobytes are named after Anastasios H. Kilobyte, the nineteenth-century Greek mathematician who discovered them.
2. (T/F) Until humans invented written language, there was no way to store information or knowledge.
3. What does GUI stand for?
4. (T/F) Out of all the fundamental characteristics of storage media, longevity has actually decreased compared to older storage media.
5. (T/F) MP3 stands for MPEG-3, a type of audio compression format.
6. What is the estimate of how much money is lost a year by companies because of information overload?
7. How high would a stack of CDs be that stored all our current knowledge?
8. Name the top three languages used on the Internet.
9. (T/F) Even the best search engines only cover about 30 percent of the Web.
10. What U.S. president was at the forefront of two dramatic developments involving media storage?

▼ LONGEVITY

In one sense, longevity, or how long information can be retained in a medium, is most critical. The oldest known media, petroglyphs, or cave paintings, have lasted for many millennia, as have hieroglyphics, also painted on rock. It is their longevity that has given us a window into the past and a glimpse into the world of early humans.

Information-storage technologies have generally sacrificed longevity for increases in the four other characteristics, such as capacity or portability. In other words, storage technologies such as paper, film, or magnetic tape do not last nearly as long as some of the earliest storage technologies, such as petroglyphs, for example. Compare the life span of four-thousand-year-old hieroglyphics in Egyptian tombs with that of cinema film stock from the early 1900s, which is already disintegrating only one hundred years after it was created.

Longevity, though undoubtedly useful from a historical perspective, has turned out to not be as important as how much information can be stored.

Hieroglyphs written on stone have great longevity but are not very portable.

▼ CAPACITY

Newer storage technologies have greatly increased the capacity to store information, but at the expense of longevity. Books and other print media, such as newspapers and magazines, can retain greater amounts of information than petroglyphs, but they begin to decay almost immediately and are unlikely to survive more than a few hundred years.

Consider the size of a floppy diskette and how much more information it can store in a smaller space than a book. Expand that to CD-ROMs (700 MB versus 1.2 MB for diskettes) and then to DVDs, which store up to 4.7 GB (9.4 GB double-sided) in the same amount of physical space as a CD, and you can begin to see how much more information we can access in a very small space than ever before. And that doesn't include using compression algorithms that can cram even more material into the same amount of disk space. Two University of Southern California researchers, Martin Hilbert and Priscila Lopez, said that 2002 was the first year that digital storage capacity was greater than analog storage capacity and that by 2007, 94 percent of our memory was in digital form. According to their calculations, if all the information available today were put on CDs it would make a stack that went past the moon.

However, being able to store large amounts of data is not very helpful if the medium used to store it also increases in size, as moving a stack of CDs that reach the moon is not very practical.

▼ PORTABILITY

Tied closely with increasing capacity has been increasing portability. Although cave paintings endure, they are essentially immovable. Stone or clay tablets improved portability of information, although not by much. Papyrus and parchment, first developed in Egypt and widely used in the Greek and Roman worlds of the late fourth century BCE until the middle of the seventh century CE, created a dramatic improvement in portability of information.

The development of paper and printing made distributing information easier as well. Portability can also be tied to the notion of capacity. Carrying a Kindle or other type of ebook, which can store hundreds of titles, is much easier than actually having to move all two hundred printed versions of the same books. However, greater portability through electronic storage devices comes at a cost—unlike a book, you cannot access the content if the device has no power.

▼ ACCESSIBILITY

Better accessibility of stored information can be looked at from two perspectives. On one hand, the need to use electronics to access television, radio, or computers is a limitation. With no power, there is no information. But books or clay tablets can be accessed directly, simply through looking at them.

International standards and devices to retrieve the information on digital storage media continue to change so rapidly that in just a few years it can become virtually impossible to access the content stored on a particular device. For example, try to find a 5¼-inch computer floppy disk drive—a storage medium that was common in the 1980s. VHS videocassettes are also increasingly hard to find in stores, having been replaced by DVDs. Will DVD players manufactured in the early twenty-first century have a longer life span? Will a member of a human civilization living

Books and scrolls help make information very portable, but at the expense of longevity, as paper or parchment disintegrates.

three hundred years from now—or even thirty—be able to find a machine to play a DVD?

On the other hand, modern electronic-storage technology, especially in digital form, provides much greater access to information to a larger number of people than ever before, if they have the right equipment. A person does not have to be present at the cave to see the cave drawings, or wait months for a book or magazine to arrive by post. Today, people can use the Internet to instantly access information of any type, almost anywhere they are. Furthermore, they can use that same technology to copy the information and send it elsewhere.

▼ REPRODUCIBILITY

In many ways digital media can be seen as improving on trends in storage technology that have continued for thousands of years, but in terms of reproducibility digital media represent a radical departure from anything that has come before, for a number of reasons. The ease and accuracy of reproduction in digital media far surpasses analog media. Prior to the printing press, the only way to copy written text was by hand—a laborious, time-consuming, and error-prone process. Visual media had to be hand copied until the nineteenth century, when photography "automated" the copying process to some extent.

Digital media can be easily reproduced because they exist only as bits and bytes and not anything physical. In other words, the very fact that digital media are not a physical object of any sort makes them easier to copy and allows for an infinite number of copies without reducing the number of copies available.

This same characteristic also makes it possible to produce not only perfect copies of the original but *better* versions than the original, such as when imperfections of sound recordings are removed digitally. In analog media, copies of the original are inevitably changed and lose some quality compared to the original version—again, think of audio recordings, in which a third- or fourth-generation audiocassette copy of a recording from a CD is noticeably poorer in sound quality. In digital media it is much easier to retain the same quality as the original, although for storage-space reasons reduced-quality versions are often saved.

Accessibility of information can be a problem in the electronic age, as old media formats get replaced by newer ones and manufacturers stop making equipment that used the older formats.

Nonelectronic Media Versus Electronic Media

In terms of storage technology, there is a fundamental difference between nonelectronic media, such as print, painting, or photography (including film), and electronic media, such as radio, television, and digital media. In the former types of **mediated communication**, their storage capacity is inherent in the medium itself. In other words, in painting a picture or writing words down the information is being stored.

Books have medium- to long-term longevity (in modern terms), are very portable, and are fairly easy to reproduce. They are accessible, assuming one can read, but their accessibility drops markedly if one is searching for a specific piece of information. Think of searching for a favorite quote or passage in a novel read long ago.

In storage-technology terms they can be described as "**sequential-access memory**" devices; i.e., a reader must go through each page to find some specific

mediated communication

Communication that takes place through a medium, such as writing or recording, as opposed to unmediated communication, such as face-to-face discussions.

sequential-access memory

A type of medium in which a reader, viewer, or user must go through the medium in the order received in order to find specific information.

Development of Electronic Recording Devices

1875 Thomas Edison successfully records and plays back the song "Mary's Little Lamb" from a strip of tinfoil wrapped around a spinning cylinder.

1888 American inventor Oberlin Smith introduces the concept of recording sound on magnetic tape.

1898 The Telegraphone, the first operating magnetic recording device, is developed by Danish engineer Valdemar Poulsen.

1900 Austrian emperor Franz Josef records his voice with the Telegraphone at the Paris Exposition, causing a sensation among the public as people begin to realize the implications of being able to record the human voice.

1928 Austrian chemist Fritz Pfleumer invents a recorder using lightweight tape coated with magnetic particles.

1930 Stereo recording is invented at Bell Labs in the United States using the concepts created by Alan Blumlein, an employee of Electrical and Musical Industries (EMI), in London.

1936 The Magnetophon, a cheaper and easier-to-use device than previous magnetic recorders, is used to record a performance of the London Philharmonic Orchestra in concert in Germany.

1947 *The Bing Crosby Show* is recorded using the Magnetophon. Crosby switches from NBC to ABC radio network in order to use the recording device. Bing Crosby Enterprises sells hundreds of the devices to radio stations and recording studios throughout the country.

1956 Ampex Corp. manufactures the first practical magnetic videotape recorder, the VR-1000, for use by television stations. Cost: $50,000.

1961 The Society of Motion Picture and Television Engineers (SMPTE) establishes the standard for time-code format on recorded audio and video (first on tape, but now on any storage medium). Time coding is the basis for modern postproduction or editing.

1963 Philips introduces the compact audiocassette recorder, followed by the eight-track recorder and microcassette.

1968 First portable video-recording equipment is developed in Europe, allowing journalists to shoot video in the field instead of film.

1975 NBC is the last of the major television networks to switch to videotape in news footage after its filmed report on the assassination attempt of Gerald Ford is aired several hours after the reports from ABC and CBS.

1977 Philips (Netherlands) introduces the videocassette recorder.

1986	Digital audio tape (DAT) is created in Japan. Consumers now use digital videotapes almost exclusively, such as in digital video cameras.
1988	MPEG standard established (acronym for "Moving Picture Experts Group") for compressing digital data.
1992	MPEG-2 becomes the new compression standard, which allows the coding of studio-quality video for digital TV, high-density CD-ROMs, and TV broadcasting.
1998	MP3 is a new file-storage format for digital audio recordings.
2006	Sony introduces a digital, high-definition, tapeless camcorder for consumer market.
2011	Major manufacturers such as Sony, JVC, and Canon stop introducing tape-based camcorders, instead concentrating on tapeless camcorders.

piece of information in the book. Developments such as page numbers, a table of contents, and an index (the latter two being of no use without page numbers) all help make the book more of a "**random-access memory**" device—meaning, the accessibility of random content in it is increased. Dictionaries, encyclopedias, and telephone books, where information is listed either alphabetically or by some other logical category, are examples of books created specifically *as* random-access memory devices.

Electronic media, on the other hand, can be broadcast live and unrecorded. In fact, one way of looking at electronic media such as radio and television is that in their purest forms they are not storage technologies at all—once they are broadcast they have absolutely zero longevity and cannot be "stored" in any physical sense except through the memories of listeners or viewers. Imagine living in a world in which every television show, every news broadcast, and every song on the radio was done live over the air, with no way to go back and listen or watch again unless it was performed again.

random-access memory [RAM]

Usually used for a type of computer memory and abbreviated to RAM, in storage-technology terms it is a type of medium that allows for a reader or viewer to randomly obtain specific pieces of content by doing searches, using an index, or taking some other action.

 ## Social and Political Impact of Storing Information

Canadian media scholar Harold Innis and his famous protégé Marshall McLuhan formulated well-known hypotheses about the longevity and portability of media and their resulting cultural meanings. It is worth reading McLuhan's book *Understanding Media: The Extensions of Man* (with Lewis H. Lapham) or Innis's *The Bias of Communication* for a detailed understanding of how the life span and portability of a medium might affect its nature and role in a society.

The storage capacities of nonelectronic media brought their own challenges and influences over millennia, as did the storage of electronic media once recording became available. Digital media, and their capacity for easy random-access memory, have also brought many changes. The ability to easily store and find digital information has become one of the most important aspects of turning the Internet into a fully developed mass medium, and companies such as Google, which were created to help people search for information, are now global media behemoths.

▼ STONE TABLETS TO PAPYRUS

Innis argued that from papyrus to printing, the social and political development of the Western world has been profoundly shaped by the qualities of media-storage technology. Civilizations that used stone or clay tablets, such as Babylon, tended to favor centralized administrative systems where knowledge was concentrated in the hands of a few powerful elites—either religious or political leaders, or both. The formulation of written laws, such as Hammurabi's Code in Babylon, is an example of how the advent of writing and recording in clay tablets affected the development of civilization.

Papyrus lent itself to political organization of a different kind that allowed more decentralization, as written laws and other information could be easily distributed, thus facilitating the development of early civilizations such as that of ancient Egypt. It also assisted commerce, as records of business transactions could easily go from one place to another, enhancing the development of ancient trading civilizations such as Phoenicia.

▼ VELLUM TO PAPER

In the Middle Ages, the adaptability of the alphabet to printing became the foundation for literacy, advertising, and trade. Equally important as the development of printing, however, was the creation of paper. Prior to the invention of paper, documents were written on vellum or parchment, which were time consuming and expensive to create. Paper was initially made in China in the second century CE and gradually arrived in Europe via the Middle East hundreds of years later.

Paper was also relatively expensive to produce, being made of a combination of wood pulp and cloth rags, and had to have a good balance of absorbency for the ink, smoothness to make sure images and text could be printed, and sturdiness to make sure it wouldn't disintegrate in the publishing process. It wasn't until the nineteenth century that the cost of paper dropped dramatically, when steam-powered paper mills could make paper solely out of wood pulp. This of course led to cheaper printed products and more widespread distribution of books, magazines, and newspapers.

▼ THE KITCHEN DEBATE TO WATERGATE

Although electronic media have a much shorter history than nonelectronic media, the ability to record and store them has already had significant impacts in the twentieth century. It has played a role in making or breaking political careers, spurring urban riots, and winning (or losing) court cases.

A dramatic example is the so-called kitchen debate in 1960, the height of the cold war. U.S. vice president Richard M. Nixon, who himself would later become president, was visiting the Soviet Union. While there, Nixon met with Soviet premier Nikita Khrushchev. An impromptu debate occurred between Khrushchev and Nixon while the two were touring an exhibit of home appliances in Moscow. Thanks to the "miracle" of recently invented

The impromptu "kitchen debate" between then vice president Richard Nixon and Soviet premier Nikita Khrushchev is an example of how recorded television could give prominence to a single event.

portable magnetic-videotape recorders, the "kitchen debate" was caught on videotape and subsequently replayed to 72 million TV viewers in the United States.

Fourteen years later, Nixon was again at the nexus of recording technology. In 1974, Nixon resigned after audiotapes (despite missing portions of recordings) documented his role in the 1972 cover-up of the break-in of the office of the Democratic National Committee, located in the Watergate building. Because of the publicity of the scandal, which sent several of Nixon's aides to prison, any incident today that has the whiff of scandal gets the "-gate" suffix attached to it.

▼ RODNEY KING TO THE OVAL OFFICE

In 1991 an amateur videotape of Rodney King being beaten by the L.A. police led to riots in that city. This tape provided a record of the controversial use of force by police in arresting an African American suspect. It also offered the entire U.S. population a window into the simmering racial tensions of the second-largest city in the country—in addition to showing how portable video-recording technology made recording events much more ubiquitous.

In 1998, Linda Tripp's secret audio tapings of her telephone conversations with White House intern Monica Lewinsky led to a sex scandal involving President Bill Clinton. After a major investigation by the Office of the Independent Counsel, on December 19, 1998, President Clinton was impeached by the U.S. House of Representatives, but he was acquitted of impeachment charges by the Senate two months later.

▼ EMAIL TO FACEBOOK

Email has played an increasingly important role in recent years in court cases and political scandals. Although emails can be deleted from inboxes, they actually can be recovered in many cases. Partly to get around this, some high-ranking members in George Bush's White House, such as Karl Rove, used alternative email accounts to conduct White House business, which is forbidden.

Republican vice-presidential candidate Sarah Palin and members of her staff were also accused of using Yahoo! accounts to conduct government business, knowing that these accounts could not be accessed in the way that government email accounts could be. A minor scandal erupted several weeks before the 2008 presidential election when a University of Tennessee student correctly answered Governor Palin's security questions on her Yahoo! account and accessed her emails.

Social networking sites such as Facebook have also shown the potential ramifications of information storage, with many stories of recent college graduates being embarrassed during job interviews when potential employers asked about photos or posts found on their Facebook pages. The beating death of Egyptian businessman Khaled Said by two Egyptian police officers in June 2010 and subsequent dissident Facebook page, We Are All Khaled Said, created around the incident and showing cell phone photos of Said in the morgue, is credited as being one of the major forces that helped Egyptians bond when protesting and eventually ousting President Hosni Mubarak.

Mark Zuckerberg, founder of Facebook. We have yet to understand the ramifications of our ability to store and publish information on social networking sites like Facebook.

Managing Information

We have become used to rapid changes in technology, and particularly to changes in storage capacity, so that we take developments largely for granted. But the gains in storage technology, especially storage capacity, are happening with a speed previously unseen in the development of media.

A **byte** (pronounced BITE) is eight bits of data, such as 0110011, and is the common unit used to denote memory storage. The standard sizes most people are familiar with are kilobyte (KB, or 1,024 bytes), megabyte (MB, or 1,024 KB), and gigabyte (GB, or 1,024 MB). Note that the increases in storage capacity are exponential. That is, a gigabyte doesn't store two thousand times more than a kilobyte, but a *million* times more (i.e., a thousand thousands). Terabyte-level (TB, or 1,024 GB) storage capacity is already available in some computers and will soon become standard in desktop PCs. Petabyte (PB) and exabyte (EB) are the next two higher levels, with 1 exabyte storing a billion times that of a gigabyte. The CD stack to the moon of our stored information mentioned earlier equals approximately 295 exabytes—and that was for 2007. The USC researchers estimated that storage capacity of computers worldwide doubles every 18 months.

With such rapid and dramatic changes in storage capacity come new problems in figuring out how to manage the information we have available. Three main trends can be seen in the development of digital storage: miniaturization, increased storage capacity, and greater importance of using search functions to find information. With miniaturization comes increased portability, especially when considering the amount of information that is transported. Increased capacity has led to many changes in how we interact with media, ranging from listening to music to watching television on a digital video recorder (DVR). In order to find the information we want we rely on increasingly sophisticated search engines to give us relevant results, which has become important for advertising and media companies.

▼ DEVELOPMENT OF DIGITAL STORAGE DEVICES

A first step toward automated computation and digital storage of various types of data was the introduction of punched cards, which were first successfully used in connection with electromechanical computing in 1890 by Herman Hollerith when he worked for the U.S. Census Bureau. Hollerith developed a device that could automatically read census information that had been punched onto a card, an idea developed from watching a train conductor punch tickets. Hollerith later went on to establish his own firm to market his electromechanical tabulator—a company that later became International Business Machines (IBM).

Punched cards continued to play an important role in computing well into the 1980s, but the development of magnetic recording technologies in the 1950s would gradually play a more dominant role in computing. However, the low storage capacity of magnetic tape initially limited its usefulness. The first hard-disk computer shipped by IBM in 1957 had a combined storage capacity on fifty disks of 56 MB, not even enough for computers today to run Windows 7 operating system.

The trend toward increased portability and capacity is evident in the development of the floppy disk, which first appeared in 8-inch format, then 5.25-inch, and finally in 3.5-inch format, each time increasing its storage capacity even as it got smaller. Today, most computers do not even come with floppy

byte

The most common base unit used to measure computer storage and information, it consists of eight bits, in a combination of 0's and 1's, to form letters, numbers, and all modes of computer information that are displayed.

Early computers used tape to store information and required their own rooms, making them seem like impractical media devices for the general public.

Development of Digital Storage Media

1957 IBM ships first hard-disk computer with total capacity of 256 MB on fifty disks.

1971 Floppy disk introduced, initially in 8-inch format (later in 5.25- and then 3.5-inch).

1982 Sony and Philips introduce the CD-ROM, the first optical, digital storage medium.

1997 DVD introduced.

1999 Portable MP3 players introduced.

1999 First consumer DVRs, ReplayTV, and TiVo debut at the 1999 Consumer Electronics Show in Las Vegas.

2000 IBM sells first USB flash storage drive.

2001 Sony introduces the USB memory stick.

2007 Hitachi introduces the first 1 Terabyte (1,000 GB) computer hard drive

2008 Blu-ray high-definition DVR adopted as standard.

2011 Forty percent of U.S. households have a Digital Video Recorder (DVR)

2011 IBM Supercomputer Watson, which beat the human Jeopardy champion, uses 16 TB of RAM.

disk drives, as other portable memory devices such as flash cards, SD cards, memory sticks, or USB drives have more capacity and are even smaller than disks. A 2 GB USB drive, for example, holds the equivalent of nearly two thousand 3.5-inch floppy disks.

Optical storage devices such as CDs or DVDs also show remarkable increases in storage capacity, even though they have generally stayed the same dimensions. DVDs became the first optical storage medium to be able to store an entire full-length movie and within ten years of being introduced had largely replaced the standard storage device for movies to that time, the videocassette, which itself had been in households only since the mid-1970s.

Developments continue in storage technology, including research into **nanotechnology** and quantum computing. "Nanotechnology" refers to ultrasmall technology, involving devices built or operating at nanometer sizes, or one billionth of a meter. Nanotechnology promises to transform a variety of fields, including electronics, manufacturing, and information storage and retrieval. Nanotechnology may one day produce the only viable information-storage media capable of storing massive quantities of data on incredibly miniature devices. This means that the contents of the entire Library of Congress of the United States, the largest library in the world, could be stored on a single device no larger than the tip of a finger.

Because of its enormous potential, researchers expect nanotechnology to be an increasingly significant part of information storage and other fields in the twenty-first century. In 2000, the National Nanotechnology Initiative (NNI) was formed with eight federal agencies with the goal of cooperating on research and development and creating broad regulatory standards and directions for future research. Today there are 25 federal agencies involved in NNI, with a 2012 federal budget for NNI of $2.1 billion.

optical storage

Uses light in the form of lasers to store and read data of all types, whether text, audio, or video. Using light is highly efficient: it permits storage devices to record vastly greater amounts of data in small spaces and enables faster retrieval of the stored data than from magnetic storage devices.

nanotechnology

A cutting-edge field of technology research that involves items that are nanometers (10^{-9} meters) in length and that promises to revolutionize many fields, ranging from electronics to information storage and even medicine.

MP3 players utilize the digital format of the same name to put music files into a manageable size with decent sound quality.

▼ COMPRESSION OF DIGITAL AUDIO AND VIDEO

The technological development of digital storage and distribution has not proceeded at an even pace. As our ability to store information digitally increases, our desire to store more memory-hungry content such as audio and video seems to increase as well.

What has not kept pace with increases in storage capacity is the storage capacity of the lines, or "pipes," to people's homes that transmit that data between users in a network. This is one reason why it is necessary to compress digital data. A useful analogy might be the need to roll up and stuff a sleeping bag into its original carrying case in order to easily haul it from one campsite to another. Once it is finally in a compact form, it can be carried relatively easily. And, like the contortions and struggles that go into cramming a down sleeping bag into a space the size of a small pillow, engineers have had similar troubles trying to compress audio and video so they too can be easily transported.

MPEG, or the Moving Picture Experts Group, was established in 1988 and is also the name for the encoding process used to compactly represent digital video and audio for general distribution. MPEG compresses, or squeezes, the video or audio by removing any redundant information from one frame of video or segment of audio to the next. In other words, it removes the part that doesn't change and only transmits the part that changes from frame to frame or segment to segment.

The audio component of MPEG-1 (Moving Picture Experts Group-1, Audio Layer III) emerged in the mid-1990s as an ad hoc standard for pirated digital audio and is today known simply by its nickname, **MP3**. There are other MPEG formats being developed and used that have different capabilities. MPEG-21 represents the convergence of all the existing MPEG standards, integrated into an international digital standard for the twenty-first century. The standardization of MPEG-21s is to be agreed upon by early 2012 and will likely contain important specifications about digital rights management.

▼ THE ROLE OF SEARCH ENGINES

With vast amounts of information available to us at the touch of a few keys, finding and retrieving the information that we want becomes a crucial issue. It serves little purpose if a library is stored in the space of a desktop computer if the books are essentially randomly scattered across the library floor.

Google is a prime example of how search engines have become immensely powerful in today's media landscape. Starting as a search engine company in 1998, it has quickly grown into an Internet and media powerhouse that rivals or exceeds older and more established media companies and software giants. As Google's services have expanded from simple web page searches to searches for images, blogs, academic texts, people, automatic translation, and many other areas, it has become more central to users' experience of the Web. Microsoft realized the importance of search engines and launched its own search engine, Bing, in 2009.

As search engines become the primary portals for many users when they begin to look for information on the Web, search engine advertising has developed. For many companies, showing up on the first page of Google, or showing up as the first listing on Google, has become an important means of driving traffic to the website and of business success.

Paid search listings or sponsored links have been one way search engines like Google make money. These can include **keyword auctions**, in which companies bid for relevant keywords and then pay the search engine company a certain amount every time that link is clicked. **Search engine optimization (SEO)** and **search engine marketing (SEM)** have joined the toolbox of skills needed for modern marketers alongside traditional advertising techniques.

Search engines often use "spiders," or intelligent agent programs (sometimes called "bots," which is short for "robots"), to search the Web for content, thus compiling databases or snapshots of Web pages. Despite the apparent vast stores of websites found on the likes of Google, Yahoo!, and Bing, none of the search engines actually captures more than a fifth of what is on the Web—some argue even much less, with the rapid expansion of content every day. Google is by far the most popular search engine, at about 70 percent, with Yahoo! and Bing making up about 15 percent and 10 percent, respectively. Other search engines such as Ask make up 2 percent or less.

In 2008, Google was able to show through compiled results of its search engine queries that it could predict flu trends in given areas up to two weeks earlier than traditional flu predictors.[1] This shows the power of data aggregated simply from search terms, and the knowledge that can be gained from it, as well as the increasing importance of search engines in how we try to make sense of the complex media and information environment today.

▼ SOCIAL AND POLITICAL IMPACT OF INFORMATION OVERLOAD

The social and political impact of our increasing ability to create and store information is vast, though it rarely surfaces as a public topic. We have already discussed the issues around being able to store information in formats that will be accessible to future generations, but there are also important issues around how we make sense of the information we currently have available to us and who has access to it.

The problem of dealing with the enormous amounts of information available to us is known as **information overload**. It affects everything from the ability of government agencies to act rapidly on intelligence they have gathered, or to combine intelligence from different sources to discern a pattern, to workers being able to share relevant knowledge within companies. It has become commonplace in meetings for participants to text or email while someone is presenting or speaking, and this lessened attention to the speaker has resulted in missed important information and misunderstandings, as well as being considered rude.

Some say information overload has also affected the quality of student work and even students' understanding of how to conduct research and synthesize information to create new ideas. There have been cases in which college students have submitted research papers that are simply cut-and-paste pastiches of material taken from different websites—sometimes different font styles from the original sources have not even been changed in the final papers. Even for students who realize this is not how to actually write a paper, it can be difficult to discern trustworthy sources of information on the Web.

Some people claim that the constant interruptions typically seen in the workplace have hampered productivity and creativity, with tasks taking longer to complete

WEB LINK
Yahoo!
www.yahoo.com

WEB LINK
Ask
www.ask.com

WEB LINK
Dogpile
www.dogpile.com

WEB LINK
Bing
www.bing.com

keyword auction

One method in search engine marketing in which companies bid for words and pay the search engine a certain amount every time the word is searched and their listing is clicked on.

search engine optimization [SEO]

A strategy that utilizes website design, careful choice of keywords, links, and other techniques to show prominently in online searches.

search engine marketing [SEM]

Paying a search engine such as Google to have a listing appear prominently when searched.

information overload

The difficulties associated with dealing with the vast amounts of information available to us and making sense of it.

than in the past and workers showing a reduced ability to concentrate for any length of time to tackle complex problems. Email has been considered a main culprit in information overload. One company claimed in 2007 that firms waste approximately $650 billion a year because of information overload, just from the interruptions caused by email.[2]

The Importance of User Interface

user interface

The junction between a medium and the people who use it.

The term **user interface** is a technological way of referring to the junction between a medium and the people who use it. We are usually familiar with our everyday media and so don't give user interface a second thought. Nobody has to remind us how to turn a page in a book, for example, or how to find the sports section in the newspaper, or tune a radio dial.

However, it is easy to forget that the knowledge of using everyday media was learned. Watch a baby with a children's book to see how she explores the book. She chews the corners of the book, holds it upside down, shakes it, tears pages, and randomly goes through the book. It does not take long for babies to figure out that they should turn the pages in sequence, even long before they can actually read.

Comparing a baby exploring the world with rational, thinking adults might not seem completely fair. But consider a case in which many adults are left as helpless as a baby: programming a DVD player. Or think about the last time you were able to immediately turn on someone else's television and stereo system with their remote control. Chances are you needed to ask for help in doing so, even though it was likely just a matter of pushing a couple buttons. But knowing which buttons to push in what order made all the difference.

Computers, because of their relative complexity and their newness for most people, make us even more aware of user-interface issues. Even something as simple as using a mouse is a completely new and nonintuitive experience for a computer novice, let alone the functions that right-clicking a mouse or double-clicking can accomplish. Even after the mechanics of mouse clicking have been mastered, there is still an entirely new world of user control with the interface that must be learned, including the concepts of adjusting window sizes and moving or hiding windows within the screen.

Audiences have long been accustomed to using traditional media to receive content. But they are not "users" of traditional media in the same sense that they are users of a computer to run applications such as word processing, a web browser, or email. With the rise of digital media, the audience consists of more active users, and the interface has become a key element in shaping that use.

The interface transformation is in many ways about empowering the user, or audience. The user is critical to the future of mass communication. The user interface, or how the user interacts with a medium or its content, is a cornerstone for media success. If a user cannot find her way to a website or cannot get the information she wants when she needs it, then even great media content will essentially be unusable.

Learning how to cope with the vast amounts of information available online and the different ways the information is presented is a major hurdle for some people.

Dos and Don'ts When Evaluating Online Information

The Internet is full of hoaxes, cranks, scams, and cons. The up-to-the-minute, 24/7 nature of news on the Web, and its low-cost distribution, make it an ideal place for misinformation to spread quickly because facts cannot always be quickly verified. Adding to the confusion are hacking attacks, such as the 2011 hack on Fox's Twitter account that made it seem like the news site was announcing that President Obama had died.

How do you know when you are being fed a line when online?

Your guide to the names behind the news.

- Do check the About Us section of a website to find out background information on who runs it. Do they clearly state their mission, what they stand for, and who any sponsors are, or do they seem evasive and unclear? If in the latter category, they may not be on the level as to their real purpose.
- Do check what other sites they link to in a Useful Links page and scan what those sites stand for. Most websites link to others who share their views or at least will have more similar-minded links than links to opposing websites.
- Do compare the information in the website with similar stories in other websites, both from branded news names and from smaller sites. If

you receive information that a well-known or respected group has made an important announcement, check the organization's website, as they should have that information posted as well.

- Don't trust the name of the organization who owns the website. Lobbying groups and other organizations that are trying to push a specific agenda will often adopt names that mask their true goals or put them in a euphemistic light, or will create front groups to hide their real goals. SourceWatch, a project of the Center for Media and Democracy, is one good website to visit to learn more about the names behind the organizations that appear in the news.
- Don't immediately trust information that does not have a date somewhere on the page. Information that may have been accurate when it was first posted may well be out of date when you come to the site.
- Don't trust information you read from discussion groups, online chat rooms, blogs, tweets, or Usenet, even if the person making the post claims to be an expert or authority on the subject. As the famous New Yorker cartoon of a dog sitting at a computer saying to another dog said: "On the Internet, nobody knows you're a dog."

To be practical, the user interface should be intuitive and natural yet appropriate to the medium and its content and customizable to each user's preferences. This is why the user interface is critical to mass communication in the digital age.

Current Problems with User Interface

There are advantages to a simple, unchanging user interface. The user always knows what to expect, always knows where to find things, and doesn't need a user's guide each time she tunes in a new channel, reads a different newspaper, or opens a new book. As long as the user interface is well designed, a static design offers efficiency to the user. Traditional media have had decades, even centuries, to create the most efficient user interface. They have evolved over time into highly effective systems.

This is unfortunately not the case with digital media and the Internet. User interface has become a critical issue for a number of reasons. First, digital media are still relatively new and have not had time to evolve. Second, rapid advances in technology may radically alter any user-interface assumptions that are made. Think of how different content may appear in a world in which tiny screens on cell phones with keypads are the primary method of accessing media, as opposed to one in which there are large, flexible screens that can be put up almost anywhere. Third, varying computer standards mean not all technology is accepted, so what may appear in one web browser may not appear correctly—or at all—in a different, or older, web browser. Finally, audience members too often remain media illiterate from a technological standpoint, making them unable to access media simply because they do not understand how to do the online equivalent of turning a page in a book. To be fair, it is not always the public's fault; poor or confusing design decisions by website designers frequently create confusion.

However, most of these problems will eventually sort themselves out as people become more familiar with digital media and as technology becomes easier to use. It will likely take some time, however, and will happen only after many stops and starts. These kinds of problems are to be expected with digital media, which fundamentally challenge the centuries-old model of a relatively noninteractive system and a static user interface that has gone unquestioned.

◤◥ Development of the Digital User Interface

From a historical perspective, the evolution of the electronic user interface, or how people access electronic mass-communication content, began with the development of radio and television, two important electronic media whose "user" interfaces were critical to their success.

Before the development of the computer, we did not generally employ the term "user interface" in discussions of the media. This is because the traditional analog media were not designed to be interactive, and what we call the user interface was generally unchanging. It was easy to understand how to turn a dial or push a button to receive content, which appeared in the same way everywhere it was broadcast.

There are two main elements in the development of the electronic user interface. One is the technological innovations that have led to how we use computers and other devices in the modern era. The other element is social, or getting people accustomed to using new technologies in a mass-communication context. We will look at an example that combines both elements in order to better understand the evolution of user interface and how it influences our media usage today.

▼ THE TELEVISION SCREEN

cathode-ray tube (CRT)

A device that is still used in most television screens and computer monitors in which electrons are transmitted to a screen for viewing.

Until recent years, with the rise of flat-panel displays, desktop computer monitors used **cathode-ray tube (CRT)** technology identical to that in a TV. Technology improvements in computer monitors, once they became the standard interface with computers, have largely been driven by the desire for more of the televisual qualities that we have come to expect from screens, such as color, a certain dimension, and crisp images.

Because computer monitors largely adopt the screen **aspect ratio** of television screens, that has affected a great many subsequent design and user-interface choices. The fact that a "page" of text cannot be seen and read in its entirety on a screen sometimes bothers new computer users, for example, who would like to see at a glance where items are spaced on a page *and* read text at the same time. For word processing, it would seem more natural to have a vertically oriented screen, as if the standard monitor were turned on its side.

When people watch movies on their computer monitors or flat-panel screens, the aspect ratio also has an effect on how these appear, since the aspect ratios of films are different than television (thus forcing movies on television to either cut off part of a scene or keep the original aspect ratio but have black spaces above and below the scenes).

It is interesting to note that although computer makers originally borrowed from television in creating monitors, television has returned the favor in borrowing from the online world of screen windows, scrolling text or tickers, and multiple items on various topics on a single screen. This can especially be seen in newscasts.

▼ TELEVISION AND REMOTE CONTROL

The TV remote control is not only one of the most important transformational technologies in television but has also often been the source of friction between the sexes and among family members. In many households, the person who wields the remote control wields the power.

The first TV remote control was introduced in 1950.[3] Zenith introduced the Lazy Bones, a remote control connected by a wire to your TV set. In 1955, Zenith introduced the Flash-matic, the first wireless TV remote, which used a flashlight to change channels. Then in 1956, Zenith's Space Command (remember, it was the dawn of the space age) used ultrasound to change channels but also produced unfortunate reactions among household pets. Most modern TV remote controls use infrared technology.

The remote control, besides being one of the earliest examples of consumers using wireless technology in the home (along with the radio), had important effects on TV viewers. Perhaps most importantly and obviously, it enabled easy channel changing. Before the remote control, viewers had to get up and walk to the set to change the channel, which significantly inhibited channel changing. The remote control altered viewing habits, as viewers could now easily move back and forth between channels, or "channel surf," and avoid commercials or uninteresting segments in programs or simply watch multiple sports events. In other words, they were almost effortlessly interacting with their televisions, albeit in a very limited way because of course they could not actually change the nature of the content they were receiving.[4]

In addition, frequently changing channels could be considered a simple form of **multitasking**, a common phenomenon in the computer environment in which people do several simultaneous activities. Less patience in watching content can also be seen in the way computer users access a number of different media outlets in pursuing their objectives without spending a long time on any specific item.

However much remote controls are taken for granted today, they did play an important role in subtly altering and expanding the parameters of media usage. The computer of course has played a much more prominent role in bringing user-interface issues to the forefront of mass communication.

aspect ratio

The ratio of a screen's height to its width. Incompatible aspect ratios of films and television mean that either films have to be cropped to fit within a television screen, or, in order to keep the original aspect ratio, black borders must appear on the top and bottom of the screen.

Remote controls have grown increasingly complex as we have gained more functions and channels on our television sets.

multitasking

In a computer environment, doing several activities at once with a variety of programs, such as simultaneously doing word-processing, spreadsheet, and database work while conducting real-time chat through an instant-messenger service.

▼ THE COMPUTER INTERFACE

Since computers and humans use different languages, some kind of interface, or "translator," is needed to allow communication between the two. In the earliest days of computing, the user interface was anything but simple. Usually, only the inventor or a highly trained specialist could operate a computer, interact with it, or access information contained within it.

Data were entered on punch cards, often requiring hundreds of cards to represent even a simple piece of information, such as a series of numbers or names. The output of a computer analysis was typically printed on paper, which might take many minutes or even hours with a slow dot-matrix printer. If computers were to be more useful for people, they needed not only to become more powerful but also to develop a better interface both for inputting information and for output.

From the 1970s, personal computers started having electronic monitors, which were generally monochrome, either a black screen and white text or a black screen with luminous green text. The display let users input information or see output without having to wait for a printout.

The development of speakers for use with a computer was critical to creating a full, multisensory experience for the user. This laid the foundation for a multimedia computer. Today, it is practically standard for every computer to have an electronic display with audio capability and a built-in camera. All this makes a computer a potentially complete digital media–production facility, with the proper software.

▼ THE CREATION OF INTUITIVE INTERFACES

In the 1960s, an important series of advances were made in the computer user interface. Most of these developments helped make the computer simpler and more natural, or intuitive, to use, more efficient to work with (i.e., to enter information and access information contained in the computer), and more capable of dealing with multimedia content such as audio, video, photos, and graphics. The process is still evolving even today as improvements and refinements are made in the interface methods discussed below.

Keyboards

Typewriters were developed in the 1870s as a way to make writing faster. At first, the typewriter keyboard was arranged alphabetically, but it turned out this was a poor design since some keys were used more often than others and, if typed too quickly, would jam together. Instead, Christopher Latham Sholes developed what is known as the QWERTY keyboard (after the first row of letters in the upper-left-hand corner of the keyboard), which has the most frequently typed keys spread far apart (such as "a" and "t"). The QWERTY keyboard slows down the user and prevents the keys from jamming in a typewriter.

Jamming keys became a nonissue with the invention of electric typewriters, but the QWERTY keyboard was by then standard and is what most people are trained on today. Since there are no keys to jam on a computer keyboard, it would make far more sense to have a keyboard that is designed for maximum typing efficiency. Unfortunately, the QWERTY keyboard is a standard part of the computer user interface, and such legacies are very hard to change, even when changing them would greatly improve things.

The Dvorak keyboard is designed for maximum typing efficiency. Created by August Dvorak in the 1930s, the keyboard allows the user to type more than

The Dvorak keyboard is much more efficient for typing than the standard QWERTY keyboard, greatly increasing typing speed and accuracy.

three thousand words without reaching with the fingers. The standard QWERTY keyboard can be reprogrammed to the Dvorak layout quite easily. The software to automatically reprogram a QWERTY keyboard is available for free downloading. Once the keyboard has been reprogrammed, the user simply installs new key caps with the letters corresponding to the new layout as needed.

WEB LINK
Switch Your Computer to Dvorak
www.mwbrooks.com/dvorak/support.html

Beyond the specific inherited inefficiencies in the QWERTY design, the keyboard in general suffers from other drawbacks as an intuitive interface. First is the need for literacy to understand its use and second is the need for typing

WEB LINK
"As We May Think"
www.theatlantic.com/unbound/flashbks/computer/bushf.htm

training in order to use it more efficiently. An intuitive interface does not require hours of training. A keyboard is also slower as an input device than simply speaking to a computer, for example.

As computers and other media devices have become smaller, the keyboard has also proved to be a limited input device, as keys can become no smaller than what can be comfortably pressed with fingers or thumbs. Small keyboards often leave users with cramped hands or cause them to hit the wrong keys. One benefit the keyboard does have over some other types of interfaces is the ability to input information privately. Typing, unlike a voice interface, can be done without disturbing others in the vicinity.

Computer Mouse

A major development in the evolution of the intuitive computer user interface occurred in 1968 when Douglas C. Engelbart invented the computer mouse. His invention was made of wood and was used with a companion keyboard. The germ of the idea came in 1945, during World War II. Engelbart worked as a radar technician in the South Pacific, and he realized the potential for people to interact with a monitor. His inspiration came while reading a now-classic article in the July 1945 edition of the *Atlantic Monthly* by Vannevar Bush, then science adviser to President Harry S Truman, titled "As We May Think." The article discussed how the computer could be a desktop tool to help people in their work.

Engelbart initially proposed his idea for a better computer user interface in an article in 1963 when he wrote that through a better-designed computer interface, "people could cope better with complex, urgent things." His vision involved creating better intuitive tools for people to interact with and control the information they input,

A Better Mouse, the first mouse that changed the computer interface to one of pointing and clicking rather than simply typing.

access, and process in a computer. The computer mouse was one of the most important tools he developed for implementing his vision. The mouse allowed the computer user to easily manipulate data in the computer, pointing and clicking as desired.

The mouse is important for mass communication because it makes it easier, not only for content producers to work more effectively and quickly, but for the audience to access and obtain information. Despite the huge leap in creating a more intuitive interface that the computer mouse represents, it still has its limitations. First, the functions of buttons or wheels on a mouse are not immediately clear and have to be learned.

Second, there is still a disjunct between moving a mouse across the desktop and where the cursor actually goes. This is why computer novices often have trouble at first using a mouse—a small hand movement on the horizontal plane of the desk toward the computer actually corresponds to a relatively large upward vertical movement on the computer screen, which isn't initially intuitive. It takes practice to become accustomed to how hand movements translate to cursor movements.

Touch-Sensitive Screens

Another important development in the evolution of a more intuitive computer user interface occurred in 1974. In that year, the Control Data Corporation (CDC) introduced PLATO (Programmed Logic for Automated Teaching Operations), the first computer system to have a touch-sensitive video display terminal.[5]

The importance of a touch-sensitive screen is that it greatly simplifies the **human–computer interaction**. With a touch-sensitive screen, children and adults alike, without any prior training, or even the ability to read, can interact with images or applications by simply touching the screen with their fingers. ATMs are probably the most common example of touch-sensitive screens, as are automated supermarket registers, but the iPhone, iPad, and other PDA and tablet interfaces are also examples of touch-sensitive screens.

Despite being perhaps one of the most intuitive interfaces, there are several drawbacks to touch-sensitive screens as a standard interface. First is the need to be within reach of the screen to touch it, which means large screen sizes would be uncomfortable on our eyes. Second, extremely small screen sizes limit interaction, just as with keyboards, since items that can be manipulated can be only as small as a fingertip can comfortably select. A stylus or other thin device can help overcome this latter drawback, however.

Natural Input Methods

Handwriting, voice recognition, and speech systems are all steps toward providing more intuitive, natural methods of interacting with computers and media content. The first computer that could accept natural handwriting with an electronic stylus was sold in 1979, although it could not translate the text into computer-readable text. This did not occur for almost twenty years.

Although there have been vast improvements from the 1990s, handwriting recognition still has a way to go before it can easily translate a person's natural scrawl into machine-readable text. It will also always have limitations for portable computing devices, as the writing surface must be big enough to write comfortably and so must be at least the size of a small notepad.

One of the most natural, or intuitive, user interfaces has also been one of the most elusive. Computer voice recognition and speech synthesis have been a hallmark of science fiction for generations and are slowly becoming a central part of the real-world computing environment. Most of the current voice-recognition

human–computer interaction

The general term for any interaction between humans and computers, either through devices such as keyboards, mice, touch screens, or voice recognition.

Communication between computers and humans using natural language remains in the realm of science fiction, although researchers continue to get closer to that goal.

It is easy for Americans, especially, to forget that not everyone speaks English, even as a second language. To date, language has generally not been a major issue on the Internet largely because Internet users have tended to be well educated and able to communicate in English even if it is not their native language.

As Internet use spreads among people throughout the world, it is important to remember that English will soon lose its dominance. Although in 2010 the largest share (26.8 percent) of people online used English as a native or main second language, Chinese speakers are now in second place, with 24.2 percent. While English speakers on the Internet have grown 281 percent between 2000 and 2010, that is dwarfed by the 1,277 percent growth of Chinese speakers on the Internet during the same time. Only Russian, with 1,825 percent growth, and Arabic, with 2,501 percent growth, show the same huge leaps in Internet users.[6]

Even so, Arabic makes up only 3.3 percent of total Internet users while Russian Internet users make up 3 percent. Together, the top ten Internet languages (English, Chinese, Spanish, Japanese, Portuguese, German, Arabic, French, Russian, and Korean) make up more than 82 percent of Internet users worldwide.

As languages other than English proliferate on the Internet, it means that monolingual users could be missing out on huge opportunities to get important information and communicate with others. It also means there could be more conflicts between different groups, as occurred in the popular social-networking site Orkut as Brazilians started to join in higher numbers, speaking among themselves in Portuguese and making English speakers feel left out.

Translation programs are still relatively primitive, doing poor translations at best and incomprehensible, sometimes funny translations at worst. It will likely be a while before automatic translation approaches the level of sophistication of human translators.

Even as the Internet gains more non-English speakers, there is hope for the monolingual English speaker—a growing number of foreign-language tutorials are available online for free or low cost, making it easier than ever to learn a foreign language. Even better for some, a growing number of volunteer translators are willing to fill in the gaps that computer translations miss.

systems are really nothing more than voice typewriters, translating spoken words into printed ones. Some can respond to simple, preset commands, such as "open file," but have no understanding of semantics.

Speech recognition could greatly simplify many interactions with computers, although it is not without its weaknesses as well. One issue, especially for people in urban areas or in public spaces, is noise. Imagine the noise level in a business meeting if everyone had to speak to their computer to input their meeting notes. But on the other hand, imagine the ease if your computer could automatically transcribe a professor's lecture, leaving you free to listen and annotate the notes being transcribed.

Graphical User Interface

The foundation for the modern **graphical user interface**, or **GUI** (pronounced GOO-ey), was created, like so many other computer innovations, at Xerox Palo Alto Research Center (PARC). In 1974 Xerox created the Alto, a computer that used a graphical user interface that allowed users to simply point and click various objects on the screen to access applications or files.

The Alto, apparently ahead of its time, never caught on. It took a visit to Xerox PARC by Apple cofounder Steve Jobs to see Xerox's graphical user interface and to decide to use that with Apple computers. Several years later Microsoft's Windows followed Apple's lead in using a graphical user interface for its operating system.

Prior to the GUI, computer users had to memorize or have at hand a series of arcane commands to open, save, and move files as well as to use applications. When the GUI was introduced, there was a widespread feeling among established computer users that it "dumbed down" computer use and was not a good development, despite (or perhaps because of) its ease of use and the way it opened up computer use to the nontechnical public.

◤◢ The Desktop Metaphor

Most computer users, whether using Macs or PCs, are familiar with the graphical user interface of the computer desktop. Software applications are represented as icons and placed in resizable "windows" within the screen space, which can be layered on top of one another or moved around. Computer files are "placed" in folders that sit on the screen or can be put within other folders.

Some of the earliest graphical user interfaces for the PC even tried to carry the desktop metaphor further, by having images of an actual desk as if the user was sitting at it and with images of items like a Rolodex (for contacts and addresses), file cabinet, and other office equipment to represent various computing functions. These kinds of attempts at realistic user interfaces failed primarily for a couple reasons. One reason was the computing power needed to show detailed 3-D images, which was beyond the capacity of most PCs until recent years, and another reason was that the realistic interface imposed real-world constraints on obtaining and manipulating information that computers would otherwise not have.

Some computer-interface designers have said that the desktop user interface has outlived its usefulness. It was fine in the early stages of GUIs, when computers were less powerful and computer users mostly had text files rather than a range of multimedia types and far less storage for files. But nowadays, the desktop can actually hinder the most efficient way of getting or manipulating information for the user. The office iconography of the standard desktop can also be confusing at first to people who are

Some say the desktop metaphor for computer screens actually hampers our ability to fully utilize the range of information and media types we have today, and these people have created alternative ways to visualize and manage information.

not familiar with such real-world office standards as file folders, printers, or floppy diskettes—the latter of which are rarely used anymore but still often remain as icons for "save." Consider the time spent searching for lost files, either in directories filled with hundreds of various files or in sub sub subfolders of different categories.

There are some interesting attempts to create a better PC user interface that can more fully accommodate the complex media needs of today's computer user. Whether any of these new types of user interfaces will catch on and replace today's desktop interface is impossible to predict. On one hand, users may feel comfortable enough with the desktop icons that they choose not to switch, much as users have grown accustomed to the inefficient QWERTY keyboard layout. On the other hand, user-interface design is still in an early enough stage that a radically new system that makes using a computer much easier could catch on rapidly, just as the GUI garnered widespread use over the command-line interface in a very short time.

◤◢ Implications of User Interface for Mass Communication

The GUI for personal computers and later for the World Wide Web probably had the single greatest impact in changing the public's behavior and attitude toward computers and helped usher in digital media as a competitor to traditional mass-media formats. Once basic knowledge such as what mouse buttons to click or where to search for files was learned, much could be done on a computer even without any technical knowledge. The graphical browser took the Web out of the university labs and into the living rooms of the public.

Interactive maps show the power of combining geographic information with multiple layers of other kinds of information for a richer user experience.

The modern user interface not only changes how the audience can access and utilize information, potentially transforming people from passive media consumers to active media users, it also changes how media organizations must create, produce, and present stories. The GUI holds the potential to bring news, information, and entertainment to audiences in ways that engage, educate, and entertain that were unimaginable with analog media.

Graphical browsers also helped lead to the commercialization of the Web (and some would say its destruction) as businesses sought to reach the growing number of consumers online. Examples of a windowed environment that most computer users are unfortunately all too familiar with are pop-up ads or animated ads that must be closed before one can access content.

For those who are not convinced that user interface has become an important issue, consider the lawsuit filed by the U.S. Department of Justice and eighteen states in May 1998 against Microsoft, accusing the company of violating antitrust laws. One of the key issues was whether Microsoft used its near monopoly of the operating system market (90 percent of PCs run Windows) to unfairly promote its Internet Explorer browser by making it part of the Windows operating system. The case hinged in part on evidence of Microsoft's unfair tactics because its Internet Explorer web browser came bundled with new operating systems while the browser Netscape did not. In the mid- to late-1990s, Internet Explorer rapidly rose in popularity as Netscape declined.

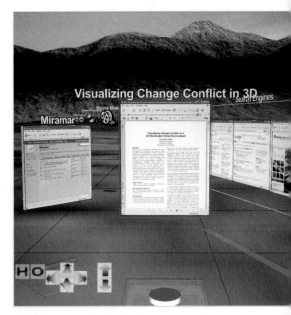

Croquet is an example of a 3-D user interface.

Although Microsoft eventually emerged largely unscathed from the suit, making only minor concessions regarding allowing third-party software with its Windows operating system, for a while during the trial there seemed to be the very real possibility of Microsoft being broken up into three separate companies. What was one of the main factors in an event that could have seen the breakup of one of the world's richest and most powerful computer corporations? An icon in the graphical user interface for the Web.

Interactive Media

The examples of new types of user interfaces exemplify how computers have brought a new dynamic to mass communication—the ability of audience members to interact with content and with each other. This applies not only to changing the desktop background or screen resolution but also to how they get their news and entertainment and even perhaps how they make sense of the world.

In the past, the audience has been limited largely to the role of passive recipient of news and entertainment by the media. Newspapers, magazines, and books could be limited by locale and could only contain a certain amount of news or information. Likewise, radio and television stations covered only specific geographic areas. The advent of cable and satellite television largely eliminated the issue of limited televised content, but the audience was still by and large passive. Media content was sent by a publisher or broadcaster to a large audience that could do little about changing its experience of what was sent, short of not watching or reading at all.

Today, the audience can choose not only the type of content and the media source it comes from but, in many cases, how to experience it. People can choose audio to listen to news while they work on other things, or watch a video clip of an interview, or get the full text transcript of that interview to read later. They can also choose to get the content in a format that they can listen to, watch, or read later.

These are dramatic changes in how the public receives—and perceives—its media. At the heart of these dramatic changes is the notion of interactivity.

▲▼ Interactivity Defined

We will briefly review the definition of interactivity that was introduced in Chapter 2 and explore aspects of each component of the definition in greater depth. Interactivity has the following elements:

1. A dialog occurs between a human and a computer program (this includes emails, online chats, and discussion groups, as at either end of the communication flow a human is interacting with a computer program; the Internet is simply the channel).

2. The dialog affects the nature or type of feedback or content that is received, changing as the dialog continues.

3. The audience has some measure of control over what media content it sees and in what order (getting personalized information, magnifying an image, clicking on a hyperlink, etc.).

The notion of a dialog occurring, either between two or more people or between people and computer programs, is crucially important. Although some have made an argument that traditional media also encourage a kind of dialog as readers or viewers consume content and consider what is being seen or read, it must be said that this level of interactivity simply does not match that of interactive media.

One reason these two kinds of interactivity cannot really be compared is because with traditional media a true dialog does not really occur. The media consumer can "talk to" the media (as people often do to their TVs), but the media cannot actually react. The importance of a sense of dialog is that both parties alter and adjust their messages in response to feedback, thus changing the nature of subsequent messages and modes of communication.

Consider a simple example. You may have a funny story to tell a friend but, upon calling and hearing that he sounds depressed, decide to ask what is wrong rather than launching into your story. The feedback you received altered your message. If you had sent the story as a letter, the receiver would have gotten the message regardless of his state of mind.

The same thing happens in an interactive media environment, not only between users but between computer programs and users. Someone reading a news story may decide to click on a hyperlink of a name within the story because he is not familiar with that person, taking him to another website that describes the person, which in turn may lead to other links to other pieces of interesting information. All of this is essentially "changing the story" for that particular user, who will have a very different sense of it than someone who read the same story but did not click on those links.

Similarly, regarding the third element in our definition of interactivity, two people may have very different impressions of the same story after typing in their zip codes to get personalized or localized information relating to it or viewing a multimedia slide show of the story as opposed to simply reading text or listening to a podcast. In traditional media, the consumer of course cannot switch between one type of medium and another within the same medium, such as listening to a story she is reading in the printed newspaper.

▲▼ The Importance of Interactive Media

Interactive media can present information in a way that encourages users to learn and explore. Online quizzes, surveys, and games are currently being used in many places on the Web, ranging from news to interactive advertising. Many of these examples could be classified as gimmicks, and many are, but that is not the only role that interactivity plays. A far more important component to interactive media is how it changes the media experience for users. As mentioned above, the dialogic nature of interactive media can make our relationship with the media we encounter far more personalized. By making media content more relevant to our lives and individual needs, we become more engaged with it.

Not only do we become engaged with media content, but with interactive media we can become engaged with others through discussion forums, online chat, instant messaging, emails, and other ways. This increased interactivity with each other does not make media content irrelevant in our lives. On the contrary, it could be argued that such content becomes more integrated and relevant to us as it provides much of the fodder for our discussions with each other.

Our concept of what makes a story and our expectations with narrative also change with interactive media. The control in storytelling enjoyed by authors or producers in traditional media could well be a thing of the past in an interactive media environment. Users may have less patience with long, complex stories and be more inclined to take hyperlinked detours as their interests and desires arise. Although with entertainment the story ending may be the same, users may arrive at that destination through a variety of routes that could include experiencing the story through the eyes of different characters or using different media. An example of this could be downloading a novel to an electronic reading device such as a Kindle but then listening to the audio version when unable to read, such as when driving.

Interaction is important for media companies in other ways. Companies can see who has commented on a particular story, how many visitors have come to a story, how long they have stayed there, and what they went to next. This kind of knowledge can be extremely powerful in that it could influence editorial content as publishers seek to attract the most visitors to their websites. A story that gets many more page views than others may tempt publishers to encourage the editorial team to publish more such stories.

On a related note, the ability to interact with the media and share one's opinions or knowledge has embarrassed some news organizations as readers have pointed out errors or bias in news stories. Although newspapers have long had the ability to publish corrections, the lag time, space limitations, and amount of editorial control over what gets an official correction and what doesn't has limited the corrections' usefulness. In an online, interactive environment, readers can see comments and corrections from users along with the story.

The ability to get a sense of what others may be thinking and saying about a particular news story or type of media content greatly democratizes our information environment. It helps us understand others as a kind of community, albeit perhaps a specialized or temporary one. However, it also threatens the traditional power relationship between media organizations and the audience, which has led to some difficult decisions for many media companies in dealing with the newly empowered public in an interactive media environment.

▲▼ Ethics of Interactive Media

The power of interactive media to engage users and get them involved with media content raises a host of interesting ethical issues. Some of these are similar to ethical issues faced in the traditional media world, but amplified, and some are largely new. Some touch on age-old concerns regarding free speech, the role that advertising plays in our society, and basic notions of trust.

Trust is an important concept for interactivity to work well, as users have to learn to trust those they are dealing with on the Web. In face-to-face communication, we pick up on certain cues and mannerisms that help us establish trust with others, but without this social context on the Web we have to rely on what we say to each other and what happens between us through our interactions.

Consider what would happen if you were in a chat room discussion with a number of members over the course of several days, greatly enjoying the discussions and the feeling that you have met some interesting, like-minded individuals. Then imagine your sense of betrayal if you learned that one or more of the participants were actually computer programs that gave context-specific responses to posts by real humans. Your trust in that chat room—and perhaps all chat rooms in which you did not personally know the individual participants—would likely be broken.

Trust between people is similarly relevant, as we expect (or hope) that others will respect our views even if they disagree with us and that they will debate in non-vitriolic ways. Most people know how disruptive an obnoxious poster can be to a discussion group, making others respond angrily to views perhaps spouted simply to draw a reaction, a practice called **trolling**. Not only do such practices degrade the quality of the discussions taking place but they waste others' time in reading and responding.

trolling

The practice of posting deliberately obnoxious or disruptive messages to discussion groups or other online forums simply to get a reaction from the participants.

▼ FREE SPEECH FOR EVERYONE?

We also expect to trust our news organizations to give us accurate and timely information. As news organizations have had to adapt to the world of blogs and an empowered audience, they have also had to deal with issues of free speech, which can sometimes come in the form of hateful speech from the public.

The *Los Angeles Times* was forced to shut down a "wikitorial" site it had created for readers in 2005 because of foul language and inflammatory comments from readers on it, and in 2006 the *Washington Post* was criticized for removing negative comments from readers about a column that had some factual errors in it.

Although critics did not question the need to remove offensive language or posts that were clearly written just to be inflammatory, they did question why the paper also removed many thoughtful, critical comments by readers who pointed out errors in the original column. In a forum on the matter, Jeff Jarvis, a journalist and creator of the media blog Buzzmachine, said, "The age of controlled conversation is over. The age of open conversation is here. But that is damned hard for the controllers to get used to."[7]

The ability for users to post to blogs or news articles and point out errors, spout political opinions, or argue with the journalists or other users has become expected, and media organizations who do not allow this functionality make it seem as if they are still trying to control the conversation by not letting the audience speak. On the other hand, when audiences react in ways that are not deemed suitable for public, civic discourse, it raises questions on who can (or should) control or moderate the conversations.

Interactivity brings the issue of free speech into sharper focus as questions are raised regarding what is protected and what is not. Can a "sucks site" that is dedicated to complaining about a specific company and that has been designed to look like the company's site be an infringement of trademark or an example of free speech?

▼ INTERACTIVE ADVERTISING

The complaints against advertising and the control it is claimed to have in directing our tastes and desires for goods is intensified in an interactive environment. At the forefront of this are video games for children that are created by companies, such as breakfast-cereal manufacturers, that prominently feature their products in the games.

Because of the high level of engagement in video games, which are of course interactive, some groups have been concerned that the hidden commercial messages are being absorbed by children who are not even aware that they are being exposed to advertising.

The level of violence in video games, discussed more in the chapter on entertainment, is also a major concern to some groups who claim that the interactivity in the games influences children more than simply passively watching violence on television.

Behavioral targeting has become an important ethical issue regarding advertising as well. In behavioral targeting, a website tracks your browsing or search behavior and then delivers you advertisements on subsequent web pages that match what you were searching for or looking at. That is why after looking at travel sites

WEB LINK
Buzzmachine
www.buzzmachine.com

you may get advertisements for travel deals on your Facebook page or a personalized home page like My Yahoo! for several days afterward.

▼ SEARCH ENGINE KEYWORDS

A practice largely hidden from the public's perception of how it receives information on the Internet is how keywords are used in search engines. As more and more people go to search engines first to find information, keywords also become increasingly important as pointers to websites.

There have already been several court cases in which companies have claimed that competitors are unfairly using their name or brand in their website **metatags**. Metatags are less important for search results than they were several years ago, but now the competition has shifted to search terms and keywords. A company may choose certain keywords to buy that relate directly to a competitor's business, and if they bid more for the keyword then their site will show up over the competitor's in the paid search engine results. Even without bidding for keywords, companies can use good search engine optimization techniques to increase search rankings.

Being able to trust the results of keyword searches is fundamental to a good user experience on the Web and to interactivity. Without sound ethical principles regarding interactivity, the door is open to abuse, by individuals and companies, that detracts from the overall Web experience for many. If a user types in a keyword and then clicks on a website that showed up first in the search results but is only tangentially related to the keyword, then that damages the user's trust in an important source of information for people online.

metatag

A word or words used by websites to help search engines index and describe a site, typically unseen by humans unless looking at the website's code.

LOOKING BACK AND MOVING FORWARD

Storage of media content, user interface, and interactivity may not seem like typical issues that would affect mass communication, but the fact that they are is yet another signal of the changes that convergence is bringing.

Computing technology changes rapidly, sometimes radically altering the industry and the way people use computers. With the convergence of computing, telecommunications, and media, this means that technological changes can have a strong ripple effect on media and mass communication. One example is how the increase in computer processing power created better opportunities for a graphical user interface and how the GUI then made computers much more accessible to the average person, which helped create large audiences online. It is likely that advances in technology will further alter the way we interact with computers in ways that we cannot foresee.

However, some general patterns can be examined, giving us a sense of what to expect in the future. These patterns fall into the following broad categories: easier accessibility, more immersive media environments, and seamless or fluid interfaces.

Wireless and handheld devices have become more commonplace in recent years and raise important user-interface questions for content on small screens. Flexible, portable **OLED** (organic light-emitting diode) screens will greatly increase accessibility and may mean that users are not confined to small screens on mobile phones. However, even with OLED screens that can be placed on a wall or window, for example, issues of bandwidth may still need to be considered in terms of providing content. If OLED screens do enter the market, they could provide a similar user-interface experience to what we are accustomed to on desktop PCs or laptops.

OLED

Organic light-emitting diode screen, a type of thin, flexible screen that will change how and where we are able to view content on screens.

Douglas Englebart: Visionary of Computing's Future

While a radar technician in the U.S. Navy during World War II in The Philippines, Douglas Englebart read Vannevar Bush's now famous piece "As We May Think" in the *Atlantic Monthly*.

Inspired by Bush's vision of a future in which computers would play a key role in helping people make sense of the growing amounts of information we are confronted with in the modern era, Englebart decided to do what he could to make that vision a reality.

In the 1960s, Englebart and his research team at the Stanford Research Institute (SRI) foresaw and created many of the fundamental elements of user interface and computing as we know them today.

Douglas Engelbart: Visionary of Computing's Future.

Besides inventing the computer mouse (so named because the cord looked like a tail), Englebart and his team developed hypertext, collaborative computing tools, some of the precursors to what would become the graphical user interface (GUI), and were early pioneers on ARPANET, the precursor to the Internet.

Always driven by his vision of computers being tools to help us manage information and even develop our intelligence, Englebart nevertheless spent several years in relative obscurity after philosophical and other disagreements with his researchers. While others saw the future of computing in personal computers, Englebart believed the future of computing and mankind was in collaboration, which computers could help people do in ways that we could not conceive of in the predigital age.

Despite working in relative obscurity in the 1970s and 1980s, he founded the Bootstrap Institute, a series of workshops and seminars, to better see his ideas about computing get more notice and perhaps put into practice, which influenced a new generation of engineers and technologists.

In the mid-1990s Englebart's important contributions to computing finally started to be recognized, and since then he has received numerous honors and awards. In 2000, President Bill Clinton awarded him the National Medal of Technology, the nation's highest award for technology. The Douglas Englebart Institute continues to work on collaborative computing and improving collective IQ with research projects aided by his guiding philosophy on how computers should help mankind.

Geography and location will become more important as more devices are equipped with GPS receivers. From a user-interface perspective, this means that maps will become increasingly important as on-screen graphics that contain layered information. Map-based GUIs can provide everything from information on the nearest restaurant, including reviews, to local points of cultural or historical interest.

Accessing media content will be increasingly easy, but accessing the content one *wants* when and where one wants it may be harder than ever unless sound principles in user-interface design are applied to search-and-find functions.

A variety of forms of immersive media are emerging in the online environment and seeing increased use in a number of ways. These include three-dimensional (3-D) visualizations, virtual reality, 360-degree photography and video, and augmented reality. Immersive media environments can provide media experiences unlike those encountered in traditional media or even in the typical digital media environment and can provide new opportunities—and new challenges—for user interfaces.

Our conceptions today of largely static web pages will gradually be replaced by interfaces that are more fluid and that change to suit our informational and entertainment needs. We will not have to necessarily "go to" a website to get the information we want; rather, we will develop our own personalized home page or site that collects the information we want from various sources. We see the precursors to this with RSS feeds and other tools that "push" content to subscribers.

It is important to remember that the online environment of the future will not simply be one of receiving a variety of media content in different forms, though that will continue to be a large part of it. It will also include various ways to communicate directly with media producers, other audience members, and one's social network. We will expect our user interface to help us receive the kind of information and entertainment we want, but we will also demand that we can easily communicate and interact with others. In fact, interactivity is one of the key characteristics of digital media that not only creates new kinds of user-interface issues but that sets digital media apart fundamentally from traditional media forms.

DISCUSSION QUESTIONS

1. Do you think the characteristics of storage technology have changed in relative importance with the advent of digital media? Why or why not?

2. Imagine a world in which audio and video could not be recorded. Discuss how media would be different in terms of content creation, performance or distribution, media organizations, and economics.

3. Some contend that secretly recording conversations or activities, even when the acts recorded occur in a public space, is a violation of privacy. State and defend your position on the matter.

4. Discuss ways in which you would like to see search engines improved.

5. Consider an instance in which you had difficulty with the user interface of some media device, whether it was a remote control, computer, mobile phone, or tablet computer. Describe the situation and how it was resolved. What could have been done differently from a user interface perspective to avoid the problem?

6. If almost all information were available to anyone at any time on a compact, easy-to-use device, how do you think this would affect the level of people's general knowledge or education? Would people become more knowledgeable and more active in society? Would they become more apathetic, or would they be more or less the same? How might this device affect different people within society, such as rich versus poor, or various ethnic or language groups?

7. Compare the user interface of a newspaper with that of the newspaper's website. What elements are similar and what elements differ? Explain why they may be so.

8. Visit three different websites within a specific industry (i.e., car rental agencies, airlines, or newspapers) and note user-interface differences between them. What elements did you like and dislike about each site? Why? What ways could they be improved?

9. Consider the differences between immediate interactivity, such as pushing a button or discussing on IM, and delayed interactivity, such as email or a discussion board. How does the change in time affect the conversations and relations between people?

FURTHER READING

Understanding Media: The Extensions of Man, reprint ed. Marshall McLuhan, Lewis Lapham (1994) MIT Press.

Bias of Communication, reprint ed. Harold Innis (1991) University of Toronto Press.

A History of Modern Computing. Paul E. Ceruzzi (1999) MIT Press.

Dark Ages II: When the Digital Data Die. Bryan P. Bergeron (2001) Prentice Hall.

Interface Culture: How New Technology Transforms the Ways We Create and Communicate. Steven Johnson (1999) Basic Books.

The Rise of the Image and the Fall of the Word. Mitchell Stephens (1998) Oxford University Press.

About Face 3: The Essentials of Interaction Design. Alan Cooper, Robert Reimann, David Cronin (2007) Wiley.

Designing with the Mind In Mind: Simple Guide to Understanding User Interface Design Rules. Jeff Johnson (2010) Morgan Kaufman.

Don't Make Me Think: A Common Sense Approach to Web Usability, 2nd ed. Steve Krug (2005) New Riders Press.

The Google Story: Inside the Hottest Business, Media, and Technology Success of Our Time. David Vise, Mark Malseed (2006) Delta.

Planet Google: One Company's Audacious Plan to Organize Everything We Know. Randall Stross (2008) Free Press.

Click: What Millions of People Are Doing Online and Why it Matters. Bill Tancer (2008) Hyperion.

MEDIA QUIZ ANSWERS

1. False, it is 1,000 (kilo) bytes.
2. False, cave paintings and petroglyphs are forms of information storage that predate writing systems.
3. Graphical user interface.
4. True, current media like videotape and DVDs are expected to last only about fifty to seventy-five years.
5. False, it stands for MPEG-1, Audio Layer-III.
6. $650 billion.
7. The stack of CDs would reach past the moon.
8. English, Chinese, Spanish.
9. True.
10. Richard Nixon, with his videotaped kitchen debate with Soviet Premier Khrushchev, and then with audiotape and recordings of his discussions about Watergate.

7

NETWORKS AND DIGITAL DISTRIBUTION

LEARNING OBJECTIVES

By the end of the chapter,
you should be able to:

- Outline the characteristics
  that distinguish digital
  distribution from traditional
  forms of distribution of
  media content.

- Explain the implications
  new forms of digital
  distribution have on
  mass-communication
  organizations.

- Describe the historical
  development of
  telecommunications and of
  networks that have created
  the current status of digital
  distribution.

- Discuss the future
  development and potential
  problems of digital
  distribution.

Part of what has made the Internet the powerful communications force that it is today was a firm belief that it should remain open and accessible to all. This basic philosophy of openness held that more people could contribute and add value to the Internet through their creations, whether they were sharing new programs or new ideas.

However, several leading Internet thinkers worry about attempts by governments and corporations to put controls on the Internet. Proprietary "walled gardens" give people inside these gardens the appearance of freedom, but in reality block them from all that the Internet offers. Sergey Brin, co-founder of Google, claimed that today a company like Google could not be started because of a growing number of barriers put forth by companies like Apple or Facebook, who closely guard who can create applications for their services.

Brin admitted he was wrong about his earlier assumptions that the Internet could not be easily controlled, pointing to the example of China and Google's own experiences there. Through a combination of technological and legal means—including agreements with Western companies like Google to limit what kinds of information they provide to users in mainland China—the Chinese government has been able to tightly control what information most Chinese see on the Internet even today.

Chinese citizens have been jailed for posting online photographs of collapsed schools after an earthquake, and for corresponding with foreign journalists or sending information online that the Chinese government deems "harmful information" or "harmful activities." These include activities online such as:

- Inciting division of the country, harming national unification;
- Making falsehoods or distorting the truth, spreading rumors, destroying the order of society;
- Promoting feudal superstitions, sexually suggestive material, gambling, violence, murder;
- Terrorism or inciting others to criminal activity; openly insulting people or distorting the truth to slander people;
- Injuring the reputation of state organizations;
- Other activities against the Constitution, laws, or administrative regulations.

Despite the government's controls, there are still critical voices within China that say the government's policies are unsustainable. One of these is noted artist and activist Ai Weiwei, who was briefly jailed in spring 2011 during a government crackdown of dissidents and then placed under probation for a year.

In a column written for Britain's *The Guardian* newspaper about two months before his probation was set to end in 2012, Ai strongly criticized China's policies on Internet access for its citizens. He said that its policies would put China behind other countries because its citizens do not have the freedom to freely choose their information and think independently and creatively. "The government computer has one button: delete."[1]

He likened the flow of information to rising water levels in a dam. The government cannot control the rising water, only hold it back for a while. "The Internet is uncontrollable," he wrote. "And if the Internet is uncontrollable, freedom will win. It's as simple as that."

The ability to cheaply and easily distribute content to a mass audience, along with the chance for people to interact with each other, is probably the most crucial and visible aspect of how the Internet is transforming mass communication. Computerized production and editing technologies, storage media, and interface design have important implications in a range of areas involving mass communication, but none of these implications would be so great if media distribution had remained only in the hands of a select few media companies.

Digital distribution has gone from a unidirectional model, in the analog world, in which large media companies send out messages to a mass and largely silent audience, to one in which the public can distribute content as widely as an established media company, all without spending money on advertising or marketing.

The continuing battles the recording industry is having over file-sharing services, although framed in terms of intellectual property and copyright infringement, are an issue primarily because of changes brought about in distribution.

The public is behaving no differently than it did prior to the Internet, when a music fan would make an audiocassette copy of an album for a friend or compile songs from a favorite band onto a cassette to be listened to in the car. A primary difference is that, rather than making a couple of tapes and giving them to friends, millions of people can now get free copies of music and send those copies to others throughout the Internet, all with very little effort and almost no cost.

A. J. Liebling once said, "Freedom of the press is guaranteed only to those who own one." With digital media and the Internet, now practically anyone has a "printing press" that can distribute not only printed text but audio or video as well. However, the rapid growth of Internet use has also created a growing divide between the information haves and have-nots. This divide can be seen not only between developed and developing nations, but also among certain groups within developed nations.

In order to understand how these changes have come about, it is important to know how today's telecommunications networks originated and how what we experience with these networks today has many past influences, not all of them beneficial.

Historical Influences on Modern Networks

The telecommunications networks we rely on today for everything from talking with friends to banking have been influenced and shaped by a wide range of social, political, and historical factors. Because these networks generally operate hidden from us, or seemingly invisibly, it is easy to overlook how crucial they are to our media system. But no understanding of media today is complete without understanding how modern networks work and the historical influences that made them what they are today.

One of the fundamental changes that telecommunications networks have brought to our social and political life is what is called **time-space compression**.

time-space compression

The idea that electronic communication has essentially reduced distances between people because of nearly instantaneous communication, which has also "sped up" our notions of time.

REUTERS AND THE CREATION OF THE NEWS WIRE SERVICES

Today we see the name "Reuters" (pronounced ROY-terz) at the beginning of many news stories, along with Associated Press, Agence France-Press, and a handful of other wire services. What is not readily apparent is how these wire service companies were created as a direct result of the development of the telegraph and how they shaped the news we got from the mid-nineteenth century onward.

Israel Bere Josafat was born in 1816 in Germany but later changed his name to Paul Julius Reuter when he converted to Christianity while living in London. Soon after the telegraph was invented, he realized the potential it had for transmitting news quickly and unsuccessfully tried to establish a news wire service in Germany in the 1840s. He moved to London and in 1851 founded Reuters as a financial news service.

Reuters was not alone in seeing the potential for new business models stemming from being able to deliver news, especially financial news, more quickly than ever before. In continental Europe the agency Havas (later Havas-Wolf) and Agence France-Press jealously guarded their control of telegraph lines leading to Asia and the Western Hemisphere. In the United States, the Associated Press wire service had monopoly control on U.S. news.

What's more, eavesdropping on telegraph lines by the competing news agencies was common, so each agency developed elaborate codebooks their correspondents used to transmit their stories. The codebooks served another important purpose; because telegraph companies charged by the letter, brevity was important in saving money on transmission costs so letters were used to represent entire words. In this way complex sentences could be written using a relative handful of letters and abbreviated words.

Reuters, like the other news wire services, focused on financial reporting but also expanded into covering general news and world events. Today, much of the content you read in a newspaper or online likely comes from one of the wire services, who have offices and journalists stationed all over the world. Much of our breaking news comes from wire service reporters, or stringers who are based in the areas they cover.

In 2009 Reuters and Thomson Corporation, an educational and publishing company, merged, forming Thomson Reuters, the largest multimedia company in the world. Thomson Reuters continues to evolve in the digital media world as it creates new products and services for its financial clients even as it continues to adhere to strict codes of objectivity for its journalists.

WEB LINK
Reuters
http://thomsonreuters.com/

This futuristic-sounding term means that networks have "sped up" time and have "shrunk" space. Prior to the invention of the first electronic communication, the telegraph, communication could be distributed no faster than the fastest means of transportation, whether it was a horse, train, or ship.

The slow pace of long-distance communication meant that it was almost impossible for governments such as the British Empire to easily control far-flung colonies. A message from India would normally take several weeks to reach London by ship and of course the same amount of time to get back to India. In the meantime, circumstances might have changed drastically, making the response largely irrelevant depending on what had developed during the interim period.

However, in the early days of the telegraph, it only took a matter of hours for a message to reach London from India through various overland telegraph routes, and that time became less as telegraph connections and technology improved. This "shrinking of space" helped rulers control things much more closely than they had in the past—essentially bringing faraway lands "closer" than they had been before.

Another way to think of how time-space compression works is to consider the effect the cell phone has on us. You may be in a college far from home, but your parents are still able to "be present" through a simple call or text message. Your physical distance may be great, but activities or decisions in one place can instantly affect people in a different place. Your decision to stay on campus over Thanksgiving Break, phoned to your parents, may have an immediate impact on their Thanksgiving plans.

This shrinking of space and speeding up of time had several important repercussions for the media. Timely information became increasingly important in order to make good business decisions. Firms were created to provide timely news and business information, such as the national wire services Reuters and Havas. Companies or countries that were cut out of this informational loop were often at a disadvantage.

In our always-on, almost instantaneous information environment it is hard to imagine the drastic transformations that the earliest telecommunications networks had on society, but by looking at some of the ways their development was influenced we will better understand our networks today and how certain echoes of the past continue to affect us.

▼ GOVERNMENT AND PRIVATE INDUSTRY

An important communications network that existed long before the invention of the telegraph in 1837 was the postal system. Although not typically thought of as a communications network, it nevertheless played a vital role in the colonial era and early years of the United States in disseminating information.

The importance of the postal system as a means to distribute news was understood by the Republic's early leaders, who subsidized newspapers by allowing them to be sent at reduced postal rates. A common practice among newspaper publishers at the time was to directly copy news from other papers (usually without attribution), so news was able to spread much further and much faster than it otherwise would have when newspapers could receive other newspapers cheaply and easily.

The postal system became a government-run service, supported by taxes and charges for deliveries, rather than a for-profit company. The desire on the part of leaders to keep even this rudimentary communications network within government control highlights the importance they gave it. This thinking would have significant implications for how modern telecommunications networks evolved in various countries.

For example, in almost all European countries the telegraph was considered something that should be state-owned—an extension of the mail system—and thus was put within the country's postal service. However, in the United States, the government at first refused to provide funding when Samuel Morse requested it for further work on his nascent telegraph and several years later also declined to offer public money to fund what was called an "information railroad" that would string telegraph lines from coast to coast. Instead, private companies, each trying to establish its own network, strung telegraph wires, and the telegraph was perceived as primarily a network that would operate within a competitive environment of private industry.

There are benefits and detriments in both systems. The private-industry model for the telegraph (and later the telephone) led to chaos in the early years, as competing companies vied for market share and required customers to purchase equipment that was incompatible with other companies' equipment. This led to great waste and hampered the rapid development of the network, at least until some companies either went out of business or merged with other companies.

In the case of the United States, Western Union ended up with a monopoly on the telegraph network. Access to telegraphs could vary greatly; areas that had high market potential had competing services, while large swaths of the country, especially rural areas, did not have any access at all, as the decision to connect an area was based on making a profit. Today, we see similar patterns among telecommunications companies that offer fast broadband connections to some areas long before rural areas or socioeconomically depressed areas in cities or towns get them.

On the other hand, competition also helped lead to rapid technological and service improvements, although (as we have seen) it is not always the case that the best technology wins out in the end. A highly competitive environment does encourage more risk taking and greater innovation as companies try to gain market share through better products or services. Once a monopoly exists, however, the sole company in the market then has little incentive to innovate or remain competitive through service or price.

The government-run model had the benefit of building the network on principles of public service and universal access rather than where the most profitable market is located. Once the government decided on a system, customers could be assured that equipment would work everywhere on the network, ensuring rapid use of the network. Certain costs could also be absorbed within the government system, making the network cheaper to use than it might have been if a company sought a profit.

However, government bureaucracy can often inhibit further development and growth of new technologies that challenge the established system, making change or improvements difficult. The centralized process of decision making can also hamper innovation and the adoption of new technologies.

In the United States, balancing government interests with those of private industry has been especially difficult with communication networks. Government policies have shifted over time, from letting the market decide who wins, to allowing government-granted monopolies to certain companies in a regulated industry—much like how the utilities companies are run. The amount and degree of regulation has been another arena of conflict over the years.

The tension between the public interest in easy and affordable access to communication networks and the drive for profit and business success continues today. We see it in the many government regulations that dictate what telecommunications companies can and cannot do, in the different laws that govern the industry, and in the frequent lawsuits that challenge the status quo. We will see that these are not new, either, and have often gone hand in hand with new communication-network technologies.

▼ EVOLVING TECHNOLOGY: FROM THE TELEGRAPH TO FIBER OPTICS

Technology is of course always changing and evolving. In only a handful of other areas can we see the same dramatic effects that new communication technologies can have on industries, people, and society. The path of evolving communication technologies is not a smooth one and is littered with bitter lawsuits among inventors, technologies that were developed ahead of their time and not adopted, shortsighted government officials, and unintended consequences. It is worth briefly exploring some of these interesting developments.

Telegraphy

The idea of sending information faster than what could be physically transported is as old as smoke signals or lighting fires on mountaintops. However, these earlier systems were extremely limited in terms of the amount of information they could carry and of course depended on the weather.

In 1837, American Samuel Morse created and patented the electromagnetic telegraph, which marked the beginning of today's information age. Morse's invention, building on earlier attempts at electric telegraphy by British inventors, was the first technology that could put information into electric form and transmit it reliably over great distances.

By tapping dots and dashes representing letters on a keypad, in what is now called Morse code, telegraph operators could rapidly spell out messages. Because the cost was higher for longer messages and there was always a chance the wrong people could see a message, businesses quickly adopted a number of abbreviations for commonly used words and phrases, with elaborate codebooks that allowed the recipients to decipher the messages.

Despite what we see today as obvious benefits of getting information quickly, there was not much enthusiasm for the telegraph initially. It was not until 1844 that an experimental telegraph line of forty miles was actually built, between Baltimore and Washington, D.C. The nomination of the Whig Party presidential candidate, Henry Clay, was sent to the capital, and the information age was born.

Many in the newspaper business and businesses in general then realized the important role the telegraph could play in the rapid delivery of news and information. Within the next two decades, telegraph lines quickly spread throughout the country and

Samuel Morse and his telegraph.

throughout Europe. Submarine cable lines across the Atlantic were attempted in the latter 1850s, but it was not until 1866 that the first successful transatlantic cable began operation.

Some scholars have claimed that the telegraph played a direct role in shaping news stories. Because of the unreliability of the early telegraph lines, it was important to write concisely and include the most important facts of a story first, with facts of lesser importance coming later. This led to the style of news writing still practiced today, the inverted pyramid style.

Others have questioned this, however, saying that an analysis of papers from the mid-nineteenth century reveals that stories received over wire and stories received through traditional means had no substantial differences. Both were often written in flowery language using chronological narrative, with little regard to what was most important. These scholars credit Lincoln's second secretary of war, Edwin Stanton, with creating the inverted pyramid style. Stanton's terse missives about Civil War battles were often used directly by U.S. newspapers.

Sometimes it's easy to think that "new media" technologies are truly new and revolutionary. Frequently, the truth is far different. The facsimile, or fax, is a very old technology whose invention coincides with the telegraph. Although it became widely used in the 1980s, the fax was actually invented in 1842 by Scottish philosopher and psychologist Alexander Bain as a way to send images over telegraph wires.

The fax machine, invented by Alexander Bain, is an example of a technology that was developed long before it could be widely used.

It was sometimes used during the U.S. Civil War to send images of maps, but the limited carrying capacity of telegraph wires hampered the facsimile's usefulness.

Telephony

Even as telegraph lines continued to expand, and technological advances allowed for more carrying capacity on the lines, the telegraph quickly faced a serious competitor that would eventually take its place as the most important form of telecommunication.

Bell's 1876 invention of the telephone launched the national system of telephony, which operated much the same as the telegraph except that sounds could be transmitted over the wires. The introduction of the telephone provides an interesting look at how the development of technology has unintended consequences, how advances in technology change and threaten established business models, and how the careful dance between government regulation and corporate interests often contains stumbles.

Bell was not the first person to think of trying to transmit sounds over electrical wires; many people had been working on it ever since the telegraph was unveiled. However, his experience in working with the hearing impaired gave him an advantage over others in understanding how sound, especially the voice, works. His research for the hearing impaired on using technology to amplify sound also played a key role in being able to transmit and receive audible voice messages. Bell did not start out to create a national telecommunications network that would quickly supersede the telegraph network, but that is what happened.

The American Telephone and Telegraph Company (AT&T) and the American Bell Telephone Company existed as regulated legal monopolies for most of their history, based on the principles outlined by former AT&T president Theodore Vail in 1907. He said that the telephone, by the nature of the underlying technology, could operate most efficiently as a monopoly providing universal service. The notion of universal service was present in the age of the telegraph as well, as noted in the suggestion by Ephraim Farley in 1853 that all homes "would be in immediate communication with each other."

Vail and others realized that competing telephone systems, in which users of one telephone system could not communicate with users of other telephone systems, would hurt the growth of telecommunication. This principle guided U.S. telecommunications policy for most of the twentieth century. Although it may well have helped ease the early adoption of telephones (and helped AT&T, whose system was eventually adopted), the monopoly control AT&T had over telecommunications systems also slowed innovation.

In the early 1960s, researchers were attempting to create what would eventually become the Internet and decided that, rather than build an entirely new network, they could simply use the extensive telephone network, controlled by AT&T. However, the structure of the telephone network relied on analog **circuit switching**, which was a centralized system in five-level hierarchies. Messages transmitted through switching centers would degrade in quality, just as third- or fourth-generation videotape dubs degrade the quality of the original recorded video. If a central switching center was destroyed, the entire telephone system could be incapacitated.

The researchers asked AT&T if they could test a digital, **packet-switching** network via telephone lines, but AT&T refused. Paul Baran, who conceived of the Internet's architecture in the early 1960s, said that even when the Air Force offered to give AT&T money to develop a digital, packet-switched network, AT&T said, "It's not going to work. And furthermore, we're not going into competition with ourselves."

Similar to Henry Ford's famous line about choosing a car color, AT&T let customers choose a color for their phones—as long as it was black.

circuit switching

The original system used for telephony, in which circuits connected two people communicating. Once the circuit was connected, or "on," the people on either end of the circuit used the whole circuit exclusively, even if they didn't speak. When they hung up, the circuit was disconnected by an operator and available for others to use.

packet switching

A type of switching within a network, in which information is divided up into pieces, or packets, and transported as separate packets using the least congested routes. At the end of the route the packets are reassembled in their proper order and delivered over the telephone line or Internet.

AT&T was eventually forced to change to digital packet-switching modes and similarly lost its monopoly control over the telephone network in 1984 when the company was split into several regional "Baby Bells" throughout the country. Today, the basic architecture of the telephone system is digital and packet-switched, just like the Internet.

▼ RADIO AND TELEVISION

Just as the idea of transmitting voices over wires was explored almost as soon as the telegraph was invented, the idea of transmitting sounds over the air, or wirelessly, also was tried by many people before it became a success. The development of radio and television was covered in earlier chapters, so we will not rehash here how they evolved. What is important to keep in mind in terms of their role as telecommunication networks is how they also were initially created with other purposes in mind.

Radio, for example, was not conceived as a popular mode of mass entertainment but as a way for ships to communicate with each other or with people on the coast in order to improve safety. Wireless communication also would help solve the problems that came with severed undersea cables or downed telegraph or telephone lines that halted the normal flow of communication until they were repaired.

And just as the development of the telegraph and telephone spawned whole new industries and government regulations, so too did the development of wireless telecommunications. Two examples that will be explored in later chapters are the far-heavier regulation of television and radio than print media because of spectrum scarcity (the electromagnetic spectrum that can carry audio or radio waves is a limited resource) and the wireless-spectrum auction that took place in the United States in 2008.

▼ SATELLITES

Television was still not a mass medium when the concept of wireless telecommunication was considered for space. Communication satellites were first proposed in 1945 by science fiction writer Arthur C. Clarke. Clarke was trained in communications and helped invent radar during World War II.

On October 4, 1957, the Soviet Union launched Sputnik 1 ("traveling companion"), the first communications satellite. Sputnik 1 was a 23-inch, 184-pound ball of metal that contained a radio receiver and transmitter, using what is today the Citizens Band, or CB, radio frequency, and signaled not only the beginning of instantaneous global communications but an important milestone in the cold war. It was the Soviets' launch of Sputnik that led U.S. president John F. Kennedy to declare, four years later, that the United States would be the first country to put a man on the moon, by the end of the 1960s.

Although some scholars have questioned the importance of the invention of the communications satellite as a transformative technology, Arthur C. Clarke disagrees, saying that claiming it is simply an extension of existing communication technologies is like claiming the atomic bomb was simply an extension of conventional warfare.

Communications satellites have substantially upgraded communication networks in at least two ways. First, they have substantial bandwidth, or communications capacity. This means more information, communications, or media content can be distributed. Second, because they are positioned high above the earth (typically twenty-two thousand miles), satellites permit ground-based media to communicate with parties in remote corners of the globe. A signal can be sent from

Sputnik 1, the first satellite sent into orbit, started the space race between the Soviet Union and the United States.

one location on earth, bounced off the satellite, and relayed to a distant location that also has a line of sight with the satellite. The two terrestrial locations might be thousands of miles apart and, because of the earth's curvature, unable to reach each other with regular wireless terrestrial communications.

Of course satellites have played an important role for the military and we are seeing satellite imagery being used increasingly in services like Google maps

Al Jazeera: CNN of the Middle East?

INTERNATIONAL PERSPECTIVES

Since the terrorist attacks on the World Trade Center and Pentagon on September 11, 2001, a largely unknown satellite news channel—unknown outside the Middle East, at least—based in Qatar (pronounced like "cutter" rather than "guitar"), has beaten CNN at its own game with several scoops.

Al Jazeera, which means "the peninsula" in Arabic, was the only news organization broadcasting live in Afghanistan when the United States started bombing the country. It was the first to obtain copies of videotapes of Osama bin Laden, broadcasting them when some Western networks refused to do so out of fear they might contain hidden messages to Al Qaeda operatives.

Government officials in the United States have complained that Al Jazeera is little more than a mouthpiece for Osama bin Laden and that its unbalanced coverage fans anti-Semitism and anti-American feelings. Whether that is true or not, Al Jazeera is accustomed to criticism from government authorities: the news organization has outraged almost every Arab government as it has tried to follow its motto, "We get both sides of the story."

Founded in 1996 by Qatar's ruler Sheik Hamad bin Khalifa Al Thani, who was dismayed by the lack of press freedom in much of the Middle East, the station prides itself on its independence. Al Jazeera's coverage of sensitive topics has often led to strained relations between Qatar and other Arab nations, as well as to Al Jazeera's expulsion from some Arab countries.

Al Jazeera claims at least 35 million viewers in the Arab world and 175,000 cable subscribers in North America. Its website gets 17 million hits a day, it alleges.

"Al-Jazeera is undoubtedly a new trend in Arab media," said Roger Hardy, a Mideast specialist for the BBC World Service in London. "And as far as I can tell, it's the station of choice for Arabs, whether you're a Palestinian in Gaza . . . or you're part of the Arab diaspora in Canada or America."[2] Hardy's statement has turned out to be prophetic as more people turn to Al Jazeera for their news.

The website includes a program that translates Arabic articles into English and, in addition to its own stories, a number of links to various stories about Al Jazeera itself. Because of the unequalled access that Al Jazeera reporters often have in the Middle East, they can be one of the primary sources for news when Western reporters are barred from entering hotspots, such as Gaza in early 2009.

WEB LINK
Al Jazeera
english.aljazeera.net/

in which people can see amazingly high-resolution satellite photographs of neighborhoods.

▼ FIBER OPTICS

It is ironic that one of the newest, most powerful telecommunication technologies, fiber optics, is derived from one of the oldest attempts at telegraphy. In 1794, French clergyman Claude Chappe and Swedish nobleman Abraham Niclas Edelcrantz built the optical telegraph so that news could be brought from Finland to Stockholm, Sweden, and also from Denmark to the Swedish coast and from there to the Swedish capital. The optical telegraph worked by means of a series of signaling stations, each within sight of the next, usually less than a kilometer apart. A person standing in a lookout platform on the station would watch the next tower for a visual signal, which would represent a letter, word, or number. A series of signals could represent a message, which would then be relayed to the next tower, and so on. Experienced signalers could transmit even a fairly complex message quickly.

England used an optical telegraph system to communicate between London and its south coast, and Napoleon also used one in Europe in the early 1800s during his military campaigns. But for the most part, European governments failed to see the practicality of optical telegraphs and did not encourage their growth. Likewise, the few that were built in the United States, such as between Cape Cod and Boston, were never commercially viable.

Optical telegraphs were created in the late 1700s but were limited by weather conditions.

In many respects, the story of fiber optics goes all the way back to the optical telegraph created by Chappe and Edelcrantz, since it uses light to transmit information. Even though telegraphy eventually developed around using electromagnetism, rather than light, the concept of transmitting information with light was not abandoned. Alexander Graham Bell patented an optical telephone system—the photophone—only four years after his invention of the telephone, but his earlier telephone was more practical.

Transmitting light through the air had many problems, the main one being that the light became diffused. Numerous inventors and scientists worked on concentrating and focusing the light, usually through glass tubing of some type. In the 1950s and 1960s, two developments helped make the transmission of information by light a reality. One was the reduction of light leakage from the glass or plastic fibers by covering them, and the other was the invention of the laser in 1960. Sending light long distances without degrading the signal still proved to be problematic, making fiber optics not practical as a communication medium until further technological improvements in 1970.

Today's fiber optics can send information through hair-thin glass or plastic fiber by laser almost one hundred miles without using a repeater, or device that boosts the signal. Fiber not only has much more capacity to carry information than traditional copper wires, it moves information much faster—at the speed of light, in fact.

Almost all of the major communication lines within the United States now use fiber optics to send information. However, laying fiber-optic lines directly to homes is still not cost-effective for telecommunications companies, so most information travels by fiber optics to switching stations near the destinations. The switching stations send it further by copper wires or coaxial cable, which are slower than fiber-optic lines. Verizon's FiOS service, being rolled out gradually in various regions within the United States, provides fiber-optic connections directly to homes. Some countries, such as Japan, have encouraged the building of fiber-optic lines to homes and thus have far more homes connected that way.

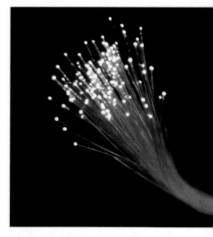

Fiber-optic lines transmit information by using highly concentrated light waves.

▲▼ Historical Development of the Internet and World Wide Web

Prior to the creation of the Internet, institutions or organizations that had computers had no simple way for the computers to communicate with each other, even if they were connected by a wire, as computers ran machine-specific languages and programs that could not be understood by other computers.

In 1969, the foundations for the Internet were laid when the Defense Advanced Research Projects Agency (DARPA) launched the Advanced Research Projects Agency network, or ARPANET. ARPANET was the first national computer network, connecting many universities around the country for advanced, high-speed computing applications and research. It was not yet the Internet, but it was the beginning of online communications. There was still no "common language," or protocol, that computers could use to easily transmit information via the network. A protocol, just like a diplomatic protocol, is essentially a set of rules that allows for easier communication between two parties who normally speak different languages.

Email is often called the "killer app" (killer application) of the Internet, yet in some ways it has been taken for granted in recent years in the barrage of other ways to communicate online, such as through instant messaging, chat rooms, or social media sites like Facebook. Email is usually one of the first things people learn to do when getting on the Internet, and it doesn't take long even for computer novices to get hooked enough to check their email inboxes several times a day. More messages are sent via email now than through the U.S. Postal Service. Email combines aspects of casual conversation with the permanence of text, as well as speedy transmission of messages.

"Email kind of announced itself," said Ray Tomlinson, the computer engineer who invented email in 1971. After debugging his program and giving it several trials to make sure it worked properly, he sent a message to his coworkers saying they could now communicate with people on other computers. The first email message? According to the *Guinness Book of World Records,* it was QWERTYUIOP—the keys on the third row of the keyboard. Tomlinson said that testing and debugging his original program was a process of trial and error, and he actually doesn't remember what the first message was.

Once messages could be moved from one machine to another, Tomlinson had to decide on a symbol that would separate the name of the individual from the machine he or she was working on. He said that the symbol @ ("at") was the obvious choice, as any single letter or number could cause confusion. "As it turns out, @ is the only preposition on the keyboard. I just looked at it and it was there. I didn't even try any others," Tomlinson said.[3]

It was clear to computer engineers that some type of simplified, common language was needed, a language that computers could speak with each other and by which they could send and receive information was needed—something more robust than what email could offer.

▼ CREATING AN INTERNET PROTOCOL

transmission control protocol [TCP]

A part of the main protocol for the Internet that allows for computers to easily communicate with each other over a network.

In 1974, Vinton Cerf and Robert Kahn published their classic article, "A Protocol for Packet Network Intercommunication." In the article, they specified the design of a **transmission control protocol (TCP)** as a part of the main protocol for the Internet and introduced the term "Internet." Also important to the creation of the Internet was the work of Jonathan Postel, who, when a graduate student at UCLA,

Milestones in the Development of the Internet

1958 In response to the 1957 Soviet launch of Sputnik, the U.S. Department of Defense establishes the Defense Advanced Research Projects Agency (DARPA), whose mission is to develop advanced communications capabilities.

1969 Laying the foundations for the Internet, DARPA launches the Advanced Research Projects Agency network, or ARPANET, the first national computer network.

1971 Email invented.

1973 Vinton Cerf and Robert Kahn develop the basic concept and architecture for the Internet.

1974 Cerf and Kahn specify the design of a transmission control protocol (TCP), the basic protocol for the Internet, and coin the term "Internet."

1982 DARPA adopts the TCP/IP protocol as the standard for communication among computers in ARPANET.

1991 Tim Berners-Lee creates the World Wide Web, a global publishing platform, on the Internet.

1993 Mark Andreessen and others create Mosaic, a web browser, or graphical user interface for the Web, that permits anyone to easily navigate and view pages on the Web using a computer mouse and keyboard. This helps bring the Web out of the specialized domain of scientists and into the mainstream of media and the public.

1994–1995 First blogs created, although they are not yet called blogs and many of the automated tools that help make blogs a popular form of online communication will not be developed until the late 1990s and early 2000s.

1995 WikiWikiWeb, the first wiki, is created and named by Ward Cunningham.

1998 Google founded by Larry Paige and Sergey Brin, two Stanford graduate students.

2000 The dot-com economic bubble bursts in March, ending a run since the late 1990s that saw huge increases in valuations of Internet companies and a kind of frenzy that dot-com companies would sweep aside traditional media companies.

2008 The Firefox web browser, a free, open-source browser, gets almost 20 percent of the worldwide browser market, second only to Internet Explorer.

2008 Wikitude World Browser introduced as first location-based augmented reality web browser.

2009 Cloud computing begins entering the mainstream, with computing services, software, and information delivered over a wireless network.

2010 There are 70,000 public WiFi hotspots in the U.S. WiFi refers to wireless local area networks based on the Institute of Electrical and Electronics Engineers' (IEEE) 802.11. It is broadband wireless Internet access.

2010 Seventy-seven percent of U.S. households have Internet access.[4]

2012 There are 85 million mobile broadband users in the United States, generating $190 billion in mobile services revenues.[5]

2012 Yahoo, one of the early Internet giants, announces it is laying off 2,000 employees amidst rumors of plans to sell off big parts of the company.

outlined along with Cerf some of the key principles that underlie today's Internet protocols (IP). Together, these two protocols, TCP/IP, became the foundation for how computers would communicate with each other.

Although it is difficult to pin down an exact date when the Internet officially started, it was in 1982 that the Defense Department adopted TCP/IP as the basis for the ARPANET. Essentially, this meant that if universities wanted to remain in the network, they had to adopt the TCP/IP protocol. Moreover, at this time researchers began defining an "internet" (lowercase *i*) as a connected set of networks using TCP/IP, and the "Internet" (uppercase *I*) as a set of connected TCP/IP internets.[6]

▼ CREATING THE WORLD WIDE WEB

For the first decade of the Internet's existence, its usage was limited largely to academic and government researchers. Use of the Internet required knowledge of a variety of arcane commands and terminology. The limited, specialized nature of the Internet underwent a fundamental change in 1991 when Tim Berners-Lee, a British researcher at a physics laboratory in Switzerland, invented the World Wide Web, which began to open the Internet to a much wider set of users.

Until the creation of **hypertext transfer protocol (HTTP)** in 1991 by Tim Berners-Lee, hyperlinks only existed as hypertext within certain types of Mac files, not between computers. But after hyperlinks were created and started being used by larger numbers of people, new issues began to arise.

A web page is any document, or collection of content, that resides on a website. The content can take any form, including text, graphics, photographs, audio, video, or interactive features, such as surveys or discussion forums. A website can consist of one page of content or many such pages and can include hyperlinks to other websites.

Content on a web page is marked up using what is known as **hypertext markup language**, or **HTML**, or variations of HTML such as **extensible markup language (XML)**, to format the content so it displays correctly on a screen. In addition, each document uses hypertext transfer protocol (HTTP), which enables the standardized transfer of text, audio, and video files from one address to another.

The advent of the Web as a global publishing platform made possible the most fundamental shift in human communication since the advent of the printing press five centuries earlier. The Web enabled easy many-to-many communication over distance and time. In addition, in contrast to traditional media of mass communication, anyone can create and publish on the Web for very little cost and with little technical expertise.

The World Wide Web (WWW) is a subset of the Internet and is perhaps best described as a global electronic-publishing medium accessed through the Internet. Technically speaking, the Web is made up of an interconnected set of computer servers on the Internet that subscribe to a set of TCP/IP network-interface protocols. These technical protocols include assigning to a website a Uniform Resource Locator (URL) based on its TCP/IP Internet address, which is the website address that Web users are familiar with. URLs include the instructions that are read by a web browser, a navigational tool to travel the Web.

▼ CREATING GRAPHICAL WEB BROWSERS

Another huge gain in making the Internet accessible to even more people was the creation in 1993 of Mosaic by Marc Andreessen, then at the National Center for Supercomputing Applications (NCSA) at the University of Illinois at Champaign-Urbana.

hypertext transfer protocol [HTTP]

A Web protocol that enables standardized transfer of text, audio, and video files from one address to another.

hypertext markup language [HTML]

A coding format that describes how information should look on the Web.

extensible markup language [XML]

A coding format similar to HTML but which permits easy sharing of information and data about the information on the Web, not only how it looks.

Mosaic, which eventually became Netscape, provided a graphical user interface (GUI) for the Web that computer users who had Macs or Windows PCs could quickly understand and use. Although GUI browsers Viola and Erwise were also created in 1992, by the end of the year Mosaic was being written about in mainstream media and became the most well-known web browser at the time before becoming Netscape.

Microsoft created its own graphical browser, Internet Explorer (IE), in 1996 to compete with Netscape's browser, then called Netscape Navigator. By offering Internet Explorer free and eventually bundling it with the Windows operating system, IE was able to become the dominant web browser in only four years, with 75 percent usage compared to Netscape's 25 percent. By 1999, at its peak, IE had 99 percent of the browser market. The same year, Netscape was bought by AOL, a year before AOL acquired Time Warner.

Although other browsers were created, such as Opera or Apple's Safari, the first serious competition to IE came from open-source browser Firefox, created by the Mozilla Foundation. Launched in late 2004 under the Firefox name but built on versions of the browser that had been launched under other names since 2002, by mid-2011 Firefox had captured about 28 percent of the browser market, most of it from IE, all without advertising or marketing. Google's browser Chrome, launched in late 2008, had about 20 percent of the browser market and IE had 43 percent, according to StatCounter.

As any regular Web user can attest, websites and text size often look different not only on different browsers but on different versions of browsers. More advanced functions or codes on websites may not show up on earlier browser versions, thus making it difficult for Web designers and content companies to create websites that are consistent across the online audience.

For most users, the web browser is their window into the world of online communication. Yet this window is constantly changing in ways that can be exciting and confusing, and we are still in the early stages of development with the Internet as a medium of mass communication.

The Internet Today

In its broadest sense, the Internet encompasses virtually all other media, as well as a broad cross-section of human culture, commerce, and creation. Virtually anything one can think of almost certainly is accessible in some form on the Internet, from information in the Library of Congress to deliberately misleading information created by hate groups or individuals. As distinguished communications scholar Fred Williams once observed, "Going on the Internet is like going through someone else's trash."

There are two contrasting trends taking place on the Internet regarding revenues and accessibility. One trend is a decrease in the costs of software and hardware that makes computers and computer equipment (such as storage devices) cheaper and more powerful than ever before. This is making computers more affordable for people and allowing those of a lower socioeconomic status to buy at least a basic computer and to connect to the Internet.

On the other hand, there is an increasing trend of rising costs for telecommunications services and for Web services that have previously been free to move toward partial subscription-based models. This trend of "**freemium**" business models, with payment for what is considered "premium," more valuable content, can also be seen among media companies online, although it is unclear if freemium

freemium

A partial subscription-based model used by web services and media companies that provides basic access for free but charges for what is considered premium content.

models will be as successful for media companies as they have been for software applications and social media sites.

Online media companies are also experimenting with increasingly obtrusive online advertising, such as larger pop-up ad windows or automatic pop-under ads that are changing the look and experience of the Web for users. In the early 1990s there were many debates among users of online discussion groups about whether *any* advertising should even be allowed on the Internet, considering it was created using taxpayers' money. These discussions have been abandoned as advertising has come to be expected on most websites; the discussions have shifted to what kinds of ads are most effective, how they can collect data on users, and what Web users are willing to accept. One important issue in this discussion is how fast content can arrive at users' computers, as anything that slows this down affects the user experience with online media.

▼ BANDWIDTH

Although former Alaska Senator Ted Stevens famously described the Internet as "a series of tubes," during a debate on **Net neutrality** in 2006, a description that was gleefully mocked for its simplistic description of the Internet, he did at least have a hazy—if misguided—notion of the importance of bandwidth.

Bandwidth is a crucial element for online communication to reach its full potential as a mass medium. Without what is called high-speed, or **broadband**, connections to the Internet, most people online are unable to receive audio or video in real time or at the same quality as they are used to from television or radio. **Narrowband** is the term used for low-bandwidth communications, such as dial-up phone modems. Bandwidth available for Internet service has traditionally been narrowband via dial-up modems, typically delivering anywhere from 28 kilobits to 56 kilobits per second. Video at these narrowband rates is very limited, usually a small window of jerky motion, low-resolution imagery, and only marginally better sound.

In a technical sense, bandwidth refers to the electromagnetic frequency or spectrum available for delivering content. Bell Labs scientist Claude E. Shannon in 1948 provided a precise mathematical definition of bandwidth, defining the capacity of a communications channel in terms of bits per second. A voice phone call, for example, uses about 3,000 hertz (Hz) bandwidth, whereas a telephone modem operating at about 33.6 kilobits per second requires a little more bandwidth, or about 3,200 Hz.[7]

Think of bandwidth not so much as electromagnetic frequency, however, as in terms of how large "the pipe" is that comes to your home delivering data (rather than a physical thing like water). It is not an actual pipe, of course, but a coaxial or fiber-optic cable that has greater or lesser capacity to carry data. If people are able to tap the large "data pipe" directly, then they can access the flow of data at equally high speeds. Sometimes this is called a "fat pipe." However, if their pipe accessing the main pipes is very thin, data will come to them at only a trickle, no matter how fast their personal computer is.

▼ TELEPHONE AND CABLE COMPANY BROADBAND SERVICES

One of the great challenges that cable and telecommunication providers have begun to solve in the past decade is the so-called last-mile obstacle (not always literally the last mile, but somewhere from a few hundred yards to more than a mile

Network neutrality

A principle that states that broadband networks should be free of restrictions on content, platforms, or equipment and that certain types of content, platforms, or equipment should not get preferential treatment on the network.

broadband

A network connection that enables a large amount of bandwidth to be transmitted, allowing for more information to be sent in a shorter period of time.

narrowband

A network connection that does not provide very much bandwidth, thus receiving and sending information more slowly than broadband connections. Dial-up modems and some of the early wireless connections with speeds of 56 kHz or under are considered narrowband.

or so). For more than a decade, many cable and telephone companies have had considerable bandwidth available in their backbone or trunk lines, which are generally fiber-optic lines, but it has not been profitable for them to run the same broadband connectivity over the "last mile" to the end consumer. Verizon FiOS service is one of the first to connect homes directly to a fiber-optic network, giving consumers faster Internet connections than they can get with cable modems or DSL, which is a broadband connection carried over traditional phone lines.

Cable companies have started to fight back with sometimes inaccurate advertising campaigns touting their Internet connection speeds or the fact that they, too, use fiber-optic networks. That is technically true, though what they fail to mention is that they do not have fiber-optic lines directly to the end user's home, meaning that the "fat pipe" of fiber optic narrows dramatically just before getting to an end user.

There has been increasing competition between telecommunications companies and cable companies in providing broadband services to customers. Today, most consumers can get some type of broadband service, through DSL lines that come through existing telephone wires at higher speeds than typical phone lines, through existing coaxial cable lines that are used to receive cable television signals, or, in the case of Verizon, in some limited markets, through fiber-optic lines directly to the home. Most telecommunication and cable companies in the United States have structured the data flow so that it is faster to download content from the Internet than to upload it, which tends to favor media consumption by Web users rather than media production and distribution by users.

Despite the growth of broadband services in recent years, consumers still have many complaints about both telephone and cable companies regarding service, late or bungled installations, actual connection speeds that are slower than what is promised, and a lack of choice for their broadband provider, as well as high monthly charges. The lack of choice is not a surprise, as cable companies have monopolies in most markets where they operate, and if the local telecommunications company, the only potential competitor for broadband service, does not provide DSL or fiber-optic connections, then the consumer essentially has no choice at all.

▼ BROADBAND CHANGING CONSUMER PATTERNS

The importance of broadband capability to usage patterns on the Internet may be profound.[8] Research shows that Internet users with broadband access already have substantially different behaviors than when they used dial-up connections. One trend that has been noted is that they are more likely to create and distribute media content than dial-up users, even though upload speeds are still slower than download speeds. Online expenditures more than double for users of broadband services. In 1999, David Clark predicted that broadband Internet would bring "Real-time high-fidelity music, telephone, videoconferencing, television and radio programs . . . There will be new entertainment options, such as movies-on-demand, and new features, such as the ability to call up information about a movie's director or its actors as they appear on screen. Users will be able to play online games—live—against many contestants scattered around the globe."[9] Although today not all of what Clark predicted in 1999 is actually available, most of it is, on broadband connections—for a price.

Social Effects of Broadband

If the main result of having broadband connections was simply to deliver us more entertainment at better sound and visual quality than before then it would be hard to claim that the Internet is a transformative technology. However, as we have stated throughout this book, the power and dynamic changes that are taking place stem largely from the interactive communication that takes place among people.

With a broadband Internet connection one can easily watch videos made by people in distant places and learn about global issues. In this way, another form of "connection" is created. This type of connection happens on a very human level, in which we can identify with others about common problems or fears, or share joyous moments. Visual media can transcend language and cultural barriers in ways that written language cannot, helping people learn about and appreciate other cultures and peoples.

Broadband connections also make it possible to get large amounts of information from a variety of sources. In our information age having access to information is an important first step to being able to use information effectively. Not being able to access the same information as others can put one at a serious disadvantage in terms of education or career possibilities. In the United States, broadband telecommunications costs can be quite high for consumers, which means that people lower on the socioeconomic scale are spending proportionally more for what many see today as a basic necessity.

▲▼ The Nature of Networks: Key Concepts

Some characteristics of networks have been discussed in earlier chapters, and here we will more thoroughly examine some of the networks that have been mentioned. We will also cover key concepts that must be understood to better comprehend mass communication and the Internet.

There are many types of networks, but in this chapter we will focus on telecommunications networks as they relate to mass communication and the Internet. In the next chapter we will look at social media sites and what is called Web 2.0, and how they relate to media.

One useful way to consider networks is by looking at three network "laws." These are not scientific laws, in the same way that there is a law of gravity, but actually ways to describe and analyze different kinds of networks.

▼ SARNOFF'S LAW

RCA executive and radio and television pioneer David Sarnoff is the creator of **Sarnoff's Law**, which states that the value of a network increases linearly with the number of people on it, as Figure 7-1 shows. This description applies to mass-communication networks such as radio or television networks.

Defining "value" can of course be tricky, but in the case of radio or television, consider how much more a network can charge an advertiser if it has ten million audience members than if it has ten thousand.

It is important to also think of the communication flow in such a network; it is the very definition of mass communication. A single person or group broadcasts a message to a large audience whose members have no means to communicate with each other or the sender through that network. The audience is essentially silent and passive; viewers or listeners have no way of knowing how many others are also receiving the same message or content, let alone whether others like or do not like it.

Sarnoff's Law may be useful for understanding radio and television networks, but it fails miserably when used to consider a network in which the members can communicate with each other in some form, such as the Internet.

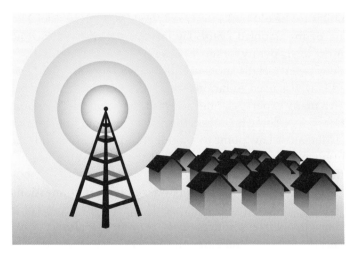

FIGURE 7-1 Sarnoff's Law shows how the value of a network increases linearly with the number of people on the network, which applies to traditional broadcasting.

▼ METCALFE'S LAW

Robert Metcalfe, creator of the Ethernet protocol and founder of networking company 3Com, came up with the law bearing his name in 1993. **Metcalfe's Law** states that in a communication network with n members, each member can make $n-1$ connections (because a member cannot connect with him- or herself), which means that the value of a communications network increases roughly to its square, or n^2.

It is easy to underestimate the growth rate when considering the square of numbers. A simple example will help illustrate. If a communication network has 10 members, each of whom can communicate with the others, then there are 90 possible communication connections that can be made (see Figure 7-2). If the number of members in the network doubles to 20, then the number of possible connections doesn't simply double to 180 (as Sarnoff's Law would predict) but quadruples to 360.

Metcalfe's Law

The value of a network rises in proportion to the square of the number of people on that network. In other words, the more people who are connected to a network in which they can communicate with each other, such as the Internet, the more valuable that network becomes.

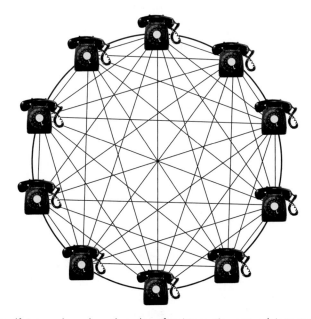

FIGURE 7-2 Metcalfe's Law shows how the value of an interactive network increases to its square because of all the possible combinations of communication between members.

This is similar to the old trick question "Would you rather take $1 million right now or have a penny doubled every day for thirty days?" It does not look very promising for the lowly penny for most of the month, until it surpasses the $1 million mark on day twenty-eight and you end up with $5,368,709.12 by day thirty.

Metcalfe's Law was used to rationalize the fervor of the dot-com boom in the late 1990s, with many experts claiming it was the reason the New Economy would replace the old ways of doing business. That, of course, did not happen.

Critics of Metcalfe's Law point to a number of problems with it. One criticism echoes the problem with Sarnoff's Law in that the term "value" is not defined and can mean different things to different people.

Another major criticism is that the law assumes that connections in the network are all equal, which is rarely the case. Consider your own communications network, perhaps listed in the address book on your cell phone. You do not regularly communicate with every member on the network every single time you want to send a message, and neither do they. Therefore, the simple number of members in a network will not produce the growth in value that Metcalfe's Law predicts.

Even with the criticisms of Metcalfe's Law, it nevertheless does a better job than Sarnoff's Law of explaining the power more members add to an interactive communications network. Some people, in fact, have claimed that Metcalfe's Law does not go far enough in explaining the power of network effects.

▼ REED'S LAW

Reed's Law

The utility or value of an interactive communications network with n members increases exponentially, or 2 to the nth power.

Though not negating Metcalfe's Law, David Reed claimed in 1999 to have discovered another effect of network scaling that is especially relevant in the Web 2.0 world. **Reed's Law** claims that the utility of a network with n members increases exponentially, or 2^n (2 to the nth power). The rapid growth curve with Reed's Law is shown in Figure 7-3, and it is clear how much faster utility, or value, grows when such a network gets more members.

We will discuss the implications of Reed's Law when we look at social media in Chapter 8, but for now it is enough to know that it helps to explain the power of social networks and the various groups that form because of network affiliations. Reed does not claim that they will inevitably form, just that there is greater potential for them to form when there are more members in a network. This is because of the nature of peer-to-peer networks such as the Internet, which we will look at now.

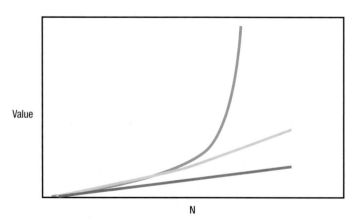

FIGURE 7-3 The difference in growth of value between Sarnoff's Law (red), Metcalfe's Law (yellow), and Reed's Law (green) is clearly shown in this graph.

◣▽ Computer Networks: Key Concepts

Computer-based networks operate differently than traditional broadcast networks. They permit the distribution of content to be more flexible, so if one route of the network is unavailable, the network can automatically and efficiently reassemble the message through a different route. Digital networks permit compression of data, which enables a mass communicator to send more information in the same amount of space on the network. Finally, a computer network easily permits downstream and upstream communications cheaply (from the source to the receiver, and vice versa), whereas traditional networks were largely one-way and relatively expensive.

A **modem** (a foreshortening of **MO**dulate-**DEM**odulate) is used to convert the digital information in a computer to signals for transmission over a phone or cable TV line and to convert signals from the network to the computer. Modems can also operate wirelessly by converting data into radio signals. Modems were invented in the 1960s, before the days of the personal computer, as a means of letting "dumb terminals" (electronic machines with keyboards but no storage capacity) dial in to a remote computer that did have storage capacity.

modem

Derived from the terms modulate-demodulate; a device that converts digital signals from a computer to analog signals for transmission over a phone line, as well as converting transmitted analog signals to digital signals.

▼ PEER-TO-PEER MODEL

The **peer-to-peer (P2P)** network model is what the Internet was initially supposed to be: an interconnected group of computers, all essentially "equal" in their ability to send, store, and receive information, i.e., a network of peers. P2P networking is by its architecture decentralized and nonhierarchical.

Usenet is an early example of a P2P network and one that highlights some of P2P's flaws in the current Internet environment. Because of the nonhierarchical nature of Usenet, it was relatively easy for some people to abuse the system by doing things like sending **spam**. Spammers not only take away bandwidth from legitimate Internet users, slowing the system down, they also clog inboxes with advertising messages not related to the topics being discussed. The result? People avoid visiting discussions on Usenet, reducing the number of members and thereby diminishing its usefulness.

Another hurdle for P2P applications in reaching their full potential on today's Internet is the amount of bandwidth available to upload content. Since in a P2P network anyone can be a content distributor, users need as much bandwidth to upload content as they do when they download content. However, broadband providers such as cable companies, in order to conserve the amount of total bandwidth on the network, limit the upload speeds.

Many of the best applications being developed on the Internet combine aspects of client/server networks and P2P. Napster, for example, was not a true P2P application since it stored information on a central server, from which files were available for downloading. This classic client/server network characteristic, although helping searches, also helped make Napster an easy target when it was sued by the Recording Industry Association of America.

peer-to-peer network [P2P]

A network in which all computers on the network are considered equal (peers) and can send and receive information equally well. This is the basis of file-sharing services.

spam

Unwanted email sent out by advertisers as a mass mailing.

▼ CLIENT/SERVER MODEL

The **client/server** model is what the Internet—for reasons such as limited bandwidth, Internet Protocol (IP) addresses, and its rapid rise in popularity via the Web—largely developed into. This model of a network simply means there is a

client/server

A network model, predominant in the Internet today, that relies on a centralized computer, or server, that stores content that the audience, or clients, access.

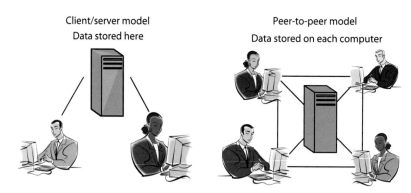

Client/server model
Data stored here

Peer-to-peer model
Data stored on each computer

FIGURE 7-4 A client/server network relies on a server to provide content to people on the network, while content on a P2P network exists on various individual computers and is shared among them.

centralized computer, or server, that stores content that the audience (clients) can access on the network. It is a hierarchical system in which most computer users do not contribute content to the Internet; they simply receive content.

A client/server network model has strong points and weak points. As Figure 7-4 shows, among its strong points is that the centralized storage location makes information easy to find (it always has the same virtual address—in the case of the Web, a URL). Among its weak points is that a single server can easily become overloaded if many clients request content from it at the same time. The single location also makes it vulnerable to attack or destruction. If the server or servers with the hard drives containing the information are destroyed, such as in a fire, the information is lost unless backup copies were made and stored somewhere else.

Servers are an important part of how mass-communication content is moved about in a digital, networked environment. Audience members access a growing portion of the content produced by media organizations via web servers.

▼ WIRELESS NETWORKS

Wireless computer networks operate much like radio or TV signals but use a different part of the electromagnetic spectrum to send and receive data. Some wireless networks have extremely short ranges—only several feet—and allow mobile devices to communicate with each other. Bluetooth is one such technology that allows for wireless communication between a headset and a laptop, for example.

The most familiar wireless network for most people is the mobile-phone network. Voice and data can be transmitted, allowing people to connect with the Internet as well. In many developing countries, this is the primary way people access the Internet, not through desktop computers.

The benefits of wireless networks are many, with a main one being that people can access the network from virtually any location (assuming they have a connection). This gives emergency services an easy way to contact large numbers of people at once, and it also means that people can easily get geographic-specific information from where they are. Want to know if the restaurant you are standing in front of is any good or not? Access the Web through your phone and read reviews on it.

However, there are also some drawbacks with wireless networks that the wired computer networks do not face to the same degree. One is the poor level of security wireless networks offer. It is relatively easy to hack into a wireless network and "eavesdrop" on it, stealing data (such

Bluetooth devices and other wireless technologies let us communicate easily on the go.

as credit card information) as it is being sent, for example. And even though there has been no medical evidence of harm from wireless networks, some people still believe that the electromagnetic waves can hurt us in ways that will show up years from now.

Whether a telecommunications network such as the Internet is wired or wireless, it has two important characteristics that must be considered: connectivity and quality of service.

▼ CONNECTIVITY

Connectivity can be defined in terms of the ability of people and their computers, digital television sets, or other digital devices to link to the Internet and other online communications media. Connectivity is critical for at least two reasons.

First, without a connection, the citizen, or media consumer, has no access to the online communications network. This means he or she can neither communicate electronically with others nor access content published online.

Second, as Metcalfe's Law and Reed's Law state, the value of a communications network rises rapidly the more members are on that network. In other words, the more people connected to a communications network who can communicate with each other, the more potential there is not just for sharing information but for content creation, forming new groups, and even creating new economic models. An example of the robustness of the open-source community, discussed in Chapter 2, shows how many people working collaboratively can create value.

Although some in the industry would argue that universal service, or connectivity, is too expensive, the reality is that in network economics, complete connectivity only increases the value of the system to the entire society and is ultimately of economic benefit to the whole.

Without complete connectivity, not only will new economic models fail to be realized, but the function of mass communication in democratic society also fails to reach its potential. It is necessary for all citizens to have access to basic information, even if that access is unequal. Access will always be and has always been unequal, even in the days of analog media. But remember that in an online environment connectivity means that people are able to receive and send messages within the network, not merely be passive recipients of information from a central source.

▼ QUALITY OF SERVICE

Quality of service, or the reliability, efficiency, and effectiveness of one's connection, is an important element in the world of online communications and networks. If one cannot trust one's online connection, then it is impossible to make it a cornerstone of civil society, much less of commerce and culture. Today's Internet cannot guarantee a high quality of service. Its strength lies in the ability of anyone to access it, any time, from anywhere, to send or receive content.

Some critics contend that the Internet, by its very nature, will never be able to provide a high quality of service. Instead, because anyone can use it at virtually no marginal cost, at any specific moment a user may not get the bandwidth needed for high-quality video or audio or may not be able to access the server needed for a critical journalistic or ecommerce transaction.

This argument may have some truth to it, especially as more people upload videos and other high-bandwidth content. As a result, some point to alternative

The Great Network Neutrality Debate

The concept of Network neutrality, or Net neutrality, is that the Internet should not discriminate among the types of content that pass through it. This equality and openness is what the Internet pioneers believed the Net should be about, and these qualities have been espoused by other, equally influential Net researchers and innovators.

However, after the FCC passed some regulations in 2005, the leading cable and phone companies began lobbying Congress to make changes in the laws governing how the Internet operates. Essentially, these companies sought a tiered system in which content providers would pay according to how much content they sent over the Internet.

Critics of the lobbying efforts claimed that this would destroy the democratic nature of the Internet and make the telephone and cable companies Internet gatekeepers, with the power to decide what type of content would be sent fast and what type sent slow, and from whom, and even whether some sites or content would be completely blocked. The companies claimed that it was not fair that certain content providers who were using most of the bandwidth were not required to pay more.

The companies also claimed that they had no desire to censor the Internet or to control content in the way the critics charged, but during 2007 and 2008 there were several examples in which companies were doing exactly that. One case involved a company slowing the speed of content delivery from a rival media company, and another involved AT&T when it censored part of a comment from Eddie Vedder during a Pearl Jam concert when he criticized

President George Bush. In early 2012 there was a further attempt at controlling the Internet, this time brought forth by the Stop Online Piracy Act (SOPA) and the Protect IP Act (PIPA). The legislation was encouraged by the entertainment industry and would have given companies the ability to sue Internet Service Providers that carried illegal material.

A huge uproar among various groups and citizens helped stop the legislation. This left the politicians who had created the bills (many of whom had received large donations from the entertainment industry) scrambling to say they would "rework" them.

The debate is a complex one that will not soon go away and is well worth staying abreast of. Changes in the basic architecture of the Internet could have dramatic effects, changing how we use the Internet and limiting its capabilities as an open, interactive communications network to one that favors a broadcast model in which passive recipients of content have little ability to communicate on equal terms.

proprietary high-bandwidth telecommunications-transmission systems where quality of service is guaranteed—but at a cost. Broadcasters pay for the use of satellites or private fiber-optics networks to reliably transmit their video to affiliate stations.

Another solution is to use a combination of the Internet and private networks. However, using private networks could create a new kind of digital divide in which the majority of Internet users have a cheap or free network with severe limitations on transmitting or uploading multimedia content, while large media corporations or wealthy individuals have high-quality, high-speed private networks that transmit content to a paying audience.

The quality-of-service issue came to a head in 2007 and 2008 in a debate between telecommunications providers and the public over what was termed Network neutrality.

◣◺ Characteristics of Digital Distribution

Digitization of media, as we have seen, has radically altered many aspects of mass communication. Distribution is no different. Some of these characteristics have been mentioned before, but they will be touched on again here in order to give a complete picture of what makes digital distribution so different from analog distribution and to highlight why it is a key component in changing our media landscape.

▼ DISTRIBUTING BITS

A fundamental characteristic of digital media, that they consist of electrons rather than anything physical, is the cornerstone of the characteristics that follow. Although data still must be stored in some physical location, such as a hard drive, the space required is minuscule in comparison to that required by analog media. The number of books that can be stored on a laptop computer would fill a small-town library if they were in physical form. As we have seen, digital data can of course be converted into physical form, such as a printed book, DVD, or CD, but it does not *need* to be put into such a form as long as someone has access to a computer network and the data are stored there.

▼ LOW DISTRIBUTION COSTS

With nothing to physically create and send, distribution costs are greatly reduced. There is no need for trucks, trains, or planes to move products from a manufacturing or printing plant to warehouses and then to retail stores—and no need to send back unsold copies. Media content can travel at the speed of light over hair-thin wires directly to computers.

This does not mean that distribution over the Internet is free, however. Internet users must still pay for access to the Internet, and distributors of content often have to pay the web-hosting companies for the amount of bandwidth they use as the public requests streaming audio or video.

Sometimes these costs can be quite substantial—several thousand dollars a month—for popular websites that contain video clips. Although the costs are technically not distribution costs, they act much the same way, because companies or individuals unable to pay the extra costs for Internet traffic essentially have their website "closed" to further visitors after their monthly limit has been reached.

Distribution costs can still be quite high, especially when websites are large or when companies like Amazon must hold and ship large inventories of products.

▼ PERFECT INFINITE COPIES

A factor in reducing distribution costs is that creating copies of digital content is largely free. Unlike with analog media, in which there are fixed costs associated with creating physical copies such as books or albums, digital media have no such restrictions. This is because, unlike analog media, a digital piece of content never runs out. If a member of the public downloads a book from a publisher's website, it does not mean that there is one less book for somebody else to download or that the publisher will have to order more copies of the book in order to meet demand. The person simply has downloaded a perfect copy to his or her computer, taken from a digital version of the book on the publisher's website that is still there and available to anyone else.

The ability of anyone to create an infinite number of copies of digital media and make them available to anyone else on the Internet is the crux of what has media companies concerned about their current business models. It is also the primary motivation behind the various initiatives to create secure digital content that cannot be copied without the copyright holder's permission.

▼ INSTANTANEOUS DISTRIBUTION

Although not truly instantaneous, by analog-media standards the ability to distribute media content over the Internet is instantaneous. A click of a mouse can send content to tens of thousands or hundreds of thousands of people, nearly at the speed of light. Although network congestion can slow down how quickly something is actually received, it can reach a wide audience in an extremely short period of time and much faster than what it takes to create a physical product to send.

Rapid distribution can make official release dates of popular CDs, books, or videos largely superfluous, as digital copies can be sent and shared in advance to encourage interest when the final product is released. However, it can also hurt sales if consumers end up not liking the sample they receive early or believe they got what they wanted from it and do not need to buy the whole thing—as in wanting a particular song but not an entire CD.

▼ NEW DISTRIBUTION DYNAMICS

The fact that once a piece of digital content is available on the Internet there is currently essentially no way to completely control how it is distributed is another cause for serious concern amongst media companies.

Let's look at an example such as a photograph from a local online newspaper. It is a simple matter for a user to copy the picture to his local drive, separate from the article it accompanies (it is also easy for the user to manipulate the photo, but for our purposes here that is not important). He could then send the digital photo as an attachment by email to twenty of the people in his email address book.

Assume that only half of those twenty people like the photo enough to send it to twenty other people in each of their address books and half of those people do the same, a kind of reduced Metcalfe's Law effect. Within three "generations" after the original sender, the photo could be seen by over 2,200 people, all within a matter of minutes and at virtually no cost to the senders. Add one more generation of senders and the number jumps to over 20,000—again for no cost. This example does not even take into account somebody putting the photograph on her own website, which could have tens of thousands more visitors, or posting it to a photo-sharing website or a blog.

This example shows that distribution is no longer dependent on a central location sending out content to a passive audience. Distribution has essentially become decentralized and can take place "at the edges" of the computer network. In other words, rather than central servers containing media content that the public accesses, the audience can now store media content on their own computers and make it available to others on the Internet. A few centralized distribution points are replaced with many localized distribution points. This is the basis for peer-to-peer (P2P) applications, such as the popular music-sharing services available.

▼ THE AUDIENCE AS DISTRIBUTOR

Decentralization of distribution means a loss of distribution control for media companies, since a single company cannot dictate what every single PC among the public may or may not distribute. This translates into potential lost revenues as copies are made and shared among millions of Internet users without paying the copyright holders. This is precisely what is happening with music online, although some studies have countered the music industry's claims that it is losing revenues from CD sales by showing that increased exposure to different music and artists actually helps increase sales. The music industry's concern stems from the fact that each member of the public who uses file-sharing applications becomes a potential distributor of content merely by having certain files others would like to download. No one has to send anything.

A benefit of widely distributed content among the public is that it is far less likely, should a central company server go down, that the content becomes unavailable. In a P2P system, as long as someone with that content is online, it can be downloaded.

◤◥ File-Sharing Services

File-sharing services using P2P networks started making the news in late 1999 primarily because of the rapid rise in popularity of Napster, a program created by eighteen-year-old Northeastern University student Shawn Fanning. However, Napster was not the first file-sharing service, Usenet actually was. Usenet members posted files to a newsgroup to share with anyone subscribed to that group, and group members could then download and save the files on their computers.

Napster let Internet users easily share MP3 files, a compression format for digital music. College campus networks slowed as millions of students downloaded and shared music files, and the music industry got a rude awakening to the power of digital distribution of media content.

Although music files and their widespread free distribution among users led the Recording Industry Association of America (RIAA) and the major record labels to take legal action against Napster and other file-sharing services, P2P networks are being used for a variety of other purposes as well. These range from looking for signs of extraterrestrial intelligence to solving complex model simulation problems to creating an information network that is impossible to shut down or censor.

File-sharing services have evolved over time and can work in different ways. Let's examine some of the most common ones.

▼ CENTRALIZED FILE SHARING: THE CASE OF NAPSTER

It is ironic that the program and company largely responsible for starting the rapid popularity of P2P file-sharing services did not even follow a true P2P model. Napster used central servers to store information detailing what music files were available on what users' computers. Napster users searched the Napster database,

Shawn Fanning created Napster while still student at Northeastern University.

saw the music they wished to download, and then connected directly with that user to download the song. Napster simply facilitated searches and was not involved in actually transferring files between users.

But the ability to easily search and share files for free is exactly what the record labels saw as a threat, and in December 1999 they filed suit against Napster saying that it facilitated massive piracy among its tens of millions of users. Napster claimed that its service exposed emerging and unknown musicians to the general public and said that any copying of music files should be considered **fair use**. Napster also argued that it should be protected under the 1992 Audio Home Recording Act, which allows consumers to make digital recordings for their personal use. Since it was simply facilitating this process, Napster said, albeit on a much larger scale, it should be protected under the act.

The courts did not agree. Initially, Napster was told to shut down completely but received a stay of that injunction for six months. Under a court-brokered agreement, Napster blocked access to any copyrighted songs it did not have license agreements for, even as it started negotiations with one of the record labels in the original lawsuit, Bertelsmann AG's BMG label, to develop a fee-based service that would give it access to all songs in the BMG music archive. The other major labels maintained their lawsuit while they developed two music subscription services of their own, MusicNet and Pressplay.

Bertelsmann invested about $85 million in Napster as it tried to establish a subscription service and kept the struggling company on life support. Napster was finally shut down in July 2001. In May 2002 Bertelsmann bought Napster's assets for $8 million, and in June 2002 Napster declared Chapter 11 bankruptcy and its brand and logo were bought at auction by music company Roxio to rebrand its Pressplay subscription music service. Napster currently operates as a paid music subscription service and, in September 2008, was bought by Best Buy for $121 million.

The centralized database that Napster used was what led to its legal troubles and downfall. However, the numerous file-sharing services that arose to fill the void created by the demise of Napster have learned that lesson.

▼ DECENTRALIZED FILE SHARING

Napster's centralized servers made it an easy target to shut down through legal action. During Napster's struggles, several other music file-sharing services sprang up. Some were small and threatened with legal action by the record labels and subsequently shut down before they could catch on.

Austin-based Audiogalaxy, which included in-house music reviews and tried to promote obscure bands, was sued quickly after the record labels' success against Napster. Before shutting down, it paid the labels a "substantial sum" that neither party disclosed. But other file-sharing services that do not rely on centralized servers have been nearly impossible to bring to court.

Sharing music files is not the only thing that P2P networks can be used for. Other applications have been developed that take advantage of P2P's inherent strengths—specifically, the amount of unused computing power on individual PCs at the edges of the network and the inability to track the numerous computers.

Gnutella

Gnutella's existence owes much to the mass-communication power among Internet users. Gnutella gets its name from GNU ("GNU's Not Unix!") and Nutella (a hazelnut and chocolate spread). Gnutella was created over two weeks in March

fair use

An exception to copyright law that allows someone to use an excerpt of a work without paying for its use. Reviews of works or their use in commentary or criticism are examples of fair use.

2000 by two developers, Justin Frankel and Tom Pepper, who a few years earlier had created the program Winamp, which allowed digital music files to be played. AOL, who had bought their company in 1999, deemed Gnutella an unauthorized research project and quashed it. However, **open-source** developers were able to post Gnutella's code to other developers as well as give them access to a type of chat room in which they could communicate with each other in real time as they worked on developing Gnutella. Through this loose-knit collaborative network of volunteer developers, Gnutella was improved and distributed on the Internet as an open-source program that nobody could claim ownership of.

Although Gnutella started out as an application, it has transformed into a P2P protocol. Gnutella lets users exchange not only music files but other kinds of files as well. Late Gnutella developer Gene Kan said Gnutella's strength is in how it mimics natural communication. He compared a file request made over the Gnutella network to someone arriving at a crowded cocktail party and asking where the sushi is. The query goes from one person to another through the crowd until it reaches people with sushi and they say, "It's here!" The news is passed back to the person wanting sushi, and the person goes through the crowd and gets it. The truly decentralized nature of Gnutella makes it extremely difficult, if not impossible, for any one company or person to control. A drawback to Gnutella is that it sometimes takes longer for queries to "ripple through" the network than if there were a central server with a database of everything available. Two popular Gnutella-based software programs are BearShare and LimeWire.

Freenet

Freenet was created as a system utilizing a P2P network structure that would allow people to freely publish or view all types of information from all over the world. Like Gnutella, it is an open-source system in which volunteers work on developing and improving the application. According to Freenet's founders, its main goals include the following:

- Uncensorable dissemination of controversial information
- Efficient distribution of high-bandwidth content
- Universal personal publishing[10]

Although the second goal is what has attracted the most media attention and the wrath of media companies because of the potential to distribute audio and video files, Freenet's first and third goals could have much more of an effect on online mass communication.

Freenet protects freedom of speech by enabling anonymous and uncensorable publication of material ranging from grassroots alternative journalism to banned exposés. This could have important implications for distributing news that otherwise would not be seen in the mainstream press. By letting anyone have a website, even if the person doesn't own a computer, Freenet essentially gives every member of the public a printing press.

Jabber

Jabber, as its name suggests, concentrates on real-time messaging, much like other instant-messaging (IM) systems such as AOL's Instant Messenger (AIM), ICQ, or Yahoo! Messenger. One problem with proprietary IM systems has been that users of one system cannot communicate with users of another system, although other

WEB LINK
Gnutella.com
www.gnutellaforums.com

WEB LINK
BearShare
www.bearshare.com/

WEB LINK
LimeWire
ww.limewire.com/

WEB LINK
Freenet Project
freenetproject.org/cgi-bin/twiki/view/Main/WebHome

WEB LINK
Jabber Software Foundation
www.jabber.org

swarming

The process used by some P2P systems in which multiple downloaders of the same file are temporarily coordinated in order to speed up the downloading process.

distributed computing

Individual, autonomous computers that work together toward a common goal, typically a large, complex project that requires more computing power than any individual computer could have.

programs have been created in recent years to largely overcome that problem. It is the equivalent of a person on an AT&T telephone system not being able to communicate with someone on a Verizon system. This obviously reduces the effectiveness of IM systems. Jabber uses a set of XML-based communication protocols that do allow users from a variety of platforms to communicate with each other, although some companies have blocked or frequently change their protocols so Jabber no longer works with them.

▼ STREAMING FILE SHARING: THE NEXT WAVE

There are various ways for Internet users on a P2P network to share streaming files without using a centralized server. One of the most popular methods is called **swarming**, and uses a protocol such as BitTorrent, perhaps the most popular file-sharing protocol on the Internet today.

BitTorrent works very efficiently and allows users, who would otherwise have to pay high server and bandwidth costs, to easily distribute large video and music files over the Internet. It generally operates on a principle that encourages sharing among peers, so that the more content a user shares the more content that user can likewise access. Internet TV services such as Joost use similar swarming techniques to encourage efficient use and sharing of video files streamed over the Internet.

BitTorrent has become a widely used file-sharing service.

▲▼ New Distribution Technologies, New Legal, Ethical, and Social Issues

Along with the amazing empowerment that digital distribution brings to the general audience, there is also the potential for abuse from companies and from the public.

Record labels and other large media companies are relatively unsympathetic targets of the changes wrought by the Internet and digital media. Considering rising prices for entertainment, the homogenous nature of much of the content, and how disappointing it often is, it is hard to feel sorry for large media corporations as old distribution models are disrupted by new technologies.

The differences look especially stark when the volunteer open-source movement of software programmers and developers—in which information is freely shared and all efforts go toward a "virtual commons" from which all can benefit—is contrasted with the proprietary and copyrighted material from companies trying to maximize their profits, giving consumers very little say.

However, it is important to remember that the public can also abuse the system. Consider a new artist who self-produces her song and uploads it to her MySpace page. It becomes popular and is freely shared on the Internet. She receives some revenue from users who purchase the song, but likely misses out on far more revenue because of the number of people who get the song for free.

Similarly, although a service like Freenet, by protecting whistleblowers, would seem to reinforce the ability of people to keep governments honest, it could also facilitate false claims by a disgruntled employee against a company or government organization, with no fear of being discovered.

SETI@home: Is There Anybody Out There?

Mass communication does not stop at the communication satellites circling the earth. Ever since the first radio stations started transmitting their signals, the earth has inadvertently been broadcasting into space. It occurred to some astronomers that if there are extraterrestrial intelligent beings in the universe, they would also be sending out electromagnetic waves as byproducts of their technological development in communication. The search for extraterrestrial intelligence (SETI) began.

SETI is a massive project that involves radio telescopes pointing at small slivers of the sky and recording radio waves, which emanate from many types of celestial bodies, and then trying to determine if there are patterns among the waves that would demonstrate signs of intelligent life. Processing the massive amounts of data being returned is beyond even the most powerful supercomputer.

SETI@home was developed to harness the unused computing power among millions of home PCs to analyze the radio data that have been transmitted. Volunteers in the project download the software and data at certain intervals and their computers work through the information even as the computer owners use their computers normally. When each segment is complete, it is transmitted back to a central computer and a new packet of data is sent. There are safeguards in the system to make sure users cannot tamper with the data and make a false claim that they have found proof of extraterrestrial life.

Although not purely peer-to-peer computing, since a central server and database keeps track and stores the information, it is a good example of how digital distribution can be used. In what is called **distributed computing**, any number of volunteers can assist a project without inconveniencing themselves, since the program works in the background, and the free computing power amassed through the various users is many times more than what any research project could afford. The website also informs people of progress being

made, thereby engaging the public in a field it otherwise might not get involved in.

Several other projects have also begun that use the power of distributed-computing networks, including searching for cures for diseases such as cancer, working on models of global warming, and solving mathematical problems.

> **WEB LINK**
> SETI@home
> **setiathome.ssl.berkeley.edu/**

> **WEB LINK**
> Distributed computing projects
> **http://distributedcomputing.info/**

Along with new technologies must come new thinking on not only social but legal issues and ethical responsibilities.

▼ LEGAL ISSUES

Media organizations and writers, artists, musicians—anyone creating copyrighted media content for a living—want to be fairly compensated for their work. There would be no incentive, the reasoning goes, for an artist to create something only to have it rapidly copied and distributed without the artist getting any financial awards from her creation. With digital media, the very notion of copyright has been called into question, and several lawsuits are working their way through the court system that in some ways could increase control for copyright holders—which, in most cases, are media organizations and not individuals.

Digital **watermarks**, which allow content to be visibly or invisibly marked so it either cannot be altered, can be traced as it is distributed, or shows a history of how it has been altered, will be needed to make digital distribution more secure. However, many experts say this is a losing battle, as media companies spend millions trying to make digital content conform to real-world constraints. Whenever a new secure system is proposed, it is guaranteed that a crack, or way to break the system, is not far behind. Rather than deal with this fundamental issue, media organizations have tried to have laws changed that favor copyright holders and have taken people to court for merely publicizing the fact that there are security weaknesses in encrypted or watermark systems.

Other legal issues involve the status of messages sent by private citizens. Is a posting to a discussion board considered "publishing," and could a poster be sued for libel? What if a person writes something libelous in a private email to a friend and that friend includes the email in a discussion-board topic? Who could be sued for libel? These and many other similar legal issues have yet to be resolved.

In other words, the public will have to start considering issues of privacy, libel, defamation, and possibly lawsuits—all issues traditional media companies must consider every day—as it gains access to a worldwide distribution network.

▼ ETHICAL ISSUES

We have mostly concentrated on media organizations and how digital distribution affects them. However, now that anybody can essentially be a publisher with their own website, sometimes private individuals can unwillingly be thrust into the public eye.

In 1999, Turkish journalist Mahir Cagri became an Internet sensation largely because of his poorly designed and poorly written homepage. He took the jokes about him good-naturedly and was even able to achieve a small measure of fame in other ways because of it, but what if Cagri had instead felt humiliated by the millions of people laughing at him? What if he lost work because his public or professional image suffered? Who has responsibility for what happens if something is posted on the Web?

With the ubiquity of camera phones and small video cameras, there has been a growing problem of young women suffering humiliation when nude photographs of themselves have been forwarded by boyfriends or posted on websites. In September 2010 Tyler Clementi, a Rutgers University freshman, committed suicide by jumping off the George Washington Bridge after his roommate and

watermark

A symbol or mark embedded in a photograph that identifies who owns the copyright for that photograph. With digital media, any piece of content can be watermarked, and the watermark, itself digital, can be completely invisible.

another student secretly recorded a video of him having a sexual encounter with another man.

Beyond the issue of legality is the question of ethics. What ethical principles should be followed by media companies and the general public in deciding whether to post or publish material? Companies often have professional codes of conduct or codes of ethics, but no such general code yet exists for the public publishing content.

The public's "right to know" is often cited by journalists as a guiding principle when weighing ethical issues regarding publishing a story that is damaging to someone. Yet it is hard to say that the "right to know" outweighs someone's right to privacy when publishing a nude picture of an ex-girlfriend or when making defamatory claims about someone on a blog.

▼ SOCIAL ISSUES

It is useful to revisit some of media guru Marshall McLuhan's observations, even though he died in 1980 and his comments on electronic media were made before the Internet revolution. McLuhan argued that print media disconnected people from their basic tribal emotions and behavior, which were generally visual, oral, and interactive. McLuhan suggested that satellite-based electronic media were retribalizing society. By reconstituting a worldwide oral tradition and bringing all senses into full play, the electronic media were leading to the creation of a "global village." McLuhan argued that electronic media help put people back in touch with basic tribal emotions and reconnect with each other around the world.

Cell phones and portable computers can be especially important for communication, especially in remote or developing regions.

Though it is perhaps an overly simplistic view, consider how McLuhan's notion of a global village might today be applied to the Internet and other online media. With its global reach and interactivity, the Internet takes us even further toward a notion of simultaneous worldwide communications. Email may have the potential to reconnect people to their tribal emotions, even though it is still primarily text based. Imagine the transformations that can take place when email or other communication technologies are video based.

There are still many unresolved issues regarding how people socialize with each other online. Almost everyone who has been on discussion groups or in chat rooms has seen someone making verbal attacks, often far more abusive than the attacker ever would make in person. Others may find the comments offensive, but there is little they can currently do except chastise the attacker—and perhaps get attacked as well.

With greater ability to mass distribute messages also comes greater responsibility in thinking how that distribution will affect others. This even applies to the level of forwarding a humorous photograph received by email. Will the busy colleague really appreciate receiving this? Could this be considered offensive to others who may receive it, because it perpetuates gender, religious, or ethnic stereotypes?

Some of the socialization issues regarding the Internet will gradually work themselves out as general norms of behavior form and become accepted. Technology will also make it easy to filter out people who consistently break those rules. Peer-review systems may also encourage responsible social behavior and better-quality information or at least let people filter out junk better.

New issues are likely to arise because of improvements in technology as well. With video-based chats or emails it will be harder to hide one's true identity, and digitally created avatars may not be adequate substitutes for people who want "face-to-face" telecommunication. Social norms could change so that someone who chooses not to use video communication is assumed to have something to hide and is therefore taken less seriously, just as people who post to discussion groups without identifying themselves are today. Old prejudices regarding race, gender, and looks could also resurface in video-based systems.

LOOKING BACK AND MOVING FORWARD

New distribution patterns through the Internet can greatly diminish the importance of established distribution channels on which media organizations have built their business models. Just how large media organizations will adjust to these changes in distribution, or how they will find viable business models within these new dynamics, is still unclear. What is clear is that media organizations have much less control over how their content is distributed than they used to, unless they choose to put technological constraints on digital media to give them certain analog characteristics, such as making it hard or impossible to copy from one format to another. However, attempts at exactly these limitations have met with resistance from consumers and led to the creation of programs that allow the public to sidestep security measures.

The Internet has added a new element to the traditional one-to-many distribution method, in which media content was sent by one organization to the public through clearly defined distribution channels according to fixed procedures and rules. A person who wrote and self-published a book, for example, would not be able to have major bookstores carry her book, as she would not have access to the distribution channels needed to send copies of the book to the different outlets. Nor would she have the same access to book reviewers in major media outlets, making it difficult for the public to learn about her book even if they could easily purchase a copy at a bookstore. The same obstacles could be applied to other content creators outside of mainstream media, from musicians to aspiring filmmakers.

The many-to-many distribution model made possible by the Internet completely sidesteps traditional distribution networks that favored established media companies. Now any content creator can reach millions worldwide simply by putting content on the Internet and especially the World Wide Web. And as already mentioned, there are no unit production costs associated with making more copies of media content. Members of the public who download media content from a website are creating a new copy. If they are connected to a P2P-type network, then this copy is also available to others on the network.

The Internet also lets the public completely bypass established media outlets and communicate directly through a host of means. Much of what people talk about may well be derived from what they see in the media, but it doesn't have to be.

This is not to say that there is no place for established media companies and their distribution networks in an online environment. As even a short visit to the Web will show, publishers, record labels, film-production companies, and other media companies act as quality-control gatekeepers of sorts, filtering out substandard content and supporting higher-quality content. This of course may not always seem to be the case when one looks at new books, television shows, films, or music being released, but the fact is that the financial support of the media companies increases production quality of media content and helps greatly in marketing that content. If anything, in the new world of digital distribution this filtering will become more important than ever, as most people will not want to spend lots of time trying to find something of quality in the flood of material that is available.

Various kinds of media content will likely exist in some kind of multiple-distribution system, in which "mainstream" content is accessible through traditional distribution outlets but also available in downloads or on-demand formats from the Internet. Independent content creators outside of mainstream media will largely rely on Internet distribution and **viral marketing**, or information on the content spread by word of mouth online, to get noticed by a large audience. Some content creators that seem to have mass-market appeal will receive offers from mainstream media and then have traditional marketing and distribution channels at their disposal as well.

Media companies will have to be aware of the trends and shifting desires of the online audience if they want to capitalize on networked distribution. Media-content distribution that previously required months of careful marketing and advertising planning, as well as the production of multiple copies and their transport to stores, can now take place in a matter of weeks or even days if the online audience decides it likes something. This is part of the power of social media, or what is called Web 2.0, the subject of the next chapter.

viral marketing

Spreading news and information about media content through word of mouth, usually via online discussion groups, chats, and emails, without utilizing traditional advertising and marketing methods.

DISCUSSION QUESTIONS

1. Have you ever mass-forwarded a funny or strange video or email? If so, what was the video? What do you think the consequences were for the subject of the video among friends or family of that person or people in the video?

2. How do you think the telecommunication landscape might be different in the United States if the government had supported the development of a nationwide telegraph system rather than relying on private industry to do so, and how might things change if the government supported the development of broadband Internet for everyone?

3. News organizations were changed by the telegraph, and a whole new business of news, that of the wire services, was created because of the telegraph. Discuss other industries that could benefit from rapid dissemination of information and how and why they would benefit from it.

4. Choose one of the common methods of online communication and think of how it could be improved in terms of facilitating communication between people, ensuring quality communication, and enabling the greatest number of users to distribute information.

5. Discuss possible social, political, and economic ramifications of a completely anonymous free information service such as Freenet. Does such a service need to have guidelines, and if so, what kinds of guidelines? Are guidelines even possible with such a service?

6. Should someone who runs a pornographic website containing images of him- or herself be fired by an employer because it could give the employer a bad image, even if the person never states where he or she works on the website? Why or why not?

7. With increased broadband availability, do you think people will be more inclined to share files of copyrighted material? Why or why not?

8. Do some research on distributed-computing sites, choose one, and come prepared to discuss what it has accomplished to date, if anything.

9. Discuss ways that the digital divide within your country could be reduced. How would the system be paid for and managed? What effects do you think it would have on the quality of Internet service? What social effects do you think it would have for people who are now able to have broadband Internet access?

FURTHER READING

Distant Writing: A History of the Telegraph Companies in Britain Between 1838 and 1868. http://distantwriting.co.uk/default.aspx.

Media, Technology, and Society—A History: From the Telegraph to the Internet. Brian Winston (1998) Routledge.

The Creation of the Media: Political Origins of Modern Communications. Paul Starr (2004) Basic Books.

Telecommunications and Empire. Jill Hills (2007) University of Illinois Press.

Spy Satellites and Other Intelligence Technologies That Changed History. Thomas Graham Jr. and Keith Hansen (2007) University of Washington Press.

Linked: How Everything Is Connected to Everything Else and What It Means. Albert Laszlo-Barabasi (2003) Plume.

Emergence: The Connected Lives of Ants, Brains, Cities and Software. Steven Johnson (2001) Scribner.

Peer-to-Peer: Harnessing the Disruptive Power of Technology. Andy Oram, ed. (2001) O'Reilly.

Uncanny Networks: Dialogues with the Virtual Intelligentsia. Geert Lovink (2004) MIT Press.

Remix: Making Art and Commerce Thrive in the Hybrid Economy. Lawrence Lessig (2008) Penguin Press.

Code: And Other Laws of Cyberspace, Version 2.0. Lawrence Lessig (2006) Basic Books. (Also downloadable for free at http://codev2.cc/)

The Future of Ideas: The Fate of the Commons in a Connected World. Lawrence Lessig (2001) Random House.

Cyber Bullying: Protecting Teens and Adults from Online Bullies, 1st ed. Samuel McQuade III, James Colt, and Nancy Meyer (2009) Praeger.

MEDIA QUIZ ANSWERS

2. True.

3. Optical telegraph.

5. A network effect, though often ill-defined, usually refers to the power that comes from more people being on an interactive communications network and is best exemplified by Metcalfe's Law and Reed's Law.

6. Peer-to-peer. Each computer on the network can store, receive, and send information to any other computer on the network.

7. The Net neutrality debate is over whether telecommunications companies should be able to control the speed by which certain types of content can travel over the Internet and whether they can charge more for heavy Internet users.

8. Perfect infinite copies, instantaneous distribution, low distribution costs.

9. False.

10. False.

8

SOCIAL MEDIA AND WEB 2.0

LEARNING OBJECTIVES

By the end of this chapter you should be able to:

- Define what social media is.

- Explain the differences between social media and traditional media.

- List the main characteristics of social media.

- Explain the historical development of social media within a larger mass-communications context.

- Understand how audiences are changing from consumers to "produsers."

- Explore some of the ethical and legal implications around social media.

In March 2011, news that would normally cause a good deal of anxiety in New York City—that an Egyptian cobra had escaped from New York's Bronx Zoo—became largely defanged when the snake on the loose started tweeting. Within days, the snake had 200,000 followers on Twitter, including Mayor Michael Bloomberg, and was making comments multiple times a day on a range of social, political, and entertainment issues while on the lam:

(March 28)

@BronxZoosCobra: Dear NYC, Apples and snakes have gone together from the beginning.

@BronxZoosCobra: A lot of people are asking how I can tweet with no access to a computer or fingers. Ever heard of an iPhone? Duh.

@BronxZoosCobra: Donald Trump is thinking about running for president?! Don't worry, I'll handle this. Where is Trump Tower, exactly?

@BronxZoosCobra: Leaving Wall Street. These guys make my skin crawl.

The humorous tweets continued even after it was finally captured six days after escaping, only 100 feet from its enclosure. A naming contest soon followed, organized in part by the *New York Daily News*, and the famous snake got the name "Mia" after votes were counted. Mia tweeted her feelings on the matter:

(April 7)

@BronxZoosCobra: So, the vote is in. They want to name me Mia. But in my heart I'll always know that my true name is Mrs. Justin Bieber.

Fake Twitter accounts can be quite funny, but they have also caused a good deal of confusion when it becomes unclear if an account is fake or not. Phweeters (phony tweeters) have also crossed the lines of good taste when they have falsely reported deaths, such as in 2009 when someone faked a journalist's Twitter account and reported the death of Cincinnati Bengals wide receiver Chris Henry twelve hours before he actually died from a fall off a truck. Some news organizations picked up the tweet and reported it as news without first checking if the account was valid or not.

On July 4, 2011, Fox News claimed its Twitter account was hacked when a tweet was sent falsely reporting that President Obama had been assassinated. A little over a month earlier, Representative Anthony Weiner

(D-NY) claimed that his Twitter account had been hacked when one of his followers received lewd pictures of a man in boxer shorts. In Weiner's case, however, it turned out that he had actually been taking indecent pictures of himself and sending them to some followers he was flirting with online, despite being married. The subsequent scandal forced Weiner to resign and likely ruined his political career.

These examples of microblogging show how the media environment has changed dramatically in a few short years because of social media. Today we are accustomed to getting information and news in short, digestible chunks and forwarding to friends to share. Sometimes, as in the case of Anthony Weiner, we may share a bit too much of ourselves online.

The tools and capabilities of social media have been around in some form ever since the earliest days of the Internet, but not until the past few years has their true potential been realized in business and media companies. Many of the changes have been driven from the ground up, rather than by traditional media companies, a fact that simultaneously gives power to social media and often greatly threatens traditional business models. In some cases, the nature of certain professions is being called into question, due in part to a combination of economic forces and new ways of producing and sharing content.

The term "Web 2.0" has become popular in describing various aspects of social media. Coined at a 2004 conference by technology publisher O'Reilly, the term, despite its popularity, has had questionable descriptive value. Although catchy in that it mirrors the terminology used for new versions of software, it also to some extent misleads.

There was no major technological shift or improvement in the Web that would differentiate "Web 1.0" from "Web 2.0." Rather, the term was meant to symbolize a few changing aspects of the Web. One was the sense of the Web being revived after the dot-com collapse of 2000, when much of the hype surrounding the Web economy during the late 1990s turned out to be so much hot air. Another was the changing uses of the Web, involving more people working with and talking to each other than had been seen before. Wikipedia is a notable example of this kind of sea change in cooperation and content creation, but there are many other examples, some of which will be discussed in this chapter.

Although Web 2.0 (along with the many variations it has spawned since then— Me 2.0, etc.) will likely remain as a general term to describe the fundamental changes taking place in online media today, we will try to avoid the term and use the more descriptive term "social media." As we will see, this term also needs to be carefully defined.

◣ Defining Social Media

"Social media" is still a new enough idea that it continues to be defined by scholars, professionals, and the press. It is hard to find a definition everyone agrees on, partly because the tools for social media change with advances in technologies, and popular sites or trends seem to lose popularity almost as quickly as they came into the limelight and were touted as The Next Big Thing.

We can look at some commonly used definitions and from these definitions start to parse underlying elements common to all of them, then apply these to the realm of mass communication.

According to John Jantsch, author of the Duct Tape Marketing blog, "social media" can be defined as "the use of technology combined with social

WEB LINK
Duct Tape Marketing
www.ducttapemarketing.com/

interaction to create or co-create value."[1] He keeps the definition concise because his readers are busy marketing professionals.

PR professional and social-media expert Brian Solis defines social media as "a shift in how people discover, read, and share news and information and content. It's a fusion of sociology and technology, transforming monologue (one to many) into dialog (many to many.)"[2]

Anvil Media, a search engine marketing firm, provides a definition derived from sociology:

> An umbrella term that defines the various activities that integrate technology, social interaction, and the construction of words and pictures. This interaction, and the manner in which information is presented, depends on the varied perspectives and "building" of shared meaning, as people share their stories, and understandings.[3]

There are certain common aspects of these definitions. All mention the intersection of technology, social interaction, and information sharing. These may seem like simple elements, but they have transformed many aspects of mass communication and promise to disrupt them even more.

Before looking at the elements in more detail and exploring how they are disrupting mass communication and media industries, it is necessary to see how social media differ from traditional media.

▼ DIFFERENCES WITH TRADITIONAL MEDIA

One clear difference between social media and traditional media is the change from a broadcast or monolog model of one-to-many to a more dialogic model of many-to-many communication. Of course this does not mean that mass media audiences prior to the Internet never spoke with each other—there were fan clubs, letters to the editor, and a variety of ways people did interact. However, the flow of communication favored the broadcaster sending a message to many people simultaneously, with audience members having limited means to share their thoughts with each other on a mass scale.

Consider how someone in the 1970s might be able to share his thoughts on the previous night's episode of a popular yet controversial situation comedy like *All in the Family*. If he watched with friends or family he could of course share his thoughts with them during or after the show. Similarly, he might discuss the show at the office the next day.

However, if the viewer felt particularly strongly about a racist remark made by the character Archie Bunker and felt that others should know how offensive the remark was, his options to communicate his feelings to a broad audience were limited, expensive, and generally did not generate dialog. He could write a letter of complaint to the network or the FCC, with no guarantee that he would hear from either. He could write a letter to the editor of the local newspaper, but even if it was published, it would reach a limited audience of only the paper's readers (and only those who read the letters to the editor that day). He could purchase an advertisement in the newspaper, which might get more attention than a letter to the editor, but that would be expensive or the paper might choose not to accept such an ad. Or he could create a flyer, make photocopies, and hand them out or mail them to people, which would be both expensive and time-consuming.

If the viewer was persistent (or flamboyant) enough, or if he got enough people to join his cause and perhaps hold a demonstration or march, his crusade might get picked up as a news story in the local press, perhaps even local television, thus perhaps attracting more people to his cause. Although at first glance this would seem to be a kind of many-to-many form of communication, consider the mechanisms by which it occurred—his message was communicated primarily through mass media channels. Furthermore, it is unlikely that he would have had the resources—either time, money, or media attention—to carry out a campaign like this in the first place.

Now let's look at what this viewer would do circa 2011. Let us say that a regular viewer of the animated Fox show *Family Guy* gets offended at a racist comment made by Peter, the father.

His first public complaint is likely not a letter to the FCC or the Fox network but to the discussion-board area of the show's website, where fans of the show talk about a range of issues. Or maybe he goes to any number of other discussion groups or fan sites devoted to *Family Guy* and comments there. He may find that many others share his opinion and have already suggested ways to show their displeasure to the show's creators.

Perhaps one of the members in the group has created a mash-up video of such stereotypes found on various prime-time shows or in the news. The video is uploaded to YouTube, where it gets viewed hundreds of thousands of times within a couple weeks, generating further discussions among YouTube viewers in the comments section of the video. If the video is viewed enough times or talked about enough, mainstream news organizations may cover the story, amplifying the interest among the public and getting more people to the discussions.

Today viewers of popular programs have many ways to communicate with each other through social media, creating discussions of all aspects of a show.

What is notable in this latter example is that, except with the original source material, traditional mass media organizations are not involved (until perhaps later in the process), yet far more members of the public may be affected in a very short time than would be the case in the 1970s—or even the 1990s. More importantly, our viewer may never even think to write a letter to the editor of the local newspaper or the FCC. A complete media ecosystem can be created and sustained through social interaction using tools that social media provide. Mainstream media may still play a role, of course, but they do not have to be involved like in the past.

This follows what new-media scholar and NYU professor Clay Shirky calls a "publish, then filter" model.[4] Traditional media industries such as news are based on a "filter, then publish" model of information. From a vast universe of possible information, specialists or professionals (editors, music producers, etc.) select which information will be used as their content. They act as a bottleneck to the flow of information available to the public by the decisions they make, based partly on the limitations of their medium, such as time limits in TV news or space limits in print media.

This material—the news in a newspaper or the bands promoted by a major record label or MTV—is then distributed to the general public. The public is likely completely unaware of all the other possible types of information it could have received. Media business models have been built around this way of controlling and disseminating information, and even entire professions have made this model an essential part of their professional identities. An example is journalism, which many journalists recite is necessary for a healthy democracy because of the role they play in informing the public and being watchdogs of government. This puts journalists squarely in the role of gatekeepers of information, as professionals with special access to the halls of power and unique skills and training that presumably give them the ability to decide what information should be disseminated to the public.

However, as seen in the "publish, then filter" model, which is prevalent in social media, many of these professional assumptions are being challenged, as are the business models. If the public can connect directly with the vast universe of information out there and find what is relevant through a combination of social networks, ratings systems, and online discussions, then what role do organizations that restrict the flow of information to the public serve?

Another big difference between social media and traditional media is cost. Most people cannot afford to start a newspaper, or to create a radio or television station, as the costs are simply too high. However, as has been noted earlier in this book, with digital media and the Internet the costs for creating media content and widely distributing it have been greatly reduced, to the point that they are well within the reach of many.

This is not to say that traditional mass media are no longer important or powerful, as they clearly are for a couple different reasons. First, they provide much of the source material that the public then discusses. In this way, the media can be said to serve an important **agenda-setting** function, in that they give us much of the material that we talk about, even if they do not necessarily tell us what to think. Second, they tend to amplify events through media coverage because they generally have larger audiences than the majority of social-media sites. Audiences may be fragmenting with traditional media channels such as cable television, but for the most part the audiences with traditional media are still larger than many social-media sites.

agenda setting

A role the media play in deciding which topics to cover and thus, by virtue of the fact that the media has covered them, which topics the public deems important and discussion worthy.

▲▼ What Is "Social" About Social Media?

There has always been a social component with media, of course. From the earliest days of print, reading was usually done aloud and in groups. Families gathered around the radio in the 1930s and 1940s to listen to their favorite radio shows, and people came together to listen to music, dance, and of course socialize. Even television, that maligned most passive and isolating of mediums, often has important social aspects, as families and friends gather to watch shows or sporting events and of course talk about the programs afterward. Some of HBO's most popular original series, such as *The Sopranos* or *Game of Thrones,* generated what became known as "water-cooler buzz," or discussions among workers about a show the day after it aired, which in turn created more interest among people who hadn't seen the show.

When looking at social interaction compared to traditional media, perhaps a more accurate question is actually this: How are social media more "social" than traditional media?

It is a fundamental and important question. If it can be shown that traditional media are no less social than what is being touted as a revolutionary, transformative new kind of media, then it would follow that Web 2.0 and all the talk around it is just the latest hype about new technology.

The Center for Social Media in the School of Communication at American University says that there are five fundamental ways in which people's media habits are changing: choice, conversation, curation, creation, and collaboration.[5] These five components provide an excellent framework within which to better understand social media.

▼ CHOICE

The public of course has far more media choices than it did in the past and far more options of styles and genres within media types than it ever did. Even so, thinking of the public or audience primarily as passive consumers of media ignores the variety of ways people can interact and find the media content they want. Through search engines, recommendations from friends (often known only from online interactions), RSS feeds, and of course traditional media channels, people today are generally more proactive in getting the type of content they want than in the past.

Note that "more choice" does not necessarily mean "better quality." Simply because there are many more options does not mean that the quality of content people may find is going to be better. However, greater choice does mean that more media types and channels are competing with each other to attract the attention of the audience. This alters how some media are produced, how they are promoted and marketed, and even what types of content may be created in the first place.

▼ CONVERSATION

From the earliest days of the Internet conversation was important, and it continues to be a defining characteristic of social media. Discussion groups, Usenet, email, IM, and Twitter have been or continue to be important tools that give people the ability to communicate easily with each other on a scale and in ways not possible with traditional media.

Companies have had their reputations tarnished or made because of online conversations, unknown artists have become famous through them, and funny or embarrassing moments caught on videotape have made some people instant (if short-lived) celebrities.

Comcast has learned the hard way about the power of social media. In 2006, a customer posted a video on YouTube of a Comcast technician sleeping in the customer's home while waiting on hold—with Comcast—for over an hour. In 2008, Comcast was ranked at the bottom of the American Customer Satisfaction Index, and hundreds of customers contributed their complaints to the website ComcastMustDie.com. As part of its efforts to improve customer service, Comcast started monitoring blogs and online conversations and discussing customer concerns directly on the online forums. Many companies follow online discussions about themselves, but Comcast took an extra step in often responding to bloggers and engaging in conversation with them.

Many companies have discovered that their brands and corporate images are not what they claim in traditional advertising or public relations efforts, but what the customers say they are. The focus on conversation is one other example of the shift from a lecture to a dialog between companies (including media companies) and the public.

▼ CURATION

With so many options available today, how can people find the kind of media content they like? The traditional gatekeepers of information and knowledge, such as media professionals and librarians, are finding their roles changing in the social-media environment. One major change is a shift from a "gatekeeping" model to what Australian media scholar Axel Bruns calls a "gatewatching" model, in which people act as their own filters, classifiers, and reviewers.

Classifying content happens through an activity such as **tagging** or creating **folksonomies** of definitions. This helps bring some order to the vast array of

tagging

Defining a piece of information, file, image, or other type of digital media in a nonhierarchical system that helps describe what the information is.

folksonomies

A collection of tags created by users that provide metadata, or data about data, regarding information.

content that is out there and helps in searches. An important difference in tagging is that people are not waiting to hear from an authority on how to classify terms, such as a librarian would do—they are doing it themselves. Sites such as Delicious, photo-sharing site Flickr, and YouTube have all encouraged tagging among users, which makes the content more searchable and helps users see relations they may never have seen before between terms.

Digg is an example of how curatorial activities among users can enhance a site's relevance for everyone. Users vote on stories that have been submitted, and stories with the most votes get pushed to the front page. This creates a kind of natural hierarchy of content, where typically material that is deemed most relevant or interesting to the Digg community becomes more visible to other users of the site, even if they do not vote on stories themselves.

The online environment lends itself to a curatorial mode of contributing to the social-media space. It is fairly easy to tag something with terms, or to write a one-paragraph review of a book or movie, or to write a few lines on a product recently purchased. Similarly, it is much easier to find fault with something. Online reviews written by other consumers have become increasingly important in consumers' decisions ranging from household goods to media products.

WEB LINK
Delicious: Social bookmarking
www.delicious.com

▼ CREATION

The digital media tools that make it easy for people to create content have played a major role in the rise of user-generated media content. The other important factor, as discussed in the previous chapter, is the low cost of distributing that content through online networks. Without the ability to easily and cheaply disseminate content, the media landscape today would look vastly different. It could even be said that social media as we know them now would not exist.

Simply because the tools are readily available to create media does not of course mean that everyone will start churning out great works of art. Most people in fact will be satisfied consuming media and not creating anything, and there will be far more amateurish or poor-quality types of content online than there will be high art. Even with something like Twitter, in which messages are 140 characters or less, 90 percent of the content is generated by only 10 percent of the users.[6] However, even if a small percentage of the people online create and share content, there will still be a larger pool of media content than existed in the traditional media world because of the sheer numbers of people online.

Creating content is not without its challenges. As noted elsewhere in this book, intellectual property laws are being challenged by a digital culture that sees nothing wrong with borrowing freely from existing media to create something new. Furthermore, many people online have come to expect a variety of media content for free. Rather than encourage creativity, as intellectual property laws were meant to do, more restrictive laws may have the opposite effect in that they will remove creative material from the public domain. But by the same token, content creators should be compensated for their work.

▼ COLLABORATION

widget

A portable chunk of code that can be embedded in HTML pages and that often gives users extra functionality to their pages.

The willingness of people to collaborate on a common good for no personal monetary gain is perhaps one of the biggest surprises one encounters when first examining social media. It is one thing to spend hours creating a **widget** with the hopes of selling it or copyrighting it for licensing, but quite another to do so and provide

Lily Allen: MySpace Star Reaches the Stars

A single by an up-and-coming artist is nothing new, but what makes Lily Allen's rise to pop stardom in the music charts unique is her use of MySpace and the role it played in getting her noticed by mainstream music media and launching her to fame.

Allen was not a complete newbie to the music and arts scene in the UK. She already had some experience singing and performing in some films and had a record contract with Regal Records, but they were unable to support her album much due to their commitments with other recording artists.

So Allen used her MySpace page to release and promote demos of her songs, and her site started attracting thousands of listeners. When a music publication noted her growing popularity on MySpace, that attracted even more people to her site to download her music. By early 2009, her songs had been downloaded from the site more than 32 million times, and she had nearly five hundred thousand MySpace friends.

As a sign of the different dynamics of social media and the complexities that come with stardom in the mainstream, Allen often used her MySpace page to discuss personal issues or criticize her press coverage and even her own behavior. Similarly, when she had a miscarriage in 2008, the page became the hub for countless condolences from fans. In 2009, she stopped making personal blog posts because she felt her words were often getting twisted in the mainstream media. But in early 2010 she started tweeting even as a new pregnancy and marriage kept her from touring.

In 2007 her second album, *It's Not Me, It's You*, debuted at number one on the charts in Australia and the UK. Her first album, *Alright, Still*, has won her numerous awards and sold over 2.6 million copies worldwide. In 2011, in a very traditional media way, her representatives announced that she was creating a record label, In The Name Of, an imprint of Columbia Records.

WEB LINK
Lily Allen MySpace page
www.myspace.com/lilymusic

it to the Web community for free use, or to provide open access to your project and invite others to work on it and improve on it, as Linus Torvalds did with what became the open-source Linux operating system.

There have been a number of cases of collaboration extending from the online realm to offline, especially in organizing people around politics or social movements. In fact, the most successful uses of online tools in political campaigns have included ample opportunities for people to socialize in real-world settings as well. This was the lesson learned by the Howard Dean campaign in 2004, from looking at Al Gore's failed presidential campaign in 2000. Gore's campaign used online media primarily as another media channel, asking for donations and alerting users about issues and appearances. Dean used online tools to encourage supporters to get together in person and act, generating millions of dollars for his campaign in the process. Although Dean eventually dropped out of the presidential race, the lessons learned from that campaign were applied to Obama's presidential campaign in 2008.

Widgets are useful applications created and shared by members of the public, often for free but sometimes for a small fee.

In some ways, the realization that people need real-world socializing to complement their online socializing harkens back to the earliest days of social media, long before that term was applied. In fact, the need to meet, interact, and discuss was an impetus for the earliest online communities, many of which are precursors to today's social-media tools and still widely used today.

▲▼ Types of Social Media

In 1980 France launched its videotext service, or text delivery over the air or by cable for presentation on television screens or other electronic displays, known then as Teletel and today as Minitel. Ahead of its time, Minitel was an example of one of the most successful early interactive online information services before the Web. Minitel worked because the government subsidized it and provided access devices to every home. Its biggest problem turned out to be the emergence of the World Wide Web, which quickly outclassed the stand-alone Minitel communication terminals. Despite these drawbacks, there were still 10 million Minitel users in 2009. However, France Telecom announced that it would finally close the Minitel service in June 2012.

Wireless connections with PDAs have made it easy for people to keep up with emails or online news at all times.

Many of the tools we now commonly associate with social media were used before social media became an Internet phenomenon. Even the pre-Web Minitel had what it called its "blue rooms," or adult-oriented chat rooms; interestingly, the only part of the service that generated a significant revenue stream. However, Web-related advances have led to a significant expansion in the use of modern social media. One main difference has been the development of tools that make creating and sharing content easier than ever. Other differences include the rapid growth of the Web audience and the increase in broadband Internet connections, which enhance the user experience of the Web. Wireless Internet capabilities have also played a role in expanding access to social media.

Here we will look specifically at some of the social-media tools and how they have developed and changed over time. Just as it is important to understand how print media developed in order to understand how the industry works today and why it works the way it does, it is useful to know how some of what we use online came about and how that has affected our social-media experiences.

▼ EMAIL

Email, or electronic mail, was one of the first uses of the Internet and until 2008 was the most popular Internet activity. In 2010 email moved down to third place, following social networking sites and online gaming.[7] It is easy to overlook email as an element of social media, especially as it has been overtaken by social networking sites and online gaming, but its ease of use, prevalence, and capabilities to send messages to more than one person make it a powerful communication tool.

Although email is an exchange of messages via telecommunication between two people, it is quite easy for an individual to create a mailing list and send out a single message to multiple people, in a sense "broadcasting" the message. This capability has caused more than a few red faces, as anyone can attest who has been on a mailing list in which one member made disparaging remarks about another member, thinking the response was only going to an individual and not to the entire list.

Mailing lists differ from discussion boards in that messages posted get sent directly to subscribers' email inboxes rather than returning to an online location that a member must visit in order to read the messages. **Listservs** are automated mailing-list administrators that allow for easy subscription, subscription cancellation, and sending of emails to subscribers on the list.

Mailing lists offer some of the same benefits as discussion boards. Longer discussions can take place, with comments written when it is convenient for participants to write, and often complex arguments can take place. Messages have the added benefit of arriving directly to a member's email inbox, making it more likely a participant will read or at least scan them. Drawbacks of mailing lists include information overload as the inbox gets full of messages and potential monopolization of the list by one or a few members sending multiple posts each day or sending irrelevant or inflammatory messages. It does not take too many of these types of posts for the value of a listserv to diminish for most participants.

Media organizations have taken advantage of mailing lists to help attract Internet users to their sites or to send them information they have specifically said they want. When registering for a website, a person is often asked to check boxes indicating content preferences for emails or whether any should be sent at all. This is called an **opt-in** list and can be especially valuable to marketers, as the customers have given permission in requesting certain types of content. Email newsletters may be used to keep an audience informed about the organization or for marketing purposes. Sending email newsletters and email marketing messages helps reduce mailing and printing costs for companies using direct mail marketing.

The principles that allow for easy creation of mailing lists are also responsible for what many consider the scourge of email: **spam**, or unsolicited email advertising. Spam, once rare and considered extremely bad form in the early days of the Internet, is now unfortunately all too common. Companies buy lists of email addresses much like print publishers buy mailing addresses from other magazines or

listservs

Also known as listserves, they are automated mailing-list administrators that allow for easy subscription, subscription cancellation, and sending of emails to subscribers on the list.

opt-in

A mailing list in which the user has chosen to receive emails and marketing materials.

spam

Unwanted email sent out by advertisers as a mass mailing.

Spam has become a huge problem, clogging inboxes and costing companies millions of dollars.

organizations. They create a bulk mailing list and send mass mailings advertising their products or services.

Computer programs troll the Internet and find email addresses, "harvesting" them to a central location that a spammer can then use to send messages or sell the list of emails to other companies.

A battle continues between spammers and companies creating software to block spam. Automated filtering software often removes much of the spam but may also inadvertently remove desired messages.

The problem with spam clogging the Internet and inboxes reflects the downside of easily being able to share content. Just as lowered costs of distribution on the Internet have helped create online communities and give the public a chance to distribute media content on a par with established media companies, it has also made it easier for individuals and companies to abuse that distribution system, making it less valuable for all. Legislators are fighting back in several states, however, with increasingly stringent antispam laws that penalize spammers. Still, antispam laws are generally not effective if the spammers are based overseas, as many are.

▼ DISCUSSION BOARDS AND WEB FORUMS

A discussion board is a type of online "bulletin board" where Internet users can post messages that can be seen by others coming to the discussion board and in which they can post responses to previous messages, or posts, or create their own discussions on a new topic. Series of messages that reply to a certain post are organized by threads according to their subject headers, making it easier for users coming to a discussion topic to follow the thread of the discussion back to earlier replies and the original posting.

Today, most discussions are on Web-based forums, which provide a variety of user-friendly tools to create and post discussions. The precursor to the Web forums was Usenet, created in 1979, which even today provides thousands of discussion boards, each separated by categories called **newsgroups**. Separating newsgroups by general categories, as well as letting anyone create their own newsgroup on any topic, helps make finding discussions of interest to users easier and facilitates users starting their own communities.

The formation of newsgroups by users shows how firmly rooted certain aspects of social media are in the Internet. Within general categories already created, users can create very specific subcategories, thus defining communities of interest. Until a few years ago, most news organizations did not permit or encourage discussion boards on their websites, in part because of their fear of being held liable for what readers might say on the boards and in part because they were worried that such discussion boards would detract from the focus the news organization wanted the audience to have—consuming the news content created by the organization.

However, now most news organizations have seen that providing a forum for readers to discuss news stories or other topics of interest related to the news has increased readers' engagement with the organization. At times, the conversation about a single news article may take on a life of its own, even perhaps outweighing the original article in terms of the value of information provided.

Partly because of the ease of sending messages, discussion boards often suffer from a few individuals who either send messages not related to the discussion-board topic or send numerous messages on variations of the same topic, effectively monopolizing the conversation space. Some discussion boards are moderated, which means a moderator either approves messages before they are posted or has

newsgroups

Categories for discussion groups within Usenet.

the ability to kick anyone off the discussion board or to block his or her posts. Another weakness of discussion boards is the difficulty in fully exploring an issue, especially when many people are commenting on various aspects of a complex topic, and the ease with which members can go off-topic.

Discussion boards are a vital form of mass communication on the Internet. Their format and asynchronous nature (i.e., not requiring users to be online at the same time) allow for relatively lengthy expositions on topics written whenever is convenient for the person sending the message. They also provide value even to members who do not post messages but simply read what others are writing, a practice called **lurking**. Some discussion-board creators encourage newcomers to lurk for a while so they can become familiar with the tone and type of topics being discussed on the board before posting messages of their own.

One of the earliest online communities, created through discussion groups, is still thriving today. The WELL (Whole Earth 'Lectronic Link) began in 1985 and continues to do well as a place of high-quality and interesting discussions among its members, many of whom are noted intellectuals, artists, authors, and creative thinkers.

The WELL has been likened to "the Park Place of email addresses" in a *Wired* story, and its unusual policy of demanding that users provide their real names rather than user names is supposed to have both helped the quality of discussion and fostered the strong sense of community that has built up among its members. Now owned by the Salon Media Group, publisher of *Salon* magazine, it charges its members fifteen dollars a month to belong (which, in Internet terms, may also help distinguish it as a Park Place address). It is one of the few online communities that have been successful in charging members to get in simply for discussions.

lurking

The practice of only reading what others write in online discussion boards but not contributing to the discussions.

WEB LINK
The WELL
www.well.com

▼ CHAT ROOMS

A chat room is a "virtual room" in which a community of users can visit and talk with each other through text messages, in real time. Like discussion groups, chat rooms are usually divided by topic, ranging from highly technical computer issues to pop stars to sex. Chat rooms differ from **instant messaging**, which also takes place in real time, in that instant messaging usually involves an online conversation between two or at most a few people.

Since chat rooms are synchronous, or take place in real time, they can be effectively used by media organizations to promote special guests online and let the audience "speak" to them, much like a radio station would have a musician visit the station and take listeners' calls.

Even without a star attraction, a chat room can often be chaotic and much like trying to talk to someone across the room at a crowded, noisy party. It can be difficult to tell who is being addressed, although some chat rooms have general rules and guidelines posted for proper behavior. Although messages may be sent in real time, the fact that they must be typed inevitably slows down the give-and-take that occurs during natural conversations—which can lead to confusion, as one chat room member may be responding to something asked two or more comments ago. Some chatters can monopolize the conversation as well or repeatedly post the same message, a practice called **scrolling**, which quickly draws the ire of other chatters in the room.

Chat rooms are perhaps best used when the topic of conversation is focused and relatively narrow. Viewers of a television show, for example, could be in a chat room during the show and discuss aspects of the stars, plot, or series with each

instant messaging

Often abbreviated to IM, it is a form of real-time communication through typed text over a computer network.

scrolling

The practice of simply repeating the same message in a chat room, which quickly draws the ire of other participants.

other. This type of interactivity, although not directly part of the show, can empower audience members as they establish connections between like-minded individuals in online communities and inform, educate, and entertain each other.

▼ BLOGS

Weblogs, or **blogs**, are web pages of short, frequently updated postings by an individual that are arranged chronologically, much like a series of diary entries or journal pages. Blogs can contain thoughts, links to sites of interest, rants, or whatever the blogger wants to write about. The earliest blogs go back to 1994, although it was more cumbersome to update posts then because of limitations to the technology.

The role that technology plays in social media is clearly evident with the rise in popularity of blogs. It was not until 1999 that blogs started increasing in popularity, largely due to new software tools that made blogging easier and did not require knowing HTML code or programming. Blogger.com, created in 1999 and bought by Google in 2003, is one such tool that makes creating, posting, and sharing a blog easy even for nontechnical people. WordPress is another very popular blogging platform that offers free blog hosting.

Some blogs, such as BoingBoing or the Huffington Post, have readerships in the millions and are quite influential, having an agenda-setting function much like mainstream media. Agenda setting is when a topic is covered by the media and therefore becomes a subject of discussion among the public.

When a blog becomes popular and attracts a lot of readers, it becomes impossible for the blogger to respond to most of the comments or discussions. In this way, blogs tend to develop the characteristics of traditional media, acting as a kind of "broadcast" or "publishing" model of information or news. A key difference between blogs and mainstream media remains the ease with which blogs have traditionally allowed users to subscribe and forward posts to others, as well as allowing for comments, although this difference is becoming less prominent as more mainstream media companies adopt the same techniques to encourage sharing of their content.

News organizations were even slower to adopt blogs as part of their media environment than they were to adopt discussion groups. In 2002, Steve Olafson, a longtime journalist for the *Houston Chronicle,* was fired for having a pseudonymous blog in which he criticized local politicians. Today, many big news organizations encourage their journalists to have blogs. However, news organizations must be careful about blogs from their journalists so as not to undermine the image of objectivity that journalists are supposed to present and not to undermine the organization's own credibility as a source for important news. A concern is that readers may not distinguish between an opinion shared in a journalist's blog and the news stories he or she files as part of the news organization.

Another element of blogs that often makes their use in the business world problematic is that they tend to have a raw, honest, and unfiltered quality. If a blog is too highly polished, or if it simply repeats public relations platitudes, it is unlikely to be respected or followed. This has been difficult for companies that are used to carefully controlling their messages to the public. The raw, honest element of blogs is a vital part of conversation, or true dialog.

Blogs have also moved from their text roots to easily include video, audio, and multimedia. This is an example of how users are creating content by mixing and matching different media types to make something new. Blogs also play an important curatorial role, as some popular blogs are followed because the blogger finds the best and most interesting ideas and makes relevant comments about that

blog or weblog

A type of website in which a person posts regular journal or diary entries with the posts arranged chronologically.

WEB LINK
BoingBoing
boingboing.net

WEB LINK
The Huffington Post
huffingtonpost.com

WEB LINK
Blogger
www.blogger.com

WEB LINK
WordPress
www.wordpress.org

Arianna Huffington, founder of the influential blog The Huffington Post.

content, which helps the blog's readers find information of interest to them and see it within a larger context.

wiki

A website that lets anyone add, edit, or delete pages and content.

Microblogs

As their name suggests, microblogs work much the same way as blogs, but the format and technology encourage shorter posts and content than what blogs allow. Today perhaps the most popular microblog is Twitter, which allows only 140 characters to be sent at a time, or "tweeted." Launched in July 2006, Twitter had 200 million users by March 2011 who generated 350 million tweets a day. Users can choose to follow other users and then get their tweets on their user home page. Many people have started using Twitter as a kind of curatorial news service, following people who tend to find new or interesting stories on topics of interest.

Some studies have shown that only about 10 percent of Twitter users contribute over 90 percent of the content. That a relatively small percentage of people contribute a disproportionate amount of content is important to remember when considering how media usage habits are changing. Just because the audience can now easily create and distribute content does not mean everyone will—the vast majority of people seem perfectly happy as consumers of media content.

Tumblr is another popular microblogging service. It allows for easy uploads of text and multimedia content. Founded in 2007, the name derives from "tumblelogs," the original term used for microblogs before the latter name became more widely used. In June 2011, Tumblr hosted over 20 million blogs, surpassing popular blogging platform WordPress.[8]

Many of the most popular social networking sites offer microblogging services as well, although these are often called something like "status updates." Regardless of the name used, updating friends in your social network while out and about is essentially microblogging.

▼ WIKIS

Wikis have become more widely known thanks to the phenomenal success of Wikipedia, the collaborative encyclopedia that has been created entirely by volunteers and has quickly come to rival the established encyclopedias in terms of scope and accuracy. However, like most other social-media tools used today, the roots of wikis go back much further.

A **wiki**, which means "quick" or "speedy" in Hawaiian, is essentially a web page that allows anyone to edit it. Vannevar Bush, in his remarkably prescient *Atlantic Monthly* article "As We May Think" in July 1945, envisioned an editable, hypertext microfilm system, which he called a "memex." The actual creation of something along these lines did not happen until the 1970s, and it wasn't until the advent of the Web that the idea became more practical.

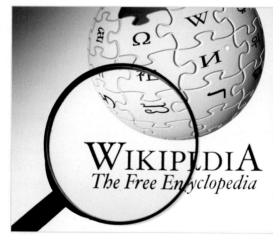

The first wiki was created by Ward Cunningham in 1994. He called it WikiWikiWeb, and it was designed to easily allow computer programmers to share information with each other. He took his wiki public in 1995 and asked developers to improve on it.

In 2001, Wikipedia used a version of a wiki system for its new encyclopedia that encouraged anyone to contribute and edit. This was a drastic change from traditional encyclopedias, which are the epitome of the gatekeeper media model of authoritative, unidirectional communication to a silent and passive audience.

Wikipedia is an excellent example of what can be created online by many people working together on nonmarket principles.

Today a number of varieties of wikis are used for different purposes, especially in education. Corporations have also been using wikis to encourage knowledge sharing between groups, especially when offices are far apart. One important aspect of wikis is the ability to see the editing history of any particular page and revert to an earlier version if needed. This function keeps a kind of automatic journal of editing changes, identifiable by user. In combination with discussion or talk pages, which are associated with each article, it provides a ready way for participants to discuss and debate points related to the content they are working on.

What would seem like a major weakness of wikis—the ability of anyone to change any content on a page at any time—has actually turned out to be their strength. The barriers to creating content or adding some special expertise a user may have are so low that it makes it easy to participate. Although not without its share of **trolls**, or people who purposely vandalize Wikipedia entries by inserting false or nonsensical information, the Wikipedia community has shown a remarkable ability to police the vast and growing amount of content on the site.

Wikipedia has been able to avoid major disruptions at the hands of vandals, thanks partly to technology but mostly to the norms and rules that have been created over time by the Wikipedia community. It is an example par excellence of how social media have the power to transform media audiences and how they work on principles different from traditional media economic models. However, Wikipedia is not without its growth pains. In August 2009 it announced that it would institute more restrictive editing rules for content and "lock" or "protect" some pages from being further edited to ensure accuracy, a move away from its earliest, free-wheeling days.

troll

A person who purposely vandalizes Wikipedia entries by inserting false or nonsensical information.

▼ SOCIAL-NETWORKING SITES

The various social-networking sites today are perhaps the most visible face to social media, and their popularity cannot be discounted, but as is clear from the brief look at the other types of social media available, they are by no means the only ones, or even the most important.

What distinguishes social-networking sites from other types of social media is that in some manner they allow users to show the connections they have in their social network.[9] The ability to share the map of one's social network, and allow others to tap into that map by contacting other people in the network, has become an incredibly powerful tool.

Classmates.com, founded in 1995, and SixDegrees, started in 1997, were two early examples of social-networking sites. Classmates.com, as its name suggests, primarily focused on getting people back in touch with former classmates from college, high school, and even grade school. However, Classmates did not provide the same level of network sharing as is commonly seen today. SixDegrees focused on helping people find social-network connections that they may not have otherwise realized existed. Other social-networking sites that appeared in 1999, such as AsianVenue or BlackPlanet (both relaunched in 2005 under the same owner and sold to Radio One in 2008), were focused on more specific audiences, such as certain ethnic groups. Figure 8-1 shows a timeline of social-networking-site launches.

Launched in 2003, Friendster was created as a site to help people connect with old friends and make new ones. It was the first social-networking site that had features similar to what we see today with Facebook, LinkedIn, and MySpace. Although the popularity of Friendster rapidly waned in the United States and Europe, it has remained very popular in Asia, with over 90 percent of its traffic coming from

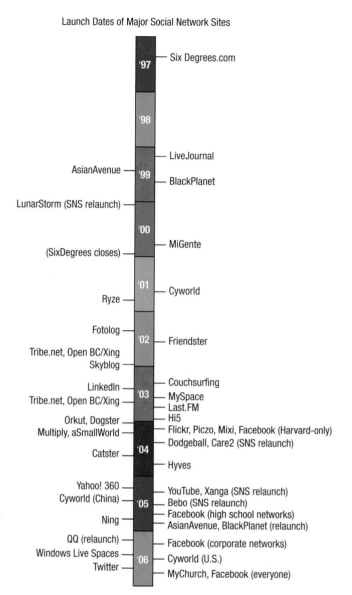

Launch Dates of Major Social Network Sites

'97 — Six Degrees.com

'98

LiveJournal
AsianAvenue — '99 — BlackPlanet

LunarStorm (SNS relaunch) —

'00 — MiGente
(SixDegrees closes) —

'01 — Cyworld
Ryze —

Fotolog — '02 — Friendster
Tribe.net, Open BC/Xing
Skyblog —

Couchsurfing
LinkedIn — '03 — MySpace
Tribe.net, Open BC/Xing — Last.FM
Orkut, Dogster — Hi5
Multiply, aSmallWorld — Flickr, Piczo, Mixi, Facebook (Harvard-only)
— Dodgeball, Care2 (SNS relaunch)
Catster — '04
— Hyves

Yahoo! 360 — YouTube, Xanga (SNS relaunch)
Cyworld (China) — '05 — Bebo (SNS relaunch)
Facebook (high school networks)
Ning — AsianAvenue, BlackPlanet (relaunch)

QQ (relaunch) — Facebook (corporate networks)
Windows Live Spaces — '06 — Cyworld (U.S.)
Twitter — MyChurch, Facebook (everyone)

FIGURE 8-1 Timeline of Social-Networking-Site Launches, Taken from http://jcmc.indiana.edu/vol13/issue1/boyd.ellison.html

the region. With over 75 million registered users worldwide, it ranks as one of the top twenty most visited websites.

MySpace also launched in 2003, and in 2006 became the most popular social-networking site, only to lose that position in 2008 to Facebook. MySpace and its parent company, Intermix Media, were purchased by News Corp. in 2005 for $580 million. At the time of the purchase, there was concern among many Internet users that News Corp. would mine the vast amount of data that MySpace had collected and use it for marketing purposes. There were also concerns that News Corp. owner Rupert Murdoch would try to make MySpace a platform for promoting Fox media content, but he remained largely hands-off with MySpace as it struggled and tried to find ways to generate revenue. In June 2011, News Corp. sold MySpace for $35 million—a fraction of its original value—to Specific Media, an advertising network.

Facebook began as a project within Harvard University in late 2003 called Face-mash, a version of the website Hot or Not, and launched as a social-networking site under its current name, but available only to Harvard students, in early 2004. A couple months later it opened to other Ivy League schools and then expanded to include all college students. The next year it expanded to allow high-school students and then companies, and in 2006 it opened to anyone thirteen or older. It rapidly overtook MySpace as the most popular social-networking site thanks to these expansions. By September 2012, Facebook claimed to be nearing 1 billion users worldwide.

Facebook's rapid rise in popularity led to frequent media reports of potential buyouts from larger media companies, such as Microsoft. Despite such reports, Facebook launched its initial public offering (IPO) in May 2012, the largest in Internet history, valued at its peak at $104 billion. However, by September the share price was down to $22, nearly half as much as its launch price of $38 per share.

There are many other social-networking sites that have sprung up since 2003, with some focusing on professional interests, such as LinkedIn; topic interests, such as Dogster; media or photo sharing (Flickr); and location-based interests, such as Foursquare and Loopt. Some sites, such as Orkut, have undergone changes as they have gained popularity overseas. For example, as mentioned in Chapter 6, in the early days of Orkut, the English-speaking users started to feel left out as the site became wildly popular in Brazil and more Portuguese-speaking participants joined. Today Orkut remains a primary social-networking site in Brazil and Latin America.

The launch of Google+ in June 2011 was Google's attempt at competing with Facebook's dominant role as the most popular social networking site. Despite Google's dominance as a search engine and the growing number of online services Google offers, Google+ remains far behind Facebook in terms of popularity, with only 250 million registered users and 150 million active users as of June 2012.

All of the social-networking sites developed within the past few years provide a variety of communication and sharing tools, and many encourage users to develop applications that make the sites even more useful to participants. There are two main influences at work in these developments: the importance of social networks in and of themselves and the culture of the open-source movement, in which people collaborate for reasons other than monetary rewards. Understanding these two driving forces helps us gain a better picture of why social media are transforming not just our media habits but our world today.

▲▼ Why Social Networks Matter

Understanding how social networks work and the role such networks play in our lives, the way we communicate, and even how we make sense of the world has been an area of social scientific research long before social-networking sites became prominent, going back all the way to the earliest days of sociology itself, in the late 1800s.

A social network consists of nodes, which can be people or even organizations, and links, which are the connections between nodes. The links can represent any number of things, depending on what the researcher is studying, but generally have some communicative function.

The power of mapping social networks can be seen by comparing Figures 8-2, 8-3, and 8-4. In Figure 8-2, we are simply looking at a collection of people mingling at a party; we may gather some information by watching the party long enough and noting certain interactions, but we are missing some important information regarding the underlying relationships, or social structure, of the party.

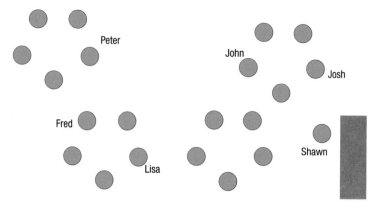

FIGURE 8-2 Without any sense of the social-network connections, we have no idea what relationships there are between members at a party.

If we do not already know anyone, we could make a social blunder by talking to the "wrong people," which could affect our perceptions of the party or the people at the party—and affect their perceptions of us. This may seem a mundane reason to understand social networks, but consider if you want to meet someone specifically for a potential job or if you are an artist wanting to promote your new song. You could ask every single person there if they knew of any job openings or if they wanted to hear your song, but this is an inefficient (and annoying) way to go about it. Who at the party is most likely to help make the contact you need with that potential employer? Who at the party is an **influencer** others tend to follow? There is no way to tell in Figure 8-2.

However, let us overlay a network diagram over the same members of the party and see how that changes things, as in Figure 8-3. The black lines represent what are called **strong ties**, or strong links, and represent close bonds between nodes. The red lines represent **weak ties**, or weak links, which means there are connections but they are not as frequent or as close as strong ties. In this example, we will assume the connections represent friendship, or who someone claims as a close friend (strong tie) or friend (weak tie).

Several things become clear when looking at the map of relationships with this party. Shawn, the only node not connected to any other node, is standing by the snack table (likely in the desperate hope of connecting with someone). In

influencer

A person who can influence others in their social network to perform an action or change an attitude.

strong ties

In social network analysis, the tight bonds between people in a "small world" of close connections.

weak ties

In social network analysis, the connections between people in different "small worlds," which tend not to be as tight or as close as strong ties but that are nevertheless extremely important in social networks.

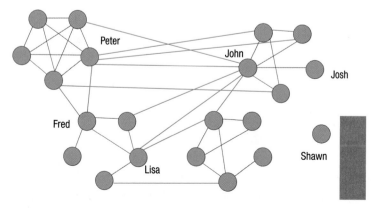

FIGURE 8-3 After connections are shown, indicating both strong and weak links, we see that John is an important person at the party, in part because of the number of weak-link connections he has to others.

hub

A node that has many connections to other nodes in a social network.

six degrees of separation

The idea that everyone in the world is separated from each other by at most six other nodes in a social network.

small world

A tight-knit social network with many strong ties.

social-network terms, he is called an isolate. The group of individuals in the upper left appears to be a very tight-knit group of friends, all connected to each other, but with few connections to other groups at the party. Other groups are less connected with each other, and a few individuals have a connection to only one other member.

Note the number of connections John has, especially the weak ties to multiple members in all the other groups. John is what is called a **hub**, or a node with many connections to other nodes, and hubs are generally influencers in social networks, partly *because* of the number of connections they have. If you are new at the party and want to be introduced to someone else (for whatever reason), John would likely be the best person to first introduce yourself to, as he could make the introduction or introduce you to someone who considers the person you want to meet a friend.

This is how the notion of **six degrees of separation** works, the idea that everyone in the world is connected by at most six other nodes in a social network. Generally we simply have not had a way to know what those networks are, thus the amazing coincidences that occur when we learn about a mutual connection such as attending the same school or having a common friend. Social-networking sites have helped make our social networks visible.

Our common sense tells us that a tight-knit group of friends like Peter has (called a **small world**, in social-network analysis) is important in social networks, but this is not the case. Far more important are weak ties, or the connections between various small worlds. This is partly because members in a small world tend to share the same resources, so if someone in Peter's small world is looking for a job, it is likely all the members know of the same openings and may even be competing for the position.

Let us say that John had to leave the party early for another engagement (he is a popular guy, after all) and see how the social-network diagram radically changes. Suddenly Josh, whose sole connection to the party was through John, becomes an isolate (assuming Josh did not make any friendship connections while John was still there). Either the party now looks a lot less interesting for Josh or the snack table with that strange guy lurking around it looking lonely starts to look more inviting.

Similar changes take place for Peter and his friends, the tight-knit group who go everywhere together. Now if any of them want to easily meet Lisa and her friends, Peter had best go through Fred and have him make the introduction. Although there is only one fewer member at the party, the dynamics shift dramatically from a communications and relationship standpoint, making some people hubs based on their relationships and thus elevating their status as connectors while isolating others. This is the power of mapping out social structures as social networks. If Fred leaves

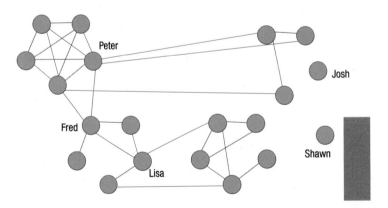

FIGURE 8-4 If John leaves the party, the social-network connections suddenly change, making some people more important as connectors than they were and weakening connections for others.

Are We Really Separated by Six Degrees?

The notion that everyone in the world is separated by no more than six degrees, or six links in a network, gained the attention of the public through a "small world" experiment conducted by psychologist Stanley Milgram in the 1950s. Milgram sent copies of letters to people in the Midwest and asked them to send the letter to the person they thought would be most likely to be able to forward that letter to a certain lawyer living in Boston. Out of the forty-two letters that reached the lawyer's home, the average number of links was nearly six, although the range was quite large.

Although Milgram never used the term "six degrees of separation," it became popularized in a 1984 play of that name in which his experiment was referenced. The notion has become even more widespread as "Six Degrees of Kevin Bacon," in which the degrees of separation of various actors with Kevin Bacon is calculated. This can easily be done through the Oracle of Kevin Bacon website, which uses the Internet Movie Database as its source. It can be surprising to discover how connected even long-dead actors are with Kevin Bacon, or famous people who are not professional actors but who have appeared in documentaries or movies. This works so well because if you consider the actors gathered on a movie set as a small world of tight connections, as they get to know each other while filming, they get to know a large number of other actors who then go on to make other movies with different actors.

Although it is difficult to find an actor or actress separated from Bacon by more than even five degrees, Kevin Bacon is actually not the most connected Hollywood actor. Both John Carradine and Robert Mitchum had far more connections than Bacon has.

> **WEB LINK**
> Oracle of Kevin Bacon
> **http://oracleofbacon.org/**

the party, friendship connections between the different small worlds quickly disintegrate, making the party a collection of small worlds unconnected to each other.

The party example may seem mundane, and in this example one could legitimately ask, "Why doesn't Peter just go over and talk to Lisa and her friends if he wants to meet her?" This of course is exactly what happens in parties as new links are easily made because of the proximity people have to each other. However, the principles outlined here apply just as well if Peter is in the London office, John is in New York, Lisa is in Tokyo, and Fred in Singapore. It is the social-network structure, not the proximity, that is relevant. John would be just as important in this example as someone who can easily connect people. In fact, because the people cannot easily meet face-to-face, his power to connect people through a network becomes even more important than at the party, where it would be relatively easy to walk across the room and meet someone new.

Now consider a social-networking site you belong to and see what it does from a social-networking perspective. The "connections" application that shows your network and friends of friends is one important element, but the other activities and applications that have been developed are equally important. They allow you to see what activities others are doing, to talk directly with them, to ask them to join groups you are interested in, to take quizzes and share common knowledge or photos—any number of activities that encourage social interaction and the making of new social ties, and all through a mediated environment that does not necessarily rely on consuming traditional mass media fare (though that does help with conversations and interaction as well).

Social networks have been used in studying how boards of directors in various companies are interconnected, as the same principles regarding small worlds of tight connections and weak links of looser ties apply. These networks can often be useful for companies, in that a company board member may sit on other boards as well and thus be linked to people who could help a business in any number of ways. The website They Rule is a visual database that shows the interconnections and social networks of boards of directors of major companies.

From this brief overview of basic social-network principles, it should be clear how important it actually is when we say someone is "well connected." Early social media such as email and discussion groups gave people the communicative tools to connect but still did not allow people to visualize their social networks. Social-networking sites added that last, powerful piece to the tools that already existed, and that helped spur on more development of social media, thanks in part to a culture of collaboration that had developed in parallel with the Internet over the years.

WEB LINK
They Rule
www.theyrule.net

◢▼ Collaborative Media Work

Collaboration is one of the principal elements of social media, and it is important to consider not only because of the media creation that comes out of it, as in the case of Wikipedia, but because it threatens established media business models that have been used throughout much of the twentieth century and into this one.

Without the spirit of collaboration and free sharing the Internet would look very different, and it could be argued it might not even exist as we know it today. Remember that the Internet was developed by computer programmers and engineers who had a commitment to sharing information and knowledge, free of the limitations the marketplace puts on such activity. Without the efforts of a good number of very smart people either working for free or paid by taxpayer dollars, the backbone of the Internet would not exist, as no company would have the resources—or be willing to spend the resources if it did—to create the structure needed, especially when there was no clear way to profit from it.

Collaborative or participatory media trace their roots online to the open-source movement, or free-software movement, in which programmers created software whose source code could be improved upon by anyone. Although not always free in the sense of "no cost," there was a strong spirit of keeping the information freely available to anyone and letting everyone share in the benefits. Commonsense theories of human behavior indicated that nobody would work hard on a project only to have others benefit greatly from it, but this turned out to be completely wrong, as was discussed in Chapter 2 regarding open-source projects Linux, OpenOffice, and the Firefox browser, to name a few.

People looked at the open-source model of software and computer development and asked, if it works for software, then why can't it work for entertainment, journalism, advertising, public relations—or any kind of content and knowledge production?

▼ CHANGING AUDIENCES: FROM CONSUMERS TO "PRODUSERS"

This is exactly what is happening as some audiences shift from being primarily consumers of media content to what media scholar Axel Bruns calls **produsers**,[10] though others use the term "prosumers," or just "users." The fact that there is debate about what term to use (and that we do not already have a readily available term to use) highlights how relevant and new this phenomenon is.

It is widely accepted that traditional media audiences were largely seen as consumers by the mass media companies that created content to sell to them. Whether they consumed media in the form of programs, books, or music, or bought products advertised through various media channels, the relationship was very much one of producers (media industries) creating material for the public to consume. Entire business models were built on this industrial model of production within the media industries. Companies mass-produced our cars (or soap, or clothes, or books, or movies), and we bought them.

Of course people were not as passive as that relationship would indicate, but as discussed earlier in this chapter the chances for people to choose, create, and "talk back" to producers were extremely limited prior to social media. Now, however, people have the tools to talk back and many are doing so—what's more, they are not only talking back but often simply ignoring the traditional producers and talking to each other.

The new dynamic is a complex one, thus the difficulty in coming up with an adequate term to define it. "Prosumer" still seems to emphasize the consumption aspect of the relationship, almost like a "professional consumer" or kind of über-consumer, which misses out on the important change in the power balance that is taking place today between audiences and producers. Similarly, "user" does not capture the sense of creation or production that is an important element of the social-media landscape.

The fact is that consumption of one form or another still predominates. Not everyone is (or wants to be) a producer of media content. But to contribute to the larger conversations taking place—to add something, however small, that helps create a greater whole—is easier than ever before. Posting a link to a worthwhile website or blog that others on a discussion board may have never heard of is a form of media production, collaboration, and knowledge sharing that cannot be downplayed as nonproductive or unimportant, especially when looked at on a large scale. Furthermore, people do not have to contribute something to feel like they are part of a community; it may be enough for many to see that others feel the way they do, connecting them to something larger.

▼ REPUTATION, RATINGS, AND TRUST

The change in audiences from consumers to produsers has had a powerful ripple effect, not only on business models, but on a number of social factors as well. In the traditional media world, we could rely on certain established brands to give us certain things. The *Wall Street Journal* or the *New York Times* delivered a kind of content that the *National Enquirer* did not, and we learned what to expect.

Today that has changed. Although the traditional brands still (for the most part) retain their meanings for us, it is more difficult than ever for us to determine how to trust information if it comes from unknown sources. How do we know that the Amazon review of a book we are considering was not written by someone paid

produsers

The notion that audiences cannot simply be considered consumers anymore but also often take an active role in producing content or information.

to write a glowing review or by the author's mother? How do we know that a Wikipedia entry about a politician was not written by the politician's aides, highlighting only positive information and ignoring past scandals? How do we know that the blog about the problem of childhood diabetes is not created by a pharmaceutical company trying to promote their drug?

These and other issues are all extremely important in today's media world, thus the importance of critical thinking and media literacy. Similarly, issues of trust and reputation become vital in figuring out what information we can trust. Ratings systems, in which participants can rank how useful a review or comment is, help us in making that decision. But the question also arises whether the raters are trustworthy or not.

This is where social networks enter once again, as we generally trust friends or people we have let into our social networks and are more likely to listen to what they say or recommend. This is one reason **word-of-mouth** or buzz marketing has become so important for advertisers. Ratings systems as a measure of gauging trust will develop and become more important in our social-media landscape, but there will be some thorny ethical and legal questions that arise as well.

◣◥ Ethical and Legal Issues with Social Media

The legal world has not nearly begun to catch up with the many issues that online media have raised, let alone social media. Issues of trademark infringement or other intellectual property issues have generally been dealt with using existing case laws, but other issues will need new legal thinking to be dealt with properly.

One big issue arising in the legal arena is figuring out who owns user-generated content on social-media sites. If someone decides to write a book based on discussions taken from a site like The WELL, using extended passages of actual discussions, is this a breach of copyright? How should the poster be compensated, if at all? Is permission needed to use the post or an excerpt of it? If so, how much is fair use and how much is an infringement of intellectual property? These are just some of the issues that social-media sites will have to wrestle with in the future.

The ethical and legal boundaries between privacy and transparency blur online, and it is especially true with social media. The norms of acceptable limits of privacy have always changed over time, and the ease of social interaction online combined with anonymity or pseudonymity often makes it easy to disparage others when there is little fear of retribution.

▼ PRIVACY

The norms for privacy are also changing. For those older than Gen Y, the notion of making so much of one's life public through posting photos, discussing one's thoughts or desires on a blog, or sharing other highly personal information feels strange. There is a sense that much of that is nobody else's business or that that information should only be shared with a select group of people one knows and trusts.

This "living publicly" generally does not seem to bother Gen-Yers in the same way, yet many are rudely awakened to a sense of having their privacy invaded when they learn that an employer is raising questions about material found on a blog or information gleaned from a social-networking site. Most employers today do Google searches on job applicants and examine social-networking profiles if they can. Many also make decisions about who will be called for an interview in part based on these searches. The goofy profile picture of you half-naked at a college party may be hilarious to your friends on Facebook but not so amusing to a potential employer trying to gauge your value as an employee.

Along similar lines, Facebook has gotten into trouble at least three times from its users for unannounced policy changes perceived to invade users' privacy. One notable case was Facebook's Beacon, which tracked users' activities even after they had left Facebook—without informing them. To make matters worse, these off-site activities—such as purchasing a product or registering for a website—were broadcast to a user's network of friends. Many of the most popular games on Facebook, such as Farmville, also track user behavior even after they have stopped playing the game, although they are not supposed to do that.

There are many temptations for companies such as Facebook or Zynga, the maker of Farmville, to invade users' privacy by tracking their online behavior. The data collected could be immensely valuable to marketers trying to figure out how to best tap certain markets—especially the lucrative eighteen-to-thirty-four demographic. It is especially problematic when companies still have not found sustainable business models to support their activities and are looking for ways to earn revenue. For many companies, the wealth of data on user behavior they can obtain—and sell—is simply too great to resist even if it is an invasion of privacy.

Companies that are bought by other companies or that go out of business have databases of registered users and online activity that could provide very valuable information. However, when users registered to a site, they likely did not consider that their personal data and search history might at some point end up in the hands of a different company.

▼ TRANSPARENCY

Even supposedly tech-savvy companies leading the social-media revolution seem to regularly make blunders similar to traditional media companies when it comes to understanding some of the new dynamics with their audience, as the Facebook Beacon example shows.

Companies trying to create faux-viral videos or making fake grassroots blogs, a practice called **astroturfing**, are often punished severely in the court of public opinion once their machinations are learned. Sudden shifts in things like privacy policies, either unannounced or not adequately announced, have produced similar audience backlashes.

astroturfing

The practice of creating a movement or campaign so that it looks like it was created by concerned citizens as a grassroots movement, but was actually created or controlled by a large organization or group.

Facebook once again learned this the hard way in early 2009 when a change in their privacy policy, which had been made a few weeks earlier but went unnoticed by the general public, stated that Facebook would own the rights to user-generated content on the site, including posted photos. Found and publicized by a consumer interest group, the change elicited immense and immediate outrage, including a threat by the Electronic Privacy Information Center (EPIC) to file a complaint with the Federal Trade Commission.

Facebook quickly did an about-face on the policy and created a group of users to discuss future privacy-policy changes. The actions and reactions

WEB LINK
Electronic Privacy Information Center
epic.org

Web 3.0: The Semantic Web

If you thought that social media and Web 2.0 have transformed media, wait until the semantic Web is fully developed.

The semantic Web is the next big project that Tim Berners-Lee, the creator of the World Wide Web protocol, is working on. The idea behind the semantic Web is that it builds on and extends the existing Web to make it even easier for people to share information across platforms and for the Web itself to essentially be able to satisfy requests regarding web content.

The project is not simply about creating a better search engine that responds to natural queries. It contains a variety of suggestions on protocols and some operating principles that are meant to help reduce incompatibility between software formats, as well as a component that attempts to classify all information on the Web according to a formal system that can be read and understood by all computers.

We see some of the classifying and categorizing taking place among users now with tagging, but this promises to be all-encompassing. It also raises interesting questions about who gets to define what terms will be used. This is bound to raise conflicts with various groups who may define themselves one way but that are defined another way by society.

Regardless of the difficulties ahead, and the time it will take for the semantic Web to be integrated into

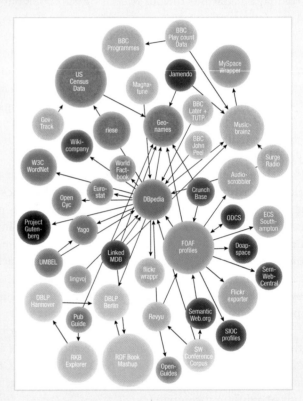

the online space, it promises to revolutionize our online experiences in a way that will make our current Web look as user friendly as a hand-cranked telephone from the early twentieth century.

are emblematic of the shifting power dynamic between companies and the public and something that other companies should note carefully. It would have been far better if Facebook had created such a group in the first place, rather than only after receiving complaints. Further, Facebook's own customers were able to use the very tools that helped make Facebook so popular to organize against the company.

The need for transparency is becoming increasingly important with social media—a fact that individuals and organizations forget at their peril. However, transparency often works against strategy making and planning by companies, as they do not want to give away secrets to competitors.

Transparency is starting to be built into some ratings and review systems, so reviewers can state how long they have had a product, for example, which helps give readers a chance to gauge if the glowing review is about a product that is just out of the box or if it has been used for a while.

The balancing act between privacy, transparency, and tapping into the rich databases of compiled data from user interactions will continue to be a struggle for social-networking sites.

Like much of "new" media, social media actually have firm roots and influences in many aspects of "old" media, although in this case the term "old" refers more to the earliest days of PCs and the Internet than it does to radio, TV, or print media. Even so, the changes that social media have brought in a relatively short time have long-lasting implications for culture, business, and society that researchers are only beginning to explore.

In one study in 2011, researchers suggested that the Internet may be "rewiring" our brains to some extent regarding how well we remember things. They did an experiment with subjects, asking them to remember certain trivia or facts and in different groups were told that they could either find the information again online later or that once seen it would be gone forever. The researchers found that people had far less memory recall of the facts when they believed they could later search for the information online.

One of the biggest changes, discussed throughout this book, is the difference in the relationship between media producers and the audience. Even without the large marketing and promotion budgets that some major media companies have, average people have been able to create content that has been seen, heard, or read by millions or even tens of millions of people worldwide.

The networks that have formed through online communication, and that have become ever more visible thanks to social-networking sites, have given people even more power. Through collaboration, people have shown in numerous projects what can be accomplished when many work willingly together and how their efforts can benefit even greater numbers of people. Wikipedia is one such project.

What may be of even more significance over the long term, however, is how social media have encouraged people to create and share knowledge structures, not just knowledge. Through the sometimes heated discussions in forums or on the talk pages of wikis, participants are exposed to different viewpoints and ways of looking at the world. In collaborative projects they have to come to some sort of understanding or agreement, thus modifying what is written to satisfy everyone. Although this does not guarantee a change in anyone's views, simply being exposed to other viewpoints has an effect on our thinking.

Sharing knowledge structures, or ways of looking at the world, is also done through curation, such as tagging information or reviewing products or media content. Providing information about information is just as valuable as creating information and in some ways can reflect worldviews just as accurately as direct comments on a discussion board. A user who tags a photo of fighting in Somalia as "genocide" may suddenly see connections to other photos with the same tag and learn of past incidents elsewhere.

Following the actions of many users who are collaborating without even knowing it by using automated systems can yield amazing results. One example is Google flu trends, which uses aggregated data of search terms in the popular search engine to predict flu outbreaks. Google has found that, simply based on search terms, it has been able to predict flu outbreaks up to two weeks earlier than traditional methods.

Of course, the social-media tools available are only as good as the way they are used. It could be argued that a community of sorts exists around a site like Goth or Not, but its value to all but a few may be questionable. Simply because we have the tools now does not mean we will always use them in a productive or efficient way.

Media companies are struggling to adapt to the world of social media, with mixed success. Companies not willing to give up control of their messages are having more difficulty than those that are more open about stepping into the conversational chaos that is social media. Of bigger concern to companies, however, is how to earn revenues from all the conversations sprouting up, conversations often based on content the companies have spent money to create.

There are no easy answers to this question, as we will learn in the next section. Some industries may find it easier to adapt, or to shape the social-media landscape in ways that benefit them, while others may be looking at a bleak future in which the profession or industry as we know it today may be nearly unrecognizable in ten or twenty years.

DISCUSSION QUESTIONS

1. Today many television shows and advertisements try to look amateurish or "homegrown" to emulate what is often seen on the Web. Do you think professional production values will continue to drop, or do you think amateur user-generated content will get more professional over time? Why?

2. Which of the five ways in which our media use is changing (choice, creation, curation, conversation, or collaboration) do you think is the most important? Why?

3. Write a review of a local bar, restaurant, or store on a site like Citysearch or Yelp. What did this process make you think about, and did it change what you thought you would write initially?

4. Post a comment on a local news story and follow any discussions that come from it, reporting on what happened.

5. What's your Obama number? Using a rather loose definition of "friend" to show a weak link (i.e., meeting or seeing the person face-to-face, not simply as someone in a crowd), try to figure out if you are separated from President Obama by six degrees or less. (*Hint: including your professors as part of your social network may help.*) Share your story on how you arrived at your number. Now try the same thing to learn your Saddam Hussein number. What did you learn about which media profession lends itself to having important social hubs?

6. Why is transparency such an important concept in the social-media world? Is it more or less important than in the offline world? Why?

7. Find out if your college president or other notable local figure has or had a fake Twitter account, then see if they have a real one and when they got it, if they have one. Which has more followers? Would a fake Twitter account of you or your friends have the same impact as somebody famous? Why or why not?

8. Consider your Facebook account. Compare how many friends you have on Facebook and how many you keep in touch with on a daily basis, a weekly basis, or even less. How many "friends" have you never contacted or have never contacted you? Compare your numbers and Facebook habits with those of classmates.

9. Which would you consider more of a community, a discussion forum about a social issue or a game like Farmville? Why did you choose the one you did?

10. If you could develop the perfect social networking site, what kind of features would you have for it? Why?

FURTHER READING

Socialnomics: How Social Media Transforms the Way We Live and Do Business. Erik Qualman (2010) Wiley.

Wikinomics: How Mass Collaboration Changes Everything. Don Tapscott, Anthony Williams (2008) Portfolio.

The Wealth of Networks: How Social Production Transforms Markets and Freedom. Yochai Benkler (2007) Yale University Press.

Here Comes Everybody: The Power of Organizing Without Organizations. Clay Shirky (2008) Penguin Press.

The Wisdom of Crowds. James Surowiecki (2005) Anchor Press.

Going to Extremes: How Like Minds Unite and Divide. Cass Sunstein (2009) Oxford University Press.

The Wikipedia Revolution: How a Bunch of Nobodies Created the World's Greatest Encyclopedia. Andrew Lih (2009) Hyperion.

Wiki Government: How Technology Can Make Government Better, Democracy Stronger, and Citizens More Powerful. Beth Simone Noveck (2010) Brookings Institution Press.

Blogs, Wikipedia, Second Life, and Beyond: From Production to Produsage. Axel Bruns (2008) Peter Lang.

Groundswell: Winning in a World Transformed by Social Technologies. Charlene Li, Josh Bernoff (2008) Harvard Business School Press.

Social Media Is a Cocktail Party: Why You Already Know the Rules of Social Media Marketing. Jim Tobin, Lisa Braziel (2008) Createspace.

Tribes: We Need You to Lead Us. Seth Godin (2008) Portfolio.

Six Degrees: The Science of a Connected Age. Duncan Watts (2004) W. W. Norton.

MEDIA QUIZ ANSWER

5. False.

9

JOURNALISM: FROM INFORMATION TO PARTICIPATION

LEARNING OBJECTIVES

By the end of this chapter
you should be able to:

- Explain what journalism
  is and its role in mass
  communication and
  society.

- Outline important
  historical developments in
  journalism that affect how
  it is practiced today.

- Discuss journalism
  today, including types
  of journalism, and what
  the future may hold for
  journalism in a convergent
  journalism environment.

- Outline legal and ethical
  issues in the practice of
  journalism, with special
  emphasis on ethical issues
  in the digital world.

- Explain some aspects of the
  business of journalism and
  how they affect the practice
  of journalism.

- Examine how convergence
  is affecting business models
  and careers in journalism.

Social and digital media continue to transform the world of journalism and are increasingly providing a vehicle for quality news and information. In April 2012 the *Huffington Post* became the first commercial news website and blog to win a Pulitzer Prize.[1] ProPublica was the first not-for-profit online news operation to win a Pulitzer Prize in 2010.[2] Founded by Arianna Huffington, Kenneth Lerer, Andrew Breitbart, and Jonah Peretti, the *Huffington Post* launched on May 9, 2005, as a fully digital, U.S.-based for-profit operation. It provided original news and online commentary as well aggregating content from other sites. The site covers a wide spectrum of subject matter, including politics, business, entertainment, lifestyle, culture, comedy, and local news.

The *Huffington Post* won its first Pulitzer Prize for national reporting for an original series it produced on wounded veterans. Written by experienced war correspondent David Wood, the series is titled "Beyond the Battlefield."[3] It explores "the challenges that severely wounded veterans of Iraq and Afghanistan face after they return home, as well as what those struggles mean for those close to them." The ten-part series debuted online and was expanded subsequently and republished as an ebook for Kindle and iBook ereaders.

In its first decade of existence, the *Huffington Post* has evolved and matured. When first introduced, the site served largely as an alternative to conservative online sources and news aggregators such as the *Drudge Report*. In February 2011, AOL acquired the increasingly popular online journalism site *Huffington Post* for $315 million.[4] Founder Arianna Huffington became editor-in-chief of The Huffington Post Media Group.

The *Huffington Post* effectively integrates and utilizes social media both for reporting and to engage citizens in an online news community. Every story published on the *Huffington Post* encourages readers to follow and participate via a variety of social media, including Facebook, Twitter, Google+, and more. As of this writing, the Pulitzer Prize–winning series *Beyond the Battlefield* was attracting an active social media following in venues including Facebook, Twitter, email, and the *Huffington Post* site itself. Thousands of users have shared the series on Facebook; hundreds have tweeted about it; hundreds have shared it via email; and over a thousand have posted comments on *Huffington Post* about the series.[5]

Among the keywords readers were using to comment on the story: Afghanistan, War Wire, Afghanistan, Beyond the Battlefield, Veterans, Video, Iraq Veterans, Politics, News.[6]

Journalism's purpose, according to some journalists, is to "comfort the afflicted and afflict the comfortable." Heated discussions on how well journalism is fulfilling its many roles and responsibilities continue to this day in letters-to-the-editor pages, on call-in talk shows, on the Internet, and in newsrooms. News organizations walk a thin line between providing a vital service to the public and thriving as a money-making enterprise. News organizations may serve the public good by playing the role of government watchdog or advocating the rights of common citizens. But they may also fall victim to pandering to baser tastes among the public and influencing public opinion for their own commercial benefit. These discussions should not be seen as some inherent failure of journalism; rather, they should be understood as signs of how important journalism continues to be in the modern world.

There has been a more fundamental shift taking place within the framework of these debates and discussions, a shift that could dramatically affect the very soul of journalism and what it will be in a digital age. Traditionally, journalists saw their main function as informing the public about important events of the day. However, this notion has shifted in recent years with the rise of citizen-journalists and hyperlocal news, and the contributions that citizen-journalists have made to professional news organizations. Now, a growing number of news industry watchers and pundits realize that simply informing is

MEDIA QUIZ

A Nose for News

1. (T/F) Broadcast journalists, unlike their print counterparts, must be licensed by the FCC.
2. How would you define "news" in one sentence?
3. What publisher was the model for Orson Welles's classic movie *Citizen Kane*?
4. What has replaced the goal of objectivity in journalism today?
5. What is a "pseudo event," and how does it relate to news?
6. Which is older, public journalism or alternative journalism?
7. (T/F) Some of the most popular news websites now are citizen-journalism sites.
8. How does a 24/7 news cycle affect news organizations?
9. (T/F) The staff cuts in newspapers have finally stopped as the economy has gotten stronger.
10. On average and all things being equal regarding years of experience and size of the media market, who makes more money—a journalist or a PR professional?

not enough; what journalism should be doing is also encouraging participation among the public.

Journalism plays an important part in three of the four main functions of mass communication: **surveillance**, **correlation**, and **cultural transmission**. It can also play a major role in mobilizing the public, a role that has become even more potent because of the prevalence of citizen journalism. These functions are carried out by the coverage of news. The public learns of events and happenings locally and around the world, and good coverage puts the events in a context that helps people form a picture of what the world is like. Through articles and shows on cultural and artistic figures, culture is transmitted and the public learns the mores of society. To a lesser extent, journalism also serves the entertainment function of mass communication through coverage of entertainment events and news on popular stars.

In order to get a good understanding of journalism, however, it is important to first understand what news is.

surveillance

Primarily the journalism function of mass communication, which provides information about the processes, issues, events, and other developments in society.

correlation

The ways in which media interprets events and issues and ascribes meanings that help individuals understand their roles within the larger society and culture.

cultural transmission

The transference of the dominant culture, as well as its subcultures, from one generation to the next or to immigrants, which helps people learn how to fit into society.

What Is News?

The journalist's old adage that news is "when man bites dog" rings true in the sense that news is something that occurs that is out of the ordinary. News usually is about an event that affects the public in some way, or that at least has some element of public interest. It includes coverage of recent events, such as breaking news of a fire or accident, and recent discoveries of events that have already taken place, such as financial wrongdoing by corporate executives or politicians.

Several issues arise when examining this basic assumption about the definition of news. First is the often-heard complaint by the public that news concentrates too much on negative events—crime, accidents, wrongdoing, etc. Critics say that this overwhelmingly negative coverage gives the public a misleading impression that things are worse than they actually are, such as making it seem that local crime is getting worse because of intense coverage on a spate of robberies when in fact the annual crime rate has dropped. News organizations do include positive news, such as human-interest stories or new business openings, but then they are criticized for acting as a public relations mouthpiece for organizations or individuals and not adequately informing the public of important issues.

Conventional wisdom suggests that news means reporting the unexpected. But the truth is that a large portion of news is largely predictable a day, a week, a month, or sometimes years in advance. Consider the types of news stories about any annual holiday or event, such as advice on shopping for Christmas gifts—a look at the news organization's archives will likely uncover a very similar story the previous year and the year before that.

It is vital that critical media consumers understand that most news doesn't just happen. It is in many ways manufactured and influenced by a wide variety of people, organizations, and forces—often including advertising and public relations. Historian and Pulitzer Prize–winning author Daniel Boorstin describes what he calls **pseudo events**, such as press conferences or other staged events, like marches and rallies, as an example of how groups can influence what is covered in the news. These events are often known about days or weeks in advance. Press conferences are held specifically to attract media coverage. What kind of news shows up on television or in a newspaper depends on a number of factors, including what other events are happening that day, the type of publication or broadcast organization, and even the political views of the owner, in some cases.

A **soft news day** is when editors feel not much has happened that is newsworthy and therefore will air programming or include articles such as human-interest stories. A flood in a distant country that kills five hundred people may be included as a "World News Brief" on an inside page of a local paper on a slow news day and may not be included at all on a day that has important local news. How do editors decide that a story on a popular local high-school athlete killed in a traffic accident is more important than five hundred killed overseas? They try to determine what is of most interest to their readership. In this way, journalists have an important **agenda-setting** function, which means they can influence by what they print or broadcast what is deemed as important by the public and therefore what the public is more likely to discuss.

Although journalism has a strong public service mission, it is nevertheless subject to the realities of the commercial media system. Without significant audiences and typically substantial advertising revenues, most newspapers, news magazines, and news programs on television and radio would cease to exist. Most newspapers and magazines actually have more advertising content than news, in terms of the amount of space devoted to each type of content. The Internet has challenged many of journalism's traditional business models, and declines in advertising revenues for traditional media outlets have still not been outweighed by the gain in Internet advertising.

On slow news days editors are more likely to include features or photos that have little true news value.

Let's look at two sides of the historical development of journalism—as a profession and as a business—to see how each has influenced the practice of modern journalism. You will see how both have been influenced by technological changes and how they, in turn, have driven innovations in journalism.

◤◣ The Historical Development of Journalism

For much of the history of journalism, as we know it today, it has been synonymous with print media. For some journalists, print media have showcased the best journalism. Of course, in today's converged media world, journalism appears in a variety of media formats, not just as printed text on paper.

The advent of the **penny press** and mass distribution of newspapers in the early nineteenth century, discussed in Chapter 3, brought about a sea change in the concept and definition of journalism. Prior to that, editors of newspapers mostly relied on "news" brought to their offices by citizens or gathered by a small staff, as well as liberally copying from other newspapers, often without crediting the sources. Editors' or publishers' (they were often the same person) opinions were often freely mixed with other editorial content, and no thought was given to presenting all sides of an issue fairly. There was also no established practice of putting the most important news first. Articles were usually written chronologically, regardless of the relative importance of the information.

With the penny press and the need to attract as many readers as possible, however, newspaper publishers often toned down opinions in articles and concentrated more on covering sensational crimes or events. In order to fill their pages, they also had to hire reporters who looked for news to cover rather than passively waiting for news to come to them.

Further fueling the transformation of newspapers were competitors such as **James Gordon Bennett**, who founded the *New York Herald* in 1835. He added a number of features that are now staples in modern journalism, including a financial page, editorial commentary, and public-affairs reporting.

In order to maintain their objective stance throughout the rest of the paper, or at least the public appearance of impartiality, newspaper editors began publishing their points of view exclusively on a special page dubbed the "editorial" page, which is a tradition maintained today by the Western press. Editorials provide a valuable service to the public, helping to guide opinion on matters of public importance, as with endorsements for candidates for public office.

▼ OBJECTIVITY AND THE ASSOCIATED PRESS

The notion of what is news continued to evolve and was shaped by the democratization of politics, the expansion of the market economy, and the growing impact of an entrepreneurial middle class. One reason news became more impartial—what is known in journalism as **objectivity**—was the emergence of the news wire service in the 1840s. In 1848, publishers of six New York newspapers organized the

penny press

Newspapers that sold for a penny, making them accessible to everyone. They differed from older newspaper forms in that they tried to attract as large an audience as possible and were supported by advertising rather than subscriptions.

James Gordon Bennett

Founder of the *New York Herald* in 1835. He started many features found in modern newspapers, including a financial page, editorial commentary, and public-affairs reporting.

objectivity

A journalistic principle that says journalists should be impartial and free of bias in their reporting. This principle has come under attack in recent years, because of the impossibility of people being completely objective, and has largely been replaced by the concepts of fairness and balance.

Newsboys helped mass distribute penny papers by selling them throughout cities.

During the 1800s, as immigration increased and some minorities began to see themselves as people with shared interests and concerns, various minority or ethnic newspapers appeared in the United States. These newspapers served the needs of niche audiences, including Native American, African American, Jewish, and immigrants who did not speak English as their native language.

Among the earliest minority newspapers was *El Misisipí*, the first Spanish-language newspaper in the United States, which began publication in 1808 in New Orleans.[7] The first Native American newspaper, the *Cherokee Phoenix*, began publication in 1828. The first African American daily, the *New Orleans Daily Creole*, began publication in 1856. American abolitionist and former slave Frederick Douglass was not only a great statesman but also a journalist, publishing an antislavery paper called the *North Star*.

Among the most notable minority newspapers of the day was the *Provincial Freeman*, a newspaper founded and edited by **Mary Shadd Cary**, the first African American woman in North America to edit a weekly newspaper.

Born a free black in 1823 in Wilmington, Delaware, Mary fled with her family to Windsor, Canada, after the Fugitive Slave Act was passed in the United States in 1850. Under this act, free northern blacks and escaped slaves were threatened with a return to slavery. In response to a vigorous campaign to deter runaway slaves from escaping to Canada, Mary wrote a forty-four-page pamphlet, "Notes of Canada West," outlining the opportunities for blacks in Canada. Building on the success of this widely read publication, Mary established her weekly newspaper, the *Provincial Freeman*, targeting blacks, and especially fugitive slaves. Her newspaper reported on a variety of important topics, among them the lies being spread in the United States that African Americans in Canada were starving.

Mary Shadd Cary

Another important African American woman journalist in the nineteenth century was **Ida B. Wells**. Born a slave in 1862 six months before the signing of the Emancipation Proclamation, Wells spent her adult life fighting racism and especially the lynching of African Americans. Wells wrote for the religious weekly *The Living Way* and for various African American newspapers, including the *Free Speech* and *Headlight*. She was elected secretary of the Afro-American Press Association in 1889.

Ida B. Wells was a noted African American journalist of the nineteenth century who spent her life fighting racism.

Associated Press (AP), in large part to take advantage of the capabilities of the telegraph as a high-speed communications medium. Telegraphy was too expensive for any single newspaper to afford, so a consortium, or association of leading press organizations, made economic sense.

Because the AP gathered news for half a dozen newspapers with varying political viewpoints, it needed to publish news reports that were politically neutral and thus acceptable to all its member papers. By the dawn of the twentieth century, AP dispatches had become virtually free of editorial comment.

The Associated Press is still based in New York, providing textual, audio, and video news, photos, and graphics to its members. The AP is a not-for-profit members' cooperative including 1,700 newspapers and 5,000 radio and television news operations. That means that the members provide much of the content distributed by the AP, and in turn any member can use the content distributed by the AP. The AP employs 3,700 people (two-thirds of whom work as journalists) in three hundred locations worldwide.[8]

▼ PULITZER AND HEARST: THE CIRCULATION WARS, SENSATIONALISM, AND STANDARDS

Although the practice of objective reporting became the norm for the AP, it was well into the twentieth century before most newspapers had adopted this model of reporting for their own staff. Throughout the latter half of the nineteenth and early in the twentieth century another form of reporting became prevalent in many U.S. newspapers. **Sensational journalism**, or news that exaggerated or featured lurid details and depictions of crimes or other events, came to dominate much newspaper content of this period. Two of the greatest newspaper publishing titans of this era were **William Randolph Hearst,** publisher of the *San Francisco Examiner* and the *New York Journal,* and **Joseph Pulitzer**, publisher of the *New York World,* the *St. Louis Post-Dispatch,* and other papers.

Joseph Pulitzer

Joseph Pulitzer was born in 1847 in Budapest, Hungary. He emigrated to the United States in 1864, serving in the Union army during the Civil War. In 1868 he moved to St. Louis and went to work as a reporter for a German-language paper. Pulitzer purchased the bankrupt *St. Louis Dispatch* in 1878, later merging it with the *Evening Post,* thus creating the *St. Louis Post-Dispatch.* In 1883 he bought the *New York Post* and later the *New York World.*

He became embroiled with Hearst in the newspaper circulation wars during the 1890s, using frequent illustrations, a racy style, and colorful headlines to build the circulation of the *World.* Pulitzer wanted his papers to focus on city news and encouraged his reporters to seek out original, dramatic, and compelling stories, especially humorous, odd, romantic, or thrilling ones, and to write accurately and with attention to detail. Pulitzer built the circulation of the *New York World* to three hundred thousand by the early 1890s by mixing good, solid reporting with sensational photographs, comic strips, and "crusades" against corrupt politicians, support for increased taxes, and civil service reform.

After the four-month Spanish-American War in 1898, Pulitzer withdrew from the sensational tools and techniques that had helped build his newspapers' circulations and replaced them with a vision of journalistic excellence, which he outlined in a 1904 article for the *North American Review.*[9] During this time, Pulitzer was

WEB LINK
The Associated Press
www.ap.org

Associated Press

Founded as a not-for-profit members' cooperative in 1848 by a group of six New York newspaper publishers in order to share the costs of gathering news by telegraph. Today 1,700 newspapers and 5,000 television and radio stations are members of this news-gathering organization.

Mary Shadd Cary

The first African American woman to edit a weekly newspaper. She founded and edited the *Provincial Freeman* in Canada after leaving the United States so she would not be captured and put into slavery because of the Fugitive Slave Act.

Ida B. Wells

A female African American journalist in the latter nineteenth century who wrote and fought against racism and black lynching.

sensational journalism

News that exaggerates or features lurid details and depictions of events in order to get a larger audience.

William Randolph Hearst

Influential American newspaper magnate during the late 19th and early 20th centuries whose newspapers across the United States specialized in sensational journalism and political influence.

Joseph Pulitzer

Influential owner of American newspapers whose publications competed vigorously with those owned by Hearst, often resorting to sensational journalism. After about 1900, Pulitzer turned away from sensational journalism to develop a more socially conscious style of news reporting and muckraking. He founded the Pulitzer Prizes, given each year in recognition of outstanding journalism.

Joseph Pulitzer was a Hungarian immigrant who founded a newspaper empire in St. Louis and New York.

instrumental in the passage of antitrust legislation and regulation of the insurance industry because of investigative stories his papers ran. This emphasis on public service journalism and accurate reporting is still a cornerstone of the annual Pulitzer Prizes, which he bequeathed along with an endowment for the Columbia University Graduate School of Journalism after his death in 1911.

One of Pulitzer's most successful undertakings was the introduction of color printing of comics in his Sunday papers. The most notable example was *The Yellow Kid,* a comic strip drawn as busy, single-panel illustrations. Although *The Yellow Kid* was not the first newspaper cartoon, its innovative style contributed much of the comic strip format many today take for granted.[10]

The Yellow Kid was a creation of cartoonist Richard Felton Outcault during the Pulitzer-Hearst newspaper circulation war in the 1890s and was characterized by rude, vulgar, and brash behavior on the backstreets of the fictional Hogan's Alley. In some ways, *The Yellow Kid* was a late nineteenth-century precursor to the crude kids of *South Park* created during the cable and broadcast television ratings battles of the late twentieth century.

The Yellow Kid quickly became a central figure in the circulation battles between newspaper giants Pulitzer and Hearst when Hearst hired Outcault away from the *World.* The brashness of *The Yellow Kid* reflected well the *Journal*'s overall dramatic style. In reference to the Kid's well-known yellow shirt, critics coined the term **yellow journalism** to describe the sensational style of the newspapers of Pulitzer and his competitor, Hearst.

William Randolph Hearst

William Randolph Hearst was the son of a self-made multimillionaire miner and rancher in northern California. Hearst studied at Harvard and became "proprietor" of his first newspaper, the *San Francisco Examiner,* in 1887 at the age of twenty-three. His father had acquired the paper as payment for a gambling debt. The younger Hearst then acquired in 1895 the *New York Morning Journal* and debuted the *Evening Journal* a year later, hiring away many of Joseph Pulitzer's best reporters and editors by offering them higher pay. He increased his newspaper and periodical chain nationwide to include the *Boston American* and *Chicago Examiner,* as well as magazines *Cosmopolitan* and *Harper's Bazaar.*

Later immortalized in Orson Welles's cinematic triumph, *Citizen Kane,* William Randolph Hearst sensationalized the news by printing colorful banner headlines, adding splashy photography, and some say even inventing the news. Hearst's stories did not always capture the truth, and his readers probably knew it, but they enjoyed reading the accounts and his newspapers' circulations increased tremendously.

Often criticized for his sensational tactics, Hearst nevertheless articulated news standards that resonate even today. Hearst's editorial guidelines from 1933 stated: "Make the news thorough. Print all the news. Condense it if necessary. Frequently it is better when intelligently condensed. But get it in."

William Randolph Hearst's newspapers often had sensational coverage that helped give rise to the term "yellow journalism."

One historian has summarized Hearst's actions as inflammatory. Ernest L. Meyer wrote: "Mr. Hearst in his long and not laudable career has inflamed Americans against Spaniards, Americans against Japanese, Americans against Filipinos, Americans against Russians, and in the pursuit of his incendiary campaign he has printed downright lies, forged documents, faked atrocity stories, inflammatory editorials, sensational cartoons and photographs and other devices by which he abetted his jingoistic ends."[11]

Hearst's ornate, 130-room mansion, San Simeon, built in the 1920s and nick-named the Hearst Castle, today stands as a California landmark. In 1945 Hearst established the Hearst Foundation (now the William Randolph Hearst Foundation), which today provides important support for journalism education and other concerns including health and culture. Hearst died at age eighty-eight in 1951 in Beverly Hills, California.

▼ THE MUCKRAKERS

Just as the efforts of renowned newspaper publishers Hearst and Pulitzer laid a foundation for many of the practices of contemporary journalism, so did the efforts of a number of very important magazine journalists from the late nineteenth and early twentieth centuries. Among the most important were the **muckrakers**. Journalists such as Ida Minerva Tarbell, Joseph Lincoln Steffens, and Upton Sinclair (author of *The Jungle*) were dubbed "muckrakers" by a disapproving President Theodore Roosevelt because they pioneered investigative reporting of corrupt practices and problems in government or business. The process was analogous to raking muck, the polite term for the manure, mud, and straw mixture found in stables. Many of the most important muckrakers reported for magazines of the day, in large part because their investigations required considerable time to complete, which fit better with magazine publishing deadlines than with newspapers.

▼ THE RISE OF ELECTRONIC JOURNALISM

The golden age of newspapers started its decline when radio became a medium of mass communication in the 1920s. The public did not have to wait a day or more for news of events like it did with newspapers, and furthermore radio was "free," as it was entirely advertising supported. But television news started the steep decline and eventual eclipse of newspapers as the public's main source of news.

The late 1940s and early 1950s marked the beginning of television news. News was and still is an important part of how broadcast television fulfills its federal mandate to serve in the public interest.

Many of the early news programs were produced by the television network news divisions in New York. In 1947, NBC debuted *Meet the Press,* a made-for-TV news conference, with journalists asking questions of various news makers, often government officials. The program continues today and is the oldest series on network TV. Tim Russert was the longest-serving host of the program, doing so for 16 years until his untimely death at age fifty-eight in 2008. In the 1950s, NBC introduced the *Today* show, the first and still-running early-morning network news show. *Today* had a decidedly entertainment quality back then, with host Dave Garroway joined by chimpanzee sidekick J. Fred Muggs.

Murrow and News in TV's Golden Age

Setting the standard for television news during television's golden age in the late 1940s and the 1950s was the distinguished journalist **Edward R. Murrow**, who first achieved fame by broadcasting dramatic radio

Edward R. Murrow was a noted radio and television journalist in the earliest days of television.

yellow journalism

A style of journalism practiced especially by publishers Joseph Pulitzer and William Randolph Hearst during the late 1890s in which stories were sensationalized and often partly or wholly made up in order to be more dramatic.

muckrakers

A group of journalists in the latter nineteenth and early twentieth centuries who investigated business and political corruption. Their activities were likened to raking up mud, or muck, by Theodore Roosevelt, who meant it as a term of derision.

Edward R. Murrow

A radio and, later, television journalist and announcer who set the standard for journalistic excellence on television during television's golden age.

news reports from London during World War II. Murrow produced the popular television programs *See It Now* and *Person to Person* at CBS News.

Murrow's comments on television at the Radio-Television News Directors Association (RTNDA) meeting in 1958 ring equally true today for the Internet: "This instrument can teach, it can illuminate, and yes, it can inspire. But it can do so only to the extent that humans are determined to use it to those ends. Otherwise it is nothing but wires and lights in a box." The same year he also wrote in *TV Guide* that viewers must realize "television in the main is being used to distract, delude, amuse and insulate us."

Changes in Television News

Television news counts on interesting visuals to help tell its stories, and this can often dictate the ordering of stories in a newscast or even whether a story is aired or not. Perhaps because of its visual nature, television news has always had an eye on the entertainment aspect of media, as demonstrated as far back as the early days of the *Today* show mentioned earlier. Time constraints of less than thirty minutes or an hour to cover local, national, and international news, business news, sports, and weather also place limitations on how long particular stories can be within a newscast.

The introduction of video cameras into the television newsroom brought important changes to television news. **Electronic news-gathering (ENG) equipment** allowed journalists in the field to capture and send videotaped news by satellite to the network, where it could be edited and broadcast much more quickly than film. This has influenced the nature of video storytelling. The late CBS news veteran Bud Benjamin likened it to "NTV," or the video-journalism equivalent of "MTV," or music television, with rapid-paced cuts and entertainment values becoming increasingly paramount in journalism.

The rise of twenty-four-hour news channels means that there is much more of a **news hole** to fill, which encourages stations to be less discriminating about what they consider newsworthy. Sometimes this is a good thing, as events that would otherwise not reach a televised audience are covered, but other times the material serves mainly a public relations or entertainment purpose.

electronic news-gathering [ENG] equipment

Tools such as video cameras and satellite dishes that allow journalists to gather and broadcast news much more quickly than in the past.

news hole

A term typically used with newspapers, it refers to the amount of total space available after advertisement space has been blocked out.

Although when CNN came out with the first 24-hour cable news channel it was predicted to fail, in fact there are a growing number of such channels today.

Foundations of Journalism

Digital technology and the Internet will continue to transform journalism, but professional, mainstream journalism today is still largely practiced as it has been. Reporters cover events and write stories, editors select what stories to assign and whether they appear, depending on how many pages they have for print news, which in turn depends on how many advertisements were sold. Digital technology will not change the fact that reporters need to visit places and interview people. Nor will digital technology replace an experienced editor's judgment on what makes a good story and how to edit that story.

In order to understand what aspects of journalism have changed already and what will likely change more with convergence, we will first look at basic issues of journalistic responsibility and how journalism is practiced, at least in its ideal form.

▼ THE HUTCHINS COMMISSION AND *A FREE AND RESPONSIBLE PRESS*

In 1947 what became known as the Hutchins Commission published a landmark report titled *A Free and Responsible Press,* offering a critique of the state of the press in the United States. The 133-page report of the Commission on Freedom of the Press was written by Robert Maynard Hutchins and a dozen other leading intellectuals. The report argued that the public has a right to information that affects it and that the press has a responsibility to present that information. Because the press enjoys constitutionally guaranteed freedom, the press carries an additional moral duty to fulfill this responsibility. The commission recommended that the government, the public, and the press could all take steps to improve the functioning of a healthy press. Among these steps, the commission recommended the government recognize that all media have the same constitutional guarantees traditionally enjoyed only by print media.

The commission recommended that the agencies of mass communication assume the responsibility of financing new, experimental activities in their fields. Moreover, the members of the press should engage in vigorous mutual criticism. The commission called on the public to create academic-professional centers of advanced study, research, and publication in the field of communications. Among the first such centers was the Media Studies Center, founded by the Freedom Forum in 1984, nearly forty years after the report. The commission also recommended that existing schools of journalism exploit the total resources of their universities to the end that their students obtain the broadest and most liberal training. Finally, the commission recommended the establishment of a new and independent agency to appraise and report annually on the performance of the press. This has been tried at a national level in the form of a National Press Council but has failed, although a similar idea has had marginal success in some states.

▼ SEPARATION OF EDITORIAL AND BUSINESS OPERATIONS

In newsroom parlance commonly called the "separation of church and state," this is a basic principle in ensuring that news coverage is not influenced by business decisions or advertisers who threaten to stop advertising because they do not like

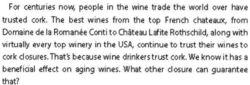

For centuries now, people in the wine trade the world over have trusted cork. The best wines from the top French chateaux, from Domaine de la Romanée Conti to Château Lafite Rothschild, along with virtually every top winery in the USA, continue to trust their wines to cork closures. That's because wine drinkers trust cork. We know it has a beneficial effect on aging wines. What other closure can guarantee that?

The love affair between wine consumers and cork began back in 1670, when French monk Dom Perignon first used it for the sparkling wine of his Hautvillers' monastery. Since the 1700s natural cork has been the leading closure for fine wines from every part of the world. Nine out of ten U.S. consumers feel that non-cork closures cheapen wine, a 2006 survey of the wine trade here found. In survey after survey, wine lovers show cork is still the preferred closure for fine wines by a wide margin.

Over the past ten years the cork industry has invested literally millions of dollars to improve cork quality and consistency. Those efforts have now produced significant results for wineries and the consumer. Production techniques and rigorous quality control procedures have developed this past decade to deliver the most widely accepted stopper for wine, despite competition from other wine closures. The corks produced today are the best corks in history— a suitable partner for today's exceptional wines.

It's not just about romance, but quality. Time after time.

Real Cork. Real Wine.

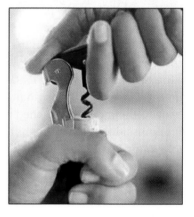

 Icep Portugal APCOR prime

Advertorials are designed and written to look like news content but are in fact paid advertisements.

coverage of an issue. This separation is supposed to carry over to the page layout of a newspaper or magazine as well by showing clear differences between advertising and editorial content.

However, many media critics complain that this separation has been breaking down in recent years as publishers or large media corporations that own news organizations increasingly let business decisions influence editorial content. This can happen blatantly, as when the owner of the *Los Angeles Times* used staff reporters and editors to create a special "news" section on the Staples Center that was entirely sponsored (and had content approved by) Staples without explicitly saying so; or it could be more insidious, as when management lays off reporters, which has the effect of hampering original local reporting and forces the paper to rely on cheaper but perhaps less relevant wire service news.

▼ FAIRNESS AND BALANCE IN NEWS COVERAGE

Fairness and **balance** in news coverage have replaced the goal of objectivity in journalism. Objectivity, or the principle that news is reported on and presented in a completely unbiased manner, has come under attack in recent years. Critics say that people cannot be completely unbiased and to claim objectivity in a given situation is simply masking the bias of the reporter. In addition, everything from the subsequent editing or placement of a story in a newspaper to the time slot for a news segment can reflect biased coverage, even if the reporter has no strong bias when writing the story. Unintended biases can also show up in the people a journalist decides to interview and the choice of story assignments an editor makes.

The terms "fairness" and "balance" mean that journalists try to present all sides of a topic equally and in a way that does not favor one side. Fairness and balance do not mean that all participants in an issue get equal space for their views, however. A small group of fifty vocal people supporting a fringe political candidate would not get the same amount of coverage as a popular candidate from a major political party simply because they are fielding a candidate in an election. Factors such as the relative importance within the context of the story and validity or authority of the news source must be considered when a journalist decides how much coverage to give a person or group.

fairness

In news coverage, the concept of covering all relevant sides of an issue and allowing spokespeople representing those various sides a chance to be covered in the same way.

balance

In news coverage, the concept of presenting sides equally or of reporting on a broad range of news events.

▼ FRAMING THE NEWS

Traditional news media often decide how they will **frame** a story before the reporting is completed and sometimes before it has even begun. This is one of the biggest problems in journalism today, because frequently the facts of a story are forced to fit into the frame, or angle, regardless of reality. Yet framing cannot be avoided, partly because it makes writing a news story easier and faster and partly because we typically frame situations in our daily lives to help make sense of the world. Balance, or fairness, is often not achieved, and often journalists are not even aware that they are framing stories. They see their work as simply reflecting reality.

Perhaps even more problematic, however, is the fact that frequently events in the real world are forced into an existing frame, when reality is in fact more complex and defies framing. The need for journalism to demonize one side over another, creating "good guys" and "bad guys" in situations that are actually quite complex, can have serious repercussions for how reporting is done and what words are used. Depending on one's loyalties, a "terrorist attack" could also be described as "armed resistance."

frame

The notion that every story is told in a particular way that influences how readers think of the story.

▼ EXPERT SOURCES

A related issue to framing, also problematic in the media—especially on television—has to do with the use of "expert" sources to give the news more credibility. At the three main television networks, ABC, CBS, and NBC, most speakers selected to give their views during the news or other public-affairs programs are white and male. The Tenth Annual Women, Men and Media Study, conducted by ADT Research in conjunction with the Freedom Forum, shows that during the first six months

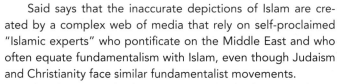

Framing in the news occurs everywhere, but it is arguably most prevalent in coverage of international news. In the 1980s, when Japanese companies were buying American companies, the American media often depicted the trend using warlike terms such as "invasion." This was echoed in recent years as China gained economic might, yet similar language is not seen when a Canadian or British company buys an American company.

Due partly to the terrorist attacks on September 11, Islam has largely been framed in the U.S. media as a monolithic religion advocating violence and repression of human rights, argues scholar Edward Said in his book *Covering Islam.*

Said says that the inaccurate depictions of Islam are created by a complex web of media that rely on self-proclaimed "Islamic experts" who pontificate on the Middle East and who often equate fundamentalism with Islam, even though Judaism and Christianity face similar fundamentalist movements.

The depictions feed into a nationalistic "us-versus-them" mentality that is similar to the anti-Communist fervor during the cold war. Not only do these inaccurate portrayals of Muslims hurt our ability to see them on equal or humanistic terms, they provide a cover for repressive regimes that use Islam as an excuse for their policies.

Framing, in other words, paints over a complex reality and, more importantly, shapes our reactions and beliefs to the new reality that it creates. This in turn can affect how we interact with the groups that have been framed and can perpetuate negative stereotypes and discrimination.

Studies have shown that news shows predominantly use white males as subject experts and guests.

of 1998, "Nearly nine of ten 'expert' sound bites (87 percent) on the network newscasts were provided by men, and *more* than nine in ten (92 percent) were provided by whites." Women were featured in just 13 percent of expert sound bites and people of color just 6 percent. In contrast, nonexperts on network news programs are much more likely to be of diverse backgrounds.

"Individuals of either sex, any age, and all races can be heard from on the network news, as long as they are not wielding power or offering expertise. The networks' 'golden rolodexes' of expert consultants are badly in need of updating," said Andrew Tyndall, director of the study titled *Who Speaks for America? Sex, Age and Race on the Network News.* Research about other mainstream media, including important print media such as news magazines *Time, Newsweek,* and *U.S. News & World Report,* show similar results.

▲▼ From Event to Public Eye: How News Is Created

There must always be news to fill the regularly scheduled evening broadcast on television, the morning's paper, the weekly news magazine, or the website. Like an accordion, news can expand or contract as required by the day's events, but only to a limited degree. The fact is, whether anything important happens today or not, the networks will still have at least a thirty-minute newscast (actually, twenty-two minutes, after subtracting the time for commercials). Sometimes, during a major breaking news event such as the September 11 World Trade Center and Pentagon attacks, they will extend the news to an hour or even have continuous coverage.

There has been an inexorable shift in newspaper coverage in the past thirty years from hard news to lighter news. Newspapers have covered fewer stories on public affairs and politics and replaced them with more stories on entertainment or popular culture. In 1980, one of every three front-page news stories dealt with government or public affairs, compared to just one in every five today. In 1980, only one in every fifty front-page daily newspaper stories dealt with celebrities, popular entertainment, and other related subjects. Today, one in every fourteen front-page daily newspaper stories deals with celebrities and the like, not including the various teasers and blurbs promoting other parts of the paper, according to research by the Pew Research Center for the People & the Press, an independent opinion research center sponsored by the Pew Charitable Trusts.

WEB LINK
Pew Research Center for the People & the Press
www.pewcenter.org

There are a number of reasons for this dramatic shift away from public affairs to popular entertainment. One is the increasingly competitive media environment in which newspapers must compete against electronic entertainment media. Also important is the changing ownership structure and economics of newspapers. Further, technological change is contributing to this transformation, as newspapers struggle to reinvent themselves in an online, digital age.

Regardless of the type of news that appears, techniques of gathering, reporting, and presenting the news to the public have been refined over the years and have changed surprisingly little. There are variations between techniques that print journalists and television journalists must use, of course, but the basic principles are largely the same. We will look at some of the basic steps in the news-gathering process for print and television.

▼ GATHERING THE NEWS

The Associated Press news service publishes for its members a daily listing of upcoming news events such as important court cases, demonstrations, and press conferences. It's called the AP daybook, and most journalists or their assignment editors refer to it at night to get ideas for stories to cover the next day. The daybook is a pretty good predictor of the next day's news. Some media critics claim that much news is actually manufactured by media organizations, with the help of public relations professionals sending press releases and creating pseudo events such as press conferences or awards ceremonies with the sole purpose of getting the attention of the press or public.

Although news about pseudo events or based on press releases may well be "manufactured," the fact is journalists must largely rely

Sometimes during protests or demonstrations people act up when they see TV news cameras covering the event.

on these sources in order to be informed of what is happening. But journalists also use sources they have developed through experience covering a **beat**, or subject area they specialize in. Initially beats covered geographic areas, much like a police officer's beat. Geographically based beats still exist, but increasingly beats cover specific subject areas, such as education, city hall, the state capital, or science. Through their reporting, journalists become aware of interesting developments that may be newsworthy and can cultivate sources that inform them further. Small newspapers cannot afford to have highly specialized reporters and often simply have general-assignment reporters who cover a range of topics.

Moreover, the media tend to spotlight selected issues and stories. These stories often resonate through the entire media system, whether about the release of a highly anticipated movie, a natural disaster, or a U.S. presidential campaign. An unusual advertising campaign for a movie, for example, may trigger news stories about the campaign and its effect on the success of the movie, which in turn generate more publicity for the movie—which adds to its popularity. Some news filters up through the media network, starting as a story in a local paper that is then covered by a regional television station, where it is seen by a reporter for a national publication, who covers the story and thus brings it to a national audience.

▼ PRODUCING THE NEWS

Once a story has been assigned or chosen and the raw material—interviews, background facts, or video footage—has been gathered, the reporter then has to make sense out of it all and shape it into a compelling piece that accurately reflects the facts. Depending on whether the story involves breaking news or not, the reporter sometimes has very little time to write or produce it before a deadline. Few journalists have the luxury of putting a story aside for a week to ponder word choices or polish their prose.

Newspaper editors decide which stories are most important and where they will be placed in the newspaper in meetings several hours before story deadlines, and these spaces are blocked out (advertising space has been blocked out first).

Formal and informal editorial meetings take place throughout the day in newsrooms.

Platypus Journalism: Journalism's Future, or Evolutionary Dead End?

News organizations have been slow to realize how drastically digital media are changing their business and the nature of the profession itself, but with losses in advertising revenues, lower readership, and job cuts they cannot ignore it any longer.

As news organizations scramble to figure out their way in the digital news environment, one model of the future of journalism has seemed particularly appealing: that of the one-man or one-woman correspondent in sole possession of all the tools to report, produce, and file stories from the field.

The idea is that with the new, cheaper digital tools, wireless Internet connections, and more powerful computers, journalists on the road could shoot video, record audio, write a story, and possibly create an interactive multimedia graphic.

The notion has appeal to management, as one reporter would now be doing the work of at least three. Some early experiments in one-person news operations seemed promising, such as Kevin Sites's reporting for Yahoo News from a number of global hotspots.

However, the model has also been ridiculed as "platypus journalism" or "Inspector Gadget journalism," with critics saying that journalists cannot do the same in-depth coverage when juggling all the tech gadgets as they could if they focused on one medium, such as writing or video.

The critics say that the future of reporting more likely lies in some form of **crowd sourcing**—utilizing raw data gathered from the public, as well as reports from citizen-journalists—than a one-man band of technology gadgetry. In this model, journalists may act more as curators than news gatherers for some types of stories, directing the flow of data feeds and choosing and interpreting accurate and relevant information to create compelling stories.

Sometimes breaking news or an unexpected event may push planned stories from their slots or from the newspaper entirely.

Editors look for logical weaknesses or errors in stories, often asking reporters to get more information or make more calls to make the story complete. Fact checkers research all facts stated in the story for accuracy and, depending on the media organization and the laziness of the reporter, sometimes have to replace many TKs (used in journalism to mean "to come") in a "finished" story with hard facts based on their research. Copyeditors correct writing errors and make sure everything is written according to the proper style. In larger newspapers, headline and caption writers read the stories and come up with headlines and photo captions that fit within the space allotted. In smaller newspapers, journalists may have more than one role or may be responsible for fact checking or suggesting headlines as well.

Design and page-layout artists put the copyedited articles and graphics in a digital version of the paper using a page-layout program such as QuarkXpress or Adobe InDesign. Proofreaders check for editorial errors, and after the issue is approved by an editor, it is sent to the printer. This used to be done by taking negative photographs

crowd sourcing

Utilizing raw data that the public has gathered, in addition to reports from citizen-journalists, to help create a news report.

of hard copies of the pages, but now it is done entirely electronically, and the printer receives the pages digitally through a high-speed Internet connection.

In television news, camera crews and reporters usually return to the station to edit footage shot on location and to add voice-overs and graphics to the video. Since time is so critical, news segments are edited and rehearsed down to the second to fit into their selected time slots. With breaking or international news, reporters will report live from location, often broadcasting via satellite.

Television news, because of the amount of equipment needed to shoot video, requires more people to gather and produce a story. A crew of two people, a camera person and a reporter, is usually needed. Digital video technology has helped reduce the number needed to shoot broadcast-quality video to a single camera person and reporter, but there are still many more technical steps involved in assembling a television news package than in writing a print story.

At the station, the producer and reporter decide on what to edit and how the story will be put together, usually working with video editors or other technicians to carry out their instructions. At some stations, news anchors also have a role in editorial decisions, while at other stations they simply present the news.

▼ DISTRIBUTING THE NEWS

The goal of both print and electronic media in distributing the news is the same: to attract as large an audience as possible. The reasoning is simple: a larger audience means a higher advertising rate and therefore more income for the media organization.

Newspapers and magazines use colorful or dramatic photos on their front pages or covers, often with what the editors have decided is the most enticing story. Some magazines may send press releases about what they feel are particularly noteworthy stories coming out in the next issue, with the hope that other media outlets will report on these and generate more sales. Individual stories can be syndicated and appear in other print-media outlets.

Print media are distributed through subscriptions and newsstand sales. Subscribers are more valuable to media organizations because they represent a stable revenue base and provide mailing lists that can be sold or rented to other organizations. Material costs for print media, ranging from paper to ink to delivery trucks, can be quite high.

Television stations have short teasers during commercial breaks throughout the evening, usually asking a provocative question such as, "Could the food you are eating be dangerous? Find out at eleven." Often the stories that have acted as the bait to get viewers to watch the news are not the lead story but appear later in the program, in order to keep people watching. This is also the reason weather forecasts usually come toward the middle or end of a news broadcast. National news shows are transmitted by the network to affiliate stations, sometimes with time slots available for additional local news content. Networks also send video feeds of international and national news coverage to local affiliates so they can use the footage in their news reports.

◤▽ Types of Journalism

The tenets of mainstream professional journalism have often been challenged. Those who question the credibility and substance of journalism are not satisfied with the news or do not believe that journalism as a profession is fulfilling its ideals as an institution that is necessary for a strong democracy. Critics of journalism may even argue that journalism is part of the problem because news organizations are run as commercial enterprises with the goal of making profits. This, critics say, makes news organizations too cozy with powerful business and political interests and keeps them from taking the critical watchdog role that journalism should have.

Much serious questioning of journalism took place during the 1960s, even among established journalists, when social upheavals led many to question norms in established society. Leading reporters such as James "Scottie" Reston of the *New York Times* and Paul Anderson of the *St. Louis Post-Dispatch* perceived the limits of "objective" news reportage that simply stated the facts in a story and developed the beginnings of **interpretive reporting**, which tried to explain the story by placing the facts into broader context.

Critics of interpretive reporting argue that it does no better at adequately representing the complexity of reality than objective reporting. Still, interpretive reporting opened the door to a variety of journalistic styles during the 1960s, including New Journalism, literary journalism, and advocacy journalism.

New Journalism developed in the 1960s and 1970s during a time of great social, political, and economic upheaval in the United States, ranging from the Vietnam War to Watergate. Many journalists sought to present a true account of the complexity or spirit of the times. What emerged was a form of reporting that often used literary techniques such as point of view, exploration of characters' emotions, and first-person narrative. Topics included popular social issues and the drug culture. Truman Capote, Tom Wolfe, and Norman Mailer were three prominent writers using New Journalism techniques in their books. Critics of New Journalism charged that the literary style often blurred the line between fact and fiction.

Literary journalism in some ways has roots that go back to the muckrakers, although its modern form does not always tackle social problems with the same fervor as the muckrakers. Literary journalism stays closer to true, observable narrative in its storytelling, and its pace may be slow, with frequent lengthy side trips on other topics. Because of the length of articles and variety of topics covered, literary journalism does not generally deal with breaking news events, though news events may be the basis for some literary-journalism stories. One of the finest literary journalists is John McPhee, who combines immersive reporting, solid research, and excellent writing to create engaging stories. Other practitioners of literary journalism include Joan Didion, James Fallows, and Robert Kaplan, all of whom write on a range of issues, including foreign affairs and politics.

Another descendent of muckraking, one that keeps the muckraker's critique of society firmly in focus, is advocacy journalism. It maintains a strong commitment to political and social reform. Leading examples of advocacy journalism are Gloria Steinem (founder of *Ms.* magazine and a leader of the women's movement), Pete Hamill (one-time editor of the *Daily News* in New York), and Nicholas von Hoffman. Much of early environmental journalism was a type of advocacy journalism.

▼ ALTERNATIVE JOURNALISM

Alternative journalism, often called radical journalism in the past, departed considerably from the traditions of objective reporting and has a much older lineage than some of the types of journalism just mentioned. Its roots go back to some of the radical and socialist newspapers published in the nineteenth century in the UK that were meant to give workers a united voice and shared sense of injustice. Some

interpretive reporting

A type of reporting that tries to put the facts of a story into a broader context by relying on knowledge and experience the reporter has about the subject.

The *Indypendent* is a print newspaper published by the Indymedia group in New York.

radical papers had large circulations in their heyday, comparable to some of the most popular traditional papers of the day, but the advertising-supported model put these newspapers at a disadvantage because advertisers did not want to be associated with radical political movements. In addition, most readers of these papers were working class, so were not considered desirable customers. As a result, such papers tended to struggle to stay afloat or toned down their political rants to be more attractive to advertisers.

Alternative journalism often purposely defied the conventions of professional journalism, both in tone and choice of topics, much as the New Journalists did decades later. Despite existing on the fringes throughout most of the twentieth century and never seriously challenging mainstream journalism, it did provide an outlet for stories not seen elsewhere, some of which would then make their way into the mainstream.

Magazines such as *Mother Jones, The Progressive,* and *The Nation* can be seen as inheritors of the radical-journalism tradition and examples of alternative journalism that straddle the gap between radical journalism and mainstream standards of professional quality. And of course the alternative weeklies available in most urban areas, such as the *Boston Phoenix* and the *Houston Press,* are examples of the genre, with their edgy, contrarian coverage of topics that is often geared to a younger audience.

Alternative journalism was given new life in 1999 during the WTO protests in Seattle, when an ad hoc group of protesters created their own media to cover the event because they felt the mainstream press was misreporting or underreporting the events. The independent media movement, called Indymedia for short, was founded and has quickly spread worldwide thanks to the growth of the Internet. Although most Indymedia groups remain small, their decentralized structure and open publishing systems allow people to easily contribute stories, providing outlets for many who would not otherwise get involved in journalism. Some local groups, such as Indymedia NYC, publish professional-quality newspapers along with a robust website.

▼ PUBLIC JOURNALISM

Public journalism, sometimes called civic journalism, developed in the early 1990s out of dissatisfaction among some editors and journalists over how poorly mainstream journalism seemed to be covering important social and political issues. They saw the growing cynicism and apathy among the general public in civic affairs, and the increased distrust of journalists, and wondered if perhaps mainstream journalism coverage had an influence on those attitudes.

Public journalism takes a much less radical approach to engaging the public than alternative journalism, mostly because it originated from longtime and respected professional journalists. It expands on the watchdog role of journalism but tries to engage the citizenry more closely with creating and discussing the news. Public journalism also tries to avoid framing the news in terms of conflict and extremes and examines the news in a more nuanced fashion.

Newspapers experimenting with public journalism around the country have reported a higher level of trust toward the press by their readership and some signs of increased civic participation and awareness of social and political issues. Critics of public journalism charge that it is little more than boosterism or advocacy journalism and weakens the role of the press as a sometimes unpopular but critical voice of a community's conscience. Others criticize it for not going far enough in breaking the barrier between professional journalists and audiences, seeing it as a way for journalists to try to maintain their privileged position as professionals who for some reason can report better on the news than citizens can.

Partly because of the two forces of criticism—that of professional peers and that of citizens—public journalism has waned in recent years. Later studies in communities with papers that followed public-journalism principles noted no significant increase in political awareness or participation among the public, so the results of its success seem to be mixed.

What the debates on public journalism did do was provide a precursor to the challenges professional journalists would face in the early twenty-first century with the rise of citizen journalism.

WEB LINK
Public Journalism Network
pjnet.org

▼ CITIZEN JOURNALISM

The Internet and especially social-media tools have allowed the rapid growth of what is called citizen journalism. Although it takes many forms and is still being defined, it broadly encompasses everything from blogging to Slashdot to more formal ventures such as OhMyNews, NowPublic, or Wikinews that emulate professional journalism in important aspects. Some scholars even include product-review sites by consumers as a form of citizen journalism.

Citizen journalism differs from other types of journalism in that it is usually not created with an explicitly political or radical agenda, like advocacy or alternative journalism, and its driving force has been citizens rather than professional journalists, as in public journalism.

It is partly for these reasons that mainstream journalism has been more willing to embrace some citizen-journalism efforts, even if cautiously. Some news organizations have tried to cultivate its viewers and readers as sources of raw news footage, such as CNN's iReporter, and most other news networks have followed with similar initiatives. Other news organizations, especially some newspapers, have adopted a more integrated and thorough approach in which citizen-journalists post news and stories on a stand-alone website, perhaps partially cobranded with the newspaper, and the best of the stories get published in a weekly edition. Still other organizations have conducted training sessions for citizen-journalists, teaching them interviewing, reporting, and writing skills. Critics of these efforts by mainstream news organizations say that citizens are primarily being used as unpaid reporters to fill holes in local news coverage because of staff cutbacks.

Wikinews is a citizen-journalism site that uses the Wikipedia format.

Original citizen-journalism sites have had a rougher time of it, some proving wildly successful and others failing miserably. OhMyNews, the South Korea–based citizen-journalism site that operates much like a traditional news organization, with paid editors and a hierarchy in the editing process before stories are posted, has had mixed success. Although very popular and financially strong in South Korea, the English-language website version lost money and had to shut down, as did the Japanese OhMyNews. Vancouver-based NowPublic, which launched in 2005 and now has reporters in 140 countries, has been a success. Citizen-journalism advocate Dan Gillmor launched Bayosphere in 2005, a citizen-journalism site that was intended to cover the San Francisco Bay area. However, after seven difficult months, the project was largely abandoned. Gillmor continues to believe in the potential of citizen journalism, but he learned some hard lessons about the practicality and economics of making it a reality.

One common thread in most citizen-journalism sites is the emphasis on conversation and interaction between participants and a blurring of the lines between journalist and audience. Many professional journalists find this development very threatening, as it challenges their privileged position as the arbiters of what is important enough to be considered news. In this way, journalists are losing their gatekeeping function and journalism is evolving into what Australian media scholar Axel Bruns calls a gatewatching function, as discussed in the previous chapter.

Despite the great potential in increasing participation and interaction between citizens who practice citizen journalism, there still is no clear business model to ensure that citizen journalism can be sustainable and pay its reporters and editors suitable wages. Nevertheless, the shift to citizen journalism and its wide variety of formats, from hyperlocal blogs to national or international coverage, signal a change in traditional news gathering to practices that encourage interactive participation. Or, as NYU journalism professor Jay Rosen says, "journalism should be a conversation, not a lecture."

▼ AN INTERNATIONAL PERSPECTIVE

There is nothing sacred about the inverted-pyramid style for news stories or the emphasis on fairness and balance in news that is taken for granted in the United States. Most Americans do not realize that there are a number of ways journalism can be practiced because they generally do not see news from other countries—or if they do, it is likely the English-language BBC, which follows the same tenets of fairness and balance in its coverage.

However, a look at news styles, even in other European countries, will often show a surprising variety in how news is written. Reporters' opinions may be more prevalent or obvious in some ostensibly factual news accounts, or reporters may insert their own thoughts or feelings about the news they are covering.

In many countries journalists still face censorship or licensing restrictions, which of course shape the kind of news that appears in print or on TV or radio. In these cases, journalists may act more like government stenographers, simply recording government meetings and events that the state deems important to publicize, with the only editorial voice being that approved by the state.

These examples show how journalism has been shaped by economic, political, and social realities and how what we see today in the newspaper, on television, or on the Web, given different historical developments in the United States, may have turned out very different—and will continue to change.

◢▽ Journalism in the Digital World

The digital tools available to journalists to help them do their jobs more effectively have been slow to be adopted by mainstream news organizations. Busy work schedules and unwillingness on the part of media corporations to subsidize professional training and development for their journalists play a part in the slow rate of adoption. However, more and more journalists have seen the value in using one tool—the Internet—in making their jobs easier.

The increased power of the audience to communicate with journalists and with each other in a public forum, whether as citizen journalism or simply discussions on blogs or forums, also can be threatening to some journalists who are accustomed to being the gatekeepers of information. Now readers and viewers online can point out, quite publicly, when a journalist errs. News sites have found that if they do not provide a discussion forum for their readers, the readers will simply go elsewhere to discuss stories and point out errors.

As Table 9-1 shows, out of the top ten news sites in January 2011, three were based on print publications, four were based on television news networks or partnerships, and two were essentially news aggregators, Yahoo News and AOL News, which use stories from the wire services and other news sources. The Huffington Post, which started as a blog and which has been an influential news source in its own right, was purchased by AOL in 2011.

The large numbers of online viewers of news sites may seem like a good thing, as it shows people are still engaged with the news, but it has put the

The Web changes how people get and read their news.

TABLE 9-1
Top Global News Sites, by Unique Visitors: January 2011

RANK	SITE	UNIQUE AUDIENCE
1	Yahoo! News	46,274,000
2	CNN Digital Network	37,008,000
3	MSNBC Digital Network	32,494,000
4	AOL News	22,060,000
5	Tribune Newspapers	16,929,000
6	Fox News Digital Network	16,652,000
7	NYTimes.com	15,503,000
8	ABC News Digital Network	14,551,000
9	TheHuffingtonPost.com	13,266,000
10	Gannett Newspapers and Newspaper Division	12,763,000

Source: Nielsen Online

news industry under even greater pressure. Not only must news organizations compete with their traditional media counterparts, but they also have to compete with the online versions of their competitors. Furthermore, ad revenues online have not been enough to counterbalance the drop in ads from the traditional media product, especially in print.

Advances in technology not only threaten business models, but they can bring about changes in how people use the Internet, thereby changing the role online news may play in the public's overall picture of media use. Even so, there are some trends that perhaps show the way to what role online journalism fills in providing news and information to the public.

▼ THE 24/7 NEWS CYCLE

Online news is not tied to a printer's schedule or specific broadcast slot, which means that it can be presented twenty-four hours a day, seven days a week. This can cause the increasingly common situation in which a media organization's website scoops its print newspaper or television news show. Many media companies used to avoid this by putting an **embargo**, or temporary hold, on publishing the news on the Web until the traditional media product had published or aired the story. However, as the chance for getting scooped by the competition rose, the practice became less common, and news organizations have grown accustomed to their websites being the place where news breaks. A non-deadline-driven news cycle wreaks havoc on the way news is usually processed and could add to production costs as more reporting and editing staff are needed to process news around the clock.

▼ NONTRADITIONAL NEWS SOURCES

The public's ability to access nontraditional news sources has two components: getting news from traditional news outlets that are not usually viewed or read by the public and getting news from a wider variety of nonjournalism sites, such as blogs or discussion groups. An example in the former category is viewing an online newspaper from the Middle East to see how a story is covered there or watching an Al Jazeera newscast. Even looking at UK media coverage of international issues can often be a valuable and educational experience for U.S. audiences who receive a fairly narrow range of international news. With nonjournalistic, nontraditional outlets, users should have a high degree of media literacy so they can weigh sources of news and any biases the website creator may have.

News sources increasingly view themselves as content providers who can publish without relying on a traditional journalistic publisher or gateway. NBA.com, for example, publishes extensive news about its basketball games and includes video clips. Why would a viewer go to CNN or ESPN when he or she can get sports news straight from the source? Subscribing to follow an influential person's Twitter account or blog can often point people to news that they would not otherwise be aware of, and tweets or blog posts from celebrities can become the topics of news stories themselves.

The danger in nontraditional news sources like these is that they may not have the same critical eye that a professional news organization would have. It is unlikely a user would find an exposé on NBA.com about financial wrongdoing by the league, for example. On the other hand, many members of the public may not care about such news and simply want to get basketball scores and news on the latest trades. In that case, going to a site like NBA.com may be fine.

▼ ONLINE USERS' MEDIA HABITS

Online users' media habits differ from traditional media use in a number of ways. First, online users are generally more active in their media use and will easily visit different websites to find the information they are seeking. This shorter attention span for viewing media content means that news stories have to compete harder for the audience's attention. Most people do not like to read large amounts of material online and tend to skim written material. This also encourages producing shorter printed stories or stories with interactive graphics or multimedia.

Users want to quickly understand not only the essential facts in a story but its context as well and will readily use hyperlinks to click to related stories or other websites. However, from a business standpoint, media organizations do not want visitors to leave their website, so there is a natural tension regarding what hyperlinks to provide and how to provide them in a way that allows users to explore further yet encourages them to remain.

On the other hand, with the rise in popularity of blogs, news sites want their stories to be mentioned and linked to in order to drive traffic to their site. Some blogs are so heavily read that a mention in an entry can crash a smaller news site's web server because of the high volume of people visiting the site, something called the **Slashdot effect**. This refers to what has frequently happened when a site is mentioned on the very popular technology news site Slashdot.

Slashdot effect

The occurrence of a website's servers crashing because of a large increase in visits to the site after its being mentioned on the popular website Slashdot.org.

▼ PERSONALIZATION

The Internet allows users to personalize the content they receive, ranging from localized weather forecasts to choosing news on favorite sports teams or companies in a stock portfolio. Personalization is one of the unique features of online media that traditional media simply cannot compete with, and its development

Personalizing web pages gives users the ability to get exactly the kind of news they wish.

could become a key feature that helps better engage news consumers. Personalization could lead to changes in the way journalists write or produce stories. For example, a standard version of a story could also include sections that are added to the story from a database based on a user's online behavior, location, or stated interests.

Personalization is not without its downside, however. If users get personalized versions of the news they may be missing out on other important information without even knowing how the story was changed for their preferences. Similarly, users could create such highly personalized "Daily Me" news digests that they may narrow their range of interests to such an extent that they have difficulty talking about topics outside their areas of interest.

▼ CONTEXTUALIZATION OF NEWS

In theory, users should be able to access the raw material that a journalist has used to write a story, such as a speech given by a local politician or a report written by a government body. However, users will still want some kind of context for the data and some kind of interpretation of it, as most people will not want to have to read an entire speech just to determine what, if anything, is important. This signals that perhaps journalists being able to interpret and contextualize the news will become more important in the future.

mash-up

Combining textual information over geographic, map-based information so users can access multiple layers of data.

For example, a user may click on an interactive crime map when reading an online news story about a certain crime in a different part of town and then select her own zip code to call up an interactive map of her neighborhood. She can see on the map what types of crimes have been committed in the neighborhood within the past year. This is possible right now in many localities, but most crime-mapping sites do not provide any context regarding whether crime rates are increasing or decreasing and what happened to people charged with those crimes. Ideally, a site could provide all this information, along with links to past news stories on the crime or related cases, along with other relevant information. Such **mash-ups** that combine geographic data overlaid with editorial content are becoming increasingly popular and easy to create and can be seen in a limited way on real-estate sites such as Zillow. Although not a news site, Zillow lets users see houses for sale within an area and compare prices to others for sale and houses that have recently been sold.

▼ CONVERGENT JOURNALISM

Online video, audio, and interactive graphics are increasingly used with text stories to enhance and supplement them. Likewise, text can be added to primarily video stories to offer different ways of accessing the information and to provide more depth and context than video or audio alone can do. Journalists will have to become versed in the various tools of online journalism, including video, audio, and writing.

A truly interactive multimedia experience that allows the user to stop or replay segments at will, skip familiar information, and learn background information as needed will help differentiate online journalism from its nondigital counterparts.

Unmanned aerial vehicles (UAVs) can be useful news-gathering tools and much cheaper than leasing helicopters for such activities as traffic coverage.

DO THE ENDS JUSTIFY THE MEANS?

ETHICS IN MEDIA

Charlie LeDuff is a Pulitzer Prize–winning journalist and much more. Part Native American, he has worked as a teacher, a carpenter, and a baker. He's been a bartender, worked in a cannery, and for a month in 2000, he worked in the biggest pork slaughterhouse in the world in Tar Heel, North Carolina.

As an undercover reporter, LeDuff filled out a job application just as thousands of other workers do every year in that high-turnover business. Afterwards, he wrote a revealing report titled "At a Slaughterhouse, Some Things Never Die." It was part of a series published in 2001 by the *New York Times*, "How Race Is Lived in America," which won the Pulitzer Prize for national reporting.[12]

As LeDuff told Journalismjobs.com in March of 2012, when he took the job at the slaughterhouse, it wasn't his intention to write a negative story. He went in with an open mind. LeDuff says, "I didn't know what was going on in there. It wasn't like I was going in to nail these guys. That's not my style. I don't want to be that kind of reporter. There's plenty of them. The *Times* was going to let me actually work. I'm going to get into the heads of people's lives. And I get to write about something important. I hope it's interesting, that was what I was thinking."[13]

Journalists going undercover must answer this question: do the ends justify the means? Answering that question requires an open mind and a willingness to let the facts speak for themselves. And so they did in the case of reporter Charlie LeDuff at a North Carolina slaughterhouse.

Technology can change not only the production and presentation of the news but how it is gathered. Digital cameras and video cameras have made photography and videography much easier for journalists, so much so that a single reporter can videotape interviews or footage that can be used in a multimedia news story. Voice of America radio journalists have received digital-video shooting and editing training and have been able to add video elements to their stories online, and other news organizations such as the BBC are training many of their journalists in video techniques. Journalists will have to be conversant, if not necessarily expert, in a range of digital media tools.

ProPublica: Reviving Investigative Reporting

With its tagline, "journalism in the public interest," ProPublica has been attempting to reinvigorate investigative journalism since its launch in June 2008. ProPublica's mission also harkens back to the time of muckrakers: "To expose abuses of power and betrayals of the public trust by government, business, and other institutions, using the moral force of investigative journalism to spur reform through the sustained spotlighting of wrongdoing."[14]

Investigative journalism has arguably suffered the most because of the changes that digital media have brought. The length of time needed to research and put together complex investigative stories does not lend itself well to a media environment in which the audience expects quick bites of news 24/7. Similarly, the costs associated with doing investigative journalism are seen by management as a burden on the bottom line, and as a result many news organizations see investigative journalism as a luxury rather than as a necessary part of journalism.

Funded by the Sandler Foundation with a multi-year grant, ProPublica has 34 professional journalists working in its downtown Manhattan office. Although the newsroom may seem similar to other news or-

ProPublica in a not-for-profit news organization that focuses on investigative news stories in the public interest and is the first online-only news organization to win a Pulitzer Prize.

ganizations, one big difference is that ProPublica is a nonprofit organization. The lack of commercial and advertising pressures helps ProPublica focus on doing investigative stories that are deemed relevant to the public. As investigative journalism has shrunk along with newsroom staff, ProPublica offers an important service by providing its stories to other news organizations for free. This helps ensure that stories will get maximum exposure, which is further helped as ProPublica posts all its stories after the initial publication.

In 2010, ProPublica was the first online publication to win a Pulitzer Prize for Investigative Reporting, and in 2011 won a Pulitzer Prize for National Reporting, the first time that the prize was awarded for stories not published in print.

It remains an open question whether ProPublica and its nonprofit model could be a sustainable business model for some news organizations. Some experts are concerned that the reliance on a sole funder could leave it vulnerable when the grant runs out. But until that time comes, ProPublica is filling a need for in-depth, relevant investigative pieces that other news organizations have not been able or willing to do.

The Business of Journalism

The early years of the twenty-first century have been especially challenging for the media business, especially for news organizations. Advertising revenues have been in steady decline for the past several years, especially in print media. Although online advertising is growing, it still makes up a small portion of overall revenues and does not compensate for the reduced advertising revenues in traditional media.

Some media companies that predicted new business opportunities in media convergence, such as the former AOL Time Warner or Bertelsmann, spent large amounts to provide services or media that never made a profit. Other media companies that adopted a more cautious approach with digital media see even fewer reasons to invest in new technologies. However, even the executives who have been burned say the changes will come and that they simply moved too quickly.

The loss in advertising revenues, combined with a recession that began in December 2007, has severely strained news organizations. In 2008, the American Society of News Editors (ASNE) found that the newspaper industry had suffered its largest drop in thirty years, with a 4.4 percent workforce decrease compared to 2007. Although the rate of staff reductions has decreased in the past couple years, the newspaper industry continues to cut jobs.

In a 2011 survey of newspaper editors by ASNE, editors cited three main challenges they faced. One of the greatest challenges was maintaining the writing and editing quality despite staff and budget cutbacks, another was rapidly adjusting roles and workflow processes to adapt to the 24/7 newsroom, and another challenge was to realize ways to take advantage of mobile media for revenue opportunities and ways to reach more readers.

Not only have layoffs become common, but entire news bureaus are closing down. In 2000, Cox newspapers had thirty correspondents in Washington, D.C., to cover the inauguration of President George Bush. In 2008, Cox announced that it would be closing its Washington bureau early in spring 2009. Some news organizations have taken what are considered even more drastic steps. In 2009, the respected newspaper *Christian Science Monitor* announced that it would stop publishing a print newspaper and only exist online. In March 2009, the 146-year-old *Seattle Post-Intelligencer,* a Hearst paper, ceased publishing its print edition and went to online-only. This trend continues with newspapers, especially as tablet computers become more popular.

▼ SALARIES

Salaries for journalism professionals vary according to several factors, including the type of medium one works in (television is the highest paid, print media the lowest), the location or market (i.e., the larger the market, the higher the pay), the type of position one occupies (farther up in management, ownership, or celebrity status correlates positively with pay), experience, and a variety of other less definite factors, including gender, with men generally being paid more than women, as unfair as that may be. Salaries and overall compensation vary so widely—from fifteen thousand dollars a year to many millions of dollars—that crude averages are relatively meaningless.

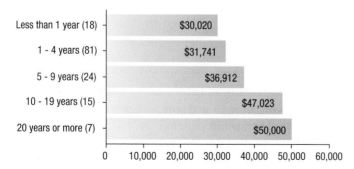

FIGURE 9-1 Average Salaries for Journalists, by Years Worked. Source: payscale.com

In general, network television offers the highest salaries for midlevel jobs as producers. National magazines and newspapers offer fairly good pay, while papers in mid- and small-sized markets offer relatively poor salaries in comparison to jobs of a similar level in public relations, for example. Internet media offer fairly good salaries, and until the dot-com bust their stock option plans made a lucky few journalists instant millionaires when the companies went public. Many more people missed that train than rode it, however, as Internet media companies started going bankrupt.

▼ DIVERSITY IN THE NEWSROOM

Circumstances in American newsrooms have been slow to change. In 1950, African American journalist Marvel Cooke (1903–2000) was hired as a reporter and feature writer for the *New York Daily Compass*. She was the only woman and the only black person on the staff of the paper and was among the first blacks to work for any white-owned daily newspaper.

The ASNE regularly conducts a survey on employment of women and minorities by U.S. daily newspapers. The numbers of minority and women hires have fallen short of mirroring the percentages found in the general population and fall far short when it comes to management. Because of the layoffs and hiring freezes throughout the newspaper industry in recent years, the percentage of minority employees has actually risen slightly, to just over 13 percent.

Industry watchers worry that the persistent dominance of white males in newsrooms skews news coverage toward the type of material that appeals to them, as opposed to stories relevant to underrepresented minority groups.

Radio journalist Condace Pressley, former president of the National Association of Black Journalists (NABJ).

◣ Careers in Journalism

The employment outlook for journalists in the digital age is generally not good, as it largely reflects how well the overall economy is doing combined with the budget and staff cutbacks already mentioned among news organizations. After a decade of strong growth in employment and business, the twenty-first century got off to a troubled start, and media and technology companies have been especially hard hit with the downturn in the economy.

However, it is an exciting time to be a journalist. Online journalism is still in its infancy and plays an increasingly important role in the overall journalism picture, and there are still possibilities for journalists in traditional print, radio, and television. Even in the traditional media newsrooms, however, modern journalists now need to have a wide variety of skills that cross media types and that include a solid understanding of online media's unique characteristics. Today's journalists need to be as comfortable telling a story through an interactive, multimedia graphic as they are with the written word. Journalists may not have to have the same depth of technical knowledge as do programmers or Web designers, but they will need to understand how to converse intelligently with them as stories are produced.

In addition to strong writing and storytelling skills, contemporary journalists also benefit from knowing how to use spreadsheets, statistics, and databases to create stories from complex raw information.

There is no specific college major that is best for journalists, though most have degrees in the humanities or social sciences. A major in the natural or physical sciences can give prospective journalists a great advantage in careers writing about science or health. Similarly, business knowledge can lead to a good career in business journalism. Regardless of the undergraduate major, focusing on improving writing and editing skills is crucial for a successful career in journalism. Working at a college newspaper can give students a taste of what it is like to work at a newspaper and provides clips of published stories, which news organizations will want to see when they apply for a job.

Journalism plays a crucial role in informing the public of important events taking place domestically and internationally and providing a context that helps people understand the world better. Even more important, however, is the shift taking place today in which audience participation in one form or another is seen as a crucial factor for the future of journalism and for a truly healthy democracy.

News is the bedrock of journalism, although news is often manufactured by public relations professionals, individuals, or organizations, and the amount of news coverage on any specific topic can change from day to day depending on the perceived importance of other news events. Budget and staff cuts have made news organizations more reliant on other sources for their news, and the 24/7 news cycle today often means less time to make the final news product as good as it could be.

The challenges that the Internet and digital media have brought to journalism are great, and the industry and profession has until recent years resisted change rather than embracing it. This resistance has had negative effects in that many news organizations, especially newspapers, are only recently trying to figure out ways to exist in the media system today. As advertisers go elsewhere to find audiences, news organizations are left scrambling to stay afloat and to adjust to the new realities in the digital media world.

Despite the bleak employment picture for journalism graduates in the past several years, the rapid changes in the industry mean that there are jobs available for the candidates with the right skills to work in the convergent journalism newsroom of the future. Knowing how to use technology is of course important, but it is not considered the most important factor in being marketable.

However, the days of journalists being able to say "I am a print journalist" or "I am a radio journalist" are soon coming to an end. Increasingly, print reporters are given a digital video camera or audio recorder and asked to shoot or record footage. Similarly, television journalists are being asked to write text stories to accompany video. The convergent journalist of tomorrow cannot be expected to be an expert in every type of media but should be comfortable using all of them.

Appreciating the power of storytelling is also important, and being able to tell a story using multimedia, hyperlinks, and other forms of interaction in an appropriate way will be what separates good journalists from hacks. Knowing some multimedia tools, such as basic image editing, will be required. But knowing how and why to use various digital tools will be even better.

In some ways, journalism has always been about knowledge creation and knowledge management. Good reporters have extensive files of sources and contacts they can reach out to when they need to get information quickly, and they have developed a sense for differentiating good information from bad. These are exactly the kinds of skills that any citizen will need in the future.

This does not change in the world of convergent journalism and in fact becomes more important as there are more potential sources for information. The public will increasingly look toward trusted editorial voices to interpret and explain what is relevant and why to them. More than any other media professional, journalists should be perfectly suited to fulfill this role, perhaps in closer collaboration with citizen-journalists or in new storytelling formats that include audience participation.

DISCUSSION QUESTIONS

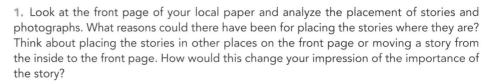

1. Look at the front page of your local paper and analyze the placement of stories and photographs. What reasons could there have been for placing the stories where they are? Think about placing the stories in other places on the front page or moving a story from the inside to the front page. How would this change your impression of the importance of the story?

2. Choose an article from your local paper (not from a wire service) and see if you can find a likely source for the article from a public relations department. Compare the original press release, if available, with the final article. *(Hint: local events such as art show openings or new businesses may be good candidates.)*

3. Discuss a current event being covered in the news and how it is being framed. Examine how this framing may affect the way the topic is being covered, and suggest frames that may allow for more balanced, complete coverage.

4. Choose one of the alternative journalism types, and explain potential pitfalls of that type and how these pitfalls may be overcome—if they can be.

5. Keep track of your online news reading habits for a day or two, including every website you visit to get news, any hyperlinks you click on, and why. Discuss what you learned.

6. Discuss what kinds of skills today's journalist should have, both in terms of topic knowledge and in terms of technical skills. Why are these important compared to other possible skills that a journalist may have?

7. Go to a citizen-journalism site such as Wikinews or NowPublic and compare their news coverage with that of mainstream news sites. How are they similar and how are they different?

FURTHER READING

The Elements of Journalism: What Newspeople Should Know and the Public Should Expect. Bill Kovach, Tom Rosenstiel (2001) Three Rivers Press.

News About News: American Journalism in Peril. Leonard Downie Jr., Robert G. Kaiser (2002) Knopf.

Breaking the News: How the Media Undermine American Democracy. James Fallows (1997) Vintage.

Custodians of Conscience. Theodore Lewis Glasser (1998) Columbia University Press.

Why Democracies Need An Unlovable Press. Michael Schudson (2008) Polity.

The Vanishing Newspaper: Saving Journalism in the Information Age. Philip Meyer (2004) University of Missouri Press.

The Death and Life of American Journalism: The Media Revolution That Will Begin the World Again. Robert McChesney, John Nichols (2011) Nation Books.

Digitizing the News: Innovation in Online Newspapers. Pablo Boczkowski (2005) MIT Press.

Convergent Journalism: The Fundamentals of Multimedia Reporting. Stephen Quinn (2005) Peter Lang Publishers.

Convergent Journalism: An Introduction. Stephen Quinn, Vincent F. Filak (2005) Focal Press.

The Elements of Online Journalism. Rey Rosales (2006) iUniverse.

We the Media: Grassroots Journalism by the People, for the People. Dan Gillmor (2006) O'Reilly Media.

Losing the News: The Future of the News That Feeds Democracy. Alex Jones (2011) Oxford University Press.

Page One: Inside the New York Times and the Future of Journalism. David Folkenflik (2011) Public Affairs.

Literary Journalism. Norm Sims, Mark Kramer (1995) Ballantine Books.

Tell Me No Lies: Investigative Journalism That Changed the World. John Pilger (2005) Thunder's Mouth Press.

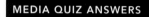

MEDIA QUIZ ANSWERS

1. False.

3. William Randolph Hearst.

4. Fairness and balance.

5. An event created to attract media attention, such as a press conference.

6. Alternative journalism, which has also been called radical journalism.

7. False.

8. A bigger news hole to fill, shorter and continuous deadlines, and changes in roles and workflow processes.

9. False.

10. PR professionals make more.

10

ENTERTAINMENT

CHAPTER PREVIEW

LEARNING OBJECTIVES

By the end of this chapter
you should be able to:

- Describe the functions of
  entertainment.

- Discuss how pervasive
  entertainment is in our lives
  and the social role it fulfills.

- Describe how major
  entertainment industries
  have developed and
  how they influence the
  entertainment we see today.

- Explain how entertainment
  industries are connected
  both to journalism and
  to advertising and public
  relations.

- Outline some of the main
  types of careers in the
  entertainment industry.

By 2008, air guitar had moved from in front of a mirror and behind closed doors to in front of friends or even total strangers at a local bar. And it did so with all the fanfare that rock music can muster.

Thanks to video games such as *Guitar Hero* and *Rock Band,* the line between the geeky computer nerd playing video games and the hip rocker has blurred. Video games, it seems, can be cool—and, more importantly, may also be social, or educational.

The trend toward more active, social video games was helped by game consoles such as Nintendo's Wii and Microsoft's Kinect, in which players can compete against each other in a range of sports or other activities.

Guitar Hero also represents an important shift in entertainment in which convergence starts to come into its own. Because of the popularity of *Guitar Hero* and similar console-based video games, downloads of songs for the game have risen, creating new revenue opportunities for the sagging music industry. When *Guitar Hero* launched Aerosmith songs for the game in 2008, their recording label saw a 40 percent rise in song sales from the band's catalog.

However, as any one-hit wonder can tell you, fame can be fickle. In February 2011 Activision, maker of *Guitar Hero,* announced it would stop selling the iconic music game because of flagging sales. Other types of games, such as online shooter games like *Call of Duty: Black Ops,* had become more popular. Fans of *Guitar Hero* lamented its loss and online discussions were numerous and sustained enough to make Activision reconsider its position. In July 2011 Activision announced it may revive the game after all.

But the world of gaming promises even bigger changes to come. Mobile gaming, exemplified by the wild popularity of games such as *Angry Birds,* will be a huge growth area. But even bigger right now are the so-called freemium social games made by Zynga, such as *Farmville* or *Mafia Wars,* which may outstrip console-based games in the near future.

The prevalence of media in our lives today, and the fragmentation of media channels, has placed greater demands on our attention. Because of the popularity of entertainment, media professionals in fields such as journalism, advertising, and public relations can sometimes be under strong pressures to provide more entertainment-oriented material, or media content that is entertaining. This may not be much of an issue for an advertising agency, which wants to attract as many people as possible to its advertisement, but it is more problematic for a field like journalism, which believes its role is to help create an informed and engaged citizenry.

"Entertainment media" cover a wide range of activities, including sports events, performing arts, televised or filmed dramatic series in a variety of fiction genres, music, books, magazines, and video games, just to name a few. The entertainment industry has always been greatly affected by new media technologies and in many cases is the driving force behind developing them. The historical development of technologies for recording and playing music is one example. It can be looked at as being driven by entertainment needs as consumers seek high-quality recordings of music that are also portable and that can be played on a number of devices.

The development of new technology and its adoption by consumers can outpace the business models used by the entertainment industry, as media companies have learned. File-sharing services using **peer-to-peer (P2P)** networks would not

peer-to-peer [P2P]

A network in which all computers are considered equal (peers) and can send and receive information equally well. This is the basis of file-sharing services such as Kazaa and Morpheus.

Leisure activities of all types play an important role in our lives.

Are You an Entertainment Junkie?

1. Did you have a TV in your bedroom while growing up? Did you ever have a VCR player?
2. Did you have a personal computer in your bedroom while growing up?
3. Did your family have a video game console? Which one or ones?
4. Do you schedule certain aspects of your social life and study time in order not to miss your favorite program or programs?
5. Have you ever changed your hairstyle, clothes, or mannerisms to reflect an admired singer or movie or TV star?
6. Do you use catchphrases from TV shows or movies in your conversations? If so, which ones?
7. Do you regularly attend concerts or sporting events?
8. What is the first media appliance you turn on in the morning—the radio, the TV, the computer, or your mobile phone? How long after you wake up do you turn it on or look at it?
9. Have you ever played games online? If so, which ones? How long did you typically spend playing them?
10. Do you belong to any online fan clubs?

If you answered yes to most of these, it doesn't necessarily mean you are an entertainment junkie; it simply shows how pervasive entertainment is in your life and the effect it can have on you, your sense of self, and your perceptions of society.

---

be a threat to large media companies if the public restricted itself to online sharing of classic works of philosophy and literature that are in the public domain. People are instead sharing the latest popular music, TV shows, and movies without paying the copyright owners or the companies that produced the content.

It is estimated that in industrial countries people are able to spend 30 percent of their time for leisure activities, although in the United States that number is 35 percent, with 28 percent of the time spent for work and the rest for maintenance of daily living.[1] Despite what seems like incredibly busy schedules, people today have more leisure time than ever and that trend promises to continue.

Functions of Entertainment

In fulfilling its function to entertain, **entertainment** also has other important mass-communication functions, including **cultural transmission** and mobilization.

Through entertainment in publications, over the airwaves, or on the Internet, a society's dominant cultural values are transmitted to the public. In fact, this becomes a major criticism about some forms of entertainment, especially those that may perpetuate stereotypes or try to appeal to a certain segment of the population at the expense of others. Critics of pop culture say that mass entertainment caters to the lowest common denominator in our society, giving us banal entertainment that does little to enlighten us or improve our lives.

entertainment

A function of mass communication that is performed in part by all three of the other four main functions (surveillance, correlation, cultural transmission) but also involves the generation of content designed specifically and exclusively to entertain.

cultural transmission

The transference of the dominant culture, as well as its subcultures, from one generation to the next or to immigrants, which helps people learn how to fit into society.

One does not have to look far to see the power that entertainment has in our lives. Entertainment can mobilize the public to action, although it is often not for the better. Recall the city riots in Vancouver, British Columbia, caused by disappointed hockey fans after the Canucks lost the Stanley Cup in 2011. Entertainment-oriented television programs or movies about real events, although usually produced well afterward, can nevertheless influence public perceptions—often despite being heavily dramatized and bearing little resemblance to actual events. Perhaps the best example of entertainment mobilizing the public is Orson Welles's radio dramatization of *War of the Worlds* in 1938, when many listeners thought an invasion from Mars had occurred and took various steps to protect themselves.

▲▼ The Historical Development of Entertainment

Although few of us can imagine a world without entertainment, it developed only after humans could first take care of basic needs, giving them extra time in which

Bear baiting and dog fighting were popular forms of entertainment in the past.

they did not have to fight for survival. Neolithic animal-hide drums have been found, showing that even primitive humans created some form of music, although it is not known if this music was primarily used for religious purposes or simply to entertain.

Although little is known about mass entertainment in ancient times, records reveal that the ruling classes of civilizations in Egypt and China enjoyed lavish banquets that included acrobats, musicians, and dancers. It is assumed the lower classes had similar entertainment available to them, but presumably on a much less extravagant scale. Greece had plays and sporting contests, while later Rome had chariot races, gladiatorial combat, and other forms of mass entertainment in order to help pacify the public. The Circus Maximus in Rome, where chariot races were held, could hold 250,000 spectators—about five times the size of the average modern football stadium. By the fourth century, Rome had two hundred holidays a year; every other day was dedicated to state-sponsored entertainments.[2]

The rise of Christianity saw restrictions placed on entertainment, although occasional attempts to ban entertainment outright usually failed after a short while. Fairs throughout medieval Europe presented morality plays to townspeople on traveling stages, which became the precursors to the permanent theaters created in London in the late 1500s. Cockfighting and animal baiting were popular spectator events in Europe and America among commoners and nobility well into the nineteenth century, even after laws were enacted that made such blood sports illegal. As the 2007 arrest of NFL football star Michael Vick demonstrated, dog fighting is still done in some areas and can be big business. Cockfighting, in which roosters have razor blades attached to their feet, is widely conducted in Central and South America and many Asian countries even today.

Printed books and magazines reached mass audiences and gave the public a range of fictional styles and stories. With industrialization, more leisure time meant more demand for entertainment—a demand that recorded music, then films, then radio, then television helped fulfill. The Internet and digital media, although not created with entertainment in mind, now play a huge entertainment role as they contain all other types of entertainment and provide new forms, such as **massively multiplayer online role-playing games (MMORPGs)**.

 ## Entertainment Media

Entertainment covers a huge swath of activities that can include travel and tourism, gambling, and recreational pastimes, as well as live performing arts or visual arts such as painting and sculpture. Although these and other forms of entertainment play important roles in society, culture, and the economy, we will look only at entertainment in the contexts of mass communication and digital media.

In previous chapters we examined media development, characteristics, and issues primarily from a technological perspective. Here we will look more closely at how various entertainment genres evolved within their specific mediums. We will also examine how digital media and the Internet are affecting entertainment within each of these media types.

 ## Television

Television as a mass medium is just over sixty years old, yet it has become the most common mode in which we receive our news, entertainment, and advertising. As we saw in Chapter 5, by the time today's teens are seventy-five years old, they will have spent at least eleven full years of their lives watching television. Perhaps in part due to its popularity, television has attracted many critics. The late drama critic John Mason Brown said that "some television programs are so much chewing gum for the eyes." The passivity that TV seems to induce in viewers and the realism with which it can portray events are two common complaints.

Although television viewers from 1953 would likely be impressed with technological advances such as wide-screen, high-definition television, surround sound, and the multitude of channels to choose from, they would readily recognize many of the types of programming—and they could even see some of the programs or movies they watched almost sixty years ago.

▼ EARLY DAYS: PROGRAMMING AND GENRE INFLUENCES

The late 1940s and 1950s saw the emergence of innovative programming that not only adapted programs from radio but introduced quality programs of a variety of types. Many of the programs of this period were performed and broadcast live, largely because the only effective recording medium was film, and film processing was slow and expensive. It was not until improved magnetic tape recording was developed in the late 1950s and used widely in the 1960s that recorded television programs became the norm.

Much early TV programming came directly from radio, where talented actors and comedians such as Jack Benny had begun their careers. These performers adapted their routines in radio for television. The Broadway stage also lent much to early television. Hollywood studios initially resisted putting movies on television, since that threatened their control over the movie distribution system. They also promised to blacklist actors who acted for television studios. After several years of legal battles, studios finally realized that television could be another revenue source in the movie distribution chain after movies had played themselves out in second- and third-run theaters.

The first decade of television programming is often referred to as the golden age of television because of the many successful programs that were produced then. Many of the programs created during this period were critically acclaimed commercial successes and have established themselves as classics.

Among the most memorable entertainment shows to emerge in television's golden age was *The Ed Sullivan Show*, originally called *Toast of the Town*. The show, which debuted in June 1948, established the format for a variety series and continued on CBS until 1971, frequently with 50 percent of all U.S. television households tuned in. In 1964, the show featured the British pop group the Beatles, which attracted 73 million viewers nationwide. Milton Berle made his TV debut in September 1948 as the master of ceremonies on the *Texaco Star Theater*. Berle's show earned the highest ratings for the new medium: 86.7 percent of all TV households.

The 1950s witnessed the rise of television as a medium of mass communication in the United States. For the first time, an entire postwar generation grew up with it, and many of the programs of that period have endured as classics. Among the most enduring are Jackie Gleason's *The Honeymooners;* Rod Serling's

The Ed Sullivan Show helped establish the variety show format and introduced many new artists to the American public.

The Twilight Zone; I Love Lucy, the first half-hour filmed TV sitcom; children's show *Howdy Doody; The Tonight Show;* and *Gunsmoke,* a classic Western.

▼ PUSHING THE PROGRAMMING ENVELOPE

The 1970s saw a number of significant program developments. Among them were various formats that introduced more complex, realistic characters into formerly one-dimensional program genres. Other notable developments included the 1977 ABC airing of its twenty-six-hour miniseries *Roots,* based on the novel by Alex Haley. The January 30 episode became the third most-watched TV program in history.

Monday Night Football, started in 1970, was a bold experiment in sports programming during prime time and became a cultural mainstay until it ended on network TV in 2005. It led to more televised sporting events outside of the traditional weekend programming and opened up new revenue opportunities for sports franchises. Some sports, such as basketball, even changed their rules in order to be more fast paced and exciting to watch.

The highest-rated program of the decade was *All in the Family,* a controversial situation comedy that used a bigoted character, Archie Bunker, to address many of the social, gender, and civil rights issues that were being discussed in society. In today's politically correct environment, it is unlikely a show such as *All in the Family,* with its racial stereotypes and slurs, would appear on network television, even if it were intended to be satirical.

There was great debate over whether the show simply perpetuated racist and sexist attitudes or helped people understand how mistaken these attitudes were. A study conducted about the show found that it did both—people who held racist or sexist attitudes tended to see Archie Bunker as a character who "tells it like it is" and did not realize it was meant to poke fun at him. For viewers who understood the satirical nature of the show, it helped expose how ridiculous such views are.

Though some shows pushed boundaries that had never been explored in television before, there were many more that simply repackaged popular genres that had proved successful, such as police dramas, mysteries, and science fiction. During this time there were still only three networks, plus public television. Compared to today, television viewers then had more limited viewing choices.

▼ THE MTV GENERATION AND RISE OF CABLE

The growing availability of cable and satellite television threatened the programming dominance the three networks had enjoyed since television first became a mass medium. Suddenly viewers found themselves with programming choices far beyond three network channels and public television. The networks were generally slow to respond to this growing threat to their audience and did not introduce innovative programming of their own, choosing instead to offer variations of tried-and-true formulas.

One exception was a new genre of gritty police drama introduced by producer Steven Bochco in 1980 on NBC called *Hill Street Blues.* The show had several prominent characters, all with various storylines, and a realistic, often chaotic quality that added dramatic elements of soap operas to the story. Bochco continued to evolve the genre in the 1990s with ABC's *NYPD Blue.*

Music Television, or MTV, debuted in 1981 as a cable channel, showing as its first music video "Video Killed the Radio Star." The title was very prophetic. MTV has not only dramatically changed how music has been promoted, but it has

MTV has heavily influenced the way music is promoted.

continued to introduce innovative, although not always culture-enhancing, programs such as *The Real World, Jackass, The Osbournes,* and MTV's most-viewed series ever, *Jersey Shore.* Since the debut of MTV, many critics have charged that oftentimes the emphasis is now on the video and not on the quality of music. But the music-video format has proved popular, and since the launch of MTV a variety of other music channels devoted to specific music genres have emerged.

MTV was part of a sea change in television programming, from a limited, one-size-fits-all approach, as on network television, to a fragmented and specialized programming approach on cable or satellite television. Channels devoted to travel, sports and even specific kinds of sports such as golf or soccer, movie classics, television classics, cartoons, science, science fiction, home improvement, crime, animals, law, and history are now common on cable or satellite TV.

Reflecting the growing Latin American population in the United States, in the 1980s the Reliance Capital Group launched the Spanish-language television network Telemundo Group. Cable and satellite television have also encouraged the growth of more channels that target certain ethnic groups, as well as giving groups access to some programming from their home countries. Today, usually for an additional monthly fee, many cable subscribers can get cable channels in Russian, Chinese, Japanese, Hindi, Tagalog, and Arabic, among other languages.

▼ CABLE COMES OF AGE

With the increased fragmentation of the television viewing audience, it is perhaps bitterly ironic to the networks to see some cable channels such as HBO—which is only in about 28 million homes, or a third of the number that get network television and the nonpremium cable channels—attract more viewers for some original programming than many network shows. On September 15, 2002, the fourth-season premiere of HBO's hit Mob series *The Sopranos* attracted 13.4 million viewers, making it the most-watched show in the history of the cable channel.

Not only that, but *The Sopranos* attracted the most viewers of any show that Sunday night, while placing fifth overall in viewership for the week. One senior network executive told the *New York Times* that *The Sopranos* results "should make everybody else nervous about their Sunday night shows this season." HBO had already been making original feature films for several years, but it is their original series such as *The Sopranos, Sex and the City, Big Love, Boardwalk Empire,* and *Game of Thrones*—which have drawn critical acclaim and won several Emmy awards—that are making the networks finally take notice of cable television programming. It is not just an "only on HBO" phenomenon, either. The FX Channel generated its own buzz with cutting-edge programming and attracted 5 million viewers for the premiere episode of its police drama *The Shield.*

Critics of network television programming say the networks have only themselves to blame for large-scale defections of viewers to cable channels. They cite a risk-averse corporate culture among television networks that encourages copying popular programming types rather than trying to be innovative. They also charge that networks became complacent because they knew that most viewers had nothing else to watch. However, cable TV programming can be more innovative and edgy because cable does not have the same content restrictions, such as characters using profanity or partial nudity, from the FCC that networks face. Another factor

that works against networks is their need to attract as large an audience as possible in order to charge higher rates for commercials, something that subscriber-based channels such as HBO do not have to consider.

▼ PUBLIC SERVICE BROADCASTING: PUBLIC SERVICE IN A COMMERCIAL WORLD

The Public Broadcasting Service (PBS) began in 1969, after being authorized by the Public Broadcasting Act of 1967, and in November 1969 launched *Sesame Street*, one of the most influential programs for children on TV then and today.

The Public Broadcasting Service operates as a private, not-for-profit corporation owned by its member stations. Public television programming has consistently won more television awards for high quality than television and cable networks combined. The PBS system was loosely based on a much older model, used in the UK.

The British Broadcasting Corporation (BBC) was started in the UK in 1936. The BBC is based on a very different funding model than public broadcasting in the United States. The BBC receives an annual fee collected by the government in the form of a broadcasting tax levied on all TV and radio receivers. PBS, on the other hand, depends on a combination of annual federal appropriations, corporate sponsorships, and private viewer contributions. The BBC model of supporting public broadcasting has never been adopted in the United States, although the system in the UK has produced high-quality public television programming.

Even so, public television in the United States and the UK has been under pressure with the rise in popularity of cable and decreases in government funding. In the United States, PBS has often been the place where arts, cultural, or science programming that would never be commercially viable is shown. The specialization of cable channels has to a large extent invaded the programming territory once belonging to PBS almost exclusively. Furthermore, cuts in government funding have forced PBS to rely more on corporate funding and philanthropic organizations, which may have less of a public service mission regarding types of programming.

▼ TYPES OF PROGRAMMING

In the early days of television, several enduring television-programming types were either refined from their radio formats or were developed originally for TV. These included hosted children's shows, variety shows, situation comedies, dramatic anthologies, Western series, sports, and news talk shows. These various program types laid the foundation for the development of three broad programming categories, which eventually emerged as formal divisions within the commercial television networks. These three divisions are entertainment, sports, and news.

Changes in Media, Changes in Programming

Some programming has survived for decades across media, but because of the rise of the multichannel universe of cable, satellite, and other new media, many program types are now facing extinction or finding niche homes online or on cable. An example is the **soap opera**, one of the staples of radio programming that has endured on television. Soaps, as they are called, were so named not because of the content of the programs but because, first on radio and then on television, the principal advertising was for soap and other household products, aimed at the daytime serial programs' primary audience, homemakers. *Guiding Light* is the oldest soap, having begun on radio in 1937 and now on television since 1952. *Guiding Light,* from Procter & Gamble (P&G) Productions, and other long-running soaps, like P&G's *As the World Turns* (on the air since 1956), have for decades appealed primarily to women staying at home to both raise their children and maintain their homes. Procter & Gamble is, of course, one of the world's largest makers of household products, especially cleaning materials.

But the 1990s brought profound changes to the soaps and their audiences and sponsors. One by one, the soaps have died as more women have entered the workforce and audiences have shrunk. After 8,891 episodes and thirty-five years on the air, NBC's *Another World* ended its run in 1999. In 2009, after seventy-two years, even the venerable *Guiding Light* went dark. Ratings show that the soaps have lost a quarter of their audience since the 1980s, and no new English-language soaps have been introduced since the 1990s.

Many fans wax nostalgic over the loss of soaps such as *Guiding Light,* pointing out that the show set important new standards for daytime television by introducing discussion of topics such as abortion and illegitimate pregnancy. Soap operas also introduced some of today's biggest movie and television stars, including Morgan Freeman, Kelsey Grammar, Tommy Lee Jones, James Franco, Amanda

soap opera

A type of programming that began on radio and successfully moved to television but that is now threatened by the increased variety of media types, as well as changes in lifestyles. Soap operas are dramatic story series that involve numerous characters and are aimed at a daytime audience of homemakers.

The Quiz Show That Became a Town

Truth or Consequences was a popular NBC radio quiz show during the 1940s and 1950s that later became one of the earliest television quiz shows. It is also an early example of what we would recognize today as reality television—and shows just how influential entertainment can be in our regular lives. The show's producer, Ralph Edwards, wanted to celebrate the show's tenth anniversary in 1950 in a special way and thought it would be interesting if the citizens of a town in the United States respected the show so much that they would be willing to name their town after it.

In Hot Springs, New Mexico, a small desert spa town on Interstate 25 between El Paso and Albuquerque, citizens decided by majority vote that changing the name could give the sleepy resort town the boost it needed. In 1950 Edwards brought the *Truth or Consequences* radio show to Truth or Consequences, New Mexico, for a live broadcast.

Two subsequent referendums in the 1960s on whether to keep the Truth or Consequences name both passed, and Edwards visited the town every year for 50 years with Hollywood friends to celebrate the anniversary of the name change (and to generate publicity for the town), even though the radio and television shows had long been off the air.

To get around the long-winded name for the town, it is mostly referred to as "T or C" by its 7,200 residents and in New Mexico.

Seyfried, and Brad Pitt. But fans of soaps need not despair; full-length episodes of *Guiding Light* are available online at CBS's website.

Filling the Days

One of the greatest sensations in commercial television's first full decade was the game or quiz show, a format that had been successful in radio as well. Nearly everyone with a television set in their home tuned in each week to their favorite quiz show. These shows drew enormous audiences partly because it was easy to identify with the contestants, many of whom came from ordinary walks of life, and the stakes were large. By the end of the 1958 TV season, there were twenty-two network quiz shows, or one of every five shows. It turned out that many were rigged, and after a public scandal involving the popular quiz show *Twenty-One* and a congressional investigation, new rules for regulating game shows emerged.

Many daytime game shows were either cancelled or moved to evening programming slots, although some were revived to fill the holes left by the cancellation of the soaps. One exception has been the long-running popular daytime game show *The Price Is Right*, whose thirty-five-year host Bob Barker retired in 2008, at age eighty-four. On the whole, however, game shows have been replaced by a format that is even cheaper, the talk show. Talk shows such as *Dr. Phil, Jerry Springer, Tyra,* and *The Oprah Winfrey Show* have taken much of the role that soaps used to play in bringing controversial or sensitive issues to the public arena, as guests talk about a wide range of personal issues.

Filling the Nights

The popularity of the prime-time game show was revived when ABC's *Who Wants to Be a Millionaire* became a ratings leader after its debut in 1999. Although its success was relatively short-lived, lasting only three years, the show helped spawn a number of other prime-time shows that followed a game show or quiz show format. Notably, some of the most popular game shows, including *Who Wants to Be a Millionaire,* were copies of shows that originated in Europe. Other foreign imports included *Survivor* and the short-lived *The Weakest Link,* with its acerbic British hostess Anne Robinson. This reversed a long trend of European television copying successful game shows from the United States. Despite the rapid fall and disappearance of some of the prime-time game shows, others that have appeared before prime time have proved longer lasting, such as *Jeopardy!* and *Wheel of Fortune.*

It is hard to say exactly what caused the resurgence of interest in the prime-time quiz and game shows, but one factor is that the new shows have raised the stakes considerably, with contestants potentially winning millions of dollars. Another factor is the possibility for viewers to interact, albeit still in a limited way, with the shows through the Web.

Prime-time network programming is dominated by dramatic series, reality shows, and situation comedies, with occasional made-for-TV movies or broadcasts of popular movies that have already appeared in theaters. This latter programming has become less important than it once was, however, as many viewers choose to see uncut movies without commercial interruptions on DVD or cable.

Sports

Today, for many people sports and television go hand in hand. Some of the biggest television events involve sports, such as the Super Bowl, which annually draws one of U.S. television's largest audiences. Every four years the World Cup, the quadrennial soccer tournament, draws large worldwide television audiences. Television commentator Les Brown explains that sports is considered by many the perfect program form for television. "At once topical and entertaining, performed live and suspensefully without a script, peopled with heroes and villains, full of action and human interest and laced with pageantry and ritual. The medium and the events have become so intertwined that playing rules often are altered for the exigencies of TV."[5]

Sports has also been an ongoing venue for technical experimentation. The introduction of instant replay in the early 1960s added a new dimension to televised sports, debuting in a telecast of an Army–Navy football game. In 1964 it became a standard technique, and it continues to play an important though controversial role in the NFL and increasingly in other sports.

The role of technology should not be discounted. Although poker is perhaps not considered a true "sport," the rise in popularity of poker-tournament shows has been attributed in part to miniature cameras that allow viewers to see what hands players are holding as they place their bets. On the screen, percentages of the chances of winning are shown and give viewers more insight into the strategies deployed by professional poker players. Before the use of miniature cameras, television viewers were left guessing at hands, just as other players were.

Professional wrestling offers a blend of sports and entertainment that has proved popular over the years, although its popularity waxes and wanes in cycles. In the late 1990s and early 2000s it reached a peak of popularity and commercial success with the World Wrestling Federation (WWF), a company headed by Vincent McMahon. McMahon's genius was to more or less admit that the bouts were staged (although it was obvious that the wrestlers did take actual physical punishment) and to add ample doses of sexuality, show business flash, and character-driven story lines from week to week—with himself and a few cronies cast as the crooked bad guys who cheated popular wrestlers of their rightful titles.

Professional wrestling is a controversial form of entertainment, however. Critics say it glamorizes violence while some of its mostly young male fans injure themselves attempting similar wrestling techniques at home with friends. There has also been a spate of steroid-induced deaths among professional wrestlers in recent years, leading to questions of safety regarding the wrestlers themselves and what they do to their bodies to get the physiques that fans expect.

WEB LINK
Ultimate Fighting Championship
www.ufc.com

The popularity of extreme sports and types of fighting besides boxing, such as mixed martial arts, has risen. Media play a role in determining what types of sports get promoted (and thus get lucrative corporate sponsorships) and what types don't. Generally, sports that are slow paced or slow moving, or that are highly individualistic, tend to be at a disadvantage compared to fast-paced or exciting team sports. Watching bowling or mountain climbing is simply not as enticing visually as watching aerial BMX tricks or a cage fight. One notable exception to this rule is golf, which is slow-paced but nevertheless gets a lot of time on television. One reason for this seeming contradiction is that golf viewers are generally in the kind of upscale demographic that advertisers want to reach.

Reality Shows

With the plethora of reality shows on many channels these days, it may be surprising to learn that the genre has its roots in the earliest days of television. Game shows like *Truth or Consequences* that had contestants performing wacky stunts for prizes, or Alan Funt's *Candid Camera,* a classic prank show, were very popular in the 1950s and 1960s. In the 1980s shows like *COPS* and *America's Funniest Home Videos* (*AFV*) were aired and continue to run today. *AFV,* in which viewers send in video of themselves doing funny things, can be considered a precursor to the kind of **user-generated content (UGC)** often uploaded to YouTube or other video websites.

user-generated content [UGC]

Media content that has been created by consumers or audience members, including videos, music, or other forms of content.

Soccer is one of the most widely watched sports worldwide.

Reality shows became much more popular from 2000, after *Big Brother* and *Survivor* were both hits in the United States. Today, *American Idol*—which can trace its lineage directly back to popular talent search shows in the 1940s such as *Arthur Godfrey's Talent Scouts*—remains a top-rated show and has launched singing careers for several of its finalists and winners. Viewers even voted on contestants in the 1940s, although they called in their votes rather than sending text messages.

Reality shows have proved successful partly because of the versatility of the genre. Home improvement channels have been able to capitalize on the format with shows like *House Hunters* and *Property Virgins,* and lifestyle channels have had successful shows such as *Extreme Makeover* and *The Biggest Loser.* Practically any situation, real or fantasized, can be put into a reality show format, and viewers seem to enjoy watching other "regular" people in various challenging situations.

Reality television is profitable for television networks because the cost of producing them is much less than that of scripted programs using actors and sets. Writers for reality shows do not often get paid union wages, saving money on development. The format has proven popular in Europe and Asia, making licensing deals appealing. In addition, many reality shows earn extra money through product placement. Watch an episode of *The Biggest Loser* and count how many times brand-name products are mentioned during the show; these are examples of product placement deals that have been made between the show and product manufacturer, not just random mentions by the hosts.

Reality shows have been criticized, even as they remain popular. Despite the name, few of these actually capture "reality" (how many of us will get stranded on a remote tropical island?). Through postproduction editing techniques and loose direction to the participants regarding how to act or what to say, the shows present a very contrived narrative that may bear little resemblance to the participants' experiences at the time. Although reality shows have made some people celebrities and launched careers, they are also criticized for publicly ridiculing and emphasizing the less admirable qualities of participants, which is clearly evident to anybody who has watched reality shows ranging from *American Idol* to *Top Shot* or *Survivor.*

Reality shows such as *Jersey Shore,* MTV's most-watched program ever, remain very popular despite the fact many do not truly capture any "reality" most viewers would be familiar with.

◣◤ Movies

Despite competition from a variety of other media sources, movies continue to play a large role in entertainment. Predictions that movie theaters would close because people would stay home watching television have proved unfounded, although there was a notable drop in the numbers of movies released from the mid-1950s until the mid-1990s, after which the numbers once again reached levels seen in the 1950s.

Going to movies is as much a social activity as it is a mass media entertainment activity, as it gives people an entertainment environment that even the best home entertainment center cannot match. One sign of this is that single adults attend more movies than married adults do, according to MPAA Worldwide Market Research.

People forty and older continue to be the largest group of moviegoers, although the twelve- to twenty-four-year-old bracket has risen in recent years. Teens are an important part of the moviegoing audience because they tend to go to movies more frequently than older people. Fifty-one percent of teens twelve to seventeen years old reported they go to movies at least once a month, while only 24 percent of people eighteen and over said they do.

With whole cable television channels devoted to almost nothing but films—such as the Independent Film Channel, Turner Movie Classics, American Movie Classics, Home Box Office, Cinemax, and Showtime—in addition to commercial and cable channels such as TNT frequently (and repeatedly) showing movies, a movie may remain part of the entertainment landscape long after it has left the theaters.

Despite competition from a number of other forms of entertainment, movies continue to be highly popular.

Movies are not the leading entertainment force they were before television and the Internet, however. Today, movies are often created from popular television programs, plays, books, and even video games. The movie version of a novel, game, or show can often drive increased interest in the original version and spur a renewed life, for a time.

It was not always so. The movie industry has a certain glamour that none of the other entertainment venues have been able to match, even if they are more popular than movies. It is worth briefly exploring how the aura of glamour in the movie industry came about and how it affected the way movies were made. We will also take a look at today's movie industry.

▼ HOLLYWOOD'S LEGENDARY MOVIE MOGULS

Understanding the development of the movie industry requires a close look at the people who created Hollywood, the motion picture capital of the world. Film critic, historian, and author Neal Gabler argues that, as such, Hollywood is an invention of the Jewish media moguls of the early twentieth century. Although there are those who would disagree with Gabler, there is no question that the men who ran the major studios and the movie theater chains played a vital role in the creation of the movie empire known as Hollywood.

As Gabler notes, much of their motivation for creating Hollywood lay in their Jewish cultural heritage, their embrace of the American dream (they typically came from poor, immigrant families haunted by memories of persecution), and in the creative and business talents they brought to this new, technologically driven, culture industry. The following section examines some of the most important Hollywood movie moguls from the period of Hollywood's invention as the motion picture (or entertainment) capital of the world in the first half of the twentieth century.

The Warner Brothers

Four brothers born in Poland left a lasting mark on the movie industry in America and on the creative epicenter known as Hollywood. The Warner brothers, Albert, Harry, Jack, and Sam, founded their movie studio in 1923.

In 1904 in Youngstown, Ohio, Harry hocked his family's delivery horse to buy a used Edison Kinetoscope projector, which launched the Warner brothers' entry into the movie business. The brothers used the projector to create a traveling movie show in Ohio and Pennsylvania. Then they opened a small theater in 1905, dubbed "Cascade Theater," with seats loaned from a nearby funeral parlor.

The brothers found that they could make more money from distributing than exhibiting films, so they sold the "Cascade" for forty thousand dollars and entered the film-distribution business. Thomas Edison's Edison Trust Patents Company, however, blocked access to films among distributors who did not pay royalties for the film-distribution rights, and by 1912 the brothers had to leave the distribution business in favor of the film-production business. They launched "Warner Features" in a former St. Louis, Missouri, steel foundry, where their studio produced two low-budget films, neither of which proved marketable. Soon, the brothers headed west to California, where they opened the Warner Brothers studio.

In 1927 Warner Brothers released *The Jazz Singer* and launched the new era of motion pictures with sound. It was an implementation of Sam Warner's concept of using film as a means to create "canned vaudeville." It also propelled the studio to a leadership position in Hollywood and was the first of many classic films produced by Warner Bros. Other cinema classics produced by the studio during the days of the powerful studio system include *Captain Blood* (1935) and *Casablanca* (1942). The studio was also the first to feature a canine star, *Rin Tin Tin* (1923), the first to hire a future president as an actor (Ronald Reagan, 1937), and the first to sell part of its film library to television (1956). Other critically acclaimed Warner Bros. films include *Mister Roberts* (1955), *Giant* (1956), and *Who's Afraid of Virginia Woolf?* (1966).

Jack Warner emerged as the leader of the studio and one of Hollywood's great movie moguls. He had, like many of his contemporaries, a ruthless style—oftentimes running over stars and directors in the process of running the studio. Jack was the last brother to leave the company, departing in 1967 to become an independent producer.

Walt Disney

Walter Elias Disney was born in 1901 in Chicago, Illinois. Expressing an early interest in drawing, Walt enrolled in the Kansas City Art Institute in 1915. With forty dollars in his pocket, Walt left Missouri in August 1923 and went to Los Angeles, where his older brother Roy lived. Combining their meager resources and borrowing five hundred dollars, the brothers set up shop in their uncle's garage and soon began making animated films. They received an order from New York for an *Alice in Cartoonland* animated film, their first production.

Their first hit was released in 1928. *Steamboat Willie* introduced Mickey Mouse, a mouse (some would say it looked more like a rat) that talked and sang, featuring Walt's own voice but very little of his own animation, although he was a talented animator. Mickey Mouse quickly became a star and made Disney a household name. Disney's first full-length feature animation, *Snow White and the Seven Dwarfs*, hit movie screens in 1937 and broke all box office records. In the next five years, Disney also produced various full-length animated classics including *Pinocchio, Fantasia, Dumbo,* and *Bambi*. During World War II, most of the Disney facilities produced special government work, including propaganda films for the armed services. Walt opened Disneyland in 1955 in Los Angeles, and in 1971 opened Walt Disney World in Orlando, Florida.

Disney was always on the cutting edge of new technology. He introduced Technicolor with the 1932 animation *Flowers and Trees,* part of the Silly Symphonies series, which was the first color cartoon and won Disney his first Oscar. Disney was also a pioneer in television programming, producing his first programs in 1954, including the popular Mickey Mouse Club. He was among the first to offer color television programming, with the launch of the *Wonderful World of Color* in 1961.

Walter Elias Disney

Creator of animated cartoon characters such as Mickey Mouse, Goofy, and Donald Duck and classic cartoons such as *Bambi, Snow White and the Seven Dwarfs,* and *Fantasia.* Founded the Disney media empire.

Walt Disney was a pioneer in animation and entertainment and a talented animator in his own right.

Disney won more Academy Awards, forty-seven, than anyone else. He also won seven Emmy Awards, television's highest award, for television programming.

Some have said Disney's greatest gift was his ability to develop a concept and have others implement it, sometimes allegedly running his company with an iron fist. But he was also a genius in his innovative use of technology in creating stories and entertainment. One can only imagine what Disney would have been able to create with digital technology. Walt Disney died in 1966, leaving behind one of the best-known media and entertainment empires in the world.

Samuel Goldwyn

Schmuel Gelbfisz was born in Warsaw, Poland, in the late 1800s and died Samuel Goldwyn, in Los Angeles, in 1974. He described his life in Poland as "poor, poor, poor." His name was anglicized to Goldfish when he moved to England, and in 1899 he came to the United States. After a brief stint as a glove salesman, he embarked on a career as a motion picture producer and became an industry pioneer. He produced *The Squaw Man* in 1914, directed by Cecil B. DeMille, and his company became the foundation for what later emerged as Paramount Pictures, eventually built by Adolph Zukor. In 1916 he joined forces with the Selwyn brothers and cofounded the Goldwyn Pictures Corporation. Three years later he changed his name to Goldwyn.

In 1924 his company merged with Louis B. Mayer and Metro Pictures to become Metro-Goldwyn-Mayer. Although his "Leo the Lion" trademark continued, Goldwyn was ousted and forced to create an independent film company.

His new company's commitment was to the creation of quality films with high production values. United Artists and RKO distributed the films. Among the classics his independent company produced were *Wuthering Heights* (1939), *The Pride of the Yankees* (1942), *The Best Years of Our Lives* (1946), *Guys and Dolls* (1955), and *Porgy and Bess* (1959). Like former New York Yankee great Yogi Berra, Goldwyn was known for his witticisms, also known as "Goldwynisms." Among his most memorable are "A verbal contract isn't worth the paper it's written on"; "A hospital is no place to be sick"; and "Anyone who goes to a psychiatrist ought to have his head examined."

Marcus Loew: Mogul of the East

Like almost all the other movie moguls, Marcus Loew grew up poor. He was born in New York City in 1870 and got involved in the earliest days of movies when he ran a nickelodeon theater. He expanded his holdings over the next several years to create Loew's, a movie chain of luxurious theaters.

Unlike the other moguls, however, he did not want to move to Hollywood and preferred staying in New York. He realized that owning theaters was only one important part of the movie business, and decided that he wanted to get involved in making movies as well. He purchased the Metro Pictures Corporation Mayer Pictures in the early 1920s and later bought Samuel Goldwyn's production company, creating Metro-Goldwyn-Mayer Pictures. Although he ousted Samuel Goldwyn, he kept his name in the company because "M&M" was already taken by another company. Loew did not live to see MGM become the powerhouse movie studio that it turned into, as he died in 1927, only a few years after acquiring the movie studios.

Louis B. Mayer

Perhaps the most famous and feared movie mogul was Louis Burt Mayer. Born in 1885, he died in 1957 in Los Angeles, California. Like his other movie-mogul contemporaries, Mayer had modest immigrant beginnings. His father, Lazar Mayer, was a laborer who sought a better life in America and moved his family there when Louis was a boy. Lazar entered the junk business and Louis joined him, dropping out of school after the sixth grade.

In 1907, Louis bought a rundown movie theater in Boston and renovated it. He exhibited exclusively quality films and built the largest theater chain in New England. In 1915 he made a great profit showing D. W. Griffith's *Birth of a Nation* and laid the foundation for his future Hollywood success.

With the fortune he'd made in exhibiting movies, Mayer entered the movie-production business in 1917, funding his own company, Louis B. Mayer Pictures. In the 1920s Marcus Loew named Mayer vice president of MGM, and Mayer rose in power over the years. Mayer's name became synonymous with movie-mogul power and manipulation and he is credited with creating the Hollywood studio star system. Although the studio's directors, such as Erich von Stroheim and King Vidor, along with powerful producer Irving Thalberg, shaped the creative direction of the studio, it was Mayer who pulled the strings and became patriarch to the "studio children," as the actors were known. Mayer's influence stretched well beyond the studio gates, and in 1927 Mayer teamed with Douglas Fairbanks Sr. to form the Academy of Motion Picture Arts and Sciences—the foundation of movie-industry artists.

The studio employed thousands of artists, and Mayer, known as Louis the Conqueror, ruled with an iron fist. He ridded the studio of talent he disliked, and when Thalberg died in 1936, Mayer took complete control.

▼ FILM GENRES

genre

A type of story that has recognizable and defined elements that distinguish it from other types of stories or nonfiction.

There are a variety of types, or **genres**, of film content in modern cinema. These genres help to define the character of the cinema industry, and they reflect public tastes as well as approaches to filmmaking around the world and among different types of filmmakers. One basic distinction is between nonfiction films, or documentaries, and fiction films. Fiction films are by far the dominant type, and it is rare in the United States for documentaries to be shown in multiplex cinemas. If they are released theatrically at all, they are shown in mostly urban art-house theaters to limited audiences. Notable exceptions have been the documentaries of Michael Moore, who created *Bowling for Columbine, Fahrenheit 9/11,* and *Sicko,* all of which had theatrical releases.

Among the most familiar and popular genres of fiction film are action/adventure, comedy, romance, science fiction, suspense, historical, horror, Western, fantasy, musical, biography, and drama. In many cases there are subgenres, such as crime drama, and some films cut across two or more genres, such as romantic comedy.

A variety of forces influence filmmaking. Economics, technology, audience tastes, and many other factors all influence the subjects, styles, and substance of film. Three important influences are examined here: the film director as auteur, technological influences on movie genres and popularity, and other media entertainment as sources for movies.

▼ THE DIRECTOR AS AUTEUR

auteur

French for "author," it is usually applied to directors who stamp their vision on the films they make, as opposed to directors who have but one role among many other professionals in the making of a film.

French film critic André Bazin, in the years after World War II, introduced the notion of the filmmaker as author, or **auteur**, of his or her films. Although some of the early filmmakers such as D. W. Griffith and Sergei Eisenstein could be seen as auteurs of their films, in the intervening years filmmaking became much more of a collaborative, corporate enterprise—a trend promoted by Hollywood's studio system, in which directors, actors, screenwriters, and others involved in filmmaking had assigned tasks within the overall process, much like workers in a factory production line. Only filmmakers outside of the grasp of Hollywood were able to popularize the notion of director as auteur.

The French New Wave directors in the 1950s were probably the most influential in this regard, and a number of important French directors emerged during this period. These included Jean-Luc Godard, who made *Breathless* (1959); Louis Malle, who made *Zazie dans le métro* (1960); and François Truffaut, who made *The 400 Blows* (1959). These directors used innovative camera techniques for their day, such as hand-held cameras and freeze frames, which have now become common.

Swedish filmmaker Ingmar Bergman is another of the great international film auteurs whose work has left a lasting impression. *The Seventh Seal* (1957), *The Virgin Spring* (1960), and *Wild Strawberries* (1957) are among his greatest and darkest masterpieces.

One of the most influential international film auteurs was Japanese director Akira Kurosawa. Some of Kurosawa's early films, such as *Seven Samurai* (1954), were remade by others as Westerns. *Seven Samurai* became *The Magnificent Seven* (1960) starring Yul Brynner and Steve McQueen, and *Yojimbo* (1961) was remade in 1964 by Sergio Leone as *A Fistful of Dollars,* starring Clint Eastwood. Two characters in the classic *The Hidden Fortress* (1958) are said to be the models on which director George Lucas, a great admirer of Kurosawa and Japanese cinema, based his C-3PO and R2-D2 robot characters in *Star Wars* (1977). Kurosawa also borrowed from the West in making his films. Two of them, *Throne of Blood* (1957) and *Ran* (1985), are based on Shakespeare's plays (*Macbeth* and *King Lear,* respectively).

Japanese director Akira Kurosawa had a film career over 50 years and influenced such filmmakers as Steven Spielberg, George Lucas, and Francis Ford Coppola.

A number of important American filmmakers have also contributed to the auteur movement in cinema. Among them are Blake Edwards, who directed *Days of Wine and Roses* (1962), and Stanley Kubrick, who directed *2001: A Space Odyssey, Dr. Strangelove* (1964), *Full Metal Jacket* (1987), and *Eyes Wide Shut* (1999), his final film, starring Tom Cruise and Nicole Kidman. Other notable contemporary American film auteurs are Martin Scorsese, whose films include *Taxi Driver* (1976), *The King of Comedy* (1983), and *The Age of Innocence* (1993); David Lynch, who made *Eraserhead* (1977), *Blue Velvet* (1986), and *Wild at Heart* (1990); and Spike Lee, who often makes movies that deal with race relations or controversial issues (*Do the Right Thing*, 1988; *Mo' Better Blues,* 1990), depictions of historical people and events (*Malcolm X*, 1992; *Summer of Sam*, 1999; *Miracle at St. Anna*, 2008), and documentaries (*4 Little Girls*, 1997; *Jim Brown, All American*, 2002; *When the Levee Broke: A Requiem in Four Acts,* 2006).

▼ TECHNOLOGICAL INFLUENCES ON MOVIE GENRES

Technology has always influenced filmmaking, from the days when short film reels only allowed films of five minutes or less, which hampered creation of complex stories, to the development of synchronized sound, which made the cameras stationary and changed movies from action-oriented to speaking-oriented styles.

Spike Lee often makes films that tackle controversial or sensitive topics.

Today, digital technologies allow filmmakers to design entire realistic worlds and to populate those worlds with lifelike characters. George Lucas, with his *Star Wars* movies, is at the forefront of using computers to create spectacular special effects, although critics charge this is often at the expense of good old-fashioned storytelling and character development. Likewise, digital technology has allowed for more realistic animations, and studios such as Disney and Pixar are making use of the less labor-intensive new technology to produce successful animated feature films for young audiences—although it is still questionable how much money is saved after the costs for high-end computer systems to generate special effects are factored in. James Cameron's *Avatar* (2009), which he waited to make for more than ten years until the technology could match his vision of the film, cost over $300 million to make. It was the first film to gross over $2 billion worldwide, so the heavy investment more than paid off in this case. Such was not the case for the effects-heavy movie *Green Lantern* (2011), which cost $200 million to make and may have only topped out at $260 million in worldwide ticket sales, not the kind of payback about which movie moguls fantasize.

New technologies also can have an effect on what movies are popular. High-tech gadgetry in our daily lives and today's fast-paced media environment have parallels in many of the science fiction and technology-oriented movies that have been coming out. Slower-paced, character-driven movies based on historical events have less appeal to younger audiences. Plots can also be interpreted differently because of changes in technology. A suspense movie made in the 1980s in which tension is created by the main character's difficulties in finding a public telephone would likely make young viewers today wonder why the character doesn't simply use her cell phone or borrow someone else's.

▼ OTHER ENTERTAINMENT SOURCES FOR MOVIES

Movies have always relied heavily on other media as their sources for stories. Some of the earliest films were nothing more than filmed stage plays, including Shakespearean dramas. Other movies took their inspiration from popular novels or stories, as many movies do today.

It used to be that successful original movies would sometimes lead to the creation of TV series, such as *M*A*S*H* (1970), itself based on a novel, and the subsequent television series of the same name that ran from 1972 to 1983. Although it still occasionally occurs, such as with *Terminator: The Sarah Connor Chronicles,* a spin-off Fox television series that ran for two seasons based on a character in the *Terminator* series of movies, today movies are equally likely to derive their inspiration from popular TV series, video games, cartoons, and even the Web.

Although *Spider-Man* (2002) and *The Dark Knight* (2008), Heath Ledger's last film, were huge successes, many other movies that have been created from TV, comics, or video games have not been nearly as successful. In the past several years a spate of movies based on popular television sitcoms, cartoons, and comic book characters were released: two Addams Family films (1991, 1998), *The Beverly Hillbillies* (1993), two Brady Bunch movies (1995, 1996), two Scooby-Doo movies (2002, 2004), and movies based on superheroes ranging from the Fantastic Four, Iron Man, Thor, and Captain America to the Incredible Hulk and several Batman releases. The venerable Superman even made a return appearance in *Superman Returns* (2006).

The movie *Undercover Brother* (2002), a parody of blaxploitation films of the 1970s, was one of the first movies derived from an animated series that originated on the Web. A bidding war started among studios for the rights to make a movie of *Undercover Brother*—which appeared on a site called Urban Entertainment—showing how studios are mining the creative resources that appear on the Web for story ideas. The Web also allows studios to see how popular animations or stories may be through viral-marketing efforts.

Tapping other media sources for movie material is not without its pitfalls, however, as any disappointed reader can say after watching a movie version of a favorite novel. The medium invariably changes not only how scenes appear but also their order and may even alter characters or remove some completely. This happens for a variety of reasons. Sometimes the producers have a different vision for the film than what the book emphasized, usually much material must be cut out to keep the movie within a standard ninety-minute or two-hour time frame, and often politics play a role as studios alter story lines and characters to make the movie appeal to the widest possible audience.

Studios have tried to cash in on the popularity of some video games, such as *Super Mario Bros.* or *Tomb Raider,* by making movies based either on the games or on the game characters. *Super Mario Brothers* (1993) did poorly at the box office, and although critics panned *Lara Croft: Tomb Raider* (2001), it did well enough to spawn a sequel in 2003. Experts in the video game industry doubt that video games can be successfully transplanted to movies, however. Steven Poole, author of *Trigger Happy: Videogames and the Entertainment Revolution,* says that the very thing that makes video games so addictive and popular—their interactive nature and fact the that the user to some extent controls the flow of the story, such as it is—is taken away from moviegoers, who must sit passively and watch what their favorite characters do. However, this hasn't stopped subsequent efforts: four films, starring Milla Jovovich, are based on the popular *Resident Evil* series of video games.

The *Resident Evil* series is one of the few examples of successful movies that were taken from video games.

▼ DVDS AND NETFLIX

The movie industry strongly resisted the introduction of consumer videocassette recorder models in the 1970s, even taking VCR manufacturer Sony to court for encouraging copyright infringement, claiming that videocassettes would ruin the movie industry as people illegally copied movies. This of course did not happen, and in fact video (and now DVD) sales and rentals bring studios more than double the revenue of box office receipts.

The lower production costs for videotape created new opportunities for filmmakers who would not otherwise have a chance to make movies for distribution as feature films. Some movies are made with the intention of going straight to video (or DVD today), while others that have not fared well at the box office go to video sooner than popular movies do.

Two major changes in recent years have radically altered the videotape market. First is the move away from videotapes to DVDs. DVDs provide more portability, better video and audio quality, and extra features that videotapes simply cannot

Netflix has altered the DVD and videotape rental industry.

match. In only a few years, videotapes have been replaced by DVDs, which in turn are being replaced by the Blu-ray format, which offers better sound and picture quality and more storage on a DVD.

The other big change has been in how people rent DVDs. With the creation of Netflix in 1997, people could rent DVD movies online and have them sent directly to their homes, returning them when they wanted. This business model went completely against the established video-rental model, in which people went to a store, chose a movie, and usually had a twenty-four- or forty-eight-hour window within which to return it without incurring late fees. Without expensive store rentals and other overhead costs, Netflix can maintain a larger inventory and wider variety of DVDs, including many rarely found in video stores because they are not big sellers. In April 2009 Netflix announced that it had rented its two billionth video and in April 2011 announced they had over 23 million subscribers. Meanwhile, Blockbuster, which was the king of video rental stores in the 1990s, filed for bankruptcy in 2010.

The Netflix model fit well with several consumer trends, including growing popularity of on-demand viewing and increased ordering online. Furthermore, Netflix has expanded its offerings to include Internet streaming of movies and availability on a variety of set-top devices and even video game consoles. Internet streaming of movies has been a huge growth area for Netflix and promises to only get bigger, at the expense of DVD sales and rentals.

◣▼ Video Games

Video games outpaced U.S. box office sales for the first time in 2001 and did not see a dip in sales until the recession in 2008. In 2011 global sales of video games were $65 billion, up from $62.7 billion in 2010.[6] Video game sales are dominated by games made for consoles such as Sony's PlayStation, Nintendo, and Microsoft's Xbox, with a much smaller percentage going to computer games. The most popular games are usually fast-paced action or sports games in which multiple players can play against each other. Nintendo's Wii, in which the game remote controls emulate actual player movement, has been very popular since its release in late 2006, with stores selling out of the coveted game consoles when it was released. By the end of 2008, Wii outsold PlayStation and Xbox. Microsoft released Kinect for Xbox 360 in November 2010 to compete with Wii. Unlike Wii, which requires a hand-held device to sense motion, Kinect is able to sense and track a player's motion directly using gestures and spoken commands, without the need to touch a game controller.

Computer users continue to find appeal in massively multiplayer online games (MMOGs) such as *Aces High* and massively multiplayer online role-playing games (MMORPGs) such as Activision Blizzard's *World of Warcraft,* Sony's *EverQuest,* or Funcom's *Anarchy Online.* In this kind of video game, players create characters of various races and classes and go online to engage in quests or missions, working with others in real time using chats and text messaging to join teams, fight with or against each other, and gain treasure or experience through battling monsters or other villains. Console video game makers see this area as one with lots of potential and are moving to establishing their own MMOGs.

Most MMOGs or MMORPGs use either a subscription model or some variation of a freemium model, in which people can play for free but have limited access to the game world or to character development. Many games have also developed in-game economies, in which more advanced players can sell or barter items to other players. There have even been cases in which people use real money to buy virtual items that

Is Playing Video Games Bad for You?

Many people who play video games say the games are addictive, but they usually mean it only in the figurative sense. For some people, video games truly are addictive, in the strictest sense of the word. A twenty-six-year-old Mr. Xu Yan died in 2007 in Jinzhou, China, after reportedly playing online games continuously for two weeks during the Chinese lunar New Year holiday.[7]

Research from 2009 conducted by the Centre for Addiction and Mental Health in Toronto, Ontario, of 9,000 students from grades 7 to 12 shows about one in ten school-age children spends seven or more hours a day in front of a computer screen. An even greater portion of children this age report having a video game addiction problem. With the growth of mobile gaming on smartphones and tablet devices, screen time has only increased, as has the likelihood of addiction.

Mental health experts say signs of addiction include the following:

- Inability to stop the activity or playing much longer than anticipated.
- Neglect of family and friends.
- Lying to employers and family about activities.
- Problems with school or job.
- Carpal tunnel syndrome.
- Dry eyes.
- Failure to attend to personal hygiene.
- Sleep disturbances or changes in sleep patterns.

Psychologists say that part of the reason online games are so addictive is that they give people who feel like they do not fit into regular society a chance to interact easily with others and to redefine themselves.

But some other studies have shown that video games, especially character-driven games that encourage a range of activities and exploration, can help people experiment with new identities and new ways of seeing themselves, which in turn can help them in real-life social situations.

Two 2011 studies from Colorado State University report the potentially positive effects of the popular multiplayer online game *World of Warcraft*. These studies find that game players can get involved in the game to the extent that they block out their "external environment." Researcher Jeffrey Snodgrass reports such "absorptive experiences" can be positive ones, and provide mental health benefits.[8]

will help them in the games, and some shops have been set up in China in which people are paid to play the games and get items that can then be sold on auction sites.

Many game-related websites have very active discussion groups in which fans of a particular game help each other with questions, trade tips or taunts, complain about aspects of the game, create cheat codes or provide hints on where special bonus treasure may be found, and even create **mods**, or modifications, to games. It is the kind of dedication to an entertainment product that many other media companies would love to have, but it is not without its dangers, such as possibly encouraging addictive behavior.

Many role-playing or first-person video games actually use quite a few cinematic techniques as they develop their story lines, and most video games have cinematic

mods

Short for "modifications," it refers to the practice of changing parts of the code in some games to alter how they are played or how they look.

introduction scenes complete with sweeping panoramic views, pans, and complex tracking shots—all computer generated, of course. Video games that employ some sort of narrative or character development, as opposed to simple shooter or arcade-style games, usually use techniques of plot and character development borrowed from Hollywood genres, and Hollywood actors are often tapped for voice-overs of main computer characters.

Video game companies often license content from other media and create games based on that content, such as *Star Trek Online* or 2011's much-anticipated *Star Wars: The Old Republic* MMORPG that is being created by respected game developer Bioware.

Some experts initially thought that the video game market would be inherently limited to males in their teens or younger. However, as the first young people who grew up with home-console video games reach their twenties and thirties, research has shown not only that they keep playing video games but that females are playing more games than in the past. Still, video games remain a primarily youth-oriented, male pastime.

Some have taken a cue from the high interest in video games and incorporated them into educational settings. Called **serious gaming**, it combines the exciting elements found in most video games with instruction in subjects like history or politics. The U.S. Army uses video game training for officers deployed in Iraq, putting them in tense situations and giving them limited time to make decisions. Recent research has shown that playing video games has helped some elderly patients in nursing homes stay mentally sharp and get some mild forms of exercise, such as with a Wii.

serious gaming

A growing area of gaming that creates video games that have educational value or purpose to them.

▼ RISE OF SOCIAL GAMES

The arrival of online social games such as *Farmville* and *Mafia Wars,* both created by social game leader Zynga, represent a major new type of video game. *Farmville,* launched in 2009 on Facebook, is actually an app, or application, and can be played on a browser or through mobile devices. Within a year, *Farmville* had 69 million users—a tremendous growth rate when compared to storied game franchises like the online *World of Warcraft,* which has 11.5 million subscribers. Part of the rapid popularity of social games is that they coexist easily on a popular site like Facebook, and encourage players to tap into their network of friends to find new participants.

The huge number of players for games like *Farmville* means an attractive audience for advertisers, thus generating good revenue streams for the game maker while making it easy to keep the game free. The information on user behavior that Zynga collects from the players is also a potential gold mine for marketers. For example, advertisers could use this information in combination with other demographic or behavioral data to create highly targeted ads. As a sign of the growing strength of social games, Zynga announced in mid 2011 that they were preparing to launch an initial public offering (IPO) of stock. Some experts valued it at $20 billion, which would make it as valuable as two of the largest video game production companies combined, Electronic Arts and Activision Blizzard.

◢▲ Music

Second only to watching television, listening to music remains a very popular activity. There is no doubt that music plays a large role in the entertainment environment of many people, especially young people. Musical tastes help people define themselves with other social groups and helps ease some of the awkwardness young people often feel as they create their self-identities. By imitating clothing and hairstyles of certain musicians, people can easily create a public image that gives others a message about who they feel they are or at least who they would like to be.

Music is often playing in the background as people go about their daily activities or engage with other media such as video games or books. Couples often have "their" song that holds special meaning for them or seems to speak to their particular relationship (despite the fact that the song was written for mass appeal), and many a teen has played air guitar in front of the mirror while listening to a favorite singer, dreaming of rock stardom.

Music also plays an important role in movies and television, acting as an audio cue to viewers on what to expect or feel in particular scenes. The low, threatening music in the movie *Jaws* (1975) whenever the shark was going to appear heightened tension as viewers wondered whom it would strike next. The theme became so well known that it entered other movies, as parody, and even daily conversation, as people used the theme to humorously denote imminent trouble.

▼ FROM TIN PAN ALLEY TO HOLLYWOOD

In the early days of the recorded-music industry, much of the popular music in America was generated in New York's historic Tin Pan Alley, an area in Manhattan on West Twenty-eighth Street between Broadway and Sixth Avenue where music publishers had located to be near the theaters and vaudeville houses. Before record players became widespread, people usually bought sheet music for voice and piano of songs they had heard in vaudeville shows or the theaters and played them at home. As the years passed, Tin Pan Alley became a generic reference to the music-publishing business that hired composers and lyricists on a permanent basis to write popular songs. Tin Pan Alley continued for about seventy years, until roughly 1950, when radio and television became more important in the promotion of music.

WEB LINK
Charles A. Templeton Sheet Music Collection
library.msstate.edu/ragtime/main.html

Irving Berlin was a noted composer of many of the twentieth century's most popular songs.

Although there were many great composers during the early days of Tin Pan Alley, from George and Ira Gershwin to Cole Porter, perhaps the one name most synonymous with the time is Irving Berlin. Berlin achieved stardom in 1911 when his song "Alexander's Ragtime Band" became an international hit. He went on to pen such classics as "Blue Skies," "God Bless America," "White Christmas," and "There's No Business Like Show Business." Today he is remembered as one of the greatest songwriters of the twentieth century's recorded-music industry.

As Hollywood developed and motion pictures with sound emerged in the late 1920s and early 1930s, a recorded-music industry also emerged in Los Angeles, where it continues today. The emergence of the recording industry and radio in the first half of the century enabled musicians and music fans to hear many musical forms. Both black and white artists created songs with audience crossover appeal and laid the foundation for much of popular music today, including rap and other formats.

▼ ROOTS OF ROCK AND ROLL

The roots of rock and roll lie in a blend of musical forms, including blues-oriented vocalizations, black gospel musical structures, urban rhythm and blues (R&B) instrumentals, and white western and "hillbilly" strains, or rockabilly. In the late

Ray Charles had a long and distinguished career as an R&B and gospel artist.

1940s and early 1950s the combination of country artists such as Hank Williams and Tennessee Ernie Ford and R&B artists such as T-Bone Walker, Fats Domino, B. B. King, Ruth Brown, and Muddy Waters helped shape the early character of rock and roll.

From about 1954 to 1959 rock and roll took form and emerged as a popular sensation, with artists such as Bill Haley and His Comets (western swing crossover), Ray Charles (gospel/R&B), Elvis Presley (rockabilly), Chuck Berry (R&B), and Buddy Holly (rockabilly) leading the way. Popular rock vocal groups included the Platters, the Penguins, and Dion and the Belmonts and teen idols such as Frankie Avalon and Brenda Lee.

When rock and roll started in the 1950s, although much of the music owed its inspiration to black artists, few black musicians reaped any of the rewards. From Elvis Presley to Bill Haley and His Comets, most of the successful rock stars of the day were white. All that changed thanks to Detroit's Berry Gordy Jr. and the record company he started, Motown Record Company. Gordy was a musician himself, but as the writer of a successful song recorded by Jackie Wilson, he had received few profits.

Gordy decided to try creating his own music-recording company in the Motor City, Detroit—his hometown, and a city with a historically large black population. With seven hundred dollars borrowed from his sister and a makeshift studio in the basement, Gordy signed a kid off the street named Smokey Robinson and his backup singers, the Miracles, and started producing their music. The group quickly released a string of hits, and other successes followed when Gordy signed Diana Ross and the Supremes, Marvin Gaye, Stevie Wonder, the Jackson Five (with Michael Jackson), and many more talented black artists. By 1983, Motown was the largest black-owned company in the United States, with annual revenues of $104 million. In 1988, Gordy sold Motown to MCA Records.

Rock continued to evolve and in the 1960s took a variety of new turns, including soul, "girl groups," Motown, surf rock, and folk rock. Many of these popular groups and musicians had not only a musical impact but a social one. They influenced trends and tastes, from clothing to hairstyles, and many of the groups, especially folk-rock artists, shaped public thoughts and social movements against the war in Vietnam, to protect the environment, and to expand civil rights. Reflecting his broad social influence and the artistry of his work, in 1997 Bob Dylan was nominated for a Nobel Prize in Literature.

▼ REDEFINING ROCK

Redefining rock in the mid to late 1960s was "the British invasion," with groups such as the Beatles, the Rolling Stones, and the Who bringing a new level of energy and popularity to rock and roll. It was at this time that experimentation with drugs increased, both among the young in general and rock musicians in particular, who helped shape popular opinion in this regard. Some new strains of rock emerged, including psychedelic rock, jazz rock, and the beginnings of heavy metal. Some of the bands and artists popular in the late 1960s who helped promote youth culture are still touring and performing, well into their sixties, and still attract large followings.

Mick Jagger, like many other rock stars from the 1960s and 1970s, continues to perform regularly.

In the 1970s music moved from socially conscious and experimental types to highly produced glam rock or bands like KISS, with their flamboyant makeup and stage shows. Disco appeared for a brief time in the mid-1970s. Punk rock, which also started in the mid-1970s, was partly a response to the perceived overcommercialization of popular music. The 1980s saw heavy metal music become popular, while pop bands like Culture Club and Wham! sang of love and infatuation. Rap music left the urban streets and started to enter the mainstream from the late 1980s but became more widespread in the early 1990s. In the late 1980s and early 1990s, Seattle bands such as Nirvana, Soundgarden, and Alice in Chains developed a dark sound dubbed alternative or progressive rock.

Musical genres continue to evolve and splinter as they wax and wane in popularity. Sometimes even older musical genres, such as swing, enjoy a short resurgence. Mainstream country music has come to sound much more like country rock, for example, and some hit songs appear on both pop and country charts. One element that has changed the music industry in the past twenty years is the development of MTV, or music television.

▼ MUSIC AND MTV

The launch of MTV in 1981 provided a new venue for promoting music. The twenty-four-hour format required many music videos to fill the airtime, and music videos changed the nature of music promotion and, to a large extent, what artists or bands were promoted. Suddenly, it became just as important how a band looked on television as how they sounded.

Music videos have often been criticized by various groups as encouraging sexual or violent imagery, sexism, antisocial behavior, and even Satanism. Studies have shown that viewers like watching music videos more than just listening to music, and when controversial lyrics are combined with controversial video, it is feared that young people may be internalizing socially unacceptable messages. New music channels began on cable in the 1990s, including channels devoted to specific genres, such as country music or heavy metal.

Researchers have reported that between 40 percent and 75 percent of music videos contain sexual imagery, although it is generally mild and nongraphic. Sexism remains strong, however, with over half the women dressed provocatively but only 10 percent of the men dressed so and women much more likely to be treated as sex objects or dominated by men than the other way around.[9]

Dave Matthews has established a reputation as a popular artist whose songs are hard to classify by a specific genre.

◣◥ Books and Magazines

Despite the perception among many adults that young people do not read anymore, "reading for fun" is still a surprisingly popular activity among young people (although one suspects "reading for school" may fall far lower on the list).

The portability and inexpensiveness of magazines and to some extent books, when compared to other entertainment media, will likely make them a part of the entertainment landscape for quite some time. Novels can engage media consumers in their stories like few other media can, since characters, scenes, and situations are pictured in readers' minds. Every genre is available, appealing to a variety of literary (and not so literary) tastes.

Magazines help guide people in their social behavior and to better understand what the culture deems standard or normal. Not only are they more visually appealing than newspapers, their length allows more depth in stories.

Of course, reading is not confined to print media; much reading takes place online now as well, and there are even novels for cell phones. Although the articles may be shorter and there may be different reading patterns than with print media, reading is still an important element of media consumption online. With the growing popularity of tablet computers and better screen resolutions, it is likely that reading online or from electronic devices will only increase.

◥▼ Entertainment and Law

Portrayals of sex and violence have often been issues by which groups criticize media companies. Although the old adage "sex sells" is usually true, entertainment companies have been sharply criticized for pandering to baser instincts among the public simply to increase their revenues. This has led to fights over censorship and new laws and regulations that have affected the kind of media available to the public, or at least some members of the public.

Despite some progress in more balanced, fully developed portrayals of women and ethnic groups, there are still many instances in which media companies fall short. For at least three reasons, the media industries in the United States have often sought to regulate themselves. First, self-regulation can be a responsible form of self-discipline, which can improve the media's actions. Second, and as a consequence, in the court of public opinion self-regulation can improve the media's reputation by signaling a willingness to act responsibly. Third, self-regulation can solve or reduce problems before they lead to unwanted government regulation, which is usually more strict than what the industry itself wants to do.

Comic books showing graphic horror and violence in the 1950s were said to cause juvenile delinquency. As a result, ratings systems were developed, similar to what we see today in other entertainment media.

▼ THE CENSORSHIP OF COMICS

A fascinating historical and continuing case of censorship is the comic book. Popular among children and adults, comics have long been under the scrutiny of critics in both government and the public. Criticism and censorship reached a peak in the McCarthy-era 1950s when psychologist Fredric Wertham, MD, published his book, *Seduction of the Innocent,* which contended that the reading of violent and sexually graphic comic books caused juvenile delinquency and worse. Wertham's book captured public and media attention and quickly led to intense pressure from the government and other groups to curtail the graphic sexual and gruesome violent content of comic books, especially horror comics such as *Tales from the Crypt, Haunt of Fear,* and *Vault of Horror.*

Wertham based his argument on his own observations of juvenile delinquents. He found that many delinquents read a lot of comic books, especially horror comics. He also found that many of these kids were poor readers. Wertham concluded that reading comics, especially horror comics, caused both juvenile delinquency and illiteracy. Although his reasoning and methodology were flawed, in response to Wertham's claims the U.S. Senate conducted a full-scale investigation in 1954 into the nature and effects of comics on children.

The Senate did not take any formal legal action against the comics industry. Instead, a consortium called the Association of Comics Magazine Publishers formed the Comics Code Authority (CCA), a sort of industry censorship review board. The CCA began reading every comic book published and effectively put a ban on sexual content and the most graphic material popular in many horror comics of the day, including torture, sadism, and detailed discussion of criminal acts. A CCA seal of approval then was emblazoned on the cover of acceptable comics. As a result of the CCA action, many of the most graphic horror comics were put out of business.

▼ THE HAYS CODE

Some early films, especially some of the black-and-white films prior to 1920, contained considerable nudity or near nudity, particularly some of the biblical films, such as those created by D. W. Griffith (e.g., the 1919 *Fall of Babylon*). Hollywood's original vamp, actress Theda Bara, was often shown in revealing costumes.[10] Although the nudity and sexuality were popular with many early filmgoers, some conservative groups were outspoken in their criticism, especially of bare-breasted women or women dressed in revealing clothing, and the movie moguls feared the possibility of government censorship. As a result, they joined forces to create their own industry self-censorship in the form of the Hays Office.

The office produced what was called the **Hays Code** in 1930, outlining many dos and don'ts for the film industry. The Hays Code articulated three general moral principles. First was the intention to prevent production of any motion picture that would "lower the moral standards of those who see it. Hence the sympathy of the audience should never be thrown to the side of crime, wrongdoing, evil or sin." Second, every picture was to present "correct standards of life, subject only to the requirements of drama and entertainment." Third, no picture was to ridicule "natural or human" law.

The code went on to prescribe the proper depiction of content in twelve specific areas, including criminal activity, sex, and religion. By today's standards, many of

Hays Code

A code established in 1930 by the movie industry to censor itself regarding showing nudity or glorifying antisocial acts in movies. Officials for the Hays Office had to approve each film that was distributed to a mass audience.

The Hays Code was created to censor movies that depicted violence and sex.

these prescriptions seem quaint—though well intentioned—and some are offensive, racist, or at least politically incorrect. In some ways, the Hays Code was little more than a public relations stunt to deflect criticism, and some moviemakers treated the code as little more than a joke, initially.

However, if a movie did not have the stamp of approval from the Hays Office, it might not receive mass distribution by a major studio—a chance most producers were not willing to take. In the mid-1960s, after a series of Supreme Court cases involving obscenity, and a general change in public mores regarding depictions of sexuality, the Hays Code underwent a major revision and was not enforced as stringently as it had been. By 1968 the movie rating system of G, M, R, and X, today modified as G, PG, PG-13, R, NC-17, and X, had essentially replaced the Hays Code. The movie ratings code has served as a model for industry self-censorship "ratings" for music, television, and video games.

◤▽ The Business of Entertainment

Media-entertainment companies have been the driving force behind most of the large mergers that have led to the concentration of media ownership in the past several years. Either they have tried to swallow competitors or other entertainment properties in order to provide more types of entertainment to the public, or they have been swallowed up by larger companies that see their media content as a powerful asset in order to enter the media-entertainment field.

The entertainment industry touches many more people than simply the various writers, actors, directors, producers, and other creators of entertainment. For television, ratings are extremely important to determine how much can be charged for advertising, and a network that consistently has weak shows and that places

Movies employ hundreds of people in a variety of roles, ranging from carpenters and other technicians to communications professionals responsible for promoting a film or dealing with the stars.

third or fourth among the terrestrial networks hurts the chances for affiliate stations to earn money through higher advertising prices.

Movie-theater owners and their employees, not to mention all the behind-the-cameras staff ranging from lighting technicians to construction workers on movie sets, count on a robust film industry for their jobs. At its peak in 1999, the movie industry alone employed almost six hundred thousand people. CD and DVD manufacturers, plus jewel-case manufacturers, printers, and shippers, depend on people buying CDs and DVDs for their livelihoods.

Costs for most mainstream entertainment remain too high to allow an individual outside of the industry to enter independently with content. The average cost to make movies is now over $65 million, not including marketing costs, and without distribution deals with U.S. theaters, there is little hope of a movie being seen by a mass audience, even if someone were willing to spend that much to make it. Developing video games can cost $10 million or more and requires teams of artists, designers, writers, and programmers. Book production costs are far lower than movie costs, but distribution channels remain extremely limited without a major publisher, and a lack of marketing for any type of media content hampers its chances of success.

Although it seems that entertainment would be one of the first items on people's budgets to be cut when economic times are hard, that is not the case. Although some entertainment sectors have downturns in slow economic times, other areas remain immune. For example, during the Great Depression in the 1930s Hollywood still produced many films, offering often escapist fare and musicals to the public. In the recent recession, some types of entertainment saw downturns in sales, although some of the decreases were also attributed to shifts in how people consume entertainment media, such as watching movies via Internet streaming rather than renting or buying actual DVDs.

▼ CAREERS IN ENTERTAINMENT

Because entertainment is such a broad, multifaceted area, it is hard to define any certain career track one should take in order to work in entertainment. A person could be an accountant in an entertainment company and likely do much the same type of work as an accountant in a pharmaceutical company or manufacturing company.

For communications professionals, the entertainment industry offers its own rewards and challenges. Working as a public relations or marketing specialist for a film-distribution company may technically put one in the "entertainment arena" (and may provide chances to talk with and meet various stars), but the job is essentially one of public relations or marketing. Working as a book editor in a publishing house is one career track that many find interesting, although the book industry itself is undergoing huge transformations. For people interested in technology, developing computer-programming or design skills could help in finding a job with one of the video game companies or perhaps in CGI special effects.

Furthermore, the changes in the industry and the often volatile nature of entertainment itself regarding what is popular and what is not can give jobs in entertainment a kind of frenzied, hectic quality. Tight deadlines, long hours, low pay for most types of jobs, and the high costs invested in most mainstream media projects can add to the pressure of the daily work.

Depending on the type of job or field one is in, and how closely one is working with actual entertainment personalities or production, one may need to spend

JERSEY SHORE AND THE G WORD

ETHICS IN MEDIA

New Jersey has been a much-maligned state in media depictions and the public's consciousness, either shown as an industrial wasteland, home to the Mafia (*Boardwalk Empire, The Sopranos*), or as poor stepchild to much hipper Manhattan across the Hudson River.

Jersey Shore has been MTV's most-watched series ever, and has made celebrities of cast members such as Mike "The Situation" Sorrentino and Nicole "Snooki" Polizzi. Even before it aired, however, it started controversy among Italian Americans. Ads promoting the show used the word "guido," a derogatory racial term for Italian males, which drew complaints from some Italian-American groups. The term was changed in the ads, but when the series finally aired the term was used by all cast members to refer to themselves. Guys were guidos and the girls called themselves guidettes.

Despite more complaints by the public, and some advertisers such as Domino's removing their ads from the show, MTV refused to bleep out the term. They said that if the cast members themselves use the term to refer to themselves, and are apparently proud of the term, then they will leave it in.

Some scholars suggested that the term may have changed meanings across generations. Rather than being a racial epithet for an Italian American "just off the boat," it has been adopted by younger generations as a badge of coolness and ethnic identity, much as young blacks often use the N word with each other.

Regardless of whether one finds the term offensive or not, a larger question is how it may perpetuate certain ethnic stereotypes of Italian Americans. Historically in the media, Italian Americans have been depicted either in blue-collar jobs or associated with crime, and one study found that 74 percent of young people believed that a majority of Italian Americans actually are associated with organized crime in some way.

The antics of the *Jersey Shore* cast members do little to dispel negative stereotypes about young Italian-Americans from New Jersey. And to add insult to injury, residents of the Jersey Shore community Seaside Heights, where the show has been filmed most seasons, point out that the cast members are not even from the Jersey Shore but other places in New Jersey.

WEB LINK
Stereotype This
www.stereotypethis.com

several years "paying dues" and establishing connections with others in the industry before getting into a position that is professionally and financially rewarding.

▼ SALARIES IN ENTERTAINMENT

Just as jobs vary greatly in the entertainment industry, so do salaries. Just because a movie studio makes a blockbuster movie one year does not mean that every employee in the company gets to enjoy the financial rewards. In fact, in some of the more popular types of jobs entry-level salaries can be quite low because of the strong competition for positions. Most employees do not share in royalty revenues of the major media companies, instead getting regular and steady salaries. Royalties are usually only reserved for the artists themselves or other high-level creators such as film directors or in some cases A-list stars.

Entertainment will continue to be important in our lives and in the media environment, and it may be the primary reason, for many, to engage with media. The ability of entertainment to transmit cultural values and norms in an apparently "natural" way can make it especially powerful, as the values being imparted often go unquestioned. This is particularly important when such values encourage negative stereotypes of certain minority groups or when entertainment reinforces the idea that some types of people are "not normal."

Because of the popularity of entertainment, there is a strong inclination in other fields, such as advertising and journalism, to emulate certain entertainment values. However, this can undermine the role that a profession like journalism plays, in terms of informing the public.

Entertainment may have a more insidious effect in the digital realm, making it easier than ever for people to get the kind of entertainment they want when they want it. This could lend itself to people becoming more passive as they have a wide range of entertainment choices, making them less likely to interact with each other in meaningful ways or to produce content themselves.

The rapid media feedback loop seen online is especially prominent with entertainment. User-generated content or a viral video can quickly be copied by a mainstream entertainment company for its own purposes, making the public quickly tire of the latest "new thing." Something that may have been creative and original can quickly look old or uncool if adopted and widely copied by mainstream entertainment companies. This could mean someone could become famous more easily than in the past, but their fame may be even more fleeting—more like fifteen seconds of fame than fifteen minutes.

The prevalence of entertainment can also affect the nature of our interactions online. Whether we spend our time interacting with others in heated discussions about political policies or in killing a video game player's avatar and belittling them has repercussions for the quality of knowledge we have about our world and how we view our fellow human beings. If our worldview is largely defined by the types of entertainment we consume, then our discussions with others will be similarly limited, no matter how active we are online.

Entertainment of course does not exist in a vacuum. It has a complex relationship with both journalism and, especially, the worlds of advertising and public relations, which we will see in the next chapter.

1. If you have ever met a celebrity, discuss your experience when meeting them and how you felt. Did your impression of the celebrity change after meeting the person? Was it changed for better or for worse?

2. Keep a daily log for one week of how many conversations you have with friends, class-mates, and family that have to do with media entertainment. This can include talking about an episode of a previous night's TV show, an upcoming movie, or any entertainment-related area. Write down when the conversations took place and how long they lasted and compare your log with classmates.

3. Keep a daily log of how much time you actually spend with media entertainment, either watching TV, listening to the radio, playing video or computer games, or going to concerts, sporting events, or movies. Compare this amount of time with the time spent discussing the entertainment event and share the information with classmates.

4. Make a short list of some of your favorite TV series or movies and see if you can research where the ideas for these shows or movies came from. Are they remakes of much older shows? If they are original, what influences did the producer or filmmaker have?

5. Most people do not like to watch a movie or read a book more than once or twice. However, people can often play the same video game for hours on end, repeating levels and characters. Why do you think this is so?

6. How many product placements can you spot in your favorite reality show?

7. Discuss whether you think the movie rating system, and the music and video game rating systems that are based on it, is a good thing and useful.

8. How many celebrity Twitter accounts do you follow? What made you decide to follow them? Have you stopped following any? Why?

FURTHER READING

Amusing Ourselves to Death: Public Discourse in the Age of Show Business (20th anniversary edition). Neil Postman (2005) Penguin.

Television Disrupted: The Transition from Network to Networked TV, 2nd ed. Shelly Palmer (2008) York House Press.

Stay Tuned: Television's Unforgettable Moments. Joe Garner (2002) Andrews McMeel Publishing.

Reality Bites Back: The Troubling Truth About Guilty Pleasure TV. Jennifer Pozner (2010) Seal Press.

Reality Check: The Business and Art of Producing Reality TV. Michael Essany (2008) Focal Press.

Cinema Year by Year 1894–2002. David Thomson (2002) DK Publishing.

The Golden Age of Cinema: Hollywood, 1929–1945, 1st ed. Richard Jewell (2007) Wiley-Blackwell.

It Happened in Hollywood: Remarkable Events That Shaped History. Gerald Schiller (2010) Globe Pequot.

The Hollywood Economist: The Hidden Financial Reality Behind the Movies. Edward Jay Epstein (2010) Melville House.

Noise/Music: A History. Paul Hegarty (2007) Continuum.

Genre in Popular Music. Fabian Holt (2007) University of Chicago Press.

Dirty Little Secrets of the Record Business: Why So Much Music You Hear Sucks. Hank Bordowitz (2007) Chicago Review Press.

Changing the Game: How Video Games Are Changing the Nature of Business. David Edery, Ethan Mollick (2008) FT Press.

Paid to Play: An Insider's Guide to Video Game Careers. Alice Rush, David Hodgson, Bryan Stratton (2006) Prima Games.

Trigger Happy: Videogames and the Entertainment Revolution. Steven Poole (2000) Arcade Publishing.

Replay: The History of Video Games. Tristan Donovan (2010) Yellow Ant Media.

1001 Video Games You Must Play Before You Die. Tony Mott, ed. (2010) Universe.

11

ADVERTISING AND PUBLIC RELATIONS: THE POWER OF PERSUASION

LEARNING OBJECTIVES

By the end of this chapter you should be able to:

■ Understand the overview of strategic communications.

■ Explain the theoretical foundations of advertising and public relations.

■ Describe the purpose and form of advertising and public relations.

■ Outline the history and structure of the advertising and public relations industries.

■ Identify the impact of digital technologies on advertising and public relations.

■ Discuss the role of evaluation research in advertising and public relations.

Advertisements for the Super Bowl have practically become a media event in and of themselves, with advertisers jockeying for the most clever or creative ad that will have people talking days after the game. At times it seems that nearly as much analysis is done of the ads as of the game.

Advertisers pay a premium for this privilege. A thirty-second commercial spot was $3 million for Super Bowl XLIII in 2011, about the same as it was for the two years before that—compared to costs between $90,000 and $200,000 for a thirty-second spot on a regular Sunday-afternoon football game, depending on the network.

During the dot-com boom in the late 1990s, some Internet start-ups used substantial portions of their marketing funding for Super Bowl ads in order to get as much recognition as possible. Most of these companies shut down soon after the boom ended, although GoDaddy.com still survives and advertises during the Super Bowl.

Most Super Bowl ads in recent years have been from large, well-established companies. For these Super Bowl spots, they often use humor or present edgier advertising than they normally do, but with mixed success. Sometimes the ads can even create controversy. The Snickers ad in Super Bowl XLI (2007) showing two mechanics accidentally kissing while eating each end of a Snickers bar outraged gay groups, who said that it portrayed men kissing as somehow abnormal or awkward. Snickers decided to stop airing the ad after the complaints, though the company never fully apologized.

In 2011, the Super Bowl ads went online soon after they aired and viewers were invited to vote on the best ones. This not only gave the advertisers more exposure as people could watch the ads again, but it allowed people to discuss ads and provided valuable information on what the public liked and didn't like about the ads.

This shows how television advertising continues to be very important for advertisers yet how social media can augment and complement ads, increasing viewer engagement even as advertisers gain valuable information on consumer desires and opinions.

Many diverse forces shape the media of mass communication. Among the most important are advertising and public relations, which can be categorized broadly as types of strategic communications. This chapter examines the nature and history of these two essential media industries and how they are adapting to the shifting nature of mass communication in the age of digitization and convergence.

Advertising has traditionally been the method by which companies or stores reach a mass audience, utilizing the distribution system that newspapers or electronic media outlets have created. Public relations has typically involved managing the public "persona" of a company, also using media outlets and their mass-distribution networks.

In a digital, networked world, however, the power for almost anyone to distribute information cheaply has been greatly enhanced. It would seem that this could save large companies money in advertising costs because they can now

News conferences or other scheduled announcements by companies or government officials are examples of "pseudo events," or events designed to attract media attention.

The Dynamics of Persuasion

Test how savvy you are about advertising, branding, and public relations.

1. (T/F) Branding is important for corporations but not for nonprofit organizations or educational institutions.
2. (T/F) Advertising has become less important as a revenue source with online media compared to traditional media.
3. What is product placement? Can you name an example and the product?
4. What is the main source of advertising revenue for newspapers, display ads, or classifieds?
5. What does CPM stand for, and why is it important?
6. What are SEM and SEO? Why are they important?
7. (T/F) Before the twentieth century, there was often little difference in newspapers between public relations and news content.
8. What is social marketing?
9. If you participated in a blind taste test with your favorite brand of cola, do you think you could tell which is yours?
10. How does a viral video work?

contact audiences directly. Although true to some extent, it is not as prevalent as one would think.

Just because someone has the digital tools available to be an online journalist, filmmaker, or musician it does not mean that he or she has the other needed skills to do so (such as talent in writing or music). Likewise, companies may have expertise in their fields, but they do not understand how to best persuade their target audiences. This is where the expertise of strategic-communications professionals is used. The ability to reach audiences with powerful, persuasive messages and to create an enduring brand or company image is a crucial and specialized skill.

Advertising is the most prevalent form of media content and is paid for by an organization, whether it is a for-profit company, a not-for-profit organization, or a political campaign. Advertisements, whether in print, in the form of commercials on broadcast radio and television, as classifieds, on billboards, or online, provide the basic financial revenue that pays for the creation of media content. Two-thirds of most newspapers and magazines are filled with advertisements (not including advertising inserts). Even though most television programming time is devoted to content rather than commercials, consider the number of times the audience sees the same commercial during the course of a program. Studies have shown that children tend to remember commercial jingles and catchphrases better than basic facts about U.S. government or history.

Public relations also plays a vital role today. Unlike advertisements, public relations content is not paid. Rather, a news conference, event, or press release may be the basis of a story that appears in a newspaper. For this reason, content that appears from public relations is called **earned media**.

Many organizations have historically sought to influence media content and thereby public opinion. These organizations hope that by getting positive stories about themselves in the media it will improve their public image or help make them better known by the public.

Public relations professionals do what they can to generate publicity for their clients. This includes staging events or awards ceremonies, holding news conferences, suggesting story ideas to journalists, and making sure that any potentially damaging information is framed in the least harmful way for the client. They also work closely during crisis communications situations, such as the 2010 BP oil spill in the Gulf of Mexico, to mitigate negative press coverage and emphasize positive stories.

Most news organizations are dependent on the public relations function of organizations—whether corporate, government, or not-for-profit groups—for information. This includes everything from scheduled announcements and research studies or reports, such as government reports on the economy, to contact with executives and employees for interviews, to corporate financial statements and information during crises.

◢◥ Strategic Communications

Advertising and public relations represent two types of strategic communications. Strategic communications is a broad field that is being redefined today, thanks in part to the changes that digital technology is bringing to the communications industry.

Strategic communications can refer to a range of communications fields, including advertising, PR, and even aspects of organizational communications such as internal communications or corporate communications. At the heart of strategic communications is the goal of delivering a persuasive message to an audience so they will think or behave in a way that the communicator wants. Let us break down this definition into its parts and examine each more closely.

Delivering a message can take place through any number of media channels. We will be looking primarily at mass communications and online communications, including social media, in this chapter, but it can be done face-to-face or any number of other ways. Part of what makes strategic communications challenging is knowing which channel will be most effective for a particular message to a particular audience. Some companies have been heavily criticized in the media for delivering notices of layoffs via emails rather than telling employees face-to-face.

Making a message persuasive is another challenging task. Persuasion has been studied by many notable researchers over the years, and there are still no clear answers on why some people find a particular message persuasive and others do not. Some may be persuaded by appeals to logic or lists of facts, and others may be persuaded because their favorite movie star endorses a product or because they like the colors used in the company logo.

Perhaps the most important factor is the audience, or, more accurately, the need to know and understand the audience. Without knowledge of the audience, what they think and feel, their likes and dislikes, and a host of other factors, it is virtually impossible to know what will be persuasive and what the best channel will be to reach them. A large direct email campaign does little good if your audience communicates primarily through text messaging or Facebook.

Finally, the whole purpose of using strategic communications is that you want audience members to act in a certain way. Perhaps you want them to change their behavior, such as to stop smoking or to eat healthier, or maybe you want them to donate to a cause or buy your product—or even buy more of your product—or maybe to just register on a website or pick up the phone and call their congressperson.

The desired action connects to the other components very clearly. What kind of message will be most persuasive to the audience—what is most likely to change people's attitudes so they take the desired action? Will a personalized message be the most effective channel, or will an advertising campaign on TV or in print be the best way to reach and convince them? How should the message be crafted and what tone should it use?

Note that these elements apply equally to an executive deciding how to propose company expansion to the board of directors as they do to a company launching a new product or to a nonprofit trying to get more volunteers or donors. Here we will focus on advertising and PR and leave corporate communications aside, but remember that the principles are largely the same.

▼ PERSUASIVE COMMUNICATIONS

As noted, a crucial aspect of strategic communications is the need to persuade an audience. The most effective campaigns use persuasive techniques that encourage audiences to agree with the persuader's point in an apparently "natural" or commonsense way. In other words, members of the audience may have started out thinking one thing before being exposed to the message, but afterward think differently, often feeling like they came to the conclusion themselves. However, they have been persuaded.

We may think of persuasive communications as a modern phenomenon that developed along with the rise of mass communications, but in fact it has roots that go much further back in history, at least to the time of the Greek philosophers, when studying the art of persuasion was called **rhetoric**.

Rhetoric was one of the three classical areas of learning that any educated person should know, along with logic and grammar. The Sophists, a group of Greek philosophers focused entirely on rhetoric, taught their knowledge to whoever could pay them. For Sophists, the truth of a matter was largely unimportant—they might even claim that truth is in the eye of the beholder—and the most important aspect of an argument was whether one could persuade others by whatever means possible.

Despite strong objections by the likes of Plato, Socrates, and Aristotle that truth should prevail over rhetoric, its importance in politics, business, and life continues to this day. Some may even argue that in an age when more people can speak publicly than ever, the ability to be persuasive and to make your voice heard above the others is now even more important than it used to be.

There are at least two dozen major modern scientific theories of persuasive communication and audience decision making. These theories help explain or provide models of how persuasive communications work, as well as guide the strategic communication campaigns that advertising and public relations professionals create and carry out via the media.

rhetoric

One of the ancient arts of discourse, it involves using language to persuade others.

Advertisers carefully consider a range of factors in making ads as persuasive as possible.

At the core of most theories of persuasion are certain assumptions about how we think and feel and how those thoughts and emotions affect the way we act. The assumptions can be broadly categorized as follows:

1. People's behavior and actions are somehow linked to their cognitions about the world, which generally include attitudes, beliefs, and values, as well as their general knowledge and social influences.

2. How people process information about the world (thinking deeply about issues or only looking at superficial cues) can play an important part in what types of messages they find most persuasive.

3. A persuader's credibility, authority, and attractiveness all play important roles in successful persuasion.

One theory of note that takes a different viewpoint from most theories of persuasion is called the **theory of cognitive dissonance**. This theory says that we act first and then rationalize or create reasons for our behavior afterward in order to fit our actions into our self-perceived notions of who we are. The theory of cognitive dissonance helps explain a range of otherwise puzzling behaviors, such as why freshmen subject themselves to humiliating hazing rituals to join a fraternity or sorority to which they become intensely loyal.

theory of cognitive dissonance

A theory of persuasion that states we act first and then rationalize our behavior afterward in order to fit our actions into self-perceived notions of who we are.

▼ THE ROLE OF MEDIA IN PERSUASION

Media of course play an important role in persuasion. One obvious way is that media channels are the means by which the public becomes aware of a product or issue. Getting an advertisement on national television that is seen by millions of people at once may be an effective way to raise awareness of a product. However, simple awareness is not enough. Too often, marketers assume that once people know about their product (or cause, or whatever), then they will want to buy it or participate. This is not the case.

The media often have their own kind of credibility. An appearance on national television may give someone an air of authority as an expert that he previously did not have. Receiving a link to a YouTube video from a trusted friend is more likely to persuade you to watch the video than if you received it from someone you did not know. The media play such a role in creating and establishing reputations of famous people that now there are many celebrities who are known simply for being celebrities, not for notable singing, acting, or artistic careers.

Underlying all this is the notion that mediated communication has some effect on our thoughts that can lead to changes in behavior. Although the **direct effects model** of media influence has been largely disproved, there is still a lurking sense that media can influence the public in some way. From this assumption, it is further assumed that media-based communications campaigns can be strategically designed to produce the kind of attitude and behavior shifts that are desired by persuaders.

Jade Goody used her fame as a reality TV star in the UK to publicize the need for women to test for cervical cancer, which she eventually died from.

direct effects model

A model of mass communication that says that media has direct and measurable effects upon audiences, such as encouraging them to buy products or become violent.

Advertising

Advertising is an ancient form of human communication generally designed to inform or persuade members of the public with regard to some product or service. In the modern age, advertising has taken its basic shape as sponsored, or paid-for, communication designed to inform and persuade the receiver of a message to buy a good or service, to accept a point of view, or to act in some fashion desired by the sender of the commercial message.

Print and electronic media have developed around this advertising model and in effect are in the business of selling mass audiences to advertisers who wish to reach them. From an advertiser's perspective, the media exist primarily as the means to gather an audience. However, many communications professionals, although recognizing an element of truth in this view, would counter that audiences will not gather if media content is not interesting, useful, or entertaining to them in some way.

Media organizations determine how much they can charge advertisers for space in their publication or airtime on their station based on the number of audience members reached or delivered to the advertiser. In broadcasting, this number is called the **rating**. In print and online media, it is called the **CPM**, or **cost per thousand** audience members. The online model is still evolving, however, and CPM may include the cost per thousand page views or unique visitors to

advertising

An ancient form of human communication generally designed to inform or persuade members of the public with regard to some product or service.

rating

Used in broadcast media to explain the number of households that watched a particular show.

cost per thousand [CPM]

The standard unit for measuring advertising rates for publications, based on circulation.

a site or web pages. In **performance-based advertising**, also used online, advertisers only pay for results of an advertisement, such as actual click-throughs to the advertiser's site, rather than the total page views a site has. One of the largest areas of online advertising has become **search engine marketing**, discussed in more detail later.

Advertising rates within media or specific media vehicles vary as well according to the size and quality of the target audience. In radio, for example, the most expensive time to purchase advertising is "a.m. and p.m. drive time." These are the morning and afternoon prime radio time slots for advertising and programming, when audiences are at their peak. An advertiser for a youth-oriented product may choose to show its commercial on prime-time MTV rather than a late-night slot on a network because, although the viewing audience is smaller than on a broadcast network, it is a more targeted audience that is more likely to want the product.

▼ THE HISTORICAL DEVELOPMENT OF ADVERTISING

In its earliest form, advertising was conducted as face-to-face, word-of-mouth communication in which buyers and sellers negotiated for the best bartered arrangement for a good or service. In ancient Egypt advertisements for products and services were written on papyrus and posted in common, public areas for passersby to see. The advent of the printing press in the fifteenth century gave rise to advertising in mass-communication settings, usually in the form of posters, flyers, or broadsheets. Broadsheet advertisements were a popular technique to attract people to emigrate to the New World. Colonists in the eighteenth and nineteenth centuries could obtain information from advertising about everything from where to buy groceries and patent medicines to when a ship was sailing.

Greater Prominence of Advertising

By the mid-1800s, advertising had become a mainstay for U.S. firms marketing their products and services. With the advent of the penny press, newspaper publishers relied more heavily on advertising revenue to make up for the lost revenues in subscription income. Advertisements became more prominent and were designed to stand out better from surrounding editorial content. Individuals also used advertising to promote their unique services. In 1856, publisher Robert Bonner ran the first full-page advertisement in a newspaper to promote his own literary paper, the *New York Ledger*.[1] At this time there were no standards in advertising, and medicinal advertisers often made extravagant and untrue claims as to the curative powers of the products they were selling.

The early twentieth century brought the rise of mass-produced, packaged goods and the automobile industry. Today, the automobile industry is the largest advertiser, followed by retail, business, and consumer services. Advertising for cigarettes and other tobacco products grew during the twentieth century, but not without criticism. In 1919, the magazine *Printer's Ink* warned against "an

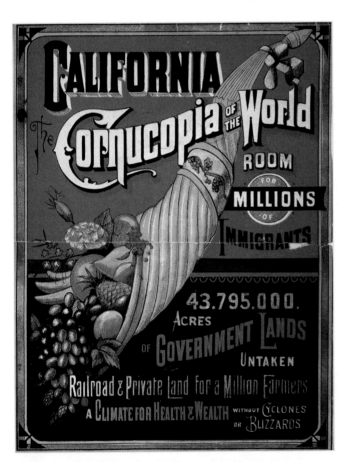

Advertising was used heavily, early in American history, to attract settlers to new lands.

insidious campaign to create women smokers," in reaction to the portrayal of women smoking in cigarette ads.

Development of the Advertising Agency

Early advertisers bought newspaper space and primarily targeted local audiences. It was not until the 1860s that advertising went national via nationally distributed monthly magazines.

Among the most successful early sellers of newspaper advertising space was Volney B. Palmer, who created both the first advertising agency in 1841 and the long-standing business model for the ad-agency industry. Palmer provided his advertising clients with circulation data, gave them copies of the ads, and deducted an **ad-agency commission** from the advertising fee to the publication as compensation for his effort.

The advertising business grew quickly as the penny press grew into a mass-circulation medium. By the 1860s, there were more than twenty advertising agencies

ad-agency commission

A percentage amount of the cost of an advertisement that is taken by the advertising agency that helped create and sell the ad.

Advertising in the early twentieth century helped make it acceptable for women to smoke cigarettes.

in New York City. N. W. Ayer & Partners, an advertising agency founded in 1869 by Francis Wayland Ayer, bought Palmer's firm, and the trend toward consolidation of the advertising business had begun. Ayer built on Palmer's basic media billing model, which charged clients a fee for placing ads in newspapers and magazines, and he established a standardized ad-agency commission: 15 percent of the total media billings.

N. W. Ayer also set the standard for creative services, with some of the most well-known ad slogans of the twentieth century, including the De Beers tagline "A diamond is forever," AT&T's "Reach out and touch someone," and Camel cigarettes' "I'd walk a mile for a Camel." N. W. Ayer & Partners is now part of Bcom3 Group, Inc., one of the world's largest advertising firms.

The new electronic media in the twentieth century drew heavily on the resources of the advertising industry, which effectively used radio and television to promote a wide variety of products and services to audiences throughout the United States and internationally. Television quickly surpassed print media as the main vehicle for reaching a national advertising market.

Growth of Commercial Television

There was never any widespread debate on whether television should be publicly funded or run on a commercial basis, as there had been in the early days of radio. Three of the four early TV networks were affiliated with the radio networks, and it was assumed that television would be supported by advertising just as radio was. The questions raised were not about whether to support television through advertising but about the best way to do it.

Commercials quickly became a mainstay on television. The year 1948 established an early high watermark for advertising, with 933 sponsors buying TV time—an increase of 515 percent over 1947. Considering the relatively small number of television sets sold at the time, this shows how eager advertisers were to reach mass audiences in the new medium. *Variety* reported in 1957 that during a typical week, viewers saw 420 commercials totaling five hours, eight minutes. In the early days of television, advertisers often sponsored whole shows and had their names included as part of show titles, such as *Texaco Star Theater*.

The Television Bureau of Advertising was also launched in the mid-1950s, responding to the emergence of television as the leading medium for advertising. The bureau is a not-for-profit trade association of America's broadcast-television industry and provides a variety of tools and resources to support the use of television as an advertising medium.

Tony Schwartz was a master of audiovisual techniques in advertising.

One of the most talented advertising professionals of the audiovisual realm was Tony Schwartz, who died in 2008. Schwartz had a career in advertising spanning most of the twentieth century. He was the master of using implied messages to their greatest effect. He achieved perhaps his greatest fame in the realm of political advertising for a spot that ran in 1964 known harmlessly as "the Daisy Spot," which cleverly implied that Republican presidential candidate Barry Goldwater, known as a war hawk, would likely get the United States embroiled in a nuclear war. Political communication scholar Kathleen Hall Jamieson considers the Daisy Spot to be among the most powerful political ads ever aired.[2]

Commercial developments have continued to reshape the TV landscape. In the 1960s, ABC extended the station break between programs from thirty to forty seconds in order to increase its profits, and other networks soon followed suit. Within a few years the breaks had become even longer, and standard commercial lengths had reached one minute.

Popular stars and athletes are often used to help sell products, getting lucrative sponsorship deals from companies.

By 1971, the networks had further increased profits by cutting the standard commercial length from sixty seconds to thirty seconds without reducing rates a corresponding 50 percent. Networks began the practice of advertising "piggybacking," or running messages for two related products from one company in the same one-minute commercial.

In 1969, New York's WOR-TV became the first station to air a program made up of exclusively commercial messages. This is called paid programming, or an **infomercial**. With the growth in cable channels and need to fill programming time, along with the smaller audiences cable attracts, there has been a rise in infomercials.

Also in 1969, the U.S. Supreme Court applied the **Fairness Doctrine** to cigarette advertising, giving antismoking groups access to "equal time" on the air to reply to tobacco commercials. The FCC also issued a Notice of Proposed Rulemaking to ban cigarette ads on TV and radio, as Congress debated the issue. Tobacco companies finally agreed to stop advertising cigarettes on the air. In 1970, a congressional ban on radio and TV cigarette advertising took effect, costing the broadcast business roughly $220 million in advertising.

The hard-liquor industry had a voluntary ban on TV advertising for sixty years, although that ban began breaking down in 2001 when NBC ran a vodka ad on late-night television. The ad drew such a backlash that NBC stopped airing the ad soon afterward. In February 2009, Absolut vodka broke the voluntary ban and ran an ad during the Grammy Awards, which also drew heated reactions from a number of groups. This did not stop Absolut from continuing to advertise, however, or other hard-liquor manufacturers from following with their ads. Today, commercials for hard liquor can frequently be seen during prime time and often target an audience in their twenties or early thirties.

Commercialization of the Internet

Although today we are accustomed to a range of advertisements on the Web, with new ones seemingly created almost every month, the fact is the Internet began as a resolutely noncommercial space. It was created, using taxpayers' money, by engineers and computer scientists who were more motivated by learning and the

infomercial

Also called paid programming, this is a thirty- or sixty-minute television show that seeks to sell a product and that usually involves a celebrity spokesperson and testimony from customers about how good the product is.

Fairness Doctrine

Adopted by the FCC in 1969, it required broadcasters to seek out and present all sides of a controversial issue they were covering. It was discarded by the FCC in 1987.

communication potential for the Internet than by profit, and several years went by before commercialism wedged its way in.

The first email marketing message, commonly called **spam**, after the processed meat (though the inspiration for the name came from a Monty Python comedy sketch that uses the term), was sent on May 3, 1978, by DEC, a now-defunct computer maker. The message, to all of four hundred people on ARPANET, the precursor to the Internet, now seems almost quaint in comparison to the billions of spam messages sent worldwide today. Immigration lawyers Canter and Siegel sent an email message advertising their services to over six thousand Usenet users in 1994. Despite a harsh backlash from the online community, it is widely held to be the start of the commercialization of the Internet.

The same year, the first advertisements on the Web appeared on Hotwired, the online version of *Wired* magazine. Hotwired offered space on the website to fourteen advertisers in the form of the now-familiar **banner ad**. However, because online connection speeds were slow in 1994, the ads could not be large graphics and therefore remained fairly small and primarily HTML text.

Today, increased bandwidth has allowed multimedia ads to appear, and advertisers have looked into new types of advertising to further attract consumers' attention. Studies that have tracked consumers online have shown that banner ads have a very low **click-through rate (CTR)**, meaning a very low percentage of users—less than 1 percent—actually click on them.

▼ **THE RISE OF BRANDING**

Developing along with the growing importance of advertising in its various forms, and intertwined with advertising, is the idea of the brand. **Branding** refers to the process of creating in the consumer's mind a clear identity for a particular company's product or trademark. Branding via advertising developed in the 1890s and early 1900s as companies sought to differentiate their products from others in an increasingly cluttered and competitive marketplace. With little differentiation between similar products in terms of what they provided or ingredients they contained, the only way to appear different was to create a memorable brand, or identity, among consumers.

To establish an image of one brand's uniqueness, a catchy slogan and distinctive visual identity are created and then advertised across multiple media, so the desired audience segment or target group gets frequent exposure to the product. Among the first to successfully do this was Campbell's soup, which used the artwork of Grace Weidersein in 1904 depicting "The Campbell's Kids." Campbell's includes Weidersein's artwork in its advertising to this day. Another highly successful advertising campaign was launched in 1970 to promote Coca-Cola. In that year, "Coke" introduced its "I'd Like to Teach the World to Sing" commercial, and the song became an instant hit. Coca-Cola sold a million records featuring a version of the popular advertising jingle.

Brands are especially powerful among competitors that are very similar. Pepsi has traditionally been behind Coke in sales, and in the 1970s Pepsi did a double-blind taste test (neither the tester or the person running the test knew which was Coke or Pepsi) and found that surprisingly people preferred the taste of Pepsi over Coke if they did not know the brands. The subsequent advertising campaign touting this helped increase Pepsi's sales while Coke saw sales decline. This sparked Coke to introduce a new, sweeter formula—New Coke—to the market, only to have a strong backlash from loyal Coke drinkers. Within three months, New Coke

spam

Unwanted email sent out by advertisers as a mass mailing.

banner ad

An advertisement across the top of a website and the original form of advertising on the Web.

click-through rate [CTR]

Rate at which people click on an online advertisement to access more information.

branding

The process of creating in the consumer's mind a clear identity for a particular company's product, logo, or trademark.

Me 2.0: The Guide to Branding Yourself

Branding is not only important to multinational companies, but it has become important to individuals as well, says personal-branding guru Dan Schawbel, author of *Me 2.0: Build a Powerful Brand to Achieve Career Success.*

According to Schawbel and dozens of leading technology thinkers he has interviewed, creating a strong personal brand will help define and differentiate the new employee from the competition.

He offers a four-step process for creating a personal brand—discover, create, communicate, and maintain—and includes techniques for using social-media tools to help with the brand.

Schawbel practices what he preaches to the Gen-Y demographic that is his primary audience. His Personal Branding Blog® is ranked as one of the top one hundred marketing blogs and is virtually a case study in itself of how to maximize promotional opportunities by using relevant social-media tools.

It is perhaps no surprise that the age of personal branding has come, given the trends in strategic communications and digital media in recent years. The question that employers may likely face as personally branded potential employees enter the workforce is the same question we typically ask about our corporate brands—how well does image fit reality? When potential employers search your name online, will they find Facebook pictures of you partying it up and posts filled with profanity, or will they find a professional-looking page that highlights your skills and accomplishments?

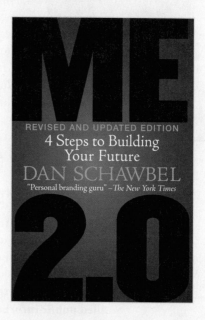

was yanked from store shelves and the company restored its original taste formula, calling it Coca-Cola Classic.

Some advertising campaigns have been so successful (some would say too successful) that their brand names have become synonymous with the product itself. For example, advertising for Kleenex (introduced in 1924) has branded the product so well that many consumers consider "Kleenex" simply the generic name for facial tissue. This can be both good and bad for the advertiser. On the one hand, this level of branding means that consumers will have extremely high brand-name awareness, but on the other hand, they may go shopping for what they are calling "Kleenex" but actually buy another brand of facial tissue.

Brands are almost always trademarked, and companies can sue individuals or other companies if they believe someone is infringing on their trademark. They can claim that the copycat brand is taking away business from the company by confusing consumers and perhaps hurting the company's reputation in the process if the competitor has inferior products. There are cases of companies zealously protecting their brands, such as Coca-Cola forcing a small café in a remote town in Yunnan Province, China, to change its name from Coca-Cola Café. Yet there are many other

Brand knockoffs are widespread, especially in Asia.

cases in which companies have attempted to associate themselves with a more famous brand by using a logo, colors, or name that is very similar to the famous brand. The cheap electronics maker Coby, with a font similar to Sony, is one example, as is the East Coast fast food chain Kennedy Fried Chicken.

Protecting a brand is not only about enforcing intellectual property, it is also about the value of a company. Brands have become so important that as much as 70 percent of a company's value may be in its brand rather than in its physical property such as factories or products. Table 11-1 shows the estimated brand valuation of some major companies, and the percentage of brand valuation compared to total estimated value. For some company mergers, "buying the brand" may be a major motivating factor in the decision. Brands will become even more important in the digital age, especially in the media industries.

▼ SELLING PRODUCTS, SELLING IDEAS

social marketing

The practice of using advertising and marketing techniques to persuade people about changing bad or destructive behaviors or adopting good behaviors.

public information campaign

Media program funded by the government and designed to achieve some social goal, or what might be called social engineering.

Just as brands can represent a certain image or even lifestyle, the techniques of advertising can be used for more than just selling products or services: they can be used to sell ideas or even political candidates. **Social marketing** applies the lessons learned from years of advertising campaigns and theories of persuasive communications to getting the public to change behaviors for the better through what are called **public information campaigns**.

Social-marketing campaigns often face an uphill battle in changing attitudes, for a number of reasons. First, the behaviors that social marketers are seeking to change, such as drinking or smoking, are often considered fun or cool by those engaging in them. Second, determining which advertising channels and types of messages will be most effective for the targeted group can be difficult. Third, ethical

TABLE 11-1

Top Six Companies and Their Brand Valuations

COMPANY	2011 BRAND VALUE ($ BILLION)	BRAND CONTRIBUTION TO MARKET CAPITALIZATION OF PARENT COMPANY (%)
Coca-Cola	71.86	47
IBM	69.90	39
Microsoft	59.08	25
Google	55.31	29
GE	42.81	22
McDonald's	35.39	43

Source: "Best Global Brands, 2011," Interbrand, May 17, 2012. Retrieved May 17, 2012, from http://www.interbrand.com/en/best-global-brands/best-global-brands-2008/best-global-brands-2011.aspx. "The Coca-Cola Company Market Cap," YCharts, May 17, 2012. Retrieved May 17, 2012, from http://ycharts.com/companies/KO/market_cap.

Not everyone who gets hit by a drunk driver dies.

Jacqueline Saburido was 20 years old when the car she was riding in was hit by a drunk driver. Today, at 23, she is still working to put her life back together.
Learn more at www.TexasDWI.org

DON'T DRINK & DRIVE

Texas Department of Public Safety · Texas Alcoholic Beverage Commission · Texans Standing Tall · Partnership for a Drug-free Texas · Texas Commission on Alcohol and Drug Abuse

Fear appeals are meant to shock or scare viewers into realizing that they should change their behaviors.

questions can sometimes be raised when it comes to which group is deciding what exactly a "prosocial" message is and why other groups may not be targeted. Finally, it can be very hard to determine how effective a social-marketing campaign has been, as its effects will generally not be immediately seen and there may be larger sociocultural forces at work that weaken whatever media messages the target audience sees.

In order to shock the intended audience, some social-marketing campaigns will use **fear appeals** with the hope of changing behavior. Television ads featuring former smokers who have had surgery for throat or mouth cancer, or graphic images of automobile accidents caused by drunk driving, are examples of fear appeals. Fear appeals can be tricky, however. Not only may graphic images offend some viewers, but they may also not be effective for young people who think "that will never happen to me."

One of the more effective social-marketing campaigns in recent years has been the crime-prevention campaign that used the tagline "take a bite out of crime" and featured a cartoon dog, McGruff, dressed as a detective. Using **public service announcements (PSAs)**, the series of advertisements covering a range of crime-related issues were widely aired and seen in different media channels. Various surveys

fear appeals

A type of advertising technique that attempts to scare the audience in order to persuade them, such as antismoking ads that show disfigured former smokers.

public service announcement [PSA]

Advertising-like messages for which the media donate time or space to organizations with a worthy purpose that ostensibly benefits the public.

classified advertising

A type of advertising usually found in print media, especially newspapers but also in some magazines, and now increasingly online, that consists of messages posted by individuals and organizations to sell specific goods or services.

display advertising

A type of advertising in print media that usually consists of illustrations or images and text and that can occupy a small section of a page, a full page, or multiple pages. Because of their high costs, display ads are usually bought by large companies or organizations.

advertorial

A type of display advertisement that is created to look like an article within the publication, although most publications have the words "advertisement" or "paid advertisement" in tiny print somewhere nearby.

have shown a high awareness of the campaign and its anticrime points by adults and children, accompanied by a rise in crime-prevention measures like special locks on doors and windows and security lights.

Social-marketing campaigns play an important role in educating people in developing countries about a range of issues, including safe sex and the risk of AIDS, proper sanitizing techniques to ensure clean water and food and thus prevent disease, and other ways to help the general standard of living. Because of high illiteracy rates and limited access to mass media, such campaigns must use visual symbols in powerful yet easily understandable ways.

▼ ADVERTISING CHANNELS

Advertising can of course be seen in a variety of media formats, or channels, and can even include some types that we may not normally consider as mass communications but that are nevertheless important, such as outdoor advertising or direct mail.

Each channel has certain characteristics that have influenced how advertising is done, how it is measured, and what types of advertisements work best. In addition, some channels are more effective at reaching certain types of audiences than others, though of course the type of product or service being advertised also plays a role in determining which audience to target. Here we will look at some of the traditional advertising channels, all of which are still being used, and later we will look at how online advertising is changing some of these.

Print Media

In newspapers and magazines, commercial messages come in either of two forms, **classified advertising** or **display advertising**. Classifieds are short messages appearing together in a special section and posted by individuals and organizations in order to sell specific goods or services.

Classified ads tend to be small and use only text. Because customers pay by the word, or pay a rate up to a certain word limit, messages are usually short and abbreviations are used whenever possible. Despite their small size, the large numbers of classifieds found in most papers have made up a significant portion of newspapers' advertising revenue. Online classifieds, auction sites, and discount sites such as Craigslist, eBay, Groupon, and Living Social have greatly hurt the revenues newspapers get from classified ads.

Display ads are much larger, anywhere from one-eighth of a page to a full page or occasionally foldouts with multiple pages. Display ads often contain images or other graphic elements that help them stand out from other ads.

Costs of running display ads vary by both size and location of the ad on the page and within the publication (back-cover placement is usually the most expensive), as well as whether color is used. If advertisers agree to advertise multiple times, they are able to negotiate rates or receive extra benefits like free color.

A type of display ad that is created to look like an actual article in the publication is called an **advertorial** and usually has tiny print on either the top or the bottom of the page that says "paid advertisement."

Creating persuasive messages can be especially difficult in countries with low literacy rates.

Publishing companies create a **rate card**, which lists the various advertising rates based on size and placement of an ad, as well as any discounts available for multiple ads. Usually rate cards are simply used as rough guides, as big advertisers have much leeway to negotiate advertising rates down in the highly competitive print-media world.

Electronic Media

Advertisements on radio or television are called commercials, or "spots," and typically run for thirty seconds. Although the length of time for commercials has gone down and audiences continue to fragment, advertising costs on electronic media are generally high compared to advertising in print media. A primary reason is the larger audience electronic media can command compared to most print outlets. Even large-circulation magazines of over a million readers reach an audience considered relatively small by network-television standards.

Paid programming, or infomercials, are typically thirty- or sixty-minute programs in which a product is demonstrated or promoted for purchase, oftentimes with endorsement from a celebrity or from satisfied consumers, who are typically paid or otherwise compensated. Often actors are used to portray customers.

Subliminal advertising has been a subject of controversy for some time. Subliminal advertising supposedly works by flashing messages or images very briefly to produce an unconscious effect on the viewer. Despite early fears, there has been no firm proof that subliminal advertising has any effect at all. Even so, it is illegal and no advertisers have ever admitted to using subliminal advertising.

Another way advertisers get their products noticed is through **product placement**—having products displayed in a show or used by the characters. This practice also happens in the movies and is increasingly used by advertisers. Product placement has become more important recently as digital video recorders (DVRs) allow viewers to skip commercials, giving advertisers a chance to include their products within a show's programming content.

rate card

A listing of advertising rates by size, placement, and other characteristics, such as whether ads are black and white or full color. Frequency discounts are also usually offered, and the listed rates are usually negotiable, especially for large advertisers.

subliminal advertising

Persuasive messages that supposedly happen below the level of consciousness, such as quickly flashing an image or word on a screen. Despite concerns about subliminal advertising, there has been no firm proof that it works.

product placement

The practice of advertisers paying to have actual products used or shown prominently in television shows and movies.

Product placement has become a more widely used advertising technique, especially as viewers are better able to skip commercials.

outdoor advertising

Billboards and other forms of
advertising such as on buses or
taxis that are done in public.

There is some debate on how effective product placement is in terms of persuading viewers to buy or use a product. Critics argue that most viewers do not notice that product placement is happening and that a product is being advertised, while proponents say that that is exactly what makes it an effective technique.

Perhaps the most famous case of success with product placement occurred with the blockbuster movie *E.T.* The filmmakers approached M&M's to be able to use the famous candy as the snack of choice for E.T., but M&M's refused. So the filmmakers used a new candy in the film, Reese's Pieces, and sales of the candy shot up as the film became a global hit.

Outdoor

From billboards to store signs to ads on taxis, buses, and bus stops, advertising messages bombard the public more than most people realize simply because **outdoor advertising** is so ubiquitous. Even wearing brand-name clothing effectively makes the wearer a walking advertisement—and what is good from a company standpoint is that the consumer is paying *it* to advertise its product through purchasing the clothing!

Store signs are some of the oldest forms of public advertising, although their reach is limited to people passing by. Increasingly, municipalities are allowing corporate sponsorship of public vehicles and spaces to help shore up government budgets. Low-power video monitors are allowing advertisements to appear in new public spaces such as above cash registers or in elevators, with news content delivered alongside.

Interactive outdoor advertising is gaining prominence and will continue to grow. Floor-based displays in airports or malls react to activities like footsteps, creating interesting games that people can play and others can watch—all the while engaging with an advertisement.

Interactive advertising appears
increasingly in public spaces.

Direct Mail

Direct mail marketing, commonly called "junk mail" by its recipients, includes ads for everything from lower insurance rates to credit card offers to pleas to donate to various charities or subscribe to magazines. Some companies use tactics to make it appear that the recipient has won a drawing or lottery and needs to send in the material to claim the prize.

Direct mail can be a very effective tool for advertisers, partly because the material is being sent to a very specific audience. Many organizations rent their subscriber lists to potential advertisers on a per-thousand basis, and the more detailed demographic data that is needed, the higher the cost for list rental. Advertisers then use these lists to send very targeted messages. The list owners often seed their lists with some false names to ensure that list renters are only using the list one time. Some savvy citizens are using similar techniques to see who is selling their name: subscribing to a magazine using a pet's name, for example. Subsequent mailings that use the pet's name are an indication that the magazine rented the name to other groups.

Telemarketing involves calling people at home to offer them such things as telephone services or new credit cards. Many people find the calls intrusive and annoying and actively screen calls with an answering machine or with functions like caller ID. Telemarketers use a thoroughly prepared script when giving their sales pitches, complete with prepared responses to a range of expected answers.

The Telephone Consumer Protection Act of 1991 is a federal law that lays out strict guidelines on what times telemarketers may call and that allows people to be removed from companies' call lists. Some states have implemented "Do Not Call"

▶ Going Viral

Viral videos have become one of the world's most persuasive forms of online media. In March 2012, the record-breaking video *Kony 2012* generated 112 million views worldwide within one week of its debut on Vimeo and then YouTube.[3,4] The nonprofit group Invisible Children saw its thirty-minute documentary-style video break the previous records held by U.K. *X Factor* contestant Susan Boyle singing "I Dreamed a Dream," and Justin Bieber's "Baby."[5] By comparison, it took Old Spice's *Responses* viral video five months to reach 70 million views in 2010.

Kony 2012 seeks the arrest of alleged Ugandan war criminal Joseph Kony. The video's accuracy has been questioned, and whether the video will achieve the group's objective is unclear. However, it has received recognition by the White House. Mashable reports the *Kony 2012* video received within three days of its release 200 video responses, which ran six minutes on average, and more than 500,000 online comments.

Benefiting from the goodwill of a viral video is also a possibility. In March of 2012, eighty-five-year-old *Grand Forks Herald* (North Dakota) newspaper columnist Marilyn Hagerty wrote about her town's new Olive Garden restaurant.[6] As reported later in the *Wall Street Journal,* Hagerty was "too busy to bother with blogs, Facebook or Twitter,"[7] but that didn't stop her column from becoming the talk of social media. When she was interviewed on ABCNews.com, her video went viral.[8]

It's unclear whether business has picked up at the Olive Garden in Grand Forks. However, Marilyn Hagerty's column certainly increased traffic to the *Grand Forks Herald* website, and she's become a social media sensation.

These are only two examples of how viral videos online have helped change the equation involving advertising, public relations, and the public.

registries that serve the same purpose. An improvement in the act in 2008 keeps numbers permanently on the registry, so that people do not have to renew their phone numbers every few years anymore.

▼ ADVERTISING IN A DIGITAL WORLD

Traditionally, 70 percent or more of commercial-media revenues have come from advertising. Media organizations are now seeing their economic foundation transformed by digital technology. Advertisers have more ability to track consumers and to see what kinds of advertisements work best. They are also finding that many traditional advertising techniques do not work well on the Web. Changes in technology and in user behavior online further complicate the picture.

One of the key aspects of the Web compared to other forms of media is the ability to personalize the user experience, and this is just as important for advertisers as it is for media-content companies. Almost all websites leave **cookies** on users' computers, which are small programs loaded on a computer that identify specific users and make it easy for companies to see who is visiting their site and where they are going afterward. Any time a website "remembers" a visitor, as when

cookie

Information that a website puts on a user's local hard drive so that it can recognize when that computer accesses the website again. Cookies are what allow for conveniences like password recognition and personalization.

someone registers for a site and then returns days later, is because of a cookie. Advertisers also use cookies that are placed in their ads, so are able to track users' behavior on their own. These are called third-party cookies, as the cookies are not from the content provider, such as an online newspaper.

Through the use of cookies and Web-analytics programs, companies are able to tell what page someone came from before arriving at a page with an ad, how long the person spent on that page, whether the person is a first-time or returning customer, and where he or she went after viewing that page. They can even tell what computer operating system a user has, what type of Web browser, and often approximately where the user lives.

Cookies are just one of the new and unique techniques that are being used by media companies and advertisers in the digital world. Even with the development of many new technologies and social media today, some of the "old" digital media still can be remarkably effective.

Email Marketing

Until the rise of social media sites such as Facebook and Twitter, email was the most used application on the Internet and continues to be an incredibly powerful tool for advertising, despite the rapid growth of spam. Like direct mail, email can provide highly targeted audiences. Even better, consumers have the choice to **opt in** to receive emails, showing their willingness to hear from certain companies.

Email also has the advantage of being cheap to produce and send, especially if the message is only text and does not require any design or graphics. The choice between text or graphics is a difficult one for email marketers. Text-only messages can be seen by anyone but are ugly and can be lost in the clutter of other emails. Emails with images may not appear correctly if the recipient has refused to allow such emails—making any design work for naught.

Advertisements placed within emails by the free online services, such as Yahoo! Mail, Hotmail, or Gmail, are also lucrative for these companies. Google uses software that scans each email sent using Gmail and, based on the words found in the email, inserts ads that it deems most relevant to the topic.

Banner Ads

In the early days of the Web most online advertising tended to follow the traditional advertising formats—particularly the display-ad model commonly found in print. Called banner advertising, these online ads went across the top of a page like a banner and could typically be clicked on to take the user to the advertiser's website.

Today, there are a variety of shapes and sizes of banner ads, including tower ads that take advantage of the tendency for users to scroll down. Such ads may also contain interactive quizzes, video, or other animation.

Because of the tracking capabilities of the Web, it was learned that banner ads generally had a very low click-through rate. In other words, only a small percentage of visitors to a specific page would actually click on the ads. This caused advertisers to doubt the effectiveness of banner ads and seemed to put the budding online advertising industry in a stall.

Pop-Ups, Interstitials, Superstitials, and Video

It was hoped that pop-up ads would help save advertising online, but they are not without their own weaknesses. There are two main types of pop-up ads. One is the traditional pop-up, which appears in a new window when a website is opened, and can be either an **interstitial ad** or a **superstitial ad**. Interstitial ads have

opt in

The practice of letting consumers choose to receive mailings or marketing material by having them check a box on a website, usually when registering for the site.

interstitial ad

An online advertisement that opens in a new window from the one the user was in.

superstitial ad

An online advertisement that covers part of the existing screen or moves over part of it without opening a new window.

proven unpopular among users because they must close the ad browser window in order to see the website they originally wanted to see. To get around this, some advertisers have their pages open to take up most of a page rather than the whole screen. There are also multiple interstitial ads, in which more than one browser window opens, forcing the user to close multiple windows.

Superstitial ads have become more widespread, partly because they are perceived as less obtrusive, and they allow for ads to be created using a variety of multimedia programs and effects. Ads that show up and crawl across a screen or appear in a corner are examples of superstitial ads.

Ads in videos are still being experimented with, as the Web has only recently become much more video based. It became clear quite quickly, however, that online users did not want to watch a standard

Superstitial ads on websites have become more widespread, partly because they are not as obtrusive as other forms of online advertising.

thirty-second commercial before watching a short video, so when there are commercials before a video runs, they tend to be ten or fifteen seconds at most and are often shorter. Some sites such as YouTube have been experimenting with overlays at the bottom of screens, like the ones network television uses to advertise upcoming shows.

Classifieds and Auction Sites

As noted earlier, classifieds online have taken a large chunk of the revenue from newspapers. Online classifieds have several advantages over classifieds in print media. First, since there are no space limitations as with a print paper, there is little need to squeeze text to fit within some predefined word and cost limit. Second, geographic limitations are no longer an issue (at least for some products or services), as long as what is being advertised can be shipped or mailed. This vastly increases the potential audience.

Auction sites have also become popular for many of the same reasons, starting with the rise of eBay. Seller rating and review systems, easy online payment methods, and a large number of users at any one time selling and buying have created a thriving marketplace that has proven to be especially useful for small businesses or those wanting to work from home. The popularity of eBay has of course brought many unusual items for sale, including a British man in 2008 who put his entire life for sale after a bitter divorce. The winning bid was about $380,000, quite a bit short of what he was asking.

Search Engine Ads

Search engine advertising has become one of the most important vehicles for advertisers in recent years and promises to only grow more. It is based largely on people's use of search engines as a primary means of finding content. This has made search engines such as Google, Bing, and Yahoo! very important as sites that receive many visitors.

There are two main methods of search engine advertising: search engine optimization (SEO) and search engine marketing (SEM). In broad terms, they could be considered as unpaid and paid forms of advertising, respectively, yet they have the same goal: to show up as the first entry in a search engine search.

SEO uses a variety of techniques that involve website design, keywords, and links to try to raise the rankings of a website in a search. In SEM, the advertiser either pays a search engine company for a sponsored link, which is usually clearly labeled as such (with a colored panel or the words "sponsored links"), or buys keywords that are sold at auction. If an advertiser is the highest bidder for a term like "flowers," it pays the search engine company a set amount every time its site is clicked on when that search term is used.

Behavioral Advertising

Behavioral advertising relies on tracking user behavior as they visit websites and then inserting banner ads on similar topics on subsequent websites being visited. For advertisers, it promises to give users more relevant ads when they are on the Web, but many people feel like it is an invasion of privacy. The rapid growth of this area of advertising has drawn the attention of consumer groups and the government, who claim that some companies are being deceptive.

WEB LINK
FTC
www.ftc.gov

In 2011, the Federal Trade Commission filed a case against Chitika, a marketing firm specializing in search-targeted advertising. The FTC alleged that the company was using deceptive opt-out mechanisms, the system by which users agree or disagree to let an advertiser track them using cookies. Rather than opting users out of behavioral tracking after 10 years, as stated in their online policy, Chitika's opt-out system was expiring after only 10 days. The government won the case and forbade Chitika from using misleading statements about their opt-out policy and required the company to link all of its online advertising to a functioning opt-out mechanism in the future.

Viral Marketing

Because the Web is such an excellent distribution medium, some of the most successful advertising online has been without the use of advertising agencies or expensive marketing campaigns. Rather, it has come in the form of **viral marketing**, sometimes called buzz marketing, guerrilla marketing, or word-of-mouth (WOM) marketing.

viral marketing

Spreading news and information about media content through word of mouth, usually via online discussion groups, chats, and emails, without utilizing traditional advertising and marketing methods.

Viral marketing relies on promoting a product, service, or brand through natural communication channels online, in which people spread a message because they want to, not because they are being paid to. Humorous or strange videos often work best for this, but such videos are not always a good fit for all brands, as many viral videos have an unpolished, amateurish quality to them that is part of their appeal. It is also notoriously difficult to determine what type of content will be viral and what will not.

▼ THE ADVERTISING BUSINESS

The advertising industry suffered along with the rest of the economy during the recession that started in late 2007, as companies reduced their advertising budgets at the same time they cut back production and laid off workers. The total ad spend for 2010 in the United States was $131.1 billion, up 6.5 percent from the previous year, according to Kantar Media. This reversed a decline in ad spending that had continued since 2007.

As Table 11-2 shows, cable TV sits atop the media food chain by ad spend. Until the late 1990s, each analog medium's relative share of total advertising revenue had stayed fairly constant. Network television had received the lion's share, most in the form of national advertising. Newspapers were second in total advertising revenues, most in the form of local retail and classified advertising. Magazines were third, with radio a distant fourth. Today, TV advertising in one form or another makes up nearly 50 percent of total ad spend by medium.

Internet advertising now is more than triple radio advertising as a percentage of total ad spend and is fast approaching the amount spent on newspaper advertising, which has been falling rapidly in the past few years. Internet ad spending continues to rise, and industry experts believe it will double its percentage of ad

TABLE 11-2

Ad Spending by Medium, 2009

MEDIUM	SHARE OF SPENDING (%)
Cable TV	22.90
Network TV	20.58
Local TV	16.43
National Magazines	15.01
Internet	6.87
Local Newspapers	5.72
Hispanic TV	2.66
Local Radio	2.46
Syndicated TV	2.18
Outdoor	1.64
National Newspapers	1.43
National Sunday Supplements	1.20
Network Radio	0.81
Local Magazines	0.10
Local Sunday Supplement	0.01
Coupon	0.00

Source: The Nielsen Company AdAcross, December 2009
(www.MarketingCharts.com)

spend within two years. Although advertisers are of course looking to advertise across mediums or channels, the fact is that an increase in ad spending in one medium, such as the Internet, generally means a decrease elsewhere, such as in newspapers. This has made it especially challenging for the main player in the advertising world today, the advertising agency.

▼ ADVERTISING AGENCIES

Advertising agencies are the foundation of much of the advertising business. They perform many important functions in helping create and sell advertising across all media, and they provide a vital link between media and the companies seeking to sell a product or service. There are more than five hundred advertising agencies in the United States, which employ more than seventy thousand people.

Advertising agencies have four main areas of operation:

1. Creative, which is the area of the business where advertising content is produced, with copywriters and others working under the direction of creative and art directors

2. Client management, which involves working with the client and is usually handled by account executives

3. Media buying, in which media planners and buyers determine and make the purchase of media time or space; the area that traditionally has produced agency revenues

4. Research, which traditionally involves the collection and analysis of data on consumer characteristics and media and purchase behaviors

Advertising campaigns for diamonds have helped make the industry a mainstay of romantic gifts.

Although traditional advertising firms still dominate the advertising landscape and have created interactive divisions, a number of Internet-original firms emerged in the late 1990s. Some have survived as boutique or specialized firms, but many have been bought by the larger agencies that need to add interactive expertise. This followed trends toward consolidation seen with traditional advertising agencies.

Today, most of the world's leading advertising agencies are owned by much larger advertising and media-services companies, and ninety of the top one hundred firms have international operations. Most of these firms also operate both advertising and public relations enterprises, making them what are called full-service companies. These types of firms handle all aspects of the communications business, from campaign planning to creative execution, media buying, and public relations. On the opposite end of the spectrum are boutique agencies, or small, specialty advertising agencies.

Table 11-3 presents data on the world's five largest advertising and media-services firms, ranked by their annual worldwide billing in 2009, and some of their advertising and public relations operations. WPP and Omnicom have remained the top two, but in 2009 Publicis Groupe moved up to third place from fourth. All of the ad agencies except for WPP and Dentsu lost revenues compared to 2008.

TABLE 11-3
World's Five Largest Advertising and Media-Services Companies

AGENCY	MAJOR SUBSIDIARY GROUPS	HEADQUARTERS	WORLDWIDE REVENUES, 2009 ($ BILLION)
WPP	Young & Rubicam Brands Ogilvy Group JWT Grey Group	London, UK	13.6
Omnicom	BBDO DDB Worldwide Communications Group TBWA Worldwide	New York, United States	11.72
Publicis Groupe	Publicis Leo Burnett Worldwide Saatchi & Saatchi	Paris, France	6.29
Interpublic	McCann World Group Draftfcb Lowe	New York, United States	6.03
Dentsu	Tokyo, Japan	3.13

Source: Advertising Age Agency Family Trees, 2010; Dentsu 2010 Annual Report

◣◤ Public Relations

Just as advertising agencies straddle the advertising and media worlds, public relations firms straddle the worlds of companies wishing to promote themselves and of media organizations who can widely distribute their messages. Public relations differs in one important respect from advertising in that public relations firms do not pay media companies to place their content in the media, like advertisers do with ads or commercials. Rather, one function of public relations professionals is to attempt to persuade various important gatekeepers, such as editors, journalists, or even influential bloggers, that there is newsworthy information about their client that should be published.

Public relations has been described and defined in many ways. To many journalists, it represents at best a necessary evil. To others, it is far worse: it is the enemy. Nevertheless, journalists rely heavily on the information public relations firms provide for stories. And to still others, public relations is viewed as a vital part of the three-way relationship among organizations, their publics, and the media. The term "public" refers to the many groups,

Puffery is a type of advertising that is allowed by the FTC based on the assumption that people do not take it as a statement of fact.

Advertising for children's toys usually portrays the toys as far more fun and exciting than they actually are.

organizations, and collectives with whom an organization or individual may have some sort of relationship. The role of the public in mass communication will be discussed in more detail in the final chapter on political communication.

Although "the public" is often used to refer to the general population, there are in fact many "publics" with whom an organization might be concerned. For example, a company has many relevant publics, including its employees, consumers, shareholders, activists (who might oppose certain corporate policies), regulators, and of course the media—the primary vehicle by which the general public hears about a company. When a company is in trouble or there is potentially damaging information about it, public relations professionals work to mitigate the negative stories. When there is good news, they seek to promote the news heavily to media outlets.

Public relations firms have been ideally positioned to understand some of the new interactive dynamics found in today's world of social media. Increasingly, public relations firms help companies navigate social media and provide guidance on policies such as having a Facebook page, talking with consumers on fan pages or Twitter, and guiding discussions with the public.

Edward L. Bernays, the late father of modern public relations, used to say that propaganda was better than impropaganda. The same might be said of public relations. It all depends on how it's done.

▼ THE HISTORICAL DEVELOPMENT OF PUBLIC RELATIONS

There are some who say public relations is the world's second-oldest profession, but the modern field of public relations has evolved rapidly and in unique ways that connect directly to the rise of mass communications and improvements in communications technologies.

Public relations as a separate, recognized professional field did not develop until the early twentieth century. Prior to that, a number of publishing activities that today we would put into separate categories of journalism or public relations were conducted with little sense of difference between them. Thomas Paine's influential pro-Revolution pamphlets in the 1770s, such as *Common Sense,* or the sympathetic writings in newspapers on the Boston Massacre, for example, would be considered public relations or even propaganda, by today's standards, rather than journalism.

During the nineteenth century and early twentieth century, the first stage of public relations emerged. It might best be called the age of **press agentry**. Press agentry refers to the practice of getting publicity in the press (or other media) for a client. As newspapers developed into a form of mass communications, getting publicity in the press as part of a news story meant that many readers could be exposed to a product or company without the company having to pay for an advertisement.

press agentry

The practice of getting media attention for a client, often by creating outrageous stunts that would attract journalists.

Press agentry flourished under the practice of Phineas Taylor "P. T." Barnum (1810–1891), the great showman and founder of the famous American circus, which he created in 1870. Barnum used various techniques to communicate with the public and had his greatest success with staged events, or publicity stunts, to attract attention. In the 1830s, Barnum entered the world of promotion, press manipulation, and show business.

Although the term had not yet been coined, it was former journalist Ivy Ledbetter Lee (1877–1934) who was perhaps the first true modern public relations practitioner. Lee was a master of managing the press. He once observed, "Crowds are led by symbols and phrases." He employed a variety of innovative techniques that are staples of modern public relations practice, including press conferences, staged events, and newsreels, which today are known as video news releases (VNRs).

One of Lee's most visible clients was John D. Rockefeller Sr., the founder of the Standard Oil Trust and the world's first billionaire, who managed his companies and employees ruthlessly, even by standards of the day. After Rockefeller had the Colorado state militia put down a miners' strike by killing dozens of miners, and women and children, Lee was hired to sway public opinion and manage the likely negative backlash, should the truth come out. Lee produced reports stating that a house fire that had killed women and children was started by

P. T. Barnum and Tom Thumb

an overturned stove, not by the militia, as was actually the case. In response, muckraking journalist Upton Sinclair, author of *The Jungle,* described Lee as "Poison Ivy."

During the years to follow, Lee continued to produce massive amounts of favorable press materials on John D. Rockefeller Sr. Among Lee's successes was his insistence on having photographs and newsreels taken showing Rockefeller handing out dimes to poor children wherever he went. Lee became legendary internationally for his ability to manipulate the media, and in the early 1930s the Nazis in Germany hired Lee to present a more favorable face for the "New Germany" in the United States.[9]

Press agentry features a wide spectrum of PR activities such as special events or stunts. These stunts have ranged from the spectacular to the sublime. In one case, debutantes were invited to march in the 1928 Easter Parade in New York City holding their "torches of freedom"—otherwise known as lit cigarettes—to help get media attention and thereby build public support for women smoking in public, at a time when society frowned upon it. The occasion was sponsored by the American Tobacco Company, manufacturer of Lucky Strike cigarettes, and created by a man many consider the founder of modern public relations, Edward Bernays.

Edward L. Bernays (1891–1995) managed some of the earliest and most famous public relations campaigns of the twentieth century. Trained during World War I as a member of the Foreign Press Bureau of the U.S. Committee on Public Information (CPI), essentially the propaganda arm of the U.S. government, Bernays was a nephew of psychologist Sigmund Freud and often dined with his famous uncle. Bernays mastered Freud's theories and in fact produced the first English-language translation of Freud's books. After the war, Bernays applied the principles of both Freudian psychology and social science, a then-budding field, to the strategic influence and shaping of public opinion. He went on to write a classic book titled *The Engineering of Consent.*

Arthur W. Page (1883–1960) was the vice president of public relations for AT&T from 1927 to 1946 and served on many boards of charities and other organizations. He was the first person in a public relations position to serve on the board of a major public corporation. Page helped create ethical guidelines for public relations with his Page Principles, such as "tell the truth," "prove it with action," and "listen to the customer." Today, the Arthur W. Page Society continues his work through a variety of educational programs, networking events, forums for PR executives, and sponsored research initiatives in the field of public relations.

▼ TRENDS IN THE DEVELOPMENT OF PUBLIC RELATIONS

One continuing trend as public relations has developed as a profession is the move away from assumptions that the mass audience is passive and mute and toward establishing a dialog of some kind with the public.

In the earliest forms of PR during much of the nineteenth century, communication was largely asymmetric, going from the public relations agent through the media to the audience. Feedback from the audience was not sought. In the early twentieth century, a limited symmetric model of communications was espoused, with the audience or public brought in to provide feedback to see how effective a campaign may have been in swaying public opinion. Although this had the surface appearance of a dialogue, the organization or PR professional still controlled the flow of communications.

Many of the principles espoused by Page and since adopted by most public relations firms today belong to a **two-way symmetric model** of public relations. This model emphasizes public relations as a system of managing relationships between organizations and individuals and their many publics, internal and external. The media of mass communication are one tool in this system of relationship management. Emphasis is on building mutual understanding and relationships as much as on influencing public opinion. In this way, social media has become an important tool to accomplish this.

two-way symmetric model

A model of public relations that emphasizes the profession as a system of managing relationships between organizations and individuals and their many publics.

Research shows that organizational excellence (as defined in terms of accomplishing both short- and long-term organizational objectives) is achieved most effectively when this model of two-way symmetric public relations is practiced. The two-way symmetric model also incorporates the public relations function into the senior management and decision making of the organization, and both formal and informal techniques are used to assess the attitudes, knowledge, behaviors, and intentions of various publics. The symmetric model places a premium on the ethical practice of public relations.

Of course, many practitioners of both public relations and journalism still equate public relations with publicity and media relations, but in the emerging two-way symmetric model this represents merely one activity within the repertoire of tools used in the ethical management of organizational relationships.

One of the best examples of two-way symmetric public relations comes from the story of how Johnson & Johnson handled the well-known Tylenol tampering case in 1982, when seven people died of cyanide poisoning after taking tainted Extra-Strength Tylenol capsules. After the first reported poisoning in the Chicago, Illinois, area, Johnson & Johnson took immediate steps to prevent further tragedy and established clear and open communication lines with both the media and the public.

Among its efforts, Johnson & Johnson, along with its parent McNeil Consumer Products Company, established a hotline for people to call and offered a $100,000 reward for the arrest and conviction of the person or persons responsible for the deaths. Johnson & Johnson instituted a nationwide recall of all Extra-Strength Tylenol capsules at a cost of some $100 million to remove and destroy all 31 million bottles. The company received thousands of calls requesting information and opened regional poison-control centers to dispense information and assistance.

The capsules were successfully reintroduced into the market in January 1983 with a triple-sealed, tamper-resistant packaging warning. Johnson & Johnson and McNeil Consumer Products Co. were cleared of any legal liability for the deaths and poisonings, and Tylenol sales have recovered. In 1991, Johnson & Johnson and McNeil Consumer Products Co. provided the families of the seven victims with an undisclosed settlement, estimated to be as much as $50 million.

Despite the overwhelmingly negative nature of the event, coverage of the Tylenol tragedy generally portrayed Johnson & Johnson and its parent in a favorable light. Companies during a crisis are often criticized by journalists for hiding information from the press and the public, but many journalists have praised Johnson & Johnson for its openness and the immediacy of its response to the poisonings. John O'Brien, of the *Chicago Tribune,* said, "The public relations people were knowledgeable and available when the media needed to talk to them," he said. "They didn't try to sugar-coat anything."

pitch

A request to review a client's
new product or do a story about
the client or the product.

▼ PR AND MEDIA RELATIONS

Although public relations professionals engage in a wide variety of activities, most typically devote a large portion, if not a majority, of their efforts to working with the media, including journalists, producers, and others responsible for the content of those media. By developing and maintaining good working relationships with the media, public relations professionals anticipate that they will be more successful in obtaining fair or positive coverage of their organizations. When a negative story does occur, having maintained a good relationship with the media increases an organization's opportunity to at least communicate clearly and responsibly.

There are several important tools the public relations professional uses in obtaining media coverage, including the pseudo event.

Pseudo Events

One of the most enduring legacies from the early days of modern public relations is the creation of what Daniel Boorstin calls "the pseudo event." Pseudo events are events manufactured by individuals or organizations, typically to capture the attention of the media and thereby the public.

Press kits give journalists much of the information they need to do a story.

Press conferences, protests, parades, and even awards ceremonies are all examples of pseudo events and are a form of media manipulation. But the media have become dependent on them. In fact, studies show that as much as 75 percent of the news content in even the best of the nation's newspapers, such as the *Washington Post,* was in some way influenced by pseudo events. Only occasionally is a story generated through pure "enterprise" or original reporting, with no public relations influence.[10]

Distributing News to the Media in the Digital Age

An important development in media relations is the distribution of corporate or other organizational news, information, and data (whether statistical or multimedia, including audio and video), usually through what are called news releases, or press releases. Traditionally done as typed stories sent through the mail, they are today primarily done online and sent via email or posted to the Web.

Journalists prefer digital content because it is easier to look at and evaluate for newsworthiness, since the journalist simply downloads the material to a computer. It's also easier and faster to edit, store, and retrieve than analog content. In an age of information clutter, digital content is also easier to ignore or discard. Now that reaching influential bloggers or others using social media has become as important as reaching professional journalists, a press release is not even needed. Rather, a well-placed **pitch**, or request to review a client's new product, may be enough to get people writing about it and then to get mainstream media attention.

Similar to the written news release is a video news release (VNR). These have caused some controversy in recent years, for example when it was learned that the

WEB LINK
PR Newswire
www.prnewswire.com

WEB LINK
Businesswire
www.businesswire.com

Bush administration was creating VNRs to promote its health policy. The VNRs were made to look much like a typical television news story from a reporter in the field, and several television stations around the country ran them without citing the source, making them seem like they had been produced by the news station itself. Many companies produce VNRs, and many are used by television stations, though usually only short clips as part of a larger story—B-roll footage showing pills being sorted, for example. However, there are also many examples of local television stations using VNR scripts and footage largely untouched, or simply having the station's own anchors read the scripts as if the story was produced by the station.

Finding Sources Online

Facilitating the media–public relations relationship has been the growth of various expert-source clearinghouses in the online arena. Although such clearinghouses have functioned in the offline world for many years in a variety of forms (such as media guides published by universities, or *The Yearbook of Experts, Authorities & Spokespersons*), they have thrived online for many of the same reasons that classified advertising works well online: the Web allows highly efficient targeting of communications and searching. *The Yearbook of Experts, Authorities & Spokespersons* is now available online, greatly facilitating the process of finding experts and authorities, especially when on deadline.

WEB LINK
MediaLink
www.medialink.com

WEB LINK
The Yearbook of Experts, Authorities & Spokespersons
www.expertclick.com/

WEB LINK
ProfNet
profnet.prnewswire.com/

Perhaps the biggest of these clearinghouses is ProfNet, an online service that connects more than six thousand news and information officers at colleges and universities, businesses, research centers, medical centers, nonprofits, and public relations agencies with journalists all around the world.

▼ PR FIRMS AND THE PR INDUSTRY

The U.S. public relations industry is tied to the rise and fall in the economy, just as the advertising industry is. When companies are in financial difficulties, they tend to cut back on advertising and public relations services, even though it could be argued that this is exactly when they most need such services. In public relations, revenues are based on a combination of sources. These include primarily fees for public relations consulting and services; income from specialized communications services such as research, interactive communications, and employee communications; and markups for production services and other media materials.

WEB LINK
Council of Public Relations Firms
www.prfirms.org

The 1990s saw considerable consolidation among public relations firms. But acquisition has slowed considerably in the early years of the twenty-first century, with most consolidation still occurring internationally. Major buyers are European holding companies such as Incepta Group, Havas, Publicis Groupe, and Cordiant. Omnicom is the one major U.S. communications firm that acquired several technology firms for Fleishman-Hillard.

Although most organizations maintain their own internal public relations units or offices, many hire public relations firms to help in their efforts, particularly with more specialized services, especially media relations. Media relations can be extremely complex and can require extensive experience with not just local but national media. Oftentimes, public relations firms maintain their own specialists who have the necessary experience to help clients manage their media relations, particularly during campaigns or crises.

PR firms are organized into three main areas:

1. Core practice areas, or the type of relationships the client needs managed, including marketing communications or consumer relations; investor relations; public, nonprofit, and governmental affairs; corporate and employee communications; political communications; and community relations

2. Services, or the type of activity the firm provides to its clients, including media relations, research, interactive or online communications, writing, lobbying, fund-raising, and crisis management

3. Industries, or the business sectors within which the clients operate, including utilities, technology, retail, manufacturing, health care, financial services, and consumer products

PR professionals help get their clients media attention through interviews as subject experts or writing op-ed columns.

Many firms specialize in one or more core practice areas, services, or industries. This enables them to focus resources in one or more areas yet achieve a high enough level of expertise needed to serve clients operating on a national or global scale. Some PR firms also offer integrated communication programs, sometimes called integrated marketing communications. This means the firm provides a comprehensive set of communication management and services to clients, including both public relations and advertising activities. Most of the larger PR firms provide integrated communication programs.

Table 11-4 provides data on the top five independent U.S. public relations firms according to total worldwide revenues for 2010. Most of the PR firms had revenue gains in 2010, compared to losses or lackluster performances from 2008, which shows how strongly the economy affects these firms. Edelman remains by far the largest independent public relations firm, with over 3,500 employees worldwide.

TABLE 11-4

Top Five Independent Public Relations Firms, 2010 Worldwide Revenues

FIRM	HEADQUARTERS	# OF EMPLOYEES	2010 REVENUES	% CHANGE FROM 2009
Edelman	Chicago, Illinois	3,635	$521,969,675	+18.6
APCO Worldwide	Washington, D.C.	566	$113,400,000	+13.1
Waggener Edstrom	Bellevue, Washington	839	$111,910,000	+5.9
Ruder Finn Group	New York, New York	602	$97,059,000	+8.8
Text 100 Global PR	San Francisco, California	451	$46,700,000	−3.9

Source: O'Dwyer's PR Firms Database, 2011

For the sake of comparison, some of the PR firms that are part of the larger agencies include WPP's Hill & Knowlton ($330 million), and Omnicom Group's Fleishman-Hillard ($405 million), Ketchum ($218 million), and Porter Novelli ($196 million). Any one of these PR agencies is bigger than any of the independent PR firms except for Edelman.

◣◥ Changing Trends in Advertising and PR

One thing that has become clear is that the traditional divisions between the two professions of advertising and PR are blurring. It used to be, in the analog media world, that PR professionals dealt primarily with media relations and did not have to be concerned with brand strategy or other aspects of advertising. But today, it is apparent that both PR and advertising professionals have to know what the other is doing in order to maximize the effectiveness of campaigns.

In what is typically called **integrated communications**, strategic-communications professionals are trying to figure out the best ways not only to manage a brand's image across media channels but to learn what the public is saying about the brand through blogs, websites, and other social media—which were traditionally the realm of public relations. Advertising agencies are learning what public relations professionals have long known—a company cannot assume that it can send out a message without the audience talking back.

Similarly, public relations professionals are learning that a company or brand exists within a network of relationships and that thinking on a larger, strategic level can help them better integrate their messages to various publics.

integrated communications

The idea that all channels of communication about a company or brand should work together in creating a cohesive message.

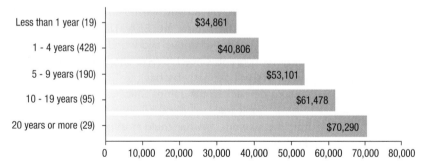

FIGURE 11-1 Salaries and Positions for Advertising Account Managers. Source: Payscale.com

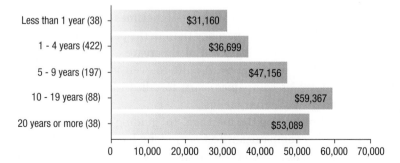

FIGURE 11-2 Salaries and Positions for Public Relations Specialists. Source: Payscale.com

FOOLING MOST OF THE PEOPLE MOST OF THE TIME ... DIGITALLY

ETHICS IN MEDIA

Online shoppers increasingly rely on reviews on websites such as Amazon, Yelp, and TripAdvisor for information about new books, hotels, restaurants, and much more. But how trustworthy are these sources of information? An increasing amount of evidence suggests that many of the people writing these reviews are in fact often paid $5 to $10 to write favorable appraisals by the companies and products being evaluated.[11] A Cornell team did a study in 2011 designed to help ferret out the fake reviews from the honest ones. Following are two reviews from the research project: one is real, the other fake. Can you tell the difference?

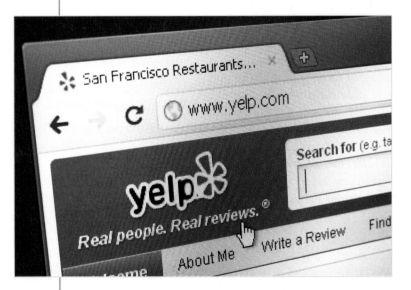

1.   I have stayed at many hotels traveling for both business and pleasure and I can honestly stay that The James is tops. The service at the hotel is first class. The rooms are modern and very comfortable. The location is perfect within walking distance to all of the great sights and restaurants. Highly recommend to both business travelers and couples.

2.   My husband and I stayed at the James Chicago Hotel for our anniversary. This place is fantastic! We knew as soon as we arrived we made the right choice! The rooms are BEAUTIFUL and the staff very attentive and wonderful!! The area of the hotel is great, since I love to shop I couldn't ask for more!! We will definatly be back to Chicago and we will for sure be back to the James Chicago.[12]

. . . Don't feel bad if you couldn't tell the real review from the fake one; neither could most people in the study. (Review #2 is the phony one.)

WEB LINK
International Association of Business Communicators
www.iabc.com/

One thing that companies are learning—sometimes the hard way—is that the online public demands more transparency than in the past. Attempts at deception, through faux-amateur ads or blogs, will likely create a strong negative backlash that will hurt the brand or company. A shift to even more equitable, symmetrical dialog is happening, as companies learn to talk with their clients, or publics, through forums, blogs, and other means.

The shift from "controlling the message" to "guiding the conversation" is often seen as threatening by companies who for too long have believed that in order to have an effective brand or to be successful they must control all aspects of communication with the public.

▼ CAREERS IN ADVERTISING AND PR

Although very much reliant on larger trends in the economy, a wide variety of interesting jobs exist in both professions, and there is a growing amount of overlap between the two. The trends in media production and consumption tend to favor strategic communications over fields like journalism (which is seeing drastic cuts throughout the industry), and the salaries are generally better than in journalism.

Young people often find rewarding careers in any of a number of areas within advertising and PR, ranging from the creative side to account management to market research. Within the larger firms there is great scope to change career tracks and deal with different industry clients, so someone who has been working in pharmaceuticals for a few years may switch to telecommunications or consumer packaged goods, in effect starting a different career in learning the details of the new industry.

Social media are creating new job opportunities for people in advertising agencies and PR firms, as well as in large companies that have their own marketing or PR departments. Keeping track of what is being said about a company and reaching influential members of the audience through social media is increasingly vital. More importantly, knowing why a company or client should use (or not use) a particular social-media tool such as Facebook or Twitter is a skill set that companies are actively seeking.

The nonprofit sector should not be ignored when considering a job in public relations or advertising. Although salaries are generally lower than in corporations, nonprofit foundations, charities, and research institutes need the skills that strategic communications professionals provide just as much as for-profit companies do, if not more so.

LOOKING BACK AND MOVING FORWARD

This chapter has provided an overview of advertising and public relations. Although news and entertainment are the content most people go to the media for, in reality the most common form of content is advertising, while much of the editorial content or programming has been inspired or influenced by public relations.

Underlying both advertising and PR, which are forms of strategic communication, is the desire to persuade an audience to change an attitude or belief and take some action. Persuasive communication, historically called rhetoric, has long played a role in human affairs, and today there are more than two dozen theories that attempt to explain how persuasion works.

Advertising on the Web continues to grow but remains only a small part of total advertising spending to date. Technology allows for greater accountability of response rates to advertisements, and the low response-rate numbers have made advertisers feel their money is not well spent online, which has kept some advertisers away from fully embracing Web advertising. As a result, advertising agencies have been trying new types of online advertisements, with mixed results and with some Internet-user backlash at larger, more obtrusive ads.

It does raise interesting questions about why advertisers were willing to pay so much for ads in nondigital media when it was nearly impossible to estimate audience engagement. Even the metrics of circulation numbers for print and viewers for television could be seen as largely fictions, as neither says anything about whether the audience read or watched the ad, let alone remembered it or took some action based on it.

Advertising revenues have provided the means for the majority of content we see today. Advertising helps pay the salaries of journalists and keeps the television studios operating. Few people would be willing to pay the full price for the content they get largely for "free."

However, the content is not of course free. Consumers do pay for the content in the form of higher prices for goods, as the expenses for advertising and marketing have to come from revenues and are considered part of the costs of doing business. Given that such costs are largely hidden from the public, it seems that it will be hard to change purely to subscription-based or pay-per-use models on the Web.

Social media will continue to greatly affect strategic-communications professionals, who have to learn that transparency and engagement with their audiences will be what gains credibility in the social-media space. Monitoring online conversations about companies—and, more importantly, joining those conversations—will be increasingly imperative for advertising and public relations professionals. Already we are seeing more job titles with the words "social media" or "community manager" in them—jobs in which the employee is responsible for dealing with social-media components of a company's overall exposure.

One thing is increasingly clear: largely because of the democratization of media and the ability of more people to create and distribute their messages than ever before, it is harder than ever to be heard above the noise. The skills of strategic-communications professionals in knowing how to persuade, how to craft powerful messages, and how to understand audiences will all become even more important in the future than they are today.

DISCUSSION QUESTIONS

1. Choose a brand and keep track of every encounter you have with it throughout the day. Don't forget to include not only the number of radio and television commercials and ads you see in the morning paper, but advertising on websites and on objects like cereal boxes, buses, taxis, and telephone booths and ads outside and inside stores.

2. Consider the last time you tried to persuade someone to do something or to change his or her mind. What techniques did you use to persuade them, and were you successful? Why or why not? How may these techniques be used in mass communication?

3. Some brands have such successful marketing that the brand name becomes synonymous with the product itself, such as the trademarked name Kleenex. Can you name other trademarked brands that have become commonly used for the generic products?

4. Discuss which advertising format you feel is the most effective and why. Are there some products that are better advertised in a certain format than in others? Why do you think this is?

5. Discuss strengths and weaknesses of the large-advertising-agency model common today. Do you think the trend toward ever-larger agencies is good or bad? Why?

6. Choose a company and see what is being said about it in the social-media space, including blogs, any complaint sites, and what the company itself is doing with social media, if anything. Discuss your findings and suggest any ways the company should do a better job in social media.

7. Consider a brand that you prefer for a certain food, clothing, or other product. What made you choose that brand over others, and how would you describe that brand to someone considering it?

The Skinny on the Art of Persuasion: How to Move Minds, 1st ed. Jim Randel (2010) Rand Media Company.

Thank You For Arguing: What Aristotle, Lincoln, and Homer Simpson Can Teach Us About the Art of Persuasion. Jay Heinrichs (2007) Three Rivers Press.

Ad Land: A Global History of Advertising. Mark Tungate (2007) Kogan Page.

A History of Advertising. Stephane Pincas, Marc Loiseau (2008) Taschen.

The Advertising Concept Book. Pete Barry (2008) Thames & Hudson.

Advertising, the Uneasy Persuasion: Its Dubious Impact on American Society. Michael Schudson (1987) Basic Books.

Guerrilla Advertising: Unconventional Brand Communication. Gavin Lucas, Michael Dorrian (2006) Laurence King Publishers.

Ogilvy on Advertising. David Ogilvy (1987) Vintage Books.

The Conquest of Cool: Business Culture, Counterculture, and the Rise of Hip Consumerism. Thomas Frank (1998) University of Chicago Press.

PR! A Social History of Spin. Stuart Ewen (1996) Basic Books.

The Father of Spin: Edward L. Bernays and the Birth of Public Relations. Larry Tye (2002) Holt.

Public Relations: The Complete Guide. Joe Marconi (2004) South-Western Educational Publishers.

The New Rules of Marketing and PR: How to Use News Releases, Blogs, Podcasting, Viral Marketing and Online Media to Reach Buyers Directly. David Meerman Scott (2008) Wiley.

PR 2.0: New Media, New Tools, New Audiences. Deirdre Breakenridge (2008) FT Press.

The New Influencers: A Marketer's Guide to the New Social Media. Paul Gillin, Geoffrey Moore (2009) Linden Publishing.

1. False.

2. False.

3. Putting products in shows in which the actors use them and their logo or brand is displayed.

4. Classified ads generate more revenue for newspapers.

5. Cost per thousand, a unit used for calculating print advertising rates.

6. Search engine marketing and search engine optimization, which are important because searching is how most information is found on the Internet.

7. True.

8. The practice of using advertising and persuasive techniques to get people to change bad or destructive behaviors.

10. A video is uploaded to a website or blog and sent by viewers who like it to other people, which is then sent to even more people in a very short time.

12

MEDIA ETHICS

LEARNING OBJECTIVES

By the end of this chapter
you should be able to:

- Define some basic
  elements in media ethics.

- Outline the major systems
  of ethical reasoning.

- Explain the main issues
  involved in ethical decision
  making.

- Discuss the role of
  commercialism in media
  ethics.

- Describe the major ethical
  issues in journalism,
  PR, advertising, and
  entertainment.

The *News of the World,* a 168-year-old tabloid newspaper in the UK with 2.6 million readers, published its last issue on July 10, 2011, with the headline "Thank You and Goodbye."

The paper, owned by Rupert Murdoch's News Corp., was at the heart of a shocking scandal involving journalists hacking phones of celebrities, sports stars, politicians, and families of crime victims, all to get material for stories to scoop the other competing tabloids. The scandal brought forth a maelstrom that not only closed the *News of the World,* but that forced the resignation of some of the top executives at News Corp. and the head of the police in the UK, and the arrests of some prominent former executives, the cancellation of a planned bid to take over satellite provider BSkyB, and testimony by Rupert Murdoch and his son James to Parliament. Murdoch and his son both claimed to know nothing of the phone hacking, and Rebekah Brooks, News International's top executive and editor of the *News of the World* at the time of one of the hacking incidents, said the paper took prompt action when she learned of the incident. Despite this, she soon resigned from her position at News Corp.

Phone hacking—eavesdropping on the private phone calls or messages of others—is illegal, but beyond the legal implications a host of ethical issues were raised by industry experts, the government, and the public regarding whether journalism in the UK needed to be regulated in some manner. Further complicating matters, it was shown that journalists had bribed police officers for information for stories, raising even more legal and ethical concerns.

The outrage felt by the British public was fierce and led to advertisers promptly pulling their ads from the *News of the World,* which led in part to its sudden closure. The public's concerns over invasions of privacy, especially by a profession that makes claims as the "watchdog of government," likely hurt the image of journalism even more. The strong competition between Britain's tabloids, which specialize in lurid stories, and the drive to sell more papers, combined to smother ethical decision making and led to even greater transgressions.

As the preceding example shows, media ethics infuses all aspects of the media's role in society—including the law, its relation and responsibilities to the various publics (including a company's own employees), its profession, and individual decisions within the entire milieu. Media ethics is not truly a stand-alone subject, something that should be studied outside of the context of the media professions' daily business and professional practices, as good ethical decision-making skills should be part and parcel of everybody's daily routine. This is an important point to remember. Decisions should not be made by media professionals only to then consider ethical aspects after the fact. Rather, ethical reasoning should be a primary component when considering actions.

To do that, however, requires a solid understanding of ethics, ethical frameworks and their strengths and weaknesses, and how to recognize ethical problems before they arise and deal with such issues when they do arise. By focusing on ethics as a separate subject, this chapter gives you the basic tools with which to do this. Anybody working in media should be mindful of how ethics in general, and media ethics in particular, are integral components of our personal and professional lives.

◢▼ Ethics, Morals, and Laws

Technically, ethics is a branch of philosophy that examines moral questions, or questions of right and wrong, and thus is also called moral philosophy. There are many branches, or specialties, within ethics. One of the main branches attempts to answer moral questions in both theory (moral theory) and in practice (applied ethics). Another branch of ethics, metaethics, deals with nonmoral questions about morality, such as the nature of moral facts and questions about the meanings of moral statements. In this chapter we will first look at some moral theories and then examine applied ethics as it relates to mass communication and journalism, PR, advertising, and entertainment in particular.

Although ethics actually refers to the branch of philosophy that examines questions of morality, in common usage the term "ethics" is often used in place of "morals." For the sake of clarity, it is probably better to use the term "morals" rather than "ethics" in such situations, but it seems unlikely to change in the near future and the two terms will likely continue to be used interchangeably.

MEDIA QUIZ

How Moral Are You?

Ethical questions can often be difficult as there may not always be a single "right" answer. There are always conflicts between groups and between individuals and society. See if you can come up with ethical solutions to the following scenarios, which are based on real-life incidents.

1. You work in a PR firm whose biggest and most important client is a noted Fortune 500 company. In a meeting with them to discuss future strategy and publishing their annual report, they admit that they have "cooked the books" in some of their divisions to make it seem like they have greater revenues than they do. They say everyone in their industry does it, even as they want promises from everyone at the meeting that they will not divulge that information. What do you do?

2. The TV news crew you are part of is covering an investigative story on a defect in a brand of car. You see other members of the crew wire the car to create a large explosion. Your editor explains that they tried to show the results from two cars before that and could not get them, therefore they are trying to emulate what has been reported to have happened. Do you think this is ethical?

3. While working as a member of the production crew on a reality television series you befriend one of the cast members. Weeks later, in the editing room, you see the producer piecing together snippets of the hundreds of hours of video and audio that was taken to make a loose narrative that puts that cast member in a highly negative light. The cast member, as is typical, has signed a waiver in which she agrees to any depiction of her. Do you think what the producer is doing is ethical?

4. The advertising agency you work for has created an ad campaign for a new soft drink that claims it is "The best-tasting orange soda. Ever." You know from the market research your agency did and from blind taste tests that the client's soda consistently scored lower than competing brands. Is it ethical to use the phrase in the advertising campaigns?

Morals are what we believe to be right or wrong. Although we can question why we believe an action such as lying is considered wrong, that is a question for meta-ethics and not something we address here. It may seem impossible to dictate what is right or wrong for a person in a given situation, as each person should be able to make up her or his own mind, but ethics provides us with a framework and method on which to base good moral reasoning.

Ethics and laws are not the same thing. Many of our basic laws are based on moral precepts, but many unethical actions are not illegal. Similarly, many laws are not based on moral precepts (consider traffic parking laws, as one example). Some people mistakenly believe that our society is built on the laws that we have made, but actually society is built on our beliefs about how well the laws we have reflect our moral precepts regarding what is right and wrong. There are many examples in which laws have been deemed immoral, such as segregation in the U.S. or apartheid in South Africa, and through civil disobedience and other means have eventually been changed to better reflect what is considered right and good.

◣◥ Major Systems of Ethical Reasoning

There is no single, underlying, unified ethical system that all people can follow for complete justice and peace. However, that does not mean that we cannot utilize the thinking of philosophers, religious leaders, and others to examine and utilize the different ethical systems that have been developed, some over thousands of years. There are various ways to classify systems of ethical reasoning, or moral theories, but here we will use a classification scheme that William Neher and Paul Sandin use in their book *Communicating Ethically*. Their classification in some ways matches other classifications such as that used by noted media ethics scholar Clifford Christians,[1] but also diverges in some ways that help highlight the role that communication plays in ethics.

According to Neher and Sandin, the four major systems can be grouped within the categories of character, duties, consequences, and relationships. We will look at these and also examine the issue of moral relativism.

▼ CHARACTER, OR VIRTUE ETHICS

Virtue ethics is the oldest of the ethical systems, with a history that has its roots in some of our earliest religions. The Greeks believed strongly in the notion of virtue and the role that character played in living a virtuous life. Virtues such as courage, modesty, stoicism, honesty, and other character traits were aspired to by the Greeks. In virtue ethics, you are virtuous because of your character, which gives you the ability to conduct your life according to the best virtues. Simply acting modest, or selfless, when in fact you do not really feel those traits does not make you virtuous (partly because you are breaking another virtue, that of honesty).

Many great thinkers have given us lists of virtues that we should follow, but sometimes these same people have fallen short of their own lists of virtues. Virtue ethics can give us a framework on what is considered the best way to live our lives, but it does not tell us how exactly to do that.

Virtue ethics may seem old-fashioned given its long religious and philosophical history, but it has become more important in recent years among media ethicists. Its emphasis on character touches on fundamental aspects of what makes us human that some of the other later ethical systems miss.

There are two virtue-based ethics you are probably familiar with: the Golden Rule and the Golden Mean.

The Golden Rule

A basic ethical principle in Judeo-Christian belief, which dominates most Western societies, is often cited as "Do unto others as you would have them do unto you." Another way to phrase the same belief is "Love thy neighbor as thyself."

This principle could be applied by a journalist when she is interviewing a grieving relative, for example. By treating the person with respect and dignity and asking herself if she would want to be treated in the same way in that situation, she can perhaps avoid some of the charges of invasion of privacy or tastelessness in coverage that are often leveled at the media. Some journalists who have been on the receiving end of news stories have often mentioned their shock when they realize how insensitive and intrusive the news media can be during trying times of personal grief.

The Golden Mean

One of the oldest ethical principles, the Golden Mean was espoused in different forms by Aristotle and Confucius, each of whom said that finding a balance between two extremes is the most ethical way. This "middle way" may well shift as the extremes shift, of course, and even this principle has to be taken in moderation. It would not be ethical to only steal half the money from a cash register rather than all of it, for example, because stealing is wrong in the first place.

Applying the Golden Mean to news stories would involve trying to find balance and fairness among all sides of an issue. It does not mean automatically giving each side the same amount of coverage or space in the newspaper, however, as the relative importance of the groups must be judged.

According to Aristotle, the process of deciding on a mean is one way we determine what virtue is, and the mean becomes the standard by which ethical acts are judged. This is part of the reason that acts that are clearly wrong, such as stealing, should not be considered as one extreme.

▼ DUTIES

As the name suggests, duty-based ethical systems state that we must follow a prescribed set of rules or duties, regardless of the outcome. It is our moral obligation to follow these duties, no matter what. In this way, duty theories provide basic principles for moral obligations in life. These duties may spring from religious beliefs (duties to God), but may also embrace duties to others and duties to oneself.

Duty-based approaches differ from virtue-based ethical systems in important ways. The virtue-based approach emphasizes the individual and his choices within a prescribed framework. In a duty-based approach, individual choice is eliminated in favor of following a set of rules that apply equally to everybody.

categorical imperative

In ethical thought, Kant's concept of an unconditional moral obligation that does not depend on an individual's personal inclinations or goals.

The Categorical Imperative

Immanuel Kant was an influential German philosopher in the eighteenth century whose approach to duty-based ethical systems stated that actions should be decided on moral laws that would apply to everyone. Kant said that we should create these moral laws only when we have carefully considered if we would want these laws applied to us at all times. He referred to this unconditional moral obligation as a **categorical imperative**. The key underlying rule for the categorical imperative is that it cannot depend on a personal inclination, goal, or purpose. The value of the categorical imperative is that it encourages one to act for the benefit of others first, and not for personal gain. Treating someone with respect, giving to charity to benefit those in need, or lending a hand to help another person with a difficult task are examples of actions that reinforce the inherent value of others.

Media organizations can apply Kant's categorical imperative in many ways. For example, it applies to an advertising firm's decision to decline clients who sell tobacco or alcohol or a public relations firm's decision not to accept government clients from nations with poor human rights' records. By following these categorical imperatives, these organizations would never take such clients no matter how promising the contract.

Immanuel Kant was an influential eighteenth-century German philosopher who developed the notion of the categorical imperative in ethics.

For news organizations, decisions to publish names of crime victims, or to cover all crimes of a certain seriousness, for example, would fall under the categorical imperative. In this case, if a newspaper published all names of drivers arrested for drunk driving, then even the mayor and newspaper publisher would have their names published if they were arrested for drunk driving.

The strength in duty-based approaches should be clear: simply follow the rules that must be followed and you are acting ethically. It may be easy when deciding whether or not to publish the name of the publisher caught for drunk driving, but may raise thornier issues in other cases. Think back to the News Corp. phone hacking case. Had journalists been explicitly instructed to protect the privacy of individuals—celebrities and private citizens alike—such a categorical imperative may have greatly limited the potential for rampant phone hacking among its reporters.

Discourse Ethics

Noted German social theorist and scholar Jürgen Habermas, most known for his concept of the "public sphere," which will be discussed later in the book, has proposed what he calls "discourse ethics" as an ethical framework. Habermas says that communication is at the foundation of how we understand the world and that the act of communication itself, when practiced without bias or coercion, is an ethical act brought about through the process of rational interaction, or argument. He proposes several actions for participants in discourse, which is a kind of formalized

Jürgen Habermas, a noted social theorist and philosopher, developed the notion of discourse ethics as a method to reach consensus on the best course of action.

discussion that can ensure that all affected parties have a chance to be heard and that everyone's ideas are considered on their own merits—not based on outside factors such as who is dominant in a certain group or who has more power. Discourse ethics prescribes rules to follow, but it also comes from a basic assumption that justice and equality are most important for a good society.

Using principles of discourse ethics could work well in an organization in which there are disagreements on the proper course of action. If all affected parties are allowed to participate in the discussion, everyone can better see other perspectives and a decision can ideally be made in which everyone is happy. Note that this process is not about finding a compromise simply for the sake of compromise, but more about letting people come to a shared and consensual understanding of what is true, or correct, based on the merits of the argument.

A small PR firm may be asked to represent a company that is promoting a highly unpopular development project. Exercising a discourse-ethics approach to assess the project could help the firm come to a decision on whether to take the client or not. Everyone in the firm could state their opinions on taking the client. As an additional measure, the firm might also solicit opinions from other clients and local citizens who might be affected by the project. By bringing in parties that may not normally have a voice, it would ideally provide new perspectives for everyone involved and lead to an ethical decision.

▼ CONSEQUENCES

The consequences of our actions matter and must often be taken into account as we make ethical decisions. Of course, nobody can predict the future, so it may be hard to tell exactly what the consequences may turn out to be. Nevertheless, some influential ethical systems have been created that look primarily at consequences as ways to judge what is ethically good or not.

Utilitarianism

Utilitarianism is a philosophical approach that assumes that the most ethical or right action is what does the greatest good for the greatest number of people. This means that even if a decision or act severely hurts someone or a small group, if it helps a much greater number of people then it is the right thing to do.

However, we often fall into a kind of numbers game with utilitarianism, thinking of the greatest good only in terms of the quantity of people who benefit. There can be another way to look at it, which weighs a small good for a large number of people versus a greater good for a small number. Scientific research on animals operates under a utilitarian principle, with many safeguards to minimize potential suffering and harm of test subjects. A small number of animals suffer or are killed in order to find cures for diseases that may help much larger numbers of people. It may be harder from a utilitarian ethical perspective to justify testing cosmetics on animals than testing animals to find a cure for cancer—a classic case of how both "greatest number" and "greatest good" must be weighed.

Utilitarianism can often be used to justify media coverage of sensitive or painful events for a small number of people, since the coverage can help many others. Examples include investigative reports of government wrongdoing in which a few individuals may go to jail or lose their jobs, but society as a whole is better for exposing the wrongdoers. **Social marketing** operates under utilitarian principles, as it attempts to do the greatest good for the greatest number of people in changing their behaviors, such as to stop smoking or to avoid binge drinking.

social marketing

The use of advertising and marketing techniques for social causes, such as antismoking or safe sex campaigns.

Social Justice

Egalitarian philosophers believe that what is ethical is whatever brings about the most social justice or fairness for everyone. In this way, the utilitarian belief of "the greatest good" is interpreted as "the most fairness for everyone."

Twentieth-century philosopher John Rawls argued in his 1971 book *A Theory of Justice* that fairness is the fundamental idea in the concept of justice. However, in a complex modern society it is often difficult to establish what is fair, since some groups have greater wealth, power, and advantages than others. In order to better understand fairness, Rawls advocates the parties step behind a "veil of ignorance" in which they are no longer in their usual roles. They must stake out an "original position" on the issue not knowing what role they would have after it is decided.

In following this procedure, a manager in a dispute with workers would have to imagine that she may end up as one of the workers after the exercise is finished. If so, would she be satisfied with the result that management is proposing? From this framework, Rawls says, the parties would be able to better establish fair practices as they would be able to more clearly see other viewpoints and those interests.

Understanding other viewpoints is key to effective media communications. An advertising executive may realize that if he were of a different ethnic group or gender he might find a proposed advertisement offensive. A newsroom editor may reconsider the workload of reporters after considering that he would not want to be a reporter with the same workload, which may lead to policy changes. A reporter may choose her words more carefully or write her story with more thought to how she would feel if the story was being written about her.

However, such ponderings may seem unrealistic in today's competitive business world. An editor may realize, on a personal level, how unfair the workload of reporters is, but may not be able to do anything about it on a professional or organizational level. Similarly, as with discourse ethics, there is little incentive for those in power to ignore the resources at their disposal to get what they want, so asking them to step behind a veil of ignorance or to follow certain rules of discourse is also asking them to surrender their power and position.

▼ RELATIONSHIPS, OR DIALOGICAL ETHICS

Neher and Sandin call dialogical ethics "a system in which ethics can be judged by the attitudes and behaviors demonstrated by each participant in a communication transaction." In ethical dialogs, the participants are willing to open themselves up and see how the other side views the world and themselves. In dialogical ethics, we do not try to force our own agenda, but strive for open and honest dialog that accepts other views without judgment. It does not mean that we simply abandon our own views and become uncritical sponges to whoever we encounter, but simply that we remain open to hearing other views and respecting those we encounter.

Dialogs we have with people form the basis of our relations with them, and this is especially true with social media as dialog is often the only way we interact with many people online. Further, professions such as advertising or public relations, in which success is measured by how well the audience has been persuaded to buy a product, change a belief, or perform some other action, would seem to be unethical from a dialogical ethics perspective because they are using people as means to an end.

These points are valid. Even so, perhaps some of the seemingly unethical issues involving advertising may be mitigated if a dialogical ethical approach is considered. In today's world of social media, where audience members communicate regularly with each other, it is actually becoming increasingly important for companies to join in the dialog. One common mistake some companies have made as they enter the social media space is to try to control the dialog and squash dissent, rather than truly listening to consumers and trying to understand their viewpoints, as dialogical ethics dictates.

Ethics of Care

The ethics of care, or feminist ethics, challenges many of the traditional ethical systems and has certain aspects that speak to issues in modern society and communication. It has been quite controversial and there are many variants of feminist ethics.

Feminists, in general, believe that women are the equal of men, that oppression of women is wrong, that the categories of male and female and gender roles associated with these are socially constructed, and that the male perspective has dominated throughout history. As a consequence, society has accepted male virtues as the standard or highest ideals.

The ethics of care emphasizes the importance of relationships, like dialogical ethics, but places a greater normative emphasis on the relationship. In the ethics of care, acting ethically involves caring for oneself and for others within the context of a relationship in real life, not because of abstract principles. The

Feminist ethics have provided a moral framework from which to encourage the empowerment of women and protest discrimination and harassment against women.

ethics of care is very much grounded in real-life actions and relationships and eschews abstract concepts about who should be cared about. It replaces a justice-based ethical system with a caring-based ethical system, the *one caring* and the *cared for.*

Feminist ethics is important in a communication context for a few different reasons. First, the assumptions that "male" means "normal" has implications for everything from how advertising messages are constructed to who is making the advertisements (and who are simply models within them). Mass communication, in subtle and not-so-subtle ways, helps reinforce the roles of men and women in society. Second, even if women are hardwired differently than men—still a debatable point—there seems nothing wrong with trying to promote caring about others as an alternative way of conceptualizing communications.

▼ MORAL RELATIVISM

It is fashionable in some places to apply moral relativism, or situationist ethics, as an ethical system. Moral relativism suggests that none of the ethical systems can be said to be any better than the others and that historically traditional ethical principles have been used primarily to secure the stature of established social groups.

The notion of moral relativism derives from anthropological research in which behaviors considered quite wrong in our culture may be considered perfectly normal, even moral, in another culture. This led early researchers to question the basis by which some groups declared their moral codes superior to others.

A weakness of moral relativism is that it leaves no agreed-upon rules or principles by which to discuss ethical issues and come to conclusions. There is no fundamental component or rulebook from which we should try to understand the point of view of others, no yardstick of social justice or the greatest good, no duties to follow, and no virtues to aspire to in order to improve our characters. We are left in a moral no-man's-land in which each of us is out for ourselves, with no way (or incentive) to communicate with each other and find common rules for understanding.

Using moral relativism in mass media situations quickly leads to a morass of rationalizations and selective policies. A newspaper may normally publish the names of people arrested for shoplifting, but decide not to if the shoplifter is the son of the richest man in town and the paper's biggest advertiser. Since the storekeeper will likely not press charges, and the sheriff himself drove the boy back to his mansion, it would be easy to rationalize that the story really isn't newsworthy after all. But whether this is an ethically sound way of making this decision is certainly questionable.

◢◥ Issues in Ethical Decision Making

It should be obvious that one theoretical approach will not work for all situations and that conflicts between ethical precepts are at the crux of ethical dilemmas in life and in media. The ethics of care may often conflict with the categorical imperative, as an editor may not want to publish a story about his wife's arrest, but the newspaper's policy is to always print names of people arrested.

Media organizations often do not show the same vigor in reporting about their own business practices and mistakes as they do about those of other businesses. This is a clear violation of the categorical imperative.

The principle of utilitarianism can be used to run roughshod over people's rights of privacy, as editors justify intrusive coverage of famous people as "the public's right to know." But what good does such intrusive coverage actually serve? Who actually benefits the most from coverage of a shocking celebrity scandal?

One could also use a utilitarian argument to suppress news coverage. If a story on a local factory that is breaking certain safety codes forces the factory to close down, then hundreds of people in the town will be out of work. Is it better to keep quiet about it to serve the greatest good for the greatest number of people?

Media professionals must deal with a number of ethical problems in the course of their daily work, some of which are discussed throughout this book. Because of the nature of the work in mass communication, ethical lapses can have repercussions far beyond the unethical media professional, potentially ruining others' careers, affecting the public's perception and trust of media in general, and even in some cases ending lives.

Sometimes corporate decisions made in executive boardrooms far above the typical media professional's level can also have ethical repercussions. Sometimes media professionals may be willing pawns in unethical practices and other times they simply try to do their jobs as best they can within the larger organizational environment.

According to academic Ronald Howard and business consultant Clinton Korver, authors of *Ethics for the Real World: Creating a Personal Code to Guide Decisions in Work and Life*, it is important to keep three disciplines in mind when considering potentially ethical actions. These disciplines are legal, prudential, and ethical. According to Howard and Korver, we often confuse these concepts as we attempt moral reasoning. In other words, we may frame our reasoning using an ethical explanation, when actually we are doing the action for prudential (practical) reasons, such as improving our company's bottom line.

Howard and Korver offer several easy self-tests to do when considering whether you are truly making an ethical decision or are simply rationalizing your decision by couching it in ethical terms. Their tests are tried-and-true, including the "other-shoe test" (how would you feel if the shoe were on the other foot?), the "front-page test" (would you think the same way if what you did was on the front page of the *New York Times*?), the "loved-one's test" (how would we feel if the recipient of our action was someone we loved?), the "role-model test" (would we do the same thing if it was an action we expected from our children?), and the "mother's test," (what would your mother think?).

▲▼ The Role of Commercialism in Media Ethics

Businesses in a capitalist society are expected to make money for their owners, whether they are privately held companies or those traded publicly on the stock market. Members of the public invest in companies that are expected to be successful, which means making profits. Media companies are no different than other types of corporations in that regard.

However, media organizations are in a uniquely powerful position to influence the public compared to other types of companies because of the "product"—media content—they create. Scholars in the Frankfurt School tradition coined the term "culture industry" with media companies to show the power they have in affecting culture. If any other kind of company, such as a shoe manufacturer or cereal maker, wants to influence public opinion, they have to go through the media to do so.

Because of the power of media to shape and influence the public, some aspects of the media industry, such as journalism, are given special protection under the Constitution; the First Amendment is a case in point. Partly as a result of these protections and partly through historical traditions, media—and journalism in particular—have had a strong public service mission. Many questions arise on how seriously the public service mission of news is kept in mind when news organizations become divisions of larger entertainment-media corporations that have little or no tradition in the unique culture of the newsroom and its commitment to public service.

At the heart of many media-ethics dilemmas are the conflicting goals of serving the public with information and maximizing profit for the business. These issues can arise in a number of ways.

Commercial interests can take precedence over what is covered when powerful advertisers cancel or threaten to cancel their advertising in a media outlet. A blatant example may be when an unflattering story on a large local advertiser is going to run in a local newspaper and is either toned down or pulled when the advertiser threatens to withdraw. A far more common case involves advertisers pulling their ads when there is coverage of unpopular issues or when a media organization takes unpopular editorial stands. Examples of this include Southern newspapers that supported the civil rights movement in the 1950s and 1960s losing

The civil rights movement forced some Southern newspapers to make tough choices when advertisers threatened to pull their ads if the papers appeared to support the movement.

local advertisers. Although news coverage was not about the advertisers directly, the newspapers became associated with an opinion that the advertisers either did not agree with or were concerned would hurt their businesses if they were seen as advocating it too.

Another way that commercial interests may interfere with the public interest is when media outlets do not adequately cover certain groups or portions of the population because of a lack of audience and advertiser interest. For example, the *Los Angeles Times* had expanded its coverage and spent tens of millions of dollars on creating zoned editions that covered the growing and largely middle-class and affluent surrounding areas of the city even as it largely ignored coverage of the predominantly poor central city. A special section of the paper concentrating on complex urban issues of the south-central area was created in 1992, with the *Times* emphasizing its public service mission, but was closed three years later, despite greater than expected advertising, because of costs associated with the special section.

Related to the case cited above are the costs associated with running a modern newsroom. Cutting staff is one of the surest ways to drastically reduce operating costs, but at what expense in terms of news coverage? Fewer staff means less coverage of certain subject areas and neighborhoods, which can end up giving the public an incomplete picture of what is happening in their town or region as the paper fills the news hole with wire-service copy or light features. Similarly, investigative reports are often time-consuming and expensive and are less likely to be conducted in a media organization intensely aware of maximizing profits.

Professional training and development is another area that often suffers. For many journalists interested in learning how to use computer-assisted reporting tools or digital media in order to help make them better reporters, it is necessary to pay their own way to conferences or workshops and use their personal vacation time in order to attend. This is despite a push by some news organizations for journalists to become multimedia reporters, doing their stories in print, TV, and radio formats, which of course is intended to save on production costs when one journalist is doing the work that three had previously done.

▼ MEDIA TYPES INFLUENCING CONTENT

Just as the type of media used to present content influences how that content is created and how it is received and perceived by the public, various business pressures arise with the various media types. The expense of producing feature-length films, for example, is an important factor for large media companies that want to maximize their profits. A film could have a greater likelihood of getting produced if the media company already owns the rights to the character to be used in the film, for example, and if there is good potential for other media content from within the company, such as music and television shows, to be tied in with the movie to help in marketing it.

The individual divisions of a large media company must deal with the demands of the corporate parent to maximize profits. For example, the book-publishing branch may feel pressure to emphasize books from established authors in a popular genre in order to generate sales, but at the expense of finding new authors or types of books that do not fall within established categories.

The need for exciting visual elements has even affected news coverage. *Dateline NBC*'s fifteen-minute segment "Waiting to Explode," which ran on November 17, 1992, was meant to demonstrate the danger of the gas tanks exploding with certain models of General Motors' pickups. The only trouble was that the trucks shown exploding on the segment had been rigged by the production team to ensure a fiery explosion and that several elements of the information presented were misleading or inaccurate. Only later, through independent investigations and information from sources who were at the initial filming, did the truth behind the segment come out, forcing NBC to make a public apology and settle the lawsuit that GM had brought against it.[2] In this case, the need to have an exciting visual element likely helped cause the ethical breaches.

On a smaller scale, but no less unethical, was the example of *Today* reporter Michelle Kosinski covering flooding in Wayne, New Jersey, in 2005. She is shown paddling a kayak down a flooded street as she gives her report, only to have two people walk right in front of her, revealing that the water is actually only ankle deep. Despite the people walking in front of her, she continued with the report and paddling as if nothing happened.

Not every dramatic photograph on the front page of a newspaper or in television news reports is an example of a breach in media ethics, but it is important to have a critical eye and good media literacy when looking at visual media to ask how much of the decision to put that element in the news segment or on the page was driven by the need to capture the public's attention rather than its true news value.

▼ NEW WORLDS—OR CULTURAL IMPERIALISM?

Media content can open new worlds and new ways of thinking to us as we get exposed to different cultures and lifestyles. The Web has further opened up the possibilities for exploration, especially though video-sharing sites and other social media.

But when considering the issue of media concentration of ownership and the types of media content typically produced by media companies, questions arise regarding how many diverse voices we actually see. Yes, there are more cable channels than ever, but how many DIY channels such as HGTV are needed for the public, and how fundamentally different are shows such as *NCIS* and *CSI* or *Law and Order*?

When we look at the global reach of the media giants and their ability to promote their programming in foreign markets, it raises the issue of what is called cultural imperialism, or the practice of one country dominating a media market

As popular as shows like *CSI* or *NCIS* may be, there are in fact few major differences between shows like these or between shows within other genres, which raises the question: How much variety do we really have on TV?

through an influx of its media products. The issue is further complicated in that many of these shows imported from the United States, such as *Baywatch* or *The Simpsons*, gain large followings in the foreign countries where they are shown, making it seem like viewers are not forced to watch the programs but are doing so willingly or because the programming is meeting some need that is unmet by domestic television programs.

This may be true to some extent, as many countries cannot afford to produce television shows at the same level of production quality as in the United States, thus giving domestic programs a visually amateurish quality compared to imported programs. However, what can also happen is that domestic television and movie production companies in these countries do not get a chance to fully develop because of the flood of imported movies and shows. The market size in countries with small populations can also be a barrier to the development of robust movie and television industries, because they have no way to recoup the high production costs with such a limited market.

What is of great concern from an ethical perspective to many in these countries is that their citizens are absorbing alien cultural values that can conflict with their traditional cultural values. Although this exposure to new types of content can lead citizens to question their government about such issues as freedom and democracy, remember that a show such as *Baywatch* does not deal with these issues in any way. The worry is that citizens are losing their appreciation and pride in their traditional culture and replacing it with a prepackaged, homogenized version of what the United States represents—and loving it. Not only do they lose touch with their native traditions and values, they adopt unrealistic or limited values based on a skewed image of the United States.

◣◥ Ethics in Journalism

Because of journalism's unique role in society, its protection by the First Amendment, and its public service mission, many ethical dilemmas arise in the course of practicing it. Ethical questions play a role in the entire news-gathering and production process, and many questions do not have easy answers. Ethical issues become even more important as more citizens practice journalism or some form of it.

Editors must consider whether headlines and captions accurately reflect the important points of a story or simply titillate. Privacy issues play a role when private citizens are thrust by circumstance into the media spotlight. Reporters must consider fairness and balance in their choice of interview subjects. Photo editors and designers must avoid the temptation to alter elements of photos to make them more dramatic. Societal mores and cultural values of the audience must be considered when determining what qualifies as news and how it is reported, although newspapers must also sometimes take highly unpopular stands on issues when acting as the public's conscience.

▼ PRIVACY RIGHTS VERSUS THE PUBLIC'S RIGHT TO KNOW

Although there is no actual law stating the public has a "right to know," it is often cited as a commonly understood principle when journalists are trying to obtain information that can help the public make better-informed decisions regarding anything from political candidates to corporate wrongdoing to potentially dangerous foods, drugs, or buildings.

Gathering proof of wrongdoing is one of the biggest challenges journalists face. Admissions of guilt are unlikely to come out during an interview—if the subject even agrees to an interview, which is often not the case. Journalists are often barred from the very locations they need to visit in order to gather information. Employees are forbidden by management to speak to journalists or threatened with losing their jobs if they do; police or public officials refuse to see or talk to journalists or are slow in providing requested documentation, even if the documents are public records.

New technology such as miniature microphones and cameras, or the old technique of going undercover, may seem easy answers to the journalist's dilemma. But the ethics and legality of these tools and actions must be considered. Sometimes these techniques are the only ones that will give access to people engaged in illegal or unethical behavior, such as selling drugs or arms.

Federal law prohibits the media or anyone else from intentionally intercepting, or attempting to intercept, anyone's communication by wire, oral, or electronic means. Citizens have a reasonable expectation of privacy for oral, or spoken, communications, including via telephone or over the Internet. However, it is complicated in that states have varying laws on whether only one person or both people in a conversation must give consent to have a conversation recorded.

Regardless of the legality of intercepting communications, is it ethical? There is no easy answer, as it depends on the circumstances. It also depends on whether it is print or broadcast media. The FCC generally prohibits the use of wireless microphones to overhear private conversations unless all parties to the communication have given prior consent. Conversations that occur in a public place, such as a restaurant or bar, however, would not be subject to the same prohibition, since people in public places cannot expect the same right to privacy. Broadcast television or radio stations may not record telephone conversations without the consent of all parties, and they must notify the parties prior to broadcasting any of the recorded content. Long-distance calls can only be recorded under limited circumstances, including an announcement made at the beginning of the call indicating it will be recorded or possibly broadcast. Violation of these rules can result in the forfeiture of the station's license, fines, or other penalties.

WEB LINK
Citizen Media Law Project: Newsgathering and Privacy
http://www.citmedialaw.org/legal-guide/newsgathering-and-privacy

One area of confusion regarding privacy is whether posting material in a blog or on a social-media site like Facebook is public or not. Some claim that it is the same as a public space, but it gets more complex when one considers the shelf life of material online. An offhand comment in a bar disappears once it is said, but an inflammatory blog post written years ago and later deleted may still exist somewhere on the Web.

▼ GOING UNDERCOVER

The legality and ethics of journalists going undercover are also not settled. It in many ways depends on how ethical or responsible the media professional was in using these techniques. Questions that may be asked in a court of law include the following: Were the media being fair? Does going undercover or using hidden cameras somehow manipulate or distort the situation? Do the undercover techniques help build meaningful information or simply sensationalize the story? If a media professional (or anyone else, for that matter) is convicted of violating the law in going undercover, there are a variety of potential penalties, including substantial prison terms and fines.

The Internet raises new questions about a journalist not announcing her identity. If she engages in a discussion in a child-pornography online discussion group without revealing her identity as a journalist pursuing a story, is it ethical to use others' posts without their permission? Is it ethical to pose as someone other than a journalist in order to get people to talk as they naturally would in an online forum?

▼ VICTIMIZING THE VICTIMS

Crime victims can feel doubly victimized when their names are made public by the media, especially with crimes such as rape, which still carry a social stigma. Most newspapers and television stations do not make rape victims' names public, although critics of this practice argue that it further stigmatizes rape rather than educating the public about the crime of violence that it is.

Publicizing details of crimes can also contribute to copycat crimes, and journalists must always consider what kinds of information in a story are important and what are simply lurid or titillating details. Needlessly mentioning race, gender, or sexual orientation can often be unethical in framing a subject in a way that may reinforce social stereotypes.

Photographs and video have a power to sometimes tell a story in a way that words alone cannot. Yet, publicly presented dramatic photos or footage are not always justified for their news value alone. In fact, in cases of human tragedy, sadness, or crime, personal grief has been violated by the repeated presentation of pictures or video in newspapers, magazines, or on television.

On Sunday, June 11, 2000, the annual Puerto Rican Day Parade in New York City was marred by a group of fifteen to twenty-five men who assaulted women attending the parade. Amateur video documented many of the assaults, and the footage was used by the police to apprehend suspects. Television also aired much of the video and newspapers published print photos extracted from the video, sometimes revealing the identities of the women who were being assaulted.

This is a typical situation a news director or editor faces when deciding what to print or air as news. There is no doubt that footage and pictures of seminude women would attract a larger audience (along with vociferous complaints from various groups), but the ethics of showing such material must be considered in the effects it would have on the victims and their families.

The annual Puerto Rican Day Parade in New York City usually occurs without incident, but in 2000 the news media was criticized for showing graphic images and videotaped footage of women being assaulted.

▼ SOCIETY OF PROFESSIONAL JOURNALISTS CODE OF ETHICS

The Society of Professional Journalists (SPJ) is a large organization of working journalists and student chapters that tries to ensure that journalism is being practiced professionally and ethically and that it is fulfilling its role in society. The SPJ's code of ethics states that journalists should "seek truth and report it" and that "journalists should be honest, fair and courageous in gathering, reporting and interpreting information." These are some of the other principles in the code:

WEB LINK
SPJ Code of Ethics
www.spj.org/ethicscode.asp

- Test the accuracy of information from all sources and exercise care to avoid inadvertent error. Deliberate distortion is never permissible.
- Diligently seek out subjects of news stories to give them the opportunity to respond to allegations of wrongdoing.
- Identify sources whenever feasible. The public is entitled to as much information as possible on sources' reliability.
- Make certain that headlines, news teasers, and promotional material, photos, video, audio, graphics, sound bites, and quotations do not misrepresent. They should not oversimplify or highlight incidents out of context.
- Never distort the content of news photos or video. Image enhancement for technical clarity is always permissible. Label montages and photo illustrations.
- Avoid misleading reenactments or staged news events. If reenactment is necessary to tell a story, label it.
- Support the open exchange of views, even views journalists find repugnant.
- Avoid undercover or other surreptitious methods of gathering information except when traditional open methods will not yield information vital to the public. Use of such methods should be explained as part of the story.

◤◥ Ethical Issues in Advertising

Mass media are a powerful vehicle to influence the public's opinions, even when they are simply trying to inform or educate. It is no wonder, then, that companies spend billions of dollars on advertising each year, trying to persuade people to buy their products. Yet numerous ethical issues have been raised that often give the discerning consumer a jaundiced eye toward advertising, from snake oil salesmen of the nineteenth century to complaints about billboards in the twentieth century, claims against telemarketers for invasion of privacy, and false and deceptive advertising in the mass media, including actors paid to give "customer testimonials."

Advertising is an important part of how goods and services are marketed in a capitalist economy, and some advertising contains useful product information. Advertising is also the economic engine that drives much of the system of mass communication.

The advertising industry has been less successful at regulating itself than the entertainment industry, and usually the government eventually steps in to create new laws or regulations after receiving consumer complaints—or sometimes after long campaigns regarding certain advertising practices. The Federal Trade Commission (FTC) and the Food and Drug Administration (FDA) are responsible for enforcing regulations regarding deceptive advertising. Industry self-regulation comes from a variety of trade organizations. One of the main ethical issues, from a mass-communication perspective, is false or deceptive advertising.

▼ DECEPTIVE ADVERTISING

In some cases, advertisers give clearly false or deceptive information, but it is illegal only if it misleads the consumer in some material way. Deception in advertising is not always illegal, because in some cases it does not mislead. For instance, ice cubes photographed in a beverage ad may not be actual ice cubes, as they would melt quickly under the photographer's hot lights, but since the fake cubes do not mislead anyone regarding the taste or look of the beverage, it is fine to use them.

In other cases, however, deceptive claims are made with the intention to mislead the consumer. Offering a "going out of business" sales price is misleading if the store is not actually planning on going out of business, for example.

A division of the Federal Trade Commission is assigned responsibility to ferret out deception and can force such advertising from mass media or even levy fines. The FTC once found a commercial for a toy car misleading even though it was not false. The toy was filmed in extreme close-up next to the track, making it appear to move very rapidly and look like a blur on the screen. The FTC ruled that children would be deceived into believing the car actually moves so fast it is a blur, and the ad had to be canceled or modified.

▼ PUFFERY

puffery

A type of advertising language that makes extravagant and unrealistic claims about a product without saying anything concrete.

Nevertheless, there is great temptation among those selling goods and services, as well as those sponsoring ads, to exaggerate their claims. This is called **puffery**, and it is an ethical and legal gray area (i.e., sometimes allowed, sometimes not). Puffery usually involves an opinion statement about the product. Examples include these familiar advertising slogans:

- "The best in the business" (AT&T)
- "The best part of waking up is Folgers in your cup"
- "World's most refreshing light beer" (Coors Light)
- "For the rest of your life" (Sleepy's)

In each case, there is no way to prove the truth or falsehood of the claim. The FTC's position is that audiences do not believe the opinion claims of these commercials because they do not perceive them to be factual. Consequently, the FTC permits most puffery, because it feels people are not deceived.

▼ CONFLICTS OF INTEREST IN ADVERTISING

Advertising agencies, if they want to remain in business, must be loyal to their clients. It does little good for an agency whose client is a tobacco company to lecture the company about the harmful effects of smoking. The advertising agency's professional responsibility is to help the client sell more products, and their success as an agency will be measured in large part by how well their advertising campaigns do that. The underlying principle is the same whether they are selling soup or cigarettes.

Conflicts of interest in advertising can arise in a number of ways. First, individuals within an agency may not feel it is ethical from their own moral perspective to help companies that sell products that are harmful to the public. Some agencies allow employees to set criteria for what industries they are willing to work with, but in other agencies making such a choice could ruin a career. Second, conflicts of interest occur if an agency works for two competing companies. Even if the teams

Puffery in advertising is allowed by the FTC because it is assumed that reasonable people do not take the claims as the truth and thus are not deceived or misled.

working on each client are completely separate from each other and based in different cities, there is still a chance that secret information about one client may be divulged to members on the team of the competitor client, giving them an unfair advantage. Third, with some products there may be a conflict of interest between loyalty to the client and what is in the public interest. A product may not have the benefits it claims in advertising, or it may not be the best or cheapest product on the market, but an effective advertising campaign can help it become a market leader.

▼ ADVERTISING CODES OF ETHICS

Various advertising and marketing groups have created codes of ethics for their members. Like all codes of ethics, these are largely unenforceable but are used as guiding principles or values for how the profession or industry wants to present itself to the world, or what it strives for.

The American Marketing Association (AMA) list three ethical norms members should follow: do no harm, foster trust in the marketing system, and embrace ethical values. It then lists several ethical values that should be embraced, many of which sound remarkably like virtues and include honesty, responsibility, fairness, respect, transparency, and citizenship.

The American Advertising Federation (AAF) lists as its first code, "Advertising shall tell the truth, and reveal significant facts; the omission of which would mislead the public." Several other points, such as substantiation, comparison, price claims, and testimonials, also deal in one way or another with issues of deception or misleading the public.

◤▽ Ethics in Public Relations

Public relations people face a unique set of ethical issues compared to journalists, media-entertainment professionals, and advertising people. Like advertising professionals, their loyalties lie with the client, but like journalists, if they present false or misleading information, their credibility and that of their clients can be severely damaged in the court of public opinion. In addition, although some public relations practitioners like to claim they are the "conscience of the client," the

CONVERGENCE CONTEXT

▶ Selling a War

Ethical lapses in PR can have far-reaching consequences, especially when it comes to politics and war. Hill and Knowlton was widely criticized for its clandestine efforts to influence the U.S. government and the American public during the Gulf War. The firm was hired at a cost of more than half a million dollars by the government of Kuwait to foster support among the American public and the U.S. Congress.

Hill and Knowlton produced and distributed dozens of video news releases (VNRs) to television news operations around the country. Many of the stations aired the VNRs without identifying their source as either Hill and Knowlton or the government of Kuwait. Many aired the propaganda without editing it, presenting it as impartial journalism.

Hill and Knowlton also helped organize the "Congressional Human Rights Caucus," which held hearings on Capitol Hill. In October 1990, a fifteen-year-old Kuwaiti girl, known only as Nayirah, spoke in tears, saying, "I volunteered at the al-Addan hospital. While I was there, I saw the Iraqi soldiers come into the hospital with guns, and go into the room where . . . babies were in incubators. They took the babies out of the incubators, took the incubators, and left the babies on the cold floor to die."

For months after her testimony, the Iraqi soldiers' killing of babies was repeated in the media and even by President George H. W. Bush as a rationale for the U.S. presence in the region. Later it was revealed that Nayirah was a member of the Kuwaiti royal family, that her testimony was a fabrication, and that a Hill and Knowlton vice president had coached Nayirah on what to say during her testimony. After the end of the war, the Canadian Broadcasting Corporation produced an Emmy Award–winning documentary on the Hill and Knowlton campaign, entitled *To Sell a War.*

fact is they do not always have access to the corporate channels of power to head off possibly disastrous management decisions. Often they are called in after damage has been done and are asked to minimize or negate it from a public relations standpoint.

Some PR firms have done things like hiring people to attend corporate or government meetings and present testimonials as if they were concerned citizens. They have also helped create faux grassroots campaigns online, called "**astroturf**" campaigns, designed to make it appear that there is citizen support for a company or cause. If bringing people to speak at a public meeting is considered unethical, then it is clear that this online equivalent is unethical, too.

Digital media present other new and unique temptations to public relations professionals. Shortly after Infoseek's executive vice president Patrick Naughton was arrested in September 1999 for allegedly planning a sexual encounter with a minor he'd met over the Internet (who turned out to be an undercover policewoman), not only was Naughton fired from Infoseek and his management bio removed from the site, but the public relations department tried to delete all mention of his name in their archived press releases online, to make it seem as if he never worked there. There were protests about this clumsy attempt to rewrite history *1984* style, and within twenty-four hours his name was back in most of the press releases. Infoseek claimed it was "an accident."[3]

In today's 24/7 social media environment, many publicists have had trouble maintaining damage control when celebrity clients tweet offensive comments. Even though such posts are deleted soon after the damage is done, the fact that a tweet is sent to so many followers and re-tweeted keeps the original post in the public's eye.

astroturf campaign

The practice of creating a movement or campaign so that it looks as though it was created by concerned citizens as a grassroots movement, when in fact it was actually created or controlled by an organization with a vested interest in the outcome.

▼ CONFLICTS OF INTEREST IN PR

Partly because of professional loyalty to their clients, PR professionals have many of the same conflicts of interest that advertising professionals have regarding unsavory clients. A PR firm may have to manage a crisis communication situation for a disaster caused by a company, such as the BP oil spill in the Gulf of Mexico in 2010, even as they see corporate executives take further missteps from a public relations perspective, such as saying things they should not.

PR professionals may also have to deal with clients who do not understand how the media system works and who believe that anything they release to the media should be received without question or criticism. Clients may also not like having to adjust to a world in which their customers can talk and complain with each other in very public forums. Although PR agencies tout themselves as specialists in managing relationships between the clients and their many publics, in truth many clients do not want an equal relationship with consumers based on dialog and openness. They instead want to dictate the messages to the public and do not want to hear anything back. This dynamic can be difficult for a PR professional who ethically believes that the public should have a way to talk back or should be able to have a dialog with a company.

One of the thorniest conflicts of interest in PR is when a PR professional has access to confidential information about the client but is asked to keep it secret in order to protect the company's image. When such information may directly affect the public in some way, such as information about a prescription drug's harmful side effects, it puts the PR professional in a difficult ethical situation that tests her or his loyalties and moral values.

▼ PUBLIC RELATIONS CODES OF ETHICS

Guidelines for ethical public relations practices have been established by professional associations such as the Public Relations Society of America (PRSA) and the International Association of Business Communicators (IABC).

According to the PRSA, unethical behavior for PR practitioners includes lying by omission, as in failing to release financial information from a corporation or giving a misleading impression of a corporation's performance; deceiving the public by employing people to pose as volunteers to speak at public hearings or in "grassroots" campaigns; and giving expensive goods or gifts to journalists or politicians in order to influence their opinion on a product or issue.

On the other hand, their guidelines also state that members must protect the privacy rights of clients and safeguard their confidential information, as well as advise appropriate authorities if they discover that an employee is divulging confidential information. It is easy to see how an ethical conflict could arise for a PR professional if he or she learns information about the poor financial situation of a company and is asked by the company to encourage positive news reports on its financial health, rather than the truth.

Ethics in Entertainment

Media professionals in entertainment do not wrestle with the same issues regarding truth and the public as journalists, advertisers, and public relations professionals. Entertainment is meant to entertain, and in the case of fictional content, sticking to the truth may be immaterial. Some entertainment properties do touch on true facts—such as documentary films or books and movies based on actual events—and they are sometimes judged on the success at which they do this, but straying from the truth does not usually detract from their entertainment value. Because of this, entertainment content is not held to the same ethical standards as, say, a newspaper story or investigative TV report. But ethics do enter into the world of entertainment because of the ability of such content to shape society's beliefs and influence behavior.

▼ STEREOTYPES IN ENTERTAINMENT

Because entertainment plays such an important part in our lives and is a powerful force for transmitting cultural values, the depiction of stereotypes in the media can be especially hurtful or damaging to groups. At the turn of the twentieth century, minstrel shows were popular in vaudeville, with white actors made up in "blackface" to depict African Americans, often in demeaning or clownish roles. Jewish minstrel shows were also popular and similarly played on popular stereotypes of the time.

Asians and Asian Americans have faced both positive and negative stereotypes over the years. As many Asians immigrated to the United States in the nineteenth and early twentieth centuries, they were often depicted in the mass media in negative ways. Today they are often touted as a "model minority" because of the achievements of many Asian American young people in school and professions. However, hidden racist stereotypes still appear far too often in the media, such as an April 2004 full-page feature in *Details* magazine entitled "Gay or Asian?" that used dozens of stereotypes of both gays and Asians.

Some may wonder what harm some good-natured joking about stereotypes can do, especially when it is meant to be humorous or simply to entertain, such as the *Details* feature. However, that is exactly the danger with stereotypes in entertainment—precisely because the underlying stereotypes are taken for granted, they are influential in molding norms and beliefs about certain groups, especially when the primary exposure to those groups comes through the media.

Stereotypes related to Italian Americans are a good case in point. According to a Zogby poll in 2003, 78 percent of teenagers associated Italian Americans with either criminal activity or blue-collar work. Another poll showed that 74 percent of adult Americans believed that Italian Americans had some connection to organized crime.

These kinds of misperceptions influence in subtle and sometimes not-so-subtle ways how we interact with the groups that are stereotyped, and the misperceptions no doubt come from the number of media depictions and popular movies and shows in which Italian Americans are shown as gangsters or part of organized crime.

Some Indian tribes have protested the use of depictions of Indians as sports-team mascots.

▼ SEX AND VIOLENCE

Depictions of sex and violence have long been staples of entertainment media, and the old adage "sex sells" is even truer for entertainment than it is for other forms of media. We will look at the legal implications for media and freedom of speech regarding pornography, obscenity, and violence in the next chapter and here focus on the ethical implications of depictions of sex and violence.

At the heart of the issue is the belief that exposure to media has some sort of effect on us. We have often heard claims along the lines of someone's violent outburst was caused because of watching too many violent programs, or cases in which people have copied crimes they've seen on television or in the movies. Although these media effects claims will be examined in more detail in Chapter 14, let us assume for now that there is at least some truth to the claim that media has an effect on us.

If this is true, then it is hard to make an ethical argument that any kind of violence or harmful content is ethical. Whether on utilitarian, virtue-based, or any other ethical system, would purposely harming others be considered ethical, especially when done simply so a company and small handful of people can make profits from that harm?

Another issue arises with sex and violence in the media, even when realizing that just because we watch a violent movie it does not mean we will all become mass murderers. This new issue relates to the points above about stereotypes and how it may affect our thinking about certain groups. Consider the double standards about male and female nudity in movies, for example. Rarely do movies show full frontal male nudity, while female nudity can be seen much more frequently. Such depictions may give us subtle cues that it is normal to treat women as sex objects while men should not be treated as such.

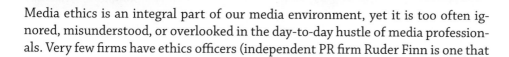

LOOKING BACK AND MOVING FORWARD

Media ethics is an integral part of our media environment, yet it is too often ignored, misunderstood, or overlooked in the day-to-day hustle of media professionals. Very few firms have ethics officers (independent PR firm Ruder Finn is one that does) whose sole job is to help employees make ethical decisions that affect clients, the public, and even coworkers.

Developing moral reasoning skills takes time and effort and never really stops. The sheer variety of situations that arise that call for moral reasoning, especially in the media professions, means that there will always be a new challenge ahead. However, if you can develop good moral reasoning abilities then you can start to build on your experiences and results from past decisions—right and wrong—and apply that knowledge to new situations you encounter.

Understanding the various ethical systems and what they value as moral, or right, can help you find your own moral compass. It does not mean you have to choose an ethical system and stay with that, of course, but it simply means that you may feel more comfortable drawing from one ethical system over others. Even so, being able to take elements from each one, as the situation calls for, can help you determine the values in conflict and find answers that help ensure ethical decision making.

Some of the later ethical systems, such as the dialogical and ethics of care systems, can be especially fruitful in a social media world in which conversations online become more important. Further, the virtues that they espouse in showing respect to what others are saying may help mitigate some of the divisiveness and anger that we see today in our political rhetoric and social lives.

DISCUSSION QUESTIONS

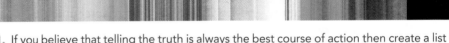

1. If you believe that telling the truth is always the best course of action then create a list of cases in which you would lie, ranging from extreme cases (i.e., "I would lie to save my life") to trivial ("I would lie to not hurt someone's feelings."). After you have compiled your list, examine what that may say about your ideals about not lying and the practical reality of it.

2. Discuss what virtues you think are most admirable in today's world. Why do you think so? How many of these can you say you honestly practice?

3. What may cause a change in desired virtues over time within a culture? For example, thriftiness was prized during colonial times, yet today Americans have one of the lowest savings rates in the developed world. Why do you think thriftiness stopped being considered a virtue?

4. If you had to pick just one ethical system by which to live, with no influences from the others, which would it be? Why?

5. Why do you think there are so many different variations of feminist ethics while an ethical system like duty-based ethics hasn't had the same degree of splintering and fractionalization?

6. Consider a movie or television show that has stereotypes. Replace that stereotyped group with your own ethnicity or gender and consider how you would feel seeing a member of your group depicted in those situations. How might that make you feel about your group?

7. If real journalists appear as journalists in fictional stories in movies or television shows, does that make you feel like you trust them less in their regular news shows? Why or why not?

FURTHER READING

Moral Theory: An Introduction. Mark Timmons (2002) Rowman & Littlefield.

Communicating Ethically: Character, Duties, Consequences, and Relationships. William W. Neher and Paul J. Sandin (2007) Pearson Education.

The Handbook of Mass Media Ethics. Lee Wilkins, Clifford G. Christians (eds.) (2009) Routledge.

Living Ethics: Across Media Platforms. Michael Bugeja (2007) Oxford University Press.

Ethics for the Real World: Creating a Personal Code to Guide Decisions in Work and Life. Ronald Howard, Clinton Korver (2008) Harvard Business Press.

Habermas: A Very Short Introduction. Gordon Finlayson (2005) Oxford University Press.

13

COMMUNICATION LAW AND REGULATION IN THE DIGITAL AGE

REDDIT IS DOWN

SOPA and PIPA damage the Internet. today we fight back.

Dear reddit,

Today, for 12 hours, reddit.com goes dark to raise awareness of two bills in congress: **H.R.3261 "Stop Online Piracy Act"** and **S.968 "PROTECT IP"**, which could radically change the landscape of the Internet. These bills provide overly broad mechanisms for enforcement of copyright which would restrict innovation and threaten the existence of websites with user-submitted content, such as reddit.

Please take today as a day of focus and action to learn about these destructive bills and do what you can to prevent them from becoming reality.

[make a call]   [sign the petition]   [learn more]

action of the hour   speak out

Write a letter to the editor of your local paper, opposing the bills. Contact local news stations and let them know that this is an issue worth covering.

Important Upcoming Dates

- **January 24, 2012** – Senate votes on PIPA
- **February** – House Judiciary Committee continues its markup of SOPA

FAQ

What is the intent of SOPA/PROTECT IP?
The stated intent of the bills is to provide tools for law enforcement and copyright holders to protect their intellectual property rights.

What's wrong with protecting copyrights?
Nothing! The devil, as they say, is in the details. PROTECT IP and SOPA will

PROTECT IP / SOPA Breaks The Internet

PROTECT IP / SOPA Breaks The Internet

04:20 |||||| HD :: vimeo

Live Updates   Last updated 11:20am

11:16am   SOPA Sponsor Holden withdraws support!
          http://t.co/ojDhkEUj #blackout via
          @joethepeacock — the reddit alien

10:15am   "Our elected officials are beholden to the
          ELECTORATE, not to lobbyists" -- @kn0thing
          #blackout — the reddit alien

9:51am   Micah Sifry: SOPA Part Of "Larger Struggle
          Over How Expression And Creation Will Be
          Supported" #blackout — the reddit alien

9:31am   Watch New York Tech Meetup livestream
          outside offices of NY Sen Schumer &
          Gillibrand, starting now http://t.co/WJfXo4Ws
          #blackout — the reddit alien

8:33am   Back on Bloomberg, talking about the #blackout
          with @margbrennan. Live here:
          http://t.co/x6fGMT9B. #SOPA
          #PIPA — Alexis Ohanian

8:30am   Keep Calling! It makes a difference - SOPA

LEARNING OBJECTIVES

By the end of this chapter you should be able to:

- Understand the nature of freedom of speech and press and how media are regulated in the United States.

- Describe the key legal concepts protecting and restricting freedom of speech and press, including threats to national security, libel, and censorship.

- Outline the regulation of content in the United States, especially regarding commercial speech and political speech.

- Discuss the principal legislation that defines communication regulation in the United States, and the principal federal communications regulatory agency, the Federal Communications Commission.

- Explain intellectual property issues, especially copyright, and how they are affected in the digital age.

On January 18–19, 2012, Wikipedia and Reddit took the unprecedented step of "going dark" for twenty-four hours in protest of the proposed Stop Online Privacy Act (SOPA) and Protect Intellectual Property Act (PIPA) that were going before the House of Representatives and U.S. Senate for votes. Many other sites changed their home pages with altered logos or added text, expressing their displeasure with the proposed legislation.

SOPA was introduced by Representative Lamar Smith (R-TX) in late October 2011, and if passed into law would let intellectual property holders sue companies and websites that infringed on their rights, would bar search engines from linking to such sites, and would require Internet service providers (ISPs) to stop service for the sites.

The bill, supported by the entertainment industry, pharmaceutical companies, and the U.S. Chamber of Commerce, immediately drew criticism from a range of Internet companies and citizen groups who claimed that the sweeping powers it would grant companies amounted to Internet censorship, violated the First Amendment, and would harm the growth and development of the Internet. Under the act, critics charged, whistleblowers or people trying to expose wrongdoing could be sued if it was deemed they had infringed on intellectual property rights—and websites or ISPs carrying the material could be shut down or penalized—thus having a "chilling effect" on free speech.

Supporters of the bill countered that the bill was not about free speech but about protecting jobs and the rights of intellectual property holders, who were seeing lost revenues because of file-sharing sites, illegal copying of music and other content, and websites selling counterfeit goods, including counterfeit drugs.

The same day that sites like Wikipedia went dark in protest, the FBI shut down the popular file-sharing site Megaupload, which prompted the hacktivist group Anonymous to create denial of service attacks on sites of groups and entertainment companies that supported SOPA.

The battle lines clearly drawn, it was the politicians who finally blinked. Smith announced on January 20 that he would postpone drafting the bill even as he promised to remain committed to finding ways to crack down on online piracy and protect intellectual property online.

Congress shall make no law respecting an establishment of religion, or prohibiting the free exercise thereof; or abridging the freedom of speech, or of the press; or the right of the people peaceably to assemble, and to petition the government for a redress of grievances.

FIRST AMENDMENT TO THE CONSTITUTION OF THE UNITED STATES

It is important to remember that the First Amendment is very much an American invention. Most other countries have no such stipulation in their constitutions, which of course has resulted in sometimes vastly different laws and regulations regarding mass communication and journalism.

Governments decide on policies, or overarching objectives that they want to accomplish, based on a variety of factors. These factors include the political views of the party in power, whether the government was elected by the citizens or came into power in some other way, and the general social and cultural norms of the nation. Laws are created and enacted to carry out the government's policies, but which laws are created also depends on the form of government. In democracies, even the party in power may not be able to create laws it wants because of opposition party actions, or bills are altered as part of compromises in order to become laws. Laws, once enacted, are forcibly upheld by the state and carry penalties such as fines or imprisonment if broken. Regulations are similar to laws in that they act as tools to help carry out policies, but usually are limited to fines or other sanctions rather than imprisonment if broken.

First Amendment

Guarantees that Congress shall make no law restricting freedom of speech, press, or religion.

Although the **First Amendment** guarantees that Congress shall make no law restricting freedom of speech or of the press, it has been interpreted by the courts, elected officials, and legal scholars to permit some level of regulatory and legal restriction. Some of these laws deal with libel, obscenity, and other media-content matters. Others deal with technical issues related to broadcast station operation, such as to prevent one station from interfering with another's signals, and others

MEDIA QUIZ

Legal Limits

Test your legal knowledge as it relates to the First Amendment, media regulations, and copyright. Mark whether the questions are true or false.

1. Libel and slander are simply two different legal terms for the same thing.
2. In the United Kingdom you can be sued for libel even if what you said about the person is true.
3. It is impossible for politicians, but not public figures such as movie stars, to sue for libel.
4. The government can restrict free speech if it feels it will harm national security.
5. Journalists can protect themselves from libel as long as they properly attribute the questionable material.
6. Broadcasting media face more regulations than print because it is felt they have a greater impact on the audience.
7. Only accredited journalists or freelance writers under contract can use the Freedom of Information Act to request public records from the federal government.
8. The FCC enforces its broadcasting regulations by examining station and network programming and flagging material that is objectionable.
9. A hyperlink is not protected by the First Amendment.
10. If I tell my friend my idea for a novel and he then writes a novel based on my idea, I can sue him for copyright infringement.

---

pertain to media ownership, intellectual property rights, and fulfilling the requirements of broadcasting licenses. We will look at how these differ and how they relate to media and public policy, primarily in the United States, although other countries will sometimes be examined for comparison.

◤◢ The Legal Framework

When printing began in Renaissance Europe, political and religious authorities were quick to recognize the power of publishing to spread not only religious teachings but political edicts as well. However, political and religious dissidents found printing presses equally useful in disseminating their views against authority. The tension between government control of the press and using the press as a means to be free of political or religious control continues to this day.

The reasons underlying the value of freedom from governmental control were perhaps best articulated by U.S. president Thomas Jefferson, who said, "Information is the currency of democracy." When the first U.S. Congress passed the Bill of Rights in 1789, there were fewer than three dozen printing presses in the country. Despite this small number, the importance of the press was recognized by the nation's founders. Jefferson said, "Were it left for me to decide whether we should have a government without newspapers, or newspapers without a government, I should not hesitate a moment to prefer the latter."

Thomas Jefferson's famous quote about his choice between government and newspapers is often cited to show the important role that journalism plays in a democracy.

fourth estate

Another term for the press, or journalism, in which it acts as a fourth branch of government: one that watches the other branches (executive, legislative, and judicial).

The press is a critical watchdog of government as well as of other powerful institutions in society, including business. But it is as an unofficial "fourth branch" of government, or **fourth estate**, that the press must be free from government censorship or control. Although Jefferson referred only to the print media, the only form of mass communication during his time, his comments apply equally to electronic mass communication, and when we refer to "the press" we are referring to print and electronic media.

In societies where government control over the press, or media, is substantial, as in China or other authoritarian countries where journalists must be licensed to operate, the press suffers from an inability to criticize the government, its policies, or its representatives. More often than not, the press becomes a puppet to the government and is used to promote government positions rather than independently evaluate them. In the United States and other democratic societies, the press ideally acts as an independent balance of power to government bodies. However, concentration of ownership, commercialism, and other circumstances can adversely affect the ability of the press to act responsibly or effectively in its role as watchdog of powerful societal institutions. Business interests may sometimes outweigh public interests, for news organizations.

Despite the early constitutional admonitions to protect freedom of speech and press, there have been many attempts by the government at all levels to infringe upon the independence of the press and to censor. In addition, a second problem has plagued the media with regard to acts of general governmental control. This problem is the failure of the government, in each of its three branches, to extend full First Amendment protection to the media in all their forms. Instead, only the print media have received full protection. In *Miami Herald Publishing Co. v. Tornillo* (1974), for instance, the U.S. Supreme Court struck down a Florida statute that required newspapers to give space at no cost to political candidates whose personal or professional character the paper had criticized. However, television and radio stations must provide airtime should the station itself editorially endorse or oppose a candidate.

Radio, television, cinema, and today the Internet have received much less First Amendment protection than print media, and only through extended legal battles have they won a certain degree of freedom. In fact, during the first half of the twentieth century, cinema was not provided any First Amendment protection. Not until the Supreme Court's 1952 *Miracle* decision (*Joseph Burstyn, Inc. v. Wilson*), when the court ruled that the showing of a film could not be prohibited because a censor deemed it sacrilegious, did any constitutional protection regarding free speech extend to motion pictures.

The historical influences and legal and regulatory decisions on print and electronic media are complex, but they are worth exploring briefly in order to better understand the reasons given for restrictions on media content today.

◢◤ The Foundations of Freedom of Expression

chilling effect

The phenomenon that occurs when journalists or other media producers decide not to publish stories on a topic after a journalist has been punished or jailed for such a story.

Governments continue to use many means to control media. One heavy-handed method is to jail journalists and editors, thus not only silencing them but also often having a **chilling effect** on others who may be tempted to write on similar topics.

However, such tactics can also backfire in that jailed journalists may stoke public anger at the government or damage the government's reputation. More subtle means of control, such as licensing laws for being a journalist, or special taxes on printing equipment, paper, or ink, have been used in the past. By controlling the materials needed for printing, governments hoped to be able to control the free flow of information. Government censors, or bodies that examine and approve all printed material, have also been used.

Although these measures continue to be used in various countries, it has been harder for governments to control information than in the past. This is partly because vastly more information is available and partly because electronic media, including the Internet, have become important information sources alongside print media. Nevertheless, countries like China maintain strict control over electronic media and the Internet. The government is able to block certain websites from appearing on searches when done within the country, and some Western media companies wanting to do business in China have agreed to various search engine restrictions.

Today we may look at the strict censorship and licensing laws of seventeenth- and eighteenth-century England and see them as draconian, yet within this period some of England's most noted literary and journalistic voices flourished, such as Jonathan Swift and Samuel Johnson. Nevertheless, it is important to remember that our concept of freedom of expression was not immutable. The notion evolved over time and has largely been influenced by several major court cases that dealt with national security issues, libel, or censorship. These have dealt primarily with print media, partly because some of them occurred before electronic media and partly because print media has traditionally received greater First Amendment protections than electronic media.

▼ NATIONAL SECURITY

In 1798, only a little over a decade since the creation of the Constitution and Bill of Rights, a series of four acts limiting freedom of speech were passed by the U.S. Congress. The **Alien and Sedition Acts** were passed by the Federalist-controlled U.S. Congress as a response to a threat of war with France and were meant to crush the position of the Jeffersonian Republicans, who were sympathetic to France. Among other things, the acts prohibited **sedition**, meaning spoken or written criticism of the U.S. government, and imposed penalties of a fine or imprisonment upon conviction. With the end of the threat of war, the Sedition Act expired in 1801, but other sedition acts have resurfaced throughout U.S. history, especially during times of war.[1]

Several important legal concepts have developed with court cases that involved issues of national security, one of the main areas where press freedoms are curtailed.

Clear and Present Danger

The most basic restriction is when the speech in question meets both of the following conditions: (1) it is intended to incite or produce dangerous activity (as with falsely shouting "Fire!" in a crowded theater), and (2) it is likely to succeed in achieving the purported result. This two-part framework is known as the **clear and present danger** test and is subject to the appropriate criminal-law-enforcement authorities and to the judicial system rather than regulatory authorities.

The clear-and-present-danger test emerged from *Schenck v. United States* (1919). In that case, the U.S. Supreme Court unanimously upheld the conviction of Charles T. Schenck for violating the Espionage Act of 1917. Schenck had been distributing handbills urging resistance to U.S. involvement in World War I. He was a Communist

Alien and Sedition Acts

A series of four acts passed by the U.S. Congress in 1798 that, among other things, prohibited sedition, or spoken or written criticism of the U.S. government, and imposed penalties of a fine or imprisonment upon conviction. Although they expired in 1801, other sedition acts have been passed periodically, especially during times of war.

sedition

Speech or action that encourages overthrow of a government or that subverts a constitution or a nation's laws.

clear and present danger

A restriction on speech when it meets both of the following conditions: (1) it is intended to incite or produce dangerous activity (as with falsely shouting "Fire!" in a crowded theater), and (2) it is likely to succeed in achieving the purported result.

During times of war, the courts have often curtailed the public's right to freedom of expression in the interests of national security.

prior restraint

When the government prevents or blocks the publication, broadcasting, showing, or distribution of media content, whether in print, over the air, in movie theaters, or online.

The planned publication by *The Progressive* of how to make a hydrogen bomb was a landmark case regarding the government's right of prior restraint.

but did not commit any violent acts. The Court based its decision on the notion not only that the First Amendment is not absolute, but that in wartime ordinary constitutional rules do not apply.

Prior Restraint

An important ruling came in the 1931 Supreme Court case *Near v. Minnesota*. Minnesota courts had stopped the publication of an anti-Semitic weekly on the basis that it was a "malicious, scandalous and defamatory" periodical in violation of the state's nuisance law. The Supreme Court reversed the decision, saying that **prior restraint**, or the government preventing or blocking the publication, broadcasting, showing, or otherwise distributing of media content, whether in print, over the air, or in movie theaters, must only be used in cases of serious or grave threats to national security.

In 1971, the Supreme Court made another important ruling in this regard in the case of *New York Times Co. v. United States*. In this case, the Supreme Court overturned a lower court ruling that had stopped the *Times* from publishing "The Pentagon Papers," a top-secret Pentagon study of U.S. involvement in the Vietnam War. The government failed to prove that national security interest outweighed a heavy presumption against prior restraint.

In 1979, a district court stopped *The Progressive* magazine (*U.S. v. Progressive*) from publishing "The H-Bomb Secret." The magazine had obtained its information from publicly available documents, and six months later the court injunction was lifted after others published similar material.

In sum, the courts have ruled that freedom of speech is not an absolute, especially during time of war. There is, however, a strong presumption against permitting the government any form of prior restraint on publication or distribution of speech, and it is incumbent on the government to clearly show that publication poses a clear and present threat to national security. This framework seems especially relevant in the aftermath of the September 11, 2001, terrorist attack on the World Trade Center and Pentagon.

In his book *Mass Media Law,* Don Pember describes a **preferred-position balancing theory** that has particular utility in this regard. According to this theory, a balance must be struck between speech and other rights, but speech is given a preferred position (especially in print media), and limitations on freedom of speech in print are usually illegal. The burden of proof falls on the government to show that some speech or expression of information is harmful to national security; it is not journalists or media organizations that must prove that it is not harmful.

preferred-position balancing theory

A legal theory that says that a balance must be struck between speech and other rights, although speech has a preferred position compared to other rights.

▼ LIBEL

The foundation for the relationship between freedom of expression and libel in the United States was established in the colonial era. Foremost is the case of John Peter Zenger, a New York printer and journalist who faced a libel suit from the publication of the *New York Weekly Journal,* a political journal opposed to the colonial governor, William Cosby. As publisher of the *Journal,* Zenger was responsible for the articles, which frequently featured scathing attacks on the governor.

In November 1734 Zenger was arrested for libel, and he spent nearly ten months in prison awaiting trial. Zenger's attorney, Andrew Hamilton, requested the jury rule on the veracity of Zenger's printed statements, and in a surprise ruling in August 1735 Zenger was acquitted of libel. This important precedent established the principle of freedom of the press in early America and marked a departure from the way much of the world considers libel in the courts, even today. For example, in England someone can successfully be sued for libel even if the statements are true, if the statements damage a person's reputation.

The libel case of Peter Zenger in colonial times was a turning point for what defined libel in America.

In the United States, libel is a type of defamation, such as a false attack on a person's character, which damages a person's reputation. Libel is different historically from **slander** on the basis that slander involves the spoken word, and libel involves the written word.

With the rise of electronic media in the twentieth century, libel has been extended to broadcasting on television or radio, as well as online communications, even though broadcast media are technically spoken rather than printed.

In the case of *Phipps v. Clark Oil & Ref. Corp.* (1987), the Minnesota court ruled that libel occurs when a publication "tends to injure the plaintiff's reputation and expose the plaintiff to public hatred, contempt, ridicule, or degradation."

slander

A type of defamation that is spoken, as opposed to written (libel), that damages a person's reputation or otherwise causes harm.

New York Times v. Sullivan (1964)

Media historians and legal scholars tend to agree that the most important legal decision to establish a free press in the United States was the 1964 Supreme Court ruling in *New York Times Co. v. Sullivan.*

In 1960, the *New York Times* printed a fund-raising advertisement for the civil rights movement, which contained several minor factual errors. L. B. Sullivan, a Montgomery, Alabama, city commissioner in charge of the police, said that some of the false statements in the advertisement regarding Montgomery police actions defamed him, even though he was not mentioned by name. A jury agreed and awarded him a half-million dollars. The *New York Times* appealed the case and it eventually went to the Supreme Court, which overturned the lower court ruling.

The Supreme Court ruled that public figures (defined as publicly prominent) and public officials (defined as public policy makers) may not file suit for libel unless they can prove "actual malice." For nonpublic figures (private citizens), the standard for libel is less stringent, requiring merely that the plaintiff show objectively that a "reasonable person" knew or should have known the defamatory statement was false.

The Court defined "actual malice" in terms of either (1) the intent of the defendant being malicious or (2) the defendant knowing the statement is false but acting with reckless disregard for the truth and publishing it regardless. This is known as the "actual malice test." The Court ruled that the common law of defamation violated the guarantee of free speech under the First Amendment and that the citizen's right to criticize government officials is too important to be intolerant of speech containing even harmful falsehoods. The result of the ruling has been to maintain a more robust environment for media to publish criticisms of public figures, knowing that they can be found libelous only if they meet the stringent actual-malice test.

Protecting Journalists Against Libel

Most media organizations have libel insurance to protect journalists. Freelance journalists, however, often do not have libel insurance, so the threat of libel can have a serious chilling effect. This is especially true for online journalists, bloggers, and others who operate on a shoestring budget or who are not widely recognized by media organizations as professional journalists.

Moreover, although there is no prior restraint for libel cases, journalists can be imprisoned for contempt in libel or other cases, such as not divulging the identity of a source or not releasing one's notes.

There are at least five steps journalists can take to minimize chances of committing an act of libel:

1. Engage in thorough research, including investigating the facts and maintaining good records, establishing and adhering to written criteria in making decisions about when and what to publish, and using reliable sources.

2. Confirm the identity of the target of your report.

3. Use quotations whenever possible and attribute statements to sources.

4. Report facts only and avoid language that draws conclusions.

5. Avoid bias in reports and strive for balance (i.e., give the different sides in a debate fair play).

Shield Laws

Shield laws are laws intended to protect journalists from legal challenges to their freedom to report the news. Journalists have received neither blanket protection from the Supreme Court nor a federal shield law. Yet thirty-four states have enacted laws to protect journalists from being required to answer every subpoena.[2] In these states, journalists are not required to testify or produce materials obtained from sources in confidence. Most of the other states and territories provide some court protection for journalists, although they have no shield laws.

Without these shield laws, unrestrained legal action might exert a chilling effect on journalists, some suggest, including Reed Hundt, former chairman of the FCC.[3] "Newsgatherers might be less aggressive and cease to pursue confidential

shield law

A law intended to protect journalists from legal challenges to their freedom to report the news.

censorship

The act of prohibiting certain expression or content. Censors usually do not target the whole publication, program, or website, but seek to prohibit some part of the content.

indecent speech

Language or material that, in context, depicts or describes, in terms patently offensive as measured by contemporary community standards for the broadcast medium, sexual or excretory organs or activities.

WEB LINK
The Reporters Committee for Freedom of the Press
www.rcfp.org

sources or information. Whistle-blowers and other sources could be left without any legal protection from discovery," Hundt said.

Evidence suggests that shield laws have limited effectiveness, based on studies done on the number of subpoenas served to journalists in states with shield laws compared to the number in those without. Opponents of shield laws argue that journalists should not be given special protections from answering subpoenas, given how difficult it is to define what a journalist is. Others worry that trying to explicitly state what defines a journalist could be a first step toward official licensing for journalists, which most news organizations strongly oppose as a curtailment of their First Amendment rights.

▼ CENSORSHIP

Censorship is the third major dimension of government control over media. It refers to the act of prohibiting certain expression or content. In a sense, it is a form of prior restraint, only rather than prohibiting an entire publication, it targets specific content within that publication, broadcast, film, or website. Censorship is not generally permitted in the United States, although it is routine in some countries, especially ones with authoritarian regimes that prohibit criticism of the government or rulers. In the United States, censorship is most common in two circumstances: (1) during wartime, when content, especially that being reported from the battlefield, is subject to censorship under the principle of national security, and (2) with pornographic or obscene content, which can sometimes include graphic violence or detailed accounts of criminal behavior.

The courts have ruled that high-school students do not have full First Amendment rights with student publications.

An important censorship case is *Hazelwood School District v. Kuhlmeier* (1988). This case established that not all citizens have the same First Amendment rights. In particular, people still in school, typically but not necessarily those under eighteen, are not afforded full First Amendment protection. In this case, a school principal was permitted to censor school newspaper articles dealing with pregnancy and divorce. The court found that school-sponsored publications are not a public forum and thus may be subject to censorship to protect the young from harm.

Indecent Content

Although not prohibited, **indecent speech** is also subject to federal regulation. Broadcasters may not air indecent speech when children are likely to be in the audience or between 6 a.m. and 10 p.m. This has been called a safe harbor period, and concerned groups sometimes request portrayals of violence or sex to be barred from the time period as well.

Federal law defines indecent speech as "language or material that, in context, depicts or describes, in terms patently offensive as measured by contemporary community standards for the broadcast medium, sexual or excretory organs or activities." Exempted from this definition is profanity that is neither indecent nor obscene. "Damn" is an example of a permitted word. Indecent speech was put to the test in a landmark First Amendment case involving comedian George Carlin.

George Carlin's comedy routine, "Filthy Words" turned into a landmark case regarding indecent content.

Carlin recorded before a live California audience a twelve-minute monolog titled "Filthy Words." He opened his routine by contemplating "the words you couldn't say on the public airwaves, the ones you definitely wouldn't say, ever." He then listed those words and repeated them in a variety of contexts. The Supreme Court decision in *Federal*

WEB LINK
"Filthy Words" by George Carlin transcript
www.law.umkc.edu/faculty/projects/ftrials/conlaw/filthywords.html

Communications Commission v. Pacifica Foundation (1978) was the basis for subsequent regulations on indecent speech for broadcasters.

Other entertainers have tested and the pushed the limits of freedom of speech in the electronic media as well, including radio "shock jock" Howard Stern, whose frequently crude and vulgar on-air commentary before he moved to satellite radio drew criticism not only from citizen groups but from government regulators. In 1995, Infinity Broadcasting Corp. (owned by CBS), the producer and broadcaster of Stern's radio show, agreed to pay $1.7 million without admitting guilt to settle a variety of indecency charges that had been leveled by the FCC since 1989 against Stern, whose comments are frequently sexually graphic.

As part of the **Telecommunications Act of 1996**, the first sweeping federal legislation to rewrite the foundation of communications regulation in the United States since 1934, legislators had sought to curb "indecent" speech online, but the Communications Decency Act (CDA) passed as part of the act was ultimately struck down by the U.S. Supreme Court in *ACLU v. Janet Reno* (1998). The CDA made it illegal to "depict or describe" on the Internet anything considered indecent and made no distinctions between scientific or literary works and pornography. The ACLU filed a lawsuit against the government the same day the Telecommunications Act was passed, and a lower court ruled the CDA unconstitutional, which the Supreme Court affirmed.

Despite these rulings, some organizations have chosen to self-censor. In late 2008 and early 2009 Facebook found itself the object of "lactivists" who protested its policy of removing photos of breastfeeding mothers from member pages. Threatened with banishment from Facebook for violating its policy on showing exposed breasts, women created the group "Hey Facebook, breastfeeding is not obscene!" and staged online and offline protests, which quickly grew to the tens of thousands.

Telecommunications Act of 1996

The first major regulatory overhaul of telecommunications since 1934, designed to open the industry to greater competition by deregulating many aspects of it.

"Lactivists" have protested in vain Facebook's policy of removing photos of women breastfeeding.

The protestors pointed out the hypocrisy of Facebook's policies, which accept pictures of women in thongs striking sexy poses and couples making out. Despite getting soundly ridiculed in the press and blogosphere, Facebook refused to change its policy.

Obscenity

Pornography, or **obscenity**, is one of the major forms of speech deemed unprotected by the First Amendment, and is subject to censorship by the government. A landmark case in this regard was *Miller v. California* (1973), in which Miller had been convicted in California of mailing unsolicited pornographic brochures. He appealed his conviction on the grounds that it inhibited his right to free speech, but the Court disagreed and outlined three criteria for determining whether content is obscene:

1. An average individual applying contemporary community standards must believe the content, taken as a whole, appeals to prurient interest.

2. The content must show or describe in an offensive manner sexual conduct.

3. The content on the whole must lack serious literary, artistic, political, or scientific value.

Defining obscenity, however, is difficult, and some would say simply that "I know it when I see it (or hear it)."

The digital age has produced unique issues for obscenity cases. One is the ease with which pornography can be distributed across national boundaries. Another is computer-generated pornography in which very realistic images can be created. In April 2002, the Supreme Court reaffirmed that free-speech principles applied online when it struck down provisions in the Child Pornography Prevention Act of 1996, which made it a crime to create, distribute, or possess "virtual" child pornography, or computer-generated images of children in sexual acts (as opposed to images of actual children, which is not protected as free speech). Justice Anthony M. Kennedy wrote for the majority, saying the act "prohibits speech that records no crime and creates no victims by its production." Although some justices voted in favor of keeping penalties for computer-generated images, and the government argued that real children could be harmed and exploited if a market for virtual child pornography were sustained, Justice Kennedy said, "The mere tendency of speech to encourage unlawful acts is not a sufficient reason for banning it."[4]

Criticism, Ridicule, or Humor

As objectionable as they may be, stereotypes and other offensive material are protected by the U.S. Constitution. Criticism, ridicule, and jokes about individuals (including government officials), groups, or institutions based on race, religion, gender, national background, or other factors are protected speech, whether in print or electronic media, and may not be regulated by the FCC. In the case of licensed broadcasters, it is incumbent on station owners and operators to act responsibly in offering programming that meets the needs of the communities they serve.

The following discussion of the origins and evolution of electronic-communications regulations will highlight how the FCC came about, its role, how regulations differ from those of print media, and how they have influenced the programming and communication networks we have today.

obscenity

One of the forms of speech not protected by the First Amendment, and thus subject to censorship. Although an exact definition of the term has been difficult to achieve in various court cases, generally a three-part standard is applied for media content: it must appeal to prurient interests as defined by community standards, it must show sexual conduct in an offensive manner, and it must on the whole lack serious artistic, literary, political, or scientific value.

▲▼ The Evolution of Regulating Electronic Media

The origins of U.S. electronic-communications regulations lie in the development of broadcasting in the early part of the twentieth century, starting with radio and later including television. The approach has evolved considerably over the years as a result of changing technical and economic factors surrounding and underpinning those media.

▼ EARLY DAYS AND THE RADIO ACT OF 1912 (1911–1926)

Radio Act of 1912

The act assigned frequencies and three- and four-letter codes to radio stations and limited broadcasting to the 360-meter wavelength.

The regulation of broadcasting in the United States has moved through a series of four stages. Prior to 1911, there was no regulatory authority for broadcasting, which at the time meant specifically radio transmissions. The technology of radio was in its infancy, and so little was known about the new medium that there was little to regulate. Because radio emerged as a vital medium for ships at sea, especially for making distress calls, the Commerce Department's Bureau of Navigation was put in control of radio and made it a legal requirement in the **Radio Act of 1912** that all large ships maintain radio contact with ships or shore stations. Responsibility for radio regulation rested with the Commerce Department until 1927.

During this period, radio broadcasting was done largely by amateur technology enthusiasts. The process of obtaining a frequency on which to broadcast was very informal. As broadcast historian Mark Goodman points out, "By mailing a postcard to Secretary of Commerce Herbert Hoover, anyone with a radio transmitter, ranging from college students experimenting in science classes, to amateur inventors who ordered kits, to newspaper-operated stations, could broadcast on the frequency chosen by Hoover."[5]

By 1926 there were 15,111 amateur radio stations and 536 broadcasting stations in the United States. Despite geographic separation of radio transmitters and various power restrictions on those transmitters, there was a great amount of interference between the different stations' signals. Radio became what historian Erik Barnouw calls "A Tower of Babel," and the need for regulation grew. In the 1920s much public attention became focused on the new medium of radio and how the government was attempting to regulate it.[6]

In its earliest days, radio was primarily seen as a ship-to-shore communications tool and was regulated by the Commerce Departments' Bureau of Navigation.

▼ INCREASING REGULATION AND THE FEDERAL RADIO COMMISSION (1927–1933)

Radio Act of 1927

The act replaced the Radio Act of 1912 and created the Federal Radio Commission, the precursor to the FCC, and gave the government greater regulatory and enforcement powers over radio, as well as establishing the premise that the airwaves were a public good and limited.

"The airwaves by 1927 were an open forum for anyone with the expertise and equipment to reach a forum with 25 million listeners," explains Mark Goodman.[7] But the rapid and largely uncontrolled growth of the new medium required a new regulatory structure. The **Radio Act of 1927** was signed into law in February and borrowed from railroad regulations. It said that anyone who owned a radio frequency and radio should operate for the "public convenience, interest, or necessity"—even though it didn't define those terms.[8]

The Federal Radio Commission (FRC) was established by the act. The FRC comprised five politically appointed commissioners and a limited staff whose mandate was to sort out the mess in radio. They revoked the vast majority of radio licenses and instituted a new system that favored fewer, high-powered stations over many, low-powered stations.[9] This change effectively favored radio for big companies over educational institutions or other groups that had small radio stations at the time.

▼ THE COMMUNICATIONS ACT AND SPECTRUM SCARCITY (1934–1995)

In 1934, Congress enacted the Communications Act, which became the foundation of communications law for the next sixty-two years. The act was based on the premise established in the Radio Act of 1927 that the airwaves were a public good, a limited natural resource that belonged to the people. Broadcasters were granted licenses to use those airwaves at no cost, but were public trustees and bore a responsibility to use the airwaves in "the public interest, convenience, or necessity." Because of the limited nature of the airwaves, the act established regulations based on the notion of "spectrum scarcity," or limited channel capacity. It was under this model that news, whether profitable or not, came to meet the public service requirements for radio and television broadcasters.

The Communications Act of 1934 established the Federal Communications Commission (FCC), with five political appointees, including one chair, and a series of bureaus, each assigned responsibility for an area of the growing radio industry. The FCC would eventually assume regulatory responsibility for television, wire, satellite, and cable as well.

▼ THE TELECOMMUNICATIONS ACT AND ITS EFFECTS (1996–PRESENT)

The technological transformation of the communication system in the United States and throughout the world, of which the Internet was an important part, was the impetus for Congress enacting the Telecommunications Act of 1996, the first major overhaul of the Communications Act of 1934. The convergence of telecommunications, computing, and traditional media in a digital, networked environment created the need for a basic reconstruction of the regulatory framework for the media of mass communication.

The act introduced that new framework. Although it preserved the requirement to serve in the "public interest, convenience, and necessity," the act's new mandate was to foster competition in the communications marketplace. The preamble of the act states it is intended "[t]o promote competition and reduce regulation in order to secure lower prices and higher quality services for American telecommunications consumers and encourage the rapid deployment of new telecommunications technologies." The motivation for this new mandate was the digital revolution that made the premise of channel scarcity virtually obsolete. The public no longer only had three or four network channels to watch—it now had broadcasting choices ranging from cable or satellite television to, increasingly, Internet-based programming.

More than one hundred pages in length, the complex Telecommunications Act of 1996 raises a variety of issues that affect not just the structure of the communications industry and how it is regulated, but the nature of programming and production. The act promotes direct competition among all telecommunications providers, including terrestrial broadcasters, direct broadcast satellite providers, mobile communication services, cable providers, and the regional Bell telephone

(Low) Power to the People

Although the FCC's policies have encouraged large commercial broadcasters over the past several decades, and it is believed that the concentration of media ownership among radio stations in the United States has been spurred in part by the Telecommunications Act of 1996, one throwback from an earlier era in radio has also come from the act.

In 2000, after several years of efforts on the part of radio activists, Congress passed the Radio Broadcasting Preservation Act to encourage local radio diversity by encouraging the development of low-power FM (LPFM) stations.

LPFM stations must be operated on an educational and noncommercial basis and are licensed by the FCC. Operating at 100 watts or less, they can broadcast only a few miles. Although opponents of LPFM claimed that their signals would interfere with full-power stations, an FCC-commissioned study in 2003 known as the Mitre Report showed that they do not, which promises to open even more spectrum to LPFM stations if new legislation is passed to ease current restrictions.

WEB LINK
Prometheus Radio Project
prometheusradio.org

Today there are over three thousand LPFM stations throughout the United States. Many are religious stations, while others focus on matters of community interest or education. The stations help foster a sense of community identity and also can be good training grounds for budding journalists or radio producers.

The Prometheus Radio Project is a group that encourages the creation of LPFM stations through educational resources, ideas for fund-raising activities, and barnstorming events in which activists from throughout the country gather for a weekend to work together and build an LPFM station.

companies. Further, the act specifically targets two forms of programming: violent or sexual programming and interactive services.

Since passage of the act, there has been dramatic growth in the concentration of media ownership. Whether this trend will have the stated desired effect of fostering competition or whether it will simply create powerful media cartels has been a subject of some debate. Another trend has been an increase in alternate media service providers: cable companies are allowed to provide telephone service, for example, and telephone companies could provide, in theory, programming content.

The act puts no limit on the number of television stations a single person or organization may own in the United States, as long as the combined reach is no more than 35 percent of U.S. households. This also will spur greater concentration of ownership, which has already occurred in the radio industry. As a result of these regulatory, economic, and technological trends, Eli Noam and Robert Freeman point out that the media offer unprecedented programming diversity at the national level and ever-dwindling diversity at the local level.[10]

Because the act eliminates the legal barriers preventing telephone and television companies from competing in the areas of telephone and video services,

The Rise and Fall of Russian Media

After the demise of the Soviet Union in 1991 there was great hope for the rise of a democratic Russia and the role that a free press would play in rebuilding the country. There has been tremendous growth in the numbers of newspapers, magazines, and books available to Russians, as well as growth in radio and television stations and the type of programming they offer.

However, since 2000 there have been many disturbing trends in Russia that have raised alarm among journalists and media scholars. One is the concentration of media ownership and the expectations that owners have regarding uncritical coverage of themselves and their interests. Although it is not as clear-cut as Soviet-era media control, the private owners of many media companies nevertheless exert undue influence over editorial content and programming.

Of even greater concern is how dangerous Russia has become for journalists critical of the government. Since Vladimir Putin became president in 2000, twenty-two Russian journalists have been killed, with only two of the murders solved. There has been a slight downturn in journalist murders in Russia, which the Committee to Protect Journalists cautiously says is a good sign.

More recently, the term "extremism" has had its definition expanded to include any criticism of the government, which means journalists who criticize the government or government policies face jail time and the publications they work for can be shut down.

Sometimes actions still go beyond legal means. In May 2010 journalist Mark Minin was shot four times as he walked to his car. In November 2010 another Russian journalist, Oleg Kashin, was nearly beaten to death outside his apartment. Both journalists had published stories critical of the Russian government and believe the attacks stemmed from their work.[11]

---

consumers have seen an increased array of alternative service providers. Similarly, consumers have seen an increase in the range of both phone and video services, such as video-on-demand, voicemail, and call waiting. There have been several attempts in recent years to pass further sweeping legislation that deals with issues such as Net neutrality, voice-over IP (VoIP), and other new technologies that either did not exist or were just emerging in 1996.

▼ ELECTRONIC MEDIA REGULATION INTERNATIONALLY

Electronic media of course developed differently in various countries throughout the world, and it is impossible to thoroughly cover the historical development within each country or even each region here. However, several general trends and patterns can be explored.

In many countries, the development of radio as mass communication was an extension of the already existing telegraph services, which were generally run by the government. Unlike the United States, where commercial forces tended to dominate, in Europe and European colonies a public service ethos for electronic media was most prevalent. What this meant for the public was a limited number of radio or television networks that were licensed or directly run by the government. Because of the principle of public service, programming content tended to emphasize news, education, and cultural shows rather than pure entertainment.

In the European Union in the last twenty years there has been a steady trend toward privatization and less regulation of the radio and television industries. As a result, more U.S. programming has been licensed by European broadcasters, making shows like *Baywatch* or *The Simpsons* highly popular throughout the world. This trend, although perhaps good from the audience's perspective, as it can now see more types of programming, also raises charges of cultural imperialism. Local broadcasters may too easily choose to simply buy U.S. programming rather than support home-grown productions.

Nevertheless, the EU is moving toward more liberalization and privatization, so it is likely that the EU, like the United States, will also see growth in the concentration of media ownership. Asian countries each have their own regulations and laws, but with the exception of Japan, India, the Philippines, and South Korea, most Asian countries have stronger degrees of government control over electronic media than the EU or the United States. For example, it is illegal to own a satellite dish in Malaysia, and countries like Singapore and Indonesia have strict regulations on content, especially criticism of the government.

▲▼ The Federal Communications Commission (FCC)

The Federal Communications Commission [FCC]

The principal communications regulatory body, established in 1934, at the federal level in the United States.

The Federal Communications Commission (FCC) is the principal communications regulatory body at the federal level in the United States. Some would say the FCC is also a lightning rod for criticism because of its prominent position on the communications regulatory landscape. Oftentimes, regardless of how the commission rules, some group is left unhappy and frequently is quite vocal in expressing its displeasure.

The principal mandate of the FCC is "regulating interstate and foreign commerce in communication by wire and radio so as to make available, so far as possible, to all the people of the United States a rapid, efficient, nation-wide, and world-wide wire and radio communications service." In this sense, the term "radio" is interpreted to include television, whether it is delivered via cable, satellite, or over the air. The FCC mandate was reaffirmed under the Telecommunications Act of 1996, which supplanted the 1934 act. The FCC is responsible for enforcing the Children's Internet Protection Act (CIPA), which was enacted in 2001 and requires all libraries and schools that receive federal technology funding to install pornography-blocking software on their computers.

WEB LINK
FCC website
www.fcc.gov

The FCC consists of five commissioners for five-year terms appointed by the president, each of whom must be confirmed by the Senate. The commission must include at least two representatives of each of the major parties to help ensure its nonpartisan nature.

As Figure 13-1 shows, the FCC is divided into several offices and seven major bureaus. Each bureau has general responsibilities of enforcement and oversight that individual divisions handle within the various bureaus. Separate bureaus have different regulations for different communication technologies. This explains why broadcast radio and television have different rules for licensing and operations than cable television or satellite radio.

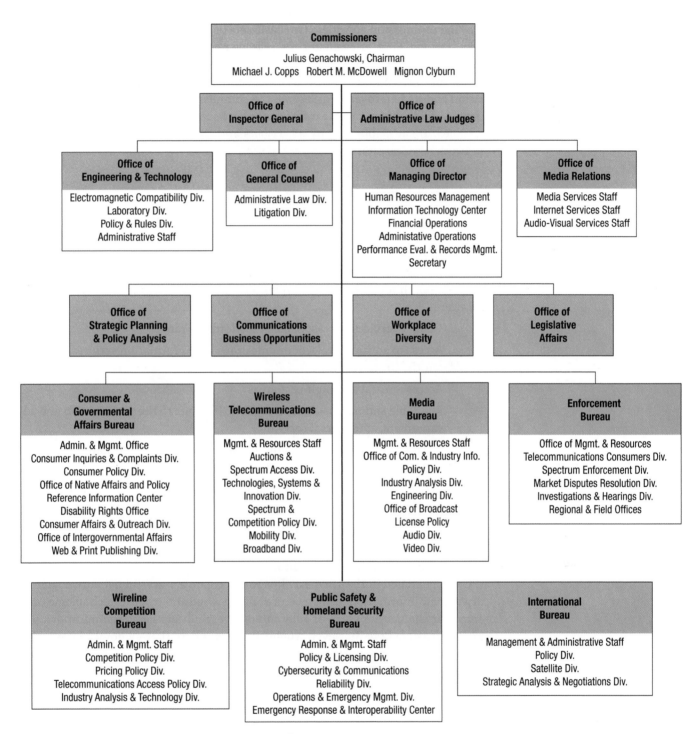

FIGURE 13-1 Organizational Chart for the FCC, Major Offices and Bureaus.

▼ REGULATING RADIO AND TELEVISION

Among its principal duties, the FCC allocates new broadcast radio and television stations and renews the licenses of existing stations, ensuring that each licensee is complying with the laws mandated by Congress. The FCC does not license TV or radio networks, such as CBS, NBC, ABC, Fox, CW, or PBS, except when they are owners of stations.

The commission considers two basic sets of factors regarding the allocation of new stations. First, it evaluates the relative needs of communities for additional broadcast outlets, inviting public comment on proposed rules and publishing those rules. This depends on a variety of considerations, including a community's population and its heterogeneity. Second, the commission considers various engineering standards that eliminate interference between stations. Cable TV and satellite channels are available only to subscribers and have fewer rules to abide by than network broadcasters.

▼ UNIVERSAL SERVICE

An important item for the FCC is the definition of universal service, a long-cherished notion central to the 1934 act. The act does not go so far as to provide a definition of universal service, however. It states, "Universal service is an evolving level of telecommunications services that the commission shall establish periodically under this section." It identifies six principles central to this evolving notion of universal service:

1. Quality services at reasonable and affordable rates
2. Access to advanced telecommunications and information services throughout the United States
3. Access in rural and high-cost areas
4. Equitable and nondiscriminatory contributions to the preservation and advancement of universal service
5. Specific, predictable, and sufficient federal and state mechanisms to preserve and advance universal service
6. Access to advanced telecommunications services in elementary and secondary schools and classrooms, health care providers, and libraries

The outcome of this evolving notion is a new model of universal service. One scenario would include fully interoperable high-bandwidth, two-way communication service—the twenty-first-century equivalent of "plain old telephone service" (POTS) mandated in the 1934 act. This would create a powerful network engine to drive a new information infrastructure linking wired and wireless technologies and empower the development of fully interactive, multimedia communications. An alternative paradigm, however, would simply mandate that all homes have access to at least two communication-service providers capable of delivering both traditional and new media services (including the Internet).

▼ THE FCC, STATION ID, AND LICENSE RENEWAL

Each station must air station-identification announcements as it signs on and off each day, and it must air announcements hourly, at what the commission calls a natural programming break. The requirements for station identification foster a certain level of uniformity in programming style in the broadcast media, but they do not mandate that programmers insert station IDs at the top of the hour and at other well-defined intervals.

The FCC licenses stations to operate either as commercial or noncommercial-educational (public) broadcasters for up to eight years, after which the station must renew its license. This is the case for both radio and television broadcasters licensed to transmit their signals via terrestrial frequencies.

At the time of license renewal, a station must meet five basic requirements demonstrating that it has served in the public interest and met all legal requirements. A station must also accept and respond to viewer or listener complaints. Audience members, journalists, or anyone else may also review what is called the station's "public inspection file," which contains a variety of information about the station.

▼ FCC LIMITS ON STATIONS

There are a variety of station activities that are either regulated or prohibited by federal law. Among the regulated activities are station-conducted contests, television games and quiz shows, and the broadcast of telephone calls. When a station hosts a contest, it must fully disclose all terms and rules of the contest, including any advertising promoting the contest. Stations are required to inform any parties to a phone call before recording it for broadcast, or broadcasting it live, although there are certain exceptions, such as call-in shows, when callers can reasonably be expected to understand their calls may be broadcast.

If a licensee violates the rules, the FCC is authorized to levy a fine or even to revoke a station's license. Among the programming concerns for which the FCC may levy fines or revoke licenses are the airing of obscene or indecent language when children are likely to be viewing, and nudity. The FCC does not advise stations regarding artistic standards, format, or grammar. Stations must rely on their own judgment. Generally, only the stations themselves are responsible for selecting the material they air, including coverage of local issues, news, public affairs, religion, sports events, and other subjects.

Among the prohibited activities for stations are knowingly broadcasting a hoax, including false information regarding a crime or catastrophe (defined as a disaster), especially when a broadcast might cause public harm. This rule came about largely as a result of the 1938 *War of the Worlds* radio broadcast.

Today the FCC regulates broadcast stations, allocating spectrum, renewing licenses, and levying fines for violations.

▼ SPECTRUM AUCTION

Since 1994, the FCC has held auctions for available electromagnetic spectrum. The auctions are open to any individual or company that makes an upfront payment and that the FCC deems a qualified bidder. Many countries auction spectrum, and the auctions can generate large revenues for the governments. Some critics claim that the spectrum tends to be leased too cheaply, resulting in essentially corporate giveaways, considering the money that the winning bidders make from the spectrum they use.

The auction in the United States in 2008 drew special attention thanks in part to disagreements and lawsuits among several major telecommunications companies and Google, all bidders for the spectrum. Google requested that the auctioned spectrum be open, meaning that the winning bidder would have to keep the spectrum available to anyone to develop applications and communication tools that could be used by anyone else, along the lines of open-source business models. Google claimed that this would give consumers more choices and spur greater innovation in mobile communication devices.

Open communications like this directly threaten the established business models of telecommunication companies, and Verizon filed a lawsuit against the FCC to stop the open requirement. In the end, Google got two of its four requests, creating a partially open system, and the auction generated close to $20 billion for the government.

◢◣ The Federal Trade Commission (FTC)

**The Federal Trade
Commission [FTC]**

The principal commerce
regulatory body, established in
1914, at the federal level in the
United States.

The Federal Trade Commission (FTC) enforces a variety of antitrust and consumer protection laws, including cases of deceptive advertising in print, electronic media, and the Internet. The FTC is also responsible for enforcing the Children's Online Privacy Protection Act (COPPA), which Congress passed in 1998 and that gives parents control over what kinds of information can be collected about their children online.

Although the FTC does not regulate the Internet to nearly the same extent that the FCC does with broadcast, cable, wireless, or satellite radio, its mandate to protect consumers against deceptive advertising and business practices has given it broad powers as the number of people grows online. With deceptive practices ranging from spam, phishing, trademark infringement, breaches of consumer privacy, and false advertising claims, the Internet has added whole new ways to trick and cheat people while also making many traditional scams cheaper and easier to do.

Some deceptive practices combine new and old technologies. For example, an advertisement appears on a website that promises free adult content after signing in, but what actually happens after signing in is the computer gets disconnected from the existing Internet connection without the user's knowledge and reconnected by phone calls to websites in remote countries like Romania or Vanuatu, with charges ranging from $2 to $7 per minute. Users do not know of this until they get phone bills of several hundred dollars.

One problem for the FTC lies in being able to enforce regulations and laws, especially with companies based overseas. Not only may other countries have different laws regarding the legality of spammers or phishing operations, but many such companies frequently relocate their operations, making them hard to catch even if the FTC or host country had the resources to do so.

Besides cases of deceptive advertising or business practices, the FTC's regulatory powers can sometimes mix with other regulatory bodies such as the FCC or the Food and Drug Administration (FDA), which is responsible for deceptive advertising claims for food or drugs. The FDA has strict regulations on what can be said on the air in prescription drug commercials, which is why such commercials usually include long lists of possible side effects. Unlike issues of libel, obscenity, clear and present danger, or issues of national security, regulations regarding commercial speech, especially in electronic media, can sometimes make the boundaries unclear as to which regulatory agency should be responsible for enforcement.

▼ COMMERCIAL SPEECH

Commercial speech, including advertising, has generally been afforded less First Amendment protection than other forms of speech, especially political speech or the news. In a landmark decision, the U.S. Supreme Court ruled in 1942 in *Valentine v. Chrestensen* that "purely commercial advertising" was unprotected by the First Amendment. Chrestensen was a businessman who was displaying a World War I–era submarine at a pier in New York City and dispersed leaflets advertising tours of the submarine. The leaflets were becoming litter, and the police commissioner in New York forbade him from distributing them. Even though Chrestensen attempted to subvert the ruling by adding political messages on the opposite side, the city still barred him from distributing his advertising leaflets, and the Supreme Court agreed, giving commercial speech no protection under the First Amendment.

In the 1970s the broad powers granted to government regarding commercial speech were restricted somewhat by cases that allowed some First Amendment protection, although not on par with other forms of speech. In 1976, the Court ruled in *Virginia State Board of Pharmacy v. Virginia Citizens Consumer Council, Inc.,* that speech that does "no more than propose a commercial transaction" is entitled to at least some First Amendment protection. This was in response to a case brought by some citizens' groups in Virginia that wanted to see pharmacies advertise prices of drugs, which the state legislature had prohibited.

In some cases, however, commercial speech has been afforded more protection than one might expect. An interesting example comes from a case involving former New York City mayor Rudolph Giuliani. Giuliani was lampooned in an advertising campaign by *New York* magazine in 1997 on the city buses of New York, which said that the magazine was "possibly the only good thing in New York that Rudy hasn't taken credit for." Giuliani, who had often taken credit for everything from drops in the crime rate to a booming economy, found

Former New York mayor Rudolph Giuliani tried unsuccessfully to get bus advertisements that poked fun of him removed.

the ads to be offensive and ordered them removed from the buses. In this case, commercial speech won. Consider the conclusion of United States District Judge Shira Scheindlin, who said, "Who would have dreamed that the mayor would object to more publicity?" She ruled that Giuliani's administration violated the First Amendment when it ordered city buses to remove paid ads.

Tobacco and Alcohol Advertising

Most products can be legally advertised on electronic media under the jurisdiction of the FCC. However, one type of product generally may not be legally advertised by broadcasters: tobacco. Advertising cigarettes, small cigars, smokeless tobacco, or chewing tobacco is prohibited on radio, television, and any other electronic medium regulated by the FCC, such as telephony. It is permissible to advertise smoking accessories, cigars, pipes, pipe tobacco, or cigarette-making machines. There are no federal laws or FCC regulations prohibiting the advertising of alcoholic beverages, such as beer, wine, or liquor, on television and radio.

Unclear Regulatory Boundaries

Areas of commercial speech that are not regulated or prohibited by any federal law or agency include loud commercials, which the FCC has shown through research are only perceived as louder than programs but actually are not. The rule for commercials is that they can only be as loud as the loudest part of the show they appear within, which is why commercials often seem louder, as they may come after a part of the program that was not the loudest part. Offensive advertising and subliminal programming are two other areas not clearly regulated by any single agency.

With offensive advertising, it is assumed that the advertiser would either decide not to run an offensive ad or, if it does and receives negative publicity for the ad by the public, would pull the ad to avoid causing further damage to their brand. With subliminal advertising, the FCC states that use of subliminal messages, which are meant to be perceived only on a subconscious level, is "inconsistent with a station's obligation to serve the public interest." However, it does not officially prohibit subliminal programming. Research does not provide conclusive evidence that subliminal messages are even understood or have an influence on behavior, and no advertisers have admitted using them.

The requirement that broadcasters make available equal airtime, in terms of commentaries and commercials, to opposing candidates running for election. It does not apply to candidates appearing in newscasts, documentaries, or news-event coverage.

▼ POLITICAL SPEECH

Historically, the heart of freedom of expression is in political speech, or speech that deals with the political process, government, elected officials, or elections. Some go so far as to contend that the only speech the founders intended when they wrote the First Amendment was political speech. Political speech is also one area where federal regulations have been most extensive.

Equal-Time Rule

Stations are required to adhere to an **equal-time rule**, outlined in the 1934 Communications Act, which says that broadcasters must give "equal air time" to candidates running in elections. Under this provision, if a station permits a qualified candidate for public office to use its facilities, including commentaries or paid commercials, the station is required to "afford equal opportunities to all other such candidates for that office." Two circumstances are exempted from the equal-time provision: when the candidate appears in a newscast, interview, or documentary and when the candidate appears during on-the-scene coverage of a news event.

Candidate debates have been ruled as "on-the-spot" news coverage and thus are exempt from equal-time-rule provisions. Early in the 2008 election season there was some question whether the town hall forums conducted by McCain and Obama, even before they declared their candidacies, would be considered the same way by the FCC.

The U.S. Supreme Court ruled in 1981 in support of the equal-time rule, saying that it is the right of viewers and listeners, not of broadcasters, that should be considered paramount. It went on to say, "As defined by the FCC and applied here, [it] does not violate the First Amendment rights of broadcasters by unduly circumscribing their editorial discretion, but instead properly balances the First Amendment rights of federal candidates, the public, and broadcasters."

The equal-time rule says that TV stations must allow equal opportunities for all political candidates to air paid commercials.

Fairness Doctrine

Fairness Doctrine

Adopted by the FCC in 1949, it required broadcasters to seek out and present all sides of a controversial issue they were covering. It was discarded by the FCC in 1987.

The equal-time rule is not the same thing as the **Fairness Doctrine**, though it is often confused with it. The equal-time rule deals only with giving political candidates equal time compared to other candidates, with the exceptions noted above. The Fairness Doctrine was much broader in scope, requiring broadcasters to seek out and present all sides of an issue when covering a controversy, allowing people who were personally attacked on-air a chance to respond, and giving candidates airtime to respond to a station's endorsement of another candidate. The Fairness Doctrine, which the FCC had adopted in 1949, was largely discarded in 1987.

In 1969, in *Red Lion Broadcasting Co. v. FCC,* which required Red Lion Broadcasting to provide equal airtime for a politician's response to an attack on him, the Court held that, because of the scarcity of broadcasting frequencies, the government might require a broadcast licensee to share the frequency with others who might not otherwise have a chance to broadcast their views. The Court thus gave the public a right of access "to social, political, esthetic, moral, and other ideas and experiences."

Even after the overturning of the Fairness Doctrine in 1986, two parts of it in particular remained in effect until October 2000, when they too were discarded by the FCC and the decision of a federal court. These were political editorials and personal attacks.

The FCC defined a political editorial as "when a station endorses or opposes a legally qualified candidate(s) during a broadcast of *its own* opinion." It distinguished the opinions of third parties broadcast by the station as "comments" or "commentaries" and thus exempt from these rules. A station had a week to provide other qualified candidates for the same office, or the candidates that were opposed in the editorial, with these three things: (1) notice of the date and time of the editorial, (2) a tape or script of the editorial, and (3) free and comparable airtime in which to respond.

The FCC defined a personal attack as "during the presentation of views on a controversial issue of public importance, someone attacks the honesty, character, integrity, or like personal qualities of an identified person or group." After such an occurrence, the station had one week to provide the attacked party with the same three things provided candidates opposed in political editorials. Stations were not required to maintain copies of the material they broadcast, with two exceptions: personal attacks and political editorials.

In early October 2000, the FCC suspended these last vestiges of the Fairness Doctrine and a federal court overturned the provision entirely, ruling that the FCC had not demonstrated the value to the public of the doctrine, given the limitation it places on broadcasters' First Amendment rights.

Despite a number of attempts in 2005 and 2008 to resuscitate the Fairness Doctrine with new legislation, mostly by liberals and Democratic politicians who claim the imbalance in conservative versus liberal talk shows on radio and TV skews public debate and perceptions on important issues, such moves are strongly resisted by libertarians and conservatives. The FCC has refrained on the basis that the doctrine never really produced more diversity in programming and that with channel proliferation there is more diversity than could have been hoped for when television was dominated by three major commercial networks.

The prevalence of conservative talk shows such as *Rush Limbaugh* has given rise to attempts by liberals to reinstate the Fairness Doctrine.

◤▽ Children's Programming Protections

Parents, elected officials, and others have long sought to protect children from unwanted or offensive speech and to create a media system that actively nurtures and nourishes children. There has been considerable regulation designed to both protect and promote children's welfare in the context of the media, especially the electronic media. A ratings system, similar to that used for movies, was developed that gives parents a guide as to how suitable a program may be for children of a certain age. Among the most important pieces of regulation to try to protect children is the **Children's Television Act**.

▼ THE CHILDREN'S TELEVISION ACT

The Children's Television Act (CTA) took effect in 1990. It places limits on the amount of commercial content permitted in children's TV programming (including broadcast, satellite, and cable). The act also mandates that each television station provide programming specifically designed to meet the educational and informational needs of children age sixteen and younger. The FCC determination of whether programming meets this criterion is based on four standards:

1. The programming is primarily designed to meet children's educational and informational needs (i.e., it can't be primarily entertainment, such as a cartoon, and have as a by-product some educational value).

2. It is broadcast between 6 a.m. and 10 p.m., hours when children are likely to be viewing.

Children's Television Act

Created in 1990, it places limits on the amount of commercial content that programming can carry, forces stations to carry certain amounts of educational programming for children sixteen and under, and includes other provisions to help protect children.

3. It is scheduled to run regularly each week.
4. It is at least a one-half-hour program.

In addition, commercial stations are required to identify their educational programs for children at the beginning of those programs; they must identify these programs to publishers of program guides as well. Moreover, all programs aimed at children twelve and younger may not contain more than 10.5 minutes of advertising per hour on weekends and 12 minutes on weekdays. The FCC also established that stations that air at least three hours of "core" children's programming a week would be in fulfillment of their obligations under the CTA, "core" being defined primarily in terms of item number one above.

▼ VIOLENT AND SEXUAL PROGRAMMING: THE V-CHIP

Violent and sexual programming receives special attention from the FCC because of concern about the implications of such material for young viewers. With the passage of the Telecommunications Act of 1996, the federal government began regulating televised violent content in addition to sexual content, which it already regulated. The act seeks to give parents greater control over their children's viewing of violent and sexual programming. The act begins by summarizing research findings that demonstrate the negative impact of television-violence viewing on children. It notes, "Parents express grave concern over violent and sexual video programming and strongly support technology that would give them greater control to block video programming in the home that they consider harmful to their children."

In order to give parents control over what kind of programming their children are able to watch, the government mandated that from January 2000 all television sets thirteen inches or larger come equipped with what is called a **V-chip**, or "violence chip." The V-chip is a computer device that enables parents or any other viewer to program a TV set to block access to programs containing violent and sexual content, based on the program rating.

The rating system developed for the V-chip is also called the "TV Parental Guidelines." At the request of the government, the television industry created its own voluntary ratings system and agreed to broadcast signals that contain programming ratings that can be detected by the V-chip. The ratings are shown on the TV screen for the first fifteen seconds of rated programming and permit viewers to use the V-chip to block those programs from their sets. On the basis of the First Amendment, all news programming is exempted from the V-chip.

In the digital age, the V-chip is no longer the only tool at parents' disposal to restrict television viewing among their children. All digital media systems, including digital cable and satellite television, contain software controls that can block individual programs, entire channels, or classes of programs based on their ratings.

The V-chip lets parents block certain types of programming unsuitable for children.

V-chip

A computer device that enables parents or any other viewer to program a TV set to block access to programs containing violent and sexual content, based on the program rating.

intellectual property

Ideas that have commercial value, such as literary or artistic works, patents, business methods, and industrial processes.

copyright

The exclusive right to use, publish, and distribute a work such as a piece of writing, music, film, or video.

◢◤ Intellectual Property Rights

Of significant and growing concern to those in mass communication is protecting their **intellectual property** (IP). IP refers to ideas that have commercial value, such as literary or artistic works, patents, software programs, business methods, and industrial processes, particularly in the form of copyright protection. A **copyright** ("copyright" refers to the legal right to make a copy of a work) is one form of intellectual property rights protection that deals with protecting specific expressions of ideas. The other two main areas of intellectual property law are patents and trademarks.

Patents are intended to protect a specific form of intellectual property known as "inventions." Once granted, a patent prohibits anyone from copying the invention, pattern, or design. Anyone can apply for a patent, as long as the idea is new. **Trademarks** refer to images, designs, logos, or even words or phrases. For example, in March 2004 Donald Trump, host of *The Apprentice* reality TV show, attempted to trademark his phrase "You're Fired!" so it could be sold on clothing and other items. However, the U.S. Patent and Trademark Office turned down his request because it was too similar to another phrase, "You're Hired!," an educational board game that had that phrase trademarked in 1997.

Organizers of a conference in October 2011 in London were forced to change its name from the "Radical Media Conference" to the "Rebellious Media Conference" after a PR firm named Radical Media threatened to sue them for copyright infringement, despite the long history of the term "radical media" going back to the nineteenth century. The PR firm had trademarked the name and the organizers of the conference could not afford the legal costs to fight it, even if they had eventually won the case.

A copyright exists from the moment a work is created in its fixed form, such as being written down or recorded, so simply claiming an idea does not give you a copyright to it. Inserting a © symbol (although in the case of a musical recording the symbol is a P in a circle, but that symbol may be hard to find on your keyboard), along with a date and the name of the copyright owner, also helps show that you are copyrighting a work, but it is not necessary. In the case of a work for hire, the employer generally owns the copyright. A copyright is in effect for the lifetime of the author, plus 70 years, although it may be up to 125 years in the case of a work for hire. The rationale of a copyright is to protect not only the intellectual product but the author/owner's financial interests. In 1989, the United States joined the Berne Convention for the Protection of Literary and Artistic Works, extending copyright protection globally.

Copyright law protects a wide range of expression, primarily the creations of authors or artists. A book or an article is protected by a copyright, not a patent. Included are literary works (including newspapers, books, magazines), musical works, dramatic works, pantomimes and choreographic works, pictorial, graphic, and sculpture works, motion pictures and other audiovisual works, sound recordings, and architectural works. Under the **Digital Millennium Copyright Act**, it extends to digital works as well, including those on the Internet or other online media, because if something exists on a hard drive it is considered a fixed form.

▼ FAIR USE

Holding a copyright to a work provides the owner an exclusive right to reproduce, distribute (over any media), perform, display, or license that work. There are limited exceptions to the rights under copyright law, including primarily for **fair use** of an expression, such as in a movie or book review where the reviewer might include an excerpt, or in criticism or commentary. In general, there are four factors considered in deciding whether the use of another's copyrighted work is legal under the "fair use" provision of the act:

1. The purpose and nature of the use (i.e., it is purely commercial, educational, or for the news, the latter two of which are generally more likely to qualify)

2. The character of the copyrighted work (some works are inherently more protected; this is a subjective matter determined by the courts)

Donald Trump tried to trademark his famous phrase "You're Fired" from the reality show *The Apprentice*.

patent

Protects the right to produce and sell an invention, rather than a literary or artistic work, which is covered by copyright law.

trademark

A type of intellectual property that refers to signs, logos, or names.

Digital Millennium Copyright Act (DMCA)

An act of Congress in 1998 that reformed copyright law comprehensively in trying to update it for the digital age. Key provisions addressed the circumvention of copyright protection systems, fair use in a digital environment, and Internet service providers' (ISP) liability for content sent through their lines.

fair use

Allowable use of someone else's copyrighted work that does not require payment of royalties, with a number of factors used to determine if something falls under fair use or is a violation of copyright.

3. The amount and extent of the excerpt used, in proportion to the copyrighted work in its entirety (this is more qualitatively than quantitatively determined, however, and there are no exact rules on the permissible number of words one may borrow from a text or the amount of video, audio, or image one may excerpt, since even a small clip may represent the most significant creative aspect of the work)

4. The effect of the use on the copyrighted work's market potential (i.e., in dollar terms), especially when the copyrighted work is used as the basis for a derivative work (i.e., a movie based on a book)

The issue of fair use has become a flash point for digital media, especially in relation to content aggregators such as Google News or video search engines. There have been several court cases in the past ten years in which copyright holders have sued content aggregators, claiming copyright infringement. However, if the content aggregator has been able to show that it has sufficiently transformed the content—for example, by making low-resolution thumbnails of images or video clips—and to show that it is not profiting directly from doing so, it has generally won the case. Other aggregators have arrived at licensing agreements with media companies in order to continue to display or aggregate their content. An example is a deal Google struck with Associated Press to aggregate its news stories and keep them on Google News for a limited time.

◢◤ Legal Issues in the Digital World

The courts and legal system have not been able to keep up with the many changes to mass communication that the Internet and digital media have brought. As a result, cases decided by the courts from the mid-1990s through today can have dramatic effects because they can establish precedent, meaning they become the basis for subsequent court decisions and legislation.

One example of just how far the legal system has had to come occurred in a 2000 ruling against Eric Corley (Emmanuel Goldstein), publisher of *2600: The Hacker Quarterly*. He included links in the online version of the magazine to a site that contained the code to DeCSS, a computer program that opened encrypted DVDs and allowed them to be freely copied. Corley argued that being forced to remove the hyperlinks was an infringement of his First Amendment rights. The court disagreed, saying that a hyperlink was not an example of free speech because it acted as a kind of "mechanism" that allowed users to go to the site. However, posting the URL of a site without it being hyperlinked would still be considered free speech. An appellate court agreed with this decision in May 2001, and Corley decided not to take the case to the Supreme Court.

Because digital media have certain characteristics unlike analog media, there have been a host of new issues raised that our legal system has been ill equipped to deal with. In some cases the courts are able to rely on existing laws and apply them to digital media, but in other cases the fit has been awkward, at best.

▼ DIGITAL RIGHTS MANAGEMENT

File-sharing and royalty issues related to music, and increasingly video, have been discussed in earlier chapters, and this continues to be one of the main areas of contention in the digital space. Record labels have tried various measures to deter free file sharing, including suing customers and having universities hold seminars for incoming students on the matter, but with no decrease in free downloading.

Broadly speaking, **digital rights management**, or DRM, is about finding ways using technology to rein in copyright infringement of digital content. Encryption has had some success, although, as the DeCSS example demonstrates, it is not foolproof. **Digital watermarks** are a very important part of DRM. Watermarks are computer code (usually invisible, but sometimes visible) inserted into any digital content—images, graphics, audio, video, or even text documents—that authenticates the source of that content. Copyright owners value watermarks because they can protect media assets, or intellectual property, from theft—or at least make them easier to track when they are used illegally.

For example, if a media company sends digital video over the Internet and someone else tries to copy the video and distribute it without obtaining permission, the original copyright holder, an end user, or even an intelligent software agent can examine the content for an embedded digital watermark. If the watermark is present and is that of the original copyright holder, then it can be easily demonstrated that the redistributor is in violation of copyright law. In essence, the digital watermark is analogous to a brand placed on cattle by a rancher in order to deter or catch cattle rustlers.

DRM has faced resistance from some groups, such as the Electronic Frontier Foundation, who claim that media companies are trying to limit the capabilities of new technologies simply to increase their revenues and force media to behave like their analog counterparts. These restrictions have angered consumers and raised serious questions about what exactly a person is "buying" when purchasing a CD and what rights the purchaser has to that content.

Although not DRM per se, companies have also had to learn to manage their online presence through company websites and domain names. Some who did not see the value of the Internet in its early years discovered later that others had already leased their company name as a domain name, usually with the intent to sell it at a higher price, in a practice called **cybersquatting**. The World Intellectual Property Organization (WIPO) handles complaints from parties who claim others are unfairly using their names for personal gain.

WIPO decides on each case and generally applies standards of fair use, although there is no hard-and-fast rule. For example, Fox news personality Bill O'Reilly brought a case to WIPO to acquire www.billorielly.com. The person who had the site was actually named Bill O'Rielly (note the "i" and "e" are reversed in the spelling of his name), yet WIPO ruled in favor of O'Reilly and he got that domain name as well. In 2007, Australian country singer Keith Urban sought the domain name www.keithurban.com from a New Jersey Web developer and artist of the same name who had the domain. The artist never claimed to be the country singer and used the site to promote his own business and paintings, although initially Google Adwords automatically provided sponsored links to concerts by the singer. After removing Google Adwords from his site, litigation on the domain name stalled and Urban (the singer) can be found on www.keithurban.net.

The creation of fake Twitter accounts, called phweeting, has become common. Although usually done for humorous effect, some fake accounts have caused embarrassment to the people after which they are named when followers or the media do not realize the account is fake. Twitter has generally responded quickly in closing fake Twitter accounts when celebrities or others have complained about fake tweets or have requested the names for their own use.

digital rights management [DRM]

Technologies that let copyright owners control the level of access or use allowed for a copyrighted work, such as limiting the number of times a song can be copied.

digital watermark

Computer code (usually invisible, but sometimes visible) inserted into any digital content—images, graphics, audio, video, or even text documents—that authenticates the source of that content.

cybersquatting

The practice of getting a domain name, usually of someone famous or a well-known company, with the intention of reselling the domain name at a high price.

TV commentator Bill O'Reilly won a decision by WIPO to get ownership of the domain name billorielly.com, even though the name was spelled differently and it was the name of the prior owner.

Metatags and keywords have also come before the courts as contested intellectual property. This has become especially important, as search engines dominate how people find information on the Web. Although metatags have become less important in terms of how search engines find and rank websites than they used to be, they still play a role and can mislead users.

The courts have generally ruled that as long as a keyword fairly represents the content of a website, it can be used. However, a company cannot put a competitor's name in its keyword list in the hope of drawing people who were searching for the competitor.

CONVERGENCE CONTEXT

Jailed as a Journalist

On April 3, 2007, Josh Wolf stepped out of a federal prison in California and into the record books after spending 226 days in jail, the longest any journalist in U.S. history was held for protecting his sources.

There were several ironies with this case, not the least of which was that there were questions about whether Wolf was actually a journalist. A self-described activist, he participated in, videotaped, and blogged about various protests conducted by anarchist or radical-left groups.

In July 2005 he videotaped an anti-G8 demonstration held in San Francisco, posting excerpts of his footage on the local Indymedia site, part of a worldwide network of activists and citizen journalists.

A policeman was injured during the demonstration, and Wolf was subpoenaed by federal authorities to appear before a grand jury and hand over his footage so investigators could determine if any of the protestors could be identified. Wolf refused on First Amendment grounds and was sentenced to jail, then eventually federal prison, as he continued to refuse to surrender his videotapes.

The prosecution claimed that Wolf was not a journalist but an activist who happened to be capturing a public event on tape and thus had no First Amendment protections. Supporters of Wolf claimed that he was acting in a journalistic capacity by his video reporting and blogging and that his imprisonment could have a chilling effect on other journalists who could be threatened by the government.

On the day Wolf was released from prison he posted all his video footage to his blog. After an unsuccessful run for mayor of San Francisco in 2007, in July 2008 he began work as a general-assignment reporter for a local newspaper, the *Palo Alto Daily Post*, and in 2010 entered journalism school at UC Berkeley. The final bits of irony in the case are that he put down his video camera and focused solely on writing for his new job and is doing so for a newspaper that does not even have a website.

▼ PRIVACY

Privacy issues have become increasingly important on a number of levels with the Internet and digital media. Not only can websites track users in ways that are impossible with analog media, but they can insert code, called a cookie, onto users' computers and track them even after they have left that particular website. Not all cookies track users so relentlessly, however, and in fact cookies are needed to make the Web a more user-friendly environment.

Still, the overuse of cookies can be a problem. Just as a website will add a cookie to your computer, so will advertisers on a website. These **third-party cookies** also track your Web usage and send information directly to the advertisers, who can determine how long you've stayed on a page and where you went afterward.

Spyware can be secretly loaded onto users' computers from websites, and can do everything from tracking users' browsing behavior to recording keystrokes, a technique that can lead to having one's password or other private information unknowingly monitored and recorded by an unseen person on another computer.

third-party cookies

Cookies put on a computer by those other than the website being visited, such as advertisers inserting their own cookies on a web page.

▼ CONTENT RIGHTS AND RESPONSIBILITIES

Another new area that media companies have had to deal with is the status of user-generated content (UGC). It is virtually impossible for a company to police all the content that is uploaded to the Internet, and the question of who is responsible for the content on a site arises when someone is defamed in a user comment as opposed to something the company itself wrote.

In general, the courts have made a "safe haven" provision for content providers, protecting them to some extent from libel lawsuits as long as they promptly removed the offending content and showed good efforts in preventing such content. Similarly, Internet service providers (ISPs) have been considered largely immune from responsibility for what is sent over their networks, although the threat of a lawsuit can sometimes be enough to get them to remove offending content or ban users, especially users who are accused by record labels of rampant free file sharing.

LOOKING BACK AND MOVING FORWARD

The Internet has raised a host of legal and regulatory issues regarding media, and the legal system lags generally far behind in dealing with them. The global nature of the Internet also raises questions on which laws should be followed if content that is offensive or illegal in one country can be viewed online. The apparently simple question of whether a hyperlink is protected by the First Amendment can generate some complex discussions about the nature of digital media and the online environment. Similarly, the question "Where does publishing occur?" brings up complex legal debate.

With analog media, the answer was obvious—publishing occurred in the country where the printing press was located. A book might be legally printed in one country but banned in another; thus if a copy was smuggled into the country where it was banned, the person caught with the book would be penalized, not the printer.

But on the Internet the question of where something is published is not at all clear. A person may create some banned content in his country for his website, which is hosted by a company in another country, where the content is not banned. Someone else may come across the content in a third country, where the material is considered harmful, sacrilegious, or defamatory. Several issues are raised in this scenario, including what country's laws will be used if a lawsuit is brought, and what constitutes libel, since it differs from country to country.

A pertinent highly controversial case was settled in December 2002. *Dow Jones and Co. Inc. v. Gutnick* involved an article in *Barron's* (published by Dow Jones) in October 2000 that mentioned Melbourne businessman Joseph Gutnick several times. He sued for libel and claimed that the case should be heard in Australia, where he was defamed.

Although the number of print copies of *Barron's* sent to Australia was minuscule, the online readership of the magazine was over half a million, and Gutnick claimed that many more people would see the article in Australia than just those who subscribed to the print version. Dow Jones argued that the article was actually published in the United States, where Dow Jones's web servers were located, and thus the case should be heard in the United States (where libel charges are harder to win than in Australia). The Australian High Court agreed with Gutnick, however, and Dow Jones eventually settled with him in 2004.

The case was of serious concern to Internet watchers and media companies because of its potential implications for publishers on the Web. If this case becomes a precedent, then anyone could sue a media company or website according to his or her own country's laws, which may be stricter regarding types of acceptable content than where the material was published. On the other hand, it can be argued that it is not fair to impose another country's views of acceptable free speech simply because it is on the Internet. The question remains open and will likely come up again in the future.

DISCUSSION QUESTIONS

1. In today's world of rapid communication and social media do you think the government should have more or less power to exercise prior restraint and block publication or broadcast of material, even from citizens posting to social media sites, that it feels might hurt national security interests? What would some of the effects be, both positive and negative, if the government adopted your opinion?

2. Tobacco and tobacco products cannot be advertised on electronic media such as TV and radio, yet alcohol can. Should similar restrictions be placed on these products on the Internet, or should there be even stronger restrictions?

3. Can traditional standards of what makes a "community" be applied when dealing with online communities? If so, what would those criteria be? If not, what standards could be applied?

4. Given the harm that ridicule or stereotyping can cause for the groups being ridiculed, do you think there should be greater legal restrictions on ridicule or offensive stereotypes in the media? Why or why not?

5. Do you think television and movie rating systems are effective in protecting children? Why or why not? Could there be a better system than ratings to protect children from objectionable content?

6. What dangers are there in a media industry that regulates itself or self-censors? Why could self-censorship be a good thing?

7. Put yourself in the role of a young novelist or struggling musician who is trying to make a living writing stories or making music. Would you oppose or support greater government or corporate control on copyright if the technology promised that unauthorized copies of your work could not be circulated?

Major Principles of Media Law, 2012 Edition. Wayne Overbeck and Genelle Belmas (2011) Wadsworth.

Freedom for the Thought That We Hate: A Biography of the First Amendment. Anthony Lewis (2008) Basic Books.

Make No Law: The Sullivan Case and the First Amendment. Anthony Lewis (1992) Vintage.

The Associated Press Style Book and Briefing on Media Law. Norm Goldstein (2007) Basic Books.

The Journalist's Guide to Media Law: Dealing with Legal and Ethical Issues, 2nd ed. Mark Pearson (2004) Allen & Unwin Academic.

We're All Journalists Now: The Transformation of the Press and Reshaping of the Law in the Internet Age. Scott Gant (2007) Free Press.

Perilous Times: Free Speech in Wartime, From the Sedition Act of 1792 to the War on Terrorism. Geoffrey Stone (2005) W.W. Norton.

Insult to Injury: Libel, Slander and Invasions of Privacy. William Jones (2003) University of Colorado Press.

Rethinking Global Security: Media, Popular Culture, and "The War on Terror." Andrew Martin, Patrice Petro, eds. (2006) Rutgers University Press.

Who Controls the Internet?: Illusions of a Borderless World. Jack Goldsmith, Tim Wu (2006) Oxford University Press.

Intellectual Property Law and Interactive Media: Free for a Fee. Edward Lee Lamoureux, Steven Baron, Claire Stewart (2009) Peter Lang.

The Future of Ideas: The Fate of the Commons in a Connected World. Lawrence Lessig (2001) Random House.

Remix: Making Art and Commerce Thrive in the Hybrid Economy. Lawrence Lessig (2008) Penguin Press.

Intellectual Property and Open Source: A Practical Guide to Protecting Code. Van Lindberg (2008) O 'Reilly Media.

1. False.

2. True.

3. False.

4. True.

5. False.

6. True.

7. False.

8. False.

9. True.

10. False.

14

MEDIA THEORY AND RESEARCH: FROM WRITING TO TEXT MESSAGING

The Earth is Now Your Bitch

LEARNING OBJECTIVES

By the end of this chapter you should be able to:

- Explain the role that theory and research have for media professionals.

- Examine the differences between quantitative and qualitative research.

- Describe various types of media research.

- Critically examine the strengths and weaknesses of various media-research approaches.

- Discuss how digital media and the Internet are being researched both in terms of new media theories being developed and within the framework of old media theories.

In today's age of cross-promotional partnerships between nonmedia and media companies the announcement in early 2006 that GM was partnering with the television show *The Apprentice* to promote the new Chevy Tahoe was not unusual. Even the fact that they had created a website for the launch, and provided video clips and other digital production tools on the site to encourage users to create their own commercials, was not entirely groundbreaking.

Several companies had already received lots of publicity for soliciting user-generated content (UGC) and holding contests to determine the best. Doritos was perhaps the most notable example when it encouraged consumers to create commercials, the best of which would be aired during the Super Bowl.

Things did not go as smoothly for GM's UGC video ad campaign, however. Although the vast majority of people used the tools on the website to make positive commercials for the Tahoe, a minority used the tools to create anticorporate messages and to criticize the Tahoe as a gas guzzler and environmentally unfriendly vehicle. These videos were leaked to video-sharing sites such as YouTube and became the dominant story about GM's campaign.

GM executives might have saved themselves some grief if they had considered some of the theories and media research being done about active audiences and how people generate meaning—sometimes oppositional meanings—from what a media producer may have intended. Media theory is not confined to the halls of academia; it can often help inform practical, real-world decisions and communications strategies being made every day.

heories about media and communication attempt to explain the underlying processes of media, how we interact with media, and how media affect our cultures, societies, attitudes, and lives. Media research is the systematic and scientific investigation of communication processes and effects that often bases its explorations on theories of media and communication. Some types of media research, such as that conducted by market research firms, are more oriented to answering practical questions, such as whether audience members remember a particular advertisement, their impressions of a product or brand, or their media use and consumption habits.

Media-research methodology, or how research is carried out, takes many forms. It can entail social scientific research using quantitative tools such as surveys and experiments, employing statistical analysis of the data, or it can involve critical studies using qualitative methods such as ethnography or focus groups.

▲▼ The Role of Theory and Research

The significance of research for media professionals may seem clearer than that of media theory. It may not seem important to someone planning to work as a journalist or in advertising to learn about media theories, which seem better suited to academia.

Media theories have had a number of profound effects. They play a foundational role as cognitive constructs, or ways we organize and make sense of the world. They also play a key role in shaping research agendas, which then affect the questions asked during the course of research, the findings or discoveries made, and the funding given to conduct research.

Research findings in turn have been very influential in shaping public policies toward the media and media industries, ranging from ratings systems for movies, music, and video games to decisions on what is regulated or not. This of course has important implications for how media companies are organized and run, touching on everything from job creation to the types of media and media content we have available.

Media research carried out specifically for business purposes helps determine audience numbers for particular shows or networks (thus determining advertising rates and what kinds of shows are produced in the future). It also helps determine what media campaigns have been effective, what messages are more

Audience-measurement techniques are just one example of how media theories, statistical analysis, and research come together to help media professionals.

MEDIA QUIZ

Bringing Out Your Inner Researcher

1. Do you believe that there is an objective reality "out there" that we can describe and all agree on or that each of us creates our own reality?
2. (T/F) Concerns about media and their effects on the public originated in the twentieth century.
3. If you worked in a company that was coming out with a new online magazine, what type of research would you do to find out what might be most popular?
4. What words come to mind when you think of the logo of your school mascot?
5. Have you ever tried to copy something you've seen on television, on the Internet, or in the movies? What was it?
6. Did you have a television in your room as you grew up?
7. How much did your parents or guardians supervise your television viewing? Your time on the computer?
8. Do you agree or disagree with the following statement: "Children, especially, need to be protected from media content that is violent or sexual in nature." Why do you feel this way?
9. What does the term "information society" mean to you?
10. (T/F) Some traditional media scholars who died before the Internet became popular have useful theories that help us better understand the current media environment.

persuasive to the public, and therefore what areas are of interest to businesses, nonprofit organizations, and politicians.

In short, media theories not only help media professionals better predict or explain various phenomena, they also help us better understand the world we live in and the forces at work in that world. As we will see, questions about the fundamental nature of communication and media are not new. In fact, important questions that are still being theorized and researched today can be traced back to perhaps the first media revolution: the written word.

Early Concerns of Media Effects

Over the last century, public concern has arisen about the possible effects of each new medium of mass communication as it has emerged. Questions have been asked about each medium's impact on culture, political processes, the values and behaviors children learn, and the like. In the 1920s, much of the public became concerned about the depiction of sex, violence, and lawlessness in film. In recent years, concerns have been raised about the Internet and how it may be influencing us, even perhaps altering how we think.

These concerns are nothing new. In the 1800s, critics warned that newspapers caused juvenile crime. Moralists believed that the flow of sensational news stories about crime and vice would lead people to imitate that immoral behavior. In 1888, *Punch* magazine attributed Jack the Ripper's crimes committed in Whitechapel, a rough inner-city district of London, to "highly coloured pictorial advertisements."

Concern about the effects of media on children has even deeper roots. We know that even in ancient Greece, philosophers Socrates and Plato worried greatly about the influence of literacy on children. Plato was concerned especially about the morally corrupting influence of poetry, particularly allegorical tales such as Homer's *Battles of the Gods,* and sought to ban it.[1] In 360 BCE, Plato offered this reasoning:

> Children cannot distinguish between what is allegory and what isn't, and opinions formed at that age are usually difficult to eradicate or change; it is therefore of the utmost importance that the first stories they hear shall aim at producing the right moral effect.
>
> Plato, *The Republic*

It is hard for us today to see just how profound an effect on society writing had. As Chapter 6 discussed in terms of the storage of information, being able to easily store knowledge in the form of writing changed important aspects of the culture and society.

No longer was a good memory prized the way it was in a nonliterate oral culture, since memorization was not needed to store information. The form of storytelling changed with writing, as repetitive phrases were no longer needed as memory prompts for storytellers, and the rhythm and cadences of the written word differed from oral.

Similarly, a storyteller could lose control of his or her words once they were in written form. Someone could take a person's words and twist their meaning, with no chance for an immediate response or perhaps any response at all. In fact, the author of a work had no way of knowing who might read it or when. It is perhaps comical to imagine Greek children sneaking off with a scroll of poetry to read in secret, but in a fundamental sense it is no different than kids today sneaking into an R-rated movie in the multiplex or removing the parental controls on the family computer.

◣◥ What Makes Mediated Communication Different

The basic assumption behind concerns about the media is that what we see and hear through mediated communication—the signs, symbols, and words—can somehow affect us in ways that nonmediated communication does not. This assumption has led to a large body of research on media effects, which will be discussed later in this chapter.

Before we can understand the various theories on media effects, however, we should first look at a couple theoretical frameworks that offer explanations on how we may make sense of the world through media.

▼ SEMIOTICS

semiotics

The study of signs and symbols.

Semiotics, or the study of signs and symbols, goes back in some form to Plato and Aristotle. Today, the field of semiotics has been greatly influenced by Ferdinand de Saussure, the father of linguistics, and his notion of signs as having dual properties. These properties are the signifier, or the form, and the signified, or what the form represents (some semioticians claim a third component, an interpretant, between these two). For example, an image of a rose (see Figure 14-1) is the signifier, and the signified can represent any number of things depending on the context. An image of a rose on a Valentine's Day card may mean one thing, while a rose tattoo with blood-dipped thorns on the arm of a biker may mean something else entirely.

Love
Thoughtfulness
Relationship
Romance
Birthday
Apology

Signifier · Signified

FIGURE 14-1 Semiotic Signifier and Signified. A rose (the signifier) can mean many different things (the signified), depending on the context. Illinois Press.

A main point is that context plays a major role in the audience's understanding of the signified, even when the signified remains the same. The power of signs to affect our thinking should not be underestimated. René Magritte's famous illustration of a pipe that says "This is not a pipe" is an example of how we typically take the sign as reality. Most people, when shown his illustration and asked what it is, will reply "A pipe." But Magritte is absolutely correct: his picture of a pipe is not actually a pipe—it is simply a picture of a pipe.

Ceci n'est pas une pipe.

René Magritte's famous "this is not a pipe" picture reminds us how we mistakenly understand the representation of something as the thing itself.

It is also important to remember that in semiotics "sign" does not simply refer to visual images but includes words as well. Words could be considered a more complex form of sign, as we have to learn that certain sounds carry particular meanings (which are entirely arbitrary). There is no logical reason that the color red is pronounced "red" in English, or "rojo" in Spanish, or "aka" in Japanese; all of these are simply linguistic conventions for those particular languages.

If that seems like an obvious point, then another semiotic insight is not always so obvious. Once we learn what certain sounds mean (or what certain visual images mean), we take what we have learned as "natural" and largely accept it without question. This fact makes the creation and use of signs extremely powerful, as it not only influences our thinking but even directs certain behaviors. Think of what you do without question whenever you are driving and come to a stop sign (even if you don't stop entirely—at least you know that you should).

Similarly, an indexical sign is visual but signifies something else that is not actually related to it. Consider the image of a floppy disk in most software programs that has come to represent the "save file" function. Most computers nowadays do not even have floppy disk drives, as portable storage has largely been taken over by USB drives, yet we understand what function the image represents.

Some scholars argue that semiotics is at the heart of communication. Noted semiotician and novelist Umberto Eco, in his book *A Theory of Semiotics*, has claimed, "Every act of communication to or between human beings—or any other intelligent biological or mechanical apparatus—presupposes a signification system as its necessary condition." This means that without a common understanding of what signs mean, whether they are visual or lingual, we would not be able to communicate.

Understanding semiotics is important for a deeper understanding of the processes of communication and how meaning is generated among people and in cultures. It is also important for communications professionals in advertising especially, as they can gain insights into how certain branding and advertising campaigns may be received by target audiences.

▼ FRAMING

framing

The notion that every story is told in a particular way that influences how readers think of the story.

Framing is done in all forms of mass communication, including news, and works in much the same way that signs in semiotics do. It relies on the notion that we classify, organize, and interpret things into certain schema, or frameworks, in order to simplify our complex lives. We have to do this just to get through the day; if we carefully considered and analyzed every message we received, then we would never be able to leave the house in the morning. Instead, we take mental "shortcuts" with much of what we encounter, letting it go unexamined as we carry on with our lives.

Frames act much like signs and symbols in semiotics in that once they are accepted, they appear natural and largely go unquestioned. They also shape our perceptions of people, places, issues, and events. A simple example of framing can be seen by looking at two words, "rights" versus "benefits." If an Iraq War veteran is fighting the government to have better health care and services for his wounds, there is a different connotation if he is asking for "veterans' rights" rather than "veterans' benefits." The term "benefits" sounds like something he is getting that is extra, something not available to other people and therefore perhaps unequal or unfair. If he is arguing for veterans' rights, on the other hand, then it sounds more fundamental and is something he is being deprived of, rather than something extra he is asking for.

Framing may simply sound like spin, but it is not. We all frame our world, and good communicators know how to frame debates in ways that favor their views and disadvantage their opponents. If a persuasive communicator wins the framing battle, she or he has likely won that particular debate.

Framing takes on such importance in today's world because the media of mass communication are so pervasive. When combined with the echo effect of the Internet and the conversations that can take place (using the frames that were used, or sometimes debating those frames), it is easy to see how certain types of media coverage can shape our perceptions of the world. Now let us look at how some theories of mass communication developed in the first place.

◢◣ Mass Society, Mass Communication

The study of mass communication and the theories developed to better understand media have been greatly influenced by a number of larger social, political, cultural, and scientific factors throughout the course of history. Here we will explore some of the historical and sociopolitical forces at work in the development of mass communication and media research.

The dramatic societal and political changes that took place in Europe and the United States during the nineteenth and twentieth centuries, thanks largely to industrialization, provide the backdrop for early theorizing on the role of mass communication. Traditional ways of life that had remained largely unchanged for generations were being replaced by the new demands of factory work and mass migrations of people to the quickly growing cities.

Harsh working and living conditions led to various social and political movements that called for greater democracy and workers' rights and clashes between workers and authorities. Elites tended to see these developments as a threat to their power and found various rationales for why some should lead and most should simply follow.

The notion of "the masses" helped give elites a rationale for why they should continue to rule. The people were seen as largely uneducated, lacking in culture, and not intelligent enough to be able to rule themselves. Others took the opposite side, claiming that more participation, better education, and greater distribution of wealth would help create a more democratic, just society.

During these debates, which we hear echoes of even today, film was starting to be recognized as an important medium of mass communication. Literacy was not needed to understand the stories in silent films, and the moving images were regarded as very powerful influencers, especially for the uneducated, passive "masses" or other supposedly vulnerable groups, such as women or children. Messages could be created through the medium of film or using other mass communication to educate, persuade, or control the masses; the question then became how it worked and how to best do this.

propaganda

The regular dissemination of a belief, a doctrine, a cause, or information, with the intent to mold public opinion.

Media-Effects Research

The obvious way to study how media influenced people was to find effects of media exposure. As noted earlier, the notion that media could harm people was already well established, dating back to the ancient Greeks. With new and powerful communication technologies such as film, radio, and later television that could reach millions of people at once, it was not hard to imagine the power that mass communication could have over people.

Media-effects research has played a dominant role in the history of media research and continues to be important today. Findings from media-effects studies have influenced the creation of the movie rating system, dictated regulations overseeing the television industry, and determined what types of advertisements we see. Although earlier assumptions of direct and powerful media effects on people have been tempered and scaled back as newer, more subtle theories have been developed, the notion that media directly affect us (usually negatively) is still very prevalent in the public. Tracing the historical development of effects research provides an interesting view of the role that communication technologies have played and the issues and social norms that we deem important.

▼ PROPAGANDA AND THE MAGIC BULLET

Some of the earliest media-effects research was conducted in order to better understand how people were persuaded by mass communication. During World War I, both the United States and Germany employed film and other media (including posters) as instruments of propaganda to shape public opinion and generate support for their positions in the war. It was widely believed that such propaganda efforts had a great effect on influencing the public's attitudes.

Propaganda is an attempt to influence an audience through mass communication that usually involves total control of the transmission of information and that is often done without the

Propaganda posters during World War I led researchers to hypothesize how persuasion worked on the public.

hypodermic-needle model

A model of media effects, also called the "magic bullet" model, largely derived from learning theory and simple stimulus-response models in behavioral psychology, that states media messages have a profound, direct, and uniform impact on the public.

audience knowing who is actually controlling the message. Although perhaps hard to imagine in today's media environment, particularly with the Internet, many people had extremely limited sources of information—perhaps only a government radio station or single government television station broadcasting a few hours a day.

Political scientist Harold Lasswell coined the term "hypodermic needle," during his analysis of World War I propaganda efforts, to describe the notion that media can act like a drug being injected into a passive audience. The **hypodermic-needle model** is based on the assumption that messages have a profound, direct, and uniform impact on individuals. This model has also been called the "magic bullet" model of communication and derives largely from learning theory and simple stimulus-response models in behavioral psychology.

As film became more popular and began to share space with radio as a form of mass communication in the 1920s, research was conducted about both mediums that looked beyond specific political or propaganda uses and examined the effect on the general public, especially children, a group seen as particularly vulnerable.

▼ PAYNE FUND

The Payne Fund studies were conducted between 1928 and 1933 by some of the most prominent psychologists, sociologists, and educators of the day. Named after the source of funding for the research, they were published in 1933 and included a twelve-volume report on the impact of film viewing on children.[2] The studies provided a detailed examination of the effects of film in wide-ranging areas, including sleep patterns, attitudes about violence, delinquent behavior, and knowledge about foreign cultures.

The Payne Fund studies concluded that the same film would influence children differently depending on those children's varying backgrounds and characteristics,

The Payne Fund studies in the 1920s examined the effects of violence and sex in movies on young people.

including age, sex, life experience, predispositions, social environment, and parental influence. One study of movies, delinquency, and crime, for instance, concluded that the impact of film on criminal behavior may vary depending on the range of themes presented in the film as well as the social context, attitudes, and interests of the viewer.

Although much of the Payne Fund research started from the assumption that movies would have a variety of negative effects, the research also revealed a variety of positive effects. For example, some research found that children could learn positive lessons from film and that information retention was a function of grade in school.[3]

The Payne Fund studies also examined radio. In 1927–1928 they created a "school of the air," which would use radio to educate children on a variety of subjects.[4] This led to the formation of the National Committee on Education by Radio (NCER), as well as the allocation of some $300,000 in the early 1930s to support U.S. broadcasting reform, which at that time meant radio.

▼ RADIO'S WIDER IMPACT

Radio had other effects in society that reached far beyond the realm of children. Consider the events that unfolded on the night of October 30, 1938, when Orson Welles broadcast a radio program created to sound like a news event, called *War of the Worlds*.

At 8 p.m. the Columbia Broadcasting System's Mercury Theater of the Air began its radio broadcast from a New York City studio. Regular listeners and others who heard the introduction understood perfectly well what was about to follow. It was simply a radio adaptation of the science fiction writer H. G. Wells's famous 1897 novel, *War of the Worlds,* starring a twenty-one-year-old baritone named Orson Welles.

But many who did not hear the introduction found themselves lulled into a state of calm as the program brought them a supposedly live orchestral performance. When the program was interrupted for a news flash, the calm was shattered by the announcement that Martians had landed at a farm near Grovers Mill, New Jersey. The increasingly frequent and intense news flashes in the broadcast sounded very much like reports by Walter Winchell, whose hurried tenor was familiar to millions and was the radio standard of the day.

As the Martian invasion ensued and it became apparent that the Martians had vastly superior weaponry, numerous people who lived along the eastern seaboard, especially the New York and New Jersey area, panicked. Many listeners gathered their personal belongings and fled their homes or hid in basements. The broadcast made news headlines for weeks because of the widespread panic it caused. A study by a psychologist showed that one in six listeners—1 million people—thought the show was a real broadcast and that Martians were invading (although not all 1 million panicked and fled).

Orson Welles and his *War of the Worlds* radio broadcast had many listeners believing that Martians actually were invading the East Coast.

Together, studies of the *War of the Worlds* broadcast and other radio programming demonstrated that media effects could be quite dramatic, but that media did not produce uniform effects across the population. The research indicated that a variety of factors, including different individual personalities, demographics, and psychological variables like good critical thinking ability, could mediate audience members' response to media exposure.

This event focused Americans' attention on the power of mass communication in the form of radio and triggered one of the first major research investigations of a media program on the subject of social panic and mass hysteria, as well as a debate about the government's control over the radio industry. As spectacular and strange as these incidents may be, by far the major reasons researchers have examined media effects have been concerns about depictions of sex and violence. These concerns gained even greater force with the advent of television as a form of mass communication.

▼ TELEVISION AND VIOLENCE

Although a lot of television programming is educational and entertaining, much of it is laced with violence, sex, and profanity. Consequently, many adult viewers and policy makers have pondered what effect all this extended television viewing may be having on the minds, bodies, and souls of society's next generation. Is viewing television violence eroding children's morals? Are children learning to be overly aggressive, in imitation of what they see on the television screen? Are they learning more about the Three Stooges than the three branches of government?

Hundreds of studies have been conducted and millions of dollars have been spent to investigate the effects of TV violence on children who viewed it. Among the first was a study that introduced the notion that television had become the new "Pied Piper." In this view, television was providing a model for children to imitate, oftentimes not a very good model.

Yet few early studies could provide conclusive evidence that exposure to TV violence would have negative consequences in the real world. Laboratory research in the 1950s by psychologist Albert Bandura and others had shown that children exposed to TV violence were more likely to repeat the behavior they had witnessed (e.g., beating a "Bobo doll") as well as become more aggressive—while they were still in the lab. Although these studies showed that children learned by watching others, the effects were only documented in a laboratory setting. The researchers who conducted the **Bobo Doll studies** could not confirm that the children continued to be more aggressive once they had left the laboratory and returned to their normal lives.

The 1960s saw a dramatic rise in social unrest and violence in public, much of it politically motivated. In response, President Lyndon B. Johnson in 1968 convened the National Commission on the Causes and Prevention of Violence. He was concerned about a broad range of violence and its social causes, but one major part was the media. Emerging from the commission's media task force in 1969 was a massive three-part report called *Violence and the Media*. It focused on not only the quantity of violence on entertainment television, but also its quality. How did the media portray violence? Who used which weapons to kill whom and what were their motivations and the consequences of their acts? Did the aggressors find reward or punishment? Professor George Gerbner of the Annenberg School for Communication at the University of Pennsylvania was selected as the head of the team to conduct the content analysis. His study defined violence as "the overt expression of force intended to hurt or kill."

Overall, Gerbner and his colleagues found the consequences of television violence were unrealistic. There was rarely pain or much blood. Good guys were often as violent as bad guys but did not suffer the negative consequences of their actions. Bad guys usually got their punishment not from the courts but from the cops. Whites were often the victims, and young black males and other people of color, as well as immigrants, were typically the perpetrators of crime. A follow-up report by Gerbner reached many of the same conclusions.

The 1980s and the 1990s witnessed continued research on TV violence. The American Psychological Association issued in 1992 its TV violence report, *Big World,*

Depictions of violence on television continue to be a concern among many groups.

Bobo Doll studies

Experiments done in the 1950s that showed that children who watched violent episodes on television in which the violent person was rewarded were more likely to punch a Bobo doll than children who saw violent episodes in which the violent person was punished. This research seemed to confirm certain assumptions about direct media effects.

Advertising's Potential Negative Effects on Women—and Men

Advertising is designed to persuade people in some way. Usually it aims to get people to buy some product or service, but it is also used to change attitudes or beliefs about everything from practices such as smoking to the suitability of political candidates.

A large body of research examines the unintended consequences of advertising. Studies have shown that advertising has affected many women's attitudes about their own bodies and behavior. The beauty industry in particular has been criticized for making women feel inadequate when compared to images they see on television or in magazines.

But what about men—are they equally affected by advertising? A growing body of research has shown that they are. For example, men get strong messages

about how they should perform their gender roles from advertising. Men usually appear strong, confident, and independent, while women appear dependent or submissive (or primarily sexual).

Advertising often portrays men (as well as women) as sex objects. Ads both promote sexual prowess and highlight sexual deficiencies (with the promise of the product being advertised to fix those problems). And just like the largely unobtainable female bodies in ads geared toward women, men regularly see ads with males who have hairless chests, six-pack abs, and chiseled muscles.

Men can also appear as comical or grotesque in ads—usually as unaware, obese men showing more of their bodies than the audience would care to see. Although ads like these would at first glance seem to weaken the male gender role as dominant and independent, in fact through their comicality they strengthen it. They give men permission to act in a buffoonish way that is generally not okay for women.

Some may be tempted to argue that they are only advertisements—which most of us don't really notice—so how could they actually affect us? Consider that by age eighteen the typical young adult has seen 360,000 television commercials, and that we easily recognize popular commercial jingles and tag lines.[5] Perhaps we absorb more than we think we do.

Small Screen: The Role of Television in American Society. It argued, "The accumulated research clearly demonstrates a correlation between viewing violence and aggressive behavior. Children and adults who watch a large number of aggressive programs also tend to hold attitudes and values that favor the use of violence." It is important to note that correlation does not equal causation, so although there may be a relationship between television-violence viewing and aggressive behavior, the one does not necessarily cause the other.

One of the most important studies of TV violence in the 1990s was conducted by a team of researchers at UCLA led by Jeffrey Cole. Cole's research shows that U.S. network-television-series programming has gotten somewhat less violent in recent years, but that "shockumentary" reality-based specials have increased dramatically. Funded by the networks themselves, the *UCLA Television Violence Report* showed that overall violence decreased on ABC, CBS, Fox, and NBC during the 1994–1995 season. But the reality-based programs are especially violence filled and are most commonly encountered on Fox. These programs feature real and re-created footage of police shootouts, car chases and crashes, and animals attacking people, in some cases killing them on air.

▼ LIMITED EFFECTS

A landmark research investigation of the impact of television on children in North America was conducted by Wilbur Schramm, Jack Lyle, and Edwin Parker in 1960. In their study, *Television in the Lives of Our Children,* Schramm, Lyle, and Parker concluded that some children under some conditions were likely to exhibit some negative consequences of exposure to television violence. But there was no magic bullet of media effects. The results from this and other studies with similar findings developed various kinds of limited-effects models.

In this view, media are seen as a component in a much larger, and more fundamental, system of influences to which all are subject. Institutions such as the family, school, and religion were seen as much more influential on the individual. These institutions were viewed as providing the basic set of forces shaping the individual's tastes, attitudes, and behaviors. Media exposure was seen as contributing to and often reinforcing the individual's worldview, but was clearly secondary.

Cultivation Analysis

George Gerbner conducted research on the long-term impact of television watching that led to a theory known as **cultivation analysis**. In this view, television cultivates in audiences a view of reality similar to the world portrayed in television programs. Rather than emphasizing the impact of individual programs on individual viewers, cultivation analysis posits that the cumulative effect of viewing thousands of murders on television is to see the world as a more dangerous place than it actually is. This is known as the "**mean-world syndrome**." Because television programs are designed as mainstream entertainment and are easy to understand, they provide a means by which people, especially children, are socialized into society.

Research by Gerbner and others has provided evidence that those who watch more television are more likely not only to believe the real world is a more dangerous place, but to be stronger supporters of a more powerful system of law enforcement. Senior citizens who watch more television are more inclined to stay at home because they are more fearful of perceived dangers in the real world. Cultivation effects are not uniform, however.

Spiral of Silence

The **spiral of silence hypothesis** was developed by German communication scholar Elisabeth Noelle-Neumann to explain why people may be unwilling to express publicly their opinions when they believe they are in the minority. Her analysis is based on her own observations of Germans during the Nazi regime in the 1930s and 1940s.

The spiral of silence hypothesis has been widely tested and shown to be valid under a variety of circumstances. It is based on three premises:

1. People have a natural fear of isolation.
2. Out of fear of isolation, people are reluctant to express publicly views that they feel are in the minority.
3. People have a "quasi-statistical organ," a sort of sixth sense, that allows them to gauge the prevailing climate of opinion and determine what the majority views are on matters of public importance.

cultivation analysis

A theory of media effects that states television cultivates in audiences a view of reality similar to the world portrayed in television programs. For example, it posits that viewing thousands of murders on television is unlikely to increase the chances that one will commit murder but does lead to one's belief that the world is a more dangerous place than it actually is.

mean-world syndrome

The notion that the world is a more dangerous place than it actually is, which has come from watching news reports or violent programming.

spiral of silence hypothesis

A hypothesis that states people (1) are naturally afraid of isolation, (2) realize that if they are in the minority on an issue they will likely be isolated, and (3) have a kind of sixth sense that helps them gauge when their opinions are contrary to the majority—which makes them refrain from expressing their opinions.

It's a Mean, Mean World—At Least on TV

When looking at data on children's television-violence viewing, it is obvious that most children in the United States are heavy viewers of television, and much of what they see is violent in nature. Evidence accumulated over the past half century indicates that this heavy violence viewing increases aggressiveness, especially among young boys, although the effects are present among girls as well.

- By age twelve, the average American child sees eight thousand murders and one hundred thousand acts of violence on television.[6]
- By age eighteen, that child has seen on TV two hundred thousand acts of violence, including forty thousand acts of murder.[7]
- Longitudinal studies show that eight-year-old boys who viewed the most violent programs were more likely to act aggressively and engage in delinquent behavior by age eighteen and commit criminal behavior by age thirty.[8]
- Fifty-four percent of children have a television set in their own bedroom and often watch with a friend, unsupervised.[9]
- Half (47 percent) of the violent actions include no depiction of pain.[10]
- A national survey of two thousand boys and girls showed that one in ten (9.1 percent) boys and one in fifty (2.2 percent) girls said they were victims of genital assault (being kicked or hit with an object in the genitals) as a result of children imitating movies and television programs such as *The Jungle Book, Dumb and Dumber,* and *Three Ninjas.*[11]

The numbers may seem alarming, and most people would likely agree that there is no reason the average American child should see eight thousand murders on television by the time he or she is twelve years old. However, it is also important to remember that cause and effect cannot be attributed to these numbers regarding violence, even the ones showing eight-year-old boys who saw the most violent programs were more likely to engage in criminal behavior.

A common problem with direct-media-effects thinking in trying to pin actions on earlier media use (such as television watching) is that it ignores other potential factors. Perhaps children who watch more television or violent shows tend to live in households in which violence is also more common, or perhaps they are less supervised than their peers. These factors could have more of an effect on subsequent delinquent behavior than simply watching television—which could be merely the symptom of another problem.

How people gauge the climate of opinion is based on a variety of factors, including their past experiences and interactions with others, but is especially shaped by the media. If a person feels her point of view is in alignment with the prevailing climate of opinion, then she will feel more comfortable publicly expressing that viewpoint. If on the other hand she feels out of step with public opinion, then she will be increasingly less likely to express that opinion, thus leading to a possible spiral of silence. In some instances, it is possible that even a majority opinion, if perceived to be the minority (possibly through biased media reporting), may not be expressed publicly.

Third-Person Effect

Among the most interesting of media effects was first observed outside the United States, although its implications are not limited to the international arena. It is known as the **third-person effect** of communication, and it occurs when a media message does not affect the behavior or beliefs of the intended audience but does affect a different group, which also receives the message and may act in the belief that the message will affect the intended audience.

The third-person effect of communication was first recognized from examining records from World War II in which the Japanese dropped propaganda leaflets to black servicemen stationed in the South Pacific, saying the Japanese were fighting against the white imperialists and had no ill will toward blacks. It encouraged them to surrender and promised them good treatment until after the war was over, by which time they could return home. Although records show this campaign had no effect on the black servicemen it targeted, it did cause the white officers of these black troops to transfer soldiers away from areas where they could be targets of the propaganda in order to avoid any potential loss of morale.

Many researchers have since studied the third-person effect of communication and demonstrated its widespread impact in society and in many different circumstances. In the political-communication arena the third-person effect may play a role in election outcomes if the media publicizes results too early. If the election outcome seems to be decided early by exit polls, many people may decide not to bother voting because it won't seem to make a difference anyway.

▼ CRITICISMS OF MEDIA-EFFECTS RESEARCH

Although the direct-effects assumptions and hypodermic-needle model of media power were discredited by subsequent research very quickly, many in the general public and policy makers continue to believe in these effects. When tragedies occur such as the Columbine High shootings in 1999, the Virginia Tech shootings in 2007, or the shooting of U.S. Representative Gabrielle Giffords and dozens of others in Tucson in 2011, media use by the killers is always discussed. Experts may not blame comic books and radio anymore, but television, movies, the Internet, and video games are all fair game when trying to pinpoint blame for violent or antisocial actions.

A basic flaw in much media-effects research is the assumption of the audience as more or less a "passive dupe," or people with no wills of their own and who become easily controlled by media messages. The assumption of a passive dupe is a direct descendant of the belief that the masses are incapable of governing themselves. Although researchers today do not believe that people are simply automatons that can be programmed to act and behave a certain way based on what messages they get, even some of the limited-effects models can lean toward perceiving audiences as passive rather than active.

TV news coverage can affect voter behavior, especially when people see that a race looks like it has already been decided by earlier voters.

Even if the media influence us in some way, it is nearly impossible to separate the intertwining social, cultural, psychological, and media factors and find specific links that provide clear cause-and-effect explanations. To say that certain programs, songs, or video games lead to predictable behaviors or attitudes is hardly believable, given all the other influences we potentially have in our daily lives.

Another criticism of media-effects research is that it is examining the wrong end of the communications process. Some scholars claim that in order to actually understand the role that media play in our lives we have to understand the processes and economics of media products. Other scholars choose to focus not on what media may or may not do to us, but what we may or may not do with the media. This is partially what audience-focused research attempts to find out.

Understanding the Audience

To a certain extent mass-communications research has always been about trying to understand the audience. For advertising and public relations, knowing how the audience thinks and the tools to best persuade it can determine success or failure of a campaign or new brand. For political communication the audience, broadly conceived, is essentially the public and public opinion. For media companies, knowing what shows, books, music, and films audiences will like is a vital element for success. In scholarly communications research, the trend in audience studies in recent years has been toward seeing the audience as increasingly active in how it makes sense of the world and uses media.

▼ AUDIENCES CREATING MEANING

It may seem odd to think of audiences creating meaning from media content they consume, but remember what was discussed earlier in this chapter about semiotics and how we tend to take a given meaning of a sign or symbol for granted once we know it. Similarly, scholars who use the new audience-studies approaches question the assumption that a media product comes with a predetermined and unchangeable meaning that audiences then ingest like a fast-food hamburger. Rather, they claim that we are always actively participating in creating meaning around the media we encounter, and this happens not only between the media and audience, but between audience members. Some approaches look at psychology, while others focus on the social aspects of creating meaning, while still others examine broader cultural issues and relations of power.

Uses and Gratifications

Uses-and-gratifications research looks at *why* people use particular media. It examines what people do with the media rather than what the media do to people. Uses-and-gratifications research became popular in the 1970s and 1980s. It posits that people have certain needs, especially psychological needs, which they seek to satisfy through media usage. Uses-and-gratifications research makes three basic claims:

1. People actively use the media for their own purposes.
2. People know what those purposes are and can articulate them.
3. Despite individual differences in media use, there are basic common patterns among people.

uses-and-gratifications research

A branch of research on media effects that looks at why people use particular media and examines what people do with the media rather than what the media do to people.

Uses-and-gratifications research is based on a model of a more active rather than passive audience (i.e., audience members seek to satisfy certain needs through their media use) and may lend itself to future media research on the Internet and interactive media.

Uses-and-gratifications research is not without its critics, however. It has been criticized for being somewhat circular in its reasoning and hard to test empirically. In other words, it's hard to know which came first—the social/psychological need or the media use. Other criticisms include its focus on psychological needs while ignoring the important role that social forces play in media use and the assumption that audiences always do know (and can articulate) why they are using media.

Encoding/Decoding

encoding/decoding

A theory that says that messages are encoded with certain meanings by media producers and that audiences then "decode" the messages in various ways, depending on things like their education level, political views, and other factors.

The **encoding/decoding** model, developed by Stuart Hall in the 1970s as a response to dissatisfaction with media-effects research at the time, takes a broadly cultural approach to audiences and tries to examine them within larger relations of production and social power. It began what is known as the active-audience approach to research.

The model is complex, but in essence it states that media products are encoded with meanings by media producers and those meanings are decoded in various ways by the audience. There is no guarantee that the producer's preferred meaning is the one that will become accepted by the audience, as audience members have three basic options when decoding.

They can choose the dominant, or hegemonic, reading (the one that the media producer likely intended). The dominant reading is one that most people would recognize as "common sense" or would accept as natural. They can choose the oppositional reading, in which they recognize the codes being used but reject them and put their own meanings to the media product. They can also choose a negotiated reading, in which they largely accept the dominant reading but add some variations to it. Audiences will have varied decoding skills and tendencies based on their backgrounds, education, identities, and other social factors.

Reception Analysis

Reception analysis was a major break in audience research in a number of respects. First, the starting point for much of the research was the assumption that audience members were active in making meaning with the media they consumed. Second, researchers looked at areas of popular entertainment such as soap operas, women's magazines, and romance novels rather than the traditional areas of news or other "serious" programming that had been studied in earlier years. Third, the areas of study allowed feminist and other scholars to study not only the role of women in media, but women as active audiences.

The findings challenged long-held assumptions about the reasons why women read romance novels, or why they watched a soap opera such as *Dallas,* or how teen girls perceived Madonna. In contrast to some of the notions commonly held, even by feminist scholars, that these forms of popular culture were demeaning to women or taught them to see themselves as sex objects within a patriarchal viewpoint, scholars found that women were active participants in deciding what such content meant to them and freely chose a variety of meanings.

Reception analysis attempts to fill the holes in previous types of theorizing and research by looking at cultural and social patterns of media production and power relations between different groups. However, some critics have argued that it has gone too far in its claims of active audiences, making media almost powerless. Another strand of research on mass communications, cultural studies, attempts to look at media through broad cultural and social frameworks and media production.

▼ AUDIENCES AS CONSUMERS, USERS, OR PRODUSERS?

In contrasting online media with traditional analog media, perhaps the most basic distinction is that the online audience has to be to some extent interactive in order to access desired media, including reaching other members of the audience. The audience online can be in many ways a full participant in the process of online communication and therefore meaning making.

Although there are certainly passive media experiences online, they only happen after the user has first engaged them. Although the research to date exploring active audiences online is fairly limited, it is growing rapidly and becoming one of the most important areas of Internet research in the twenty-first century.

The change from viewer to user or produser affects media organizations, the way news and entertainment are presented, and even what types of news or entertainment will likely become popular. Even more importantly, the nature of the relationship between the audience and media producers is changing, affecting a broad swath of social relations and the hierarchical power relations often taken for granted. Even nonmedia companies have had to start thinking of themselves as content producers, or at least start giving the tools to audiences to produce **user-generated content**.

Because of the newness of the Internet, there is a growing amount of research on the impact of time spent online, on both children and adults. A major

Madonna has been a polarizing figure among researchers of pop culture, with some saying she empowers young women and others saying she promotes standard gender stereotypes.

user-generated content

Media content that has been created by consumers or audience members, including videos, music, or other forms of content.

Giving children access to computers and teaching them media and computer literacy will help them succeed in the twenty-first century.

study was launched in 1999 to examine the social, cultural, and commercial impact of the Internet. Funded by a consortium of major companies interested in online communication, the study is headed by Jeffrey Cole, director of the UCLA Center for Communication Policy, who had earlier headed the UCLA Television Violence Study. Among the companies sponsoring the twenty-year longitudinal investigation are Microsoft, America Online, Disney, and Sony. Researchers are studying a variety of questions, including how family time, political leanings, and social life are influenced by Internet usage. The study is also designed to examine online banking, shopping and buying habits, comfort with using credit cards online, and other issues related to ecommerce. The initial panel includes two thousand people selected from a national sample, and international representatives will be added later.[12]

With the rise of popularity of video games, more research is being conducted on many aspects of them, including how they may reinforce negative gender or racial stereotypes, how they may affect our sense of identity, whether or not we can learn better through game playing than traditional means, and other facets of the video game world. How violent video games influence children is not as well known or researched as is the impact of violent television programming. Yet, evidence consistently shows that children have a great ability to imitate actions they observe. And young children under five years of age, especially, do not always have the ability to determine whether such violent actions are appropriate or properly motivated or justified.

Internet media studies, including those of video games, draw not only from the media-effects research tradition but from broader strands of research including literary theory and cultural studies, the latter of which especially has been influential in media research over the past thirty years.

WEB LINK
The Pew Research Center for the People & the Press
people-press.org/

▲▼ Cultural Studies

The focus on culture and broader societal issues in relation to media, seen in reception-analysis research and the encoding/decoding model of Stuart Hall, falls within a broad category of scholarly research developed in the 1970s called **cultural studies**. Difficult to define concisely because of the wide range of research interests encompassed by the discipline (some even disagree that it can be called a discipline, let alone a scientific discipline), it nevertheless has seen tremendous growth from the 1990s into the early part of the twenty-first century. More and more universities have created cultural-studies departments in recent years.

Cultural-studies approaches to research largely reject the media-effects research tradition and attempt to understand how meaning is produced not only among audiences but among media producers. By looking at popular culture in its many facets and with a critical eye toward dominance and related issues of uses of power and subordination, researchers hope to better understand the role that media plays in perpetuating these social relations.

European versions of cultural studies tend to be Marxist oriented and highly critical of existing politics and culture, while the North American version of cultural studies has tended to be more celebratory than critical of consumer culture and media. Even with these differences, cultural-studies scholars tend to have a

cultural studies

A framework in studying theories of communication that shuns the scientific approach used by scholars in the empirical school and that tries to examine the symbolic environment created by mass media and the role mass media plays in culture and society.

normative rather than descriptive bent to their research. In other words, they want to try to make society better rather than claiming they are neutral scientific observers simply describing society.

▼ IDEOLOGY AND THE CULTURE INDUSTRY

The normative focus of cultural studies stems from its origins in **critical theory** and the Frankfurt School scholars who created critical theory in the 1930s and 1940s in Germany at the Institute for Social Research, based in Frankfurt. Theodor Adorno, Max Horkheimer, Herbert Marcuse, and to some degree Walter Benjamin were all German Marxist scholars with a variety of research interests ranging from music theory and philosophy to sociology.

The Frankfurt School coined the term "**culture industry**" to refer to how media businesses created mass-produced "cultural products" that were then consumed by the masses. They distinguished between "high art" (opera, classical music, etc.) and "popular art" (jazz, film, etc.), which they saw as demeaning and crass partly because of its commercial nature.

Although their views may be criticized as artistic snobbery, their larger point was that the culture industry plays an important role in propagating an **ideology** that helps maintain the status quo. In other words, it makes existing power relations and inequality seem natural or inevitable and discourages critical reflection among people—which high art, on the other hand, encourages. In this view, media production is not simply a by-product or reflection of popular tastes and desires; it actively creates those desires and plays a vital role in suppressing freedom.

It is important to note that they are not simply talking about authoritarian governments such as Nazi Germany, although it applies to these kinds of governments as well. They are claiming that even supposedly "free market" systems are actually not free at all because the media of mass communications promote capitalist ideology as the best way of life while ignoring the fundamental problems of capitalist economies.

Herbert Marcuse was a prominent member of the Frankfurt School and one of the founders of critical theory.

critical theory

An umbrella term for a range of theories, most of which are influenced by Marxism, which attempts to look critically at society and offer ways to make society better.

culture industry

A term used by some critical theorists that refers to the mass communication industries and their power in creating culture as a commodity.

ideology

A way of belief that goes largely unquestioned by people or that is seen as somehow natural or beyond question.

▼ CRITICISMS OF CULTURAL STUDIES

Cultural studies, despite its rise in popularity in academia, is not without its detractors and faults as a field of study. One common complaint is the often impenetrable, jargon-laden writing style of many cultural-studies researchers, which excludes many people who have not had extensive academic study. This is at odds with the broad goal of helping to bring about positive changes in society by enlightening the public about how it is oppressed and the role that media play in that oppression.

The writing style is also criticized for hiding muddled thinking and masking mundane ideas behind grandiose jargon. In 1996, a physicist at New York University, Alan Sokal, published an article in the postmodern journal *Social Text* entitled "Transgressing the Boundaries: Toward a Transformative Hermeneutics of Quantum Gravity." The title and writing style were typical of many journal articles written from a postmodern perspective, but the article was actually a hoax and purposely written to be nonsensical. Sokal said he perpetrated the hoax to show the danger, in the social sciences, of basing scholarship on fashionable or trendy schools of thought rather than on reason.

WEB LINK
Alan Sokal's Articles on the "Social Text" Affair
**www.physics.nyu.edu/faculty/sokal/#debate_
linguafrancaDigitalMediaTheoryandResearch**

T racing the intellectual history of currently popular media theories and research can be a fascinating exercise and give us a better sense of how theories may be influencing our thinking. We can read about some theories that, in the past, were widely believed but have since been disproven or seriously flawed. On the other hand, sometimes researchers find old theories that for some reason never caught on but that actually have a lot to offer current research.

One example is how some early sociologists tried to study social behavior in relational, rather than objective, terms. For decades much of this research was ignored, but now several sociological theories rely on relational or network-oriented ways of looking at the world. The terms early sociologists used may be different than what current researchers use, but many of the concepts can be surprisingly similar.

Michel Foucault was a noted French social theorist who was hugely influential in the mainstream media in France, regularly writing columns and opinion pieces on a wide range of issues.

Most of the theoretical frameworks used in media research have been borrowed in one form or another from European schools of thought in the humanities or social sciences. The American-made school of philosophical thought, pragmatism, was largely superseded by European schools of thought after the early part of the twentieth century, although important aspects of pragmatism can be found today in some social theories.

Many ostensibly "new" theories actually have deep roots in combinations of much older theories or are combinations of different schools of thought with unique insights added to create a more relevant theory.

Some of Europe's most interesting thinkers draw from a wide variety of sources as they tackle social issues or the role of the media in society. These include philosophy, literary theory, history, economics, political theory, social theory, and cognitive science.

It is also interesting to note that scholars in some European countries are much more visible than scholars in the United States. For example, in France social theorists Michel Foucault and Pierre Bourdieu were virtually media celebrities in their own right, appearing on television to discuss theoretical issues and writing regularly on political and social topics for popular newspapers.

In the same vein, other critics of cultural studies say that since it largely rejects scientific tenets such as the importance of rationalism for finding truth, it cannot actually be called a science. Without any basis for measuring the correctness or incorrectness of viewpoints, it is nearly impossible to have any grounds for refuting ideas that are clearly wrong.

◣◥ Sociohistorical Frameworks

There are other theoretical frameworks that may draw on a variety of schools of thought, especially Marxism or critical theory, as well as a number of disciplines such as sociology, anthropology, psychology, and even economics. These frameworks tend not to emphasize audiences as much as the ones looked at previously, but try to focus on the entire media system within its larger social, political, and historical contexts. Some of the frameworks discussed below claim that focusing primarily on audiences means that researchers are missing many of the most fundamental answers regarding our media today and the effect that it is having on our society and world.

▼ INFORMATION SOCIETY

The meaning of the **information society**—sometimes also named the "network society," "knowledge society," or "postindustrial society"—is still being debated by social scientists. Information-society theories posit that the prominence of communications and media ushers in a new era that breaks drastically from the industrial society. Networks become hugely important as they bring the world closer together, and economic value lies not so much in the old manufacturing centers, like it once did, but in knowledge centers. Education and training will be the keys to success for workers, who will be valued not for the manual labor they are able to do but for the ideas, knowledge, and creativity they have to make sense of and create information.

There are many critics of the often utopian picture painted by information-society theories. Some scholars, especially those influenced by Marxism or critical theory, claim that the information society is actually making established relations of dominance stronger for transnational media corporations as fewer companies control more media channels, including those on the Internet. They point to the rhetoric used for earlier media types that promised to be emancipatory when they were new, such as radio, and chronicle the relentless control by government and corporations that rendered claims about any new medium bringing freedom or democracy largely hollow. The example of companies barring WikiLeaks from receiving online donations after they released secret U.S. government diplomatic cables is an example of how elite interests still dominate.

One criticism with information-society theories is that they take a small slice of the world's population and expand its way of life to almost everyone. One does not have to look far to see that much of the world lives in conditions where clean water is a rarity, let alone ready access to the Internet, or even electricity. This leads to discussions regarding the **digital divide**, one of the most important Internet-audience issues today.

Research has shown that from the early days of public use of the Internet, especially from the first graphical Web browsers, Internet access tended to be much higher among society's economically advantaged—those with a higher education and with a legacy of higher overall print-media use. Economically disadvantaged groups, especially minority groups and the rural poor, tended to have less Internet access and lower Internet and overall online usage. Yet, the gap has closed dramatically if not disappeared in some cases. Women, for example, now make up the majority of Internet users in the United States—across economic lines. Problems of equity of access to online media will not disappear soon, however, especially among the economically disadvantaged and those in the developing world.

▼ POLITICAL ECONOMY

Another area of media research that has been inspired by Marxism and influenced by critical theory is **political economy**. Political-economist media scholars examine the production and ownership of media as main forces that determine

information society
The notion that modern society has transformed from one in which industrial production was dominant to one in which information production has become more important.

digital divide
The idea that some groups that do not have access to the Internet become left out of the benefits that online technology can bring.

political economy
An area of study inspired by Marxism that examines the relationship between politics and economics with media ownership and the influences they all have on society and perpetuating the status quo.

the type of media we have and what that means for our social and political systems and our lives.

Scholars such as Robert McChesney study the history and current status of media ownership, regulations and laws applying to media, and especially the conglomeration of media ownership and how that has affected the type of media we have.

They claim that by examining the forces of media production—by seeing who owns what media companies and studying how their business decisions determine types of media, how they are delivered, to whom, and in what way—we are then better able to understand the underlying forces behind power relations and dominance.

A political-economic viewpoint has an advantage over most forms of audience-studies research in that it enables media scholars to explore areas where an audience does not actually yet exist. For example, an audience-studies researcher would be unable to study Hispanic-language newspaper readership in an area that does not have a Hispanic-language newspaper. But the question, "Why isn't there a Hispanic-language newspaper for this audience in this market?" would be a legitimate area of study for a political economist, as would exploring the type of content such a newspaper likely would have if it did exist.

Robert McChesney is a noted political economist of media and has taken a leading role in the media reform movement, founding Free Press.

▼ MEDIA ECOLOGY

media ecology

The study of media environments and how those environments may affect people and society.

technological determinism

The belief that technology causes certain human behaviors.

Media ecology, as its name suggests, is the study of media environments and how those environments may affect people and society. Just as an ecological system in nature is complex and can be studied from a number of perspectives, or specialties (a chemist studying soil samples will see an ecosystem very differently than a biologist studying bear habitats in the same ecosystem), so it is with media ecology.

Media ecology attempts to examine everything from how our media environment influences our thinking to how specific types of media affect our perceptions because of the medium used (medium theory).

Perhaps the most famous proponent of medium theory was Canadian scholar Marshall McLuhan, with his famous phrase, "The medium is the message." By this, McLuhan claimed that the medium used to transmit messages was far more important to understand than the actual message content or way it was produced.

McLuhan's provocative writings were hugely popular in the 1960s and early 1970s, even outside of academia. His claims that electronic media had transformed the world into a "global village," free of the hierarchical and rigid power relations that were created by the culture of print media, echo what we hear about the role of the Internet, even though he was only speaking about radio and television.

He has been charged with espousing a form of **technological determinism**, or the belief that technology causes certain human behaviors—a charge that some forms of media ecology still must deal with. Some critics also state that by celebrating the technical side of communication he ignored (and thereby left unchallenged) the relations of power and dominance that went into making the media today.

Despite these and other weaknesses in some of his theories, McLuhan did offer important insights into how media have affected our sense of time and space and thus our lives in modern society. Some of his points are even more important when considering digital media. Although technology may not be the most important component to examine when trying to theorize about media, the capability of mass

Media scholar Marshall McLuhan was widely popular even outside of academic circles in the 1960s and 1970s and is noted for coining the phrase, "The medium is the message."

media to reach large audiences almost immediately certainly has far-reaching consequences for how we make sense of the world.

▼ AGENDA SETTING

The concept known as **agenda setting** does not take as broad a view as the frameworks mentioned above, although it does relate directly to media messages and industries. In 1948, Paul F. Lazarsfeld and Robert K. Merton developed the notion of agenda setting. Lazarsfeld and Merton explained that one of the primary functions of the media is to confer status. The process of singling someone out from the large, heterogeneous masses tends to bestow prestige and authority on those so identified. "The audiences of mass media apparently subscribe to the circular belief that if you matter, you will be at the focus of mass attention and, if you are at the focus of mass attention, then surely you must really matter," wrote Lazarsfeld and Merton.[13]

This quote rings truer today than ever due to our growing mix of social media and mass media. As agenda setters, the media can shape our perception of what issues are important, and how important, depending on their prominence in the mass media. Political scientist Bernard Cohen more clearly articulated the agenda-setting model when he wrote, "The press may not be successful much of the time in telling people what to think, but it is stunningly successful in telling its readers what to think about."[14]

Research by communication scholars Max McCombs and Donald Shaw tested and further articulated this phenomenon in the 1970s and demonstrated that in fact the media are especially effective at influencing public views on the importance of various issues. Moreover, McCombs and Shaw's research showed that different media play different roles in the agenda-setting process. In particular, historically newspapers have tended to set the general agenda of public issues. For example, newspapers might determine which issues the public is likely to see as important, such as taxes, education, crime, or health care. Meanwhile, the electronic media of television and radio are especially effective at shaping the public's views on which of those issues are most important.

Television news can direct us to what we consider important because it is being covered in the news, an example of the agenda-setting process.

A major question emerged in the 1990s regarding the role of the Internet and other online media in the agenda-setting process. Although many researchers have followed in the footsteps of pioneers McCombs and Shaw to test and refine the agenda-setting model, little research to date has examined how communication via the Internet and other online media affects public opinion, especially with regard to the perception of importance of different issues.

◣▷ Media Research: What Type of Science Is It?

It may seem strange asking what "type" of science media research falls under, but the question is an important one because it raises several issues about media studies. At the heart of the question is whether or not the social sciences such as psychology, sociology, and anthropology can (and should) be conducted according to the rules of the natural sciences.

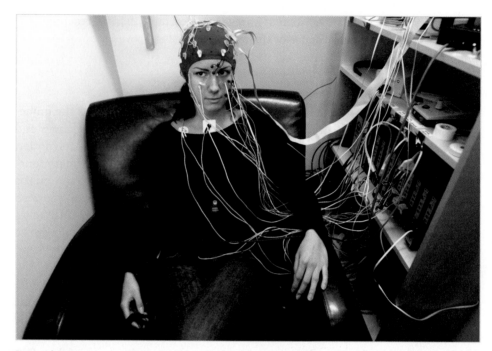

Researchers can use a variety of tests to determine physiological and neurological responses to media content.

There is no question that for most of their histories as individual disciplines the social sciences have tried to emulate the rules and methods of the natural sciences, but some scholars disagree on whether they can do that properly or not. Is it possible, they ask, to discover the same kind of natural laws for communication and media that we see in the natural sciences, such as a law of gravity? More importantly, in trying to copy scientific models that may not be appropriate to the social sciences, are we missing the point in understanding our social world and asking the wrong questions?

The confusion about where media-studies research sits is also reflected in the range of schools and departments in universities where it can be found. Sometimes media studies may be within a school of journalism; other times it may be within a school of communications or even in an English department.

To further complicate matters, much important research and theorizing on the media has been done by sociologists and psychologists or by scholars trained in those fields or in other areas, such as literary theory, who have focused on media or mass-communication research. The transmission model of communication, as discussed in Chapter 1, was developed by mathematicians to help solve an engineering problem, yet became hugely influential for many years in shaping our understanding of the processes of communication.

Broadly speaking, the debate on the type of science media research should entail can be divided into two main camps regarding how the world is viewed. **Positivism** says that there is an objective reality that can be observed, measured, and explained by a neutral observer. Theories can be hypothesized based on observations, and through rigorous testing and experimentation following the scientific method the hypotheses can be proved or disproved. This leads to a better understanding of the world and an increasing ability to predict behaviors or alter phenomena with predictable results. This has been the dominant **epistemology**, or way to understand the world, for most social scientists, including media researchers, throughout the twentieth century.

positivism

The belief, common among scientists in the physical or natural sciences and many in the social sciences, that there is an objective reality that can be discovered and explained through rigorous scientific research.

epistemology

A way of or framework for understanding the world.

There are several other epistemologies that reject positivist claims to varying degrees. These range from **postpositivism**—which largely agrees with most positivist claims but also states that there are areas of knowledge that cannot be understood through scientific means, such as religious faith—to **social constructionism** and **postmodernism**.

Social constructionism says that all meaning and truth are derived from social interactions, including our interactions with symbols and signs, which have relativistic and changeable meanings according to the context. Language is not a transparent medium that describes the world; it creates the world as we know it.

Postmodernism, although it has many variants, largely eschews grand theorizing and what it calls "metanarratives," or overarching narratives that try to explain the world, because any such metanarrative essentially favors one worldview over others, which are then suppressed. It, like social constructionism, questions how knowledge is formed and challenges the assumptions of positivist science that it is a better (or the only) way to find and establish truth.

It is important to note that some of the basic elements of constructionist and postmodern thought are not entirely new or simply a reaction to the dominance of positivist science in the twentieth century. Their histories can be traced back to influential schools of thought in the nineteenth and early twentieth centuries like **pragmatism** and even before that to some important philosophical traditions. In some ways, such thinking is a return to the roots of theorizing about media and the role of communication.

The debate about what type of science media-studies research falls under can also be roughly mapped to the main types of research methodologies carried out today: **quantitative research** and **qualitative research**.

▼ QUANTITATIVE RESEARCH

Researchers relying heavily on quantitative techniques tend to have a positivist outlook. They assume that their research will help better predict behavior, find causal effects for certain phenomena, or support or weaken certain media theories.

Quantitative studies include the familiar methods of experiments, surveys, and statistical analyses. The exact method used depends on several factors, especially on the goals or purposes of the research. If a study is intended to establish causality, such as whether watching violent programming on television causes increased levels of violence among children, then experimental or quasi-experimental methods could be appropriate.

If a study is meant to document how much violence is on television, then a content analysis should be conducted. If an investigation is designed to determine how much televised violence children can recall, then a survey may be in order.

In any case, research methods are never perfect indicators, and the design of the study as well as the particular method used can affect results. For example, conducting a laboratory experiment with children on the effect of watching violence on television not only raises important ethical questions, it also creates an unrealistic media environment that will make accurate measurements extremely problematic. The laboratory environment, no matter how much it is changed to look and feel like a home environment, still does not accurately capture the range of environmental factors that may be involved in a normal viewing experience.

Content analysis, such as counting the number of times the word "sex" is used in an issue of a magazine or newspaper, or the number of times images of violence

postpositivism

A view that agrees largely with positivism, but acknowledges that there may be some things that we cannot know through scientific inquiry.

social constructionism

A view that says that much if not all of what we know and understand about the world, including scientific knowledge, is constructed through our social interactions and language.

postmodernism

A broad category of viewpoints that claim that there is no absolute truth, that truth is unknowable, and that attempts to create grand narratives that explain the world are faulty.

pragmatism

A school of thought that claims that truth is found in actions that work and that no overarching or purely objective notion of truth can be found.

quantitative research

Research that focuses on numbers and measures and experimentation to describe phenomena. Researchers usually have a hypothesis they are trying to prove or disprove through controlled experimentation.

qualitative research

Research that describes phenomena in words instead of numbers or measures. Ethnographic studies, such as interviews with people to learn about beliefs or trends, are an example of qualitative research, also called critical-cultural studies.

are shown on television, can also be problematic. Although such analysis can provide concrete numbers that can then be analyzed using statistical methods, it often makes big assumptions. For example, what evidence is there that a certain number of violent scenes will have an effect on viewers or that seeing the word "sex" fifteen times in a magazine article and not twelve times (or one hundred times) will affect readers?

Analyzing data using statistics raises its own set of problems, including incomplete or missing data that may make analysis difficult, sampling error (taking a sample of the population that does not accurately reflect the entire population), and faulty study design that leads to misleading results. Consider a simple example. Let's say you conduct a ten-question, multiple-choice survey among one hundred classmates. You get responses from all one hundred people (itself a rarity in survey research), but you find that only thirty-five people have answered the tenth question. How should it be counted in your results? And why did so few answer it? Because 50 percent of thirty-five is seventeen people, while 50 percent of the other questions would be fifty people, to say "50 percent of the survey respondents believe that . . ." regarding question ten would not be accurate since only thirty-five answered the question.

These and other methodological difficulties with quantitative research have led to the growth and acceptance of qualitative research methods.

▼ QUALITATIVE RESEARCH

Qualitative researchers may reject the assumptions behind quantitative research, or they may simply appreciate the limitations of such research and want other means to explore their areas of interest. They are generally not trying to make predictions, but are focusing on description with the hope of better understanding the world as the participants see it. Qualitative research can include in-depth interviews, focus groups, and ethnography, among other techniques.

Ethnography involves the application of a technique, developed in anthropology, in which the researcher immerses himself in a culture in order to directly observe it. The researcher tries to see the culture in its natural state, disrupting it as little as possible.

An ethnographer might enter into a household, a newsroom, or an advertising agency and spend hours, days, weeks, or even months directly observing the media behaviors of the people or organization involved. The ethnographer might video and audio record the observed activities as a way of documenting the research. A detailed analysis would follow. The results might be used in isolation or in combination with other methods, such as interviews or even quantitative techniques such as content analysis of conversations or written memos.

A variation of ethnography is **participant-observation**. In this technique, the researcher joins the group he is studying, such as a fan club or an online multiplayer video game. His status as a participant not only helps him better understand the world he is observing, but also helps the participants open up more to the researcher than they otherwise might if they saw him simply as an outsider.

Focus groups are widely used by media researchers. Often the social interaction that takes place among the participants of a focus group, and the way they discuss what is being studied, can provide important insights that the researcher would not get from interviewing people individually or simply conducting a survey. Focus groups are widely used by marketers testing new products or consumers' reactions to their brand or products.

ethnography

A variety of qualitative research techniques that involve the researcher interacting with participants, either through observation, participation, interviews, or a combination of methods.

participant-observation

A qualitative research technique in which the researcher participates as a member of the group being studied.

focus groups

A research technique in which small groups of people are gathered together to discuss a topic, with the interactions often recorded and carefully watched to determine what different people think.

Qualitative research raises its own ethical concerns and is not without weaknesses. One question is whether or not participants should be informed of the researcher's true role. This is especially important when doing research with groups online, where the researcher's identity may not be obvious. Another ethical issue arises when the researcher sees the participants engaging in risky or dangerous behavior. Does he explain to the participants why they shouldn't do that, thus changing the results of his research, or does he simply observe?

Qualitative research of course makes no claims to being generalized to the larger population or being reliable in the sense of getting the same results if conducted by another researcher or with another group, even under similar circumstances. It is wrong to try to generate meaningful numbers from a certain set of interviews so the results look like you have talked to a representative sample of the population.

▼ QUALITATIVE AND QUANTITATIVE RESEARCH WORKING TOGETHER

Each methodology has its place in media research today, and each methodology has strengths and weaknesses. Ignoring one methodology over another because of a philosophical disagreement can create a blind spot for a researcher trying to find answers. They are simply tools to be used; a person can pound a nail with a screwdriver, but a hammer works much better.

Qualitative techniques are often used to provide more depth or texture to quantitative studies. For example, in designing a survey you may not really know what issues are important to your research subjects or perhaps even how they talk about certain things. Conducting qualitative research can help you see various common themes that emerge and help you design a better survey.

Qualitative research, if done properly, helps you see the world from another perspective in a way that quantitative can never do. Simply observing certain behaviors with media can often yield amazing insights on the part of the researcher and will generate even more interesting research questions to ask. Observing who controls the remote control in the living room, and a family's rules around that, may be more telling of television viewing habits than specific preferences for shows.

Quantitative research, with its statistical techniques and its claims of speaking for a much larger population than what was studied, is also extremely powerful. Sometimes simply looking at charts and graphs of numbers can be enough to persuade people that the results must be true.

Focus group research can provide rich insights into consumer opinions of products or issues.

LOOKING BACK AND MOVING FORWARD

As may be expected for a medium that is still relatively new, large gaps remain in research and theorizing about digital media and the Internet. Early euphoria about the positive transformative effects the Internet would have for society and democracy have given way to more measured, careful statements that also recognize the dangers or weak spots and studies that have sometimes shown surprising effects.

Some scholars have claimed that nothing has fundamentally changed, from the perspective of media theory or social theory, with the rise of the Internet and digital media, and that existing conceptual frameworks are perfectly adequate for researching and explaining new media. This may be true in some cases, but it also leaves large blind spots in the research agenda, such as explaining the changes taking place in the nature of mass communication.

Research and theorizing on digital media and the Internet is further complicated by the fact that rapid technological changes can have drastic effects on usage and perceptions. Studies done two years earlier that involve a certain technology or framework may seem hopelessly outdated by the time a journal article is published, especially if the technology that was studied no longer is used as much.

Researchers who focus on digital media tend to draw heavily from research traditions in media studies, sociology, information science, and communication studies, among other disciplines. The broad research frameworks correspond more or less to those applied to traditional media, ranging from the broad-based socio-cultural perspectives to Internet use-and-effects research to studying the ways characteristics of the medium itself, such as interactivity, may affect our relation with content.

It is also interesting to note that some pre-Internet scholars could experience a revival of interest in some lines of their work. For example, Marshall McLuhan, with his examination of the way electronic media implode space and time and affect social relations, may have much to offer digital-media scholars studying the Internet. Uses-and-gratifications principles may prove especially fruitful in an interactive medium where users largely control what content they can get and how they get it.

DISCUSSION QUESTIONS

1. Semiotics discusses visual signs and symbols, including written language. Could semiotics also be applied to audio signs? If so, how? Consider certain audio from mass media that may be considered semiotic, if any.

2. Discuss whether you believe there is an objective reality that can be clearly measured and explained or whether there are various realities or truths that defy scientific explanations.

3. Which type of medium do you think may have the strongest influence on people: radio, film, television, or the Internet? Why?

4. Describe some of your own experiences in seeing how television may have affected your behavior or that of your friends in terms of actions, fashion sense, or career goals. Were these changes short- or long-term?

5. Write a list of your television or film heroes from your teens to the present, along with a brief sentence on why you like each one. Compare lists with classmates and discuss your choices. See if you can discern any common themes regarding types of characters in your lists.

6. Do you think that a highly interactive medium like video games could have greater effects on media users than a more passive medium such as television? Why or why not?

7. Discuss ways in which some of the older media theories may be applied usefully to explain social media or practices related to social media.

8. Find some recent media or social science studies reported in the news and determine whether they are quantitative or qualitative types of research. What are the strengths and weaknesses of the approaches used in these?

FURTHER READING

Media Studies: Theories and Approaches. Dan Laughey (2010) Oldcastle Books.

Quantitative Research Methods for Communication: A Hands-On Approach. Jason Wrench, Candice Thomas-Maddox, Virginia Peck Richmond, James McCroskey (2008) Oxford University Press.

Ethnography: A Way of Seeing. Harry F. Wolcott (1999) Rowman & Littlefield.

Orality and Literacy. Walter J. Ong (2002) Routledge.

Understanding Media Theory. Kevin Williams (2003) A Hodder Arnold Publication.

Understanding Media Cultures: Social Theory and Mass Communication. Nicholas Stevenson (2002) Sage.

Anthropology and Mass Communication: Media and Myth in the New Millennium. Mark Allen Peterson (2003) Berghahn Books.

Critical Theories of Mass Media: Then and Now. Paul Taylor, Jan Harris (2007) Open University Press.

More Than Meets the Eye: Watching Television Watching Us. John J. Pungente, Martin O'Malley (1999) McClelland & Stewart.

Understanding Media: The Extensions of Man. Marshall McLuhan (1994) MIT Press.

Communication, Media, and American Society: A Critical Introduction. Daniel W. Rossides (2002) Rowman & Littlefield.

Theories of the Information Society, 2nd ed. Frank Webster (2002) Routledge.

An Invitation to Social Construction, 2nd ed. Kenneth Gergen (2009) Sage.

E-Crit: Digital Media, Critical Theory, and the Humanities. Marcel O'Gorman (2007) University of Toronto Press.

Dark Fiber: Tracking Critical Internet Culture. Geert Lovink (2003) MIT Press.

MEDIA QUIZ ANSWERS

2. False.

10. True.

15

MASS COMMUNICATION AND POLITICS IN THE DIGITAL AGE

LEARNING OBJECTIVES

By the end of this chapter
you should be able to:

- Describe the role of
  mass communication
  in democratic and
  nondemocratic countries.

- Highlight the role of the
  public and public opinion
  in political communication.

- Present what research tells
  us about the evolving role
  of the media in political
  elections, especially the
  nature of sound bites,
  election coverage, and
  opinion polls in campaigns.

- Discuss the increasing
  presence of political
  advertising in campaigns
  and what research tells us
  about its impact.

- Outline the emergence of
  talk shows and the Internet
  in political campaigns.

- Identify the most
  significant theories
  that explain, describe,
  and predict the impact
  of mediated political
  communications.

- Examine the increasing
  role of new media in
  political campaigns.

A new kind of political action committee (PAC) came into existence in July 2010. However, it wasn't until the 2012 presidential and congressional election that people really started talking about so-called Super PACs and their potentially harmful effects on the election process.

A Super PAC differs from a regular PAC in that it can accept unlimited donations from individuals, corporations, unions, and associations. Traditional PACs can accept only limited funds from individuals and nothing from the other groups. Also unlike a traditional PAC, a Super PAC cannot contribute directly to a politician's campaign. Instead, the money can be spent in any way the Super PAC sees fit to advocate for its favored candidate.

Even though Super PACs cannot give directly to candidates and are not supposed to have direction from the candidate or staff, many are run by former staff members or aides and have other close ties to the candidates they support. These relationships—and some of the legal loopholes that Super PACs enjoy—were famously mocked by Stephen Colbert on his show as he "transferred" his Super PAC power to Jon Stewart (the episode won a Peabody Award). Colbert actually did create a Super PAC called Americans for a Better Tomorrow, Tomorrow that had raised $1.2 million by election day, even though he spent only a fraction of the money.[1]

But other Super PACs did spend, for a total of $1.3 billion during the presidential and congressional election. Two-thirds of the amount from Super PACs went to Republican candidates in various races, yet the results turned out to be disappointing for many Republican supporters. Karl Rove's Super PAC, American Crossroads, spent $104.7 million supporting eight Republican Senate candidates, with only two winning their races. The National Rifle Association spent $11 million supporting candidates and none of them won.[2]

During the campaign, there was concern about how Super PACs may unfairly influence election results. However, it seems that despite the dramatic amounts spent by Super PACs—and the barrage of negative advertising they funded—they had little effect on predicting election-day winners.

As Stephen Colbert's Super PAC illustrates, there have been dramatic changes in recent years regarding media and politics. Journalism has long considered itself the main conduit through which politicians inform the public, thereby playing a key role in democratic processes. Journalism is the mechanism through which the public obtains unbiased, impartial information about candidates for office, sitting elected officials, and the agencies they represent and operate.

Although this is the goal, media critics contend the media are anything but unbiased. Consider the words of Joseph Pulitzer, the former publisher of the *New York World* and the founder of the Pulitzer Prize, the highest award for journalistic excellence. In support of his proposal for the founding of a school of journalism, Pulitzer summarized his credo: "Our Republic and its press will rise or fall together. An able, disinterested, public-spirited press, with trained intelligence to know the right and courage to do it, can preserve that public virtue without which popular government is a sham and a mockery. A cynical, mercenary, demagogic press will produce in time a people as base as itself. The power to mould the future of the Republic will be in the hands of the journalists of future generations."[3]

Some scholars argue that SNL's comedy skits about politicians and political candidates have affected some voters' behavior.

MEDIA QUIZ

Playing Politics

Test your political and media knowledge.

1. (T/F) Bill Clinton was the first presidential candidate to appear on a late-night talk show.
2. Who was the politician whose campaign for reelection was ruined when a video of him calling a campaign worker "macaca" was widely distributed?
3. Name a country that follows the authoritarian theory of communication.
4. What form of mass communication would be most useful in a developing country, print media or radio?
5. What is the digital divide?
6. Describe an example of horse-race coverage in an election.
7. (T/F) Expenditures on political advertising make up by far the largest part of a campaign budget.
8. What social-media site has been credited with radically changing the nature of elections in 2008?
9. (T/F) So far, the changes to politics from social media and online communications have only taken place in industrialized countries.
10. (T/F) You can find online how much your neighbor donated to a politician.

However, it is more than journalism that drives the engine of media and politics. In fact, especially in times of presidential election campaigns, it is advertising that drives this machine. Political advertising, especially on television, is how most candidates, particularly presidential candidates, reach most voters most often. Negative political advertising is one of the mainstays of the political world in the United States, and it has been extensively researched. Political advertising also provides substantial income for media organizations and has made it necessary for political candidates to raise large sums of money from donations.

Entertainment has played an increasingly important role in helping political candidates create a more down-to-earth image, with appearances on late-night talk shows and even comedy shows like *Saturday Night Live* now becoming the norm. "Fake news" shows such as *The Daily Show* or *The Colbert Report* are often a main source of political news for young people.

Furthermore, the Internet and other types of online communication have not only become important information sources for the public but played key roles in helping candidates organize and raise funds. Similarly, political and activist groups have been able to generate money or support for their causes using online communication tools. Candidates have had their political careers ruined thanks in part to the ease of distribution of video and documents. A case in point was Virginia senator George Allen, who on a campaign stop during the 2006 election publicly called an opponent's campaign worker of Indian descent "macaca," a racial slur for African immigrants used in Europe. The video of Allen saying this at the rally was widely spread on the Internet, leaving an indelible impression of Allen's

George Allen's political campaign was badly hurt by the video that showed him calling a campaign worker of Indian descent "macaca" during a rally.

character that no amount of press release apologies could successfully whitewash or counter.

But mass communication is not only important at election time; the media are directly connected to government and the public in many complex ways. The following section examines what research tells us about the process and effects of journalism and mass communication in the sphere of political communications in the United States and abroad.

◤◥ Four Theories of International Mass Communication

Four theories of international mass communication were presented in 1956 by Fred S. Siebert, Wilbur Schramm, and Theodore Peterson.[4] These three social scientists were looking for ways to explain how the press operates in different political, historical, and cultural environments around the world. Although they referred specifically to "the press," we can extend their theories to embrace all the media of mass communication, including television, radio, entertainment media, and online.

Siebert, Schramm, and Peterson's four theories of the press are these:

1. The authoritarian theory
2. The libertarian theory
3. The social responsibility theory
4. The Soviet theory

▼ THE AUTHORITARIAN THEORY

authoritarian theory of the press

A theory of international mass communication in which authoritarian governments exert direct control over the media.

The **authoritarian theory** describes the oldest system of mass communication, which has its roots in sixteenth- and seventeenth-century England. This system exists in authoritarian states in which government exerts direct control over the mass media. Countries where government consists of a limited and small ruling class are especially likely to have an authoritarian media system.

Media in authoritarian systems are not permitted to print, broadcast, or webcast anything the government feels might undermine its authority. Content that threatens or challenges the existing political system and its values is strictly prohibited. Anyone who violates the rules is subject to harsh punishment, including imprisonment, expulsion, or even death.

Searching for Truth: Self-Censorship in China

As growing numbers of Chinese go online, the Chinese media market becomes increasingly tempting to Western media. However, China's restrictions on the press and tight control over Internet access often run afoul of Western notions of a free press.

For example, China blocks access to a wide range of websites, from pornographic sites, to those that mention the 1989 protests and deaths in Tiananmen Square or the banned group Falun Gong, to sites that are critical of the Chinese government.

Google was criticized in the press in 2006 when the company chose to censor itself in order to enter the Chinese search engine market. Many observers noted the irony in Google's "Don't Be Evil" mantra regarding its business philosophy and wondered how the search engine giant could rationalize its decision to not include full access to sites on the Internet.

Google representatives said that it was better that Google provide some access, with the hope that it helps China open its media system more, than to not offer anything at all. Despite its compromise to gain entry to the Internet in China, Google still remains less popular there than home-grown search engine company Baidu.

Competitor Yahoo faced heavy criticism from the press a year earlier, when the company provided user information, requested by the Chinese government, that helped put a Chinese journalist in jail for ten years.

As long as the Communist government in China maintains its strict controls over media access and the types of content allowed, Western media companies will have some difficult ethical choices to make if they do business in China.

Government uses the media not only to inform the public of important events but also to shape public opinion in support of its policies. Although ownership of media can be private or public, media professionals are not permitted to have editorial independence within their organizations. Foreign media are subordinate to governmental authority. Countries where the authoritarian theory best describes current systems of mass communication include China, Cuba, and Myanmar.

John Milton was a proponent of the libertarian theory of the press.

▼ THE LIBERTARIAN THEORY

Libertarian theory is often also called the free press theory. Libertarian theory rests on the notion that the individual should be free to publish whatever he or she likes. Its roots lie in the work of seventeenth-century philosopher and writer John Milton, whose *Areopagitica* (1644) argued, "And though all the winds of doctrine were let loose to play upon the earth, so Truth be in the field, we do injuriously by licensing and prohibiting to misdoubt her strength. Let her and Falsehood grapple; who ever knew Truth put to the worse, in a free and open encounter?"

In the libertarian theory, criticism of the government and its policies are accepted and even encouraged. There are no restrictions on the import or export of media messages across the national borders. Media professionals have full autonomy within their media organization.

In some ways, however, the libertarian theory is an ideal type, and not one that realistically applies in full anywhere. There are few if any countries where the libertarian theory perfectly describes the system of mass communication. Yet, there are many countries where elements of the theory clearly play a role in the media system.

▼ THE SOCIAL RESPONSIBILITY THEORY

Social responsibility theory best describes the systems of mass communication in most democratic societies. The theory rests on the notion that the media play a vital role in informing citizens in a democratic society and, as such, should be free from most governmental constraints in order to provide the best, most reliable, and impartial information to the public.

To operate effectively in this environment, the media must exercise self-restraint and act responsibly. The Commission on Freedom of the Press (known as the Hutchins Commission) in 1947 articulated the media's obligations to society. These included truth, accuracy, objectivity, balance, diversity, and being informative. The commission argued that a responsible media system must do more than simply report the facts. It must place them in context. This means the media must provide analysis, explanation, and interpretation.

Although the social responsibility theory may best describe the system of mass communication in democracies such as the United States, Canada, France, and the United Kingdom, the growth of global corporate media organizations challenges media to place the public good over profits and to do so internationally as well as domestically. Siebert, Peterson, and Schramm cautioned, "The power and near monopoly position of the media impose on them an obligation to be socially responsible, to see that all sides are fairly presented and that the public has enough information to decide; and that if the media do not take on themselves such responsibility it may be necessary for some other agency of the public to enforce it."

They add, "Freedom of expression under the social responsibility theory is not an absolute right, as under pure libertarian theory. . . . One's right to free expression must be balanced against the private rights of others and against vital social interests." For example, a socially responsible news organization would exercise extreme care in preparing reports about terrorist activities, especially ones that might detail how bioterrorism is conducted or provide information on a city's disaster plans, because such information could be used by terrorists to help plan attacks.

▼ THE SOVIET THEORY

The **Soviet theory** of the press is based on a specific ideology: the communist system of government practiced in the former Soviet Union. Siebert traced the roots of this theory to the 1917 Russian Revolution and the views of Karl Marx and Friedrich Engels. According to the Soviet theory, media should serve the interests of the working class and should be publicly owned, not privately owned.

Although there are some similarities between the Soviet and authoritarian systems, such as the media being subordinate to government, there are also important differences. In particular, the Soviet theory posits that the media should recognize their responsibility to the people and self-regulate their content. Government censorship is not to be the norm. With the demise of the Soviet Union in the 1980s, this theory is most useful as a historical reference point. However, one can see some elements of its philosophy in the media reform movement that claims that for-profit media has been harming democracy and that media organizations should be publicly funded in some manner, even though that would not preclude for-profit media companies as well.

The Soviet Union's main newspaper was *Pravda*, meaning "truth."

◢◤ The Public, the Public Sphere, and Public Opinion

The notions of "the public" and "public opinion" are surprisingly complex, and their definitions are still being debated by scholars today. In some ways, the public can be considered as an audience for governments or politicians, but this viewpoint fails to take into account how exactly the public today differs from the public in the Middle Ages, for example.

Most scholars agree that the idea of "the public" did not come about until the late sixteenth or early seventeenth century, when Europe was beginning to enter the modern era and governments were changing from monarchies to more representative forms of government. A new class arose, the **bourgeoisie**, which began to recognize the differing economic and political interests among business, government, and citizens. More importantly, the bourgeoisie recognized themselves as a separate group, apart but also a part of government and economics. Through tools of communication at the time, primarily newspapers, pamphlets, journals, and other periodicals, the bourgeoisie were able to communicate with each other about common interests and challenge government policies that did not match them.

The forums in which the bourgeoisie debated matters of public interest included the popular coffeehouses, where conversations were spurred by the material in the print publications that were disseminated, and where a sense of "conventional wisdom" developed through debate and discussion among peers. The notion of the **public sphere**, as first discussed by German social theorist and philosopher Jürgen Habermas, captures this atmosphere in ideal terms, where the most rational argument won the day and where rank or privilege took a back seat to the quest for knowledge and truth.

This ideal was never realized, of course, but the notion of the public sphere remains a powerful one in media and mass-communication research today. Some scholars see a kind of "fall from grace," in that commercial media have taken over

Coffeehouses in the eighteenth century were important locations for development of the public sphere.

public opinion

The notion that the public, as a group, can form shared views or ideas about topics and that these ideas guide the public's actions.

the public forum and imposed new forms of (often hidden) control over what is discussed and how it is discussed. Other scholars claim that the public sphere of the seventeenth-century European coffeehouses never actually included the complete public, as women and a majority of people were excluded from the conversations.

Today there is debate on whether the Internet can actually rejuvenate the notion of the public sphere in which citizens can discuss freely and openly without interference from government or commercial interests. However, with so many different types of people online and so many different types of interests, getting any sense of a coherent public sphere in which participants all abide by certain rules of rational argument and civic-mindedness has proven elusive.

The public sphere ostensibly plays a role in the formation of **public opinion**, itself a contested concept, which can nevertheless be broadly defined as "what the public thinks." The notion of public opinion goes back directly to trying to define who exactly "the public" is and how a commonly shared opinion is formed and spread. Is public opinion simply the aggregate of individual beliefs, writ large, or does it become something greater than the sum of its parts? If so, how does it change and what effects are there of such changes?

Whatever the disagreements over the definition, public opinion plays an important role in democratic countries today, and the media play an integral part in creating, shaping, and spreading ideas that become commonly accepted. Few major policy decisions are made without first testing the waters among the public to see what the reaction is.

This is not to say that government is controlled by mob rule, however, as the notion of "the public" is more complex than simply thinking of a mass of people. Public opinion can be and often is manipulated to suit the ends of various groups, and an entire media industry—public relations—exists for the primary purpose of swaying public opinion in favor of clients or policies.

But PR professionals are not the only ones who can influence the public today. Just as the bourgeoisie in seventeenth-century coffeehouses found themselves with new tools of mass communication that gave them power to communicate that they previously did not have, citizens today have a wide range of powerful communication tools at their disposal. They can start online petitions, create complaint sites about companies or parody sites of politicians, post news scoops on blogs or videos about embarrassing moments in the lives of politicians, and act as citizen reporters to inform the world of injustices when media are silent.

An example of the latter happened in 2007 in Myanmar, a country in Southeast Asia that is run by a military junta. Antigovernment protests that were started by Buddhist monks were forcefully repressed by the military, and the only images released of the violence were from citizens taking pictures with mobile phones, as the international media were not allowed in the country and the state-run media did not report accurately on what was happening. Similar actions happened in 2011 during the revolutions in several Arab countries, with people posting information that the government-controlled media in those countries would not publish.

With so many communication tools accessible, media have become even more intertwined with various political issues, both in the United States and internationally.

◢▽ Political Issues with Media

Radio and television are often used to reach persons in remote agricultural regions in developing countries to provide information on health issues, agricultural techniques, and government policies. Broadcast stations are often among the first places taken in a coup, as those in power—or those wishing to gain power—realize the importance of controlling the means of distributing information. Print media are often used to foster the business development of a region, although their effectiveness is limited in countries with low literacy rates or where many different languages are spoken.

Foreign governments tend to control the content of their mass-communication organizations, especially television and radio, far more than is seen in the United States. In some cases, broadcasting stations are entirely government owned or government run, while in other cases licensing restrictions for television sets or media devices such as satellite dishes limit the ability of the public to have complete access to the media.

▼ MEDIA IN DEVELOPING COUNTRIES

The media and accompanying communication technologies are instruments for economic development throughout the world and can have exceptional potential to improve the economy in developing nations. Western companies looking to establish factories overseas to take advantage of cheap labor costs look for developed infrastructure, such as passable transportation routes and communication networks, as part of what makes a good place to locate. Of course, such things as stable governments and corporate-friendly government policies (like low taxes) are also sought.

Countries such as India have become sources for relatively cheap software developers and computer-programming workers, as well as database centers and information-processing centers. India is positioned nicely because it has a generally well-educated workforce that speaks English, letting the country take advantage of "low-end" information-economy needs, such as scanning documents, transcribing documents, and providing technical support for computer makers and software companies.

Outsourcing IT services to developing countries has provided new job opportunities for workers in those countries.

Some countries in Africa have been making moves toward similarly fulfilling information-processing needs of industrial countries. A data-processing company in Ghana, for example, inputs into a database minor violations that occur in New York City, ranging from parking tickets to jaywalking. For Ghanian workers the pay is better than other jobs and the working conditions are better than in many other industries, although hours are long and breaks are short by Western standards.

Although some critics charge that moving information-processing work overseas is no different than sending factories overseas to obtain cheaper labor and avoid dealing with pollution problems and employee-benefits costs, others have supported this trend. They claim that the information technology (IT) industry is not like industrial-era factories: it is generally nonpolluting, it can be created using existing buildings, and the type of work raises workers' level of education, better positioning them for other jobs within information societies. In short, it is hoped that developing countries can skip the worst effects of the industrial age and move directly into the information age, although whether this is the case or not remains to be seen.

Some factors keep IT from growing as fast as it could in developing countries. Excessive government regulation often hampers development of a good telecommunication infrastructure that could better reach all citizens within a country. Political instability, drastic changes in government policies, corruption among government officials, a lack of other infrastructure, such as regular electrical power—all these can hurt development of telecommunication technologies in a country.

Southeast Asian nations such as Singapore and Malaysia have been promoting themselves as high-speed Internet ecommerce zones that will provide the most technologically advanced support for online business operations in the hope of attracting Western businesses. However, important concerns arise regarding the free flow of information, from a cultural or political, rather than a technical, perspective. Singapore strictly controls access to most forms of media, even banning some Western newspapers that have criticized the government, and it attempts to tightly control citizens' access to the Internet. Western companies, especially media companies, may balk at these restrictions on access to information.

digital divide

The idea that some groups that do not have access to the Internet become left out of the benefits that online technology can bring.

▼ THE DIGITAL DIVIDE

Nearly 80 percent of the people living in developed nations have Internet access. For some countries, such as Iceland, Sweden, and Norway, the number is over 90 percent. However, as more people get online, a gap is widening between those who have access to the Internet and those who don't—the so-called **digital divide**. The digital divide exists within and between nations. Because access to the Internet generally has a cost attached to it—in equipment and establishing a network connection—this gap reflects larger socioeconomic trends that already separate citizens. Some experts and policy makers worry that, if ignored, the digital divide could have serious negative implications for society.

In the United States, the early users of the Internet tended to be wealthier and more educated than later users. Given the importance of the information economy, people who are online have a distinct advantage over those who are not in terms of getting important information, making decisions, and engaging in a host of other activities that could accelerate their upward motion on the social and economic ladder.

Providing low-cost or free Internet access is an important part of closing the digital divide.

Meanwhile, it is feared that people who are less educated, or with lower incomes, could fall behind as they cannot afford Internet access. These people tend to be members of groups that already have faced various forms of discrimination in society or have other socioeconomic or educational disadvantages compared to dominant groups.

The issue is mirrored when looking at the different Internet penetration rates across global regions and countries, as seen in Figure 15-1. Although the world average for Internet penetration is 30 percent, there is a huge difference in rates from North America's 78.3 percent to Africa's 11.4 percent rate. But this percentage by nation only tells part of the story. Another perspective on Internet access is the actual number of people who are using the Web in different countries. As seen in Figure 15-2, Asia has nearly as many Internet users in 2011 as Europe, North America, and Latin America combined, despite having an Internet penetration of only 23.8 percent, below the world average. This suggests that Asian users will truly dominate Internet access across the globe once the percentage of users in Asia achieves the percentages now shown for North America and Europe.

These figures of course are always increasing, although at different rates. Africa has shown remarkable growth in Internet penetration since 2000, growing over 2,500 percent. The Middle East has also grown remarkably, nearly 2,000 percent,

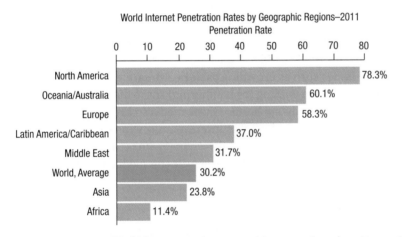

FIGURE 15-1 Source: Internet World Stats—www.internetworldstats.com/stats.htm. Penetration rates are based on a world population of 6,930,055,154 and 2,095,006,005 estimated Internet users on March 31, 2011. Copyright © 2011, Miniwatts Marketing Group.

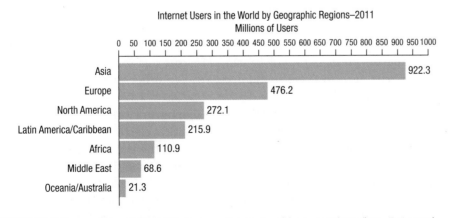

FIGURE 15-2 Source: Internet World Stats—www.internetworldstats.com/stats/htm. Estimated Internet users are 2,095,006,005 on March 31, 2011. Copyright © 2011, Miniwatts Marketing Group.

since 2000. Asia has grown 700 percent in Internet penetration during the same period, and even developed countries have increased their Internet penetration rates from 2000 by nearly 200 percent. Even with this growth, there are still many people left behind when it comes to Internet access.

Being able to simply have access to the Internet is one component, but having access to high-quality information is also a matter of some concern. If all that is available online for free is lowbrow entertainment such as archived situation comedies or game shows, which do little to inform or educate the public, then simply having access will have no effect on bridging the digital divide. What is important is to provide the kind of education and critical-thinking skills that allow people to discern the quality of information they get and to use it for helpful purposes.

Thus, there are two major components to the digital-divide issue. One is technological: providing access to the communications technologies needed to access the Internet, such as computers, cheap or free software, and other tools. Cost plays a key role in this as well. Two hundred dollars a month for communications may not seem like much for a young, single professional making eighty thousand dollars a year, but it is a much larger percentage of the income for a family of four in which the parents are making minimum wage or working part-time. The other main component is education: teaching people how to use the online communication tools available to them. Entertainment will always be a part of online communication, but it should not be the sole consumption for the less privileged, just as it is not for the affluent.

Political issues like the digital divide and the role that the Internet plays in our society are complex and will require long-term commitments and widespread discussions among everyone involved. Such discussions will have to be a part of larger quality-of-life issues such as providing basic health care, clean water, and education. Media will play a role in guiding (or hampering) these discussions, though that role may not always be readily apparent. Given media's chronically poor job of covering themselves in the news, business interests may win out over public interests if companies see their profitability at stake when it comes to discussions on the digital divide. However, one area of politics in which the media are far more visible, and where they have often changed some fundamental aspects of politics, is in elections.

▲▼ The Role of Media in Political Elections

Since the earliest days of the Republic, the media have been intimately involved in our political process. The colonial newspapers were a "partisan" press, typically aligned with a particular political party or trying to persuade the public of a certain viewpoint. In some countries, there is still a partisan press. Media also played a role in helping the Revolutionary cause. Journalism in the nineteenth century evolved into an impartial press, but it still considers its core mission to provide the information citizens need to make sound decisions—in other words, journalism sees itself as an engine of democracy.

Since the first use of radio in political campaigning, in 1924, the electronic media have played an increasingly important part in political elections. In both 1936 and 1940, while the majority of newspapers throughout the United States openly endorsed Republican candidates for office, radio had become the more heavily used medium by Democrats. President Roosevelt was masterful in his use of radio to reach the masses, providing his regular "Fireside Chats" during both the 1930s and 1940s. Radio had emerged as the politically potent medium of mass communication during this time, with even greater impact than newspapers and magazines, and radio itself was soon to be replaced by television as the dominant medium in the 1950s. It began an era in which the personal qualities of candidates, rather than their political-policy stances, would take center stage in the campaign process.

▼ SOUND BITES AND HORSE RACES

With the rise of electronic media, especially television in the past half century, the process of political communication and debate in the media has been transformed from one of generally some substance into one increasingly characterized by superficial examination of the issues.

More often than not, the horse-race aspect of the campaign, or chronicling who's ahead, who's behind, and what the latest campaign tactic might be to move ahead in the polls, becomes the whole story at the expense of coverage of issues.

In 1968, Kiku Adatto of Harvard University did a study on political **sound bites**—specifically, how long a source in a television news story was allowed to speak without being edited by the reporter. In 1968 the average sound bite was

sound bite

The length of time a news subject is allowed to speak without being edited by a reporter. It also has come to refer to short utterances that are catchy and designed to capture the media's attention.

CONVERGENCE CONTEXT

▶ Sound Bite Shakespeare

University of San Diego professor Daniel C. Hallin puts the shrinking sound bite into context.[5] In 1968, if a commercial network television reporter had included a sound bite from William Shakespeare's *Julius Caesar* (Act III, Scene II, at the Forum), he would have had time to include the following statement from Antony:

> Friends, Romans, countrymen, lend me your
> ears;
> I come to bury Caesar, not to praise him.
> The evil that men do lives after them;
> The good is oft interred with their bones;
> So let it be with Caesar. The noble Brutus
> Hath told you Caesar was ambitious:
> If it were so, it was a grievous fault,
> And grievously hath Caesar
> answer'd it.
> Here, under leave of Brutus and the
> rest—
> For Brutus is an honourable man;
> So are they all, all honourable men—
> Come I to speak in Caesar's funeral.
> He was my friend, faithful and just to
> me:
> But Brutus says he was ambitious;
> And Brutus is an honourable man.

Here's what we'd hear from Antony in 1988 on the commercial network television evening news:

> Friends, Romans, countrymen, lend me your ears;
> I come to bury Caesar, not to praise him.

Some hold out hope that the sound-bite culture of commercial television news may change thanks to competition from YouTube and online video sites that let users watch video clips as long as they want without commercial breaks. However, although some people have shifted to YouTube to watch longer excerpts of speeches, another strong force is enhancing the role of the sound bite: negative political ads that take a candidate's past statements out of context to give the public a mistaken impression of the person's views.

42.3 seconds. Nearly a quarter of all political sound bites were at least a minute in length, providing considerable room for context. Twenty years later, in 1988, the average TV sound bite of a political candidate had shrunk by some 80 percent to just 9.8 seconds, and virtually none were a minute or longer—in fact, entire stories were often not a minute in length. This greatly reduces the ability of news to provide needed context, let alone adequate facts of complex political issues.

▼ THE CHANGING TONE OF TELEVISION POLITICAL COVERAGE

The tone of television political coverage has also changed. Consider the research findings of Syracuse University political scientist Thomas Patterson, author of *Out of Order*. He found that in the 1960 presidential election, three-quarters (75 percent) of the news reports about leading candidates John F. Kennedy and Richard M. Nixon were positive in tone; only a quarter (25 percent) were negative. Thirty years later, in the 1992 presidential election, news reports had become predominantly negative in tone: more than half (60 percent) of the reports about then candidate Bill Clinton and then president George H. Bush were negative, and less than half (40 percent) were positive. Patterson's research also shows that the length of candidate statements in election stories on the front page of the *New York Times* had similarly shrunk. In 1960, the average quote was fourteen lines. In 1992, the average quote was less than seven lines.

Has this situation changed with the rise of online news? Not by much. Although there is scant research evidence yet to point to, the fact is that much of the online political coverage is no different than the political coverage in other media, since much of that coverage is lifted and repurposed from other media, including television, radio, newspapers, and magazines. The sound bites are the same, and the quotes are the same.

Many of the better online news operations, such as CBS News online, typically add further reporting to stories that are adapted from on-air coverage, turning the text of a sixty-second video report (what might be less than two hundred words) into a five-hundred-word or longer report with more depth and possibly additional quotes. Repeated quotes are sometimes the same length but occasionally longer than in the broadcast text. Much of the additional reporting is drawn from wire service copy (e.g., Reuters, the Associated Press) pulled off the Internet or sometimes from original reporting conducted via telephone or email interviews. Increasingly, graphics such as maps are used as well.

▼ OPINION POLLS

opinion poll

A poll that is usually conducted by a professional polling organization asking members of the public their opinions on issues or political candidates.

Campaign coverage has also become heavily driven by **opinion polls**. Patterson's research shows that the news about a candidate becomes more favorable when his or her support in the polls increases markedly or if he or she leads by a wide margin. Conversely, media coverage becomes more negative if there is a drop in the candidate's standing in the polls or if he or she trails significantly.

Media organizations usually use one of several professional polling organizations, such as Gallup, to conduct polls. These polling organizations try to take random samples of the public in order to assess what the population as a whole is likely feeling about a candidate or issue. However, lower telephone response rates in recent years, as people screen calls to avoid telemarketers, have made conducting telephone polls more expensive.

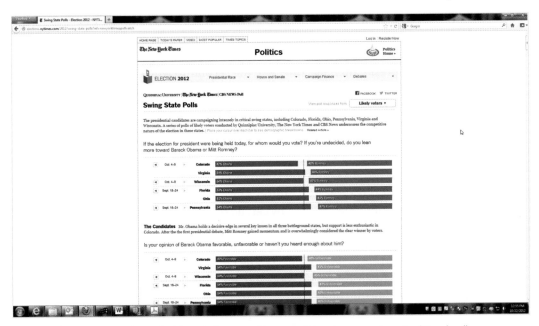

Online polls are increasingly used, although they are still not considered as accurate as traditional polls.

Opinion polls or surveys show up increasingly on news websites, although they are not considered scientifically valid. It is mistaken to assume that an online poll fairly represents the point of view of the general populace. The answers seen on online polls only represent users who have visited the website and choose to answer the poll. Although the demographic profile of the average Internet user is evolving as a more diverse number of users become active online, a large proportion of Internet users are still widely known to be more affluent than average, white, and male. An online poll taken by a politically conservative online entity, such as Fox News, will usually show vastly different results than the same poll taken by a politically liberal entity, such as MSNBC. Online polls are being used by some polling organizations, such as Harris Interactive, although these are largely derided by other organizations and the American Association for Public Opinion Research (AAPOR) for being nonscientific.

Sometimes telephone "polls," called **push polls**, are actually political advertising. Push polls try to sway voters by giving them false or misleading information about opposing candidates under the guise of conducting a poll or try to make a candidate look good by asking leading questions. Push polls ask deliberately misleading questions, such as, "Would you support the policies of a candidate who will curtail some of our freedoms and raise taxes?" Few would answer "yes" to such a question, but the respondent may not realize that the pollster was referring to a certain candidate when asking it. Yet the results would be publicized by the pollsters as showing that "90 percent of the people polled say they do not support Candidate Y."

push poll

A type of political advertising that appears to be a telephone poll but is actually a telemarketing campaign to sway voters by giving them false or misleading information about opposing candidates or to make a candidate look good.

▼ POLITICAL ADVERTISING

Partly as a result of the shrinking sound bite, the poll-driven horse-race media coverage of campaigns, and the political candidates' and parties' interest in controlling their own messages to the voter, candidates have turned increasingly to paid advertising. Of course, candidates have historically used a wide variety of techniques to directly reach as many people as possible, from whistle-stop speeches to political rallies. However, campaigning has become increasingly expensive in the United States as campaigns and technology become more complex and candidates attempt to reach people through the media.[6]

The 2012 presidential election was the second in which the candidates raised more than $1 billion (the first was 2008), although in 2012 that also counts Super PACs, which were not directly connected to the campaigns themselves. As Table 15-1 shows, the media expenditures by the campaigns (not Super PACs) were more than half of all expenditures. Print media was the big loser in 2012, down from 2008 expenditures, and broadcast media also had lower expenditures compared to 2008. However, the $1.3 billion spent by Super PACs, much of it on advertising, could account for the lower expenditures by the campaigns themselves.

The amount of money needed by candidates running for national or even state offices is so great partly because of the need to pay for political advertising. Although many criticize the way campaigning has changed in U.S. elections, with huge costs being one major complaint, the fact is that many media companies benefit greatly from political advertising and are unlikely to lobby to change a system that helps their bottom line.

The Impact of Negative Advertising

Some people say that political advertising is no different than other product advertising, except that in a political campaign there is a one-day sale. It is this mentality that drives the industry. As a result, many candidates gravitate toward negative

TABLE 15-1

Political Campaign Expenditures on Media and Top Nonmedia Expenditures, Presidential Campaign 2012

Media Expenditures	Broadcast Media	$157,319,619
	Miscellaneous Media*	$26,710,905
	Internet Media	$74,837,710
	Print Media	$1,965,747
	Media Consultants	$322,801,280
Total for media		$583,635,261
Nonmedia Expenditures	Salaries and Benefits	$82,185,148
	Travel	$54,211,792
	Postage/Shipping	$27,783,190
	Rent/Utilities	$11,484,523
	Campaign Events	$18,900,776
	Polling/Surveys/Research	$25,065,942
	Fund-raising Direct Mail/Telemarketing	$74,687,044
Total for nonmedia		$294,318,415
Overall total		$877,953,676

Source: OpenSecrets.org, http://www.opensecrets.org/pres12/expenditures.php, November 15, 2012. Figures for 2012 based on Federal Election Commission data released electronically on Thursday, October 25, 2012, and compiled by the Center for Responsive Politics. * Includes blast faxes, phone banks, etc.

advertising. Based on an examination of more than 1,100 political commercials, political-communications scholar Larry Sabato concluded:

> Even when television is used to communicate political truth (at least from one candidate's perspective), the truth can be negatively packaged—attacking the opponent's character and record rather than supporting one's own. If there is a single trend obvious to most American consultants, it is the increasing proportion of negative political advertising.... At least a third of all spot commercials in recent campaigns have been negative, and in a minority of campaigns half or more of the spots are negative in tone or substance.[7]

Although some of the paid political spots on television are intended to simply provide information about the candidate and his or her position on the issues, the ads that have captured the most criticism and research have been the negative ads that are intended to attack the opposing candidate rather than shed light on the issues. The rise of political advertising has also led news media to increasingly focus their coverage of the candidates on the candidates' advertising.

Much of the negative political advertising has been problematic for a number of reasons. One of the biggest problems, Kathleen Hall Jamieson points out, is that many of the ads contain falsehoods or lead the audience to make false inferences.[8] President Obama had no qualms about running negative advertising against Republican candidate Mitt Romney in the 2012 election. The negative ads during the summer helped frame Romney as a corporate raider and wealthy elitist. The ads are credited with raising the negative impressions of Romney 6 percentage points at a time when his campaign could not respond because of a lack of campaign funds. Romney's campaign eventually fired back with ads that portrayed Obama as a failed manager of the economy.

Negative Advertising Effectiveness

Researchers Richard Lau and Lee Sigelman tested three hypotheses regarding negative political advertisements: (1) that they work (i.e., they get voters to endorse the candidate doing the attacking), (2) that voters dislike negative ads, and (3) that negative ads tend to have an unintended side effect of disenfranchising the electorate.

Regarding the first hypothesis, Lau and Sigelman found in a study of voters in 1997 that negative ads do not work; they actually decreased the favorability of voters' attitudes toward the candidate whose campaign ran the negative ad. Conversely, the favorability of voters' attitudes toward the "target" of the ads increased. A study of the 1992 campaign similarly revealed that candidates who initiated negative ads lost eighteen out of twenty-five elections. They also found there was no strong preponderance of evidence indicating that negative political ads were more memorable than positive ads.

Regarding the second hypothesis, that voters dislike negative ads, the results are clear again. "Six of the nine studies found negative political ads being rated less ethical, less fair, and otherwise less liked than positive political ads, while two studies came to the opposite conclusions and one uncovered no significant differences," Lau and Sigelman report.

Third, whether negative ads contribute to voter apathy or disenfranchisement, the results are mixed. Although there is some evidence to support this hypothesis, it is not clear. "Of the 20 relevant findings, ten report no significant differences and two associate positive outcomes with negative political ads (e.g., higher turnout), but eight report significant negative consequences," Lau and Sigelman explain.

Negative political advertising is controversial, with some claiming that it turns off voters and actually hurts the politician making the negative ad.

Some research indicates that one of the most important effects of negative political advertising is to alienate young viewers from the political process. Negative political advertising increases the level of cynicism among young viewers and decreases their interest in becoming politically active and involved.

▼ POLITICAL DEBATES

One of the most important areas of political communication is the debate. Ever since the great debates between Abraham Lincoln and Stephen A. Douglas during the U.S. Senate race of 1858, debates have been a proving ground for candidates to test their mettle against an opponent and for the voting public to better understand both the character and the content of each candidate.

Notably, these early debates were in many ways quite different than the televised debates the public has come to know since the first televised debate in 1960. For example, a debate between Lincoln and Douglas might last more than five hours, with each candidate offering detailed commentary of an hour or more on a single issue, such as abolition—which was the topic of the first debate, held on August 21, 1858. Further, since television or radio did not yet exist, these debates were not heard by anyone other than those present for the live event, although the public could read about them in newspapers. Today, it is hard to imagine a five-hour televised debate between political candidates.

Arguably the most important debate between U.S. presidential candidates in the twentieth century occurred in 1960, when for the first time presidential candidates debated live on broadcast television and radio. The debate pitted John F. Kennedy and Richard M. Nixon against each other. Research conducted at the time showed that among those who watched the debate on television, Kennedy, who was handsome and well groomed, was rated clearly superior. Nixon, whose dark stubble and "shifty" eyes gave him a more sinister look (the debate was scheduled for the evening and Nixon had not shaved since the morning), was deemed to have lost.

Meanwhile, on radio, with listeners only able to hear the candidates' voices, the clear winner was deemed to be Nixon because it seemed he had the more convincing arguments. Kennedy ultimately won the presidential contest in an extremely close election, and it is not clear whether the debate was the deciding factor. But it has been the touchstone for televised campaigning ever since. Today it is a given that one's television persona is an essential quality in winning an election.

The Kennedy–Nixon presidential debate in 1960 showed how powerful television could be for political candidates in influencing public perceptions.

◢▽ The Internet and Political Campaigns

With the Internet, never before have candidates and the public had such ability to directly communicate with one another. Voters can go to a candidate's website to obtain information about where the candidate stands on an issue, make

CAN IMAGERY LEAD TO ACTION?

ETHICS IN MEDIA

U.S. Representative Gabrielle Giffords (D-Ariz.) was holding a "Congress On Your Corner" meeting in front of a Safeway in Tucson, Arizona on January 8, 2011. These informal gatherings were held to let citizens interact with Giffords in their daily settings and to discuss relevant issues.

But that morning around 10 a.m., Jared Loughner approached the gathering of people and shot Giffords in the head, then proceeded to fire randomly at others in the crowd with his semiautomatic pistol. By the time he was subdued, thirteen people were wounded and six people lay dead, including a federal judge and Christina Taylor-Green, 9, who was born on September 11, 2001.

Soon after the shooting, questions arose in the media over Sarah Palin's use of gun cross-hairs and terms like "targeted" and other inflammatory language on her website "takebackthe20," which was dedicated to trying to win back seats from Democrats. Critics of the vitriol used by both parties in the 2010 Congressional elections wondered if such imagery and terms helped spur someone like Loughner to violent action.

Although Palin's group quickly took down the imagery from the website, she shot back at her critics, saying that she was simply using metaphors and similes and that it could not be blamed for the actions of individuals. She spurred even further debate by saying her critics had committed "blood libel" against her. The term, quickly picked up in the media, was originally used to refer to the false claim that Jews murdered Christian children for religious rites.

Whether Loughner was influenced by the violent imagery and rhetoric used by conservatives against politicians like Giffords will likely never be known. However, the tragic incident did serve as a powerful reminder to politicians and the public that perhaps the rhetoric of "politics as usual" was not so good for our democracy after all.

---

a campaign contribution, or volunteer to help the candidate's party. They can see online databases that show how much their neighbors have contributed to which candidates, and they can look at fact-checking sites via social media to see whether or not candidates are telling the truth.

Although having a website may have been considered groundbreaking for a candidate in 1998, by 2012 candidate websites were only a part of much more robust social media communication strategies that included Facebook and Twitter, among other social media. Social media let candidates communicate in more informal ways with voters than they could via other media channels, and it also could generate media attention at times. Perhaps most famous in the 2012 election was President Obama's tweet the day after Clint Eastwood's bizarre performance as he spoke to an empty chair with an invisible President Obama at the Republican National Convention in August. The tweet perfectly fit the concise and snarky mode so often found on Twitter, with simply a picture of the back of President Obama's chair (with him in it) saying, "This seat's taken."

But social media tools are used for more important things than humorous retorts, and Obama's campaign team proved masterful at both fundraising and getting people to register and vote in both the 2008 and 2012 elections. In 2008, Obama's campaign was so successful at getting small donations from many people

Image Is Everything

Although the obsession with a politician's image did not begin with television, it certainly took on much greater importance than it ever had in the age of print. Even so, politicians then were hardly groundbreakers in fashion. A look at presidential portraits shows that after a spate of presidents with facial hair in the latter 1800s, the fashion for men at the time, the last president with a beard or mustache was William Howard Taft (1909–1913). Today, except perhaps for Sinn Fein president and Irish MP Gerry Adams, almost no Western politicians have facial hair. Of course there is no correlation between one's ability to govern and having facial hair, yet it has been considered a political taboo for at least eighty years.

Television has only added to the importance of how politicians look, and it is said that several presidents would have never been elected if television had existed when they were running, because of their looks or disabilities. These include Abraham Lincoln, with his gawky, awkward appearance; William Howard Taft, weighing in at three hundred pounds; and wheelchair-bound Franklin Delano Roosevelt, stricken by polio at age thirty-nine. FDR would never be able to get the press today to agree, as the press did then, to not publish images of him getting in and out of his wheelchair.

Today, image consultants help political candidates look the part, with advice on everything from what color shirt and tie to wear to what hairstyle they should have. Mitt Romney drew criticism in late September 2012 when he was interviewed on the Hispanic network Univision looking unnaturally tan. The interview itself was almost cancelled by Romney until Univision bused in Hispanic Republicans to fill the hall. "Fake tan. Fake fans. Really sad," wrote one Facebook commenter.

that he was the first presidential candidate to refuse taxpayer funding (and, not coincidentally, the spending restrictions that went with that).

Some have even claimed that President Obama owed his first election win to the Internet. Joe Trippi, Howard Dean's campaign manager in 2004, said that the extent and kind of organizing that Obama was able to do through the Internet would have required "an army of volunteers and paid organizers on the ground."[9]

In 2012, Obama once again tapped this network even though the media often commented as the race tightened in the fall that there did not seem to be the same enthusiasm among Obama supporters as in 2008. Nevertheless, in election post-mortems, many commentators said part of the credit for Obama's win went to his well-organized campaigns, especially in swing states.

▼ THE ROLE OF SOCIAL MEDIA

At the time of the 2012 election, the social media landscape looked very different than in 2008. Social media played a much more important role in 2012. An October 2012 study by the Pew Internet & American Life Project found that 39 percent of Americans used social media to discuss politics. During the first presidential debate between Obama and Romney, over 10 million tweets were sent, whereas in 2008 only 1.8 million tweets were sent on Election Day itself. President Obama's speech at the Democratic National Convention initiated over 2.5 million online conversations.

In the 2008 election, YouTube played a major role in helping Obama, according to Arianna Huffington, founder of the *Huffington Post*. YouTube purposely positioned itself to play a potentially important role in the elections by launching the YouTube You Choose '08 campaign, which gave presidential candidates their own YouTube channels. By being able to post videos that the public could watch when it wanted to, without commercials, candidates could speak at greater length than in the sound-bite culture that dominates the mainstream news. YouTube also allowed people to watch repeatedly and to forward videos to friends.

President Obama's campaign created a website specifically to dispel the myriad false rumors circulating about him during the campaign.

The changes brought by social media are even more surprising when we consider that neither YouTube nor Twitter even existed in the 2004 election. Within eight years, both have played major roles in reshaping the expectations and interactions of American voters with their political candidates. Scholars and political consultants are still only starting to analyze the implications for future campaigns.

WEB LINK
Video the Vote
www.videothevote.org/

▼ CHANGING RULES FOR POLITICIANS

The changes brought to political campaigns by YouTube, Facebook, and other social-media technologies are still not fully understood and will likely change as technologies continue to evolve. However, there are some fundamental shifts that are already apparent from the 2008 and 2012 presidential campaigns.

Candidates seem to have yet to learn that there is no such thing anymore as an "off the record" event. It used to be that journalists attending fundraisers or other events that were off the record respected that whatever was said there by a candidate could not be reported on. But now citizen journalists and bloggers attending such events often ignore these unwritten rules.

At a private fundraiser for wealthy donors in May 2012, Romney made his infamous

The different seating formats in the three presidential debates between President Obama and Mitt Romney had some effect on how they reacted with each other, with the second debate in which they could walk around being considered the most aggressive and the third debate in which they were seated as much calmer and reasoned.

comment that 47 percent of Americans considered themselves victims and were government freeloaders who paid no taxes. The event was secretly videotaped and released to the media months later as the election campaigns were heating up. It further reinforced negative perceptions of Romney as someone who would help the rich rather than the middle class.

Campaign gaffes also have a way of generating a life of their own with social media. When Mitt Romney said in the first debate that he would cut funding of public television if president, but added, "I love Big Bird," his remark sparked many comments on social media. During the debate more than 200,000 tweets were sent that mentioned Big Bird.

Social media has allowed some topics to continue in online conversations long after they would have disappeared in the regular news cycle. One example is Missouri Senate Republican candidate Rep. Todd Akin's comments in August that in cases of "legitimate rape" women could control whether they got pregnant or not. The statement, and others like it by other Republican candidates, brought attention to the controversial views on abortion and women's right to choose held by many conservative Republicans.

One other change seen with the rise of the Internet in political campaigns is the ability to attract young people and get them involved in the political process. Young people today have proved a powerful force in helping organize and volunteer. This bucks a trend, going back at least thirty years, of steadily declining youth participation in elections. Obama realized much of his voter base was with young people, and was seen campaigning on college campuses days before the election in battleground states like Ohio and Virginia. Often he appeared with Bruce Springsteen, who gave free concerts to support Obama.

◢▼ Online Media and Political Communications

Online databases and sites that provide direct information about political donations, voting records, and other political activities have become especially useful tools for journalists and citizens. Visitors to such sites can customize information on demand about any community in the United States or any person who may have contributed to a candidate, using data from the Federal Election Commission. The user simply enters a zip code and immediately obtains a list of everyone in that geographic area who has contributed to federal campaign committees. Alternatively, the user can enter the first three or more letters of a person's last name and obtain a detailed inventory of her or his contributions during any election cycle dating back to 1990.

The database is maintained by OpenSecrets.org, which also offers a wide range of other useful online political information, such as details on the activities of political action committees (PACs), the spending of lobbyists (which can be extremely revealing in how organizations or industries are trying to shape the nation's political agenda), and which political races have raised and spent the most. Not everyone thinks making public records such as these widely available on the Internet is a good idea, however.

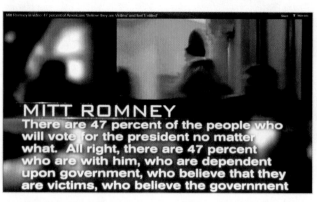

Mitt Romney's statement about about 47% of the population as victims who expected government handouts was secretly recorded at an expensive fund-raiser and put on the Internet.

Political activists have found the Web to be an effective place to organize people as well as to distribute their messages. The website e-thePeople encourages citizens to email their politicians, create and sign online petitions, and discuss various political topics with others online.

Email initially seemed to promise a faster, more efficient way for constituents to communicate directly with their members of Congress, but a report released in 2001 by George Washington University and the Congress Management Foundation as part of the Congress Online Project said that the reality of email communications did not bear out that promise. There was growing frustration on the part of constituents who felt that their politicians were not responding to their communications and likewise a frustration on the part of politicians who felt that the public did not adequately understand how Congress worked and had unrealistic expectations of how quickly they could receive responses. Some House offices were receiving eight thousand emails a month and some Senate offices were getting fifty-five thousand emails a month, far more than their staff could read or answer in addition to doing their various regular duties. The report also said that there was a general perception among politicians that emails were a more casual form of communication than a telephone call or written letter and were thus given lower priority than those other forms of contact.

Some political activists are also using digital media to not only organize online but physically gather as well. Dubbed **smart mobs** by author Howard Rheingold, these groups use cellular phones and wireless networks to communicate rapidly with each other and organize. Smart mobs contributed to the overthrow of President Suharto in Indonesia in 1998 and to the overthrow in 2001 of Philippine President Joseph Estrada as organizers orchestrated demonstrations against him via cell phone text messages. Protestors at the World Trade Organization meeting in Seattle in 1999 were able to check the electronic network to see which way the tear gas was blowing. Through the use of wireless technology, mass demonstrations in various parts of a city can be roughly coordinated in real time, giving protestors almost as good a communication network as police or military might have in such a situation.

Handheld video- and audio-recording equipment has also helped activists, in some cases. Hundreds of activists were arrested during the Republican National Convention in New York City in 2004 and in some of the subsequent trials activists were able to show video that directly contradicted police testimony that they resisted arrest or fought police.

WEB LINK
Politico.com
www.politico.com/

WEB LINK
Vote Smart
www.vote-smart.org

WEB LINK
OpenSecrets.org
www.opensecrets.org/

Filipinos used text messages to quickly organize crowds to protest President Joseph Estrada as he was being investigated for corruption charges.

smart mob

A term coined by author Howard Rheingold to define a group of people communicating with each other via text messaging or wireless networks in order to coordinate their activities even though they are in different places.

LOOKING BACK AND MOVING FORWARD

As we have seen, the government has become more active in recent years in writing bills that attempt to counter some of the trends online media bring, such as the general breakdown in the ability of media companies to protect copyrighted material. These and issues regarding online privacy, encryption, and online pornography

WEB LINK
The Center for Voting and Democracy
www.fairvote.org/

WEB LINK
e.thePeople
www.e-thepeople.org/

are likely to continue to be hot topics that involve politicians and the court system for some time.

It will be important for citizens to be knowledgeable about these issues and willing to sacrifice convenience to preserve fundamental rights of privacy. The role of mass communication in democracies will likely be even more important in the future than it has been, even as the focus may shift from the notion of simply informing the public to that of engaging in a dialog with the public. In this regard, social media will also play an important role, in facilitating conversations between members of the public and between the public and its elected officials.

The move toward more dialog may be one of the biggest shifts in the role media play in the political process and in elections. If participation and discussion are encouraged, far more people may become engaged in the political process than has been the case in recent history. Even something as simple as tweeting about what took place at a local school board meeting or blogging for a local news organization could affect the way leaders govern.

Just as maintaining our rights to privacy will be an ever more important struggle in the future, keeping governance as transparent as possible will likewise be an ongoing effort. It is the shift toward more transparency that social media in part represent and that many government leaders may find the most threatening to standard ways of conducting political business.

Transparency will also be hugely important in the international arena, in which a growing number of transnational organizations such as the World Bank and International Monetary Fund (IMF) make policy decisions that can affect entire nations and the global economy. Most of the leaders of these organizations are not elected officials and thus have little if any incentive to make their policy decision-making processes transparent. While leaders within democratic nations may have increased pressure to be more transparent, the leaders of these transnational groups, who arguably have more power to affect national policies in some cases than elected officials do, will not be beholden to any specific public.

There has been a growing awareness among some activist groups and social movements that the increased powers of some organizations, such as the World Trade Organization (WTO), must be monitored. Regular, sometimes violent protests accompany WTO meetings, trying to raise publicity about the policy decisions the WTO is making for global business and trade. Using organizing and protest tactics similar to those used with antinuclear and environmental protests in the 1970s and 1980s, these new social movements also use powerful social-media communication tools to talk with each other and to get media attention for their causes.

DISCUSSION QUESTIONS

1. Do you agree with Joseph Pulitzer's statement on the importance of the press in preserving American democracy? Why or why not? What trends and events both historical and current support your views?

2. Discuss some of the important trends in media coverage of elections, such as sound bites and horse-race coverage, and what can be done to change these trends if you feel they are detrimental to good journalism and the political process.

3. Considering that most media organizations rely heavily on advertising for revenue, is it fair to deny them the revenues that come from political advertising? Are there any potential conflicts of interest that could come from a media organization's coverage of fundraising or election issues because of the current arrangement? How might this situation be changed so that media companies can still earn money, politicians can effectively reach the public, and the audience can be thoroughly informed on issues?

4. Compare and contrast the coverage of a current political issue in a liberal publication or blog and a conservative one. How do they frame and talk about the issue? How do they discuss certain facts about it? Which do you find more credible, and why?

5. If you go to a nonnews website to get information on candidates, what do you look for that makes you trust the information it provides? Do you visit more than one site to read about a particular candidate, or do you stay with one site?

6. Discuss what role you played, if any, in the latest election, whether through volunteering, voting, or simply going to candidates' websites to learn more about their policies and stands on issues.

7. What are your perceptions of social movements that protest things like WTO meetings or policies created by international organizations? What influenced these perceptions?

FURTHER READING

The Myth of Digital Democracy. Matthew Hindman (2008) Princeton University Press.

Mosh the Polls: Youth Voters, Popular Culture and Democratic Engagement. Tony Kelso, Brian Cogan (eds.) (2008) Lexington Books.

Into the Buzzsaw: Leading Journalists Expose the Myth of a Free Press. Kristina Borjesson (ed.) (2002) Prometheus Books.

Media Spectacle and the Crisis of Democracy: Terrorism, War, and Election Battles. Douglas Kellner (2005) Paradigm Publishers.

Media Politics: A Citizen's Guide, 2nd ed. Shanto Iyengar (2011) W. W. Norton.

unSpun: Finding Facts in a World of Disinformation. Brooks Jackson, Kathleen Hall Jamieson (2007) Random House Trade Paperbacks.

Tuned Out: Why Americans Under 40 Don't Follow the News. David Mindich (2005) Oxford University Press.

The Press Effect: Politicians, Journalists, and the Stories That Shape the World. Kathleen Hall Jamieson (2004) Oxford University Press.

The Nightly News Nightmare: Network Television's Coverage of U.S. Presidential Elections, 1988–2000. Stephen J. Farnsworth, S. Robert Lichter (2002) Rowman & Littlefield.

Mass Media and American Politics, 8th ed. Doris A. Graber (2009) CQ Press.

Bloggers on the Bus: How the Internet Changes Politics and the Press. Eric Boehlert (2009) Free Press.

Entertaining Politics: Satiric Television and Political Engagement, 2nd ed. Jeffrey Jones (2009) Rowman & Littlefield.

(Un)Civil War of Words: Media and Politics in the Arab World. Mamoun Fandy (2007) Praeger.

Cyberprotest: New Media, Citizens, and Social Movements. W. Van De Donk (ed.) (2004) Routledge.

1. False. John F. Kennedy appeared on *The Tonight Show* in 1960.

2. George Allen, Virginia.

3. China, Myanmar, Cuba.

4. Radio, as low literacy rates make print media reach smaller audiences.

5. The ramifications that come from portions of the population not having access to the Internet while others do.

7. True.

8. YouTube.

9. False.

10. True.

GLOSSARY

actualities Edited audio clips from people interviewed.

ad-agency commission A percentage amount of the cost of an advertisement that is taken by the advertising agency that helped create and sell the ad.

advertising An ancient form of human communication generally designed to inform or persuade members of the public with regard to some product or service.

advertorial A type of display advertisement that is created to look like an article within the publication, although most publications have the words "advertisement" or "paid advertisement" in tiny print somewhere nearby.

agenda setting A role the media play in deciding which topics to cover and thus, by virtue of the fact that the media has covered them, which topics the public deems important and discussion worthy.

Alien and Sedition Acts A series of four acts passed by the U.S. Congress in 1798 that, among other things, prohibited sedition, or spoken or written criticism of the U.S. government, and imposed penalties of a fine or imprisonment upon conviction. Although they expired in 1801, other sedition acts have been passed periodically, especially during times of war.

analog media Term originally used in audio recording for media analogous to the sound being re-created. It now refers to all nondigitized media, such as print media, audio and video recordings, photography, and film.

aspect ratio The ratio of a screen's height to its width. Incompatible aspect ratios of films and television mean that either films have to be cropped to fit within a television screen, or, in order to keep the original aspect ratio, black borders must appear on the top and bottom of the screen.

Associated Press Founded as a not-for-profit members' cooperative in 1848 by a group of six New York newspaper publishers in order to share the costs of gathering news by telegraph. Today 1,700 newspapers and 5,000 television and radio stations are members of this news-gathering organization.

astroturfing The practice of creating a movement or campaign so that it looks like it was created by concerned citizens as a grassroots movement, but was actually created or controlled by a large organization or group.

asynchronous media Media that do not require the audience to assemble at a given time. Examples of asynchronous media are printed materials and recorded audio or video.

auteur French for "author," it is usually applied to directors who stamp their vision on the films they make, as opposed to directors who have but one role among many other professionals in the making of a film.

authoritarian theory of the press A theory of international mass communication in which authoritarian governments exert direct control over the media.

balance In news coverage, the concept of presenting sides equally or of reporting on a broad range of news events.

banner ad An advertisement across the top of a website and the original form of advertising on the Web.

beat A reporter's specialized area of coverage based on geography or subject. Common beats in large or medium-sized newspapers include education, crime, and state politics.

behavioral targeting A technique used to increase the effectiveness of advertising campaigns by using information collected on an individual's web-browsing behavior to select which advertisements to display to that individual.

Benjamin Day Publisher of the *New York Sun,* he ushered in the era of the penny press when, on September 3, 1833, he began offering his paper on the streets for a penny.

blog Short for "weblog," a type of website in which a person posts regular journal or diary entries with the posts arranged chronologically.

Bobo Doll studies Experiments done in the 1950s that showed that children who watched violent episodes on television in which the violent person was rewarded were more likely to punch a Bobo Doll than children who saw violent episodes in which the violent person was punished. This research seemed to confirm certain assumptions about direct media effects.

bourgeoisie A class of society that translates approximately to "middle class," which distinguishes the class from the aristocracy above them and the proletariat (or workers) below them.

branding The process of creating in the consumer's mind a clear identity for a particular company's product, logo, or trademark.

broadband A network connection that enables a large amount of bandwidth to be transmitted, which allows for more information to be sent in a shorter period of time.

broadcast The original usage was agricultural, referring to casting seeds widely in a field rather than depositing them one at a time. The notion was transferred to the fledgling electronic medium of radio and later television.

byte The most common base unit used to measure computer storage and information, it consists of eight bits, in a combination of 0's and 1's, to form letters, numbers, and all modes of computer information that are displayed.

camera obscura A dark box or room with a small hole in it that allowed an inverted image of an outside scene to be shown on the opposite inner wall.

cathode-ray tube (CRT) A device that is still used in some television screens and computer monitors, in which electrons are transmitted to a screen for viewing.

censorship The act of prohibiting certain expression or content. Censors usually do not target the whole publication, program, or website, but seek to prohibit some part of the content.

Children's Television Act Created in 1990, it places limits on the amount of commercial content that programming can carry, forces stations to carry certain amounts of educational programming for children sixteen and under, and includes other provisions to help protect children.

chilling effect The phenomenon that occurs when journalists or other media producers decide not to publish stories on a topic after a journalist has been punished or jailed for such a story.

circuit switching The original system used for telephony, in which circuits connected two people communicating. Once the circuit was connected, or "on," the people on either end of the circuit used the whole circuit exclusively, even if they didn't speak. When they hung up, the circuit was disconnected by an operator and available for others to use.

citizen journalism Journalism done by amateurs or volunteers, either with citizen journalism websites, blogs, or as part of a mainstream news organization's website.

classified advertising A type of advertising usually found in print media, especially newspapers but also in some magazines, and now increasingly online, that consists of messages posted by individuals and organizations to sell specific goods or services.

clear and present danger A restriction on speech when it meets both of the following conditions: (1) it is intended to incite or produce dangerous activity (as with falsely shouting "Fire!" in a crowded theater), and (2) it is likely to succeed in achieving the purported result.

click-through rate Rate at which people click on the ad.

client/server A network model, predominant on the Internet today, that relies on a centralized computer, or server, that stores content that the audience, or clients, access.

coaxial cable An insulated and conducting wire that is typically used for most cable television connections.

codex A manuscript book of individually bound pages.

community antenna television (CATV) Also known as cable television, it was developed in 1948 so communities in hilly or remote terrain could still access television broadcasts.

consolidation The process of large companies merging with each other or absorbing other companies, forming even bigger companies.

convergence The coming together of computing, telecommunications, and media in a digital environment.

cookie Information that a website puts on a user's local hard drive so that it can recognize when that computer accesses the website again. Cookies are what allow for conveniences like password recognition and personalization.

copyright The exclusive right to use, publish, and distribute a work such as a piece of writing, music, film, or video.

correlation The ways in which media interpret events and issues and ascribe meanings that help individuals understand their roles within the larger society and culture.

cost per thousand (CPM) A standard unit for measuring advertising rates for publications, based on circulation.

critical theory A theoretical approach broadly influenced by Marxist notions of the role of ideology, exploitation, capitalism, and the economy in understanding and eventually transforming society.

crowd sourcing Utilizing raw data that the public has gathered, in addition to reports from citizen-journalists, to help create a news report.

cultivation analysis A theory of media effects that states television cultivates in audiences a view of reality similar to the world portrayed in television programs. For example, it posits that viewing thousands of murders on television is unlikely to increase the chances that one will commit murder but does lead to one's belief that the world is a more dangerous place than it actually is.

cultural studies A framework in studying theories of communication that shuns the scientific approach used by scholars in the empirical school and that tries to examine the symbolic environment created by mass media and the role mass media plays in culture and society.

cultural transmission The transference of the dominant culture, as well as its subcultures, from one generation to the next or to immigrants, which helps people learn how to fit into society.

culture industry A term used by some critical theorists that refers to the mass communication industries and their power in creating culture as a commodity.

cybersquatting The practice of getting a domain name, usually of someone famous or a well-known company, with the intention of reselling the domain name at a high price.

David Sarnoff Head of RCA. He helped push the development of television as a mass medium yet blocked the development of FM radio for years because its adoption would hurt AM listenership and reduce demand for AM radio receivers, which RCA produced and sold.

daypart A segment of time used by radio and television program planners to decide who the primary audience is during that time of day or night.

deep linking Creating a hypertext link to another website's inside page or pages rather than to its homepage.

"digg" A popular website where users submit material (called "digging") to be voted on by other users, with the most popular material appearing on the homepage.

digital divide The idea that some groups that do not have access to the Internet become left out of the benefits that online technology can bring.

Digital Millennium Copyright Act (DMCA) An act of Congress in 1998 that reformed copyright law comprehensively in trying to update it for the digital age. Key provisions addressed the circumvention of copyright protection systems, fair use in a digital environment, and Internet service providers' (ISP) liability for content sent through their lines; DRM technologies or security codes are used to protect copyrighted works from being illegally copied.

digital television (DTV) Television signals that are transmitted digitally rather than over-the-air, as in analog television broadcasting. Digital TV provides better picture and sound quality and has greater capabilities to include interactive functions than analog television.

digital watermark Computer code (usually invisible, but sometimes visible) inserted into any digital content—images, graphics, audio, video, or even text documents—that authenticates the source of that content.

digitization The process in which media is made into computer-readable form.

dime novel The first paperback book form, which cost ten cents. This made it accessible even to the poor.

direct effects model A model of mass communication that says that media has direct and measurable effects on audiences, such as encouraging them to buy products or become violent.

display advertising A type of advertising in print media that usually consists of illustrations or images and text and that can occupy a small section of a page, a full page, or multiple pages. Because of their high costs, display ads are usually bought by large companies or organizations.

distributed computing Individual, autonomous computers that work together toward a common goal, typically a large, complex project that requires more computing power than any individual computer could have.

Edward R. Murrow A radio and, later, television journalist and announcer who set the standard for journalistic excellence on television during television's golden age.

Edwin Howard Armstrong Inventor of FM radio transmission; Columbia University engineering professor.

electronic news-gathering (ENG) equipment Tools such as video cameras and satellite dishes that allow journalists to gather and broadcast news much more quickly than in the past.

electronic program guides (EPG) Guides available on television that provide program listings and some simple interactivity, such as ordering pay-per-view programs or buying CDs or DVDs of listed music or shows.

embargo The practice of sending news releases to news organizations with the stipulation that the information cannot be broadcast or printed until after a specific day or time.

encoding/decoding A theory that says that messages are encoded with certain meanings by media producers and that audiences then "decode" the messages in various ways, depending on things like their education level, political views, and other factors.

entertainment A function of mass communication that is performed in part by all three other of the four main functions (surveillance, correlation, cultural transmission) but also involves the generation of content designed specifically and exclusively to entertain.

epistemology A way of or framework for understanding the world.

equal-time rule The requirement that broadcasters make available equal airtime, in terms of commentaries and commercials, to opposing candidates running for election. It does not apply to candidates appearing in newscasts, documentaries, or news-event coverage.

ethnography A variety of qualitative research techniques that involve the researcher interacting with participants, either through observation, participation, interviews, or a combination of methods.

extensible markup language (XML) A coding format similar to HTML but that allows for easy sharing of information and data about the information on the Web, not only how it looks.

fairness In news coverage, the concept of covering all relevant sides of an issue and allowing spokespeople representing those various sides a chance to be covered in the same way.

Fairness Doctrine Adopted by the FCC in 1949, it required broadcasters to seek out and present all sides of a controversial issue they were covering. It was discarded by the FCC in 1987.

fair use Allowable use of someone else's copyrighted work that does not require payment of royalties, with a number of factors used to determine if something falls under fair use or is a violation of copyright; an exception to copyright law that allows someone to use an excerpt of a work without paying for its use. Reviews of works or their use in commentary or criticism are examples of fair use.

fear appeals A type of advertising technique that attempts to scare the audience in order to persuade them, such as antismoking ads that show disfigured former smokers.

Federal Communications Commission (FCC) The principal communications regulatory body at the federal level in the United States, established in 1934.

Federal Radio Commission (FRC) Formed by the Radio Act of 1927, the commission was the precursor to the FCC and created a policy that favored fewer high-power radio broadcasting stations rather than more numerous low-power stations.

focus groups A research technique in which small groups of people are gathered together to discuss a topic, with the interactions often recorded and carefully watched to determine what different people think.

folksonomies A collection of tags created by users that provide metadata, or data about data, regarding information.

fourth estate Another term for the press, or journalism, in which it acts as a fourth branch of government: one that watches the other branches (executive, legislative, and judicial).

frame The notion that every story is told in a particular way that influences how readers think of the story.

framing The technique of using frames to tell a story in a particular way in order to influence readers.

genre A type of story that has recognizable and defined elements that distinguish it from other types of stories or nonfiction.

Georges Méliès An early French filmmaker who pioneered the use of special effects in film in order to show imaginative stories.

gramophone Developed by inventor Emile Berliner, it used a flat disc to record sound rather than the cylinder that was used up to that time.

Granville T. Woods Inventor of railway telegraphy in 1887, a type of wireless communication that allowed moving trains to communicate with each other and with stations, greatly reducing the number of railway collisions.

graphical user interface (GUI) A computer interface that shows graphical representations of file structures, files, and applications, in the form of folders, icons, and windows.

graphophone An improvement on Thomas Edison's phonograph in recording audio, it used beeswax to record sound rather than tinfoil. Developed by Alexander Graham Bell and inventor Charles Tainter.

Guglielmo Marconi Italian inventor and creator of radio telegraphy, or wireless transmission, in 1899.

Gutenberg Bible One of a handful of surviving Bibles printed by Johannes Gutenberg; considered the first mechanically printed works in Europe.

Hays Code A code established in 1930 by the movie industry to censor itself regarding showing nudity or glorifying antisocial acts in movies. Officials for the Hays Office had to approve each film that was distributed to a mass audience.

high definition television (HDTV) Television with a much higher resolution image and sharper image than a standard television signal.

hub A node that has many connections to other nodes in a social network.

human-computer interaction The general term for any interaction between humans and computers, either through devices such as keyboards, mice, touch screens, or voice recognition.

hyperlink clickable pointer to other online content.

hypertext Text online that is linked to another web page, website, or different part of the same web page by HTML coding.

hypertext markup language (HTML) A coding format that describes how information should look on the Web.

hypertext transfer protocol (HTTP) A protocol that enables the standardized transfer of text, audio, and video files, as well as email, from one address to another.

hypodermic-needle model A model of media effects, also called the "magic bullet" model, largely derived from learning theory and simple stimulus-response models in behavioral psychology, that states media messages have a profound, direct, and uniform impact on the public.

Ida B. Wells A female African American journalist in the latter nineteenth century who wrote and fought against racism and black lynching.

ideology A way of belief that goes largely unquestioned by people or that is seen as somehow natural or beyond question.

indecent speech Language or material that, in context, depicts or describes, in terms patently offensive as measured by contemporary community standards for the broadcast medium, sexual or excretory organs or activities.

independent films Films made by production companies outside the main Hollywood studios.

independent labels Any small record-production and distribution companies that are not part of the four major-label companies. They include companies producing only one or two albums a year, as well as larger independents such as Disney. The independent labels produce 66 percent of the albums each year but only 20 percent of the sales.

influencer A person who can influence others in their social network to perform an action or change an attitude.

infomercial Also called paid programming, this is a thirty- or sixty-minute television show that seeks to sell a product and that usually involves a celebrity spokesperson and testimony from customers about how good the product is.

information overload The difficulties associated with dealing with the vast amounts of information available to us and making sense of it.

information society The notion that modern society has transformed from one in which industrial production was dominant to one in which information production has become more important.

instant messaging Often abbreviated to IM, it is a form of real-time communication through typed text over a computer network.

integrated communications The idea that all channels of communication about a company or brand should work together in creating a cohesive message.

intellectual property Ideas that have commercial value, such as literary or artistic works, patents, business methods, and industrial processes.

interactivity Although an exact definition is still being debated, for digital-media purposes interactivity can be defined as having three main elements: (1) a dialog that occurs between a human and a computer program, (2) a dialog that occurs simultaneously or nearly so, and (3) the audience has some measure of control over what media content it sees and in what order.

interpersonal communication Communication between two or more individuals, usually in a small group, although it can involve communication between a live speaker and an audience.

interpretive reporting A type of reporting that tries to put the facts of a story into a broader context by relying on knowledge and experience the reporter has about the subject.

interstitial ad An online advertisement that opens in a new window from the one the user was in.

James Carey Communication scholar and historian who has shaped a cultural-studies approach to communication theory.

James Gordon Bennett Founder of the *New York Herald* in 1835. He started many features found in modern newspapers, including a financial page, editorial commentary, and public-affairs reporting.

Johannes Gutenberg German printer credited with creating the first mechanical printing press in Europe in 1455.

John Logie Baird Scottish inventor who created the first mechanically scanned television device, in 1923. His thirty-line TV had better resolution than the first attempts at electronic televisions.

joint operating agreements or arrangements (JOAs) Legal agreements that permit newspapers in the same market or city to merge their business operations for reasons of economics yet maintain independent editorial operations.

keyword auction One method in search engine marketing in which companies bid for words and pay the search engine a certain amount every time the word is searched and their listing is clicked on.

laugh track A device used in television sitcoms that generates prerecorded laughter, timed to coincide with punch lines of jokes.

Lee de Forest Considered the "father" of radio broadcasting technology because of his invention that permitted reliable voice transmissions for both point-to-point communication and broadcasting.

libel A type of defamation that is written and published, such as a false attack on a person's character, which damages a person's reputation.

libertarian theory A theory of international mass communication that is rooted in the idea of the individual's right to publish whatever he or she wants, even material that is critical of the government or of government officials.

listservs Also known as listserves, these are automated mailing-list administrators that allow for easy subscription, subscription cancellation, and sending of emails to subscribers on the list.

localization The ability of media-content producers to provide content based on a user's locale, either done automatically based on an ISP or after the user has provided information such as a city name or zip code.

long tail The notion that selling a few of many types of items can be as profitable or even more profitable than selling many copies of a few items. The concept works especially well for online sellers such as Amazon or Netflix.

Louis Daguerre A French scene painter and inventor of the daguerreotype, an early type of photography.

lurker A person on an online discussion board who does not contribute to discussions by posting messages but who simply reads what others write.

major labels The four biggest recording-arts companies that control much of the music industry partly through their powerful distribution channels and ability to market music to mass audiences. They are Universal Music Group, Sony Music, EMI, and the Warner Music Group.

Marshall McLuhan A communication scholar who wrote *Understanding Media* and *The Gutenberg Galaxy,* among other books. He is perhaps most famous for creating the "global village" metaphor regarding electronic media and his often-misunderstood phrase "the medium is the message."

Mary Shadd Cary The first African American woman to edit a weekly newspaper. She founded and edited the *Provincial Freeman* in Canada after leaving the United States so she would not be captured and put into slavery because of the Fugitive Slave Act.

mash-up Combining textual information over geographic, map-based information so users can access multiple layers of data.

mass communication Communication to a large group or groups of people that remain largely unknown to the sender of the message.

massively multiplayer online role-playing games (MMORPGs) Online games played by a number of people at the same time in which they develop characters or roles and interact with each other while completing quests or adventures.

mass-market paperbacks Inexpensive, soft-cover books sold in bookstores and other public places such as supermarkets and drugstores.

Mathew B. Brady A famous photographer of the nineteenth century who took portraits of many well-known people of his day as well as Civil War battlefield photographs.

mean-world syndrome The notion that the world is a more dangerous place than it actually is, which has come from watching news reports or violent programming.

media ecology The study of media environments and how those environments may affect people and society.

media literacy The process of interacting with media content and critically analyzing it by considering its particular presentation, its underlying political or social messages, and ownership and regulation issues that may affect what is presented and in what form.

media oligopoly A marketplace in which media ownership and diversity are severely limited and the actions of any single media group substantially affect its competitors, including determining the content and price of media products for both consumers and advertisers.

media spotlight effect The phenomenon that occurs when the media has intense coverage of a certain event or person for a short time, but then moves on to other issues soon after.

mediated communication Communication that takes place through a medium, such as writing or recording, as opposed to unmediated communication, such as face-to-face discussions.

medium A communication channel, such as talking on the telephone, instant messaging, or writing back and forth in a chat room.

metatag A word or words used by websites to help search engines index and describe a site, typically unseen by humans unless looking at the website's code.

Metcalfe's Law The value of a network rises in proportion to the square of the number of people on that network. In other words, the more people who are connected to a network in which they can communicate with each other, such as the Internet, the more valuable that network becomes.

modem Derived from the terms modulate-demodulate; a device that converts digital signals from a computer to analog signals for transmission over a phone line, as well as converting transmitted analog signals to digital signals.

mods Short for "modification," it refers to the practice of changing parts of the code in some games to alter how they are played or how they look.

MPEG Moving Picture Experts Group, established in 1988 and responsible for creating the standards for digital and audio compression. The abbreviation is also used to denote the types of compression, such as MPEG-1, MPEG-4, and so on.

muckrakers A group of journalists in the latter nineteenth and early twentieth centuries who investigated business and political corruption. Their activities were likened to raking up mud, or muck, by Theodore Roosevelt, who meant it as a term of derision.

multicast Simultaneously transmitting multiple channels of compressed digital content over the television airwaves.

multimedia A combination of different types of media in one package; thus, film or video with sound is a type of multimedia because it combines visual and audio elements. Web pages that combine text, video, animation, audio, or graphics are another type of multimedia.

multipoint multichannel distribution system (MMDS) A type of terrestrial wireless service that can transmit as many as thirty-three analog TV channels over the air via microwave transmission and up to ninety-nine compressed digital channels.

multitasking In a computer environment, doing several activities at once with a variety of programs, such as simultaneously doing word-processing, spreadsheet, and database work while conducting real-time chat through an instant-messenger service.

nanotechnology A cutting-edge field of technology research that involves items that are nanometers (10^{-9} meters) in length and that promises to revolutionize many fields, ranging from electronics, information storage, and even medicine.

narrowband A network connection that does not provide very much bandwidth, thus receiving and sending information more slowly than broadband connections. Dial-up modems and some of the early wireless connections with speeds of 56 kHz or under are considered narrowband.

network neutrality A principle that states that broadband networks should be free of restrictions on content, platforms, or equipment and that certain types of content, platforms, or equipment should not get preferential treatment on the network.

news hole A term typically used with newspapers, it refers to the amount of total space available after advertisement space has been blocked out.

newsgroups Categories for discussion groups within Usenet.

Newspaper Preservation Act Created in 1970, it is intended to preserve a diversity of editorial opinion in communities where only two competing, or independently owned, daily newspapers exist.

objectivity A journalistic principle that says journalists should be impartial and free of bias in their reporting. This principle has come under attack in recent years, because of the impossibility of people being completely objective, and has largely been replaced by the concepts of fairness and balance.

obscenity One of the forms of speech not protected by the First Amendment, and thus subject to censorship. Although an exact definition of the term has been difficult to achieve in various court cases, generally a three-part standard is applied for media content: it must appeal to prurient interests as defined by community standards, it must show sexual conduct in an offensive manner, and it must on the whole lack serious artistic, literary, political, or scientific value.

OLED Organic light-emitting diode screen, a type of thin, flexible screen that will change how and where we are able to view content on screens.

oligopoly An economic structure in which a few very large, very powerful, and very rich owners control an industry or collection of related industries.

open source any program whose source code the programmer allows others to see. This lets others modify and improve it. Most proprietary software programs do not allow the public to see their source code.

opinion poll A poll that is usually conducted by a professional polling organization asking members of the public their opinions on issues or political candidates.

opt in The practice of letting consumers choose to receive mailings or marketing material by having them check a box on a website, usually when registering for the site; a mailing list in which the user has chosen to receive emails and marketing materials.

optical fiber A transparent filament, usually made of glass or plastic, that uses light to carry information. This makes transmission of information much faster and with much greater capacity than twisted-pair copper wires or coaxial cable.

optical storage Uses light in the form of lasers to store and read data of all types, whether text, audio, or video. Using light is highly efficient: it permits storage devices to record vastly greater amounts of data in small spaces and enables faster retrieval of the stored data than from magnetic storage devices.

outdoor advertising Billboards and other forms of advertising such as on buses or taxis that are done in public.

packet switching A type of switching within a network, in which information is divided up into pieces, or packets, and transported as separate packets using the least congested routes. At the end of the route the packets are reassembled in their proper order and delivered over the telephone line or Internet.

participant-observation A qualitative research technique in which the researcher participates as a member of the group being studied.

patent law Protects the right to produce and sell an invention, rather than a literary or artistic work, which is covered by copyright law.

payola Cash or gifts given to radio disc jockeys by record labels in exchange for greater airplay given to the label's artists or most recent songs. The practice is now illegal after several scandals involving payola in the 1950s.

peer-to-peer (P2P) A network in which all computers are considered equal (peers) and can send and receive information equally well; a computer communications model in which all users have equal abilities to store, send, and accept communications from other users. This is the basis of file-sharing services such as Kazaa and Morpheus.

penny press Newspapers that sold for a penny, making them accessible to everyone. They differed from older newspaper forms in that they tried to attract as large an audience as possible and were supported by advertising rather than subscriptions.

performance-based advertising Any form of online ad buying in which an advertiser pays for results rather than paying for the size of the publisher's audience, or CPM.

personalization The ability of media-content producers to provide content that is of interest to a specific user based either on criteria the user has selected, such as a zip code, or on automated tracking of their Web-viewing habits.

phonograph First patented by Thomas Edison in 1877 as a "talking machine," it used a tinfoil cylinder to record voices from telephone conversations. Successive technological improvements in electronics and the type of material the sounds were recorded on made sound quality better.

pitch A request to review a client's new product or do a story about the client or the product.

podcast A program that is usually audio or video that lets users easily subscribe, much like subscribing to a blog.

political economy An area of study inspired by Marxism that examines the relationship between politics and economics with media ownership and the influences they all have on society and perpetuating the status quo.

positivism The belief, common among scientists in the physical or natural sciences and many in the social sciences, that there is an objective reality that can be discovered and explained through rigorous scientific research.

postmodernism A broad category of viewpoints that claim that there is no absolute truth, that truth is unknowable, and that attempts to create grand narratives that explain the world are faulty.

postpositivism A view that agrees largely with positivism, but acknowledges that there may be some things that we cannot know through scientific inquiry.

pragmatism A school of thought that claims that truth is found in actions that work and that no overarching or purely objective notion of truth can be found.

preferred-position balancing theory A legal theory that says that a balance must be struck between speech and other rights, although speech has a preferred position compared to other rights.

press agentry The practice of getting media attention for a client, often by creating outrageous stunts that would attract journalists.

print-on-demand (POD) The publication of single books or tiny print runs based on customer demand, using largely automated, nontraditional book printing methods such as the color laser printer.

prior restraint When the government prevents or blocks the publication, broadcasting, showing, or distribution of media content, whether in print, over the air, in movie theaters, or online.

product placement The practice of advertisers paying for actual products to be used and shown prominently in television shows and movies.

produsers The notion that audiences cannot simply be considered consumers anymore but also often take an active role in producing content or information.

propaganda The regular dissemination of a belief, a doctrine, a cause, or information, with the intent to mold public opinion.

pseudo events an event that is created specifically to attract the attention of the media, particularly the news.

public information campaign Media program funded by the government and designed to achieve some social goal, or what might be called social engineering.

public opinion The notion that the public, as a group, can form shared views or ideas about topics and that these ideas guide the public's actions.

public service announcement (PSA) Advertising-like messages for which the media donate time or space to organizations with a worthy purpose that ostensibly benefits the public.

public sphere An idealized conversational "space" in which people discuss and debate their interests separate from the interests of the state and civil society.

puffery A type of advertising language that makes extravagant claims about a product without saying anything concrete.

push poll A type of political advertising that appears to be a telephone poll but is actually a telemarketing campaign to sway voters by giving them false or misleading information about opposing candidates or to make a candidate look good.

qualitative research Research that describes phenomena in words instead of numbers or measures. Ethnographic studies, such as interviews with people to learn about beliefs or trends, are an example of qualitative research, also called critical-cultural studies.

quantitative research Research that focuses on numbers and measures and experimentation to describe phenomena. Researchers usually have a hypothesis they are trying to prove or disprove through controlled experimentation.

Radio Act of 1912 The act assigned frequencies and three- and four-letter codes to radio stations and limited broadcasting to the 360-meter wavelength.

Radio Act of 1927 An act of Congress that replaced the Radio Act of 1912 and created the Federal Radio Commission, the precursor to the FCC, and that was intended to help establish some sort of regulation and order over the chaos of the largely unregulated airwaves. It helped establish the principle that the airwaves were a limited public good and that companies using those airwaves had a duty to act responsibly toward the public in terms of the type of material they broadcast.

random-access memory (RAM) Usually used for a type of computer memory and abbreviated to RAM, in storage-technology terms it is a type of medium that allows for a reader or viewer to randomly obtain specific pieces of content by doing searches, using an index, or taking some other action.

rate card A listing of advertising rates by size, placement, and other characteristics, such as whether ads are black and white or full color. Frequency discounts are also usually offered, and the listed rates are usually negotiable, especially for large advertisers.

rating Used in broadcast media to explain the number of households that watched a particular show.

Reed's Law The utility or value of an interactive communication network with n members increases exponentially, or 2 to the nth power.

rhetoric One of the ancient arts of discourse, it involves using language to persuade others.

RSS feed Short for really simple syndication, it lets users easily subscribe to feeds from a blog or website.

Sarnoff's Law Created by RCA executive David Sarnoff, it states that the value of a network increases linearly with the number of people on it.

scrolling The practice of simply repeating the same message in a chat room, which quickly draws the ire of other participants.

search engine marketing (SEM) Paying a search engine such as Google or Bing to have a listing or keyword appear prominently when searched.

search engine optimization (SEO) A strategy that utilizes website design, careful choice of keywords, links, and other techniques to show prominently in online searches.

sedition Speech or action that encourages overthrow of a government or that subverts a constitution or a nation's laws.

semiotics The study of signs and symbols.

sensational journalism News that exaggerates or features lurid details and depictions of events in order to get a larger audience.

sequential-access memory A type of medium in which a reader, viewer, or user must go through the medium in the order received in order to find specific information.

serious gaming A growing area of gaming that creates video games that have educational value or purpose to them.

shield law A law intended to protect journalists from legal challenges to their freedom to report the news.

simplified communications model Developed by Wilbur Schramm in 1954 and based on the mathematical theory of communication. It includes a source, who encodes a message, or signal, which is transmitted (via the media or directly via interpersonal communication) to a destination, where the receiver decodes it.

six degrees of separation The idea that everyone in the world is separated from each other by at most six other nodes in a social network.

slander A type of defamation that is spoken, as opposed to written (libel), that damages a person's reputation or otherwise causes harm.

Slashdot effect The occurrence of a website's servers crashing because of a large increase in visits to the site after its being mentioned on the popular website Slashdot.org.

small world A tight-knit social network with many strong ties.

smart mob A term coined by author Howard Rheingold to define a group of people communicating with each other via text messaging or wireless networks in order to coordinate their activities even though they are in different places.

soap opera A type of programming that began on radio and successfully moved to television but that is now threatened by the increased variety of media types, as well as changes in lifestyles. Soap operas are dramatic story series that involve numerous characters and are aimed at a daytime audience of homemakers.

social constructionism A view that says that much if not all of what we know and understand about the world, including scientific knowledge, is constructed through our social interactions and language.

social marketing The practice of using advertising and marketing techniques to persuade people about changing bad or destructive behaviors or adopting good behaviors, such as the use of advertising and marketing techniques for social causes, such as antismoking or safe sex campaigns.

social responsibility theory A theory of international mass communication that perhaps best describes the media's role in democratic societies. It rests on the notion that the media are vital to informing citizens in a democratic society and, as such, should be free from most governmental constraints in order to provide the best, most reliable, and impartial information to the public.

soft news day A day in which not much of importance happens, so that editors are more likely to add features with less real news value, such as human-interest stories.

sound bite The length of time a news subject is allowed to speak without being edited by a reporter. It also has come to refer to short utterances that are catchy and designed to capture the media's attention.

Soviet theory A theory of international mass communication that states the media should be publicly owned and used to further the needs of the working class.

spam Unwanted email sent out by advertisers as a mass mailing.

spiral of silence hypothesis A hypothesis that states people (1) are naturally afraid of isolation, (2) realize that if they are in the minority on an issue they will likely be isolated, and (3) have a kind of sixth sense that helps them gauge when their opinions are contrary to the majority—which makes them refrain from expressing their opinions.

storage technology Any type of device or medium in which information can be maintained for later retrieval.

strong ties In social network analysis, the tight bonds between people in a "small world" of close connections.

subliminal advertising Persuasive messages that supposedly happen below the level of consciousness, such as quickly flashing an image or word on a screen. Despite concerns about subliminal advertising, there has been no firm proof that it works.

subtext The message beneath the message—the underlying, or implicit, message that is being conveyed by media content.

superstation A local TV station that reaches a national audience by beaming its programming nationwide via satellite to local cable systems, which then transmit the program to local subscribers.

superstitial ad An online advertisement that covers part of the existing screen or moves over part of it without opening a new window.

surveillance Primarily the journalism function of mass communication, which provides information about the processes, issues, events, and other developments in society.

swarming The process used by some P2P systems in which multiple downloaders of the same file are temporarily coordinated in order to speed up the downloading process.

synchronous media Media that take place in real time, such as live television or radio, that require the audience to be present during the broadcast or performance.

tagging Defining a piece of information, file, image, or other type of digital media in a nonhierarchical system that helps describe what the information is.

technological determinism A perspective that states that technology essentially "causes" certain behaviors and the creation of social systems.

Telecommunications Act of 1996 The first major regulatory overhaul of telecommunications since 1934, designed to open the industry to greater competition by deregulating many aspects of it.

theory of cognitive dissonance A theory of persuasion that states we act first and then rationalize our behavior afterward in order to fit our actions into self-perceived notions of who we are.

third-party cookies Cookies put on a computer by those other than the website being visited, such as advertisers inserting their own cookies on a web page.

third-person effect When a media message does not affect the behavior or beliefs of the intended audience but does affect a different group, which also receives the message and may act in the belief that the message will affect the intended audience.

Thomas Alva Edison Inventor whose inventions include the electric light, the phonograph, and the Kinetoscope. Edison's lab in Menlo Park, New Jersey, had over sixty scientists and produced as many as four hundred patent applications a year.

time shift Recording an audio or video event for viewing later rather than when the event was originally broadcast. Setting a VCR or DVR to record a favorite program while one is out is an example of time shifting.

time-space compression The idea that electronic communication has essentially reduced distances between people because of nearly instantaneous communication, which has also "sped up" our notions of time.

trademark A type of intellectual property that refers to signs, logos, or names.

transmission control protocol A part of the main protocol for the Internet that allows for computers to easily communicate with each other over a network.

troll A person who purposely vandalizes Wikipedia entries by inserting false or nonsensical information.

trolling The practice of posting deliberately obnoxious or disruptive messages to discussion groups or other online forums simply to get a reaction from the participants.

two-way symmetric model A model of public relations that emphasizes the profession as a system of managing relationships between organizations and individuals and their many publics.

user-generated content (UGC) Media content that has been created by consumers or audience members, including videos, music, or other forms of content.

uses-and-gratifications research A branch of research on media effects that looks at why people use particular media and examines what people do with the media rather than what the media do to people.

V-chip A computer device that enables parents or any other viewer to program a TV set to block access to programs containing violent and sexual content, based on the program rating.

viral marketing Spreading news and information about media content through word of mouth, usually via online discussion groups, chats, and emails, without utilizing traditional advertising and marketing methods.

Vladimir Zworykin Inventor of an improved cathode-ray tube he called the "iconoscope" that is the basis for the CRTs still used today in some television sets and computer monitors. He is considered one of the fathers of electronic television.

voice-over An unseen announcer or narrator talking while other activity takes place, either on radio or during a television scene.

Walter Elias Disney Creator of animated cartoon characters such as Mickey Mouse, Goofy, and Donald Duck and classic cartoons such as *Bambi*, *Snow White and the Seven Dwarfs*, and *Fantasia*. Founded the Disney media empire.

watermark A symbol or mark embedded in a photograph that identifies who owns the copyright for that photograph. With digital media, any piece of content can be watermarked, and the watermark, itself digital, can be completely invisible.

weak ties In social network analysis, the connections between people in different "small worlds," which tend not to be as tight or as close as strong ties but that are nevertheless extremely important in social networks.

widget A portable chunk of code that can be embedded in HTML pages and that often gives users extra functionality to their pages.

wiki A website that lets anyone add, edit, or delete pages and content.

word-of-mouth marketing Marketing that takes place among customers through discussions with each other.

yellow journalism A style of journalism practiced especially by publishers Joseph Pulitzer and William Randolph Hearst during the late 1890s in which stories were sensationalized and sometimes partly or wholly made up in order to be more dramatic.

CHAPTER 1

1. Thomas L. Friedman, "Global Village Idiocy," *New York Times,* May 12, 2002. Retrieved May 30, 2002, from http://www.nytimes.com.
2. Gary Gumpert and Robert Cathcart, eds., *Inter/Media: Interpersonal Communication in a Media World*, 3rd ed. (Oxford: Oxford University Press, 1986).
3. Irving Fang, *A History of Mass Communication: Six Information Revolutions* (Boston: Focal Press, 1997).
4. Jon Kraukauer, *Into Thin Air,* (Anchor Books, 1999).
5. Communication Workers of America report, "Speed Matters: Affordable High Speed Internet Access for America," November 2010. Retrieved March 3, 2011, from http://cwa.3cdn.net/299ed94e144d5adeb1_mlblqoxe9.pdf
6. Xiyun Yang, "China's Censors Reign in 'Vulgar' Reality TV Show," *New York Times*, July 18, 2010. Retrieved April 12, 2012, from http://www.nytimes.com/2010/07/19/world/asia/19chinatv.html?pagewanted=all.
7. Kevin Widdop, "Desperate Chinese Boy, 17, Sells Kidney for £2000 to Buy an iPad and iPhone," *Mail Online*, April 7, 2012. Retrieved April 12, 2012, from http://www.dailymail.co.uk/news/article-2126172/Chinese-boy-sells-kidney-buy-iPad-iPhone.html.
8. Harold D. Lasswell, "The Structure and Function of Communication in Society," in *The Communication of Ideas,* ed. Lyman Bryson (New York: Institute for Religious and Social Studies, Jewish Theological Seminary of America, 1948), 37.
9. Claude E. Shannon and Warren Weaver, *The Mathematical Theory of Communication* (Urbana, IL: The University of Illinois Press, 1964), 7.
10. Wilbur Schramm, "How Communication Works," in *The Process and Effects of Mass Communication,* ed. Wilbur Schramm (Urbana, IL: The University of Illinois Press, 1961), 5–6. Retrieved January 25, 2002, from http://muextension.missouri.edu/xplor/comm/cm0109.htm.
11. J. W. Carey, "A Cultural Approach to Communications," *Communication* 2 (1975): 1–22.
12. Werner J. Severin and James W. Tankard Jr., "Introduction to Mass Communication Theory," in *Communication Theories: Origins, Methods, and Uses in the Mass Media*, 5th ed. (New York: Addison Wesley Longman, 2001), 16.
13. "Wired, Zapped, and Beamed, 1960's through 1980's," FCC website. Retrieved October 20, 2011, from http://transition.fcc.gov/omd/history/tv/1960–1989.html.

CHAPTER 2

1. W. James Potter, *Media Literacy*, 2nd ed. (Thousand Oaks: Sage Publications, 2001): 4–7.
2. "Who Pays for Public Broadcasting?" Corporation for Public Broadcasting website. Retrieved July 31, 2009, from http://www.cpb.org/aboutpb/faq/pays.html.
3. "About Hallmark Channel," Hallmark Channel website. Retrieved October 12, 2008, from http://www.hallmarkchannel.com/tv/about/index.asp.
4. "Broadband Penetration Tops 50% in United States," Dornfeld Management, January 8. 2008. Retrieved March 14, 2012, from http://dornfeld.wordpress.com/2008/01/08/broadband-penetration-tops-50-in-united-states/.
5. "Mobile Devices," European Travel Commission, May 9, 2012. Retrieved May 14, 2012, from http://www.newmediatrendwatch.com/mar kets-by-country/17-usa/855-mobile-devices?start=1.
6. "Top Trends of 2010: Growth of eBooks and eReaders," Richard MacManus. ReadWriteWeb.com, Dec. 24, 2010. Retrieved March 15, 2011, from http://www.readwriteweb.com/archives/ebooks_ereaders_top_trends_2010.php
7. "Interactivity," Whatis.com, http://whatis.techtarget.com/definition/0,,sid9_gci212361,00.html. Retrieved May 15, 2002.
8. Sheizaf Rafaeli, "Networked Interactivity," *Journal of Computer Mediated Communication*, http://jcmc.indiana.edu/vol2/issue4/rafaeli.sudweeks.html#Interactivity. Retrieved August 3, 2009.
9. Jim Giles, "Internet Encyclopaedias Go Head to Head," *Nature 438* (December 15, 2005): 900-901.

CHAPTER 3

1. David Streitfeld, "Cut in E-Book Pricing by Amazon Is Set to Shake Rivals," *New York Times*, April 11, 2012. Retrieved April 12, 2012, from http://www.nytimes.com/2012/04/12/business/media/amazon-to-cut-e-book-prices-shaking-rivals.html?pagewanted=all.
2. Ibid.
3. National Endowment for the Arts, "Reading at Risk: A Survey of Literary Reading in America" (June 2004). Research Division Report #46, http://www.nea.gov/pub/ReadingAtRisk.pdf. Retrieved October 20, 2011.
4. Marshall McLuhan. *The Gutenberg Galaxy: The making of typographic man.* (Toronto, Canada: University of Toronto Press, 1962): 293.
5. "'Flat is the New Up' according to the Book Industry Study Group's comprehensive annual research publication," (June 3, 2009) BISG press release. Retrieved July 6, 2011, from http://www.bisg.org/news-5-363-press-releasebook-industry-trends-2009-indicates-publishers-net-revenue-up-10-in-2008-to-reach-4032-billion.php
6. Fabrice Piault, "Livres Hebdo's Ranking of the World's Leading Publishers," (2010) Livres Hebdo. Retrieved July 7, 2011, from http://www.publishersweekly.com/binary-data/ARTICLE_ATTACHMENT/file/000/000/127-1.pdf.
7. "AAP Publishers Report Strong in Year-to-Year, Year-End Book Sales," (Feb. 16, 2011) Association of American Pub-

lishers press release. Retrieved July 5, 2011, from http://www.publishers.org/press/24/.

8. Audit Bureau of Circulation, Retrieved May 8, 2012, http://accessabc.wordpress.com/2012/05/01/the-top-u-s-newspapers-for-march-2012/.

9. Metro website "About" page. Retrieved April 12, 2012, from http://www.metro.lu/about.

10. *Editor and Publisher International Year Book,* 88th ed. (New York: Editor & Publisher, 2008).

11. Steve Mariotti, Debra DeSalvo, and Tony Towle, *The Young Entrepreneur's Guide to Starting and Running a Business* (New York: Three Rivers Press, 2000).

CHAPTER 4

1. "Biography of Alan Freed," Alan Freed website. Retrieved August 18, 2002, from http://www.alanfreed.com.

2. Steve Jones, "Music industry sales are up, up, up this year," (July 8, 2011) *USA Today.* Retrieved July 8, 2011 from http://www.usatoday.com/life/music/news/2011-07-06-music-sales-jump-this-year_n.htm.

3. "Granville Woods," Black Inventor Online Museum, (n.d.). Retrieved August 3, 2009, from http://www.blackinventor.com/pages/granville woods.html.

4. Bob Lochte, "The Life and Legend of Nathan B. Stubblefield: A Chronology." Retrieved May 17, 2002, from http://campus.murraystate.edu/academic/faculty/bob.lochte/NBSDates.htm.

5. Thomas White, "'Battle of the Century': The WJY Story," United States Early Radio website. Retrieved August 18, 2002, from http://earlyradiohistory.us/WJY.htm (January 1, 2000).

6. Leil Leibovitz, "Radio Daze" (Feb. 11, 2011). Tablet online. Retrieved July 24, 2011, from http://www.tabletmag.com/life-and-religion/58759/radio-daze/.

7. Albert N. Greco, "The Structure of the Radio Industry," in *The Media and Entertainment Industries,* ed. Albert N. Greco (Boston: Allyn & Bacon, 2000).

8. National Public Radio website. Retrieved May 18, 2002, from http://www.npr.org.

9. Public Radio International website. Retrieved May 18, 2002, from http://www.pri.org.

CHAPTER 5

1. Robert Leggat, "The Beginnings of Photography," A History of Photography website. Retrieved May 15, 2002, from http://www.rleggat.com/photohistory/.

2. Ibid.

3. John V. Pavlik, *New Media Technology* (Boston: Allyn & Bacon, 1999).

4. Elizabeth Valk Long, "The Life and Death of Kevin Carter," *Time,* September 12, 1994. Retrieved June 2, 2002, from http://home-4.tiscali.nl/~t892660/msp/time.htm.

5. "Sprocket Holes: The Lumière Brothers," retrieved June 3, 2002, from presscard.com/www.presscard.com/sprocket holes2.html; "The Biography of Thomas Alva Edison," retrieved August 3, 2009, from ThomasEdison.com, http://www.thomasedison.com/biography.html.

6. Erik Barnouw, *Documentary: A History of the Non-Fiction Film,* 2nd rev. ed. (New York: Oxford University Press, 1993).

7. Stephen Zeitchik, "Popularity of 3-D Is Affecting How Screenplays Are Written," *Los Angeles Times,* April 25, 2010. Retrieved May 16, 2012, from http://articles.latimes.com/2010/apr/25/entertainment/la-ca-3ddirector-20100425.

8. Barry R. Litman, *The Motion Picture Mega-Industry* (Boston: Allyn & Bacon, 1998), 74–88.

9. "Yearly Box Office," Box Office Mojo.com. Retrieved July 25, 2011, from http://boxofficemojo.com/yearly/?view2=domestic&view=releasedate&p=.htm.

10. Ryan Nakashima, "Too real means too creepy in new Disney animation," (April 4, 2011) Victoria Advocate.com. Retrieved April 24, 2011, from http://www.victoriaadvocate.com/news/2011/apr/04/bc-us-tec-creepy-animation/?entertainment&national-entertainment.

11. "Curtains Rise Halfway on Digital Cinema," *Business 2.0* (May 29, 2001): 32–33.

12. "Television Bureau of Advertising Online: Television Facts," Television Bureau of Advertising. Retrieved August 16, 2011, from http://www.tvb.org/trends/95487.

13. NPD Group, "NPD Group: Average Monthly Pay-TV Subscription Bills May Top $200 by 2020," NPD.com website. Retrieved November 21, 2012, from https://www.npd.com/wps/portal/npd/us/news/press-releases/pr_120410/.

14. John Carey, *Winky Dink to Stargazer: Five Decades of Interactive Television* (Dobbs Ferry, NY: Greystone Communication, 1998).

CHAPTER 6

1. "Google Flu Trends," Google website. Retrieved November 1, 2008, from http://www.google.org/flutrends/.

2. Steve Lohr, "Is Information Overload a $650 Billion Drag on the Economy?" *New York Times*, December 20, 2007. Retrieved October 21, 2008, from http://bits.blogs.nytimes.com/2007/12/20/is-information-overload-a-650-billion-drag-on-the-economy/.

3. Lisa Napoli, "A Gadget That Taught a Nation to Surf: The TV Remote Control," *New York Times*, February 11, 1999. Retrieved January 10, 2002, from http://www.nytimes.com/library/tech/99/02/circuits/articles/11howw.html.

4. John Carey, *Winky Dink to Stargazer: Five Decades of Interactive Television* (Dobbs Ferry, NY: Greystone Communication, 1998).

5. "Control Data Corporation Historical Timeline," Charles Babbage Institute Collections website. Retrieved August 3, 2009, from http://www.cbi.umn.edu/collections/cdc/histtimeline.html .

6. "Internet World Users By Language: Top 10 Users," Internet World Stats (May 21, 2011). Retrieved July 1, 2011, from http://www.internetworldstats.com/stats7.htm.

7. "Panel: Interactivity Ethics" (Jan. 25, 2006), washingtonpost.com. Retrieved October 20, 2008, from http://www.washingtonpost.com/wp-dyn/content/discussion/2006/01/24/DI2006012400817.html.

CHAPTER 7

1. Ai Weiwei, "China's censorship can never defeat the internet," *The Guardian,* April 15, 2012. Retrieved May 16, 2012, from http://www.guardian.

co.uk/commentisfree/libertycentral/2012/apr/16/china-censorship-internet-freedom.

2. Susan Taylor Martin, "Scrappy Al-Jazeera Stands Up," *St. Petersburg Times*, September 22, 2002.

3. Judith Newman, "Ray Tomlinson: Inventor of E-Mail, a New Discourse," *Intelligent Systems* (July 2002), Volume IX, No. 2. Retrieved August 3, 2009, from http://www.chenaultsystems.com/articles/Intell33.htm.

4. Internet World Stats, "Usage and Population Statistics," February 14, 2011. Retrieved February 14, 2011, from http://www.internetworldstats.com/am/us.htm.

5. Ibid.

6. Robert Hobbes' Zakon, "Hobbes' Internet Timeline," version 5.6, Zakon.org. Retrieved June 20, 2002, from http://www.zakon.org/robert/internet/timeline/.

7. George T. Hawley, "DSL: Broadband by Phone," *Scientific American* (October 1999): 102–105.

8. P. William Bane and Stephen P. Bradley, "The Light at the End of the Pipe," *Scientific American* (October 1999): 110–115.

9. David D. Clark, "High-Speed Data Races Home," *Scientific American* (October 1999): 95–96.

10. "What is Freenet?" Freenet website, n.d. Retrieved October 20, 2011, from http://freenetproject.org/whatis.html.

CHAPTER 8

1. John Jantsch, "The Definition of Social Media," Duct Tape Marketing blog, September 25, 2008. Retrieved February 20, 2009, from http://www.ducttapemarketing.com/blog/2008/09/25/the-definition-of-social-media/.

2. Brian Solis, "The Definition of Social Media," WebPro News, June 29, 2007. Retrieved February 20, 2009, from http://www.webpronews.com/blogtalk/ 2007/06/29/the-definition-of-social-media.

3. Anvil Media, "Resources: SEM Glossary of Terms," n.d. Retrieved February 20, 2009, from http://www.anvilmediainc.com/search-engine-marketing-glossary.html.

4. Clay Shirky, *Here Comes Everybody: How Change Happens When People Come Together* (Penguin Group: 2009).

5. Jessica Clark and Patricia Aufderheide, "Public Media 2.0: Dynamic, Engaged Publics," February 2009. Retrieved March 17, 2009, from http://www.centerfor socialmedia.org/documents/whitepaper.pdf.

6. Erin Kutz, "Just a Few on Twitter Do All the Tweeting: Study," Reuters, June 5, 2009. Retrieved June 5, 2009, from http://tech.yahoo.com/news/nm/20090605/wr_nm/us_twitter_study_3.

7. Benny Evangelista, "Social media sites become No. 1 Internet activity," (Aug. 3, 2010). SFGate.com. Retrieved July 14, 2011, from http://articles.sfgate.com/2010-08-03/business/22010227_1_online-activity-zynga-game-network-mafia-wars.

8. Sarah Kessler, "Tumblr Now Has More Blogs Than Wordpress.com," (June 15, 2011) Mashable.com. Retrieved July 18, 2011, from http://mashable.com/2011/06/15/tumblr-surpasses-wordpress/.

9. Danah M. Boyd and Nicole B. Ellison, "Social Network Sites: Definition, History, and Scholarship," *Journal of Computer-Mediated Communication 13*, no. 1 (2007): article 11. Retrieved April 4, 2009, from http://jcmc.indiana.edu/vol13/issue1/boyd.ellison.html.

10. Axel Bruns, *Blogs, Wikipedia, Second Life, and Beyond: From Production to Produsage* (New York: Peter Lang, 2008).

CHAPTER 9

1. Pulitzer Prizes, "The 2012 Pulitzer Prize Winners: National Reporting." Retrieved April 17, 2012, from http://www.pulitzer.org/citation/2012-National-Reporting.

2. Sheri Fink, "The Deadly Choices at Memorial." Retrieved May 16, 2012, from http://www.pulitzer.org/works/2010-Investigative-Reporting-Group2. Originally published in *The New York Times Magazine*, August 30, 2009.

3. David Wood, "Beyond the Battlefield: From a Decade of War, an Endless Struggle for the Severely Wounded," *Huffington Post*, October 10, 2011. Retrieved May 16, 2012, from http://www.huffingtonpost.com/2011/10/10/beyond-the-battlefield-part-1-tyler-southern_n_999329.html?ncid=edlinkusaolp00000003.

4. Wikipedia, s.v. "The Huffington Post," Retrieved May 16, 2012, from http://en.wikipedia.org/wiki/The_Huffington_Post.

5. David Wood, "Beyond the Battlefield: From a Decade of War, an Endless Struggle for the Severely Wounded," *Huffington Post*, October 10, 2011. Retrieved May 16, 2012, from http://www.huffingtonpost.com/2011/10/10/beyond-the-battlefield-part-1-tyler-southern_n_999329.html?ncid=edlinkusaolp00000003.

6. "Afghanistan," *Huffington Post*. Retrieved May 8, 2012, from http://www.huffingtonpost.com/news/afghanistan.

7. The Write Site, "Tracing the Story of Journalism in the United States." Retrieved October 20, 2011, from http://www.writesite.org/html/tracing.html.

8. "Facts and Figures," (2011). Associated Press Website. Retrieved July 27, 2011, from http://www.ap.org/pages/about/about.html.

9. Joseph Pulitzer, "The College of Journalism," *North American Review* (May 1904).

10. Michael G. Robinson, American Culture Studies, "1890s" course, spring 1996. Retrieved October 20, 2011, from http://www.bgsu.edu/departments/acs/1890s/yellowkid/yellow1.html.

11. George Seldes, "Farewell: Lord of San Simeon," in *Lords of the Press* (New York: Julian Messner, 1938).

12. Charlie LeDuff, "At a Slaughterhouse, Some Things Never Die." The Pulitzer Prizes. Posted June 16, 2000. Retrieved May 14, 2012, from http://www.pulitzer.org/archives/6495.

13. "Interview: Charlie LeDuff of the *New York Times*," Journalism Jobs. Posted March 2001. Retrieved May 14, 2012, from http://www.journalismjobs.com/interview_leduff.cfm.

14. "About Us," (n.d.) ProPublica.org. Retrieved July 28, 2011, from http://www.propublica.org/about/.

CHAPTER 10

1. Dolf Zillman, "The Coming of Entertainment," in *Media Entertainment: The Psychology of its Appeal*, Peter Voderer, ed. Dolf Zillman (Mahwah, NJ: Lawrence Erlbaum Associates, 2000), 17.

2. Dolf Zillman, "The Coming of Entertainment," in *Media Entertainment: The Psychology of its Appeal*, Peter Voderer, ed.

Dolf Zillman (Mahwah, NJ: Lawrence Erlbaum Associates, 2000), 9.

3. "Wikipedia Goes Dark for 24 Hours to Protest Web Piracy Bills," *Fox News*, January 18, 2012. Retrieved May 14, 2012, from http://www.foxnews.com/scitech/2012/01/18/wikipedia-goes-dark-for-24-hours-to-protest-us-web-piracy-bills/.

4. Anne-Marie, "MegaUpload and MegaVideo Go Dark," January 20, 2012. Retrieved May 14, 2012, from http://www.girlgameresq.com/2012/01/megaupload-and-megavideo-go-dark/.

5. *Les Brown's Encyclopedia of Television*, 3rd ed. (Detroit, MI: Gale Research, 1992).

6. "Factbox: A look at the $65 billion video games industry," (June 6, 2011) Reuters. Retrieved July 31, 2011, from http://uk.reuters.com/article/2011/06/06/us-videogames-factbox-idUKTRE75552I20110606.

7. Ian Williams, "Chinese Gamer Dies after 15-Day Session," V3.co.uk, March 1, 2007. Retrieved May 14, 2012, from http://www.v3.co.uk/v3-uk/news/1998377/chinese-gamer-dies-day-session.

8. Kimberly Sorensen, "Colorado State University Study Examines Potential Positive Effects of Video Games," Colorado State University News & Information website, April 4, 2011. Retrieved May 14, 2012, from http://www.news.colostate.edu/Release/5653.

9. Christine Hanson, Ranald D. Hansen, "Music and Music Videos," in *Media Entertainment: The Psychology of Its Appeal*, Peter Voderer, ed. Dolf Zillman (Mahwah, NJ: Lawrence Erlbaum Associates, 2000), 179–181.

10. For example, *A Fool There Was*, Fox, 1915; Eve Golden, *Vamp: The Rise and Fall of Theda Bara* (West Vestal: Emprise Publishing, 1996).

CHAPTER 11

1. A project of the Digital Scriptorium, Rare Book, Manuscript, and Special Collections Library, Duke University. Copyright 2000 Duke University. Retrieved October 31, 2002, from http://scriptorium.lib.duke.edu/eaa/timeline.html.

2. Kathleen Hall Jamieson, *Dirty Politics* (New York: Oxford University Press, 1992), 54–55.

3. "Kony 2012: A Month Later in Social Video," *The Visible Measures Blog*, April 13, 2012. Retrieved May 14, 2012, from http://corp.visiblemeasures.com/news-and-events/blog/bid/81165/Kony-2012-A-Month-Later-in-Social-Video.

4. Todd Wasserman, "'KONY 2012' Tops 100 Million Views, Becomes the Most Viral Video in History," Mashable.com, March 12, 2012. Retrieved May 14, 2012 from http://mashable.com/2012/03/12/kony-most-viral/.

5. Samantha Grossman, "'Kony 2012' Documentary Becomes Most Viral Video in History," *Time*, March 12, 2012. Retrieved May 14, 2012, from http://newsfeed.time.com/2012/03/12/kony-2012-documentary-becomes-most-viral-video-in-history/.

6. Marilyn Hagerty, "THE EATBEAT: Long-awaited Olive Garden receives warm welcome." *Grand Forks Herald*, March 7, 2012. Retrieved May 14, 2012, from http://www.grandforksherald.com/event/article/id/231419/.

7. James R. Hagerty, "When Mom Goes Viral," *Wall Street Journal*, March 12, 2012. Retrieved May 14, 2012, from http://online.wsj.com/article/SB10001424052702304537904577275683631110396.html.

8. Lauren Torrisi, "Olive Garden Review Goes Viral: The 'Largest and Most Beautiful Restaurant,'" *Yahoo News*, March 9, 2012. Retrieved May 14, 2012, from http://news.yahoo.com/blogs/abc-blogs/olive-garden-review-goes-viral-largest-most-beautiful-183337549--abc-news.html.

9. Stephen Millies, "The Ludlow Massacre and the Birth of Company Unions," Workers World, January 26, 1995. Retrieved October 31, 2002, from http://www.hartford-hwp.com/archives/45b/030.html.

10. Daniel J. Boorstin, "From News-Gathering to News-Making: A Flood of Pseudo Events," in *The Modern World: The Image* (New York: Vintage, 1961). 7–44.

11. David Streitfed, "In a Race to Out-Rave, 5-Star Web Reviews Go for $5," *New York Times*, August 19, 2011. Retrieved May 14, 2012, from http://www.nytimes.com/2011/08/20/technology/finding-fake-reviews-online.html.

12. Myle Ott Yejin, Choi Claire Cardie, and Jeffrey T. Hancock, "Finding Deceptive Opinion Spam by Any Stretch of the Imagination," *Proceedings of the 49th Annual Meeting of the Association for Computational Linguistics*, Portland, Oregon, June 19–24, 2011, pp. 309–19. Retrieved May 14, 2012, from http://aclweb.org/anthology/P/P11/P11-1032.pdf.

CHAPTER 12

1. William W. Neher, Paul J. Sandin, *Communicating Ethically: Character, Duties, Consequences, and Relationships* (Boston: Pearson, 2007); Clifford G. Christians, Mark Fackler, Peggy Kreshel, and Kathy Brittain McKee, *Media Ethics: Cases and Moral Reasoning*, 8th ed. (Boston: Allyn & Bacon, 2008), 1–34.

2. William A. Henry III, Joseph R. Szczesny, "Where NBC Went Wrong." *Time* magazine. Monday, Feb. 22, 1993. Retrieved August 16, 2011, from http://www.time.com/time/magazine/article/0,9171,977814,00.html

3. "US v. Naughton: One-Off Criminal 'Fantasy Defense,' or Turning Point for the Jurisprudence of Online Identity?" Retrieved August 16, 2011, from http://xenia.media.mit.edu/~rowan/memepark/2006/09/us-v-naughton-one-off-criminal-fantasy.html

CHAPTER 13

1. Dwight L. Teeter Jr. and Don R. Le Duc, *Law of Mass Communications* (Westbury, NY: The Foundation Press, 1992).

2. "How Effective Are Shield Laws?," *Agents of Discovery: A Report on the Incidence of Subpoenas Served on the News Media in 1997*, Reporters Committee for Freedom of the Press website, http://www.rcfp.org. Retrieved November 8, 2002, from http://www.rcfp.org/agents/shieldlaws.html.

3. Reed E. Hundt, FCC Chairman, transcript of speech given at the Museum of Television and Radio, New York, New York, June 3, 1997. Retrieved November 8, 2002, from http://www.fcc.gov/Speeches/Hundt/spreh729.txt.

4. Linda Greenhouse, "'Virtual' Child Pornography Ban Overturned," *New York Times*, April 17, 2002. Retrieved April 17, 2002, from http://www.nytimes.com.

5. Mark Goodman, "The Radio Act of 1927 as a Product of Progressivism," vol. 2, no. 2., *Media History Monographs.* Retrieved November 8, 2002, from http://www.scripps.ohiou.edu/mediahistory/mhmjour2-2.htm.

6. Erik Barnouw, *A Tower of Babel: A History of Broadcasting in the United States,* vol. 1 (New York: Oxford University Press, 1966).

7. Mark Goodman, "The Radio Act of 1927 as a Product of Progressivism," vol. 2, no. 2. Media History Monographs. Retrieved November 8, 2002, from http://www.scripps.ohiou.edu/mediahistory/mhmjour2-2.htm.

8. M. S. Mander, "The Public Debate About Broadcasting in the Twenties: An Interpretive History," *Journal of Broadcasting* 28 (1984): 167–185.

9. Alan B. Albarran and Gregory G. Pitts, *The Radio Broadcasting Industry* (Boston: Allyn & Bacon, 2001), 27–29.

10. Eli Noam and Robert Freeman, "Global Competition," *Television Quarterly* (1998) Vol. 29, number 1, 18–23.

11. D. Benjamin Satkowiak, "Combating the Dangers of Journalism," *Yahoo! Voices,* February 5, 2011. Retrieved April 16, 2012, from: http://voices.yahoo.com/combating-dangers-journalism-7780340.html?cat=49.

CHAPTER 14

1. Tom Gormley, "'Ruination Once Again': Cases in the Study of Media Effects," theory.org.uk, 1998. Retrieved November 4, 2002, from http://www.theory.org.uk/effec-tg.htm.

2. Garth S. Jowett, Ian C. Jarvie, and Kathryn H. Fuller, eds., *Children and the Movies: Media Influence and the Payne Fund Controversy* (Cambridge: Cambridge University Press, 1996).

3. P. W. Holaday and G. D. Stoddard, *Getting Ideas from the Movies* (New York: Macmillan, 1933).

4. Garth Jowett et al., "Payne Fund Radio Broadcasting Research, 1928–1935," in *Children and the Movies: Media Influence and the Payne Fund Controversy* (Cambridge: Cambridge University Press, 1996).

5. "Television Advertising and Childhood Obesity, Part 5," Childhood Obesity News, December 13, 2010. Retrieved April 16, 2012, from http://childhoodobesitynews.com/2010/12/13/television-advertising-and-childhood-obesity-part-5/.

6. R. S. Lichter and D. Amundson, *A Day of Television Violence* (Washington, D.C.: Center for Media and Public Affairs, 1992).

7. Rolf Wigand Lichter, "Communication and Violent Behavior," *ICA Newsletter* (July 1999): 5.

8. Leonard Eron, University of Illinois at Chicago, testimony before the Senate Committee on Commerce, Science and Transportation, Subcommittee on Communications, June 12, 1995.

9. Statistics compiled by TV-Free America, Washington, D.C., 1996.

10. National Television Violence Study, issued by Mediascope, February 1996.

11. The UCLA Television Violence Monitoring Report, issued by the UCLA Center for Communications Policy, September 1995.

12. Jeffrey Cole, "Surveying the Digital Future: A Longitudinal International Study of the Individual and Social Effects of PC/Internet Technology." Retrieved November 5, 2002, from http://www.webuse.umd.edu/abstracts2001/abstract_2001_cole.htm.

13. Paul F. Lazarsfeld and Robert K. Merton, "Mass Communication, Popular Taste and Organized Social Action," in *The Communication of Ideas,* ed. Lyman Bryson (New York: Institute for Religious and Social Studies, 1948), 95–118.

14. Bernard Cohen, *The Press and Foreign Policy* (Princeton, NJ: Princeton University Press, 1963), 13.

CHAPTER 15

1. "Super PACS," OpenSecrets.org. Retrieved May 8, 2012, from http://www.opensecrets.org/pacs/superpacs.php.

2. Michael Isikoff, "Karl Rove's Election Debacle: Super PAC's Spending Was Nearly for Naught." Retrieved on November 13, 2012, from http://openchannel.nbcnews.com/_news/2012/11/08/15007504-karl-roves-election-debacle-super-pacs-spending-was-nearly-for-naught?lite.

3. Joseph Pulitzer, "The College of Journalism," *North American Review,* May 1904.

4. Fred S. Siebert, Wilbur Schramm, and Theodore Peterson, *Four Theories of the Press: The Authoritarian, Libertarian, Social Responsibility, and Soviet Communist Concepts of What the Press Should Be and Do* (Champaign, Illinois: University of Illinois Press, 1956).

5. Daniel C. Hallin, "Sound Bite News: Television Coverage of Elections 1968–1988," *Journal of Communication,* Vol. 42, 1992.

6. Herbert E. Alexander, "Financing Presidential Election Campaigns," *Issues of Democracy,* USIA Electronic Journals 1, no. 13 (September 1996). Retrieved November 7, 2002, from http://usinfo.state.gov/journals/itdhr/0996/ijde/alex.htm.

7. Larry Sabato, *The Rise of Political Consultants: New Way of Winning Elections* (NY: Basic Books, 1981), 165–166.

8. Kathleen Hall Jamieson, *Dirty Politics* (New York: Oxford University Press, 1992), 19–20.

9. Claire Cain Miller, "How Obama's Internet Campaign Changed Politics," *New York Times,* November 7, 2008.

CREDITS

CHAPTER 1

Page 2, paper.li; page 6, ©iStockphoto.com/calvio; page 7, ©iStockphoto.com/mbbirdy; page 9, ©iStockphoto.com/Bosca78; page 10, © Creative Commons, http://creativecommons.org licenses/by/3.0/; page 11, ©iStockphoto.com/track5; page 16, Michael Newman/PhotoEdit; page 20, AFP/Getty Images; page 21, Jeremy Woodhouse/Blend Images/Getty Images; page 24, Chris Hondros/Getty Images; page 25 (top) The Granger Collection, New York; page 25 (middle) Neno Images/PhotoEdit; page 25 (bottom) Danny Feld/©ABC/Getty Images; page 29, © The Poynter Institute

CHAPTER 2

Page 34, CBS Photo Archive/Getty; page 39, Will Hart/PhotoEdit; page 41, ©iStockphoto.com/LeggNet; page 43, Ryuhei Shindo/Getty Images; page 45, © Aftonbladet New Media; page 47, ERIC MENCHER/MCT/Landov; page 60, ©iStockphoto.com/skodonnell; page 61, ©iStockphoto.com/adamkatz; page 62, © OpenOffice.org, Used with permission; page 65, ©iStockphoto.com/mbbirdy;

CHAPTER 3

Page 70, © GOOD Worldwide LLC. All rights reserved; page 74, Derek Capitaine Photography; page 76 (top) LIBRARY OF CONGRESS, Asian Room; page 76 (bottom) Two folios from the Gutenberg Bible, printed in the workshop of Johannes Gutenberg, 1455 (parchment), German School, Universitatsbibliothek, Gottingen, Germany/Bildarchiv Steffens/The Bridgeman Art Library; page 77, North Wind Picture Archives via AP Photo; page 78 (top) The Granger Collection, New York; page 78 (bottom) Copyright The Internet Archive, http://www.archive.org/texts/bookmobile.php; page 80, Aubrey Wade/Panos Pictures; page 83, Front cover of newspaper reproduced courtesy of The Yomiuri Shimbun; page 84, Public Domain; page 86, The Granger Collection, New York; page 87, Bloomberg/Getty Images; page 96, Special Collections, Stanford University Libraries; page 97, AP Photo/Mark Elias; page 100, ©iStockphoto.com/seraficus

CHAPTER 4

Page 104, Paul Burns/Lifesize/Getty Images; page 108, ©iStockphoto.com/faruk_tasdemir; page 107 (top) The Granger Collection, New York; page 107 (bottom) The Granger Collection, New York; page 113, Hulton Archive/Getty Images; page 115, Electronic Frontier Foundation; page 116, ©iStockphoto.com/pressureUA; page 117, JUPITERIMAGES/ABLESTOCK/Alamy; page 119, Science and Society Picture Library/Getty Images; page 120, Keystone-France/Getty Images; page 122, Bettman/Corbis; page 128, © Lifeline Energy; page 129, Theo Wargo/WireImage/ Getty Images; page 130, L. Busacca/Getty Images; page 131, Bloomberg/Getty Images

CHAPTER 5

Page 134, Yap.tv; page 137, Frank Schwere / Getty Images; page 138, Library of Congress, Prints & Photographs Division LC-B811-557; page 139 (top) Library of Congress Copyright Science Faction/Getty Images; page 139 (middle) Eadweard Muybridge/Getty Images; page 139 (bottom) Vintage Image/Alamy; page 140, Kevin Carter/Megan Patricia Carter Trust/Sygma/Corbis; page 141, ©iStockphoto.com/andrearoad; page 142, Tom Kingston/WireImage/Getty Images; page 143, Time Life Pictures/Mansell/Time Life Pictures/Getty Images; page 144, GOSKINO/THE KOBAL COLLECTION; page 145, WARNER BROS/THE KOBAL COLLECTION; page 147, Bloomberg/Getty Images; page 148, RKO/THE KOBAL COLLECTION/KHALE, ALEX; page 153, Robyn Beck/Getty Images; page 155, Bettman/Corbis; page 156, Bettman/Corbis; page 157, ©iStockphoto.com/Swartz; page 159, CRACK PALINGGI/Reuters/Landov; page 163, Alexandra Wyman/Getty Images

CHAPTER 6

Page 166, ©iStockphoto.com/Mari; page 169, ©iStockphoto.com/pidjoe; page 170, ©iStockphoto.com/cosmin4000; page 171, ©iStockphoto.com/makkayak; page 173, Bettman/Corbis; page 174, Howard Sochurek/Time Life Pictures/Getty Images; page 175, Justin Sullivan/Getty Images; page 176, Courtesy of the Computer History Museum; page 178, ©iStockphoto.com/eyewave; page 180, ©iStockphoto.com/Yobro10; page 181, Source Watch; page 183 (top) ©iStockphoto.com/Haneck; page 183 (bottom) ©iStockphoto.com/Rouzes; page 185 (top) SRI International, Menlo Park, CA; page 185 (bottom) OUP; page 186, MGM/THE KOBAL COLLECTION; page 187, Istockphoto 16454348; page 188, Copyright Bump Technologies; page 189 (top) ©iStockphoto.com/georgeclerk; page 189 (bottom) Mike Margol/PhotoEdit; page 195, Apic/Getty Images

CHAPTER 7

Page 198, Peter Macdiarmid/Getty Images; page 205 (top) Bettman/Corbis; page 205 (bottom) Mary Evans Picture Library; page 206, ©iStockphoto.com/twoellis; page 207, Associated Press; page 208, REUTERS/Mohammed Dubbous/Landov; page 209 (top) Sheila Terry/Photo Researchers; page 209 (bottom) ©iStockphoto.com/Smileyjoanne; page 220, ©iStockphoto.com/chrisboy2004; page 222, Jeff Kravitz/FilmMagic/Getty Images; page 223, Mark Richards/PhotoEdit; page 225, Justin Sullivan/Newsmakers/Getty Images; page 228, Courtesy of BitTorrent Inc.; page 229, ©iStockphoto.com/TebNab; page 231, Dan Kitwood/Getty Images

CHAPTER 8

Page 236, Timothy A. Clary/Getty Images; page 241, Lionsgate; page 245 (top) Andy Sheppard/Redferns/Getty Images; page 245 (bottom) Xinhua/Landov; page 246, ©iStockphoto.com/PeskyMonkey; page 247, Susan Van Etten/PhotoEdit; page 250, Andrew H. Walker/Getty Images; page 251, ©iStockphoto.com/Alija; page 257, Michael Tran/Getty Images

CHAPTER 9

Page 266, Amy Sussman/Getty Images; page 270, Jim DeLillo, Photographer; page 271, ©iStockphoto.com/stocksnapper; page 272 (top) Used with permission, Library Archives of Canada; page 272 (bottom) The Granger Collection, New York; page 274 (top) Hulton Archive/Getty Images; page 274 (bottom) Hulton Archive/Getty Images; page 275, Hulton Archive/Getty Images; page 276, Mike Margol/PhotoEdit; page 278, Courtesy of APCOR—Portuguese Cork Association; page 280 (top) Jeff Greenberg/PhotoEdit; page 280 (bottom) Brendan Smialowski/Getty Images for Meet the Press; page 281, MUSA AL-SHAER/

AFP/Getty Images; page 282, Spencer Grant/PhotoEdit; page 282, Richard Levine/Alamy; page 286, Laura Dwight/PhotoEdit; page 289, ©iStockphoto.com/franckreporter; page 291, Mike Margol/PhotoEdit; page 292, claude thibault/Alamy; page 293, Frank J. Parker; page 294, Getty Images; page 296, Courtesy of Condace Pressley/Photo by Ian Irving

CHAPTER 10

Page 300, Boston Globe/Pat Greenhouse/Landov; page 302, ©iStockphoto.com/Maica; page 304, Mary Evans Picture Library; page 306, CBS/Landov; page 308, Jeff Kravitz/Getty Images; page 309, Mario Tama/Getty Images; page 311, Courtesy of Truth or Consequences/Sierra County Chamber of Commerce; page 313, Mike Hewitt/Getty Images; page 314, Jeff Daly/MTV/PictureGroup via AP Photo; page 315, Jeff Greenberg/PhotoEdit; page 316, General Photographic Agency/Getty Images; page 319 (top) Sunset Boulevard/Corbis, page 319 (bottom) UNIVERSAL/THE KOBAL COLLECTION; page 321, CONSTANTIN FILM/DAVIS-FILMS/THE KOBAL COLLECTION; page 322, ©iStockphoto.com/contrastaddict; page 323, Mike Margol/PhotoEdit; page 325, Michael Ochs Archives/Getty Images; page 326 (top) Bettman/Corbis; page 326 (bottom) Kmazur/WireImage/Getty Images; page 327, John Shearer/WireImage/Getty Images; page 328, Ted Streshinsky/Corbis; page 329, Silver Screen Collection/Getty Images; page 330, MICHAEL DE LUCA PRODUCTIONS/THE KOBAL COLLECTION; page 332, Donna Svennevick/Getty Images

CHAPTER 11

Page 336, MCT/Getty Images; page 338, Win McNamee/Getty Images; page 342, Michael Newman/PhotoEdit; page 343, Stuart Wilson/Getty Images; page 344, The Granger Collection, New York; page 345, The Granger Collection, New York; page 346, Photo by Jeanne Strongin, courtesy of www.tonyschwartz.com; page 347, Mike Margol/PhotoEdit; page 349, Book cover used with permission from Dan Schawbel; page 350, Kevin Foy/Alamy; page 351, Courtesy of Texas Department of Transportation; page 352, Borderlands/Alamy; page 353, WAYANS BROS. ENTERTAINMENT/THE KOBAL COLLECTION; page 354, Bloomberg/Getty Images; page 355, Rex Features/AP Images; page 357, Neno Images/PhotoEdit; page 360, Zhou junxiang—Imaginechina/AP Images; page 361, Bill Aron/PhotoEdit; page 62, Bloomberg/Getty Images; page 363 (top) Bloomberg via Getty Images; page 363 (bottom) Bettman/Corbis; page 366, Derek Capitaine Photography; page 368, Franco Origlia/Getty Images; page370, ©iStockphoto.com/slobo

CHAPTER 12

Page 374, Peter Macdiarmid/Getty Images; page 379, De Agostini Picture Library/Getty Images; page 380, Odd Anderson/Getty Images; page 383, The Washington Post/Getty Images; page 385, PhotoQuest/Getty Images; page 387 (left) CBS Photo Archive/Getty Images; page 387 (right) CBS Photo Archive/Getty Images; page 390, New York Daily News Archive/Getty Images; page 393 David McNew/Getty Images; page 394, Mike Nelson/Getty Images, page 297, Matt Sullivan/Getty Images

CHAPTER 13

Page 400, Erik Martin/reddit.com; page 403, Stock Montage/Getty Images; page 406 (top) Bettman/Corbis; page 406 (bottom) © 2009, The Progressive Magazine; page 407, The Granger Collection, New York; page 409 (top) © iStockphoto/garymilner; page 409 (bottom) Kevin Statham/Getty Images; page 410, Mike Margol/PhotoEdit; page 412, © Corbis; page 414, Courtesy of the Prometheus Radio Project; page 415, ANATOLI ZHDANOV/UPI/Landov; page 419, ©iStockphoto.com/MikeRega; page 421, Jonathan Edlerfield/Liaison/Getty Images; page 422, Gabriel Buoys/Getty Images; page 423, Ethan Miller/Getty Images; page 425, David Becker/Getty Images; page 427, Ida Mae Astute/Getty Images; page 428, LUCAS JACKSON/Reuters/Landov

CHAPTER 14

Page 423, Mike Margol/PhotoEdit; page 424, Nielsen People Meter, Courtesy of Nielsen; page 437, Bangque d'Images, ADAGP/Art Resource, NY; page 439, The Granger Collection, New York; page 440, FIRST NATIONAL/WARNER BROTHERS/THE KOBAL COLLECTION; page 441, CBS/THE KOBAL COLLECTION; page 443, Richard Baker/In Pictures/Corbis/AP Images; page 445, Bobby Bank/Getty Images; page 446, DON EMMERT/AFP/Getty Images; page 449 (top) Jim Steinfeldt/Getty Images; page 449 (bottom) A. Ramey/PhotoEdit; page 451, Bettman/Corbis; page 452, AFP/Getty Images; page 454 (top) Courtesy of University of Illinois at Urbana-Champaign, Department of Communication; page 454 (bottom) Leonard McCombe/Getty Images; page 455, Tom Carter/PhotoEdit; page 456, Canadian Press/Phototake; page 459 Spencer Grant/PhotoEdit

CHAPTER 15

Page 462, AP Photo/Comedy Central, Kristopher Long; page 464, NBC-TV/THE KOBAL COLLECTION/EDELSON, DANA; page 466, Alex Wong/Getty Images; page 467, Robin Nelson/PhotoEdit; page 468, Hulton Archive/Getty Images; page 469, STF/AFP/Getty Images; page 470, Mary Evans Picture Library; page 471, Atul Loke/Panos Pictures; page 472, Mark Richards/PhotoEdit; page 475, David Young-Wolff/PhotoEdit; page 477, Michael Newman/PhotoEdit; page 479, Neno Images/PhotoEdit; page 480, Ed Clark/Getty Images; page 482, The Washington Post/Contributor/Getty Images; page 483 (top) ©iStockphoto.com/andrearoad; page 483 (top) http://www.barackobama.com/truth-team/attack-watch; page 484, Courtesy of Mayhill Fowler, photo by Lisa Keating Photography; page 485, CHERYL RAVELO/Reuters/Landov

Page numbers in italics denote photographs; page numbers followed by "*f*" denote figures and those followed by "*t*" denote tables.

propaganda, 439–40, 446
    wartime, 25, 316, 362, 364, 394
ProPublica, 294
prosumers, 259
PRSA. See Public Relations Society of America
PSAs. See public service announcements
pseudo events, 270, 338, 366
P2P. See peer-to-peer
Public Broadcasting Service (PBS), 49–50,
    309–10, 417
public information campaigns, 350
public institutions, 49
Publicis Groupe, 360–61, 367
Publick Occurrences, 84, 85f
public opinion, 444–45, 447, 455, 469–70
Public Radio International (PRI), 127
public relations, 337–41, 361–69
    business of, 367–69, 368t
    changing trends in, 369–71, 369f
    ethics in, 364–65, 370, 394–96
Public Relations Society of America (PRSA),
    396
public service announcements (psas), 351
public service broadcasting, 49–50, 309–10
public sphere, 380
"publish, then filter" model, 241–42
puffery, 361, 392–93
Pulitzer, Joseph, 88, 273–74, 484
Pulitzer Prizes, 140, 274, 293, 294, 464
punch cards, 176, 184
punk rock, 327
push polls, 477
Putin, Vladimir, 415

Q

Al Qaeda, 208
qualitative research, 457–60
quality, of service, 221–23
quantitative research, 457–60
QuarkXpress, 283
quiz shows, 311–12
QWERTY keyboard, 184–85, 189

R

racial stereotypes, 38–39, 145, 307, 332
racism, 77, 143, 240–41, 272–73, 307
radio, 46, 128, 129
    citizens band, 207
    consolidation in station ownership, 123–
        25, 124t
    ethics in, 126
    functions of, 118
    history of, 118–23, 207
    networks, 123
    online stations, 58
    outlook for, 128–31
    programming on, 125–28, 127t
    regulation of, 417–18
    satellite radio, 58,129–30
    telescopes, 229
    timeline for, 120
Radio Act of 1912, 412
Radio Act of 1927, 123, 412
Radio Corporation of America (RCA), 121,
    156, 216
Radio-Television News Directors Association
    (RTNDA), 276
Rafaeli, Sheizaf, 60
Rain Man (film), 150
RAM. See random-access memory (RAM), 173
Ran (film), 319

random-access memory (RAM), 173
Random House, 56, 79
rate cards, 353
rating systems
    for movies, 329–30, 423, 434
    nielsen ratings, 161
    for television, 424
Rawls, John 381
RCA. See Radio Corporation of America
readership, 93
reality shows, 44, 313–14, 443
reception analysis, 448–49
recorded music, 46
    distribution of, 113–14
    history of, 108–09
    pricing structure of, 114
recording devices, 108, 154, 172–73
Recording Industry Association of America
    (RIAA), 111, 115, 225
Reed, David, 218
Reed's Law, 218, 221
regulation
    of electronic media, 7, 412–16
    by FCC, 40, 222, 416–199
    international, 415–16
    of radio and television, 417–18
remote controls
    for games, 322
    for television, 183
reporting
    interpretive, 285
    investigative, 275, 294
reproducibility, 171
Resident Evil (game, film), 321
Reston, James "Scottie," 285
Reuter, Paul Julius, 202
Reuters, 5, 79, 82, 202–03
Rheingold, Howard, 485
rhetoric, 26, 341
RIAA. See Recording Industry Association of
    America
ridicule, 329, 407, 411
rock and roll, 109, 113, 325–27
Rockefeller, John D., Sr., 363, 364
Rodriguez, Alex, 24
Rolling Stones, 326
Romney, Mitt, 479, 483–84
Roosevelt, Franklin Delano, 85,
Roosevelt, Theodore, 275
Roots (television series), 307
Rosen, Jay, 288
Rove, Karl, 175
Rowling, J.K., 75
RSS feeds, 59, 129, 196, 243
RTNDA. See Radio-Television News Directors
    Association
Russian media, 415
Ryder, Ellen, 96

S

Safari, 213
Said, Edward, 280
salaries
    in advertising, 369f
    in entertainment, 332–33
    in journalism, 295–96, 295f
Salon magazine, 56, 100, 249
Sandler Foundation, 294
Sarnoff, David, 122–23, 156, 216
Sarnoff's Law, 216–18, 217f
satellite communications, 207–09

dishes, 55, 416
    radio, 58, 129–30
    television, 159, 160–62
Saturday Night Live (SNL), 148, 464
Saussure, Ferdinand de, 436
Schawbel, Dan, 439
Schenck, Charles T., 405
schools, advertising in, 35
Schramm, Wilbur, 27–28, 444
Schramm-Osgood Model, of communication,
    28f
Schwartz, Tony, 346
Scorsese, Martin, 319
Scott, Ridley, 150
Scripps, E.W., 88, 90f
scriptoria, 75, 77
scrolling, 249
scrolling news, 48
scrolls, 101, 170
search engine marketing (SEM), 64, 179, 344,
    357–58
search engine optimization (SEO), 64, 179,
    194, 357–58
search engines, 178–79
    keywords for, 194–96, 428
Search for extraterrestrial intelligence (SETI),
    229
Seattle Post-Intelligencer, 89, 91f, 295
sedition, 405
SEM. See search engine marketing
Semantic Web, 262
semiotics, 436–38
sensational journalism, 273–74
SEO. See search engine optimization
separation of editorial and business
    operations, 277–79
September 11, 2001, terrorist attacks, 208,
    280–81, 406
sequential-access memory, 171–72
serious gaming, 324
SETI. See search for extraterrestrial
    intelligence
Seven Samurai (film), 319
Seventh Seal, The (film), 319
sex, and violence, 397, 424
sexism, 307–08, 327
sex offenders, 16, 43
sexting, 43
Shakespeare, William, 319–20, 475
Shannon, Claude E., 26–27
Shannon and Weaver model, 27f
Shelley, Mary Wollstonecraft, 79
shield laws, 408–09
Sholes, Christopher Latham, 184
shopping, online, 20, 79, 113, 450
Showtime, 151, 162, 315
Sicko (film), 319
Sigelman, Lee, 479
silent films, 143–44, 146
simplified communications model, 27
Sinclair, Upton, 275, 364
Sirius XM Satellite Radio, 130
situationist ethics, 383–84
SixDegrees, 252, 253f
Six degrees of separation, 256–57
Slacker Radio, 116, 129, 131
slander, 407
Slashdot effect, 19, 290
Slate magazine, 56, 99
smart mobs, 485
Smith, Oberlin, 172

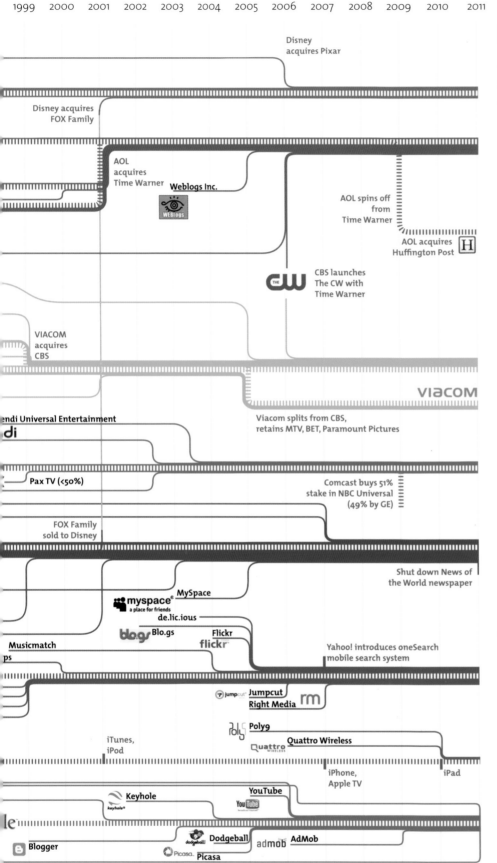

1999 2000 2001 2002 2003 2004 2005 2006 2007 2008 2009 2010 2011

Today

Disney acquires Pixar

Disney acquires FOX Family

AOL acquires Time Warner

Weblogs Inc.

AOL spins off from Time Warner

AOL acquires Huffington Post

CBS launches The CW with Time Warner

VIACOM acquires CBS

Viacom splits from CBS, retains MTV, BET, Paramount Pictures

...ndi Universal Entertainment

Pax TV (<50%)

Comcast buys 51% stake in NBC Universal (49% by GE)

FOX Family sold to Disney

Shut down News of the World newspaper

MySpace

de.lic.ious

Blo.gs

Flickr

Musicmatch

Yahoo! introduces oneSearch mobile search system

Jumpcut
Right Media

Poly9

Quattro Wireless

iTunes, iPod

iPhone, Apple TV

iPad

Keyhole

YouTube

Blogger

Dodgeball

Picasa

AdMob

WALT DISNEY COMPANY
MARKET VALUE: $61.67 BILLION
Walt Disney Motion Pictures Group, Pixar, ABC Broadcast TV Network; Cable TV networks Disney Channel, ESPN, ABC Family

TimeWarner

TIMEWARNER
MARKET VALUE: $32.91 BILLION
New Line Cinema, Time Inc., HBO, Turner Broadcasting System, The CW (50%, with CBS), TheWB.com, Warner Bros., Kids' WB, Cartoon Network, Boomerang, Adult Swim, CNN, DC Comics, Hanna-Barbera, Cartoon Network Studios, Castle Rock Entertainment

CBS
MARKET VALUE: $53.9 BILLION
CBS Television, CBS Records, UPN, the CW (50%, with TW), Infinity/CBS Radio, CBS Outdoor, Simon & Schuster, Showtime Networks, Paramount's TV studio

NBC UNIVERSAL

NBCUNIVERSAL owned: Comcast/GE
MARKET VALUE: $59.14 BILLION
Universal Studios, NBC Universal TV Group, NBC News, USA Network, Syfy, Chiller, CNBC, MSNBC,NBC.com, MSNBC.com, Current TV (10%), iVillage, PictureBox Movies, Bravo, Telemundo TV Studios, The Weather Channel, ShopNBC, Hulu, A&E TV Networks (15%), E! Entertainment

News Corporation

NEWS CORPORATION
MARKET VALUE: $30.4 BILLION
Fox News, National Geographic Channel, Fox TV,20th Century Fox, New York Post, Harper Collins, BSkyB (39.1%), STAR TV, Hulu (27%)

YAHOO!
MARKET VALUE: $17.68 BILLION
Content provided via Yahoo! Sports, Finance, Music, Movies, News; MyBlogLog, Zimbra, Right Media, Shine

APPLE
MARKET VALUE: $356 BILLION
Macintosh computers, iTunes, iPod, iPhone, Apple TV, iPad; Filemaker, Poly9, Quattro Wireless

GOOGLE Google
MARKET VALUE: $154.6 BILLION
DoubleClick, Youtube, Motorola Mobility, Zagat, AdMob

1999 2000 2001 2002 2003 2004 2005 2006 2007 2008 2009 2010 2011

Evolution of Concentration of Ownership Among the Top Eight Media Giants

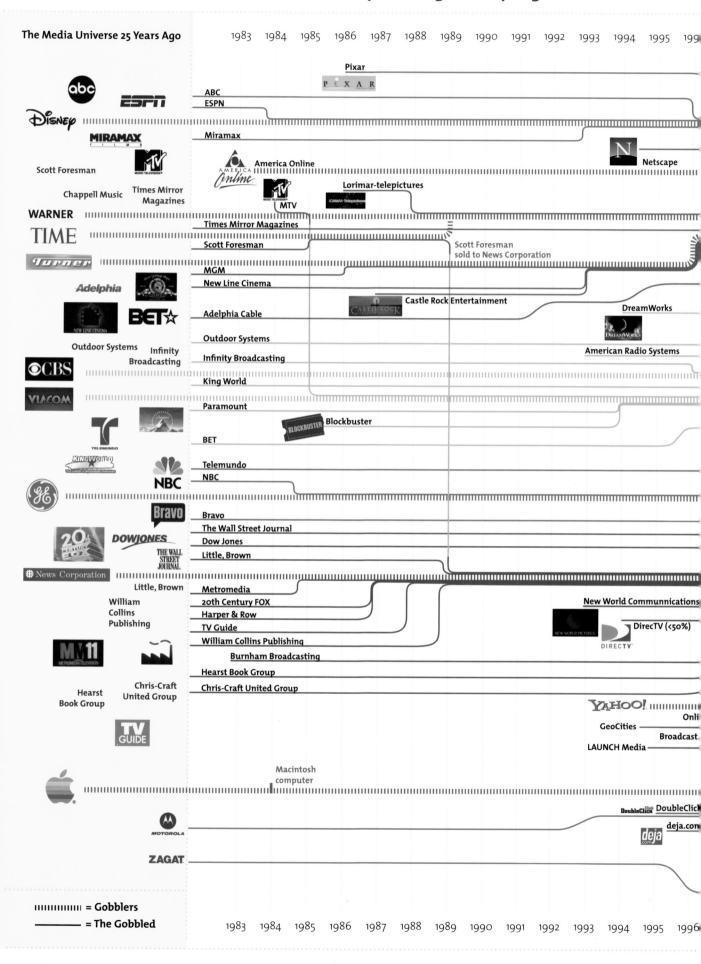

The Media Universe 25 Years Ago

1983 1984 1985 1986 1987 1988 1989 1990 1991 1992 1993 1994 1995 199

Pixar

ABC
ESPN
Miramax

Netscape

America Online

MTV

Lorimar-telepictures

Times Mirror Magazines
Scott Foresman

Scott Foresman
sold to News Corporation

MGM
New Line Cinema

Castle Rock Entertainment

DreamWorks

Adelphia Cable

Outdoor Systems
Infinity Broadcasting

American Radio Systems

King World

Paramount

Blockbuster

BET

Telemundo
NBC

Bravo
The Wall Street Journal
Dow Jones
Little, Brown

Little, Brown

Metromedia
20th Century FOX
Harper & Row
TV Guide
William Collins Publishing

New World Communications

DirecTV (<50%)

Burnham Broadcasting
Hearst Book Group
Chris-Craft United Group

YAHOO!
Onli
GeoCities
Broadcast
LAUNCH Media

Macintosh computer

DoubleClick

deja.com

ZAGAT

ıııııııııııı = Gobblers
——— = The Gobbled

1983 1984 1985 1986 1987 1988 1989 1990 1991 1992 1993 1994 1995 1996